Fodor's

BELGIUM

4th Edition

WITHDRAWN

Where to Stay and Eat for All Budgets

Must-See Sights and Local Secrets

Ratings You Can Trust

Fodor's Travel Publications   New York, Toronto, London, Sydney, Auckland
www.fodors.com

FEB 12 2009

FODOR'S BELGIUM

Editor: Alexis C. Kelly

Writers: Cillian Donnelly, Karina Hof, Tim Skelton, Nicola Smith

Production Editor: Astrid deRidder
Maps & Illustrations: David Lindroth, *cartographer*; Bob Blake, Rebecca Baer, *map editors*; William Wu, *information graphics*
Design: Fabrizio La Rocca, *creative director*; Guido Caroti, Siobhan O'Hare, *art directors*; Tina Malaney, Chie Ushio, Ann McBride, Jessica Walsh, *designers*; Melanie Marin, *senior picture editor*
Cover Photo (Outdoor cafes in Market Square, Bruges): Bob Krist
Production Manager: Amanda Bullock

4th Edition

ISBN 978–1–4000–0881–0

ISSN 1553–9164

SPECIAL SALES

This book is available at special discounts for bulk purchases for sales promotions or premiums. Special editions, including personalized covers, excerpts of existing books, and corporate imprints, can be created in large quantities for special needs. For more information, write to Special Markets/Premium Sales, 1745 Broadway, MD 6-2, New York, New York 10019, or e-mail specialmarkets@randomhouse.com.

AN IMPORTANT TIP & AN INVITATION

Although all prices, opening times, and other details in this book are based on information supplied to us at press time, changes occur all the time in the travel world, and Fodor's cannot accept responsibility for facts that become outdated or for inadvertent errors or omissions. So **always confirm information when it matters,** especially if you're making a detour to visit a specific place. Your experiences—positive and negative—matter to us. If we have missed or misstated something, **please write to us.** We follow up on all suggestions. Contact the Belgium editor at editors@fodors.com or c/o Fodor's at 1745 Broadway, New York, NY 10019.

PRINTED IN THE UNITED STATES OF AMERICA

10 9 8 7 6 5 4 3 2 1

Be a Fodor's Correspondent

Your opinion matters. It matters to us. It matters to your fellow Fodor's travelers, too. And we'd like to hear it. In fact, we need to hear it.

When you share your experiences and opinions, you become an active member of the Fodor's community. That means we'll not only use your feedback to make our books better, but we'll publish your names and comments whenever possible. Throughout our guides, look for "Word of Mouth," excerpts of your unvarnished feedback.

Here's how you can help improve Fodor's for all of us.

Tell us when we're right. We rely on local writers to give you an insider's perspective. But our writers and staff editors—who are the best in the business—depend on you. Your positive feedback is a vote to renew our recommendations for the next edition.

Tell us when we're wrong. We're proud that we update most of our guides every year. But we're not perfect. Things change. Hotels cut services. Museums change hours. Charming cafés lose charm. If our writer didn't quite capture the essence of a place, tell us how you'd do it differently. If any of our descriptions are inaccurate or inadequate, we'll incorporate your changes in the next edition and will correct factual errors at fodors.com immediately.

Tell us what to include. You probably have had fantastic travel experiences that aren't yet in Fodor's. Why not share them with a community of like-minded travelers? Maybe you chanced upon a beach or bistro or B&B that you don't want to keep to yourself. Tell us why we should include it. And share your discoveries and experiences with everyone directly at fodors.com. Your input may lead us to add a new listing or highlight a place we cover with a "Highly Recommended" star or with our highest rating, "Fodor's Choice."

Give us your opinion instantly at our feedback center at www.fodors.com/feedback. You may also e-mail editors@fodors.com with the subject line "Belgium Editor." Or send your nominations, comments, and complaints by mail to Belgium Editor, Fodor's, 1745 Broadway, New York, NY 10019.

You and travelers like you are the heart of the Fodor's community. Make our community richer by sharing your experiences. Be a Fodor's correspondent.

Bon Voyage!

Tim Jarrell, Publisher

CONTENTS

MAPS

ABOUT THIS BOOK

OUR RATINGS

Sometimes you find terrific travel experiences and sometimes they just find you. But usually the burden is on you to select the right combination of experiences. That's where our ratings come in.

As travelers we've all discovered a place so wonderful that its worthiness is obvious. And sometimes that place is so unique that superlatives don't do it justice: you just have to be there to know. These sights, properties, and experiences get our highest rating, **Fodor's Choice**, indicated by orange stars throughout this book.

Black stars highlight sights and properties we deem **Highly Recommended,** places that our writers, editors, and readers constantly praise for consistency and excellence.

By default, there's another category: any place we include in this book is by definition worth your time, unless we say otherwise. And we will.

Disagree with any of our choices? Care to nominate a place or suggest that we rate one more highly? Visit our feedback center at www.fodors.com/feedback.

BUDGET WELL

Hotel and restaurant price categories from ¢ to $$$$ are defined in the opening pages of each chapter. For attractions, we always give standard adult admission fees; reductions are usually available for children, students, and senior citizens. Want to pay with plastic? **AE, DC, MC, V** following restaurant and hotel listings indicate whether American Express, Diners Club, MasterCard, and Visa are accepted.

RESTAURANTS

Unless we state otherwise, restaurants are open for lunch and dinner daily. We mention dress only when there's a specific requirement and reservations only when they're essential or not accepted—it's always best to book ahead.

HOTELS

Hotels have private bath, phone, TV, and air-conditioning and operate on the European Plan (aka EP, meaning without meals), unless we specify that they use the Continental Plan (CP, with a Continental breakfast), Breakfast Plan (BP, with a full breakfast), or Modified American Plan (MAP, with breakfast and dinner) or are all-inclusive (including all meals and most activi-

ties). We always list facilities but not whether you'll be charged an extra fee to use them, so when pricing accommodations, find out what's included.

Many Listings	
★	Fodor's Choice
★	Highly recommended
⊠	Physical address
↔	Directions
⬥	Mailing address
☎	Telephone
🖷	Fax
⊕	On the Web
✉	E-mail
☞	Admission fee
⊙	Open/closed times
Ⓜ	Metro stations
▭	Credit cards

Hotels & Restaurants	
🏨	Hotel
⇙	Number of rooms
⚲	Facilities
⫟⊙⫟	Meal plans
✕	Restaurant
⬦	Reservations
⬈	Smoking
⏣	BYOB
✕🏨	Hotel with restaurant that warrants a visit

Outdoors	
⚐	Golf
⬠	Camping

Other	
☾	Family-friendly
⇨	See also
⊠	Branch address
☞	Take note

WHAT'S WHERE

1 **Brussels.** In Belgium, all roads lead to Brussels—and this goes for the railroads and airlines, too. Brussels is now the capital of the European Union. In many respects, it's a thoroughly modern city, with shining steel-and-glass office blocks jostling Gothic spires and Art Nouveau town houses.

2 **Brugge.** Famed as the birthplace of Flemish painting, Brugge's museums display some of the finest masterpieces of Jan van Eyck, Memling, and Hieronymus Bosch. Just 60 mi from Brussels, you can contemplate its weathered beauty in the dark mirror of its peaceful canals. North of Brugge, you'll reach the resorts of the North Sea coast, where you can stroll the wide, gleaming beaches and try some of the country's best seafood.

3 **Gent.** In the 15th century, Gent, located 35 mi from Brussels, was among the richest cities in Europe, and the aura of that golden age still seems to emanate from its opulent merchants' homes, and cathedrals.

4 **Antwerp.** Vibrant and hip, Antwerp has an unmistakable buzz that permeates the entire city. While the city has grown and modernized apace—today it's a major port and diamond center 29 mi from Brussels—it

preserves a great deal of yesterday's glories. These days, the predominance of Antwerp style is in the realm of avant-garde clothing design, as shown in the city's Mode Museum.

5 **The Meuse & the Ardennes.** Perhaps more than any other part of Belgium, the Meuse Valley—in the south, bordered by France and Luxembourg—is marked by human efforts toward survival and protection. Signs of the great Belgian craft of metalwork are everywhere, especially in Dinant, squeezed between the river and the cliff side, and in 17th-century Namur. The symbol of Walloon independence and pride is Liège, hard hit by the international steel crisis but still an important industrial center. En route to the French border, the Ardennes is a favorite vacation spot for Belgians, who are drawn to the region's forested hills, threaded with streams.

GREAT ITINERARIES

HAUTE CUISINE & COUNTRY AIR: 8–10 DAYS

The peripatetic gourmet chooses overnight stops to ensure that each evening meal is a feast. It is a bonus that many of the finest small hotels with outstanding restaurants are in out-of-the-way places that you might not otherwise visit. This kind of travel obviously does not come cheap.

Days 1–2: Antwerp

Kick off your trip with a French-inflected dinner at Antwerp's 't Fornuis. While exploring the city the next day, be sure to stop for lunch or coffee at De Foyer before dining at Neuze Neuze.

Day 3: Gent

Should you feel peckish while exploring the city, stop into Etablissement Max for a crispy waffle. Jan van den Bon is worth seeking out, but if you need to whip up an appetite, consider cycling out to the village of Sint-Martens-Latem for a prix fixe at Auberge du Pêcheur.

Day 4: Brugge

Decide between the inventive menu at De Karmeliet, a formal French experience at De Witte Poorte, and seafood at De Visscherie. Break up your culinary agenda by taking a short canal trip round the pretty medieval town.

Day 5: Oostende and Knokke-Heist

Nothing whets an appetite like sea air, so head for the coastal resorts. Spend the day exploring the resorts that makeup Knokke-Heist: Knokke, Heist, Alberstrand, Het Zoute, and Duinbergen. This is an area of dunes, beaches, ocean, wildflowers, and golf courses. There's also shopping along the Kustlaan or the 375-acre Het Zwin, a nature reserve and bird sanctuary, to explore. End the day in royal style with a night at Oostendse Compagnie, a beachfront villa with a noteworthy contemporary restaurant.

Days 6–10: Brussels

Go out with a bang. Try the superb French cuisine at Comme Chez Soi, the Sea Grill for seafood, Maison du Boeuf for steak and people-watching, or In 't Spinnekopke for unfussy, truly local cooking. Save some room for the simple pleasures of fresh frites from a stall and a trip to a top chocolatier on the Grand'Place or the Grand Sablon.

By Public Transportation

Train service is thorough and convenient, connecting all the major towns in the country. Bus connections are possible between some towns, such as Brugge and Gent, but are generally less convenient than the trains. A good tram service connects the resort towns along the coast; the trams run every 15 minutes from Easter through September. Renting a car is also easy to do, although roads to the coast are often plagued with traffic jams during the summer months. You could also undertake some cycling; Flanders is especially easy biking territory.

ANCIENT CRAFTS OF THE LOW COUNTRIES: 7 DAYS

The extraordinary flourishing of decorative crafts in the Low Countries during the Middle Ages was the result of the rulers' insatiable appetite for ornamentation, an appetite shared by local gentry and wealthy burghers. The clothing and jewelry lovingly depicted in 15th-century Flemish paintings indicate the high standards of the artisans of the era, whose traditions continue.

Day 1: Brussels

Start your tour with a crafts crash course, courtesy of some of the finest examples of Belgian tapestry, from the 14th to the 16th centuries, on view in the Musées Royaux d'Art et d'Histoire; lace and needlework are on view in the Musée du Costume et de la Dentelle.

Days 2–3: Antwerp

Diamonds are big business in Antwerp, where the origins and history of diamond cutting are shown at the Provinciaal Diamantmuseum. Diamondland, where you can also see diamond-cutting demonstrations, is one of the world's most spectacular diamond showrooms.

Day 4: Brugge

Brugge is intimately associated with lace making, and there are shops selling everything from lace souvenirs to works of art. The best place to get a real understanding of the craft is the Kantencentrum, incorporating a museum and a lace-making school.

Day 5: Liège

The Val Saint-Lambert glassworks in Seraing, on the outskirts of Liège, is one of the finest in the world; you can visit the showroom and watch glassblowers in action. The factory outlet offers great values.

Days 6–7: Brussels

Return to the capital for a final round of shopping and ogling, whether for antique or contemporary lace, tapestries at the Textilux Center, or vintage *brocante* at one of the weekly markets. Check the concert schedule of the Hôtel de Ville—you might be able to hear a performance in the Gothic Hall, which is hung with priceless Brussels and Mechelen tapestries.

TIPS

If you decide to sample Brussels's famous seafood dishes, beware of the area around Rue des Bouchers, behind the Grand'Place. The alleyways packed with fish restaurants may look charming, and the waiters entertaining, but prices are often vague and over inflated. Many tourists have been caught out by an unexpectedly large bill. A safer bet is to try the more refined Ste-Catherine area which used to be where fishermen uploaded their catches from a now-covered-up canal. The area also boasts a large choice of fish restaurants.

If you would rather enjoy a beer away from the tourist-laden Grand'Place, walk five minutes to the St. Gery area, just behind the bourse (money exchange). The small square of bars has a much more authentic atmosphere and is popular with locals.

To get around Brussels easily and cheaply, buy a ticket for 10 journeys for €11 at any metro station. One ticket journey lasts for one hour, no matter how many modes of transport are required. Taxis are also relatively cheap and most central locations can be reached for around €10.

By Public Transportation
There's direct train service between all the cities on this itinerary.

QUINTESSENTIAL BELGIUM

The Art of Brewing

Belgian brewing took off in the early Middle Ages, when hops cultivation was introduced and monasteries got in on the act. Today some of the country's top beers are still produced by monasteries, the best known being the Trappist beers. *(See "What Is a Trappist Beer?" in Chapter 1.)* Lambics, fruit beers, "white" or wheat beers, dark brown ales, seasonal beers—a plain lager seems drab in such company. Beer lists in pubs and restaurants run from the dozens into the hundreds. Some breweries have guided tours and tastings; the smaller, family-run operations will give you the best sense of the local traditions.

Avant-Garde Fashion

The first rumblings of a substantial Belgian "fashion culture" came with the 1960s provocateur Ann Saelens and the artistic presentations of Yvette Lauwaert, but it was the "Antwerp Six" in the late 1980s that put Belgium on the global fashion map. They were all graduates of the Antwerp Academy of Fine Arts, which has continued to groom designers known for their creativity and impeccable workmanship. *(See "Antwerp à la Mode" in Chapter 6.)* Today's Belgian designers—Raf Simons, Véronique Branquinho, and Olivier Theyskens—have picked up the thread of individualism. Some, like Theyskens, work for venerable international couture houses while others stick to their native country. There are several Belgian museums dedicated to textiles and clothing including the Mode Museum, in the same building as the fashion department of Antwerp's Academy.

Belgium, with its complicated mix of cultures and languages, is often overlooked on traditional tours of the European continent. But visitors to the small Benelux country are sure to discover a wealth of national treasures that will not leave them disappointed.

Mussels & Beyond

Simply put, Belgians love food. In this culture, preparing food and sharing a meal are all something to be lingered over and savored. As it shares borders with the Netherlands, Germany, and France, Belgium absorbed enough influences to create a traditional cuisine known for its creativity and high quality. Belgian food combines French cooking's finesse with a German- and Dutch-style appreciation for unaffected, homey fare. When people think of Belgian food, though, they often conjure up one particular image: a steaming pot of mussels. Served with fries, mussels are virtually a national dish. (Though these days, the shellfish often come from the Netherlands.) Belgian food is often not highly spiced. Instead, dishes can include rich amounts of butter or cream; are braised in beer; or get a flavorful kick from mustard or dried fruit.

Chocolate Delights

It would be almost criminal to visit Belgium and not try a generous sampling of the country's world-famous chocolates. With more than 2,000 chocolatiers spread across almost every town and village, you'll have no choice but to succumb to the mouthwatering indulgences. Some chocolatiers still make their delicious products by hand, and the process can be viewed at the Musée du Cacao et du Chocolat in Brussels. While you're in Brussels, head to the Grand'Place or the smaller Grand Sablon to sample the best melt-in-your-mouth pralines from some of Belgium's most prestigious chocolate brands—Leonidas, Marcolini, Godiva, and Neuhaus. Those lucky enough to be in Brugge in the spring can experience the annual chocolate festival. *For an in-depth look at Belgian chocolate see "Chocolate Country" in Chapter 3.*

IF YOU LIKE

Medieval Architecture

The medieval architecture in Belgium has survived the test of time. Highlights include Brugge's Church of our Lady, with its towering brick spire; Gent's Gravensteen castle; the cobblestone lane of Vlaeykensgang; and Brussels's Grand'Place.

Brugge. Known as the "Venice of the North," Brugge is considered one of the most beautiful cities in Europe. Strolling through the maze of winding, cobbled alleys, alongside its winding canals and over its romantic bridges, it's easy to see why UNESCO included the entire medieval city center on its World Heritage list.

Gent. Much is medieval in Gent, and remarkably well-preserved. Fine examples include the Saint Bavo Cathedral with its famous altarpiece, the belfry, the Gravensteen castle, and the architecture along the old Graslei harbor.

Antwerp. Antwerp's Onze-Lieve-Vrouwekathedraal is the most breathtaking religious monument in the country. But a stroll down the narrow cobblestone lane of the Vlaeykensgang will get you as near as can be to being in the Middle Ages—without having a slops bucket emptied on you from on high.

Brussels. Everything you've heard about the Brussels Grand'Place is true. The spectacular 15th-century town hall is a stunning example of medieval Flemish architecture, and the surrounding guild houses complement it beautifully—it's just a pity the prices in the cafés are as over-the-top as the buildings!

Belgian Beer

Beer is your entrée to authentic Belgian culture, but with 450 different varieties to choose from, it may be difficult to know where to begin. Belgium has enjoyed an enviable reputation for its specialty beers since the Middle Ages and modern connoisseurs can indulge in flavors ranging from raspberry beer to chocolate-and-white and brown beers, Trappist beer, and the beer Belgium is most famous for—Lambic.

Drie Fonteinen. If trying a real Lambic, Gueuze, or Kriek is high on your tasting list, than this brewery is for you. Located in the tiny village of Beersel, the brewery also serves a Flemish-style dinner, which you can work off by walking to the nearby 15th-century castle.

Abbaye d'Orval. Unfortunately the brewery at this abbey is off-limits to the public, but you can taste the dry, bitter brew at the nearby Hostellerie d'Orval or L'Ange Gardien, which you'll pass on your way to the abbey.

Brasserie d'Achouffe. This artisanal brewery started out as a hobby for the owner and his brother-in-law. Today it's an internationally respected brewery that produces some flavorful beer like La Chouffe. If you're lucky to visit in December or January, try the N'Ice Chouffe.

Notre-Dame de Scourmont. The monks at this Trappist brewery produce Chimay, some of the country's tastiest and most potent beer; they also make really good cheese. The abbey is off-limits to the public, but you can try the beer and cheese at the nearby Auberge de Poteaupré.

Art

"The Art Cities of Flanders" is a phrase that conjures up images of Gent's proud spires and medieval Brugge. In the 15th century, these were among the richest cities in Europe, and the aura of that golden age still seems to emanate from their cloth halls, opulent merchants' homes, and cathedrals.

Groeningemusem. If you're looking for a crash course in Flemish Primitives and their successors, this museum is one-stop shopping. Two to see: Jan van Eyck's amazingly realistic *Madonna with Canon Van der Paele* and *Moreel Triptych,* one of Hans Memling's greatest works.

The Atomium. One of Brussels's most distinctive landmarks, the Atomium—a 335-foot-high structure—represents an iron crystal magnified 165 billion times. The nine steel spheres are connected by 20 passageway tubes and form a striking image on the Brussels skyline. Created by Andre Waterkeyn for the 1958 Brussels World's Fair, the Atomium now plays host to a variety of exhibitions.

The Horta House. Hidden off the beaten track in the St. Gilles district is another of Brussels's treasures. The Horta House is a tribute to the Art Nouveau style and the celebrated work of one of Belgium's most acclaimed architects, Victor Horta.

Gent Altarpiece. Visit St. Bavo's Cathedral to see Jan van Eyck's *Adoration of the Mystic Lamb,* which is considered to be one of the most influential and beautiful paintings of the Middle Ages. Visitors can listen to a detailed explanation about each panel of the intricately painted altar through a headset in their own language.

Battlefields

As the site of numerous battles during World War I and World War II, any trip to Belgium should include one of the country's infamous battlefields.

Ardennes American Cemetery. Spanning 90 acres, this cemetery in Neuville-en-Condroz contains the graves of 5,328 U.S. servicemen, many of whom died in the Battle of the Bulge.

In Flanders Fields. This museum offers insight into the horrors of the Great War, giving an accurate picture of its scale and the harshness of the battles.

Passchendaele. The Memorial Museum Passchendaele 1917 gives an overview of the five battles of Ieper using authentic memorabilia. Visitors can walk through a German trench and descend into a 20-foot-deep British headquarters dugout. At the end of your visit, don't miss the haunting bugler's rendition of "The Last Post" every day at 8 PM at the towering Menin Gate.

Waterloo. Waterloo, the site of the famous 1815 showdown between Napoléon Bonaparte and the Duke of Wellington is another popular battlefield. Ride through the historic fields in a 4WD truck or visit the interactive panorama that re-creates the sights and sounds of a turning point in Europe's history.

IF YOU LIKE

Celebrations

Whether it's music festivals, all-night parties, offbeat celebrations, or some other raucous event, Belgium's citizens know how to have a good time. Check out On the Calendar for more events.

Gentse Feesten. This 10-day celebration (⊕*www.gentsefeesten.be*) of indulgence was originally intended to curb summer drinking by workers in Gent. However, it seems to have had the opposite effect, and includes music making, entertainment, and assorted happenings in the streets of the city, and a world-class dance music festival that lasts until the wee hours.

Carnival. Celebrated in early February with great gusto, the festivities at Binche—with its extravagantly costumed *gilles*—and at Tournai and Charleroi—each of which has its own style and verve—are especially great. Mardi Gras (Shrove Tuesday) and the preceding Sunday are the high points.

Summer Music Festivals. Summer heats up with some of Belgium's most important rock festivals. Rock Werchter (⊕*www.rockwerchter.be*), a multiday outdoor concert, pulls in major acts like R.E.M. and Tricky. Axion Beach Rock is held in the seaside town of Zeebrugge. Dour Music Festival (⊕*www.dourfestival.be*) brings cutting-edge DJs and alternative bands to the heart of rural Wallonia.

Nuit Blanche. Brussels stays up for this mid-October night's dream (⊕*www.nuitblanchebrussels.be*), during which musical and cultural events go on until 6 AM.

BEATING THE EURO

Below are suggestions for ways to save money on your trip, courtesy of the Travel Talk Forums at Fodors.com.

Transportation

"In Flanders, people under 26 can buy a Go Pass for the train. You pay around €46 for 10 one way rides. The rail pass for over 26 are €71 and also usually a good deal, for instance from Leuven to Gent is €12. Using the pass as an adult you save €4 on that one trip. If you're using the buses and trams, buy a de Lijn kaartje. You get 10 rides for €8 vs. €1.60/ride when paying on the bus. The card works on buses and trams all over Flanders. They are widely available—at the grocery store, newspaper stands, etc."
—mgbleuven "

Book a hotel that offers free bike rental. A ride around Bruges is fabulous. And don't pay for parking. There are free parking lots along the ring road and then it's less than a 10 minute walk to the Market Square."—pommefrites

Food & Drink

"Take your frites to any of the bars lining Place Jourdan and they'll happily serve you a beer to accompany them. (The bars that let you bring your frites in have a little sign in the window). You can eat your fries at the pavement tables or inside most establishments."—hanl

"In Brussels, avoid the restaurants around the Grand'Place. You can eat much, much better for the same amount (or less) at the wonderful non-chain restaurants in residential neighborhoods like the Chatelain/Tenbosch area of Ixelles."—BTilke

Lodging

"You can get good deals on hotels in Brussels when the European parliament is in recess."—hetismij

"The coast is less crowded and a lot cheaper to visit in the spring or the fall. However, avoid school holidays (around Easter, All Saints, and Christmas) as the prices go up again and the crowds re-appear."—MyriamC

"We rented an apartment. There was a minimum of 4 nights but it was only €130 per night and everything was extremely convenient."—gregeva1

Sights

"The maritime museum in Antwerp has an (largely covered) outdoor section that's free. It's especially great for kids, and there's even a specially constructed play structure that's made along the lines of a boat."—Therese

"In Brugge, the museum pass is a very good deal: €15 for any 5 museums. The Royal Museums of Fine Arts in Brussels (which include both the Ancient Art Museum & Modern Art Museum) only charges €5 for admission. An excellent deal considering its huge collection of Flemish Primitives paintings and its Surrealism paintings."—yk

ON THE
CALENDAR

ONGOING September–December	Every year, **Europalia** (☎*02/507–8550* ⊕*www.europalia. be*), held mainly in Brussels, honors a different country with exhibitions, concerts, and other events amounting to a thorough inventory of its cultural heritage.
WINTER December	The **European Christmas Market** in the Grand'Place in Brussels presents the traditions and products of many different European countries.
January	Brussels's **International Film Festival,** which is pushing its way onto the international agenda, takes place across the capital.
SPRING April	**ArtBrussels** (☎*02/402–3666* ⊕*www.artexis.com/artbrussels/ index.html*) brings dozens of up-and-coming contemporary-art dealers to the capital.
Easter	On Easter Monday, the **Cavalcade de Jenmappes,** a traditional costumed procession, is held in Mons.
Late April–early May	The **Royal Greenhouses** (☎*02/513–0770*), at Laeken Palace near Brussels, with superb flower and plant arrangements, are open to the public for a limited period.
May	On Ascension Day, **De Heilig Bloedprocessie** (*[Procession of the Holy Blood]* ☎*050/44–86–86*) in Brugge is one of the oldest and most elaborate religious and historical processions in Europe. Early seat reservations are recommended.
	Brussels hosts the **KunstenFESTIVALdesArts** (☎*02/219–0707* ⊕*www.kunstenfestivaldesarts.be*), a three-week international celebration of contemporary drama, dance, and music.
	Brussels Jazz Marathon (☎*0900/00606* ⊕*www.brusselsjazz marathon.be*) encompasses gigs and informal sessions in more than 60 clubs and pubs, plus outdoor concerts in the Grand'Place, Grand Sablon, and place Ste-Catherine.
	The **Ducasse** held in Mons on the first Saturday and Sunday following Whitsunday is a fantastic citywide festival including a procession of the relics of the town's founding saint and an enactment of St. George's battle with the dragon.
SUMMER June	Fashionistas head to Antwerp for the **Antwerp Academy Fashion Show** (☎*03/205–1890* ⊕*www.modenatie.com*), which presents the work of the annual graduates of the acclaimed design school.

July	The **Ommegang** (☎ 02/548–0454 ⊕ www.ommegang.be) takes over Brussels's Grand'Place. It's a sumptuous and stately pageant reenacting a procession that honored Emperor Charles V in 1549. Book early if you want a room in town during the festivities.
	Belgium's National Day is celebrated in Brussels with a military march, followed by a popular feast in the Parc de Bruxelles and brilliant fireworks.
	Bouillon takes a step back in time during the **Medieval Village Fair**, featuring markets, parades, and tournaments.
August	Dinant honors its native son, Adolphe Sax, with the annual **Saxophone Festival.**
	Bathtubs of all shapes and sizes float through Dinant during the annual **Bathtub Regatta** (☎ 082/222–129).
	In Brugge's **Reiefeesten** (*Canal Festival* ☎ 052/21–39–56), events from the city's past are re-created alongside the romantic canals. It is celebrated every third year; the next takes place in 2010.
AUTUMN September–October	The **Annual Meeting of Hot Air Balloons** takes place just outside of Tournai, attracting thousands of visitors.
	The **Festival van Vlaanderen** (*Festival of Flanders* ☎ 09/293–9494 ⊕ www.festival.be) brings hundreds of concerts to all the old Flemish cities.
	On **National Heritage Day** (☎ 02/511–1840) buildings of architectural or historical interest throughout Belgium that are not normally accessible to the public open their doors.
	Gent's **Flanders International Film Festival** (☎ 09/242–8060 ⊕ www.filmfestival.be) is the most important film festival in the country. It screens the work of new Belgian talent as well as of international directors.
November	The **European Community Challenge** (☎ 03/326–1010) in Antwerp is a major event on the international tennis circuit, with a diamond-studded racquet worth $1 million available to anyone who wins the event three times in five years.

WHEN TO GO

The best times to visit the country are in the late spring—when the northern European days are long and the summer crowds have not yet filled the beaches, the highways, or the museums—and in fall. The stereotype of overcast Belgian skies is not unfounded, and early spring and fall do get quite a bit of rain, but the weather can change dramatically in the space of a few hours.

Because Belgians take vacations in July and August, these months are not ideal for visiting the coast or the Ardennes, but summer is a very good time to be in Brussels, Antwerp, or Liège. In summer you will also be able to get a break on hotel prices; on the other hand, this is also vacation time for many restaurants.

Climate
The following are average daily maximum and minimum temperatures in Brussels.

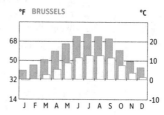

Belgian Beer

WORD OF MOUTH

"All Belgian beers are good and quite distinctive. Experiment! Be advised though, they vary from strong to very strong. A bottle of Trappist beer at lunchtime might require a bit of a lie-down afterwards."

—stfc

"My favorite Belgian beers depend on circumstances. If I'm only having one or two, then Westmalle or Grimbergen will be right up there. I like Gordons in the winter, nice, dark & heavy, and in the summer I'll take a Kriek (Timmermans for choice) to cut my thirst. If I'm having a few beers in the evening, then Palm Special is the beer of choice. With a meal, something like a Maes pils is nice."

—doonhamer

Updated
by Cillian
Donnelly

BREWING'S PLACE IN BELGIUM'S CULTURAL pantheon can't be overstated. No other country offers so many distinct and sophisticated styles of beer, each suited to a particular taste, occasion, or meal.

TOURING & TASTING BEER IN BELGIUM

ITINERARIES

Many visitors to Belgium come specifically for beer tours of the entire country. However, it's also rewarding (as well as easier) to incorporate visits to breweries, famous beer cafés, and other beer-related sights into the general itinerary for your trip. All of Belgium's major cities have interesting beer-related attractions either within their boundaries or nearby.

This chapter is organized by region, so you can match up places located near the cities you'll be visiting; you can stop on the way from one city to another, or make a detour to visit a brewery or abbey and have lunch in a beer café. Here are some options:

Brussels should be your first stop. There's a beer museum on the Grand'Place and several charming cafés with lots of specialty beers. Since Brussels is situated in the middle of the country, any excursion is feasible on a day trip—even the most remote place listed here, the monastery of Orval, is only 180 km (112 mi) away. You might consider side trips to nearby Leuven, where Stella Artois is brewed, or to a small authentic Gueuze brewery, or even to the Trappist monastery of Chimay.

From **Antwerp** you could visit the De Koninck brewery or Bierhuis Kulminator, a café with 550 beers on its list. From Antwerp, it's an easy trip to Het Anker in Mechelen or the Trappist monastery in Westmalle. From **Gent,** take a trip to the Liefmans or Roman breweries in Oudenaarde. **Brugge** might be the starting point for an excursion to the abbey in Westvleteren or breweries in Roeselare and Poperinge. The city of **Liège** is about an hour and a half from the monasteries in Orval and Rochefort.

TRAPPIST BEER

If you have—as many do—a particular interest in the Trappist monasteries and their delicious beers, you'll have to crisscross the entire country and travel almost 400 mi in order to visit them all. It would probably be better to pick just one or two. A trip to Westvleteren or Achel is special because the beer is so hard to come by (however, fans of Westvleteren should check before going: the monks do run out of stock). Rochefort is located near the World War II sites in Belgian Luxembourg, and a drive to Orval or Chimay is worthwhile because of the scenery and the idyllic location of these abbeys.

BREWERY VISITS

Brewers are proud to have visitors witness their craftsmanship and experience the magic of the intricate brewing process. Except for the Trappists, most Belgian breweries are open to the public. Don't expect

Helpful Beer Web Sites

1

⊕ www.beerparadise.be. The Association of Belgian Brewers' web site contains an interactive map of Belgium pointing out the location of beers and breweries.

⊕ www.trappistbier.be. A personal site dedicated exclusively to Belgian Trappist beers, with a history of each beer.

⊕ www.dma.be/p/bier/beer.htm. A list of beers from the Benelux region (Belgium, the Netherlands, and Luxembourg), with entries on pubs, breweries, and beer clubs.

⊕ www.ratebeer.com. A site where beer fanatics rate beers from all over the world.

⊕ www.beeradvocate.com. A site dedicated to beers from all over the world. Gives information on types and styles and offers ratings as well.

old-fashioned factories with men stirring boiling kettles; most of the brewing process is automated, and all breweries are now well equipped with modern technology.

Visiting a local brewery guarantees a more personal experience and might be more enjoyable than touring a large industrial one. However, if you do prefer the latter, head for Stella Artois in Leuven—their kettle room is especially impressive. If you fancy a small brewery, Drie Fonteinen in Beersel or Martens in Bocholt are good experiences. The former makes unique fruit-flavored beers and has a charming café and restaurant; the latter houses a museum depicting the history and process of beer making.

Tours usually cost €5 or €6 and take you through the different stages of the brewing process—from the storage and treatment of raw materials to the heating and adding of flavors to the final bottling. A drink, and sometimes cheese, is also included. Groups should book tours at least two weeks in advance; individuals should always check the opening hours and group size restrictions beforehand. Information on tours can be found on the Web sites mentioned in this chapter or on the site of the Union of Belgian Brewers (⊕ *www.beerparadise.be* ☎02/511–4987).

BEER PUBS AND CAFÉS

Most breweries own one or several bars in their immediate neighborhood. Some are worth a visit, such as the cafés near the Trappist monasteries. They are moderately priced, know exactly how beer should be served, and sometimes have an extra kind of beer that isn't found anywhere else. The prevalence of beer cafés also means that you don't necessarily need to travel to remote parts of the country to taste a specific beer. It's possible to order an Orval beer on the North Sea coast or drink a Rodenbach in the Ardennes. Moreover, the cafés are usually in places worth visiting for the scenery alone.

STOCKING UP

Want to bring some of your favirote brews home? **Beer Mania** (✉ *chaussée de Wavre 174-176, Brussels* ☎ *02/512–1788* ⊕ *www. beermania.be*) stocks over 400 beers and will arrange worldwide shipping for large purchases.

Thanks to excellent distribution, most Belgian beers are widely sold in regular grocery and liquor stores; there are specialty shops, but you'll pay a premium. You can also buy directly from breweries when you visit. Belgian beer can even be ordered over the Internet: Web sites like Beermania and Belgianshop deliver the goods to your doorstep. Just remember that you can only take a limited amount home with you, so check customs regulations before you board.

Lambic, Gueuze, Kriek, or other fruit-flavored beers are the best bets for bringing home. Trappist brews are sometimes hard to find or else very expensive; for Achel and Westvleteren, you'll probably need to go to a specialty store, or the abbeys themselves.

Suppliers Belgium Beers (✉ *Reynderstraat 2/1, Antwerp* ☎ *03/226–6853*). **De Hopduvel** (✉ *Coupure links 625, Gent* ☎ *09/225–2068*). **Terclavers** (✉ *Mechelsestraat 203a, Leuven* ☎ *016/20–20–00*). **Beermania** (⊕ *www.beermania.be*).

BRUSSELS & ENVIRONS

BRUSSELS

The capital is an excellent starting point for beer lovers. Not only are interesting places in the rest of the country generally no more than an hour's drive away, but there is much to enjoy right here. There's a beer museum in the heart of the city on the Grand'Place, and numerous cafés with exhaustive beer menus are scattered around town. *For more details see Chapter 3, Brussels.* Some especially worthwhile cafés are A La Mort Subite, the art deco café Falstaff (near the Grand'Place), the stylish belle epoque Hotel Métropole, and Chez Moeder Lambic, located somewhat outside the city center.

Although there's only one traditional brewery left, Brussels has historically been the home of Lambic beer. The eight other Lambic breweries are in the Pajottenland region, to the west of Brussels.

VISITING & TASTING

MUSEUMS **Brewers House.** In the 16th century, the original brewers' guild headquarters was on the Grand'Place in Den Gulden Boom; nowadays, the Belgian Brewers Association's home is in an 18th-century mansion on the same square. The upper floors are closed to the public, but in the cellar you'll find a small museum containing tools from the original Hoegaarden brewery as well as a high-tech video installation in four languages that provides an excellent overview of the brewing process. The entrance fee includes a glass of beer, which changes every week. ✉ *Grand'Place 10, Lower Town* ☎ *02/511–4987* ⊕ *www.beerparadise. be* 🖅 €4 ⊙ *Daily 10–5.*

Musée de la Gueuze/Museum van de Gueuze. It hardly seems right to call this a museum; since 1900, this brewery, otherwise known as the Cantillon brewery, has produced Lambic and specialty beers. Although Lambic is the quintessential Brussels beer, this is, sadly, the only Lambic brewery left in Brussels (the others are in the Zenne Valley, to the southeast of Brussels). Created through spontaneous fermentation (fermentation begun by natural yeast molecules in the air, versus artificial cultures), it is the basic ingredient in many popular Belgian beers, such as Gueuze (an effervescent blend of Lambics), cherry-flavored Kriek, and raspberry-flavored Framboise. Only organically grown grains are used for production. On tours, available in English, you'll see the works, from the aging containers to the bottling machines, and have a tasting. Many commercially brewed Lambics bear scant resemblance to the real thing, so drink up while you're here. ⊠*rue Gheude 56, Anderlecht* ☎*02/521–4928* ⊕*www.cantillon.be* ⬜€*5* ☉*Weekdays 8:30–5, Sat. 10–5.*

WHERE TO DRINK

A La Mort Subite is an authentic Brussels café that has preserved its turn-of-the-20th-century atmosphere. Young and old, students and businessmen, regulars and tourists gather around the wooden tables and are served by waiters who speak the authentic, endangered Brussels dialect, which mixes French and Dutch. The beer list isn't very large, but it covers some winners: Lambic, Gueuze, and Kriek from the Brussels region, and four of the six Belgian Trappist beers. Snacks include *kip kap* (a plate of assorted cold cuts), *kop* (meat from a pig's head), and bread with *platte kaas* (creamy white cheese). ⊠*Montagne aux Herbes Potagères 7* ☎*02/513–1318.*

BEERSEL

13 km (8 mi) south of Brussels.

In the market square of the small village of Beersel, you'll find one of the eight remaining traditional Lambic brewers in the Pajottenland region. This is a popular day trip for beer lovers and a stop on most beer tours.

GETTING HERE & AROUND

There are several trains an hour from Brussels to Beersel; the trip takes 40 minutes, including a transfer in Halle. By road, take the southern side of the circular R0 in the direction of Charleroi and get off at exit 14, which will lead you straight to Beersel.

VISITING & TASTING

Fodor'sChoice **Drie Fonteinen.** Be prepared to taste unfamiliar beers at this meeting ★ place for devotees of real Lambic, Gueuze, and Kriek. Drink them while consuming a copious, Flemish-style dinner. Call in advance to visit the brewery. Afterwards, aid your digestion by taking a walk to the nearby 15th-century castle. ⊠*Hoogstraat 2A* ☎*02/306–7103* ⊕*www.3fonteinen.be* ☉*Closed Tue. and Wed.*

What Is a Trappist Beer?

Trappist beer has been called the champagne of Belgium, and for good reason. Produced in small quantities, in tightly controlled environments, Trappist beers have been lauded as exceptionally flavorful and complex, far more refined than their commercial counterparts.

But how did it all begin? Belgium's abbeys have a long brewing tradition, established long before specifically Trappist beers became affiliated with the country. St. Arnold, an 11th-century monk and founder of the Abbey of Oudenburg in Brugge (now called the Abbey of Steenbrugge), is Belgium's patron saint of brewing. Legend has it that, during a plague, St. Arnold dipped his crucifix into a brew kettle and encouraged the people to drink boiled beer rather than the contaminated water. Belgium's brewers now pay homage to St. Arnold at an annual church service in Brussels.

The first Trappist beers were brewed in the Abbaye de la Trappe, a monastery in Normandy founded in 1664 by Benedictine monk Armand-Jean Le Bouthillier. The monastery became known simply as *Trappist* rather than by its full name of "Order of the Reformed Cistercians of Strict Observance." The French Revolution uprooted these monks and forced them into exile, with some eventually settling in Belgium.

Now the Trappist appellation refers exclusively to beers made in one of Belgium's Trappist monasteries, following the strictest of Benedictine principles. Belgium has a dozen Trappist monasteries, only six of which brew beer: Rochefort in Namur, Orval in Luxembourg, Chimay in Hainaut, Westvleteren in West Flanders, West-malle near Antwerp, and Sint-Benedictusabdij in Achel on the Dutch border. (The last, Achel, is a new contender, having produced their first beer since World War I in 1999.) These cloisters produce a total of 20 beers, identifiable by a logo specifying "Authentic Trappist Product."

Although Trappist beers may be generally characterized as yeasty, sweet, fruity, and strong, each of the six monasteries brews a unique product. Beer from Orval, for instance, has a dry, citrus quality, and is golden amber in color with a slightly cloudy, foamy head, while Rochefort ale is plum-colored and full, with a creamy head. Chimay is fruity and blond or brown.

Since Trappist beers have gained worldwide attention, modern commercial beer companies have tried to cash in on the beers' popularity by using images or names with Trappist connotations. To protect their products from imitators, the monastery breweries established the International Trappist Association in 1998 and registered the word Trappist as a legal denomination of origin. The association formalized the conditions for Trappist beer: it must be brewed in a Trappist monastery, under the supervision of monks, and the majority of the revenue must be dedicated to charitable works. A hexagonal insignia noting "Authentic Trappist Product" now marks all true Trappist brew. Once you get your hands on a Trappist beer, read the side of the bottle for directions on how to pour it and the best temperature for consumption.

LEUVEN

26 km (16 mi) southeast of Brussels via the E40 or E314 highway.

Leuven (Louvain), like Oxford or Cambridge, is a place where underneath the hubbub of daily life you sense an age-old devotion to learning and scholarship. Its ancient Roman Catholic university, founded in 1425, was one of Europe's great seats of learning during the late Middle Ages. The city was pillaged and burned by the Germans in 1914; 1,800 buildings, including the university library, were destroyed. They were rebuilt with gifts from American universities only to be bombed again in 1944. In the 1960s, intercultural tensions caused the old bilingual university to split into separate French-language and Flemish-language schools. French speakers moved their university south of the linguistic border to the new town of Louvain-la-Neuve; the Flemish speakers remained in Leuven.

GETTING HERE & AROUND

Leuven is a 20-minute drive from Brussels on the E40 highway to Liège. There are several trains an hour from Brussels; the trip takes 30 minutes.

ESSENTIALS

Visitor Info Province of Vlaams Brabant (⊠ *Provincieplein 1, Leuven* ☎ *016/26–76–20* ⊕ *www.vlaamsbrabant.be*).

VISITING & TASTING

BREWERIES **Stella Artois.** Leuven is considered the beer capital of Belgium, and Stella Artois the premier institution of Belgian brewing. The brewery is a mammoth building with a sleek, modern exterior. Contemporary facilities may characterize the brewery today, but beer has been made here since 1366, originally under the name Den Horen (the horn, which can still be seen on the label). Master brewer Sebastien Artois took over the operation in 1717, and the barley beer Stella Artois was launched in 1926. Now you can size up the enormous modern vats as a tour takes you through the entire brewing process. It's best to make tour reservations three weeks in advance. ⊠ *Vaartkom 33* ☎ *016/24–71–11, 016/24–70–61 reservations* ▣ *€6* ⊗ *By reservation only, weekdays 9, 10:30, 1:00, 2:30, 4;00 and 6:30.*

Domus. Tucked into a back street off the Grote Markt, this café adjoins the tiny Domus brewery, famous for its honey beer. The place is casual, the clientele on the young side, and the decor authentically rustic: craggy old beams, a brick fireplace, a labyrinth of separate rooms, dusty bric-a-brac, and paisley table throws. The menu includes traditional dishes such as black-and-white pudding with apples. ⊠ *Tiensestraat 8* ☎ *016/20–14–49* ▭ *AE, MC, V.*

ALSO WORTH SEEING

★ **Stadhuis.** Every Flemish town prides itself on its ornate, medieval stadhuis (town hall). This one is the work of Leuven's own architectural master of Flamboyant Gothic, Mathieu de Layens, who finished it in 1469 after 21 years' work. It's a miracle that it has been so well kept;

because it was occupied by German staff, it escaped the fires of the invading Germans in 1914, and a bomb dropped at its entrance in 1944 luckily didn't cause much damage. You'll need to stand back from it to appreciate fully the vertical lines in the mass of turrets, pinnacles, pendants, and niches, each with its own statue. The interior contains some fine 16th-century sculpted ceilings. Tours are given in Flemish and English.

Be sure to nip across the street to the **Sint-Pieterskerk,** where you can see two masterpieces by 15th-century Flemish painter Dirk Bouts. ⌧ *Grote Markt 9* ☎ *016/21–15–40* ⌧ *€2* ☉ *Oct.–Mar., tours daily at 3; Apr.– Sept., tours weekdays at 11 and 3, weekends at 3.*

MUSIC FESTIVALS

There's more to Leuven than learning and beer. During the first weekend of July, the small town of Werchter, 8 km (5 mi) north of Leuven, hosts **Rock Werchter** (⊕ *www.rockwerchter.be*), a four-day outdoor festival that draws many major international acts. On Friday evenings in July, there are concerts all over town, and in mid-August, the city turns its center over to **Marktrock** (⊕ *www.marktrock.be*), a weekend-long music festival. Access to shows is free or inexpensive, and dozens of bands fill the historic center's squares.

HOEGAARDEN

16 km (10 mi) southeast of Leuven, 40 km (25 mi) east of Brussels.

At the end of the 19th century there were 35 breweries near Hasselt; sadly, only one remains. However, De Kluis does brew Belgium's most famous wheat beer. De Witte van Hoegaarden is a blond, slightly effervescent, thirst-quenching beer, which tastes best on a hot summer day.

Also worth a visit are the 25 different **gardens** near the rococo church in the center of town. ⌧ *Houtmarkt 1* ☎ *016/79–78–43* ⊕ *www. detuinenvanhoegaarden.be* ⌧ *€5* ☉ *Daily 10–sunset.*

GETTING HERE & AROUND

From both Leuven and Brussels, take the E40 towards Liège and get off at exit 25. Hoegaarden is another 5 km (3 mi) to the south. There is still no direct train to Hoegaarden. A service runs from Brussels Central at 34 minutes past each hour to Tienen, the nearest stop.

VISITING & TASTING

WHERE TO DRINK

Het Kouterhof. If you're wondering why the floor of this brasserie is made of cobblestones, it's because its former inhabitants were cattle. The farm was converted into a large café in 1986, and now welcomes locals and cyclists from nearby towns. If it's too dark inside (cows don't need a view), take a seat outside. The regular Hoegaarden and the special Grand Cru are good choices, and if you're hungry, a *waterzooi* (Flemish stew with chicken or seafood) will do the job. ⌧ *24 Stoopkensstraat* ☎ *016/76–74–33* ☉ *Fri.–Sun. 11–11, Mon.–Thurs. 11–8.*

History of Beer in Belgium

Though its origins lay in the Middle East 10,000 years ago, it was the Romans who introduced the art of beer making to Western Europe. Its success spread quickly, and from the 5th century on, monks held a monopoly on brewing, supplying innkeepers and nobility with beer.

During the Middle Ages, power shifted towards the guilds, which stimulated the rise of breweries, gradually turning beer into a popular drink. The number of breweries increased dramatically over the years and beer became a cultural staple—as can be seen in many paintings by 16th-century painter Pieter Bruegel.

At the end of the 18th century, the aftermath of the French Revolution caused a serious decline. Many monasteries and their breweries, such as the abbey in Orval, were destroyed, a blow from which they recovered only slowly. Better times for beer were ushered in at the end of the 19th century; inventions by Louis Pasteur

guaranteed better conservation and increased its overall quality. By 1900 there were over 3,000 breweries in Belgium. Unfortunately, just after this peak, the Great War, the economic crisis of the 1930s, the Second World War, and the growing popularity of other alcoholic beverages from the 1950s combined to weaken the industries. There were 755 breweries left in 1946, and now there are only about 100.

The market has forced many Belgian breweries to merge, creating internationally successful conglomerates such as Inbev, which owns Stella Artois, Hoegaarden, and now also Anheuser-Busch, among others. On the other hand, small breweries and local brands have recently emerged in every corner of the country. Although the consumption of beer as a whole may be on the decline, the production of these special regional beers is on the rise.

—By Dirk Blancke

ANTWERP & ENVIRONS

ANTWERP

VISITING & TASTING

BREWERIES **De Koninck.** Antwerp's last remaining brewery is hidden between a crisscross of heavily trafficked roads. Things were quieter at the beginning of the 19th century, when Joseph Deconinck bought De Plaisante Hof (The Pleasant Garden), originally an inn, and turned it into the brewery that soon became Antwerp's pride and joy. Arrange visits by phone or Internet at least one month in advance; you'll get a general introduction, take a tour of the brewery, and taste two beers. ⊠*291 Grote Steenweg, Middelheim* ☎*32/18–40–48* ⊕*www.dekoninck.be* ⏰*Mon.–Sat. by reservation.*

Moortgat. "Shh, we're having a Duvel" reads the sign outside this ultramodern industrial brewery. Moortgat has produced its signature strong (8.5%), foamy, blond beer—along with six others—since Albert Moortgat began importing yeast from Scotland in the 1920s. You'll find Duvel (Devil) in almost every café in Belgium; the name's meaning will become clear after your third glass. Groups of at least 10 can reserve a tour. Breendonk is situated along the A12 motorway between Antwerp (23 km [14 mi]) and Brussels (27 km [17 mi]). The **Fort van Breendonk** *(See Chapter 2, Historic Battlegrounds)* is along the same road and worth a detour. ⊠ *58 Breedonkdorp, Breendonk* ☎ *03/860– 9400* ⊕ *www.duvel.be* ⌫ *€4* ⊙ *Weekdays.*

WHERE TO DRINK

Bierhuis Kulminator. This famous Antwerp bar pours 550 different kinds of beer, including EKU-28, known as the strongest beer on earth. ⊠ *Vleminckveld 32–34, Oude Stad* ☎ *03/232–4538* ⊙ *Closed Sun.*

'T Waagstuk. In a 16th-century warehouse near the river Schelde, this modest-looking café, with a red-tile floor, wooden tables, and a canopy of beer glasses hanging from the ceiling, has welcomed beer lovers since 1983. In addition to serving many specialty beers, they organize seminars for beer devotees. ⊠ *Stadswaag 20, Oude Stad* ☎ *03/225–0219.*

MECHELEN

28 km (17 mi) north of Brussels.

Mechelen (Malines in French), north of Brussels, is a small, peaceful gem that has preserved its medieval and Renaissance past but that, unlike Brugge, is never overrun with tourists. As the residence of the Roman Catholic Primate of Belgium, it's an important ecclesiastical center. It's also a center of vegetable production: the town and its environs are known for *witloof,* the Belgian delicacy known elsewhere as chicory or endive, and asparagus, whose stalks reach their height of perfection in May.

GETTING HERE & AROUND

Mechelen is situated almost exactly between Brussels and Antwerp. By car it is easy to reach from both cities via the E19 highway. Hourly trains from Brussels get you there in 20 minutes.

VISITING & TASTING

BREWERY **Het Anker.** The first document referring to the brewery dates from 1369, making it one of the oldest breweries in Belgium. Touring this small, intimate brewery, the birthplace of Mechelen's pride and joy, the dark, sweet Gouden Carolus (Golden Charles) beer, you can witness every stage of the beer-making process. Tours in English, for a minimum of 12 people, must be arranged in advance. The brasserie next to the brewery serves five different kinds of Gouden Carolus and several beer-seasoned dishes at affordable prices. In 2005, they introduced a new beer created especially for women, the Margriet. A modest 22-room hotel is part of the brewery complex, so devoted beer fans can spend the night (€93). ⊠ *Guido Gezellelaan 49* ☎ *015/20–38–80* ⊕ *www. hetanker.be* ⌫ *€3.50 with beer tasting, €8.70 with beer and food* ⊙ *Tours only by appointment.*

CLOSE UP

How Beer Is Made

1

Although much attention is given to the subtle intricacies of wine production, the beer-making process is actually just as complex and nuanced. The main ingredients are barley (or wheat for wheat beer), water, hops, and yeast. Other ingredients, such as herbs or fruit, may be added during the brewing process. The quality and taste of each ingredient and the way they are mixed and treated influences the final outcome.

Generally, the first step is to soak barley in water to cause germination, which creates chemical changes that are useful in the brewing process later on. At just the right moment, germination is stopped and the barley is roasted in a kiln. The roasted barley is then thrown into a giant kettle and heated with water. The length of time that the barley is left to stew with

the water—not how long the barley is roasted, as many think—ultimately determines the strength or body of the beer. The barley is then removed and hops (a small flowering plant that grows on vines and is the ingredient that makes beer taste bitter) is added for flavor and aroma.

After this process, the resulting liquid, called "wort," is ready to be fermented. To do this, yeast is added, which will, depending on the type used, sit at the top of the tank or sink to the bottom. Once the yeast has been filtered back out of the tank (in the case of many wheat beers, it isn't removed—thereby giving it its characteristic cloudy complexion and yeasty aroma), the beer will usually sit for another few weeks until it is bottled or kegged.

WHERE TO DRINK

Borrel Babel. The smallest café in Mechelen is in the charming Sint-Romboutshof, behind the cathedral. Different varieties of jenever are the potent specialty. ⊠ *Nieuwwerk 2* ☏ *015/27–36–89.*

ALSO WORTH SEEING

Fodor$Choice ★ **Sint-Romboutskathedraal.** Completed in the 1520s, this cathedral represents a magnificent achievement by three generations of the Keldermans family of architects, who were active in cathedral building throughout Flanders. The beautifully proportioned tower, 318 feet high, was intended to be the tallest in the world, but the builders ran out of money before they could reach their goal. Inside are two remarkable 40-ton carillons of 49 bells each. Carillon playing was virtually invented in Mechelen (the Russian word for carillon means "sound of Mechelen"). The best place to listen to the bells is in the Minderbroedersgang. Chief among the art treasures is van Dyck's *Christus an het Kruis* (Crucifixion) in the south transept. The remains of the cathedral's namesake, Sint-Rombout (St. Rumbold), are hidden in the high altar. ⊠ *Grote Markt* ☏ *015/29–40–37* ☉ *Apr.–Oct., daily 9:30–5:30; Nov.–Mar., daily 1:30–4:30; check tourist office for tower tours; carillon concerts Sat. and Mon. 11:30 AM, Sun. 3 PM.*

WESTMALLE

33 km (21 mi) northeast of Antwerp, 75 km (50 mi) northeast of Brussels, 15 km (10 mi) west of Turnhout.

One of the main attractions of the vast Campine region to the northeast of Antwerp, the rich woods and fields of Malle (the municipality made up of Oostmalle and Westmalle) draw thousands of cyclers and walkers each year.

Bikes can be rented close to the abbey at **Eikelspark** (✉ *Antwerpsesteenweg 506* ☎ *03/383–0958*).

At **Arnauts** (✉ *Molendreef 9* ☎ *03/312–3269*) you can take a tour through Malle on a hooded wagon. However, most visitors to Westmalle come because of the abbey's internationally renowned Trappist beer.

GETTING HERE & AROUND
From Antwerp, take the N12 in the direction of Turnhout for 26 km (16 mi); the abbey of Westmalle will be on your left. From Brussels take the E19 highway to Antwerp, get off at exit 6 and follow directions to Turnhout, which will lead you to the N12.

VISITING & TASTING
ABBEY **Abbey of Our Lady of the Sacred Heart.** A magnificent lane, bordered by oak trees, leads you from the highway to the beautiful abbey. Founded in 1794, it owes its fame to the brewery where the famous Trappist beer has been made since 1836. Fruity and spicy, the red-brown Dubbel (Double) is the only Trappist beer available on tap (all others are bottled). The creamy, golden Tripel (Triple), called the mother of all Tripels, was the first of its kind in 1934. A sign on the door warns that the abbey is "only accessible to relatives of the monks"; however, individuals looking for a silent retreat are welcome and should contact the *gastenbroeder* (guest monk). ✉ *Antwerpse steenweg 496* ☎ *03/312–9209.*

WHERE TO DRINK
Café Trappist. Across the street from the abbey is this large brasserie, where you can order enormous plates of Trappist cheese to accompany your beer. Cheese and beer are for sale for take-away or to eat in the restaurant (as are regional maps with bike and walking routes). ✉ *Antwerpse steenweg 487* ☎ *03/312–0502.*

LIMBURG PROVINCE

ESSENTIALS
Visitor Info **Toerisme Limburg** (✉ *Willekensmolenstraat 140, Hasselt* ☎ *011/23-74-50* ⊕ *www.toerismelimburg.be*).

HASSELT

77 km (46 mi) southeast of Antwerp, 82 km (49 mi) east of Brussels, 42 km (25 mi) northwest of Liège.

Limburg's principal town has busy shopping streets, innovative museums, and a cathedral with the de rigueur carillon. In mid-October, it hosts an annual weekend festival for its signature drink, jenever. In the late 1990s, the ring road around the old town center, which followed the line of the medieval city walls, was revamped; now called the "Groen Boulevard" (Green Boulevard), it's lined with trees and has a wide pedestrian walkway. This, plus the free city bus service and a handful of pedestrian-only blocks, makes Hasselt particularly easy to navigate.

GETTING HERE & AROUND
Hasselt is a straight drive, almost as the crow flies, from Antwerp on the A13/E313 motorway (which continues to Liège); from Brussels, take the E40/A2 via Leuven to Exit 26, then the E313 for the last few miles. There are hourly direct trains from Antwerp's Centraal Station to Hasselt (1 hour, 5 minutes) and from Brussels (1 hour, 30 minutes).

VISITING & TASTING
MUSEUM   The **Nationaal Jenevermuseum** perpetuates Hasselt's slightly raffish distinction of having had jenever as its major industry. The museum dates from 1803 and includes one of the country's oldest surviving distilleries. On a tour of the installations, you'll see a computer animation of the production process and such changing exhibits as vintage jenever-advertising posters, before ending in the paneled tasting room. You can sample jenever of various ages, flavors, and proofs from two dozen Belgian distilleries. ⊠ *Witte Nonnenstraat 19* ☎ *011/24–11–44* ⊕ *www.jenevermuseum.be* 🖃 *€3* 🕙 *Apr.–Oct., Tues.–Sun. 10–5; Nov.–Mar., Tues.–Fri. 10–5, weekends 1–5.*

WHERE TO DRINK
't Stookerijke. A convivial and attractive bar, this is *the* place to continue your education in jenever—the owner is an expert. It's behind the cathedral. ⊠ *Hemelrijk 3* ☎ *011/22–63–48.*

FESTIVALS
During the third weekend in October, Hasselt celebrates jenever with a giant festival. This popular feast includes exhibitions, second-hand bazaars, music in the squares and streets, and a race to appoint the best waiter in town. It may not be Belgium's most important cultural event, but it's a pleasant way to experience the flamboyant local atmosphere.

ACHEL

43 km (27 mi) north of Hasselt, 41 km (25 mi) east of Geel.

Achelse Kluis is the most recent abbey to produce Trappist beer. It was founded in 1686 and originally housed a community of hermits.

Monks from Westmalle founded the present abbey in 1846. For over a century they committed themselves mainly to farming and craftsmanship. In 1999 the monks began producing highly fermented beer, making their abbey Belgium's sixth Trappist brewery. You'll recognize Achel Blonde 8 (the number refers to the percentage of alcohol) by its white cap, and Browne 8 by its golden one. Achel Extra is a slightly stronger brown variant. Achel's beers are not yet as widely available as some of the other Trappist beers such as Westmalle, Rochefort, and Chimay, but you can buy them here in the modest shop next to the abbey. A six-pack costs €7.52.

GETTING HERE & AROUND

Achel is a tiny village in the northeast corner of Belgium on the Dutch border. From Brussels take the E40 in the direction of Liège; jump on the E314 in Leuven and keep following directions to Aachen (Germany) until exit 29; take the N715 to Hechtel; from there it's a few kilometers to the center of Peer on the N73; finally, take the N748 through the woods to Achel. From Antwerp take the E313 towards Hasselt; get off at exit 23; follow the four-lane N71 to Overpelt; crisscross towards Neerpelt; take the N712 toward Hamont and follow Achel at the crossroads with the N748. There is no train service.

VISITING & TASTING

ABBEY Like all Cistercians, the monks of **Achelse Kluis** are very keen on their privacy and tranquility, but unlike other abbeys, visitors are not totally excluded. Anyone can join in prayer seven times a day, from the night office at 4:30 until day closure at 8:30. It's a unique opportunity to witness the monk's piety in the seclusion of their church. A tour of the monastery is possible for €50 by appointment, but only for groups. There's even a guesthouse for people who want to retreat in silence. The fee of €28 covers a simple room, three meals, and two coffee breaks a day. You'll also find a shop, a bookstore, and an art gallery stuffed with religious items. The adjacent cafeteria, where you can, of course, taste their Trappist brews, is open every day from 11 to 6 in summer and from noon to 5 Tuesday to Sunday in winter. ⊠ *De Kluis 1* 🕾 *011/80–07–66* ⊕ *www.achelsekluis.org.*

NEAR ACHEL

On the N762 from Hamont to Bree, 15 km (10 mi) southeast of Achel, lies Bocholt, home of **Brewery Martens**. The somewhat characterless village may or may not be worth a detour, but the brewery does host an appealing museum depicting the history and process of brewing. Martens makes beers (Sezoens and Quattro) that are popular mainly in the province of Limburg. You can taste Martens beer in the adjacent inn **De Bierketel**, which is—so it's said—secretly connected to the kettles in the brewery. ⊠ *Dorpstraat 53, Bocholt* 🕾 *089/48–16–76* ⊠ *€5* ⊗ *July and Aug., daily, 1–6; Sept.–June, by appointment.*

FLANDERS

OUDENAARDE

30 km (20 mi) south of Gent.

Once an important center for tapestry making and silversmithing, Oudenaarde is now a quiet provincial town on the banks of the Schelde river.

The Gothic town hall on the spacious Markt and the beguinage are worth a visit, as is the **Centrum Ronde van Vlaanderen** (⊠ *Markt 43* ☎ *055/33–99–33* ⊕ *www.crvv.be* ✉ *€7.50*), an interactive museum honoring the cyclists who rode the annual tour. For a taste of rural Flanders, visit the region to the north of Oudenaarde. Small villages (like Mullem or Wannegem) with cobblestone streets and old cafés are hidden among the woods and fields.

GETTING HERE & AROUND

From Brussels take the E40; at the crossroads in Zwijnaarde (near Gent) follow the E17 towards Kortrijk for 5 km (3 mi) and get off at exit 8 to get on the N60. There is also frequent train service. From Brussels Midi, the trip takes 45 minutes, and from Gent, 30 minutes.

VISITING & TASTING

BREWERIES **Liefmans.** This small brewery is a bit outside of town, towards Aalst. Visits are possible (only by appointment), but make sure you get a peek at the magnificent Baudelot hall no matter what. Several tasty beers are made here, including the soft, dark Oud Bruin, the newer and stronger Jan van Gent, and the very sweet Kriek and Frambozen bier (cherry and raspberry beer). ⊠ *Aalststraat 200* ☎ *055/31–13–91* ⊕ *www.liefmans. be* ✉ *€3* ☉ *Visits and lunch by appointment.*

Roman. A family brewery since 1545, Roman is now run by the 12th generation of Romans. In addition to the traditional Romy pils and wheat and brown beers, in 1990 it added to its list Ename, a rich and delicious abbey beer. ⊠ *Hauwaart 105* ☎ *055/45–54–01* ✉ *€4* ☉ *Group visits Tues.–Thurs., by appointment.*

WHERE TO DRINK

A nice place to taste some of Liefmans's beer, along with 30 other types of Belgian beer, is **De Mouterij** (⊠ *Meerspoortsteeg 2* ☎ *055/30–48–10* ⊕ *www.demouterij.com*), a former malt factory near the Markt. The menu provides abundant and inexpensive dishes such as *everzwijnstoofvlees* (stew of wild boar) and *vispannetje* (fish casserole). It's closed on Wednesday.

WESTVLETEREN

138 km (86 mi) west of Brussels, 94 km (58 mi) southwest of Gent, 46 km (29 mi) west of Kortrijk.

Although Westvleteren is considered by some to be the best beer in the world, it's neither mass-produced nor widely distributed, and hence isn't available in regular stores. Almost the only place to get it is right here. Cars regularly line up outside the doors of the abbey in order to stock up. The limit is 10 cases per car, but due to the demand, people often drive away with much less. The monks only produce enough beer (4,800 hectoliters) to support themselves and their good works; several times a year they run out of stock. If you'd like to buy their Trappist beer, call to check the availability (☎057/40–10–57) before you go. Beer is sold daily 10–noon and 2–5, except on Friday, Sunday, holidays, and during the first two weeks of January.

GETTING HERE & AROUND
From Brussels, take the E40 towards Gent, switch to the E17 towards Kortrijk, follow the A19 to Ieper, and then take the N8 towards Veurne for another 15 km (9 mi) before reaching Westvleteren on your left.

VISITING & TASTING
ABBEY **St. Sixtus Abbey.** The abbey was founded in 1831 by Jean-Baptist Victoor, a hermit who lived in the fields and woods to the west of the small village of Vleteren. The brewery was started eight years later and grew rapidly until 1945, when the then Dom, Gerardus Deleye, decided to cut down production. Twenty-nine monks still live here, devoting themselves to prayer, study, and manual labor. They produce three kinds of Trappist beer: Blonde (5.8%), Eight (8%), and Twelve (10.8%). Blonde is made from three kinds of regional hops and has a slightly bitter taste. Eight is sweeter and fruity. Twelve, sometimes called the Flemish Burgundy because its excellence equals that of Burgundian wine, has a strong malt flavor and is one of the most potent Belgian beers. ✉*Donkerstraat 12.*

WHERE TO DRINK
Café in de Vrede. The original café across the street from the abbey was demolished in the 1990s and replaced by a big, modern, and somewhat characterless building. The large barroom serves the three kinds of Westvleteren Trappist beer and accompanying snacks. In the west wing, the claustrum (the monks' barracks) gives a view on life in the monastery and depicts the history of the brewery. A small shop sells beer (when in stock), cheese, pâté, and other local products. ✉*Donkerstraat 13* ☎*057/40–03–77* ⊘*Closed Fri., first 2 wks in Jan., last 2 wks in Sept., wk after Easter, and Thurs. in Oct.–Mar.*

ROESELARE

100 km (62 mi) west of Brussels, 73 km (45 mi) southeast of Gent, 40 km (25 mi) south of Brugge, 24 km (17 mi) northeast of Ieper.

Roeselare is twice as large as the nearby city of Ieper, yet it draws far less attention. It may not have as many historical points of interest, but a walk through the city is quite enjoyable, as is a visit to its local brewery.

GETTING HERE & AROUND

From Brussels (or Gent), take the E40 towards Gent and Brugge and get off at exit 11. Follow the N37 to Tielt, where you'll take the N35 to Roeselare. From Brugge, get on the E403 towards Kortrijk and get off at exit 8.

VISITING & TASTING

BREWERY **Brouwerij Rodenbach.** A fruity, mild brown beer has been made here since 1836. It owes its taste to the yeast and the oak barrels in which the beer ferments. A visit will give you an insider's view on the brewing process. ⊠*Spanjestraat 131–141* ☎*052/24–28–36* ⊕*www.rodenbach.be* 🎟*€5* ☉*July and Aug., Tues.–Thurs. 1:30; groups by appointment.*

POPERINGE

11 km (7 mi) west of Ieper on N38.

In addition to its importance in World War I history, Poperinge is in the capital of Belgium's main hop-growing region, the so-called "Hoppeland Route."

GETTING HERE & AROUND

Poperinge is a short drive from Ieper on the N38, a straight, four-lane road through fields and small villages. You can also take a train from Brugge, but as you have to switch in Kortrijk, the trip takes 1½ hours.

VISITING & TASTING

BREWERY **Brouwerij van Eecke.** This small local brewery in Watou, a picturesque village on the Belgian–French border, brews three kinds of beer: the amber-colored abbey beer Het Kapittel; the somewhat sour Witbier; and, most popular, the sweet, honey-like Hommelbier. Make an appointment online or over the phone to visit. Every summer from July through mid-September, Watou turns into a cultural magnet, offering poetry and art on every street corner. ⊠*Douvieweg 8, Watou* ☎*057/42–20–05* ⊕*www.brouwerijvaneecke.tk.*

MUSEUM **Nationaal Hopmuseum.** The museum uses tools, audiovisuals, and photos to explain just about anything you ever wanted to know about hops. ⊠*Gasthuisstraat 71, Poperinge* ☎*057/34–66–77* ⊕*www.hopmuseum. be* 🎟*€1.50* ☉*Mar.–Nov., Tues.–Fri. 10–6, weekends 2–6.*

BELGIAN LUXEMBOURG

ESSENTIALS
Visitor Info **Province of Belgian Luxembourg Tourist Office** (✉ *quai de l'Ourthe 9, La Roche-en-Ardenne* ☎ *084/41–10–11* ⊕ *www.ftlb.be).*

ROCHEFORT

128 km (79 mi) southwest of Brussels, 55 km (34 mi) southeast of Liège.

It's a pity that the **Abbaye de St-Remy** (about 3 km [2 mi] north of Rochefort), where the delicious 6°, 8°, and 10° Trappist beers are brewed, isn't open to the public. It's possible to spend a period of reflection within the walls, but tourists are not welcome—the 15 remaining monks are firm about this. The monks preserve an austere life, talking only when necessary, for example. The recipe for the beer remains a mystery. We know that they use water from a monastery well and that coriander and sugar candy are added during the brewing process. But really, the only thing we know for sure is that their beers taste heavenly.

GETTING HERE & AROUND
From Brussels, follow the E411, toward Luxembourg, and get off at exit 23. Direct trains run hourly from both Namur (40 minutes) and Liège (75 minutes) to Jemelle, the nearest railway station to Rochefort, about 3 km (2 mi) east. From Jemelle, buses 29 and 166a make the short journey to Rochefort in about five minutes. Both run about once an hour.

VISITING & TASTING
WHERE TO DRINK
Limbourg Café. The first owner of this tranquil tavern originated from the Flemish province of Limburg, hence its name. The café, serving the three kinds of Rochefort Trappist, has preserved the grandeur of a Belgian bar at the beginning of the 20th century. The restaurant, on the other hand, is very modern, with inexpensive yet excellent food. Try the homemade foie gras or the *côtes de porcelet à la Trappiste* (pork chops with beer). ✉ *pl. Albert 21* ☎ *084/21–10–36* .

Le Luxembourg. You may have trouble choosing between the 26 Belgian beers on the list of this café-restaurant in front of the Hôtel de Ville. However, since you're in Rochefort, your best bets are the sweet 6% or more bitter 10% Trappist with a side order of cheese. Look for a seat on the sunny terrace in summer. In winter, ask for a table near the fireplace and order a grilled *filet pur* (sirloin) or *côte à l'os* (T-bone steak). ✉ *pl. Albert 19* ☎ *084/21–31–68* ⊕ *www.leluxembourg.be.*

ORVAL

29 km (18 mi) southeast of Bouillon, 190 km (118 mi) southeast of Brussels.

Orval, a few kilometers from Belgium's border with France, is a tiny town hidden in the forest. One major attraction is the draw here: the magnificent abbey and its famous Trappist beer.

GETTING HERE & AROUND

By Belgian standards, Orval is very remote. From Brussels take the E411 towards Arlon. Get off at exit 26 and follow the N40 to Neuf-château. There, take the N85 which will lead you through pines and beeches to Florenville. Finally, the N88 leads to the Abbey of Orval in the forest of Merlanvaux.

VISITING & TASTING

Fodor's Choice
★   **Abbaye d'Orval.** Although all six beers are brewed by monks from the same order, each has a distinct taste. Without a doubt, the Abbaye d'Orval makes the most distinctive of all. It's dry and bitter—even a bit sour—and due to its low alcohol content (6.2%), it's an excellent thirst quencher. Some argue that Orval doesn't resemble a classic Trappist at all and betrays its German and English influences. In fact, the first brewings in the 1930s were based on the then-popular British ale style and were supervised by a German brewer. The name Orval, "golden valley," refers to the dark orange color of the beer.

Founded by Italian Benedictines in 1070, and once one of Europe's richest and most famous monasteries, the Abbaye d'Orval flourished for 700 years before being destroyed by French troops in the aftermath of the French Revolution. The abbey was rebuilt between 1926 and 1948 under the supervision of Marie-Albert Van der Cruyssen, a monk and builder from Gent who started the brewery in 1931 in order to finance the rebuilding project. The brewery and most of the monastery's buildings are closed to the public, but there are several ways to experience the solemn atmosphere inside the abbey's walls. You can attend one of the eight daily liturgical services (contact the gatekeeper at the entrance) or visit the medieval and 18th-century ruins of the original abbey. The tomb of Wenceslas, first Duke of Luxembourg, is in the choir of the abbey church, and the gardens contain the spring where Mathilde, Duchess of Lorraine, once dropped her wedding band, only to have it miraculously returned by a trout. (Mathilde's magical fish is the abbey's trademark symbol, and it is said that this spring, from which the monks draw the water to make the beer, is partly responsible for the beer's particular flavor.) A film in English describes life in the monastery. The 18th-century cellars house a small museum that explains the abbey's architecture and displays some religious art. For €30 a night you can enjoy the monks' hospitality in one of the guestrooms; call 061/32–51–10 for more information. ✉ *Villers-devant-Orval* 🕾 *061/31–10–60* 🌐 *www.orval.be* 💷 *€4* 🕑 *Mar.–May, daily 9:30–6; June–Aug., daily 9:30–6:30; Sept.–Feb., daily 10:30–5:30.*

WHERE TO DRINK

Hostellerie d'Orval. The summer crowds come here for an Orval beer with a slice of Orval cheese. It's open all year. ⊠*rue d'Orval 14, Villers-devant-Orval* ⚓*About 2 km (1 mi) from the abbey* ☎*061/31–43–65.*

L'Ange Gardien. On the road towards the abbey, every visitor passes L'Ange Gardien (The Guardian Angel). There's a nice view of the abbey's entrance from the terrace, which is heated in cold weather. Orval cheese and beer are available, and the accompanying glass can be purchased here as well. ⊠*rue d'Orval 3* ☎*061/31–18–86.*

ALSO WORTH SEEING

If you've already come all the way out here, you should take a detour to the beautiful little village of **Torgny,** about 7 km (4 mi) southwest of Virton. Its houses, with their yellow stone walls, blue-painted windows, and shallow, red-tile roofs, are reminiscent of Provence in France. The 6th-century ruins of a Roman villa lie 1,000 yards southwest of the village.

HOUFFALIZE

27 km (17 mi) southeast of La Roche-en-Ardenne, 102 km (63 mi) south of Liège, 152 km (94 mi) southeast of Brussels.

This adorable mountain village is a place for clean air and family fun. There's something here for all ages and all activity levels—from biking and hiking to fishing and boating.

VISITING & TASTING

BREWERY The **Brasserie d'Achouffe,** a fast-growing artisanal brewery with a whim-
★ sical elf for a mascot, is a family affair. What started as a hobby for Chris Bauweraerts and his brother-in-law, Pierre Gobron, has now become an internationally respected brewery featuring unusual, flavorful beers. Stop in for a tour and a tasting, or visit their gift shop. If hunger strikes, the attached restaurant ($) serves fresh trout and unbeatable rabbit stew; it's closed Wednesday. ⊠*Achouffe 32* ☎*061/28–94–55* ⊕*www.achouffe.be* 🎫*Tour €5* ⚓*Reservations essential* ▤*MC, V* 🕙*Tours weekends at 10:30; shop Thurs.–Tues. noon–9.*

HAINAUT AND NAMUR PROVINCES

BINCHE

16 km (10 mi) east of Mons, 62 km (37 mi) south of Brussels.

Binche is the only remaining walled city in Belgium. Two dozen towers and solid medieval ramparts enclose a small, sleepy city that wakes up during carnival season when the Gilles (local jesters) fill the streets.

GETTING HERE & AROUND

From Brussels, travel on the E19 towards Mons, get off at exit 21 and follow the N55 straight to Binche. Direct hourly trains from Brussels take an hour.

VISITING & TASTING

BREWERY **Brasserie La Binchoise.** Zip around the corner from the Musée International du Carnaval et du Masque for a characteristically Binchois experience: a trip to the brewery. It's a charming brick building with a bowered court-yard. If you make a reservation in advance, you can tour the brewery to see the works and get a sample of suds. The *Rose des Remparts* is a refreshing, raspberry-flavored light beer, while *Spéciale Noël* is a spicy, potent winter special. A small museum sketches the history of the use of brewing machinery and breweries in the region. You can get a bite (char-cuterie, beer-marinated eel in summer) and try some of the brews at the restaurant ($–$$), open on Friday night and on weekends. ⊠*Faubourg St-Paul 38* ☎*064/33–61–86* ⊕*www.brasserielabinchoise.be* ⊠*Tour €3* ⊗*Tour by reservation only. Restaurant Fri.–Sun.*

ALSO WORTH SEEING

★ The **Domaine de Mariemont** started out in the early 17th century as a hunting park for Mary of Hungary. A few castles were built here over the centuries, each destroyed by war or fire; now the keystone building is a modern museum with rich art and archaeology exhibits. The collec-tion spans Greco-Roman and Egyptian artifacts, Asian decorative arts, and interests closer to home (Tournai porcelain, local archaeological finds). Don't miss Rodin's statue of the *Burghers of Calais,* one of a few that were cast during the artist's lifetime. Save some time to wan-der through the park—it's beautifully laid out, dotted with sculptures and picturesque 18th-century castle ruins. You can get an audioguide in English for the museum and park. ⊠*chaussée de Mariemont, off N59, 5 mi (8 km) north of Binche, near Morlanwelz* ☎*064/21–21–93* ⊕*www.musee-mariemont.be* ⊠*€4* ⊗*Oct.–Mar., Tues.–Sun. 10–5; Apr.–Sept., Tues.–Sun. 10–6.*

CHIMAY

50 km (30 mi) south of Charleroi, 122 km (76 mi) south of Brussels.

The boot-shaped Botte du Hainaut region is rich in wooded valleys, villages, châteaux, and lakes. Towns here are small and untouristy. At the bottom of the "botte" is Chimay, a small town where time seems to have come to a standstill, but which still has a few surprises up its sleeve. It has a château, a mostly 16th-century church, a nearby mon-astery, decorous classical music concerts—and a racetrack for car and motorcycle races (June through August). Chimay was also the home of Froissart, the 14th-century historian whose chronicles furnished the background information for many of Shakespeare's plays.

Hainaut Festivals

In addition to its heavenly Trappist beers, the Botte du Hainaut, the boot-shaped region south of Charleroi, is known for its extravagant annual festivals. Two of the most popular, the Carnaval de Binche and the Ducasse de Mons, draw crowds into the hundreds of thousands. If you happen to be in Belgium during one of the festivals, they're worth a day trip from Brussels.

The **Carnaval de Binche** is said to have been sparked by a week of festivities held for the visit of Charles V in 1549. Today, the carnival is taken very seriously by the Binchois and there are strict rules of conduct. The festivities begin on the Sunday before Ash Wednesday, when hundreds of men turn out in costumes, some as *mam'zelles* (in belle epoque women's clothing) and many as *gilles*. Only the most upstanding residents whose families have lived in Binche for generations can be gilles—the signature figures of the Carnaval. They're costumed in identically smooth, mustached masks, green glasses, and large white decorative collars. Two days of music and partying later, at dawn on Mardi Gras, a solitary drummer marches to the home of the head gille to escort him out into the street. They dance to the home of the next gille and so on until there are perhaps 100 men doing a slow, shuffling dance to the ancient tunes of the musicians who, like the gilles, gradually join the procession. They troop down to the *hôtel de ville* to be welcomed by the burgomaster, and reappear after lunch in enormous ostrich-plumed hats to toss out oranges to the crowds, then gather in the Grand'Place for music and dancing. The day ends with fireworks, but the gilles continue dancing through the night. Traditionally, they drink nothing but champagne.

You can get a taste of the spirit of the Carnaval at the **Musée International du Carnaval et du Masque,** which has an impressive collection of masks and costumes from all over the world. You can see a video of Binche's own Carnaval—as well as watch people working on the next year's costumes. ✉ *rue du St-Moustier 10* ☎ *064/33–57–41* ⊕ *www.museedumasque.be* 💶 *€5* ⊙ *Tues.–Fri. 9:30–5, weekends 10:30–5.*

Every June, Mons (16 km [10 mi] west of Binche) bursts at the seams with revelers during its annual festival, the **Ducasse de Mons.** Begun in the 14th century by grateful souls who survived a plague, the Ducasse is so exuberant that the local church officials asked that it not be celebrated during the Easter religious observances. The festival is a hodge-podge of events. It's officially opened with the Descente, which presents the relics of St. Waudru to the burgomaster. The relics are paraded through town on an ornate 18th-century carriage, which is then pushed up a sloping street, a massive effort called the Montée du Car d'Or, to return to the saint's namesake church. Symbolically, Mons is thus reestablished. The Combat de la Lumeçon, an enactment of the story of St. George and the dragon, is the highlight of the festival; it's held on the Grand'Place. The dragon's tail is topped off with a horsehair switch that brings good luck to the reveler who grabs it. But first, you have to get past the dragon's guards. St. George then finishes off the beast. Concerts, carillons, and fireworks keep the city buzzing for several days.

GETTING HERE & AROUND

There is no train station near Chimay, so you'll need to drive. From Brussels, drive to the city of Charleroi via the A54 and then take the N5 to Couvin, where you'll turn right to get on the N99. Close to Chimay, turn left on the rue des Juifs and follow this road through the woods for another 7½ km (5 mi) before reaching the abbey.

VISITING & TASTING

ABBEY **Notre-Dame de Scourmont.** The monks of this Trappist monastery (established in 1850) produce some of the best cheese and tastiest, most potent beer in Belgium. Chimay is commonly praised for its blue and red beers, colors referring not only to the label, but also to the beer itself. Red Chimay is deep red and tastes soft and fruity; its blue counterpart has a dark brown appearance, and its full, rich flavor continues to evolve through the years. They also make five different kinds of cheese. Although the abbey is not open to the public, except for retreats, you can visit the church and the gardens, where an enclosed cemetery holds the graves of former monks. ⊠ *About 7½ km (5 mi) south of Chimay* ☎ *060/21–03–27* ⊙ *Church and gardens daily 8–8; Tues.–Fri. tour at 10.*

WHERE TO DRINK

The Abbey's beer and cheese, as well as other local products can be tasted in the nearby **Auberge de Poteaupré.** Less than half a mile from the Abbey, this café and restaurant accommodates up to 260 people and has seven rooms for €100 per night. ⊠ *rue de Poteaupre* ☎ *061/21–14–33* ⊕ *www.chimay.be.*

ALSO WORTH SEEING

Château de Chimay. The château became the home of Madame Tallien, a great beauty who was known to revolutionary France as Notre Dame de Thermidor. She narrowly escaped the guillotine, married her protector, Citizen Tallien, and persuaded him to instigate the overthrow of Robespierre. Eventually, she was again married, to François-Joseph Caraman, prince of Chimay, and ended her days in peace and dignity as mistress of the Château de Chimay. The warrant for her arrest, signed by Robespierre, is preserved at the château, along with other French memorabilia, such as the baptismal robe worn by Napoléon's son, the king of Rome. There's also a florid rococo theater, designed after the theater in Fontainebleau. A château tour (available in English and French) is conducted by Princess Elizabeth, mother of the current prince of Chimay, Philippe. ⊠ *rue du Château* ☎ *060/21–28–23* ⊡ *€6* ⊙ *Guided tours Easter–Sept. at 10, 11, 3, and 4; otherwise by appointment.*

Where to Stay & Eat

✕**Hostellerie Le Virelles.** North of Chimay, in the open greenery around the Etang de Virelles, this wonderful old country inn offers simple, regional cooking in a pretty, well-weathered beam-and-copper setting. You can have trout or try the more ambitious, multicourse menu based on regional freshwater fish and game. The restaurant is closed on Wednesday and for dinner on Tuesday. The seven rooms ($), all named after field flowers, are simple, cozy, and inexpensive at €62, breakfast included. The adjacent nature reserve is great for long walks. ⊠ *rue du Lac 28, Virelles, near Chimay* ☎ *060/21–28–03* 🖃 *AE, DC, MC, V.*

🏨**Les Ardillières du Pont d'Oye.** In a beautiful, lake-dotted valley, this first-class inn ($$$) promises quiet, outdoor activities, and first-rate cuisine. You can practice your cast in the private fishing area or refine your game with the giant, outdoor chess set. The restaurant, Les Forges du Pont d'Oye ($$$$), serves fresh, inventive meals prepared by chefs (and brothers) Richard and Jean-Luc Thiry. One menu is entirely devoted to truffles. Specialties include oven-roasted pigeon and cabbage cannelloni, flavored with herbs from the garden. Some of the spacious, contemporary guest rooms have a view of the fountain; others overlook the garden. ⊠ *rue du Pont d'Oye 6, Habay-la-Neuve* ✛ *25 km (16 mi) east of Orval* ☎ *063/42–22–43* ⊕ *www.lesforges. be* 🖃 *AE, DC, MC, V* ⊘ *No lunch Tues. and Wed.*

🏨**Château du Pont-d'Oye.** Loll in the lap of luxury at this glorious 17th-century château ($$), which used to belong to the infamous Mar-

quise de Pont d'Oye, who reportedly spent her fortune on the grand balls she regularly held at the château. Each individually decorated room has oil paintings, chandeliers, thick drapes, and regal red carpets. There's a wooden chapel on the first floor, and beyond it fragrant rose gardens. The daily specials at the restaurant ($$$–$$$$; closed Mon.) could include foie gras, oysters, lobster, or quail with truffles. This hideaway can fill up quickly, so it's wise to book well in advance. Pension plans are a good deal here, but the restaurant is closed for dinner on Sunday. ⊠ *rue du Pont d'Oye 1, Habay-la-Neuve* ✛ *25 km (16 mi) east of Orval* ☎ *063/42–01–30* ⊕ *www.chateaudupontdoye.be* ⇦ *18 rooms* 🖃 *AE, MC, V.*

🏨**Jackson's Hotel.** In a modern building opposite the hospital—where you can park free on weekends—and a five-minute walk from the town center, Jackson's is pleasant, modest lodging ($) for the budget-minded. You'll find charming owners, a quiet environment, and simple, comfortable rooms (with floral-pattern curtains and bedspreads that may not be to everyone's taste). ⊠ *Brusselsestraat 110–112, Leuven* ☎ *016/20–24–92* 🖃 *AE, DC, MC, V.*

🏨**Les Volets Verts.** A converted house in the center of Binche, this friendly B&B (¢) has a warm, genteel living room and a shared garden. The four comfortable rooms can sleep from one to three people. Breakfast in the beautiful salon costs €5 more. ⊠ *rue de la Triperie 4, Binche* ☎ *064/33–31–47* ⊕ *www.lvv.net* 🖃 *No credit cards.*

Historic
Battlegrounds

WORD OF MOUTH

"We recently spent 6 nights in Belgium, and it was wonderful. We started in the little but gorgeous town of Dinant, near Bastogne, and visited the WWII monuments there. We drove, which was easy. Then 2 days in Brussels and 2 days in Bruges. Magnifique! "

—Maria_G

"Are you planning to visit the Ardennes, Bastogne, Malmedy and other sites associated with the WW2 Battle of the Bulge? I was especially interested in one of the memorials as it had my father's division listed. He was wounded in the Battle of the Ardennes. It was a very moving experience even if you know no one who fought there."

—aieger

Updated
by Cillian
Donnelly

DURING THE 20TH CENTURY, TINY Belgium was dragged not once, but twice into a conflict between the Great Powers of Europe, causing hundreds of thousands of casualties on its soil and suffering to millions of civilians. In 1914 the Allies halted the German offensive in the Western corner of the country, where soldiers from both sides dug themselves in for a trench war that lasted four years. Thirty years later, the Second World War took a decisive turn on the opposite side of the country. While major Belgian towns, harbors, and railway stations were being bombed, the last German offensive was brought to a halt in the small Ardennes village of Bastogne after the Battle of the Bulge, a bloody conflict in which many foreign (mainly American) soldiers gave their lives. Many reminders of both periods can still be seen and visited, from Flanders Fields to the slopes of the Ardennes.

WORLD WAR I

In 1914, neutral Belgium was forced into the Great War when the Germans invaded France from the north. They left a trail of destruction and atrocities throughout the country, before they were finally halted by Belgian, French, and English soldiers in Westhoek, the western corner of Flanders. It was here, on the front line forming a "bulge" (in military terms, a salient) around the city of Ieper, that almost half a million people died during a battle that lasted four years. It was the sad culmination of Flanders's bloody history, which started in 1302, when Flemish peasants defeated the French near Kortrijk, a victory still commemorated annually on July 11th.

Although only the Westhoek was left unoccupied during the First World War, the trenches dividing both sides stretched from Nieuwpoort at the North Sea, along the river IJzer, towards the city of Ieper, crossing the French border near Mesen (Messines).

Nowadays, the peaceful "plat pays," the flat countryside that haunted singer Jacques Brel's imagination, still carries the scars of that gruesome period. Every year, farmers still dig up more than 200 tons of ammunition from the fields. Monuments and memorial stones pay honor to those who gave their lives in Flanders fields, where "the poppies blow / Between the crosses, row on row / That mark our place," as Canadian army doctor John McCrae wrote in 1915. British, Canadian, Australian, and New Zealander soldiers are buried in 173 Commonwealth cemeteries around Ieper; German casualties are gathered in four graveyards; Belgians and French rest in peace in many local graveyards. Every evening at 8 at the Menin gate in Ieper, the Last Post sounds in their honor, keeping the memory of the darkest period in Flanders's history very much alive.

GREAT ITINERARIES

IF YOU HAVE 1 DAY
If you only have a day in the area, you should focus on Ieper and its surroundings. A visit to the **In Flanders Fields Museum** is the perfect introduction to this region's history. Take a walk through the city, lingering in the Grote Markt to view the Belfort, the Town Hall, and the nearby St. Martin's Cathedral. Don't forget to visit **St. George's Memorial Church** before heading for Zillebeke to see the remaining craters and trenches at **Kasteelhof 't Hooge.** Your next stop should be the **Memorial Museum Passchendaele 1917** in the center of Zonnebeke and the breathtaking **Tyne Cot** cemetery in Passendale. If you have

time, visit some other cemeteries in the area—but be sure to get back to the Menin gate in Ieper by 8 PM to witness the **Last Post.**

IF YOU HAVE 2 DAYS
Follow the above itinerary on the first day and spend the night in Ieper. On the second day, go a little farther afield, visiting **Talbot House** in Poperinge and the war memorials in **Diksmuide,** such as the **IJzertoren** and the **Dodengang.** From there, if you have time, you might wind down by heading for the coast (a 15-km [9-mi] drive). You might also visit the city of Kortrijk, which contains the Groeningeabdij Museum with its reminders of still older battles.

EXPLORING

GETTING AROUND
Traveling by train or bus is not feasible, since connections are slow and most sites are scattered around the countryside. Although many places of interest are centered around Ieper, you'll need a car to visit anywhere else. Tourist offices in all major towns can provide brochures with road maps.

ON FOOT If you limit your visit to Ieper and its immediate surroundings, you'll just need good walking shoes or a bike. The tourist office (in Ieper's Lakenhallen) will be happy to get you started on one of the many walking tours in the area.

ORGANIZED TOURS
Several companies in Ieper offer guided minibus tours through the region, ranging from basic day trips for €20 to more elaborate itineraries that include meals or accommodation. From Brugge, two companies (Quasimodo and Daytours) provide trips to the battlefield region. *(For more information see Tours in Essentials.)*

SELF-GUIDED TOURS
DRIVING ROUTES The 82-km (51-mi) In Flanders Fields Route starts in the heart of Ieper and guides you to all major places of interest. So does the IJzerfront Route, which starts in Diksmuide for a 79-km (49-mi) trip along the former front line. Blue signposts along the well-kept roads show you the way.

BIKE TOURS   The Vredesfietsroute (Peace Biking Tour) will take you on a 45-km (28-mi) trip around Ieper, toward the cemeteries in Passendale and Langemark. Bikes can be rented at the railway station on the René Colaertplein Jeugdstation in the 16 Leopold III-laan.

VISITOR INFORMATION

All of the city and regional tourist offices in Flanders have English-speaking staff. Those in the Flanders Fields region tend to be open on weekdays and one weekend day; the Ieper office, for instance, is open every day but Saturday. An area Web site, **www.toerismewesthoek.be**, includes English-language information on cycling and driving routes, local attractions, and links to World War I sites.

IEPER

124 km (77 mi) west of Brussels; 81 km (50 mi) southwest of Gent; 71 km (44 mi) southwest of Brugge.

Known as the Ypres of World War I infamy, "Wipers" to the Tommies in the trenches, and Ieper (pronounced *eeper*) to the locals, this town was the Hiroshima of the Great War. Founded in the 10th century as a popular stop on the Brugge–Paris trade route, Ieper's textile industry helped it expand into one of the region's major mercantile centers during the Middle Ages. Epidemics, sieges, repressions, and strife took their toll, and the cloth makers packed their bags in the 16th and 17th centuries. Ieper then became a quiet convent town, the seat of a bishopric, but was drawn into the crossfire of World War I three centuries later.

There were four major battles at Ieper; in the second (1915), the German army introduced a new weapon, poison gas, while the third (1917) was a particularly infamous disaster of roiling mud and horrifying casualties in which the Allies gained only a few kilometers. In the last battle in 1918, the Allies decisively broke through the German lines, finally securing the western front. Completely destroyed in the war, modern Ieper is a painstaking reconstruction of major medieval buildings—the last were laid in the 1960s. The city proudly stands as homage to the spirit of the Flemings, and to the memory of the soldiers who fell in the surrounding fields and who lie in the vast cemeteries spreading over the flat polder plains.

GETTING HERE & AROUND

From Brugge, take the E403 highway towards Kortrijk, where you get on the A19 (direction Ieper); take exit 4, and follow the N37 to the city center. If you're coming from Gent, follow the E17 towards Kortrijk and Rijsel (aka Lille, in France); south of Kortrijk, jump on the E403 (direction Brugge) for 6 km (4 mi) and take the A19 as described above. From Brussels, take the E40 towards Gent, and at the crossroads in Zwijnaarde, follow directions from Gent as described above. Hourly direct trains from Brussels get you to Ieper in 1 hour and 45 minutes. There are hourly trains from Gent and Brugge as well, but as you have to change in Kortrijk, the trip takes over an hour.

2

ESSENTIALS

Taxis **Kristof Demey** (✉*Klerkenstraat 134, Ieper* ☎*057/48–80–88*). **Taxi Leo** (✉*Dikkebusweg 37, Ieper* ☎*057/20–04–13*)

Visitor Info Ieper (✉*Stadhuis, Grote Markt 34* ☎*057/23–92–20* ⊕*www.ieper.be*).

WHAT TO SEE

Fodor'sChoice ★ The powerful interactive displays in the **In Flanders Fields Museum** preserve the terrors of trench warfare and the memory of those who died in nearby fields. The museum focuses on World War I, but expands to the universal theme of war. Computer screens, sound effects, scale models, and videos realistically portray the weapons, endless battles, and numerous casualties of the area's wars. Each visitor receives a "smart card" with details of a soldier or civilian and follows that person's fortunes throughout the war. The museum is housed on the second floor of the magnificent Lakenhallen (Cloth Hall) on the Grote Markt, a copy of the original 1304 building. If you climb the 264 steps in the square belfry, the view of turrets, towns, and fields seems endless. There are smart cards and other information in English. The museum also maintains casualty databases, which can be used by the public. ✉*Grote Markt 34* ☎*057/23–92–20* ⊕*www.inflandersfields.be* 💶*€8* ⊙*Apr. 1–Nov. 15 daily 10–6; Nov. 16– Mar. 31, Tues.–Sun. 10–5.*

St. George's Memorial Church, a small Anglican church built between 1927 and 1929, contains furnishings, decorations, and memorabilia from both world wars. Note the colorful kneelers decorated with the badges of historic regiments. Although this church is often visited as if it were a museum, remember that it is also a space for contemplation. ✉*Elverdingsestraat 1* ☎*057/21–56–85.*

Fodor'sChoice ★ About 100 yards east of the Grote Markt, the **Menenpoort** is among the most moving of war memorials. It was built near the old Menin gate, along the route Allied soldiers took toward the front line. Troops on the "Menin road" endured brutal, insistent German artillery attacks; one section was dubbed "Hellfire Corner." After World War I, the British built the vast arch in memory of the 300,000 soldiers who perished in this corridor. The names of some 55,000 soldiers who died before August 15, 1917, and whose bodies were missing, are inscribed. Since 1928, every night at 8, traffic is stopped at the Menin gate as the **Last Post** is blown on silver bugles, gifts of the British Legion. The practice was interrupted during World War II, but it was resumed the night Polish troops liberated the town, September 6, 1944. Be sure to witness this truly breathtaking experience ✉*Menenstraat.*

ANNUAL EVENTS

A walking memorial event, **Vierdaagse van de IJzer** (⊕*www.vierdaagse. be*), or Four Days of the IJzer River, organized by the Belgian Army, occurs in the third week of August. Thousands of people walk for four days in the IJzer area to commemorate the victims of the First World War.

During the first weekend of August the **Folkfestival Dranouter** (⊕*www. folkdranouter.be*) settles down in the charming village of Dranouter, 20 km (12 mi) southwest of Ieper and close to the French border. Started

in 1975, it has gradually broadened its horizons to include rock and world music, welcoming artists like Lou Reed, Ry Cooder, and Marianne Faithfull. While in Dranouter, you can visit **The Bloody Fields of Flanders** (⊠ *Dikkebusstraat 234* ☎ *057/44–69–33* ⊕ *www.bloodyfields offlanders.be* ⬛ *€6* ⊙ *Wed.–Fri. 10–6, Sat.–Sun. 11–6*), a museum about war and music in the Westhoek region.

ON A LIGHTER NOTE   The **Kattestoet** *(Festival of the Cats)* is one of Europe's most fanciful celebrations, held on the second Sunday in May in even-numbered years. A town jester throws hundreds of velvet cats from Ieper's town belfry, a custom originating centuries ago when "Cat Wednesday" marked the final day of the annual market. Until 1817, live cats were tossed to symbolize the expulsion of evil spirits, but animal lovers prevailed. Now the Kattestoet is a happy tradition, with a parade, flags flying, coats of arms displayed, and feline giants Cieper and Minneke Poes as special guests.

ZILLEBEKE

6 km (4 mi) east of Ieper.

Maple Avenue, in the tiny village of Zillebeke (which is actually part of Ieper), formed the Canadian front line in 1916. After the war, the avenue was planted with maples in remembrance of the many Canadians who fell here.

GETTING HERE & AROUND
It's hard to miss Hooge Crater when biking or driving to Menen on the N8. Hill 62 is a bit farther down a side street of the same road.

WHAT TO SEE
Kasteelhof 't Hooge is one of the few places where bomb craters can still be seen. Some of them are part of the hotel gardens *(see Where to Stay & Eat)*.

A museum, **Hooge Crater 1914–18,** has been installed in the old chapel. Items on display include bombs, grenades, rifles, and uniforms. More than 6,500 British soldiers lie in the cemetery across the street. ⊠ *Meenseweg 467* ☎ *057/46–84–46* ⬛ *€2* ⊙ *Feb.–mid-Dec., Tues.–Sun. 10–7.*

Follow the signs via Canadalaan and Sanctuary Wood to **Hill 62,** an old-fashioned museum and dusty café. In addition to photographs, weapons, and assorted objects salvaged from the battlefield, the owner has preserved some of the original trenches on his land. They were part of a tunnel complex that stretched from the coast at Nieuwpoort to the French-Swiss border (at least 600 km [400 mi]). The ground is muddy even on sunny days, so you might need boots to inspect them. ⊠ *Canadalaan* ☎ *057/46–63–73* ⬛ *€2.95* ⊙ *Daily 9:30–6.*

PASSENDALE & ZANDVOORDE

11 km (7 mi) west of Ieper on N38.

2

Passendale and Zandvoorde are two of the five villages east of Ieper that constitute the municipality of Zonnebeke, which also encompasses Beselare, Geluveld, and Zonnebeke proper. As peaceful as they may look nowadays, tucked away between the endless fields, these villages were ravaged during the heyday of the Great War. It is here that British and French troops halted the Germans in 1914. The area endured four major battles, the use of poison gas, deadly bombardments, and thousands of casualties. From July through November 1917, British troops gained 8 km (5 mi) at the cost of 500,000 men. Almost a century after the war, farmers still turn up a few shells every month, and bomb-disposal experts often have to be called. Five cemeteries, thirteen monuments, and numerous remembrance plaques are silent reminders of this bloody period in Europe's history.

GETTING HERE & AROUND

It's easy to get lost in the crisscross of roads east of Ieper—but by doing so, you'll stumble upon many reminders of the war period. The surest way is to follow the N332, which will take you straight to the center of Zonnebeke. Tyne Cot (in Passendale) is 3 km (2 mi) farther; continue on the N332, take a left onto the N303, and left again after 1 km (½ mi) onto a small winding road.

ESSENTIALS

Visitor Info Zonnebeke (Passendale) (⊠ *Ieperstraat 5* ☎ *051/77-04-41* ⊕ *www.zonnebeke.be*).

WHAT TO SEE

★ With 12,000 graves, **Tyne Cot,** a British cemetery near Passchendaele (as Passendale is written in old Flemish), is the largest and best known of more than 170 military cemeteries in the area. In its awe-inspiring austerity, it evokes the agony of anonymous and unknown losses. A significant majority of the graves here are for unidentified casualties, and a curving wall lists the names of nearly 35,000 Commonwealth soldiers killed after August 1917 whose bodies and graves vanished in the turmoil of war. A large cross stands atop one of the German pillbox bunkers for which the site was named; British troops trying to gain the ridge dubbed it a cot, or cottage.

Even though **Buttes Cemetery and Polygon Wood Cemetery,** close to the center of Zonnebeke, have fewer graves, they are no less impressive. The former, which used to be a drill ground, contains the graves of British, Australian, and New Zealand soldiers. The wood across the street, where the latter, smaller cemetery is situated, was completely destroyed during the war.

Fodor's Choice
★ Also in Zonnebeke is the **Memorial Museum Passchendaele 1917,** a must-see. Opened in 2004, it houses the largest public collection of First World War memorabilia in western Flanders. Weapons, uniforms, documents, and photographs re-create the tragedy of the Third Battle of

Ieper. You can even smell the different poison gasses that were used. The cellar holds a realistic reconstruction of a dugout, a subterranean camp that lodged soldiers during the war; it was, according to one of them, "one of the most disgusting places I ever lived in." The museum is planning several events to commemorate the 90th anniversary of the battle of Ieper in 2007. Check the Web site for more details. ⊠ *Ieper-straat 5, Zonnebeke* ☎ *051/77–04–41* ⊕ *www.passchendaele.be* ⌷ *€5* ☾ *Feb.–Nov., daily 10–6.*

In the village of Zandvoorde, 10 km (6 mi) south of Zonnebeke, are the well-kept remains of a German command bunker. It was built in 1916 and has six chilling rooms. The modest **Zantvoorde British Cemetery,** the final resting place of 1,583 men, is nearby. A memorial plaque on the Zandvoordeplaats reminds visitors that world-famous singer Jacques Brel was originally from Zandvoorde.

The largest **German military cemetery** in Western Europe can be found on the northeastern edge of the city of Menen, close to the French border. Almost 48,000 dead are honored here with simple memorial stones. From Ieper, take the N8 to the center of Menen and follow the N32 towards Roeselare; the first street on the right will lead you to the Groenestraat and the cemetery.

POPERINGE

11 km (7 mi) west of Ieper on N38.   ·

During the war, the only part of Belgium not occupied by the Germans was a small area in the southwest corner of West-Vlaanderen (West Flanders). Here, in the quiet provincial town of Poperinge, the British Army set up its headquarters, accommodating up to 200,000 men. The city has some 200 hectares of hops-growing fields in its surroundings, making it the hops capital of the country. *(See Chapter 1, Belgian Beer for more information.)*

GETTING HERE & AROUND
Poperinge is a short drive from Ieper on the N38, a straight, four-lane road through fields and small villages.

ESSENTIALS
Visitor Info Poperinge (⊠ *Stadhuis, Markt 1* ☎ *057/33–40–81* ⊕ *www.poperinge.be*).

WHAT TO SEE
In Poperinge, you'll find a rare sanctuary for combatants in World War I. The **Talbot House** was founded by Anglican priest "Tubby" Clayton and named after the younger brother of army chaplain Neville Talbot, who died in action in 1915. The mansion provided an opportunity for soldiers to get together behind the front line, regardless of rank, for mutual support and comradeship. During the war, part of the house was used for CONCERT PARTIES—opportunities for soldiers to dance and party. Photographs and art by soldier-artists are displayed, and there's a film of a staged Concert Party, but the attic chapel, where everything

remains preserved as it was, is the best place to experience the original atmosphere. Talbot House's fame spread even to the Germans, to whom it became known as a symbol of peace. ⊠ *Gasthuisstraat 43* ☎ *057/33–32–28* ⊕ *www.talbothouse.be* ☒ *€8* ⊘ *Closed Mon.*

DIKSMUIDE

23 km (15 mi) north of Ieper on N369.

Like Ieper, Diksmuide was completely destroyed during the First World War and rebuilt in its original style, which you can savor best from the Grote Markt, the spacious square flanked by brick-gabled buildings and dominated by the huge, spired St. Niklaaskerk. Even more impressive is the IJzertoren (Iron Tower) war memorial, originally from 1930, but blown up in 1946 by the resistance who regarded it as a symbol of Flemish collaboration during the Second World War.

GETTING HERE & AROUND

When leaving Ieper, cross the N38 (which leads to Poperinge to the west and Kortrijk to the east) and head for the N369. It follows the canal for 4 km (2½ mi) and then cuts through rural Flanders towards Diksmuide. Trains are not an option, but regular bus service connects both towns.

ESSENTIALS

Visitor Info Diksmuide (⊠ *Grote Markt 28* ☎ *051/51–91–46* ⊕ *www.diksmuide. be*).

WHAT TO SEE

The **IJzertoren,** a 275-foot tower, was rebuilt in 1965 to honor defenders and casualties from both world wars and represents the Flemish struggle for autonomy. The giant letters on the monument (AVV-VVK) mean "Everything for Flanders, Flanders for Christ." Flemish nationalists gather here in August for the yearly IJzerbedevaart (IJzer Pilgrimage). The 22-story tower houses a museum chronicling the two wars and the emancipation of Flanders using images, text, and sound. The top floor and the roof provide a splendid view of the entire area. In May, the two-day Ten Vrede (Go for Peace) concert draws musicians from all over the world. ⊠ *2 km (1 mi) southwest of Diksmuide* ☎ *051/50–02–86* ⊕ *www.ijzertoren.org* ☒ *€7* ⊘ *Apr.–Sept., daily 10–6; Oct.–Mar., daily 10–5.*

Two kilometers (1 mi) northwest of town you can visit the so-called **Dodengang** *(Trench of Death),* a network of trenches on the banks of the IJzer river where Belgian troops faced and held off their German adversaries for four years. It's a 20-minute walk or a short drive from the city center. Follow the N35 in the direction of Nieuwpoort, but turn right immediately after crossing the bridge over the IJzer. Make sure to dress warmly on a cold day, as the wind tends to add some extra drama by howling across the plain. ⊠ *IJzerdijk 65* ☎ *051/50–53–44* ☒ *Free* ⊘ *Apr. 1–Nov. 15, daily 10–4:30; Nov. 16–Mar. 31, Tues. and Fri 9:30–4.*

The **Vladslo German Military Cemetery** reminds visitors that the "other side" suffered terribly, as well. The bodies of 25,644 men rest here, watched over by Parents In Mourning, a sculpture by German artist Käthe Kollwitz. Kollwitz's son, who fell in 1914, is buried in front of the sculpture. The memorial is 5 km (3 mi) outside Diksmuide, on the road between the villages of Esen and Beerst.

WORLD WAR I SITES OUTSIDE FLANDERS

LONCIN

Everything at the **Fort de Loncin** has remained as it was at 5:15 PM on August 16, 1914, when a German shell scored a direct hit, killing most of the garrison. Guided tours are led from April through September on the first and third Sundays of the month at 2 PM. ✉ *Rue des Héros 15 bis, Loncin* ☎ *04/246–4425* 💶 *€5* 🕐 *Apr.–Sept., Wed.–Sun. 10–6; Oct.–Mar., Wed.–Sun. 10–4.*

GETTING HERE & AROUND

10 km (6 mi) west of Liège; 92 km (57 mi) east of Brussels.

From Brussels, take the E40 highway, get off at exit 31, and turn right onto the N3 in the direction of Liège; the fort will be on your left after 2 km (1 mi). From Liège, follow the N3 toward Sint-Truiden (St-Tronc) for about 10 km (6 mi); the fort will be on your right.

MONS

Mons, near Binche in the Hainaut region, became a flashpoint in World War I. It was here that the British Expeditionary Force first battled the Germans in August 1914. The British were outnumbered more than two to one but briefly held off the German army, before retreating and joining the French for the successful Battle of the Marne. These British troops came to be known as the "Old Contemptibles," tweaking Kaiser Wilhelm II's alleged assessment of their "contemptible little army." In World War II, further destruction was wrought by a running battle between advancing American troops and the retreating Germans.

WORLD WAR II

Although it had declared itself neutral yet again, Belgium was invaded yet again by the Germans in May 1940. It took a mere 18 days to force King Leopold III to surrender. Thousands of soldiers fled overseas to England, and some citizens managed to reach the unoccupied part of France, but most inhabitants were trapped. Food was scarce and rations strict. Dissidents, Jews, and resistance fighters were locked up in transit camps before being deported. The sinister Breendonk Fort, near Willebroek, where hundreds of people were tortured and killed, is a reminder of that period.

During the last months of the war, German V-1 and V-2 rockets as well as Allied bombs fiercely struck Belgian cities such as Antwerp and Leuven, demolishing ports, railway stations, and roads. However, the province to suffer most during Hitler's last offensive was Luxembourg.

In December 1944, nearly 77,000 American and 82,000 German soldiers were wounded or killed on the gentle slopes and in the dense forests of the Ardennes.

THE BATTLE OF THE BULGE

Although often attributed to German Commander in Chief von Runstedt, it was Hitler himself who came up with the plan for *Wacht am Rhein,* as the Germans call the Battle of the Bulge. Three German armies were to surprise the Allied troops in southeastern Belgium with a blitz offensive through the supposedly impenetrable forests of the Ardennes. Their goal was to prevent the transport of troop reinforcements and supplies, cut off the British army from the American army, force their surrender, and obtain a peace treaty on the western front. German troops would then move to Russia to concentrate on the eastern front. The plan was to reach the river Meuse near Liège within 48 hours, move on towards Namur and Brussels, and eventually take the port of Antwerp.

The attack started at 5:30 AM on December 16, 1944 and came as a complete surprise to the outnumbered Allied forces. The American units were shattered and defenses were penetrated at several points. To make things worse, about 1,500 Germans disguised as Americans caused confusion, and bad weather made Allied air strikes impossible.

The small city of Bastogne became a turning point in the Battle of the Bulge. German tanks surrounded it on December 20, trapping civilians and American soldiers. General Eisenhower ordered a counterattack, and within eight days 240,000 men were deployed to the region, eventually turning the tide. The weather cleared, allowing the Allies to bomb German strongholds and deliver supplies. By the end of December, the German tank divisions finally began their withdrawal, but it would be another month until the battle was finally won.

EXPLORING

Due to the large distances between the major sites, traveling by car or motor bike (as many do) is the best way to visit the Ardennes and its World War II relics. Bus connections are time-consuming and intricate, trains are scarce, and biking on the steep slopes is only an option if you are (or still feel like) a true athlete.

BASTOGNE

34 km (20 mi) south of La Roche-en-Ardenne, 88 km (53 mi) south of Liège, 148 km (89 mi) southeast of Brussels.

Bastogne is where General McAuliffe delivered World War II's most famous response to a surrender request: "Nuts!" Although a number of Ardennes towns were destroyed during the Battle of the Bulge, Bastogne was the epicenter.

McAuliffe's American 101st division reached Bastogne on December 19, 1944, one day before General Von Manteuffel's tanks surrounded it. The town was under constant attack, and the miserable weather made it impossible for supplies to be flown in. On December 22, the Germans asked the U.S. forces to surrender. They refused. On Christmas Eve, the defenders were close to a defeat, but relief was near. The American 42nd tank division, led by General-Major Gaffey, broke through the German lines. The next day, General Patton managed to safeguard a small corridor through the German lines toward the town. On December 26 the skies cleared and supplies were flown in, but it was another month before the last German stronghold was destroyed. To this day, a Sherman tank occupies a place of honor in the town square, named after General McAuliffe himself.

GETTING HERE & AROUND
There is no public transportation from the city center to any of the monuments. If you don't have a car, you can take a taxi or walk about 2½ mi. It is possible to visit these sights in an army jeep. Contact Willy's Jeep Tour (☎063/60–10–75). Tours cost €40.

From Liège, take the E25 towards Luxembourg and get off at exit 53. From Brussels, take the E411 and switch to the N4 at exit 18. This two-lane road leads straight to Bastogne. There is regular train service to Bastogne from most major cities, as well as bus service from major Walloon cities.

ESSENTIALS
Visitor Info Bastogne (✉ *pl. MacAuliffe 60* ☎ *061/21–27–11* ⊕ *www.bastogne-tourisme.be*).

WHAT TO SEE
The **Colline du Mardasson** *(Mardasson Hill Memorial)* honors the Americans lost in the Battle of the Bulge. The names of all U.S. Army units and the history of the battle are inscribed on the wall, along with a simple phrase in Latin: "The Belgian people remember their American liberators." Mosaics by Fernand Léger decorate the crypt's Protestant, Catholic, and Jewish chapels. From the top of the memorial you have a magnificent view of the former battlegrounds. The Colline is open all year.

The **Bastogne Historical Center,** next to the memorial monument, is built in the shape of a five-point star and is filled with uniforms, weapons, and commentary from and about World War II. Moreover, there are several American and German military vehicles, such as an authentic Harley-Davidson and a Zündapp from the Deutsche Wehrmacht. In the adjacent mini-theater, a 30-minute film in English with original footage evokes the dark December days of 1944. ✉*N84, 3 km (2 mi) east of Bastogne* ☎*061/21–14–13* ⊕*www.bastognehistoricalcenter. be* ☞*€8.50* ✿*Mar.–Dec., daily 10–4:30; Jan. and Feb. by appointment only.*

LA ROCHE-EN-ARDENNE

29 km (18 mi) north of Bastogne, 77 km (46 mi) south of Liège, 127 km (76 mi) southeast of Brussels.

The nickname "Pearl of the Ardennes" refers to La Roche's beautiful surroundings, not to the town itself. It was leveled by 70,000 shells during the Battle of the Bulge. La Roche was rebuilt quickly after the war and has become a busy tourist resort. Cafés, restaurants, and hotels line the street along the Ourthe river. On weekends and in summer they're filled with tourists taking a break from hiking, biking, skiing, or kayaking in the area.

The town shelters below the ruins of the 9th-century medieval château that stands on the hill above it. A tiny cobblestone alley from place du Marché takes you there. Admission to the site is €2.50.

In summer, the ghost of Berthe, a woman of local legend, supposedly appears at sunset.

GETTING HERE & AROUND
From Bastogne, the N834 runs through the Ardennes forest towards La Roche. From Liège, take the E25 towards Luxembourg and get off at exit 50. La Roche is another 17 km (11 mi) along the charming N89. From Brussels, take the E411 in the direction of Namur and Luxembourg; jump on the N4 at exit 18 and drive to Marche-en-Famenne; there follow the bendy N888, which will take you through the woods to La Roche. There is regular train service to La Roche from Liège and Namur; the trip takes 90 minutes, including a switch once in Ottignies.

WHAT TO SEE
A walk through the town, which is no more than a handful of small streets, immediately reminds you of La Roche's violent past. An American Pershing M46 tank stands on the quai de l'Ourthe, in front of the Hôtel de Ville. At the entrance of the town stands an MK10 British Achilles tank. A moving plaque sits at the intersection of rue de la Gare and rue Cielle, the spot where American and British troops met.

The somewhat dusty **Musée de la Bataille des Ardennes** contains an extensive selection of American, English, and German war relics, including an authentic code-deciphering enigma machine. Numerous photographs re-create life in the Ardennes during the war. ⊠ *Rue Châmont 5* ☎ *084/41–17–25* ⊕ *www.batarden.be* ☏ *€5.95* ☽ *Apr.–Dec., Wed.–Sun. 10–6; Group requests taken all year round.*

POTEAU (ST. VITH)

55 km (34 mi) northeast of Bastogne.

GETTING HERE & AROUND
From Bastogne, take the E25 towards Liège and get off at exit 50, Baraque de Fraiture—Belgium's highest point (2,093 feet). Follow the

N89 and N68 towards Vielsalm, where you'll turn right and follow the N675 to Poteau.

ESSENTIALS
Visitor Info **St. Vith** (✉ *Hauptstrasse 34* ☎ *080/28–01–30* ⊕ *www.st.vith.be*).

WHAT TO SEE
The **Ardennen Poteau '44 Museum** in the small village of Poteau (part of St-Vith) displays what started as an impressive private collection of war relics. The deRuyter family spent years looking for relics kept by civilians and visiting trade markets all over Europe to create this museum. Housed in a former customs house and adjacent barracks, the museum has lots of old weapons, vehicles, and photographs from the 14th American cavalry group, which was ambushed in December 1944. You can even be driven around the battlefield area in a half-track. You can even be driven around the battlefield area in a half-track. ✉ *Poteauerstrasse 22* ☎ *080/21–74–25* ⊕ *www.museum-poteau44.be* 🎟 *€7* ⊙ *Mid-June–mid-Sept., 1–5; Apr.–June 14 and Sept. 16–Oct., weekends 1–5; Private groups by appointment.*

AROUND LIÈGE

Relatively close to the German border, situated on the river Meuse and the Albertkanaal, the channel connecting Antwerp with Liège was of utmost strategic importance. By the end of the 19th century, 12 forts had been built in the area to keep Prussian or French invaders out. In the 1930s, another four were added in anticipation of a German invasion. Alas, these efforts failed; the fort of Eben-Emael was taken in one day, and the defense of the Albertkanaal given up after two days, allowing the German offensive passage towards Antwerp and the rest of the country.

GETTING HERE & AROUND
To reach the Fort de Battice, follow the E40 towards Aachen and head for the N3 at the roundabout (6 km [4 mi] after exit 37); the fort is 1 km (½ mi) outside Battice on the N648 towards Aubel. Henri-Chapelle is another 10 km (6 mi) along the N3: turn left just before the village of Henri-Chapelle towards Aubel; the cemetery is another 3 km (2 mi) along that road. Eben-Emael is close to the Dutch border. Take the E25 towards Maastricht (Netherlands), get off at exit 1, cross the river Meuse toward Lixhe. When you reach the N671, follow directions to Maastricht for about 5 km (3 mi). The best way to reach the cemetery in Neuville is to head for the E46 towards Marche-en-Famenne; the cemetery will be on your right in the village of Neuville-en-Condroz.

ESSENTIALS
Taxis **Liège Taxi** (✉ *rue du Cimetière 993, Liège* ☎ *0800/32–200*). Taxis **Melkior** (✉ *Quai de Rome 30, Liège* ☎ *04/252–2020*).

Visitor Info **Liège** (✉ *En Féronstrée 92* ☎ *04/221–9221* ⊕ *www.liege.be*).

GREAT ITINERARIES

2

IF YOU HAVE 1 OR 2 DAYS
Start in **Bastogne**, where the **Bastogne Historical Center**, neatly summarizing the Battle of the Bulge, will provide you with a solid historical background. After also taking in the Sherman tank on Place Mac Auliffe and the **Colline du Mardasson**, honoring the American soldiers, head along small and winding roads towards **La Roche-en-Ardenne** to witness how strongly war memories are kept alive in this small village. You might take a scenic detour to see the **Ardennen Poteau Museum** near St. Vith; otherwise, it's a pleasant 70-km (43-mi) drive through the forests towards the area around Liège. There you can visit the moving **Henri-Chapelle** cemetery and the **forts of Battice** and **Eben-Emael**, which were attacked in 1940.

WHAT TO SEE

BATTLE SITE   Built in the 1930s on a 111-acre area, 700 Belgian soldiers held out against the Germans in the **Fort de Battice** for 12 days in May 1940, while the German tanks rolled on into France. Eventually, a German stuka airplane dropped a bomb on one of the concrete blocks, killing 26 men. Heavy armory is still inside and some walls are covered with frescoes made by soldiers before the war. Unfortunately, the fort is only open to the public from March to November, usually on the last Saturday of the month at 1:30. Guided tours are possible by appointment. The fort is muddy, so be sure to wear boots. ⊠ *Rte. d'Aubel, Battice* ✛ *20 km (13 mi) east of Liège* ☎ *011/88–42–22* 🎫 *€3* ☉ *Open for tours Mar.–Nov., last Sat. of month at 1:30; other times by appointment.*

The impressive **Fort Eben-Emael** was built into the rocks after the First World War. Supposedly impregnable, it was almost invisible to the eye. However, on May 10, 1940 German gliders landed on the plateau and threw explosives down the air shafts. A day later the 700 Belgian soldiers guarding the fort surrendered to a mere 55 Germans. The fort and its equipment remain intact and can be visited. There's also a museum containing photographs and weaponry. ⊠ *Rue du Fort 40, Eben-Emael* ✛ *26 km (15 mi) north of Liège* ☎ *04/286–2861* ⊕ *www.fort-eben-emael.be* 🎫 *€6* ☉ *Mar.–Nov., 10–6 one weekend each month. Check Web site for details.*

CEMETERIES   Ten kilometers (6 mi) east of the Fort de Battice is **Henri-Chapelle,** the largest American military cemetery in Belgium. It is the resting place of 7,989 American soldiers who fell in the Battle of the Bulge. The crosses and stelae are arranged in arcs converging on the central monument, which also contains a small museum and provides a striking view over the plateau of Herve. Ceremonies are held here on American Memorial Day in late May. ⊠ *Rte. du Mémorial Américain 155, Hombourg* ☎ *087/68–71–73* ⊕ *www.henrichapelle.com* 🎫 *Free* ☉ *Daily 9–5.*

CLOSE UP

Where to Stay & Eat

IN IEPER

✕**'t Ganzeke.** A favorite of locals as well as hungry tourists, this restaurant's (¢–$$$) menu of hearty meals includes giant kebabs, steaks, and a large selection of pancakes and ice cream. ⊠ *Vandepeereboomplein 5* ☎ *057/20-00-09* ⊟ *AE, DC, MC, V* ⊘ *Closed Mon.*

✕**Old Tom.** The name of this traditional restaurant ($–$$$) is as matter-of-fact as the food; here you'll find unfussy but appetizing Flemish standards, such as beef stew with beer, river eel, and chicken waterzooi. You can also stay in one of the nine modest rooms for €68, which have a TV and bathroom. ⊠ *Grote Markt 8* ☎ *057/20-15-41* ⊕ *www.oldtom.be* ⊟ *AE, MC, V.*

▦**Gasthof 't Zweerd.** Here you'll find comfortable, well-equipped rooms (¢), some of them offering a nice view of the Grote Markt. You can dine in the cozy restaurant or grab a snack in the brasserie. ⊠ *Grote Markt 2* ☎ *057/20-04-75* ⊕ *www.gasthof-tzweerd.be* ⥲ *17 rooms* ⊟ *AE, DC, MC, V.*

▦**Regina.** In a sturdy neo-Gothic brick building directly on the Grote Markt, this fresh, comfortable hotel ($) has generous, light-filled spaces and 20 up-to-date rooms that tip their hats to various cultural figures such as Matisse and Edith Piaf. Just about everything has been upgraded except the windows. The only drawback is the traffic noise. ⊠ *Grote Markt 45* ☎ *057/21-88-88* ⊕ *www.hotelregina.be* ⊟ *AE, DC, MC, V* ⦿⦿ *BP.*

AROUND IEPER

▦**Hostellerie Mont Kemmel.** Atop Flanders's highest peak (Mont Kemmel is a classic ascent during the yearly Ronde van Vlaanderen bike tour), 16 well-appointed rooms ($) offer panoramic views over Flanders Fields. Chef Solange Bentin cooks up sophisticated specialties in the elegant restaurant ($$$–$$$$). A bar, tennis court, and golf course are all nearby. ⊠ *Kemmelbergweg 34, Kemmel* ⊹ *7 km (4½ mi) south of Ieper on N331* ☎ *057/45-21-60* ⊕ *www.kemmelberg.be* ⊟ *AE, MC, V* ⊘ *Restaurant closed Mon. and Tues., except to hotel guests.*

▦**Hotel Kasteelhof 't Hooghe.** Ever stayed in a hotel with authentic trenches, craters and bunkers in the yard? This mansion, situated on the former front line, was once the headquarters of the British army. The rooms (¢) and their view over Flanders Fields won't disappoint even the most demanding visitors. ⊠ *Meenseweg 481, Zillebeke* ⊹ *4 km (2½ mi) southeast of Ieper* ☎ *057/46-87-87* ⊕ *www.hotelkasteelhofthooghe.be* ⊟ *AE, DC, MC, V.*

▦**De Klaproos.** The name of this small bed-and-breakfast (¢) at the corner of the Tyne Cot cemetery means "the poppy." There are two bedrooms (with a third on the way), a fully equipped kitchen, a small bathroom with shower, and a terrace. Bikes are free. ⊠ *Tynecotstraat 26* ☎ *050/77-87-53* ⊕ *www.deklaproos.com* ⊟ *No credit cards.*

IN POPERINGE

✕**D'Hommelkeete.** This low-slung Flemish farmhouse ($$$–$$$$) close to the French border combines rustic and modern decor, and it's said to be the best place to experience the elusive and expensive delicacy called *hopscheuten* (hop shoots). This special treat is only available for three weeks

2

in spring, so call ahead. Braised sea scallops, warm goose liver, and venison noisettes will ease your disappointment if you arrive at other times. ⊠ *Hoge Noenweg 3* ☎ *057/33-43-65* ⊟ *AE, DC, MC, V* ⊗ *Thurs.–Sun. noon–2 and 7–9.*

IN LA ROCHE-EN-ARDENNE

✗ **Le Midi.** Food is the real reason to visit this tiny, old, cliff-side hotel; straightforward regional specialties are simply and stylishly served in the restaurant ($–$$). In season, wild game such as tenderloin of young boar in old port is superbly cooked; there's also air-dried Ardennes ham with candied onions. The eight modern hotel rooms (¢–$) have distinctly local, if not antique, furnishings. Breakfast is included. ⊠ *Rue de Beausaint 6* ☎ *084/41–11–38* ⊕ *www. hotelmidi.com* ⊟ *AE, DC, MC, V.*

▦ **Auberge La Grande Cure.** This rural hideaway is tucked outside the village of Marcourt. Proprietors Hélène and Tim Christensen make you feel like you're staying in their home. After a day exploring the countryside, settle down to a fabulous, Mediterranean-inspired 3-, 4-, or 7-course fixed-price meal ($$$$; reservations essential). The nine guest rooms ($) are simple but comfortable. You can lounge on the terrace in summer, or warm yourself by the fireplace in the library in winter. ⊠ *Les Planesses 12* ☎ *084/47-73-69* ⊕ *www.lagrandecure.be* ⊟ *AE, DC, MC, V.*

▦ **Claire Fontaine.** Set on a gorgeous bluff, this family hotel ($–$$) has a string of parlors lined with eccentric bric-a-brac. The 28 spacious, modern rooms have magnificent views, as does the bustling restaurant ($$–$$$). If you like seafood, order the crayfish and trout with almonds. Meat-eaters will enjoy the veal sweetbreads. ⊠ *Rte. de Hotton 64* ☎ *084/41-24-70* ⊕ *www.clairefon taine.be* ⊟ *AE, DC, MC, V* ⦿| *BP.*

▦ **Les Genêts.** At this romantic old mountain inn, each of the eight rooms ($) have stenciled wallpaper and a homey mix of plaid, paisley, and chintz. Picture windows take in valley views on two sides. The restaurant ($$–$$$) serves traditional dishes. ⊠ *Corniche de Deister 2* ☎ *084/41-18-77* ⊕ *www.lesgenetshotel.com* ⊟ *AE, DC, MC, V* ⊗ *Closed July 1–15, 3 wks in Jan.*

IN BASTOGNE

✗ **Wagon-Restaurant Léo.** Originally a tiny, chrome railroad diner, this local institution has spilled over across the street into the chicly refurbished Bistro Léo. The restaurant ($–$$) serves huge platters of Belgian standards while in the bistro, quiche, and homemade lasagna are the fare. In 2003, Wagon Léo opened At Home, a comfortable, modern hotel, right next to the restaurant on Pl. MacAuliffe. The 14 rooms ($) are very spacious and all have three single beds. ⊠ *Rue du Vivier 8* ☎ *061/21-14-41* ⊟ *MC, V.*

▦ **Best Western Hotel Melba.** A walking path to the Bastogne Historical Center begins right behind this modern chain hotel ($), which is also a couple of minutes' walk from place MacAuliffe. The 34 rooms don't have much character, but they're roomy, bright, and comfortable. ⊠ *Av. Mathieu 49–51* ☎ *061/21-77-78* ⊕ *www.hotel-melba.com* ⊟ *AE, DC, MC, V.*

The **Cimetière Américain des Ardennes** is the final resting place for 5,328 soldiers of the U.S. First Army division who fell in the Ardennes at the Siegfried Line and around Aachen. The memorial, decorated with an immense American eagle, contains a nondenominational chapel. Giant maps on the walls depict the history of the war. Ceremonies are held here on American Memorial Day in late May. ⊠ *Rte. du Condroz 164, Neuville-en-Condroz* ✛ *20 km (13 mi) southwest of Liège* ☏ *04/371–4287* ⊕ *www.abmc.gov* 🎫 *Free* ☉ *Daily 9–5.*

WILLEBROEK

23 km (14 mi) north of Brussels, 27 km (17 mi) south of Antwerp.

GETTING HERE & AROUND
Breendonk is almost exactly halfway between Antwerp along the A12.

ESSENTIALS
Visitor Info **Willebroek (Breendonk)** (⊠ *Saaasplein 18* ☏ *03/886–2286*).

WHAT TO SEE
Belgium was not spared the horror of Nazi concentration camps, as can be witnessed in the **Fort van Breendonk** in Willebroek. In this camp, 3,500 people including resistance fighters, political prisoners, and Jews, were incarcerated, ill-treated, and tortured. By means of an audioguide you're taken through the sinister, seemingly endless corridors. The torture chamber and the execution site, with its original poles and gallows, are truly horrifying. ⊠ *Brandstraat 57, Willebroek* ☏ *03/860–7525* ⊕ *www.breendonk.be* 🎫 *€6* ☉ *Daily 9:30–5:30.*

Brussels

WORD OF MOUTH

"I know that plenty of people simply love Bruges, but personally I enjoyed my time in Brussels more. Seemingly more activity, people watching, and so on."

—Dave

"I was in Belgium last fall and visited Antwerp, Brugge, and Brussels. I loved Belgium, what a gorgeous country, and Brugge is a beautiful village."

—bombasticlife

Updated by
Nicola Smith

BRUSSELS' VIBRANT, COSMOPOLITAN ATMOSPHERE AND multi-cultural beat make it much more than simply the administrative hub of Europe. For all its world-class restaurants, architecture, and art, though, the city keeps a relatively low profile, so you'll have the breathing room to relish its landmarks, cobbled streets, and beautiful parks.

Brussels started life as a village towards the end of the 10th century. Over the next eight centuries, it grew as a center for trading and crafts, and was alternatingly ruled by everyone from local counts of Leuven, the Burgundians Philip the Good and Charles V, to the Spanish and later Austrians. Despite its history of occupation, after 1815 the city resisted Dutch attempts to absorb it, and 1830 saw the uprising that finally gained Belgium its independence.

At the end of the 19th century, Brussels was one of the liveliest cities in Europe, known for its splendid cafés and graceful Art Nouveau architecture. That gaiety, however, was stamped out by German occupation during the First and Second World Wars. Still, the city made a comeback little more than a decade later, its reemergence on the international scene heralded by the World's Fair and the Universal Exposition of 1958. It became the European Economic Community's headquarters that same year, a precursor to its hosting of the EU's administrative and political arms.

As a by-product of Europe's increasing integration, international business has invaded the city in a big way since the 1960s. The result: city blocks of steel-and-glass office buildings set only a few steps from cobbled-street neighborhoods featuring hallmarks of the city's eventful past. Over the centuries, Brussels has been shaped by the different cultures of the foreign powers that have ruled it. It has learned the art of accommodating them and, in the process, prepared itself for its role as the political capital of Europe. In 1989 the Brussels region became autonomous, on a par with Flanders and Wallonia. The city is technically bilingual, though French is the dominant language. Now, diversity is the capital's greatest strength; one-third of the city's million-strong population are non-Belgians, and you're as likely to hear Arabic or Swedish spoken on the streets as French or Flemish.

ORIENTATION & PLANNING

ORIENTATION

While Brussels technically includes 19 communes, or suburbs, most sights, hotels, and restaurants are clustered in the center, which encompasses Lower Town and Upper Town. To the south, is the posh area of Ixelles and the cluster of European institutions, along with the museums of the Cinquantenaire park. To the west of the center lies St-Gilles, with its mix of Art Nouveau architecture and immigrant areas around the Gare du Midi. (The area north of St-Gilles, Forest, is a similar amalgam, though it's more residential.) Farther west you'll find Erasmus's

TOP REASONS TO VISIT BRUSSELS

Eat, Drink, and Be Merry. Beer and fries is really the classic combination and there's no better place to taste the two than Brussels.

Rub Shoulders With Diplomats. The "capital of Europe" plays host to the vast bureaucracy of the European Union institutions—the European parliament, Council, and Commission.

Be a High Culture Vulture. Home to the Musée des Instruments de Musique (MIM), Centre Belge de la

Bande Dessinée, Brussels's comic strip museum, and the Musée d'Art Ancien, just to name a few, you could spend all your times soaking up the sights. There's even a €15 combo pass to help you do it.

To Market, To Market. Every day of the week guarantees at least one lively market where stalls sell everything from olives and fruit to antique furniture and dog-eared books.

house in the industrial area of Anderlecht. The green communes of Jette and Laeken lie to the north.

CITY CENTER
Most sights, hotels, and restaurants are clustered in the center, which encompasses the lovely Grand'Place and Sablon squares, the two royal palaces, the old quarter of Les Marolles, and the urban chic of the places St-Géry and Ste-Catherine. Locals simply call this the *centre,* but the tours here distinguish a Lower Town and Upper Town.

LOWERTOWN Also known as the heart of Brussels, this area is literally the lower section of the center and includes the area around the Grand'Place and the Bourse.

UPPER TOWN A steep slope leads up to the Upper Town, around rue de la Régence, place Royale, and the Sablon squares.

CINQUANTENAIRE & SCHUMAN
Just east of central Brussels you'll find the buildings that make this city the "capital of Europe," as well as a number of museums and an attractive park, which surround Brussels' version of the Arc de Triomphe, known as the Cinquantenaire arch.

IXELLES
Fine examples of Art Nouveau and Art Deco architecture decorate this posh neighborhood that runs along either side of avenue Lousie just south of the city's center.

NORTH OF THE CENTER
The northern part of the city is a little seedy and run-down, but beyond that you'll find green suburbs with lots of character and some of the city's best tourist attractions, including the Atomium building.

PLANNING

TAKE IT ALL IN

1 Day: Wander the narrow, cobbled lanes surrounding the square and visit the graceful, arcaded Galeries St-Hubert, an elegant 19th-century shopping gallery. Head down rue de l'Etuve to see the Manneken Pis, the famous statue of the little boy urinating. Walk to the place du Grand Sablon to window-shop at its many fine antiques stores and galleries. If it's a weekend, enjoy the outdoor antiques market. Have lunch in one of the cafés lining the perimeter, and don't forget to buy chocolates at one of the top chocolatiers on the square. Then head to the Musée d'Art Moderne and the Musée d'Art Ancien. End with dinner on the fashionable rue Antoine Dansaert or have a drink in one of Grand'Place's many cafés.

3 Days: Kick off your stay with the exploration outlined above. On your second day, start at the Parc de Bruxelles, a formal urban park that originated as a game park. Check out the elegant place Royale across the street and then head to the Musée des Instruments de Musique, which houses one of Europe's finest collections of musical instruments. Hop a tram to avenue Louise in Ixelles for a little shopping and lunch along place du Chatelain. After lunch, visit architect Horta's own house, now the Musée Horta, on rue Américaine. If you crave more art and architecture, go to the Musée David-et-Alice-Van-Buuren. If you crave lighter entertainment, head towards the Gare du Midi and visit the Musée de la Gueuze to see how Lambic beer is brewed the old-fashioned way. For dinner head to place Ste-Catherine for a feast of Belgian seafood specialties. Later, check out the many cafés and bars that crowd the narrow streets around the Bourse.

On Day 3, take the metro to Schuman and walk past the cluster of EU buildings on your way through Parc Cinquantenaire to the Autoworld museum, which houses a fantastic collection of vintage cars. Catch a tram to Tervuren and the Koninklijk Museum voor Midden Afrika/ Musée Royal de l'Afrique Centrale, a legacy of Belgium's role in the Congo, including objects and memorabilia from explorers. Relax in the surrounding park before heading back into town for another fine dinner. Another option would be to visit some of the famous sights and towns on the border of Brussels. First on the list is Waterloo, the battlefield that changed the course of European history, where you can explore the Musée Wellington, the Butte de Lion, and the Champ de Bataille field. Next, head for Gaasbeek, where you'll find the Gaasbeek Château and scenery straight out of a Bruegel painting.

EAT RIGHT, SLEEP WELL

The Brussels restaurant scene is a lively mix of haute cuisine, hearty Belgian favorites, and food from all over the world. The top Brussels restaurants rival the best Parisian restaurants; so, alas, do the prices. But one of the joys of the city is the quality and value of its smaller, neighborhood restaurants. You'll find everything from tapas bars to African buffets, as well as excellent and affordable bistros and plenty of good Vietnamese, Italian, and Portuguese restaurants.

Prix-fixe menus are often an especially good bargain. Menus and prices are always posted outside restaurants. Don't feel that you're under an obligation to eat a three-course meal; many people order just a main course. If you don't want two full restaurant meals a day, there are plenty of snack bars for a light midday meal, and most cafés serve sandwiches and light hot meals both noon and night. And, of course, at almost any hour, you can grab tasty double-fried frites with mayonnaise for dipping from mobile *frituurs* around the city.

Local lunchtime starts at 12:30 and continues until 2; people generally take their time over several courses. Restaurants fill for dinner around 8 and stay busy for several hours. Although locals tend to take dining out seriously, you don't need to dress too formally; jackets and ties are required only at the most exclusive restaurants. Reservations are always recommended, but you can usually get a table on short notice. Many restaurants close completely for the months of July and August, when the owners and staff take their vacations. Check the Web site ⊕*www.resto.be*, where you can search Belgian restaurants by city and type of cuisine.

As the capital of Europe, Brussels attracts a large number of high-powered international visitors—one in two travelers is here on business—hence, a disproportionate number of very attractive luxury hotels have been built to accommodate them. Their prices are higher than what most tourists would like to pay, but on weekends and during July and August, when there aren't many business travelers, prices can drop to below €150 for a double room, even in the most upscale hotels. As a rule though, always negotiate a price: the listed rate is rarely applied in practice in the larger hotels.

Happily, new hotels catering to cost-conscious travelers, priced at less than €100 for a double, have also been constructed over the last few years. They may be less ostentatious, but they're squeaky-clean and offer as much attention to your comfort as the palatial hotels. Of the various neighborhoods, the Upper Town has the fewest less-expensive options. Brisk with businesspeople and diplomats, the EU quarter has a number of efficient, good-value hotels that often lie almost empty on weekends, making it possible to grab a deal. The international chains are sprinkled across the city, clustered to its south or near the Gare du Nord, with easy access to the airport.

Small, family-run inns and cutting-edge boutique properties are thin on the ground here. Instead you'll find many belle-epoque hotels that were occupied during World War II, abandoned mid-century, and then fought their way back to center stage. These generally have an appealing combination of evocative period architecture or decor and high-tech amenities. In a handful of places, patina or an individual, quirky style provides a change of pace from the glossy international chains.

There's also an accommodations service that arranges overnight stays in private homes: **Bed & Brussels** (⊠*rue Gustave Biot 2, Etterbeek* ☎*02/646–0737* ⊕*www.bnb-brussels.be*). Through this company, you can stay with a host family for €40 to €90 a night, including breakfast.

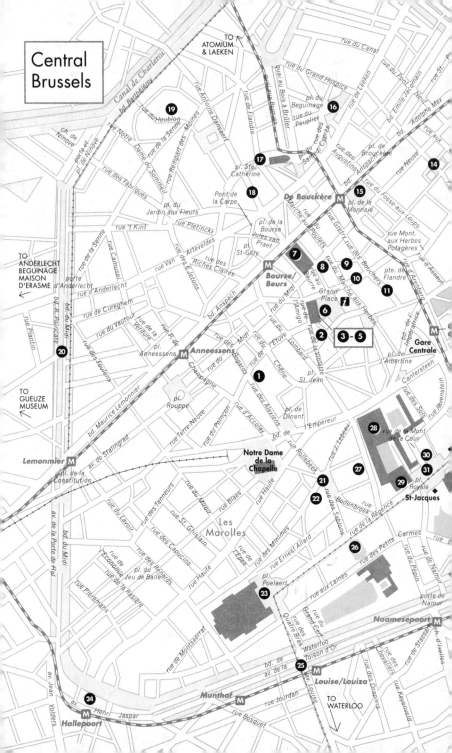

Central Brussels

TO ATOMIUM & LAEKEN

Canal de Charleroi

bd. Barthélémy

ch. de Ninove

porte et pl. de Ninove

TO ANDERLECHT BEGUINAGE MAISON D'ERASME

TO GUEUZE MUSEUM

rue du Houblon

rue Antoine Dansaert

rue Notre Dame du Sommeil

rue des Fabriques

rue de Flandre

rue de la Senne

rue du Rempart des Moines

rue des Fabriques

rue de la Senne

rue 't Kint

rue de Laeken

quai au Bois à Brûler

quais aux Briques

pl. du Jardin aux Fleurs

rue Pletinckx

rue du Canal

rue du Grand Hospice

ph. du Béguinage

rue du Peuplier

rue des Sœurs Noires

rue des Augustins

pl. des Barricades

bd. Emile Jacqmain

rue Neuve

rue aux Choux

Adolphe Max

19

16

17

18

pl. Ste. Catherine

Pont de la Carpe

De Bouckère

pl. de la Monnaie

15

14

Marché aux Poulets

rue du Fossé aux Loups

pl. de Brouckère

bd. Anspach

pl. de la Bourse

Jules van Praet

pl. St-Géry

rue Grétry

rue Neuve

rue Mont. aux Herbes Potagères

Bourse Beurs

7

8 **9**

10

11

pte. de Flandre

rue d'Assaut

rue du Marché aux Herbes

Grand Place

6

i

2

3–5

Gare Centrale

M

Anneessens

M

rue de l'Etuve

rue Lombard

pl. St. Jean

pl. de l'Albertine

Canterstein

rue des Sols

rue Ravenstein

1

pl. de Dinant

bd. de l'Empereur

Notre Dame de la Chapelle

rue de Rollebeek

28

rue de la Mont. de la Cour

30

31

29

pl. Royale

St-Jacques

Lemonnier

M

pl. de la Constitution

av. de Stalingrad

pl. Rouppe

rue Terre-Neuve

bd. Maurice Lemonnier

rue du Poinçon

21

27

rue Bodenbroek

22

rue des Sablons

rue de la Régence

Les Marolles

rue des Tanneurs

rue du Miroir

rue Blaes

rue Haute

rue des Capucins

rue St. Ghislain

pl. du Jeu de Balle

rue des Renards

rue de l'Economie

rue de la Rasière

rue Pieremans

rue des Minimes

rue de l'Epée

rue Ernest Allard

pl. Poelaert

26

rue des Petits Carmes

rue du Pépin

porte de Namur

23

rue aux Laines

rue du Grand Cerf

Naamsepoort

rue de Namur

av. de la Porte de Hal

bd. du Midi

av. de la Porte de Hal

rue de Montserrat

bd. de Waterloo

Toison d'Or

25

av. Louise

TO WATERLOO

av. Jean Volders

24

av. Henri Jaspar

Hallepoort

M

Munthof

M

rue Jourdan

rue Bosquet

Louise/Louiza

M

rue des Chevaliers

rue de Stassart

rue Keyenveld

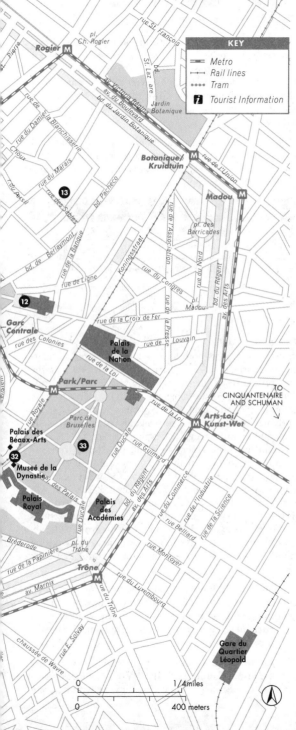

3

You submit your requests and preferences, including the number of people, whether you want a private bathroom, whether you'd prefer a quiet or a busy area, and so on; the company then provides you with a list of available choices. The host families are carefully screened; most have room to spare after children have flown the coop. Not only can you find a low-cost, high-quality place to stay, but you'll have a window into local daily life.

Service in hotels is sometimes criticized for falling short of what you'd expect in some cosmopolitan cities, with the exception of the most elite hotels. However, if you come with an open mind, a bit of patience, and a smile, you're unlikely to be disappointed.

WHAT IT COSTS IN EUROS					
	¢	$	$$	$$$	$$$$
Restaurants	under €10	€10–€15	€15–€20	€20–€30	over €30
Hotels	under €75	€75–€100	€100–€150	€150–€225	over €225

Restaurant prices are for a main course at dinner, not including tax or tip. Hotel prices are for two people in a standard double room in high season, on the European Plan (EP, with no meals) unless otherwise noted. Rates include 6% Value Added Tax plus a 9% city tax.

GETTING HERE & AROUND
The police and fire departments both have immediate-response emergency hotlines. One pharmacy in each district stays open 24 hours; the rotating roster is posted in all pharmacy windows. Driving in Brussels can be an unnerving experience. Belgians weren't required to have driver's licenses until 1979 and local driving habits are often slapdash. Drivers frequently neglect to use their turn signals, park precariously on street corners, and zoom through pedestrian crossings. The main problem for foreign drivers, however, is the rule of priority from the right. Often, even if you are on a main road, cars coming from blind corners on the right have the priority. A yellow-and-white diamond sign to your right as you approach an intersection indicates that you have the right-of-way. It's best to be extremely cautious until you get the hang of this rule. On the plus side, tunnels under busy intersections allow crosstown traffic to pass quickly. Rush hours run from 7:30 to 9 AM and 5 to 6 PM. If you plan to drive to the coast on a Friday during the summer months, leave well before rush hour, as traffic can back up for hours.

The city is surrounded by an inner and outer beltway, marked RING. Exits to the city are marked CENTER/CENTRUM. Among several large underground parking facilities, the one close to the Grand'Place at rue Duquesnoy is particularly convenient if you're staying in a downtown hotel.

The metro, trams, and buses operate as part of the same system and are run by the city's transport authority, STIB/MIVB (Société des Transports Intercommunaux de Bruxelles/Maatschappij voor het Intercommunaal Vervoer te Brussel). All three types of transport are clean and efficient, and a single "Jump" ticket, which can be used among all three systems in an hour-long time frame, costs €1.50. The best buy is a 10-trip ticket, which costs €10. Special tourist tickets are also a good value at €3.80 for a one-day unlimited travel card; €9 for three days; and €12 for five days (weekdays only). You can purchase these tickets in any metro station or at newsstands. Single tickets can be

> ### I SPY . . . PUBLIC ART
>
> Keep your eyes peeled for the public artworks in many of the city's metro stations. For instance, the Porte de Hal station has a three-story relief of skyscrapers with old-fashioned trams poking their noses out, while a huge futuristic city in rainbow hues brightens up the Montgomery station.

purchased on the bus or on the tram. Children under six accompanied by an adult travel free. You need to validate your ticket in the orange machines on the bus or tram; in the metro, you validate your card at the orange machines in the station. Metro stations have bilingual names, such as Bourse/Beurs, and are marked by signs showing a white M on a blue background. Metro trains, buses, and trams run from around 5:30 AM until 12:30 AM. One bus, the number 71 from place de Brouckère to Delta, runs until 3 AM. Brussels is a relatively safe city, but it's wise to be cautious in remote metro stations late at night.

Detailed maps of the Brussels public transportation network are available in most metro stations and at the Tourist Information Brussels in the Grand'Place. You get a map free with a Tourist Passport (also available at the tourist office), which, for €7.50, allows you a one-day transport card and discount admissions at museums.

The easiest way to ensure a cab is to call Taxis Verts or Taxis Oranges. You can also catch a taxi at cab stands around town, which are indicated with yellow signs. All officially registered taxis have a yellow-and-blue sign on their roofs. A cab ride within the city center costs between €6.20 and €12.40. Tips are included in the fare.

See the Getting Here & Around section in Travel Smart Belgium for information on travel by air, train, and car.

BANKS & EXCHANGE SERVICES

Currency exchange points cluster around the Grand'Place, while the major banks, Fortis and ING, have branches around the city. Branch hours are 9 AM to 1 PM and 2 PM to 4:30 PM. There are 24-hour ATMs, called Bancontact or Mister Cash and marked with blue-and-yellow signs, all around Brussels, though not as many as in most European cities. This is why long lines often sprout from downtown ATMs on weekend nights. Frustratingly, ATMs are often out of order and can be totally out of cash by Sunday evenings.

ESSENTIALS

Bus Station CCN Gare du Nord (⊠ *rue du Progrès 80, St-Josse* ☎ *02/203–0707*).

Emergency Contacts Ambulance and Fire Brigade (☎ *100*). **Dentist** (☎ *02/426–1026*). **Doctor** (☎ *02/479–1818*). **Police** (☎ *101*). **24-Hour English-Speaking Info and Crisis Line** (☎ *02/648–4014*).

Internet Cafés Avenue Cyber Theatre, EasyEverything (✉ *pl. de Brouckere 9–13, Lower Town* ☎ *02/311-0820* ⊙ *8 AM–11:30 PM*). **The Coffee Club** (✉ *rue du Bailli 38, Ixelles* ⊕ *www.thecoffeeclub.be* ⊙ *Mon.–Sat. 9–6*).

Public Transportation Info STIB/MIVB (☎ *02/515–2000* ⊕ *www.stib.irisnet.be*).

Taxis Taxis Oranges (☎ *02/349–4343*). **Taxis Verts** (☎ *02/349–4949*).

Train Stations Gare Centrale (✉ *carrefour de l'Europe 2, Upper Town* ☎ *02/555–2555*). **Gare du Midi** (✉ *rue de France, Lower Town* ☎ *02/555–2555*). **Gare du Nord** (✉ *rue du Progres 76, St-Josse* ☎ *02/555–2555*).

Visitor Info Tourist Information Brussels (*TIB* ✉ *Hôtel de Ville, Grand' Place, Lower Town* ☎ *02/513–8940* ⊕ *www.brusselsinternational.be* ⊙ *Weekdays 9–6*). **Waterloo Office de Tourisme** (✉ *chaussée de Bruxelles 149* ☎ *02/352–0910* ⊕ *www.waterloo-tourisme.be* ⊙ *Weekdays 9:30–5:30*).

EXPLORING BRUSSELS

Around the 1,000-year-old historic center of Brussels, a group of ring roads form concentric circles. Crossing them is like traveling back and forth across the centuries. Brussels once had a river, the Senne, but it was buried in the 19th century after becoming clogged with sewage; the absence of left and right riverbanks can make orientation in the city a bit difficult.

The center, sitting in a bowl, is sometimes known as the Pentagon, from the shape of the oldest ring road, which roughly follows the ancient ramparts. The remains of the ruins include one of the gates, the Porte de Hal, and a small patch of wall next to a bowling alley near place de la Chapelle. From the 19th-century ring road you can see the cupolas of the Palais de Justice and the giant basilica in the Koekelberg commune (to the north). In the center, the slender belfry of the Hôtel de Ville rises like a beacon.

Brussels is small enough that you can get a superficial impression of it from a car window in a single day. For a more substantial appreciation, however, you need one day for the historic city heart, another for the uptown squares and museums, and additional days for museums outside the center and excursions to the periphery.

LOWER TOWN: THE HEART OF BRUSSELS

During the latter half of the 10th century, a village began to emerge on the site of present-day Brussels. A population of craftspeople and traders settled gradually around the castle of the counts of Leuven, who were later succeeded by the dukes of Brabant.

In 1430 Philip the Good, Duke of Burgundy, took possession of Brussels, then known as Brabant. During this era, Brussels became a center

CLOSE UP

Touring Brussels

Brussels is small enough so you can easily visit many of the major sights in a day—just bring a sturdy pair of shoes. Or, you could jump on and off one of the city tour buses, which leave from the central station. All of the major train stations have good connections with other sightseeing hot spots in Belgium and major cities in neighboring countries.

WALKING TOURS

ARAU (☎ *02/219-3345* ⊕ *www. arau.org*) organizes thematic city bus and walking tours March–November, including "Brussels 1900: Art Nouveau" (every Saturday) and "Brussels 1930: Art Deco" (every third Saturday of the month). Tours with English-speaking guides include visits to some building interiors that are otherwise not open to the public. A half-day bus tour costs €15; a half-day walking tour runs €10. Reservations are recommended.

The tours run by **Chatterbus** (☎ *02/673-1835* ⊕ *www.busbavard. be*) either visit the main sights on foot or by minibus (from €15) or follow a walking route that includes a visit to a bistro (€10). The tours run from early June through September and can be given in English. Those with the right language skills can join in the French weekend theme tours between March and December.

BIKE TOURS

Pro Velo (☎ *02/502-7355* ⊕ *www. provelo.org*) takes visitors on cycling tours in and around Brussels. Tours, on themes such as "Comic Strips and Cafés," are available April–August. Tours in English operate in July and August. The cost is €8, plus €6 for bike rental. Group tours can also be arranged throughout the year at a cost of €124 for up to 20 people for a half-day tour, plus €4.95 per person for bike rental. Bikes may also be rented for independent use at prices ranging from €2.50 for one hour to €49.50 for a full week

INDIVIDUAL TOURS

Qualified English-speaking guides are available for individual tours from **Tourist Information Brussels** (*TIB* ☎ *02/513-8940* ⊕ *www.brusselsinternational.be*) in the town hall. Three hours costs €106, and up to 20 people can share the same guide for a walking tour and up to 50 people for a bus tour.

TOURS OUTSIDE OF BRUSSELS

In Waterloo, the expert guides at **Les Guides 1815** (✉ *rte. du Lion 250* ☎ *02/385-0625* ⊕ *www.guides1815. org*) can be hired to take you around the battlefield for one hour (€46), two hours (€56), or three hours (€75). Group tours in English (€3.65 per person) are weekends at 4 in July and August.

De Boeck Sightseeing (✉ *rue de la Colline 8, Grand'Place, Lower Town* ☎ *02/513-7744* ⊕ *www. deboeck-incoming.com*) operates city tours (€25.50) with multilingual commentary; they also visit Antwerp, the Ardennes, Brugge, Gent, Ieper, and Waterloo by bus. Passengers are picked up at major hotels or at the tourist office in the Hôtel de Ville on the Grand'Place.

for the production of tapestry, lace, and other luxury goods. The city's market-town past can still be seen in the names of clusters of streets in the center of town—rue du Marché au Fromage was once where cheese makers set out their stalls, and you can imagine the feathers flying on rue du Marché aux Poulets (chicken-market street).

By 1555, when Charles V abdicated in favor of his son, Philip II of Spain, the Protestant Reformation was spreading through the Low Countries. Philip, a devout Catholic, dealt ruthlessly with advocates of the Reformation. In 1568, his governor, the Castilian Duke of Alva, capped his Council of Blood (which condemned suspected heretics without trial) with the execution of the Counts of Egmont and Hoorn, leaders of a popular rebellion. A monument to them stands in the Petit Sablon square.

In 1695, on the orders of French King Louis XIV, Marshal Villeroy bombarded the city with red-hot cannonballs in retaliation for the extended siege of Namur. The ensuing fires destroyed 4,000 houses, 16 churches, and all of the Grand'Place, with the exception of the Hôtel de Ville. The buildings around the square were immediately rebuilt, in the splendor seen to this day.

In 1713 the Spanish Netherlands came under the rule of the Austrian Habsburgs. Despite the influence of Enlightenment theories on the province's governors, nationalist feeling had set in among large sections of the populace. These sentiments were quashed by neither the repressive armies of Napoléon nor the post-Waterloo incorporation of Belgium into a new Kingdom of the Netherlands. On August 25, 1830, a rousing duet from an Auber opera being performed at La Monnaie inflamed patriots in the audience, who burst onto the streets and raised the flag of Brabant. With support from Britain and France, independence came swiftly.

Since then, Brussels has undergone image upheavals almost as significant as the impact of this century's two World Wars. At the turn of the 20th century, the wide boulevards and Art Nouveau buildings symbolized a city as bustling and metropolitan as Paris. However, from the 1950s onward, Brussels became a byword for boring: a gray, faceless city of bureaucrats where cavalier neglect of urban planning created a new word—bruxellization—for the destruction of architectural heritage. Now the pace of European integration (and the wonders of the city's food and drink) has helped to restore the city's international reputation.

WHAT TO SEE

❼ Bourse. At the stock exchange, the decorative frieze of allegorical statues in various stages of nudity—some of them by Rodin—forms a sort of idealization of the common man. Trading here, as at most European stock exchanges, is via electronic computer screens, meaning that there is no longer a trading floor. Next door lies **Bruxella 1238**, an archaeological museum where you can inspect the excavation of a 13th-century church. ✉ *rue de la Bourse, Lower Town* ☎ *02/279–4355* 💷 *€3*

◷ *Guided visits from Hôtel de Ville, first Wed. of the month, 11:15*
Ⓜ *Metro: Bourse/De Brouckere. Bus: 34, 48, 95.*

⓬ **Cathédrale St-Michel et Ste-Gudule.** The twin Gothic towers and outstanding stained-glass windows of the city's cathedral look down over the city. One namesake, St. Michael, is recognized as the patron saint of Brussels, but mention St. Gudule and most people will draw a blank. Very little is known about this daughter of a 7th-century Carolingian nobleman, but her relics have been preserved here for the past 1,000 years. Construction of the cathedral began in 1226 and continued through the 15th century; chapels were added in the 16th and 17th centuries. The remains of an earlier, 11th-century Romanesque church that was on the site can be glimpsed through glass apertures set into the floor. Among the windows in the cathedral, designed by various artists, those by Bernard van Orley, a 16th-century court painter, are the most spectacular. The window of *The Last Judgment*, at the bottom of the nave, is illuminated from within in the evening. All royal weddings and christenings take place here. ✉ *Parvis Ste-Gudule, Upper Town* 📞 *02/217–8345* ◷ *Weekdays 7–7, Sat. 7:30–7, Sun. 8–7.* Ⓜ *Metro: Gare Centrale. Bus: 71, 38, 65.*

⓭ **Centre Belge de la Bande Dessinée.** It fell to the land of Tintin, a cherished
☾ cartoon character, to create the world's first museum dedicated to the
★ ninth art—comic strips. Despite its primary appeal to children, comic strip art has been taken seriously in Belgium for decades, and in the Belgian Comic Strip Center it is wedded to another strongly Belgian art form: Art Nouveau. Based in an elegant 1903 Victor Horta–designed building, the museum is long on the history of the genre but sadly short on kid-friendly interaction. Tintin, the cowlicked adventurer created in 1929 by the late, great Brussels native Hergé, became a worldwide favorite cartoon character. But many other artists have followed in Hergé's footsteps, some of them even more innovative. The collection includes more than 400 original plates by Hergé and his Belgian successors and 25,000 cartoon works; those not exhibited can be viewed in the archive. There are also good temporary exhibitions from time to time, a large comic strip shop, a library, and a lovely Art Nouveau brasserie. Most information is in French. ✉ *rue des Sables 20, Lower Town* 📞 *02/219–1980* ⊕ *www.comicscenter.net* 🎫 *€7.50* ◷ *Tues.–Sun. 10–6* Ⓜ *Metro: Botanique.*

NEED A BREAK?

Cirio (✉ *rue de la Bourse 18–20, Lower Town* 📞 *02/512–1395*) is a beautiful café with outstanding Art Nouveau decor that was once part of a classy Europe-wide chain set up in 1903 by Italian canned-food magnate Francesco Cirio. The Half and Half cocktail (half champagne and half white wine) was invented here, and is still poured with panache by the courtly waiters. Particularly cozy and twinkling in the winter, you'll get a real taste of Brussels in its turn-of-the-last-century heyday here. If you'd prefer something sweet, there are a couple of good ice-cream and waffle joints a few doors down.

⓰ **Eglise St-Jean-du-Béguinage.** Originally this elegant Flemish Baroque church served as the center for the *béguines* (lay sisters) who lived

CLOSE UP

Comic Strip Capital

Belgium is recognized the world over as the home of the comic strip. *Bande dessinée*, or BD as it's usually called, is taken very seriously here—practitioners from the Golden Age of the 1950s and 1960s are now the subjects of museum retrospectives and documentaries.

At the top of the pile is Georges Remi, the Brussels-based writer and illustrator who, under the name Hergé, created the indomitable boy reporter Tintin. These days, Tintin is a multimillion-euro industry, with books, figurines, mugs, and even a clothing line. A Tintin museum in the capital is still under discussion; until that gets off the ground, you'll have to make do with the comic strip museum (Centre Belge de la Bande Dessinée/Belgisch Centrum voor het Beeldverhaal), where local heroes Tintin, Lucky Luke, and the Smurfs feature prominently.

Another way to soak up Brussels' comic strip culture is to hit the streets: 23 walls in the city center are covered with colorful murals featuring well-known characters. Ask the Tourist Office for a map of the trail.

Finally, see what all the fuss is about by visiting one of Brussels' numerous comic book stores. Most books are in French or Dutch, but you can find some in English. Look for Benoît Peeters and François Schuitens' Obscure Cities (Cités Obscures), a series of beautifully illustrated graphic novels about a parallel universe that looks like it's been designed by Victor Horta and Jules Verne.

SHOPS

Brüsel ⊠ *blvd. Anspach 100, Lower Town* ☎ *02/511–0809* ⊙ *Mon.-Sat. 10–4:30, Sun. noon–6:30* Ⓜ *Metro: De Brouckere/Anneessens. Tram: Bourse.*

Forbidden Zone ⊠ *rue de Tamines 25, St-Gilles* ☎ *02/534–6367* ⊕ *www.forbiddenzone.net* ⊙ *Tues.-Sat. 12:30–7* Ⓜ *Metro: St Gilles. Tram: 3, 23, 55, 90.*

La Bulle D'Or ⊠ *blvd. Anspach 124, Lower Town* ☎ *02/513–7235* ⊙ *Mon.-Sat. 10:30–7, Sun. 12:30–6:30* Ⓜ *Metro: De Brouckere/Anneessens. Tram: Bourse.*

—Susan Carroll

in houses clustered around it. The interior has preserved its Gothic elements, with soaring vaults. The surprisingly different architectural styles combine to make this one of the most attractive churches in Brussels. A number of streets converge on the small, serene, circular square, which is surrounded by buildings that help create a harmonious architectural whole. ⊠ *pl. du Béguinage, Lower Town* ☎ *02/217–8742* ⊙ *Tues.–Fri. 10–5* Ⓜ *Metro: De Brouckere. Tram: Bourse. Bus: 34, 48, 95.*

❽ **Eglise St-Nicolas.** This small church, surrounded by tiny houses that seem to huddle under it, is almost 1,000 years old. Little remains of the original structure, but a cannonball fired by the French in 1695 is still lodged in one of the pillars. You can only view the exterior, as the church is closed for renovation. ⊠ *rue au Beurre 1, Lower Town* ☎ *02/513–8022* Ⓜ *Metro: De Brouckere. Tram: Bourse. Bus: 34, 48, 95.*

⓫ **Galeries St-Hubert.** There are three parts to this arcade: *de la Reine, du Roi,* and *du Prince* (of the queen, the king, and the prince). They were built in 1847 as the world's first covered shopping galleries, thanks to new engineering techniques that allowed architects to use iron girders to design soaring constructions of glass. Neoclassical gods and heroes look down from their sculpted niches on the crowded scene below; flags of many nations billow ever so slightly; and the buskers play classical music, while diffused daylight penetrates the gallery from the glassed arches. The shops, which are generally open Monday–Saturday 10–6, are interspersed with cafés, restaurants, a theater, and a cinema. ⊠*Access from rue des Bouchers or carrefour de l'Europe, Lower Town* ☎*02/512-2116* Ⓜ*Metro: Gare Centrale.*

NEED A BREAK?

A la Mort Subite (⊠*rue Montagne-aux-Herbes-Potagères 7, Lower Town* ☎*02/513-1318*) is a Brussels institution named after a card game called Sudden Death. This 1920s café with its high ceilings, wooden tables, and mirrored walls brews its own traditional Brussels beers, Lambic, Gueuze, and Faro, and is a favorite of beer lovers from all over the world. The sour, potent beer may be an acquired taste, but, like singer Jacques Brel, who came here often, you'll find it hard to resist the bar's gruff charm.

❻ **Grand'Place.** This jewel box of a square is arguably Europe's most ornate and most theatrical. It's a vital part of the city—everyone passes through at some point. At night the burnished facades of the guild houses and their gilded statuary look especially dramatic: from April to September, the square is floodlighted after sundown with waves of changing colors, accompanied by music. Try to be here for the *Omme-gang,* a magnificent historical pageant re-creating Emperor Charles V's reception in the city in 1549 (the first Tuesday and Thursday in July). You'll find here a flower market, frequent jazz and classical concerts, and in December, under the majestic Christmas tree, a life-size crèche with sheep grazing around it.

*Fodor's*Choice ★

Built in ornate Baroque style soon after the 1695 bombardment, the square's guild houses have a striking architectural coherence. Among the buildings on the north side of the square, Nos. 1–2, **Le Roy d'Espagne,** belonged to the bakers' guild. A figure of Fame perches on its cupola. **Le Sac,** No. 4, commissioned by the guild of joiners and coopers, and No. 6, **Le Cornet,** built for the boatmen, were both designed by Antoon Pastorana, a gifted furniture maker. **Le Renard,** No. 7, was designed for the guild of haberdashers and peddlers; a sculpture of St. Christopher, their patron, stands on top of the gable. **Le Cygne,** No. 9, was formerly a butchers' guild. Today, it is an elegant restaurant, but before that it was a popular tavern often frequented by Karl Marx. ⊠*Intersection of rue des Chapeliers, rue Buls, rue de la Tête d'Or, rue au Beurre, rue Chair et Pain, rue des Harengs, and rue de la Colline, Lower Town* Ⓜ*Metro: De Brouckere, Gare Centrale. Tram: Bourse.*

Hôtel de Ville. The Gothic town hall, which dates from the early 15th century, dominates the Grand'Place. It's nearly 300 years older than the surrounding guild houses, as it survived the devastating fires of 1695.

The left wing was begun in 1402 but was soon found to be too small. Charles the Bold laid the first stone for the extension in 1444, and it was completed four years later. The extension left the slender belfry off center; it has now been fully restored. The belfry is topped by a bronze statue of St. Michael crushing the devil beneath his feet. Over the gateway are statues of the prophets, female figures representing lofty virtues, and effigies of long-gone dukes and duchesses. Inside the building are a number of excellent Brussels and Mechelen tapestries, some of them in the Gothic Hall, where recitals and chamber-music concerts are frequently held. ⊠ *Grand'Place, Lower Town* ☎ *02/279–4365* ⌁*€3* ⊙ *Guided tours only, Tues. and Wed.: Dutch 1:45, French 2:30, English 3:15. Sun: Dutch 10, English 10:45 and 12:15, French 11:30* Ⓜ *Metro: De Brouckere, Gare Centrale. Tram: Bourse.*

NEED A BREAK? There are plenty of cafés to choose from on Grand'Place. But **Le Roy d'Espagne** (⊠ *Grand'Place 1, Lower Town* ☎ *02/513-0807* ⊕ *www.roydespagne.be*) is by far the friendliest and most popular. In the summer, sit out on the terrace and soak up the beauty of the square; in winter, snuggle up to the huge fire. You can expect to pay a few euros more for coffees and beers in the Grand'Place area, but most people seem to think the view is worth it.

⑲ **La Maison de la Bande Dessinée.** This museum is a celebration of Belgian cartoonists and famous characters that are brought together in constantly changing exhibitions. Lose yourself for hours enjoying the adventures of Tintin, le Petit Spirou, the Smurfs, and Boule et Bill. ⊠ *blvd. de l'Imperatrice 1, Lower Town* ☎ *02/502–9468* ⊕ *www.jije. org* ⌁*€2* ⊙ *Tues.–Sun. 10–6* Ⓜ *Metro: Gare Centrale. Bus: 29, 38, 60, 63, 65, 66, 71.*

❹ **Maison de la Brasserie.** On the same side of the Grand'Place as the Hôtel de Ville, this was once the brewers' guild. The building, also known as l'Arbre d'Or (the Golden Tree), now houses a modest **brewery museum,** appropriate enough in a country that still brews 400 different beers. There are audioguides in English. ⊠ *Grand'Place 10, Lower Town* ☎ *02/511–4987* ⌁*€5* ⊙ *Daily 10–5* Ⓜ *Metro: De Brouckere, Gare Centrale. Tram: Bourse.*

❺ **Maison du Roi.** No ruler ever lived in this House of the King; rather, it housed Charles V's administrative offices. It was built on the site of Brussels' 13th-century covered market in the 16th century, but was rebuilt in neo-Gothic style towards the end of the 19th century. Today, it houses the **Musée Communal,** a municipal museum that has some fine tapestries, altarpieces, and paintings, notably the *Marriage Procession,* by Pieter Bruegel the Elder. On the top floor you can see the extravagant wardrobe of costumes donated to clothe the little statue of *Manneken Pis* on festive occasions. It's a good idea to book your visit well in advance. ⊠ *Grand'Place 29–33, Lower Town* ☎ *02/279–4350* ⌁*€3* ⊙ *Tues.–Sun. 10–5* Ⓜ *Metro: De Brouckere, Gare Centrale. Tram: Bourse.*

❶ Manneken Pis. This cocky emblem of Brussels has drawn sightseers for centuries—but after all the hype, you may be underwhelmed by the small statue of the peeing boy, an image that launched a thousand tchotchkes. The first mention of the Manneken dates from 1377, and he's said to symbolize what Belgians think of the authorities, especially those of occupying forces. The present version was commissioned from sculptor Jerome Duquesnoy in 1619. It is a copy; the original was seized by French soldiers in 1747. In restitution, King Louis XV of France was the first to present *Manneken Pis* with a gold-embroidered suit. The statue now has 517 other costumes for ceremonial occasions, an ever-increasing collection whose recent benefactors include John Malkovich and Dennis Hopper, and his own personal dresser. On one or two days of the year, he spouts wine or beer, rather than water. A female version set up by an enterprising restaurateur, the *Jeanneke Pis*, can be found off the rue des Bouchers. ⊠ *rue de l'Etuve at rue du Chêne, Lower Town* Ⓜ *Metro: Gare Centrale. Bus: 34, 48, 95.*

❸ Musée du Cacao et du Chocolat. This modest museum devoted to cacao and chocolate gives an inside look at one of Belgium's prize products. It explains how cacao beans are grown and processed, taking you through all the stages of chocolate production. There's information available in English, and you'll get a small tasting. ⊠ *Grand'Place 9–11, Lower Town* 🕾 *02/514–2048* ⊕ *www.mucc.be* 💶 *€5* ⊙ *Tues.–Sun. 10–4:30* Ⓜ *Metro: De Brouckere, Gare Centrale, Tram: Bourse.*

❷ Musée du Costume et de la Dentelle. The costume and lace museum pays tribute to Brussels' textile-making past. Housed in four 17th-century houses and a warehouse, the museum is something of a 17th- to 18th-century fashion show, with accessories, embroidery and clothes on display, many featuring the delicate lace for which the city became famous. ⊠ *rue de la Violette 12, Lower Town* 🕾 *02/213–4450* 💶 *€3* ⊙ *Mon., Tues., Thurs., and Fri. 10–12:30 and 1:30–5; weekends 2–5.* Ⓜ *Metro: Gare Centrale.*

❿ Place des Martyrs. This square holds a monument to the 445 patriots who died in the brief but successful 1830 war of independence against the Dutch. The square itself is a neoclassical architectural ensemble built in 1795 in the cool style favored by the Austrian Habsburgs. ⊠ *rue du Persil, Lower Town* Ⓜ *Metro: De Brouckere.*

⓱ Place Ste-Catherine. If you find the Grand'Place overrun by tourists, come to this square, a favorite of locals. It's a working market every weekday from 7 to 5, where people come to shop for necessities and banter with fishmongers. There's a stall where you can down a few oysters, accompanied by a glass of ice-cold muscadet. In the evening the action moves to the old **Vismet** (fish market), which branches off from the Eglise de Ste-Catherine. A canal used to run through here; it's now reduced to a couple of elongated ponds, but both sides are lined with seafood restaurants, some excellent, many overpriced. In good weather, there's outdoor waterside dining. ⊠ *Intersection of rue Ste-Catherine, rue du Vieux Marché aux Grains, rue de Flandre, quai aux Briques, quai au Bois à Bruler, pl. du Samedi, rue Plateau, and rue*

Melsens, Lower Town Ⓜ*Metro: Ste-Catherine.*

㉔ **Porte de Hal.** Built in 1381, this gate is a unique remnant of Brussels' city walls, and in 1847 became one of the first museums in Europe. Having lost its collections to the Cinquantenaire complex in the 1870s, it now focuses on the history of Brussels. There are guided tours available. If you visit, try and catch the nearby morning market, which has particularly good flower and organic food stalls. ✉*blvd. du Midi, Lower Town* ☎*02/533–3450*

> **DID YOU KNOW?**
>
> During a performance of Auber's *La Muette de Portici* at Théâtre de la Monnaie, the national opera house, on August 25, 1830, members of the audience became so inflamed by the duet "Amour sacré de la patrie" that they stormed out and started a riot that led to the country's independence from the Dutch in a brief and largely bloodless revolution.

💶*€2* 🕐*Tues.–Fri. 9:30–5, weekends 10–5* Ⓜ*Metro: Porte de Hal.*

❿ **Quartier de l'Îlot Sacré.** Flimflam artists and jewelry vendors mingle with
★ the crowds in the narrow rue des Bouchers and even narrower petite rue des Bouchers. While many streets in central Brussels were widened as part of the preparations for the 1958 World's Fair, these tiny routes escaped being demolished after locals complained. The area was given special protection in 1959 and there are strict rules governing what changes can be made to its historic buildings. As long as you watch out for pickpockets, it's all good-natured fun in the liveliest area in Brussels, where restaurants and cafés stand cheek by jowl, their tables spilling out onto the sidewalks. One local street person makes a specialty of picking up a heaped plate and emptying it into his bag. The waiters laugh and bring another plate. The restaurants make strenuous efforts to pull you in with huge displays of seafood and game. The quality, alas, is a different matter, and there have been arrests in recent years for large-scale credit card fraud in these restaurants. *(For some outstanding exceptions, see Where to Eat, below.)* ⊕*www.ilotsacre.be* Ⓜ*Metro: Gare Centrale.*

⓲ **Rue Antoine Dansaert.** This is the flagship street of Brussels' fashionable quarter, which extends south past St-Géry and Ste-Catherine. Avant-garde boutiques sell Belgian-designed men's and women's fashions along with more familiar designer labels. There are also inexpensive restaurants, cozy bars and cafés, edgy galleries, and stylish furniture shops.

⓯ **Théâtre de la Monnaie.** Built on the site of a former mint (hence the name), the graceful hall is among Europe's leading opera stages. Tickets are relatively cheap and there are guided tours on Saturdays at noon. ✉*Between De Brouckere and Fossé-aux-Loups at rue Neuve and rue des Fripiers, place de la MonnaieLower Town* ☎*02/218–1202* ⊕*www.lamonnaie.be* Ⓜ*Metro: De Brouckere. Tram: Bourse.*

➒ **Théâtre Toone.** An old puppet theater, now run by the youthful Nicolas Geal—an eighth-generation member of the Toone family who's thus known as Toone VIII—this theater has a repertory of 33 plays, including some by Shakespeare. You won't understand a word, as per-

Money-Saving Tips

A group of arts institutions in this area has formed an alliance called the **Mont des Arts**. It includes the Musée d'Art Ancien, the Musée d'Art Moderne, the Musée des Instruments de Musique, the Musée de la Dynastie, and the Palais des Beaux-Arts. On Saturdays and Sundays you can buy a special pass which gives you entry to all the participating institutions, including occasional concerts. The pass costs €11; for information on shows and exhibits, see the Web site

⊕ *www.kunstberg.be*, which has an English translation.

Another good-value pass is the €30 Brussels Card, which gives you three days of free public transport (except airport transfers) and free entry to 30 museums, including those on the Mont des Arts. You can buy it at Brussels public transport offices in stations such as the Gare du Midi. Find out more at the Web site ⊕ *www.brussels museums.be*.

3

formances are given in the local *vloms* dialect, but it's fun anyway. There's a puppet museum (only accessible during the shows) and a great, old-fashioned bar. ✉ *Impasse Schuddeveld, off petite rue des Bouchers, Lower Town* 📞 *02/511–7137 or 02/513–7486* ⊕ *www. toone.be* 💶 *Performance €10, entrance to museum free with show* 🕙 *Tues.–Sun. noon–midnight, performance most evenings at 8:30* Ⓜ *Metro: De Brouckere.*

UPPER TOWN: ROYAL BRUSSELS

Uptown Brussels bears the hallmarks of two rulers, Austrian Charles of Lorraine and Leopold II, Belgium's empire builder. The 1713 Treaty of Utrecht, which distributed bits of Europe like pieces in a jigsaw puzzle at the end of one of the Continent's many wars, handed the Low Countries to Austria. Fortunately for the Belgians, the man Austria sent here as governor was a tolerant visionary who oversaw the construction of a new palace, the neoclassical place Royale, and other buildings that transformed the Upper Town.

The next large-scale rebuilding of Brussels was initiated by Leopold II, the second king of independent Belgium, in the latter part of the 19th century. Cousin of Queen Victoria and the Kaiser, he annexed the Congo for Belgium and applied some of the profits to grand urban projects. Present-day Brussels is indebted to him for its wide avenues and thoroughfares.

WHAT TO SEE

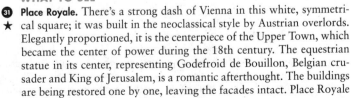

❸❶ **Place Royale.** There's a strong dash of Vienna in this white, symmetrical square; it was built in the neoclassical style by Austrian overlords. Elegantly proportioned, it is the centerpiece of the Upper Town, which became the center of power during the 18th century. The equestrian statue in its center, representing Godefroid de Bouillon, Belgian crusader and King of Jerusalem, is a romantic afterthought. The buildings are being restored one by one, leaving the facades intact. Place Royale was built on the ruins of the palace of the Dukes of Brabant, which had burned down. The site has been excavated, and it is possible to see the underground digs and the main hall, Aula Magna, where Charles V was crowned Holy Roman Emperor in 1519 and where, 37 years later, he abdicated to retire to a monastery. The church on the square, **St-Jacques-sur-Coudenberg**, was originally designed to look like a Greek temple. After the French Revolution reached Belgium, it briefly served as a "Temple of Reason." The Art Nouveau building on the northwest corner is the former Old England department store, home of the Musée des Instruments de Musique.

On or near place Royale are the **Hôtel Ravenstein** (⊠ *rue Ravenstein 3*), built in the 15th century and the only surviving aristocratic house from that period; and the **Palais des Beaux-Arts** (⊠ *rue Ravenstein 23*), an Art Deco concert hall, designed in the 1920s by Victor Horta and remarkable more for the ingenuity with which he overcame its tricky location than for its aesthetic appeal.

㉠ Kermesse du Midi. From mid-July until the end of August, all of Belgium's carnival barkers and showmen and their carousels, ghost trains, Ferris wheels, shooting galleries, rides, swings, and merry-go-rounds congregate along the boulevard du Midi for this giant and hugely popular funfair. It extends for blocks and blocks. ⊠ *Both sides of blvd. du Midi, from pl. de la Constitution to Porte d'Anderlecht, Lower Town* 🎟 *Attractions separately priced* ◷ *Daily 10 AM–midnight* Ⓜ *Metro: Porte de Hal/Gare du Midi.*

★ Les Marolles. If the Grand'Place stands for old money, the Marolles neighborhood stands for old—and current—poverty. This was home to the workers who produced the luxury goods for which Brussels was famous. There may not be many left who still speak the old Brussels dialect, mixing French and Flemish with a bit of Spanish thrown in, but the area still has raffish charm, although gentrification is in progress. The Marolles has welcomed many waves of immigrants, the most recent from Spain, North Africa, and Turkey. Many come to the daily **Vieux Marché** (flea market) at the place du Jeu de Balle, where old clothes are sold along with every kind of bric-a-brac, plain junk, and the occasional gem. For more browsing, hit the smattering of antiques shops on rue Haute and rue Blaes. This area can be sketchy at night, so you may want to leave by sunset, particularly if you're alone. ⊠ *Bordered by blvd. du Midi, blvd. de Waterloo heading southwest from Palais de Justice, and imaginary line running west from pl. de la Chapelle to blvd. Maurice Lemonnier, Upper Town* Ⓜ *Metro: Louise/Gare du Midi.*

㉜ Musée BELvue. The museum in the lovely, historic Hôtel Bellevue was renovated in 2005, and its displays given a much needed revamp. It was built in 1776 by the French architect Barnabé Guimard for wine merchant Philippe de Proft and later became a hotel. Many famous people have passed through its doors—Honoré de Balzac, Franz Liszt, and Sarah Bernhardt slept here, and the Duke of Wellington stayed just before the Battle of Waterloo. The museum charts Belgium's history from the 1830 revolution to the present day, using film, photographs, documents and objects. There's a decent café with outdoor seating in the summer. ⊠*pl. Palais 7, Upper Town* ☎*02/545–0801* ⊕*www.musbellevue.be* ⊡*€5, in combination with Palais de Charles V* ☉*June–Sept., Tues.–Sun. 10– 6; Oct.–May, Tues.–Sun. 10–5* Ⓜ*Metro: Parc. Tram: 92/94. Bus: 27, 38, 71, 95.*

3

㉙ **Musée d'Art Ancien.** In the first of the interconnected art museums, the ★ Ancient Art Museum pays special attention to the great, so-called Flemish Primitives of the 15th century, who revolutionized the art of painting with oil. The Spanish and the Austrians pilfered some of the finest works, but there's plenty left by the likes of Memling, Petrus Christus, Rogier van der Weyden, and Hieronymus Bosch. The collection of works by Pieter Bruegel the Elder is outstanding; it includes *The Fall of Icarus,* in which the figure of the mythological hero disappearing in the sea is but one detail of a scene in which people continue to go about their business. Bruegel the Younger's wonderful *Fight between Carnival and Lent* is also here. A century later Rubens, Van Dyck, and Jordaans dominated the art scene; their works are on the floor above. Look for Rubens's outstanding *The Martyrdom of St. Livinus.* The 18th-century collection on the ground floor includes the melodramatic *Death of Marat,* by Jacques-Louis David, who, like many other French artists and writers, spent years of exile in Belgium. You can forge ahead into the 19th and 20th centuries by using the underground passage that connects this museum to the adjacent Musée d'Art Moderne. There are English-language brochures and guided tours available. ⊠*rue de la Régence 3, Upper Town* ☎*02/508–3211* ⊕*www.fine-arts-museum.be* ⊡*€5* ☉*Tues.–Sun. 10–5* Ⓜ*Metro: Louise/Park. Tram: 92, 94.*

㉘ **Musée d'Art Moderne.** Rather like New York's Guggenheim Museum in ★ reverse, the Modern Art Museum burrows underground, circling downward eight floors. You can reach it by an underground passage from the Musée d'Art Ancien or you can enter it from the house on place Royale where Alexandre Dumas (*père*) once lived and wrote. The collection is strong on Belgian and French art of the past 100 years, including such Belgian artists as the Expressionist James Ensor and the Surrealists Paul Delvaux and René Magritte, as well as Pierre Alechinsky and sculptor Pol Bury. Highlights include Magritte's *The Empire of Light* and Delvaux's *Pygmalion,* and Ensor's *Skeletons Fighting for a Smoked Herring.* Notable works by non-Belgian artists include Francis Bacon's *The Pope with Owls.* There are English-language explanatory brochures and guided tours available. Note that lunch hours at this and the Musée d'Art Ancien are staggered so as not to inconvenience visitors. ⊠*pl. Royale 1, Upper Town* ☎*02/508–3211* ⊕*www.fine-arts-museum.be* ⊡*€5* ☉*Tues.–Sun. 10–5* Ⓜ*Metro: Louise/Park. Tram: 92, 94.*

30 **Musée des Instruments de Musique (MIM).** If you've ever been curious to
☺   know what a gamelan or Tibetan temple bell sounds like, here's your
FodorśChoice   chance. In addition to seeing the more than 1,500 instruments on dis-
★   play, you can listen to them via infrared headphones; you can hear musical extracts from almost every instrument as you stand in front of it.
The more than 200 extracts range from ancient Greek tunes to mid-
20th century pieces. Paintings and ancient vases depicting the instruments being played throughout history complete the experience. The
four-story museum features a complete 17th-century orchestra, a precious 1619 spinet-harpsichord (only two such instruments exist), an
armonica, a rare Chedeville bagpipe, and about 100 Indian instruments
given to King Leopold II by the rajah Sourindro Mohun Tagore. There's
a rich selection of European folk instruments, as well as creations by
the amazingly prolific Adolphe Sax. In the basement, the Garden of
Orpheus is set up for children to discover musical instruments. The site
combines one of the city's most beautiful Art Nouveau buildings—the
former Old England department store, designed by architect Paul Sain-
tenoy in 1899—with the adjoining neoclassical 1913 Barré-Guimard
building. A third building in the adjoining rue Villa Hermosa houses the
7,000 instrument reserve. The tearoom and restaurant on the sixth floor
offer panoramic views of Brussels. ⊠*rue Montagne de la Cour 2, Upper
Town* ☎*02/545–0130* ⊕*www.mim.fgov.be* ☜*€5* ☽*Tues.–Fri. 9:30–5,
weekends 10–5* Ⓜ*Metro: Gare Centrale. Tram: 92. 94, Bus: 71.*

22 **Musée Juif de Belgique.** This museum traces the history of the Jewish
faith, and the fate of its followers in Belgium. The extensive collection
includes religious objects dating from the 16th century, documents, and
books. In addition to objects that illustrate Jewish customs throughout
Europe are a number of pieces, including textiles and silver, made in
Belgium. There are excellent regular temporary exhibitions on aspects
of Jewish life. ⊠*rue des Minimes 21, Upper Town* ☎*02/512–1963*
⊕*www.jewishmuseum.be* ☜*€5* ☽*Sun.–Fri. 10–5.* Ⓜ*Metro: Louise.
Tram: 92, 94.*

27 **Palais de Charles de Lorraine.** Charles of Lorraine, who governed the
Austrian Netherlands in the 18th century, filled this 1757 building with
ornate stonework, beautiful floor art, and other delights. Now used as
the Museum of the 18th Century and the Royal Belgian library, it is
dominated by a vast staircase leading to a rotunda that is paved with
28 types of Belgian marble, a small sample of Charles's collection of
minerals. You can look around the five lavish rooms where the prince
entertained guests and see decorative and scientific objects of the time.
⊠*pl. du Musée 1, Upper Town* ☎*02/519–5311* ☜*€2.50* ☽*Daily
9–5, closed weekends in winter* Ⓜ*Metro: Park. Tram 92, 94.*

32 **Palais de Charles V.** Under the place Royale lie the remains of a mas-
★   sive palace first constructed in the 11th century, and upgraded over
hundreds of years in line with the power and prestige of Brussels' suc-
cessive rulers. Destroyed by a great fire in 1731, the palace was never
reconstructed. Parts of the palace, and one or two of the streets that
surrounded it, have been excavated and the underground site is a fascinating glimpse into Brussels' past. You can see the remains of palace

rooms and walk up the steep cobbled rue Isabelle, once the busiest street in the city. Access is through the Musée BELvue. ⊠*pl. Palais 7, Upper Town* ☎*02/545–0800* 💶*€5, combined with the Musée BELvue* ⊗*June–Sept., Tues.–Sun. 10–6; Oct.–May, Tues.–Sun. 10–5* Ⓜ*Metro: Park. Tram: 92, 94.*

㉓ **Palais de Justice.** Many a nasty comment— "the ugliest building in Europe," for instance—has been made about Leopold II's giant late-19th-century law courts on the site of the old Gallows Hill. Ugly as the building may be, the panoramic views from the balustrade facing the city center are great. Much of the Marolles district was pulled down to make way for the monstrosity, leaving thousands homeless. Visitors are only allowed into the entrance hall, where you can see the shrine to the young girls killed by notorious pedophile Marc Dutroux in the late 1980s and early 1990s. The mishandling of that case shook the country to its core and led to the resignation of several government officials, as well as an overhaul of the police department. ⊠*pl. Poelaert, Upper Town* ☎*02/508–6111* 💶*Free* ⊗ *Weekdays 9–5* Ⓜ*Metro: Louise. Tram: 92, 94.*

㉝ **Parc de Bruxelles.** This was once a game park, but in the late 18th century it was tamed into rigid symmetry and laid out in the design of Masonic symbols. On warm days, joggers and strollers circle the park (the ornamental layout doesn't invite relaxing on the grass). The huge **Palais du Roi** occupies the entire south side of the park. It was built by Leopold II in the early 20th century on a scale corresponding to his megalomaniacal ambitions. In the palace, you can proceed into the vast throne room, lit by 11 chandeliers. Don't miss the ebony-and-jewel-encrusted piano in the Louis XV music salon or the dazzling Mirror Room, where floor-to-ceiling mirrors are interspersed with marble columns. The present monarch, King Albert II, comes here for state occasions, although he lives at the more private palace in Laeken. ⊠*pl. des Palais, rue Royale, adjacent to pl. Royale, Upper Town* 💶*Palais du Roi free* ⊗*July 22–Sept. 15, Tues.–Sun. 10:30–4:30* Ⓜ*Metro: Park. Tram: 92, 94.*

㉑ ★ **Place du Grand Sablon.** "Sand Square" is where the people of Brussels come to see and be seen. Once, as the name implies, it was nothing more than a sandy hill. Today, it is an elegant square, surrounded by numerous restaurants, cafés, and antiques shops, some in intriguing alleys and arcades. Every weekend morning a lively antiques market of more than 100 stalls takes over the upper end of the square. It isn't for bargain hunters, however. Downhill from the square stands the **Eglise de la Chapelle,** dating from 1134. Inside, there's a memorial to Pieter Bruegel the Elder, who was married and buried in this church. At the eastern end of the square stands the **Eglise Notre-Dame du Sablon,** a Flamboyant Gothic church founded in 1304 by the guild of crossbowmen (the original purpose of the square was crossbow practice) and rebuilt in the 15th century. One of Brussels' most beautiful churches, its cream exterior is undergoing a restoration due to finish in 2008, and at night the stained-glass windows are illuminated from within. ⊠*Intersection of rue de Rollebeek, rue Lebeau, rue de la Paille, rue Ste-*

Anne, rue Boedenbroeck, rue des Sablons, petite rue des Minimes, rue des Minimes, and rue Joseph Stevens, Upper Town Ⓜ*Metro: Louise. Tram: 92, 94.*

NEED A BREAK?

Wittamer (✉*pl. du Grand Sablon 12, Upper Town* ☎*02/512–3742*), the best of Brussels' many excellent pastry shops, has an attractive upstairs tearoom, which also serves breakfast and light lunches. The profiteroles and crème fraîche truffles are particularly tempting.

㉖ Place du Petit Sablon. Opposite the Grand Sablon, this pretty square is surrounded by a magnificent wrought-iron fence, topped by 48 small bronze statues representing the city's guilds. Inside the peaceful garden stands a double statue of the Flemish patriots Counts Egmont and Hoorn on their way to the Spaniards' scaffold in 1568.

㉕ Place Louise. There's a certain type of young Belgian matron—tall, blond, bejeweled, and freshly tanned whatever the season—whose natural urban habitat is around place Louise. The most expensive shops are along boulevard de Waterloo. Prices are somewhat lower on the other side of the street, on avenue de la Toison d'Or, which means the Golden Fleece. Additional shops and boutiques line both sides of avenue Louise and the Galerie Louise, which burrows through the block to link avenue de la Toison d'Or with place Stéphanie. This is an area for browsing, window-shopping, movie-going, and café-sitting, but don't go expecting a bargain. ✉*Av. Louise and blvd. de Waterloo, Upper Town and Ixelles* Ⓜ*Metro: Louise. Tram: 92, 94.*

CINQUANTENAIRE & SCHUMAN: MUSEUMS & THE EU

East of the center at the end of rue de la Loi, Rond-Point Robert Schuman is the focus of the buildings that house the European institutions. During the week, the area hums with besuited politicians, lobbyists, and journalists from all over the Continent, but on weekends it's left eerily empty. The generally gray, massive buildings can make the area seem somewhat glowering. A number of vast museums and an attractive park surround Brussels' version of the Arc de Triomphe, known as the Cinquantenaire arch, planned by Leopold II for the 50th anniversary of Belgian independence in 1880. Leopold's inability to coax funding from a reluctant government meant it was not completed until 25 years later.

TIMING It's a 10-minute walk from the Musée des Sciences Naturelles to the European Parliament. From Rond-Point Schuman, it takes just under an hour to follow the walk to the Cinquantenaire museums. To walk to place Montgomery, allow around 30 minutes. The tram to Tervuren takes about 20 minutes. The area around the EU buildings empties out

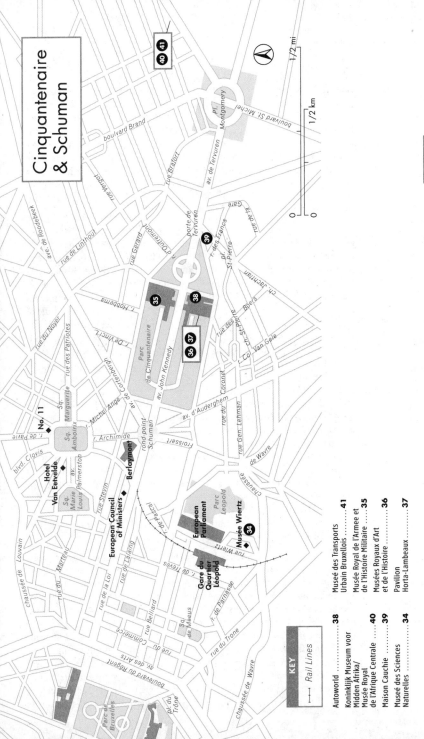

Cinquantenaire & Schuman

KEY

—⊢— *Rail Lines*

Autoworld **38**

Koninklijk Museum voor
Midden Afrika) ....

Musée Royal
de l'Afrique Centrale **40**

Maison Cauchie **39**

Museé des Sciences
Naturelles **34**

Musée des Transports
Urbain Bruxellois **41**

Musée Royal de l'Armee et
de l'Histoire Militaire **35**

Musées Royaux d'Art
et de l'Histoire **36**

Pavilion
Horta-Lambeaux **37**

significantly on weekends and can seem quite forlorn. Remember that museums, with the exception of Autoworld, are closed on Monday.

WHAT TO SEE

㊳ Autoworld. Vintage-auto fiends will find something close to paradise here. More than 450 antique cars, one of the best such collections in the world, are parked under the high glass roof of this hall. Cars used by former U.S. presidents John F. Kennedy and Franklin Roosevelt stand wheel-to-wheel with the open-topped vehicles that the Belgian royal family has been waving from for decades. Other rarities include the Minerva and other specimens from the days when Belgium had a car industry. An English-language brochure is available. ✉*Parc du Cinquantenaire 11, Etterbeek* ☎*02/736–4165* ⊕*www.autoworld. be* ✇*€6* ⊙*Apr.–Sept., daily 10–6; Oct.–Mar., daily 10–5* Ⓜ*Metro: Merode. Tram: 81.*

European Institutions. Brussels residents have an uneasy relationship with the European institutions. The European Union project brought jobs and investments to the city, but in the process entire neighborhoods were razed to make room for unbendingly modern, steel-and-glass buildings, and as more countries join the EU, more massive complexes are being built. What remains of the old blocks has seen an influx of ethnic restaurants catering to the tastes of lower-level Eurocrats; the grandees eat in splendid isolation in their own dining rooms. The landmark, star-shaped **Berlaymont** (✉*rue de la Loi 200*), reopened in 2005 after asbestos removal, is the home of the European Commission, the executive arm of the EU. The **European Council of Ministers** (✉*rue de la Loi 170*) groups representatives of the EU national governments and occupies the pink-marble Justus Lipsius building. The **European Parliament building** (✉*rue Wiertz 43*), which got caught up in controversy as France still insists on regular Parliament meetings in Strasbourg, is named Les Caprices des Dieux, or Folly of the Gods. Its central element, a rounded glass summit, looms behind the Gare du Quartier Leopold. Visitors who wish to go to the parliament can call the visitor's service (☎*02/284—2111*). For individual visitors there's an audio-guided visit Monday–Thursday 10–3 and Friday at 10 AM. There is also the chance to attend a parliamentary sitting but it's important to check times as sittings only occur every few months. ✉*Place du Luxembourg, Etterbeek* Ⓜ*Metro: Trone. Bus: 71, 95, 54, 27, 12, 21, 34, 38.*

㊵ Koninklijk Museum voor Midden Afrika/Musée Royal de l'Afrique Centrale. Stellar holdings, contemporary concerns, and a history of the jaundiced colonial mind-set make for a fascinating mix at the Royal Museum of Central Africa. Part of King Leopold II's legacy to Belgium, it holds an incredible collection of 250,000 objects, including masks, sculpture, paintings, and zoological specimens. There's also a wealth of memorabilia from the central African explorations commissioned by Leopold, most notably by Henry Morton Stanley (of "Doctor Livingston, I presume?" fame), whose archive is kept here. Some sections of the museum, such as the entrance hall, are virtual time capsules from the early 20th century, while others have been updated. The attached research center has a "Living Science" exhibition open to the public, focusing on its studies of African flora and fauna. While many parts of the museum's collection are invaluable from a scholarly point of view, they came at an incalculable cost, rooted in Leopold's brutal colonial rule. The museum has been undergoing a period of soul-searching, and is in the process of updating its exhibitions to more accurately reflect the horrific nature of Belgium's time in the Congo. The renovations are due to be completed in April 2010, the museum's 100th anniversary. There's descriptive information available in English throughout. Save some time for a walk through the museum's beautifully landscaped park. To get here from place Montgomery, take tram 44 to Tervuren. ⊠ *Leuvensesteenweg 13, Tervuren* ☎ *02/769–5211* ⊕ *www.africamuseum. be* ⌨ *€6* ⊗ *Tues.–Fri. 10–5, weekends 10–6* Ⓜ *Tram: 44.*

㊴ Maison Cauchie. Art Nouveau architect Paul Cauchie built this house for himself in 1905, using the facade as a virtual shop window for his sgraffito expertise. Sgraffito work begins with a light-color base layer; a darker color is added on top, and then, while the paint is still wet, etched with a design that allows the lighter color underneath to show through. Here, Cauchie covered the front with graceful, curving images of women playing lyres. The home's interior, only open to the public once a month, is a wonderful example of the Art Nouveau aesthetic. ⊠ *rue des Francs 5, Etterbeek* ☎ *02/673–1506* ⌨ *€4* ⊗ *First weekend of every month, 11–1 and 2–6* Ⓜ *Metro: Merode. Tram: 81.*

NEED A BREAK?

The **Maison Antoine** (⊠ *pl. Jourdan, Etterbeek*) frites stand sells the best fries in the capital, accompanied by a dizzying range of sauces. This is a great place to try Belgium's famous snack (the country's secret is frying the potatoes twice in beef tallow) and most of the bars that line the square will let you sit down and order a beer to go with your hot paper cone of frites.

㉞ Musée des Sciences Naturelles. The highlights of the Natural Sciences Museum are the skeletons of 14 iguanodons found in 1878 in the coal mines of Bernissart—these are believed to be about 120 million years old. It has a fine collection of 50,000 stones and 30,000 minerals and there are also displays on mammals, insects, and tropical shells, as well as a whale gallery. Unfortunately, there's little information in English. ⊠ *rue Vautier 29, Etterbeek* ☎ *02/627–4211* ⊕ *www.sciencesnaturelles. be* ⌨ *€7, free 1st Wed. of every month 1–4:45* ⊗ *Tues.–Fri. 9:30–4:45, weekends 10–6* Ⓜ *Bus: 34, 80.*

㊶ Musée des Transports Urbains Bruxellois. The Brussels Urban Transport Museum lines up more than 60 historic trams and buses—from horse-drawn trolleys to blunt-nosed 1950s buses. The museum also organizes visits with English commentary on historic trams Sunday morning April–October for €12. Trams depart at 10 AM for a 3½-hour ride between Woluwe and Heysel. For a break from the fumes of the history of public transport, take a walk in the adjacent Parc de Woluwe, a local favorite. If you take the tram to the museum, sit on the right-hand side and keep an eye out for the 1906–11 Palais Stoclet, a stunning geometric villa at No. 281. ⊠ *Av. du Tervuren 364b, Woluwe-St-Pierre*

☎02/515–3108 ⊕www.trammuseumbrussels.be 💶€2 or €5 including a tram ride ⊙Apr.–Oct., weekends 1:30–7.

㉟ Musée Royal de l'Armée et de l'Histoire Militaire. In the Royal Museum of Arms and Military History, you can track the evolution of military technology and equipment from the middle ages to the present day. The highlight of this vast collection, part of the Cinquantenaire museum complex, is the hall filled with 130 aircraft from World War I to the Gulf War. The World War II planes are a standout, with examples of Spitfires and Mosquitos. ⊠Parc du Cinquantenaire 3, Etterbeek ☎02/737–7833 ⊕www.klm-mra.be 💶Free ⊙Tues.–Sun. 9–11:30 and 1–4:30 Ⓜ Metro: Merode, Schuman. Tram: 81.

㊱ Musées Royaux d'Art et de l'Histoire. For a chronologically and culturally
★ wide-ranging collection of artworks, hit the sprawling Royal Museums of Art and History. The vast numbers of antiquities and ethnographic treasures come from all over the world; the Egyptian and Byzantine sections are particularly fine. Don't miss the colossal Easter Island statue. There's also a strong focus on home turf, with significant displays on Belgian archaeology and the immense and intricate tapestries for which Brussels once was famous. There's some information in English and guided tours are available. ⊠Parc du Cinquantenaire 10, Etterbeek ☎02/741–7211 ⊕www.kmkg-mrah.be 💶€5, free 1st Wed. of every month 1–5 ⊙Tues.–Sun. 10–5 Ⓜ Metro: Schuman, Merode, Tram: 81.

㊲ Pavilion Horta-Lambeaux. This pavilion in the Parc du Cinquantenaire was the first building Art Nouveau architect Victor Horta ever designed. It was built in 1889 to house a bas relief by sculptor Jef Lambeaux. But the sensual work, entitled Human Passions, was considered so racy that there was a public outcry and it was closed after only three days. ⊠Parc du Cinquantenaire 10, Etterbeek ☎02/741–7211 ⊕www. kmkg-mrah.be 💶€5 ⊙Tues.–Fri. 9:30–5, weekends 10–5 Ⓜ Metro: Merode.

IN & AROUND IXELLES: ART NOUVEAU & ART DECO

The commune of Ixelles sprung up around the avenue Louise, which King Leopold II commissioned to connect the Bois de la Cambre woodland with the city center. Art Nouveau town houses and upscale boutiques border the avenue, while tree-lined residential streets lead down to the *etangs d'Ixelles* (Ixelles ponds), with their weeping willows, ducks and swans, and endlessly circling joggers. Farther south, streets bustling with grocers and Portuguese restaurants eventually give way to the more staid European quarter, which teems with besuited bureaucrats. Brussels' sizable French-speaking black population, hailing mostly from the Republic of Congo (the former Zaire), congregates in the area of Ixelles known as Matonge. Chaussée de Wavre is the principal street for African shops, bars, and restaurants.

For a self-guided walking tour of the area that takes in Art Nouveau and Art Deco houses, start at place Vanderkindere. From here, turn right and head down avenue Brugmann, past a remarkable assortment of Art Nouveau houses. Look particularly for Brunfaut's **Hôtel Hannon,** at the intersection of Brugmann and avenue de la Jonction, and the charming redbrick Les Hiboux next door. Cross chaussée de Waterloo and head up chaussée de Charleroi, then head right onto rue Américaine to the Musée Horta to see Art Nouveau at its source. Continue on rue Américaine, then turn left onto rue du Page, crossing place du Chatelain and turning left onto rue Simonis. Take a right onto rue du Bailli, then turn left onto rue du Livourne. Turn right onto rue Paul-Émile Janson, stopping at No. 6 to see the Tassel house, also designed by Victor Horta. At avenue Louise turn right, keeping your eye open for the Hôtel Solvay at No. 224, which is generally considered Horta's finest work. (As it's a private home, you can only admire the exterior.) Cross the street and walk down rue Lesbroussart toward place Flagey. Here you can see a 1930s radio building generally called Flagey—an Art Deco gem shaped like a ship.

WHAT TO SEE

45 **Musée Constantin Meunier.** Nineteenth-century painter and sculptor Constantin Meunier (1831–1905) made his mark capturing the hardships of Belgian workers in a distinctive, realistic style. Examples of his work are displayed in his former house and studio. ⊠*rue de l'Abbaye 59, Ixelles* ☎*02/648–4449* ☜*Free* ☉*Tues.–Fri. 10–noon and 1–5* Ⓜ*Bus: 38. Tram: 94.*

43 **Musée d'Architecture.** If Ixelles's Art Nouveau houses have made you hungry for information about Brussels' architectural past, present, and future, head to the Architecture Museum. Set in a former Masonic Lodge, the knowledgeable staff and displays of documents, drawings, and photographs provide a wealth of information. The museum mounts particularly good temporary exhibitions from time to time, such as one examining the depiction of animals in architecture. ⊠*rue de l'Ermitage 86, Ixelles* ☎*02/649–8665* ⊕*www.aam.be* ☜*€4* ☉*Tues.–Sun. 10–5* Ⓜ*Tram: 81.*

41 **Musée David-et-Alice-Van-Buuren.** A perfect 1930s Art Deco interior in fine woodwork gives this museum's art collection some competition for your attention. The period made-to-order carpets and furnishings set off paintings by the Van Buurens, van Gogh sketches, and old masters including a Bruegel, *The Fall of Icarus,* one of the three versions he painted. The house is surrounded by lush formal gardens; one section, the Picturesque Garden, applies deco geometric concepts to the plantings. There's a basic brochure in English. To get here via public transit, take tram 23 or 90 to the Marianne stop. ⊠*Av. Leo Errera 41, Uccle* ☎*02/343–4851* ⊕*www.museumvanbuuren.com* ☜*€10, €5 for gardens only* ☉*Tues.–Sun. 2–5:30 by appointment for groups of up to 20* Ⓜ*Tram: 23, 90.*

44 **Musée des Enfants.** At this museum for 2- to 12-year-olds, the purpose may be educational—learning to handle objects and emotions—but the results are fun. Kids get to plunge their arms into sticky goo, dress up in eccentric costumes, walk through a hall of mirrors, crawl through tunnels, and take photographs with an oversize camera. English-lan-

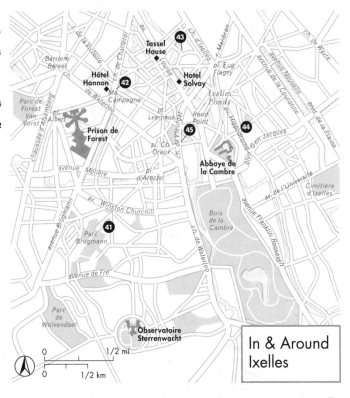

In & Around
Ixelles

guage guide booklets are available. ⌧*rue du Bourgmestre 15, Ixelles*
☏*02/640–0107* ⌖*www.museedesenfants.be* ⌑*€6.85* ✆*Sept.–July,
Wed. and weekends 2:30–5* Ⓜ*Tram: 93, 94 to the Buyl stop.*

NEED A
BREAK?

Cafe Belga (⌧*pl. Flagey 18, Ixelles* ☏*02/640–3508*)**, in an ocean-liner-like
Art Deco building, is a favorite among Brussels' beautiful people and local
TV stars are often seen here. Sip a cocktail or mint tea at the zinc bar or sit
outside and gaze at the swans on the Ixelles ponds.**

❷ **Musée Horta.** The house where Victor Horta (1861–1947), the creator
★ of Art Nouveau, lived and worked until 1919 is the best place to see
his mesmerizing interiors and furniture. Horta's genius lay in his ability to create a sense of opulence, light, and spaciousness where little
light or space existed. Inspired by the direction of the turn-of-the-20th-
century British Arts and Crafts movement, he amplified such designs
into an entire architectural scheme. He shaped iron and steel into fluid,
organic curves; structural elements were revealed. The facade of his
home and studio, built between 1898 and 1901 (with extensions a few
years later), looks somewhat narrow, but once you reach the interior
stairway you'll be struck by the impression of airiness. A glazed sky-
light filters light down the curling banisters, lamps hang like tendrils

from the ceilings, and mirrored skylights evoke giant butterflies with multicolor wings of glass and steel. Like Frank Lloyd Wright after him, Horta had a hand in every aspect of his design, from the door hinges to the wall treatments. You can reach the house by tram 91 or 92, getting off at the Ma Campagne stop. Note that you're not allowed to take photos. There's very little information in English, but you can buy books, postcards and posters in the well-equipped shop. For more examples of how Horta and his colleagues transformed the face of Brussels in little more than 10 years, ride down avenue Louise to Vleur-gat and walk along rue Vilain XIII to the area surrounding the ponds of Ixelles. ✉ *rue Américaine 25, Ixelles* ☎ *02/543–0490* ⊕ *www.horta museum.be* 🎟 *€7* ☉ *Tues.–Sun. 2–5:30* Ⓜ *Tram: 92, 81.*

NORTH OF THE CENTER

Don't be put off by the area's seedy reputation, because here you'll find green suburbs and some of Brussels' best tourist attractions. There are several sights clustered around the **Atomium** building, a model of a molecule that can be seen from all over the city. Anderlecht and Schaer-beek communes are home to a strong community of North African and Turkish immigrants, who have brought a vibrant street culture to the city. Pleasant Laeken is where the royal family spends most of its time, while Jette has a village feel and lots of amenities for children.

WHAT TO SEE

☾ ★ **Atomium.** Built for the 1958 World's Fair, the model of an iron molecule enlarged 165 billion times is one of Brussels' landmarks. It reopened in 2006 after a massive renovation that replaced its metal skin with sparkling stainless steel, spruced up its exhibition spaces, and put in a new café. Take an express elevator to the top, 400 feet up, for pan-oramic views of Brussels. To get here, pick up the 1A subway near the place Ste-Catherine and take it to the Heysel stop. The trip takes under an hour; you'll see the Atomium to your right as you get off the train. ✉ *blvd. du Centenaire, Heysel* ☎ *02/475–4777* ⊕ *www.atomium.be* 🎟 *€9* ☉ *Daily 10–7* Ⓜ *Metro: Heysel. Tram: 23, 81.*

☾ **Mini-Europe.** In a 5-acre park next to the Atomium stands an impressive collection of 1:25 scale models of more than 300 famous buildings and sights from the 25 EU countries, including a chiming Big Ben and a steaming Vesuvius. The "Spirit of Europe" exhibit celebrates the Euro-pean experiment with games and displays on themes such as diversity. From mid-July through mid-August, the park illuminates the models until 11 PM on Friday, Saturday, and Sunday. ✉ *blvd. du Centenaire 20, Heysel* ☎ *02/478–0550* ⊕ *www.minieurope.com* 🎟 *€12.40, €23.50 combination ticket with Oceade* ☉ *Oct.–Mar., daily 10–5; Apr.–June and Sept., daily 9:30–5; July and Aug., daily 9:30–7* Ⓜ *Metro: Heysel. Tram: 23, 81.*

☾ **Oceade.** Attractions at this water park include waterslides, a Jacuzzi, and a wave pool. ✉ *Bruparck, near Atomium and next to Mini-Europe, Heysel* ☎ *02/478–4944* ⊕ *www.oceade.be* 🎟 *€15.50, €23.50 combi-*

nation ticket with Mini-Europe ⊗*Feb.–Dec., Tues.–Thurs. 10–6, Fri., weekends, and holidays 10–9* Ⓜ*Metro: Heysel. Tram: 23, 81.*

Château Royal de Laeken. If your timing's right, you can get a glimpse of the plush lifestyle of Belgium's royals at their residence in Laeken. Their castle was built in 1784 in a 395-acre park north of central Brussels. The extensive steel-and-glass royal greenhouses, built in 1902, are stunning architectural feats and are home to a lush and fascinating collection of exotic plants. Sadly, the castle, greenhouses, and park are only open to the public for two weeks in April and May. Dates are set each year in February. Contact the Brussels Tourist Office for more information. ⊠*Av. Jules Van Praet 44, Laeken* ☎*No phone* Ⓜ*Metro: Heysel. Tram: 52, 23.*

La Tour Japonaise & Le Pavillon Chinois. On the edge of the royal estate at Laeken, you'll find a pair of buildings seemingly conjured up from Asia: the Japanese Tower and the Chinese Pavilion. King Leopold II was so impressed by a Japanese structure constructed for the 1900 Paris Exhibition that he bought the plans for the 125-foot Japanese Tower and had a replica built on the edge of his royal estate at Laeken. The wood doors and sculpted panels are the work of Japanese craftsmen, and the building houses temporary Japanese art exhibits. The king also ordered the construction of a Chinese pavilion next to the tower; the kiosk and most exterior woodwork were made in Shanghai. The pavilion was originally intended as a deluxe restaurant, but it now displays a collection of 17th- and 18th-century Chinese porcelain and furniture. The admission fee includes both sights. To reach the estate, you can take tram 52 or 23 (stop Araucaria), or the metro to the Heysel stop. ⊠*Av. Jules Van Praet 44, Laeken* ☎*02/268–1608 Tour Japonaise, 02/268–2156 Pavillon Chinois* ⊠*€4* ⊗*Tues.–Fri. 9:30–4:45, weekends 10–4:45* Ⓜ*Qinsert metro info.*

Basilique Nationale de Koekelberg. The fifth-largest church in the world, the basilica was built to commemorate the 75th anniversary of Belgian independence. Started in 1905, the construction was halted by the two World Wars and wasn't finished until the 1960s. The main dome of the bulky brick-faced structure is flanked by two towers. In summer you can climb to the dome for outstanding views of the city. To get here, take the metro from place Louise to the Simonis stop. ⊠*Parvis de la Basilique 1, Koekelberg* ☎*No phone* ⊠*Church free, dome €2* ⊗*Church: May–Oct., daily 8–7; Nov.–Apr., daily 8–5. Dome: May–Oct., daily 11–3* Ⓜ*Metro: Simonis.*

Anderlecht Beguinage. The Beguines, lay sisters and mostly widows of Crusaders, lived here in a collection of small houses, built between 1252 and the 17th century, grouped around a garden. Now it's open to the public, sharing a common administrative office with the Maison d'Erasme. ⊠*rue du Chapître 8, Anderlecht* ☎*No phone* Ⓜ*Metro: St Guidon.*

★ **Maison d'Erasme/Erasmushuis.** In the middle of a commonplace neighborhood in the commune of Anderlecht stands the remarkable redbrick Erasmus House, which has been restored to its condition in 1521, the year the great humanist came to Brussels for the fresh air. First editions of *In Praise of Folly* and other books by Erasmus can be inspected, and there are some extraordinary works of art: prints by Albrecht Dürer and oils by Holbein and Hieronymus Bosch. Erasmus was out of tune with the ecclesiastical authorities of his day, and some of the pages on view show where the censors stepped in to protect the faithful. ⊠ *rue du Chapître 31, Anderlecht* ☎ *02/521–1383* 🎫 *€1.25* 🕙 *Tues.–Sun. 10–5* Ⓜ *Metro: St Guidon.*

Musée Magritte. From the Maison d'Erasme, it's a short walk down rue St-Guidon to Anderlecht's St-Guidon metro station, where you can catch tram 49 to reach the Magritte Museum. The Surrealist artist René Magritte (1898–1967) lived in this house with his wife for 24 highly productive years. You can visit his studio and see a collection of original works, documents, personal effects, and photographs. Note how many of the building's architectural quirks, such as the door handles, found their way into his paintings. Take tram 49 to the Woeste stop (in Jette commune). ⊠ *rue Esseghem 135, Jette* ☎ *02/428–2626* 🌐 *www.magrittemuseum.be* 🎫 *€7* 🕙 *Wed.–Sun. 10–6* Ⓜ *Tram: 49.*

Musée Charlier. This museum was also an artist's home. Sculptor Guillaume Charlier and his friend Henri Van Cutsem were avid art collectors and asked Victor Horta to convert two houses into one to contain their treasures. It's an eclectic mix, with piles of decorative objects from the 18th to 20th centuries, an impressive collection of Belgian art, and Charlier's own realistic works vying for attention. There is an English-language audioguide. To get here, take the metro line 2 to Madou. ⊠ *Av. des Arts 16, St-Josse* ☎ *02/220–2819* 🌐 *www.charliermuseum.be* 🎫 *€5* 🕙 *Tues.–Thurs. noon–5* Ⓜ *Metro: Madou.*

WHERE TO EAT

Many of the most renowned, long-established restaurants cluster around the city center. Bustling *moules–frîtes* (mussels with fries) restaurants line the streets around the Grand'Place, while on trendy rue Antoine Dansaert there's a constant rotation of chic, eclectic eateries. Head to the commune of Ixelles, to the south, for ethnic spots and neighborhood favorites. The area around the EU institutions comes up short in the food department; there are many weekday-only sandwich shops but few restaurants of note.

LOWER TOWN

$$–$$$$ ✕ **Aux Armes de Bruxelles.** Another reliable choice among the many
BELGIAN tourist traps of the Ilôt Sacré, this kid-friendly restaurant attracts a largely local clientele with its slightly tarnished middle-class elegance and Belgian classics: turbot waterzooi, a variety of steaks, and mussels prepared every conceivable way. The place is cheerful and light, and service is friendly if frequently overstretched. A lunch menu is available for €27. ⊠ *rue des Bouchers 13, Lower Town* ☎ *02/511–5550* 🍴 *AE, DC, MC, V* 🕙 *Closed Mon.* Ⓜ *Metro: Gare Centrale.*

$$$ – $$$$
BELGIAN

✕**Belga Queen.** Any runs on this former bank are now impelled by the kitchen's modern take on traditional Belgian cuisine. A trendy crowd gathers under the 19th-century stained-glass ceiling, angling for a place at the oyster or cigar bars or a dish of *waterzooi* (a traditional Belgian stew made with seafood or chicken, vegetables, eggs, cream, and butter) cooked in a wok. This is the place to impress a date, but don't be alarmed by the unisex bathroom stalls—the clear-glass doors become opaque once they're locked. Lunch on Fridays and Saturdays has live music. ⊠ *rue du Fossé-aux-Loups 32, Lower Town* ☎ *02/217–2187* ⌕ *Reservations essential* ☰ *AE, DC, MC, V* Ⓜ *Metro: De Brouckere.*

$$ – $$$
CONTEMPORARY

✕**Bonsoir Clara.** On downtown's trendy rue Antoine Dansaert, this is the jewel in the crown of young restaurateur Frédéric Nicolay, who runs half a dozen fashionable cafés and eateries in the capital, including the Moroccan-inspired Kasbah next door. An upbeat, refined brasserie serving excellent caramelized duck as well as fish and red-meat dishes, Bonsoir Clara is best known for eye-catching decor. For instance, the back wall is entirely composed of large squares of colored glass, beautifully illustrating Brussels' stained-glass-making tradition. ⊠ *rue Antoine Dansaert 22, Lower Town* ☎ *02/502–0990* ☰ *AE, MC, V* ⊙ *No lunch weekends* Ⓜ *Metro: De Brouckere, Tram: Bourse.*

$$ – $$$$
BELGIAN
★

✕**Chez Léon.** More than a century old, this cheerful restaurant has expanded over the years into a row of eight old houses, while its franchises can now be found across Belgium and even in Paris. It's a reliable choice on the restaurant-lined rue des Bouchers—though don't expect to see any locals eating here. Heaped plates of mussels and other Belgian specialties, such as *anguilles en vert* (eels in an herb sauce) and fish soup, are continually served. ⊠ *rue des Bouchers 18, Lower Town* ☎ *02/511–1415* ☰ *AE, DC, MC, V* Ⓜ *Metro: Gare Centrale.*

$$$$
FRENCH
Fodor's Choice
★

✕**Comme Chez Soi.** Pierre Wynants, the perfectionist owner-chef of what many consider the best restaurant in the country, has decorated his bistro-size restaurant in Art Nouveau style. The superb cuisine, excellent wines, and attentive service complement the warm decor. Wynants is ceaselessly inventive, and earlier creations are quickly relegated to the back page of the menu. One all-time favorite, fillet of sole with a white-wine mousseline and shrimp, is, however, always available. One minus: ventilation is poor and it can get very smoky. Book weeks in advance to be sure of a table. ⊠ *pl. Rouppe 23, Lower Town* ☎ *02/512–2921* ⌕ *Reservations essential Jacket and tie* ☰ *AE, DC, MC, V* ⊙ *Closed Sun., Mon., July, and Dec. 25–Jan. 1. No lunch Wed.* Ⓜ *Metro: Anneessens.*

¢ – $
CONTEMPORARY

✕**Como Como.** This fun restaurant serves *pintxos* (Basque tapas) on a quirky conveyer belt. Simply grab tasty bite-sized morsels of beef, octopus, tortillas as they go past you—the bill is calculated by how many dishes you pile up in front of you. There's a great selection of Spanish wines, and very pretty desserts. ⊠ *rue Antoine Dansaert 19, Lower Town* ☎ *02/503–0330* ☰ *AE, DC, MC, V* Ⓜ *Metro: De Brouckere, Ste-Catherine. Tram: Bourse.*

¢ – $
CONTEMPORARY

✕**Exki.** Weighed down by waterzooi? Come to this low-key spot for lunch or a light supper of delicious salad, lasagna, or soup, perhaps paired with organic lemonade. The fresh food is complemented by the light, airy interior and ecologically sound wooden dishes and cutlery. Outlets are popping up all over town, but the branches on rue Nueve and chaussée d'Ixelles are the most established. ⊠*rue Neuve 78, Lower Town* ☎*02/219–1991* ⊠*chaussée d'Ixelles 12, Ixelles* ☎*02/502–7277* ⌁*Reservations not accepted* ⊟*MC* Ⓜ*Metro: De Brouckere.*

\$\$–\$\$\$
BELGIAN
★

✕**In 't Spinnekopke.** True Brussels cooking flourishes in this charming restaurant. The low ceilings and benches around the walls remain from its days as a coach inn during the 18th century. Choose from among 100 artisanal beers, then tuck into dishes made with the tipple, such as *lapin à Gueuze* (rabbit stewed in fruit beer). Go with an appetite as portions are huge. The knowledgeable waiters will recommend the best beers to go with your food. ⊠*pl. du Jardin aux Fleurs 1, Lower Town* ☎*02/511–8695* ⊟*AE, DC, MC, V* ☺*Closed Sun. No lunch Sat.* Ⓜ*Metro: De Brouckere. Tram: Bourse.*

\$\$\$–\$\$\$\$
FRENCH

✕**Maison du Cygne.** Karl Marx used to drink here when the "Swan's House" was a tavern, but now it's a place for power dining. With decor to match its impressive cuisine, the restaurant is set in a 17th-century guildhall on the Grand'Place. The paneled walls of the formal dining room upstairs are hung with old masters, and a small room on the mezzanine contains two priceless Bruegels. Typical French-Belgian dishes include steamed turbot with hazelnut-mint dressing, roast pheasant, and saddle of lamb. Service is flawless. You'll need to make reservations a few weeks in advance. ⊠*rue Charles Buyls 2, Lower Town* ☎*02/511–8244* ⌁*Reservations essential Jacket and tie* ⊟*AE, DC, MC, V* ☺*Closed Sun., 3 wks in Aug., and 2 wks over Christmas. No lunch Sat.* Ⓜ*Metro: De Brouckere, Gare Centrale. Tram: Bourse.*

\$\$–\$\$\$
ITALIAN
★

✕**Mirante.** Don't be put off by the kitsch decor; this busy and popular Italian restaurant serves the best pizzas in town, alongside specialities from Puglia. Try the Fiorentina, a spinach pizza with a raw egg yolk in its center. ⊠*rue Henri Maus 19, Lower Town* ☎*02/511–9877* ⊟*AE, DC, MC, V* Ⓜ*Metro: De Brouckere, Tram: Bourse.*

\$\$–\$\$\$
BELGIAN
★

✕**La Roue d'Or.** Bright orange and yellow murals pay humorous homage to Surrealist René Magritte in this excellent Art Nouveau brasserie. Bowler-hatted gentlemen ascend serenely to the ceiling, a blue sky inhabited by tropical birds. The good cuisine includes traditional Belgian fare—a generous fish waterzooi and homemade frites—as well as such staples of the French brasserie repertory as lamb's tongue vinaigrette with shallots, veal kidneys with tarragon and watercress cream, and foie gras. Menus in English are on hand. ⊠*rue des Chapeliers 26, Lower Town* ☎*02/514–2554* ⊟*AE, DC, MC, V* ☺*Closed mid-July–mid-Aug.* Ⓜ*Metro: Gare Centrale. Tram: Bourse.*

¢–\$
BELGIAN

✕**Le Pain Quotidien.** These bakeries–cum–snack bars are popular brunch spots on weekend mornings. They have spread like wildfire all over Europe (and even to New York and Los Angeles) with the same satisfying formula: hearty homemade soups, open-face sandwiches on farm-style bread, and bowls of café au lait, served at a communal table from 7:30 AM to 7 PM. ⊠*rue Antoine Dansaert 16, Lower Town* ☎*02/502–2361* ⊠*rue des Sablons 11, Upper Town* ☎*02/513–5154* ⌁*Reservations not accepted* ⊟*No credit cards* Ⓜ*Metro: De Brouckere. Tram: Bourse, or 92, 94 for Sablon.*

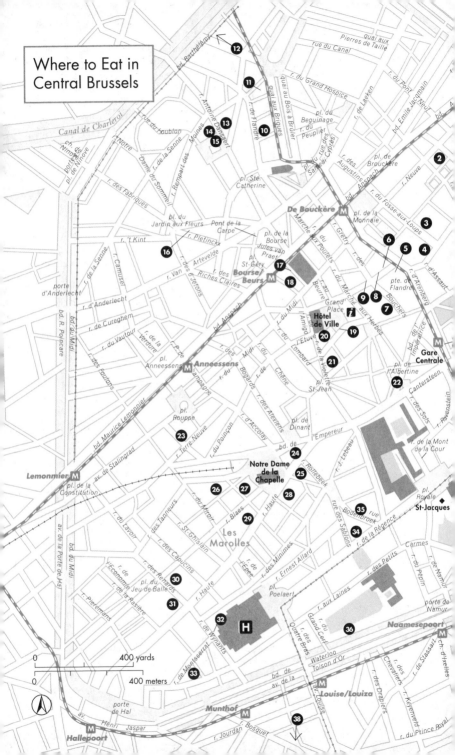

3

KEY

H Hospital

Metro

Rail

Tram

i Tourist Information

Moules the Word

Munching mussels in Brussels is one local Belgian tradition that most visitors don't pass up. The national dish is in season from September to February and most of the mussels are swept from the North Sea straight to your plate. Traditionally they are served in a large, steaming, black pot of savory broth, with a portion of Belgian frites and a large dollop of mayonnaise. The broth is usually à la marinere, a tasty sauce of white wine, shallots, parsley, and butter; occasionally the white wine is replaced by Belgian beer. Another common method of serving is à la crème, where the stock is thickened with flour and heavy cream.

Among the many fish restaurants in the maze of little alleyways behind the Grand'Place, mussels can be found in and out of season. Chez Léon on rue des Bouchers is a favorite for mussels tasting. Tourists and personalities from the world of business, culture, and politics flock to the restaurant to try one of 14 homemade mussels recipes, including the *moules speciale*, made from a secret casserole recipe.

Aux Armes de Bruxelles, also on rue des Bouchers, is another good option for indulging in mussels. But for those seeking a less-touristy location to enjoy the famous Belgian dish, place Ste-Catherine has a good reputation for delicious fish restaurants. Bij den Boer, on the Quai des Briques next to the square, is a popular treat for locals who rave about its wide range of fish specialities.

$$$–$$$$
FRENCH
★
✕**L'Ogenblik.** This small, split-level restaurant, on a side alley off the Galeries St-Hubert, has all the trappings of an old-time bistro: green-shaded lamps over marble-top tables, sawdust on the floor, and laid-back waiters. There's nothing casual about the French-style cuisine, however: wild duck with apples and pepper, millefeuille of lobster and salmon with a coulis of langoustines, saddle of lamb with spring vegetables and potato gratin. The selection of Beaujolais is particularly good. ✉*Galerie des Princes 1, Lower Town* ☎*02/511–6151* ▭*AE, DC, MC, V* ⊘*Closed Sun.* Ⓜ*Metro: Gare Centrale, De Brouckere.*

$$$$
SEAFOOD
★
✕**Sea Grill.** Dashing superstar chef Yves Mattagne presides over the kitchen of arguably the best seafood place in town. Gastronomes rub shoulders here with tycoons and aristocrats, as they tuck into king crab from the Barents Sea, Dublin Bay prawns, Brittany lobster pressed table-side, and line-caught sea bass crusted with sea salt. Inevitably, because of its hotel location, the restaurant feels rather corporate, but it's spacious and elegant, and service is impeccable. ✉*Radisson SAS Hotel, rue du Fossé-aux-Loups, Lower Town* ☎*02/227–3120* ▭*AE, DC, MC, V* ⊘*Closed weekends and mid-July–Aug.* Ⓜ*Metro: De Brouckere. Tram: Bourse.*

$$–$$$
GREEK
✕**Strofilia.** Set in a restored 17th-century warehouse with exposed-brick walls and a magnificent vaulted wine cellar, this atmospheric Greek restaurant has a good selection of hot and cold mezes to mix and match, as well as salads for vegetarians. Minced lamb kebab and pork with eggplant, tomatoes, and cheese are among the choices. It's open until 1 AM on Friday and Saturday and is a great place for large groups. ✉*rue du Marché aux Porcs 11–13, Lower Town* ☎*02/512–3293* ▭*AE,*

DC, MC, V ⊘*Closed Sun. No lunch* Ⓜ*Metro: Ste-Catherine.*

$$–$$$
BELGIAN
★
✕**Taverne Falstaff.** Students, pensioners, and everyone in-between flock to this century-old huge tavern with an Art Nouveau terrace and legendarily grumpy waiters. While the menu devotes itself to straightforward Belgian cuisine throughout the day and into the night, Cuban music and cocktails take over after 11 PM. (The kitchen is open until 5 AM on weekends.) The same group owns the next-door Montecristo Café, which is another loud, popular, late-night spot with Latin flavor. ⊠*rue Henri Maus 19, Lower Town* ☏*02/511–9877* ▭*AE, DC, MC, V* Ⓜ*Metro: De Brouckere. Tram: Bourse.*

$–$$
BELGIAN
✕**'t Kelderke.** Head down into this 17th-century vaulted cellar restaurant (watch out for the low door frame) for traditional Belgian cuisine served at plain wooden tables. Portions are huge and mussels are the house specialty, but the *stoemp et saucisses* (mashed potatoes and sausages) are equally tasty. It's a popular place with locals, open from noon to 2 AM. There are no reservations, so turn up early to be sure of a table. ⊠*Grand'Place 15, Lower Town* ☏*02/513–7344* ▭*AE, DC, MC, V* Ⓜ*Metro: De Brouckere. Tram: Bourse.*

$$$–$$$$
BELGIAN
✕**Vincent.** In a town where seafood has the upper hand on many menus, Vincent unapologetically remains a red-meat stronghold. The menu is full of Belgian specialities, like beef carbonnade (beef stew), and there are plenty of fish options, too, including mussels and cod meunière. Don't miss the hand-painted ceramic mural of fishermen at sea. ⊠*rue des Dominicains 8–10, Lower Town* ☏*02/511–2303* ▭*AE, DC, MC, V* ⊘*Closed 1st 2 wks Aug, 2 wks at Christmas.* Ⓜ*Metro: De Brouckere.*

¢–$$$
BELGIAN
✕**Viva M'Boma.** For an edgier take on Belgian cooking, visit this minimalist space in the trendy Antoine Dansaert quarter. Be brave and try the excellent *petit gris* (snails). ⊠*rue de Flandres 17, Lower Town* ☏*02/512–1593* ▭*AE, MC, V* ⊘*Closed Sun. and Wed.* Ⓜ*Metro: Ste-Catherine.*

IN & AROUND IXELLES

$–$$
FRENCH
✕**A Malte.** Located on a quiet side street near the bustling central avenue Louise, A Malte offers a cosy atmosphere with its mixture of furniture from Africa, and the Middle and Far East. Great for candlelit dinners, it also offers a quiet terrace at the back of the restaurant that's ideal for summer nights. The food is French-based, using oils and vinaigrettes rather than heavy creams, and the house specializes in finely

CLOSE UP

Brunch It

If you've skipped your hotel breakfast or gotten up early to catch the best bargains at one of Brussels' street markets, treat yourself to a little brunch at a traditional café or upscale spot.

For the best brioche in town, visit **A.M. Sweet** (✉ *rue des Chartreux 4, Lower Town* ☎ *02/513–5131*). This lovely little tearoom is run by a charming husband-and-wife team and their dog Cézanne. In addition to all kinds of tea by the Paris brand Mariage Frères, you can indulge in coffee, hot chocolate, and pastries.

For a quick bite, head to the stylish **Mundo Pain** (✉ *rue Jean Stas 20, Ixelles* ☎ *02/537–9700*). Sit outside on the terrace in the summer and indulge in a glass of rosé and some soup and sandwiches, or escape to the sophisticated interior on cold days for coffee and croissants. Don't leave without buying some bread—there are even gluten-free and organic options.

Sit in the shadow of pretty Trinity Church and enjoy a fine selection of teas at **Passiflore** (✉ *rue du Bailli 97, Ixelles* ☎ *02/538–4210*). As well as a range of Continental breakfast delicacies, the café specializes in Niçoise salads and quiches. Those with a sweet tooth can tuck into apple tart or the Passiflore crepe with raspberry and strawberry preserves.

Homesick Americans congregate in **The Coffee Shop** (✉ *rue de Stassart 131, Ixelles* ☎ *02/503–0785*) on Sunday mornings from 10 AM. It's got the works—toast, eggs any way you like them, bacon, sausages, and lots of coffee. If you're still hungry, there are even chocolate-chip muffins.

Bla Bla (✉ *rue des Capucins 55, Upper Town* ☎ *02/503–5918*) in the historic Marolles quarter serves a buffet brunch every Sunday from 11 to 3. Tuck into pancakes, scones, scrambled eggs, bacon, and sausages. This lively Mediterranean restaurant doubles as an art gallery, so it's a good spot to awaken your visual sense, as well as your appetite.

—updated by Nicola Smith

cut Argentinean beef. ✉ *rue Berckmans 30, St-Gilles* ☎ *02/539–1015* 🍴 *AE, MC, V* Ⓜ *Metro: Louise.*

$–$$$
FRENCH
★
✕**Au Vieux Bruxelles.** This Brussels institution is a fun, lively place to have dinner and a firm local favorite. The cuisine is decidedly Belgian, with *anguilles au vert* (eels in a green sauce) and hearty carbonnades on the menu, and best accompanied by a good beer. Naturally, everything is served with frites, and be sure to ask for the tasty homemade mayonnaise. If you're feeling too full to tackle a whole dessert, you can order a half portion. ✉ *rue St-Boniface 35, Ixelles* ☎ *02/513–3111* 🍴 *AE, DC, MC, V* ✆ *Closed Mon.* Ⓜ *Metro: Porte de Namur. Bus: 71.*

$$–$$$$
FRENCH
★
✕**De la Vigne à l'Assiette.** When you take into account the high quality of the food and the wine list of this homely, no-frills bistro off avenue Louise, the combination proves to be an exceptionally good value. The modern French cuisine of chef Eddy Dandrimont is embellished with such exotic flourishes as star anise sauce, and crisp angel-hair pasta atop grilled salmon. The excellent wine list refrains from the usual hefty markup. ✉ *rue de la Longue Haie, Ixelles* ☎ *02/647–6803* 🍴 *AE, DC, MC, V* ✆ *Closed Sun. and Mon. No lunch Sat.* Ⓜ *Metro: Louise.*

¢–$ ╳**Exki.** The Ixelles branch of this chain serves the same winning mixture
CONTEMPORARY of fresh and healthy salads and sandwiches. ✉*chaussée d'Ixelles 12,
Ixelles* ☎*02/502–7277* ⚞*Reservations not accepted* ▭*MC* Ⓜ*Metro:
Porte de Namur.*

$–$$$ ╳**Kushi-tei of Tokyo.** Japanese it may be, but this restaurant is sushi free.
JAPANESE Instead, it specializes in *kushiyaki* (wooden skewers of meat and veg-
etables grilled over charcoal), including chicken teriyaki. Pique your
appetite by watching the chef, on view while at work among the siz-
zling skewers. ✉*rue Lesbroussart 118, Ixelles* ☎*02/646–4815* ▭*AE,
DC, MC, V* ☉*Closed Sun. No lunch Sat.* Ⓜ*Tram: 81, 94.*

$–$$$ ╳**La Porte des Indes.** This is the city's foremost Indian restaurant—the
INDIAN creation of Karl Steppe, a Belgian antiques dealer turned restaurateur.
The gracious staff wears traditional Indian attire, and the interior is
warmed by wood carvings and a rich red-and-mauve color scheme.
A vegetarian menu is available and the daily lunch menus are good
value. Order the "brass tray" to try an assortment of specialties. ✉*Av.
Louise 455, Ixelles* ☎*02/647–8651* ▭*AE, DC, MC, V* ☉*No lunch
Sun.* Ⓜ*Tram: 94.*

$$–$$$ ╳**La Quincaillerie.** The name means "The Hardware Store," and that's
FRENCH precisely what this place used to be. It still looks the part, except now
there are tables perched on the narrow balcony, and there's an oyster bar
downstairs. It attracts a stylish, youngish clientele and offers good deals
on business lunches. The menu consists mostly of brasserie standbys, but
it's enlivened by such selections as honey-baked Barbary duck with lime,
and a glorious seafood platter. ✉*rue du Page 45, Ixelles* ☎*02/538–2553*
▭*AE, DC, MC, V* ☉*No lunch weekends* Ⓜ*Tram: 81.*

$$$–$$$$ ╳**La Truffe Noire.** Luigi Ciciriello's "Black Truffle" attracts a sophisti-
ITALIAN cated clientele with its modern design, well-spaced tables, and cuisine
★ that draws on classic Italian and modern French cooking. Carpaccio
is prepared at the table and served with long strips of truffle and Par-
mesan. Entrées may include Vendé pigeon with truffles and steamed
John Dory with truffles and leeks. In summer you can eat in the gar-
den. ✉*blvd. de la Cambre 12, Ixelles* ☎*02/640–4422* ⚞*Reservations
essential Jacket and tie* ▭*AE, DC, MC, V* ☉*Closed Sun and Mon.,
Jan. 1–10, last wk July–1st 2 wks Aug. No lunch Sat.* Ⓜ*Tram: 94.*

$$–$$$$ ╳**Le Fils de Jules.** Vivid, colorful Basque cuisine from southwest France
FRENCH is served with wines to match within the candlelit, Art Deco–inspired
setting. A well-heeled, local crowd flocks here to sup on warm foie gras
with grapes, and tartare of tuna with tapenade. ✉*rue du Page 37, Ixelles*
☎*02/534–0057* ▭*AE, DC, MC, V* ☉*No lunch Sat.* Ⓜ*Tram: 81.*

$$–$$$$ ╳**Le Pain et le Vin.** The plain-spoken name, "Bread and Wine," signals
FRENCH an equally pared-down aesthetic in this excellent restaurant. It's co-
★ owned by acclaimed sommelier Eric Boschman; hence, the cellar is
impressively deep, and wines can be ordered by the glass to accompany
different courses. The food takes the minimalist route with choices such
as risotto with asparagus and tuna steak. The large garden is a plus in
fine weather. ✉*chaussée d'Alsemberg 812A, Uccle* ☎*02/332–3774*
▭*AE, MC, V* ☉*Closed Sun. No lunch Sat.* Ⓜ*Tram 55.*

$–$$$ ╳**Les Larmes du Tigre.** This discreet restaurant near the Palais de Justice
THAI is a favorite among Brussels politicians and serves the best Thai food

in town. The red decor paired with white wicker furniture is a little jarring, but the expertly cooked food is fantastic, particularly the red curry prawns. ⊠*rue Wynants 21, St-Gilles* ☎*02/512–1877* ⊟*AE, DC, MC, V* ⊘*No lunch Sat.* Ⓜ*Metro: Louise. Tram: 92, 94.*

$-$$$ ✕**Mamy Louise.** This is one of several good-quality lunch spots on the
FRENCH pedestrianized rue Jean Stas, just off avenue Louise. With Hamptons-style decor and outdoor tables in warm weather, the varied menu includes Belgian staples like *boudin* (blood sausage), as well as quiches and salads. It's also a great place to grab a morning or afternoon coffee and a delicious slice of cake. ⊠*rue Jean Stas 12, Ixelles* ☎*02/534–2502* ⊟*AE, DC, MC, V* Ⓜ*Metro: Louise.*

¢-$$ ✕**Mont Liban.** Renowned as one of the best Lebanese restaurants in
MIDDLE- town, Mont Liban is always full of local Lebanese expats, and the
EASTERN occasional belly dancer to spice up the atmosphere. It serves a range of mouthwatering meze (hummus, tabbouleh, stuffed vine leaves, and mixed grills) at a reasonable price. Reservations are advisable as it is rarely empty. ⊠*rue de Livourne 30–32, Ixelles* ☎*02/537–7131* ⊟ *AE, DC, MC, V* Ⓜ *Metro: Louise.*

$-$$ ✕**Raconte moi des Salades.** There may be mainly salads on the menu
CAFÉ but this restaurant is not the place to start your diet. Over 30 filling, chunky combinations of salads with beef, lobster, smoked duck, and every possible mixture of ingredients, will leave you satisfied. An intricately designed floor and Aladdin lamps all help to contribute to the restaurant's quirky and artistic ambience. ⊠*pl. du Chatelain 19, Ixelles* ☎*02/534–2727* ⊘*Closed Sun.* ⊟ *MC, V* Ⓜ *Tram: 81 Bailli.*

$$-$$$ ✕**Tan.** An organic restaurant with an original flair. Tan tries to respect
FRENCH the laws of nature and human physiology with a delicious range of natural ingredients, all cooked below boiling to preserve their mouthwatering tastes. The restaurant's decor is simple and uncluttered, creating a feng-shui atmosphere. The staff is friendly and ready to explain the unique cooking techniques. The fish dishes are particularly delicious. Try the bass with black olives or the monkfish with steamed vegetables and cashew-nut sauce. ⊠*rue de l'Aqueduc 95, Ixelles* ☎*02/537–8787* ⊘*Closed Sun. and Mon. No lunch Sat.* ⊟ *MC, V* Ⓜ *Tram: 81 Bailli.*

UPPER TOWN

$-$$ ✕**Au Stekerlapatte.** In the shadow of the Palais de Justice, this down-
BELGIAN to-earth and warren-like bistro serves Franco-Belgian specialties that include cassoulet, sauerkraut, grilled pig's trotters, spareribs, and black pudding with caramelized apples. It's open until 1 AM and the waiters always seem to be able to find you a table, even if the place looks full to bursting. ⊠*rue des Prêtres 4, Upper Town* ☎*02/512–8681* ⊕*www.stekerlapatte.be* ⊟*MC, V* ⊘*Closed Sun. and Mon. No lunch Sat.* Ⓜ*Metro: Hotel des Monnaies.*

$$$-$$$$ ✕**Au Vieux Saint Martin.** Even when neighboring restaurants on Grand
BELGIAN Sablon are empty, this one is full. A rack of glossy magazines is a
★ thoughtful touch for lone diners, and you're equally welcome whether you order a cup of coffee or a full meal. The short menu emphasizes

Brussels specialties, and portions are substantial. The owner, a wine importer, serves unusually good wine for the price, by the glass or bottle. ⊠ *Grand Sablon 38, Upper Town* ☏ *02/512–6476* ⌲ *Reservations not accepted* ▭ *MC, V* Ⓜ *Tram: 95.*

$–$$ **FRENCH** ★ ✕ **Aux Marches de la Chapelle.** This very attractive restaurant, opposite the Eglise de la Chapelle near the Grand Sablon, offers brasserie fare of the highest quality, including traditional sauerkraut. One of the belle-epoque rooms is dominated by a splendid old bar, the other by an enormous open fireplace. ⊠ *pl. de la Chapelle 5, Upper Town* ☏ *02/512–6891* ▭ *AE, DC, MC, V* ☉ *Closed Sun. and 3rd wk July– 3rd wk Aug. No lunch Sat.* Ⓜ *Metro: Gare Centrale. Tram: 92, 94.*

$$–$$$ **ECLECTIC** ✕ **Bazaar.** The building along a side street in the Marolles may once have been a convent, but it now exudes a seductive allure. Candles burn in its cavernous dining room, where Moroccan lamps and sofas create intimacy in a bric-a-brac setting. It's young and fashionable; there's a disco on the lower floor on weekends. The eclectic menu includes such choices as chicken *tajine* (slow-cooked with gravy in a deep, glazed earthenware dish) with olives and lemon. Later in the evening, it becomes a lively bar. ⊠ *rue des Capucins 63, Upper Town* ☏ *02/511–2600* ▭ *AE, DC, MC, V* ☉ *No lunch. Closed Sun.–Wed.* Ⓜ *Metro: Porte de Hal, Louise. Tram: 95. Bus: 95.*

$$$–$$$$ **ITALIAN** ✕ **Castello Banfi.** The elegant place du Grand Sablon makes a fitting backdrop for this refined Italian restaurant. The high quality of the ingredients shines in such dishes as carpaccio with Parmesan and celery, red mullet with ratatouille, and an unbelievably good mascarpone. The wine list is strong on fine Chianti aged in wood. ⊠ *rue Bodenbroek 12, Upper Town* ☏ *02/512–8794 Jacket and tie* ▭ *AE, DC, MC, V* ☉ *Closed Sun. and Mon., Easter wk, Christmas wk, and last 3 wks Aug.* Ⓜ *Tram: 92, 93, 94.*

¢–$ **BELGIAN** ✕ **Eetcafe Het Warm Water.** Just above the place de Jeu de Balle in the heart of the Marolles, this café is a local institution known for its set brunches. These are rib-sticking meals, with muesli, yogurt, eggs, croissants, and some combination of cheese and ham. It's a staunchly Flemish place; the staff doesn't appreciate orders in French (English is preferable). When the neighborhood had no running water, this is where residents would come to get hot water—hence the name. Before wandering down the street to the Vieux Marché (flea market), get a snack of tasty bread and cheese or an omelet here, washed down with a bowl of *lait russe* (milky coffee). ⊠ *rue des Renards 19, Upper Town* ☏ *02/213–9159* ⌲ *Reservations not accepted* ▭ *No credit cards* Ⓜ *Metro: Porte de Hal.*

¢–$$ **ECLECTIC** ✕ **Et qui va promener le chiens?** Though we have absolutely no idea how the restaurant got it's name (roughly translated it means "And who is going to walk the dog?"), it certainly reflects the restaurant's quirky nature. Surrounded by art galleries on a narrow cobbled street close to the pretty Sablon, this restaurant beckons customers with its cozy atmosphere, soft lighting, and trendy, Asian-influenced decor. Its menu is an eclectic mix of African, Asian, Mediterranean, and Latino flavors, as is its wine list. Try the hake filet with chive sauce, or pollack with shallots. ⊠ *rue de Rollebeek 2, Upper Town* ☏ *02/503–2304.*

$$–$$$
FRENCH

✕**La Clef des Champs.** If you're being dogged by overcast days, come to this restaurant for a charming evocation of Provence. It's on a cobbled street off the place du Grand Sablon, and the blue and yellow decor is set off by watercolors, photographs, and poems by the multitalented chef and owner. Some of the edible creations include duck confit or pike and perch with a shallot-Chardonnay dressing. ⊠*rue de Rollebeek 23, Upper Town* ☎*02/512–1193* ⊟*AE, DC, MC, V* ⊘*Closed Mon. No dinner Sun.* Ⓜ*Metro: Gare Centrale.*

$–$$$
BELGIAN

✕**La Grande Porte.** A longtime artists' haunt in the Marolles area that makes no concession to fashion or style, this old place has a piano player and offhand but jovial waiters. It serves copious portions of popular Brussels specialties, such as *ballekes à la marollienne* (spicy meatballs) and *carbonnade à la flamande* (beef and onions stewed in beer). The later in the evening, the livelier the atmosphere and the greater the demand for the restaurant's famous onion soup. ⊠*rue Notre-Seigneur 9, Upper Town* ☎*02/512–8998* ⊟*MC, V* ⊘*Closed Sun. No lunch Sat.* Ⓜ*Metro: Gare Centrale. Tram: 92, 94.*

$$$–$$$$
FRENCH

✕**L'Epicerie.** Highly acclaimed chef Vincent Masson blends the traditional with the exotic, with intriguing results. Try the sea bass with cocoa, or hare in a sauce of dates, chestnuts, and oranges. ⊠*Meridien Hotel, carrefour de l'Europe 3, Upper Town* ☎*02/548–4716* ⊟*AE, DC, MC, V* ⊘*No lunch. Closed Sun.* Ⓜ*Metro: Gare Centrale.*

$$–$$$
BELGIAN

✕**L'Idiot du Village.** Don't believe the modest name of this restaurant in the Marolles; its focus on smart, well-crafted food has fostered a loyal clientele. The decor is relaxed and intimate, kitschy rather than trendy. Dishes include bass with lemon confit, and warm escalope of foie gras with pepper and vanilla. ⊠*rue Notre-Seigneur 19, Upper Town* ☎*02/502–5582* ⊟*AE, DC, MC, V* ⊘*Closed weekends* Ⓜ*Metro: Gare Centrale. Tram: 92, 94.*

$$$–$$$$
CONTEMPORARY
★

✕**Maison du Boeuf.** Red-meat lovers are drawn to the restaurant's beef dishes, especially beef tartare with caviar. There are other tempting traditional French and Belgian choices, too, mostly beef but with a couple of other choices (coq au vin, for example) as well. Upscale in every way, with gliding waiters, heavy silver cutlery, and linen tablecloths, the eatery is a favorite of politicians and high society. Caviar specialities are available, even though they aren't on the menu. ⊠*Hilton Hotel, blvd. de Waterloo 38, Upper Town* ☎*02/504–1111* ⌔*Reservations essential Jacket and tie* ⊟*AE, DC, MC, V* ⊘*No lunch weekends* Ⓜ*Metro: Louise.*

$–$$$
BELGIAN

✕**Taverne du Passage.** This Art Deco brasserie in the famous shopping arcade has been here since 1928 and remains a benchmark of its kind, serving chicken waterzooi, sauerkraut, herring, and lobster from noon to midnight nonstop. Most fun of all, however, are the roasts, which are carved before you. The multilingual waiters are jolly and the wine list is exceptional—not surprising in a restaurant owned by the president of the Belgian guild of sommeliers. Reserve a table outside if you like to watch the world go by. ⊠*Galerie de la Reine 30, Upper Town* ☎*02/512–3731* ⊟*AE, DC, MC, V* ⊘*Closed Wed. and Thurs. and June and July* Ⓜ*Metro: Gare Centrale, De Brouckere.*

CINQUANTENAIRE & SCHUMAN

$$–$$$
CONTEMPORARY
✗**Balthazar.** This chic spot is a lunchtime favorite for Eurocrats, and a dinnertime treat. The sophisticated food has a Pacific Rim flavor, such as chicken with lemongrass, but there's also a good selection of pasta dishes. ✉*rue Archimède 63, Etterbeek* ☎*02/742–0600* ⊟*AE, DC, MC, V* ⊘*Closed Sun. No lunch Sat.* Ⓜ*Metro: Schuman.*

$$–$$$$
FRENCH
✗**La Duchesse.** The eatery within the homely Montgomery Hotel is a cut above the average hotel restaurant. Chef Yves Defontaine specializes in fish but is extremely creative with whatever's on the menu of modern French cuisine. Roast fillet of bass with tarragon and grilled bacon with Guinea pepper are two specialties. ✉*Av. de Tervuren 134, Etterbeek* ☎*02/741–8511* ⊟*AE, DC, MC, V* ⊘*Closed weekends* Ⓜ*Metro: Stockel.*

NORTH OF CENTER

$$$$
FRENCH
✗**Bruneau.** Although it's outside the city center, this long-established restaurant persuades many gourmets from Belgium and beyond to flex their plastic. Meals are served in a lavishly decorated town house or in the garden in summer. The food is complex and ornate; dishes such as *coucou de malines* (chicken stuffed with truffles) are paired with thoughtful selections from the wine list. ✉*Av. Broustin 75, Jette* ☎*02/427–6978* ⊟*AE, DC, MC, V* ⊘*Closed Tues. and Wed., Aug., and 1st wk in Feb.* Ⓜ*Metro: Simonis. Bus: 49.*

¢–$
FRENCH
✗**Faubourg Saint-Antoine.** Tintin lovers will relish this restaurant, with its Hergé-related posters and bric-a-brac, including a life-sized Snowy astronaut suit. The menu changes daily, but expect traditional seasonal fish and meat dishes, including steaks and stews. ✉*Av. Albert Giraud 65, Schaerbeek* ☎*02/245–6394* ⊟*MC, V* ⊘*Closed weekends* Ⓜ*Tram: 23, 53, Train to Gare de Schaerbeek.*

WHERE TO STAY

LOWER TOWN

$$$$
★
▨**Amigo.** A block from the Grand'Place, the Amigo pairs contemporary design with antiques and plush wall hangings. Rooms are decorated in green, red, or blue, with silk curtains, leather headboards, and a mix of modern furniture and antiques. Works by Belgian artists hang on the walls, while Tintin pictures and figurines cheer up the mosaic-tiled bathrooms. If you'd like a view over the surrounding rooftops, ask for a room on one of the higher floors (these also have a higher rate). The understated luxury and polished service make the Amigo a celebrity favorite. **Pros:** conveniently located next to many of Brussels' major attractions. **Cons:** location can make it noisy, some rooms are small. ✉*rue d'Amigo 1–3, Lower Town* ☎*02/547–4747* ⊕*www.rocco fortehotels.com* ↗*176 rooms, 18 suites* ⚬*In-room: safe, Internet. In-hotel: restaurant, room service, bar, gym, parking (paid)* ⊟*AE, DC, MC, V* Ⓜ*Metro: De Brouckere, Gare Centrale. Tram: Bourse.*

$-$$$ 🏨 **Atlas.** This hotel offers unpretentious comfort and a convenient location in a building dating from the 18th century. The small rooms have cream-and-yellow walls, gray carpets, and blue-and-white furniture. Suites, on two floors, each have a kitchenette in the lounge area. Buffet breakfasts are served in the blue-and-white basement with abstract art and the exposed brick of an ancient city wall. **Pros:** good quiet location in the center of the city, cosy atmosphere, clean rooms. **Cons:** books up quickly. ✉ *rue du Vieux Marché aux Grains 30, Lower Town* ☎ *02/502–6006* ⊕ *www.atlas-hotel.be* 🛏 *83 rooms, 5 suites* ♿ *In-room: Wi-Fi. In-hotel: Wi-Fi, parking (paid)* ▭ *AE, DC, MC, V* ⍩ *BP* Ⓜ *Metro: Ste-Catherine. Tram: Bourse.*

$-$$ 🏨 **Bedford.** The hotel that preceded the Bedford at this site was frequented, according to legend, by Luftwaffe and RAF pilots in Brussels for romantic trysts during and after World War II. The current place is family run and welcoming, with marble pillars in its wide lobby, thick pink carpeting in corridors, and rooms decorated in cream, green, or pink, with cherrywood furniture. Bathrooms are small but sparkling in cream marble; 10 rooms have only showers. The location may be a little shabby, but the hotel is within easy reach of the Grand'Place. **Pros:** close to historical town center. **Cons:** in a seedy part of town. ✉ *rue du Midi 135, Lower Town* ☎ *02/507–0000* ⊕ *www.hotelbedford. be* 🛏 *326 rooms* ♿ *In-room: no a/c (some). In-hotel: restaurant, bar, parking (paid)* ▭ *AE, DC, MC, V* ⍩ *BP* Ⓜ *Metro: De Brouckere, Anneesssens.*

$$$-$$$$ 🏨 **Brussels Marriott Hotel.** This branch of the Marriott chain opposite
★   the stock exchange has a striking cream-marble lobby, and each floor has a different theme for its guest rooms. Guest rooms are done in universal corporate-travel style: cherrywood furniture, green- or yellow-striped wallpaper, and marble bathrooms. Quieter ones face an internal courtyard; those on upper floors have city views. Nearly half of the rooms are especially geared toward business travelers, with ergonomic desk chairs and no-glare lamps. **Pros:** good central location, nice bar, good breakfast. **Cons:** as a chain hotel, it lacks individual charm. ✉ *rue A. Orts 1–7, Lower Town* ☎ *02/516–9090* ⊕ *www.marriott. com* 🛏 *212 rooms, 6 suites* ♿ *In-room: safe, Internet. In-hotel: restaurant, bar, gym, parking (paid)* ▭ *AE, DC, MC, V* ⍩ *BP* Ⓜ *Metro: De Brouckere.*

$$$ 🏨 **Eurostars Sablon.** On a quiet street between the Sablon and the Grand'Place, this hotel offers spacious and attractive rooms, some with canopy beds. Some rooms are a bit dark. Suites arranged in duplex style favor comfort over corporate entertainment, with a gingham-covered sofa, a spiral staircase leading up to a tiny landing and a modern, yet classic-style bedroom in cherrywood and cream. **Pros:** good location close to the pretty Sablon area. **Cons:** the streets round the Sablon can be quiet at night. ✉ *rue de la Paille, Lower Town* ☎ *02/513–6040* ⊕ *www.eurostarshotels.com* 🛏 *32 rooms, 4 suites* ♿ *In-room: Internet, safe. In-hotel: bar, spa, gym, Internet terminal.* ▭ *AE, DC, MC, V* ⍩ *CP* Ⓜ *Metro: Gare Centrale.*

$-$$ 🏨 **Floris Arlequin Grand Place.** While the surrounding streets of the Ilôt Sacré neighborhood buzz with activity, this friendly hotel stays calm and down-to-earth. Its well-lit rooms have cream-color bamboo fittings and impressionist prints; some bathrooms have only showers. The panoramic Septième Ciel (Seventh Heaven) restaurant has views over the rooftops to the spires of the Hôtel de Ville and the cathedral. A jazz band plays in the '70s-style basement bar several nights a week. A cinema in the same arcade shows second-run and art-house movies—and gives hotel guests a discount. **Pros:** five-minute walk from Central Station. **Cons:** neighborhood can be noisy; some bathrooms only have showers. ☒*rue de la Fourche 17–19, Lower Town* ☎*02/514–1614* ⊕*www.arlequin.be* ⇆*92 rooms* ⚐*In-room: Internet. In-hotel: bar, parking (paid)* ☐*AE, DC, MC, V* ⏀*BP* Ⓜ*Metro: Gare Centrale.*

¢–$ ⚏ **George V.** Ivy-covered and quiet, this hotel fills a large house dating from 1859. Rooms, which accommodate up to four people, are simple but spacious, bright, and clean. Some have a deep shower tub rather than a full bath. The homey breakfast room has wicker chairs. Although centrally located, the hotel's on a calm residential street. **Pros:** family-run hotel, reasonable prices, close to the Brussels night life. **Cons:** some rooms are small. ☒*rue t' Kint 23, Lower Town* ☎*02/513–5093* ⇆*16 rooms* ⚐*In-room: Internet. In-hotel: room service, bar, parking (paid)* ☐*AE, MC, V* ⏀*CP* Ⓜ*Tram: Bourse.*

¢–$ ⚏ **La Vieille Lanterne.** More bed-and-breakfast than hotel, this tiny, old place of six rooms is run by the family that owns the gift shops on the ground floor. All rooms look out onto the street and the crowds that cluster round the famous Manneken Pis fountain opposite; each has a bathroom with shower only. The linoleum floors and wood furniture are cheered by pink, green, and yellow stained-glass windows. Breakfast is served in the rooms. **Pros:** good price for such a central location. **Cons:** its location near Manneken Pis makes it a noisy hectic location; no on-site parking. ☒*rue des Grands Carmes 29, Lower Town* ☎*02/512–7494* ⇆*6 rooms* ⚐*In hotel: room service, some pets allowed* ☐*AE, DC, MC, V* ⏀*CP* Ⓜ*Metro: Bourse.*

$$$–$$$$ ⚏ **Le Dixseptième.** Here you can stay in what was once the residence of
Fodor'sChoice the Spanish ambassador. The stylishly restored 17th-century building
★ lies between the Grand'Place and the Gare Centrale. Rooms surround a lovely interior courtyard, and suites are up a splendid Louis XVI staircase. Named after Belgian artists, rooms have whitewashed walls, plain floorboards, exposed beams, and suede sofas. Suites have decorative fireplaces and the honeymoon suite is particularly romantic. **Pros:** good central location, hotel has more charm than chain brands. **Cons:** some reviews complain of unfriendly staff. ☒*rue de la Madeleine 25, Lower Town* ☎*02/502–5744* ⊕*www.ledixseptieme.be* ⇆*22 rooms, 2 suites* ⚐*In-room: safe, kitchen (some), Internet, Wi-Fi. In-hotel: bar* ☐*AE, DC, MC, V* Ⓜ*Metro: De Brouckere.*

$$$–$$$$ ⚏ **Le Plaza.** Inspired by the George V in Paris, the Plaza opened in 1930 and has maintained a grandiose reputation. The public spaces have soaring ceilings and ornate chandeliers; guest rooms have imposingly heavy wooden furniture. Deluxe rooms and suites have free access to a neighboring fitness center. The bar-restaurant has a domed roof; the breakfast room is palatial. But the real treasure is the hotel's historic theater, a former cinema that is now used for conferences, banquets,

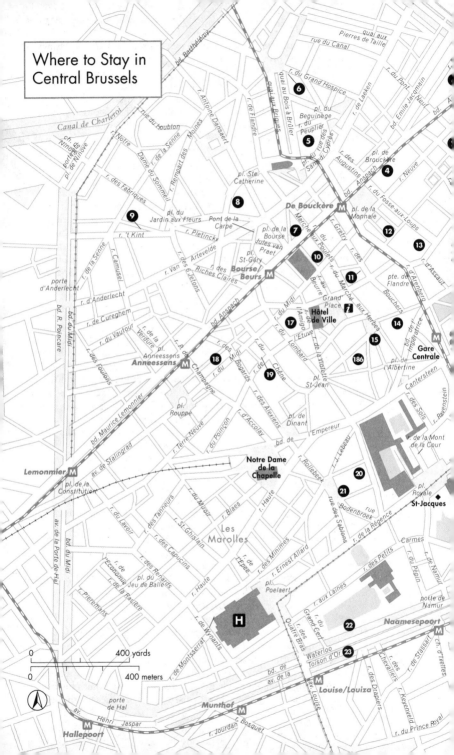

Where to Stay in Central Brussels

3

and presentations. **Pros:** good central location. **Cons:** it's not an unsafe or seedy area, but there are sex shops and lap-dancing clubs close by; parking is €30 per day. ✉ *blvd. Adolphe Max 118–126, Lower Town* ☎ *02/278–0100* ⊕ *www.leplaza-brussels.be* ✎ *93 rooms, 17 suites* ⌂ *In-room: safe, Internet. In-hotel: restaurant, bar, gym, parking (paid)* ☐ *AE, DC, MC, V* Ⓜ *Metro: Rogier.*

$–$$ ⬚ **Matignon.** Only the facade was preserved in the conversion of this belle-epoque building to a hotel in 1993. The lobby is no more than a corridor, making room for the large café-brasserie that is part of the family-owned operation. The spotless rooms are small and plain but have generous beds and large-screen TVs. Windows are double-glazed, vital in this busy spot across the street from the Bourse and two blocks from the Grand'Place. **Pros:** cheap option in the city's center. **Cons:** small lobby. ✉ *rue de la Bourse 10, Lower Town* ☎ *02/511–0888* ⊕ *www.hotelmatignon.be* ✎ *37 rooms* ⌂ *In-hotel: restaurant, bar* ☐ *AE, DC, MC, V* Ⓜ *Metro: De Brouckere. Tram: Bourse.*

$$$$ ⬚ **Métropole.** Stepping into this classic hotel, you might think you're
★   boarding the *Orient Express*. The hotel, built in 1895, exudes belle-epoque style and provides impeccable service. The lobby sets the tone, with its enormously high coffered ceiling, chandeliers, marble, Oriental rugs, and old-fashioned wood-paneled elevator, and the theme is carried through in other public spaces. The rooms, however, are understated and modern. The bar is worth a visit for its Art Nouveau decor, friendly waiters, and excellent drink selection. **Pros:** good central location; exquisite lobby; free minibar in the rooms. **Cons:** rooms could use a face-lift. ✉ *pl. de Brouckère 31, Lower Town* ☎ *02/217–2300* ⊕ *www.metropolehotel.com* ✎ *306 rooms, 17 suites* ⌂ *In-room: safe. In-hotel: restaurant, bar, gym, parking (free)* ☐ *AE, DC, MC, V* �‖ *CP* Ⓜ *Metro: De Brouckere.*

$–$$ ⬚ **Noga.** The hotel's Web site promises a "cosy, cosy, very cosy" spot,
★   and indeed it is. Opened in 1958, the Noga is packed with mementos of the Jazz Age, from table lamps to black-and-white photographs of the period. There are rooms on four floors for two, three, or four people—larger rooms have sofas—and all have bathrooms with shower only. You can rent a bike, borrow a book from the library, or even order a picnic lunch to take sightseeing with you. The hotel is in the popular Béguinage quarter, near the Ste-Catherine fish market. **Pros:** great location, inexpensive rates. **Cons:** hotel could use some updating. ✉ *rue du Béguinage 38, Lower Town* ☎ *02/218–6763* ⊕ *www.nogahotel.com* ✎ *19 rooms* ⌂ *In-room: safe. In-hotel: bar, bicycles, parking (paid), Wi-Fi* ☐ *AE, DC, MC, V* �‖ *BP* Ⓜ *Metro: Ste-Catherine.*

$$$ ⬚ **Novotel off Grand'Place.** There's no false advertising to the name; this 1989 hotel is a stone's throw from the Grand'Place. Though the facade's gables mimic those of older buildings, the Novotel has the cookie-cutter modern decor of many lodging chains. The small guest rooms come with a sofa bed and there's no extra charge for up to two children under 16. **Pros:** good central location, minutes from the Grand'Place. **Cons:** rooms facing the Grand'Place can be noisy. ✉ *rue du Marché-aux-Herbes 120, Lower Town* ☎ *02/514–3333* ⊕ *www.*

novotel.be ✈*138 rooms* ♿*In-room: safe, Wi-Fi. In-hotel: restaurant, bar, parking (paid)* ▭*AE, DC, MC, V* Ⓜ*Metro: Gare Centrale.*

$$$–$$$$ 🏨 **Royal Windsor Hotel.** Visiting dignitaries often gravitate to this hotel for its position near the Grand'Place. Many a business contact has been made in the elegant dining room, Les Quatre Saisons, and Chutney's, a colonial-style pub. Rooms are done in green with blond-wood paneling; bathrooms are small but are finished in Portuguese marble. You can get a taste of Belgian design in some rooms, which have been decked out by designers including Marina Yee and Jean-Paul Knott. Other rooms have been specially prepared to meet hypoallergenic standards. **Pros:** centrally located near the Grand'Place. **Cons:** some rooms are small, the parking fee is €25. ✉*rue Duquesnoy 5, Lower Town* ☎*02/505–5555* ⊕*www.royalwindsorbrussels.com* ✈*266 rooms, 12 suites, 1 royal suite* ♿*In-room: safe, Internet, Wi-Fi. In-hotel: restaurant, bar, gym, parking (paid), no-smoking rooms* ▭*AE, DC, MC, V* Ⓜ*Metro: Gare Centrale.*

¢–$ 🏨 **Sleep Well.** This youth hostel is bright, well-run, and conveniently located for transportation links. The basic rooms sleep from one to eight people with shared bathrooms, and you have to pay extra for sheets. The more upscale rooms in the Star section have en suite bathrooms, and pretty striped bedspreads (sheets are included in the price). There's a comic-strip mural in the lobby, a TV room, public phones, a luggage room, and lively bar with karaoke. **Pros:** cheap for a good location; bed linens and blankets available. **Cons:** streets around the metro station can be a bit sketchy at night; there are no towels or soap in the bathrooms. ✉*rue du Damier 23, Lower Town* ☎*02/218–5050* ⊕*www.sleepwell.be* ✈*82 rooms* ♿*In-hotel: restaurant, bar, Internet terminal, laundry facilities, bicycles* ▭*MC, V* ⦿*CP* Ⓜ*Metro: Rogier.*

$–$$ 🏨 **Welcome Hotel.** Among the charms of the smallest hotel in Brus-
★ sels are the young owners, Michel and Sophie Smeesters. The rooms, divided into economy, business, and first class, are as comfortable as those in far more expensive establishments. Each is strikingly decorated to evoke a certain place; the Bali and China rooms are particularly lovely, with their masks and dragon motifs. Around the corner on the Vismet (fish market), Michel doubles as chef of the excellent seafood restaurant La Truite d'Argent ($$$), where hotel guests get a special rate. The hotel is understandably much in demand, so book early. **Pros:** hotel with character and friendly staff, inexpensive on-site parking. **Cons:** hotel books up fast. ✉*rue du Peuplier 5, Lower Town* ☎*02/219–9546* ⊕*www.brusselswelcomehotel.be* ✈*14 rooms, 1 suite* ♿*In-room: safe. In-hotel: restaurant, parking (paid)* ▭*AE, DC, MC, V* Ⓜ*Metro: Ste-Catherine.*

UPPER TOWN

$$ 🏨 **Alfa Louise.** Though the edge-of-Ixelles location is near temptation—in the boutiques along avenue Louise—this hotel's attitude is strictly business. The service is briskly efficient, and the large, cream rooms have office-size desks, handy for spreading out papers. **Pros:** close to

major shopping streets. **Cons:** far from the city's historic district, no minibar, there are no refrigerators in the room (but they can be provided upon request). ✉*Av. Louise 212, Upper Town* 🕾*02/644–2929* 🖙*40 rooms* ⚴*In-room: safe, Internet. In-hotel: bar, parking (paid)* ▭*AE, DC, MC, V* ⍑⎮*BP* Ⓜ*Metro: Louise. Tram: 94.*

$–$$ 🛏**Hotel BLOOM!** This modern hotel, in the center of Brussels, has been designed to create maximum light, comfort, and space. The hotel has a unique set of colorful wall frescoes, designed by talented young artists. Some rooms offer panoramic views over Brussels, taking in the Grand'Place and the Atomium. All rooms have large windows and a comfortable chair with a footrest. **Pros:** situated close to the city's pleasant botanic gardens. **Cons:** noisy and busy because of its close proximity to some of the city's main roads. ✉*rue Royale 250, Upper Town* 🕾*02/220–6611* ⊕*www.hotelbloom.com* 🖙*305 rooms* ⚴*In-room: Wi-Fi, safe. In hotel: bar, restaurant, parking (paid), gym* ▭*AE, DC, MC, V* Ⓜ*Metro: Botanique.*

$$$$ 🛏**Hilton.** One of the first high-rises in Brussels back in the 1960s, this one outclasses most other Hiltons in Europe. The four stories of executive rooms have a separate check-in area; there are nine floors of business rooms, all decorated in warm tones. The location is great for upscale shopping, and the building, an uninspiring gray block, has a fine panoramic view over the capital. The restaurant, the Maison du Boeuf, is one of the best in town; the ground-floor Café d'Egmont stays open around the clock. **Pros:** good location between main shopping streets and historical center, nice views from upper floors. **Cons:** the building looks ugly and is located on a busy main street. ✉*blvd. de Waterloo 38, Upper Town* 🕾*02/504–1111* ⊕*www.hilton.com* 🖙*432 rooms, 32 suites* ⚴*In-room: safe, Internet. In-hotel: 2 restaurants, bar, gym, parking (paid)* ▭*AE, DC, MC, V* Ⓜ*Metro: Louise.*

$$$$ 🛏**Jolly Grand Sablon.** Part of the Sablon square's lineup of antiques shops, cafés, and chocolate makers, the Jolly offers discreet luxury behind an elegant white facade. The reception area is set within a hushed arcade of private art galleries, and there's a pretty interior cobbled courtyard. The rooms are unadventurously decorated in shades of pink, while the suites are decked out in peach. Some bathrooms have only showers, but the plush suites have whirlpool baths. Ask for a room at the back, as the square outside is often clogged with traffic and the weekend antiques market gets going at 6 AM. **Pros:** good location in the pretty Sablon. **Cons:** staff can be a bit unfriendly. ✉*rue Bodenbroeck 2–4, Upper Town* 🕾*02/512–8800* 🖙*193 rooms, 6 suites* ⚴*In-room: Internet. In-hotel: restaurant, bar, parking (paid)* ▭*AE, DC, MC, V* ⍑⎮*BP* Ⓜ*Metro: Louise, Park.*

$$$ 🛏**Radisson SAS Hotel.** Near the northern end of the Galeries St-Hubert
★ shopping arcade, this hotel has an Art Deco facade and is decorated in a variety of styles, including "Maritime" rooms with blue-and-yellow walls and wood floors. Guest rooms come equipped with handy extras, such as trouser presses and minibars that automatically replenish drinks. The greenery-filled atrium incorporates a 10-foot-high section of the 12th-century city wall and serves excellent Scandinavian-style open sandwiches. **Pros:** good breakfast, great central location, great

in-house dining option at the Sea Grill. **Cons:** hotel has a bit of a stuffy feel. ✉*rue du Fossé-aux-Loups 47, Upper Town* ☎*02/219–2828* ⊕*www.radisson.com/brusselsbe* ⇗*261 rooms, 20 suites* ⚹*In-room: safe, Internet, Wi-Fi. In-hotel: 2 restaurants, bar, gym, parking (paid)* ▭*AE, DC, MC, V* ❑*BP* Ⓜ*Metro: De Brouckere.*

\$\$–\$\$\$ ⬚**Stanhope.** This exclusive hotel was created out of three adjoining
★   town houses and continues to expand. Some rooms have high ceilings, marble bathrooms, and luxurious furniture, while others have a more modern look aimed at business travelers. Larger rooms and suites, indicated by thematic names, have individual looks and canopied beds. The Linley, for example, has furniture handmade by Viscount Linley, nephew of the Queen of England. **Pros:** friendly staff, nice rooms. **Cons:** slightly further from historical center than some hotels. ✉*rue du Commerce 9, Upper Town* ☎*02/506–9111* ⊕*www.summithotels. com* ⇗*108 rooms, 7 suites, 2 royal suites* ⚹*In-room: safe, Internet. In-hotel: restaurant, bar, gym, parking (paid)* ▭*AE, DC, MC, V* ❑*CP* Ⓜ*Metro: Trone.*

\$\$\$\$ ⬚**The Dominican.** Brussels has plenty of high-end accommodations, but it was not until the recent arrival of The Dominican that Belgium's capital could claim lodgings that combine classical beauty with modern luxury. From the smiling efficient front desk clerks to the sensuous linens adorning the plush beds, this is a hotel that understands luxury. When work must intrude, free Wi-Fi, expansive desk surfaces, and pod-style espresso machines are available, and, depending on the rooms, soaker tubs and rain-style showers. **Pros:** solid service and indulgent comforts. **Cons:** style sometimes negates efficiency, as with bathroom sinks that splash water everywhere. ✉*Rue Léopold/Leopoldstraat 9 Upper Town* ☎*02/203-0808* ⎙*02/203-0807* ⊕*www.dominican.be* ⇗*146 rooms, 4 suites.* ⚹ *In-room: safe, kitchen (some), DVD (some), Wi-Fi. In-hotel: 1 restaurant; rooms service, 1 bar, gym, laundry service, concierge, public Wi-Fi, no-smoking rooms.* ▭*AE, DC, MC, V.*

CINQUANTENAIRE & SCHUMAN

\$\$\$\$ ⬚**Hotel Eurostars Montgomery.** Business travelers are the top priority here; many of the hotel's clients zip between it and the nearby European Commission. The staff is exceptionally friendly and the five meeting rooms are well-appointed. The rooms have large writing desks and are decorated in warm Chinese colors; English-style floral; or cool, clean, colonial styles. The book-lined bar-restaurant has a wood-burning fireplace. **Pros:** close to the pleasant Cinquantenaire park. **Cons:** not within walking distance of the historical center although metro connections are good. ✉*Av. de Tervuren 134, Woluwe-St-Pierre* ☎*02/741–8511* ⊕*www.eurostarshotels.com* ⇗*61 rooms, 2 penthouses, 1 suite* ⚹*In-room: safe, Internet. In-hotel: restaurant, bar, gym, parking (paid)* ▭*AE, DC, MC, V* ❑*BP* Ⓜ*Metro: Montgomery.*

\$\$–\$\$\$ ⬚**Hotel Silken Berlaymont.**Contemporary photography inspires the Berlaymont's signature look. Each room is decorated with works of a different photographer, and the navy, black, and dark-wood furnishings are sober and smart. Attention to perspective and style are evident in the chrome, black marble, and spotlights around the hotel. Eight rooms have showers only. The green mosaic-tiled sauna, hammam, spa, and fitness center are inviting, but admission isn't included in the price. Neither is breakfast, but there's a good café on-site. **Pros:** comfortable hotel with a pleasant bar. **Cons:** located in the soulless EU quarter that is very quiet on the weekends. ⊠*blvd. Charlemagne 11–19, Etterbeek* ☎*02/231–0909* ✆*214 rooms, 2 suites* ♿*In-room: safe, Internet. In-hotel: restaurant, bar, gym, spa, parking (paid)* ▤*AE, DC, MC, V* Ⓜ*Metro: Schuman.*

$–$$ ▒ **Monty Hotel.** A stay here is like an overnight in a contemporary design
★ showroom—with breakfast in the morning. Guest rooms have ingenious lighting, like winged lightbulbs by Ingo Maurer, Mario Bellini "Cuboglass" televisions, and gray-tiled bathrooms with Philippe Starck fittings. The comfortable lounge with its tomato-red walls is peppered with equally modern-classic furniture. Unlike some boutique hotels, the Monty doesn't tip over into chilly attitude; its warmth is demonstrated at breakfast, served at a friendly communal table. **Pros:** good breakfast. **Cons:** far away from the historical center. ⊠*blvd. Brand Whitlock 101, Laeken* ☎*02/734–5636* ⊕*www.monty-hotel.be* ✆*18 rooms* ♿*In-room: Internet, Wi-Fi. In-hotel: bar, parking (paid)* ▤*AE, DC, MC, V* ▮◎▯*BP* Ⓜ*Metro: Montgomery. Tram: 23.*

$$–$$$$ ▒ **Park.** This hotel, once a private mansion, offers a rare patch of green in the city's lodging spectrum. It's across from the trees of the Cinquantenaire Park, and it has a large garden where you can organize a barbecue in summer. The comfortable rooms vary in size from enormous to standard and the executive rooms come complete with computers. The lobby evokes the colonial era with its potted palms and a bust of Henry Morton Stanley, who was dispatched by King Leopold II to explore the Congo. There's a tiny bar at the end of the reception desk. **Pros:** friendly staff, good service. **Cons:** more a business hotel than a tourist location, historical center is quite far away. ⊠*Av. de l'Yser 21, Etterbeek* ☎*02/735–7400* ⊕*www.parkhotelbrussels.be* ✆*53 rooms* ♿*In-room: Internet. In-hotel: bar, gym* ▤*AE, DC, MC, V* ▮◎▯*BP* Ⓜ*Metro: Merode.*

SOUTH OF CENTER

$$$$ ▒ **Château du Lac.** Half an hour from the city center and a good choice
★ as a peaceful base from which to visit the capital and the provinces, this mock-Florentine castle is a former Schweppes bottling plant. The contemporary rooms have walnut furniture and are decorated according to their size and location in the hotel. The restaurant turns out particularly good French and Belgian fare; it has a sweeping view of the lake to boot. Golf lovers can ask the staff to book a round on a local course. **Pros:** peaceful location outside the bustling city. **Cons:** getting to the hotel involves a half-hour train ride. ⊠*Av. du Lac 87 Genval* ☎*02/655–7111* ⊕*www.chateaudulac-belgium.com* ✆*119 rooms, 2 suites* ♿*In-room: safe, Internet. In-hotel: restaurant, bar, pool, gym* ▤*AE, DC, MC, V* ▮◎▯*BP* Ⓜ*Train to Genval station.*

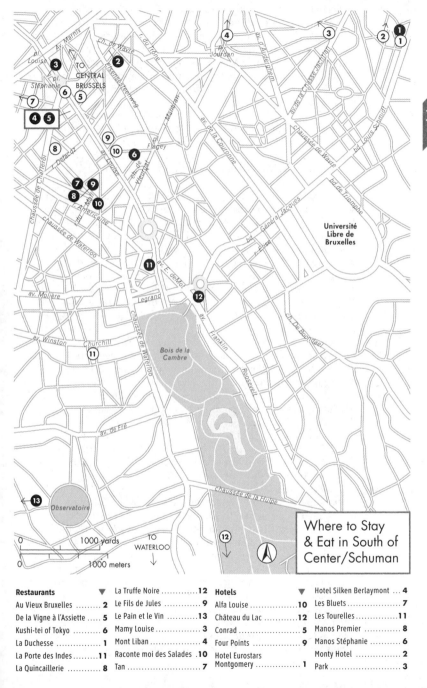

Where to Stay & Eat in South of Center/Schuman

Restaurants	▼	La Truffe Noire **12**	Hotels	▼	Hotel Silken Berlaymont ... **4**
Au Vieux Bruxelles **2**		Le Fils de Jules **9**	Alfa Louise **10**		Les Bluets **7**
De la Vigne à l'Assiette **5**		Le Pain et le Vin **13**	Château du Lac **12**		Les Tourelles **11**
Kushi-tei of Tokyo **6**		Mamy Louise **3**	Conrad **5**		Manos Premier **8**
La Duchesse **1**		Mont Liban **4**	Four Points **9**		Manos Stéphanie **6**
La Porte des Indes **11**		Raconte moi des Salades .**10**	Hotel Eurostars		Monty Hotel **2**
La Quincaillerie **8**		Tan **7**	Montgomery **1**		Park **3**

$$$$ 🛏**Conrad.** Located on the elegant avenue Louise, the classic facade of an 1865 mansion now shields the hotel's sleek interior. Rooms come in many different shapes, but all are spacious. In the stylish black-and-white marble bathrooms, baths can be filled in one minute flat. The intimate Maison de Maître restaurant is well respected, and Café Wiltcher's offers all-day brasserie dining. A branch of the exclusive English health club Champneys offers beauty treatments as well as the usual gym facilities. **Pros:** numerous heads of state passing through Brussels rest their heads here. **Cons:** a little farther from the historical town center than some hotels. ✉*Av. Louise 71, Ixelles* ☎*02/542–4242* ⊕*www.brussels.conradinternational.com* 🛏*269 rooms, 25 suites* ♿*In-room: safe, Internet. In-hotel: 2 restaurants, bars, gym, spa, parking (paid), no-smoking rooms* ▭*AE, DC, MC, V* Ⓜ*Metro: Louise. Tram: 93, 94.*

$$$ 🛏**Four Points.** This Sheraton hotel has one of the best locations in the south, as it's right on the border of Ixelles, a short walk to avenue Louise, and a few tram stops from the center. The large, bland rooms feature blond-wood furniture, a reclining chair, and good work space. You can choose from city or garden views and rent bikes to take to the Bois de la Cambre at the other end of avenue Louise. **Pros:** decent business hotel close to some nice restaurant areas. **Cons:** a 30-minute walk to the city center. ✉*rue Paul Spaak 15, Upper Town* ☎*02/645–6111* ⊕*www.fourpoints.com* 🛏*128 rooms* ♿*In-room: Internet. In-hotel: 2 restaurants, bar, gym, parking (paid)* ▭*AE, DC, MC, V* Ⓜ*Tram: 81, 93, 94 to Les Broussart.*

$$$ 🛏**Leopold.** A discreet establishment near the European Parliament, the privately owned Leopold has smallish rooms decorated in pink, cream, and gray. Bathrooms have either bath or shower. The restaurant has high, corniced ceilings; this is where European catering schools hold their annual Silver Whisk cooking competition. There is also a lunchtime brasserie and a courtyard for eating outside in good weather. **Pros:** close to lively place Luxembourg and the Royal Palace. **Cons:** a 30-minute walk to the city center. ✉*rue du Luxembourg 35, Ixelles* ☎*02/511–1828* ⊕*www.hotel-leopold.be* 🛏*111 rooms, 8 suites, 6 apartments* ♿*In-room: Internet. In-hotel: 2 restaurants, bar, parking (paid)* ▭*AE, DC, MC, V* Ⓜ*Metro: Trone.*

¢–$ 🛏**Les Bluets.** The family that runs this no-smoking hotel has filled the
★ town house with all sorts of antiques and curios, including an English grandfather clock and a screeching exotic bird in a greenery-filled conservatory. Every room is different—styles range from tastefully old-world to cluttered and kitschy—but all make you feel like a visitor in a much-loved house. The mother can be fearsome, especially if you don't respect the silence rule, but an authentic stay is guaranteed. Some rooms have bathrooms, others small shower units. **Pros:** good price for location and quality, each room has a kitchenette. **Cons:** the area can be a little unsafe in the evening; there are no safes in the room, but the hotel has a general one. ✉*rue Berckmans 124, St-Gilles* ☎*02/534–3983* 🛏*9 rooms, 1 suite* ♿*In-room: kitchen. In-hotel: no-smoking rooms* ▭*AE, MC, V* ⦿*BP* Ⓜ*Metro: Hotel des Monnaies, Louise.*

3

$ ▥ **Les Tourelles.** The mock-medieval turreted facade and wood decor of this cheerful, family-run hotel suggest an antique hunting lodge. The friendly staff members are a collective goldmine of useful knowledge about Brussels. Guest rooms are traditionally decorated in florals and pastels; the well-heated, old-fashioned breakfast room is a lovely place to start the day, especially on cold mornings. Try to get a back-facing room as the front looks out over a main road. The hotel is well connected to central Brussels by tram and street networks. **Pros:** the hotel has more character than major chains. **Cons:** it is not very centrally located, no in-room minibar. ⊠*Av. Winston Churchill 135, Uccle* ☎*02/344–9573* ⊕*www.lestourelles.be* ⇨*22 rooms* ⌂*In-hotel: parking (free)* ☰*AE, MC, V* ⊘*Closed July and Aug.* ⟦○⟧*CP* Ⓜ*Tram: 23.*

$$$$ ▥ **Manos Premier.** This sister hotel of the Manos Stéphanie is an upscale
★ choice with Italian-style terraces, a rose-filled garden populated by water fowl and songbirds and a good restaurant, Kolya. The well-appointed rooms have Louis XV and Louis XVI antiques and inviting bedspreads in green, cream, and pink. The sauna has a decadent Moroccan flavor with tiling and arched doorways. **Pros:** the garden is a pleasant oasis from the busy streets, close to some of the best shopping streets. **Cons:** slightly farther from the historical center. ⊠*chaussée de Charleroi 100–104, St-Gilles* ☎*02/537–9682* ⊕*www.manoshotel. com* ⇨*55 rooms, 15 suites* ⌂*In-room: safe, Internet. In-hotel: restaurant, bar, gym* ☰*AE, DC, MC, V* ⟦○⟧*CP* Ⓜ*Metro: Louise.*

$$$$ ▥ **Manos Stéphanie.** The marble lobby and Louis XV antiques may signal stuffy elegance, but this hotel's staff is notably friendly. The hotel occupies a grand town house, so the rooms are not rigidly standardized. All have good-size sitting areas, and those facing the street have huge windows so are especially bright. **Pros:** comfortable rooms, located near good resturants. **Cons:** slightly farther from the historical center. ⊠*chaussée de Charleroi 28, St-Gilles* ☎*02/539–0250* ⊕*www. manoshotel.com* ⇨*55 rooms, 12 suites* ⌂*In-room: Internet. In-hotel: room service, bar, parking (paid)* ☰*AE, DC, MC, V* ⟦○⟧*CP* Ⓜ*Metro: Louise. Tram: 92, 97.*

$$$ ▥ **Renaissance Brussels Hotel.** Opposite the glass giant of the European Parliament, this busy hotel generally teems with politicians (and their accompanying lobbyists) and businesspeople. The roster of amenities and services is extensive; the hotel even accepts pets. The large, bright rooms are warmed by yellow bedspreads; those to the rear overlook a shared garden. Business rooms have work spaces. Apartments, including two duplexes, can be rented for a week or more. **Pros:** close to public transportation. **Cons:** located in the business district that becomes very quiet at the weekends. ⊠*rue du Parnasse 19, Ixelles* ☎*02/505– 2929* ⊕*www.marriott.com* ⇨*243 rooms, 19 suites, 57 apartments* ⌂*In-room: safe, Internet. In-hotel: restaurant, bar, pool, gym, parking (paid), no-smoking rooms* ☰*AE, DC, MC, V* ⟦○⟧*BP* Ⓜ*Metro: Trone. Bus: 95, 12, 27, 21, 54, 22, 34, 38, 64, 80.*

$$$$ ▥ **Sofitel Toison d'Or.** Getting to the lobby of this chain hotel entails an escalator ride from a chic shopping arcade on the building's ground floor. Once there, you'll find public and guest rooms done in green and cream. Double rooms have king-size beds; bathroom telephones and

bathrobes are standard. **Pros:** great central location; walking distance from designer boutiques, antiques shops, and art galleries. **Cons:** chain hotel lacks the charm that can be found in Brussels. ⊠*Av. de la Toison d'Or 40, Ixelles* ☎*02/514–2200* ⊕*www.sofitel.com* ↪*170 rooms* ⚿*In-room: safe, Internet, Wi-Fi. In-hotel: bar, restaurant, gym, some pets allowed* ▤*AE, DC, MC, V* Ⓜ*Metro: Louise.*

NIGHTLIFE & THE ARTS

THE ARTS

Although the presence of both French and Flemish drives a wedge or two through the capital's cultural landscape, it also delivers some advantages. Both Flemish- and French-language authorities inject funds into the arts scene; one notable combined effort is the annual Kunsten Fesitval des Arts, a contemporary arts festival held in May. A glance at the "What's On" section of weekly English-language news magazine the *Bulletin* reveals the breadth of the offerings in all categories of cultural life. Tickets for major events can be purchased by calling **FNAC Ticket Line** (☎*0900/00600*).

CLASSICAL MUSIC

The principal venue for classical music concerts is the Horta-designed **Palais des Beaux-Arts** (⊠*rue Ravenstein 23, Upper Town* ☎*02/507–8200*). The complex, which also houses an art gallery and a theater, was the first multipurpose arts complex in Europe when it opened in 1928. Its Henry Le Boeuf concert hall has world-class acoustics.

Chamber music concerts and recitals are held in the more intimate **Conservatoire Royale de Bruxelles** (⊠*rue de la Régence 30, Upper Town* ☎*02/213–4137*). Many concerts are held in churches, such as the **Chapelle Protestante** (⊠*pl. du Musée, Upper Town*). The **Eglise des Minimes** (⊠*rue des Minimes 62, Upper Town*) also hosts classical performances.

Belgium is particularly renowned in the fields of early and Baroque music—look for conductors René Jacobs and Philippe Herreweghe and the Sablon Baroque Spring festival in April and May. Also in spring, the grueling **Queen Elisabeth Music Competition** (the penultimate round is at the Royal Conservatory, the final week at the Palais des Beaux-Arts), a prestigious competition for young pianists, takes place in Brussels. The monthlong **Ars Musica** (☎*02/512–1717*) festival of contemporary classical music in March and April attracts new music ensembles from around the world. The **Fete de la Musique** occurs every June, when performances featuring jazz, hip-hop, salsa, classical, and contemporary music take over the streets and bars of Brussels.

FILM

First-run English-language and French movies fill most local screens. If you can leap the language barrier, look for the latest Belgian releases; the Belgian film industry may be small but it has won international acclaim, with the two-time Palme d'Or–winning Dardenne brothers leading the pack. Most international films are subtitled in French and Flemish. Listings indicate when a movie has been dubbed (*v.o.* stands for *version originale*, undubbed with subtitles).

The most convenient movie theater complex in the Upper Town is **UGC/Toison d'Or** (⊠*av. de la Toison d'Or* ☎*0900/29930*). Another major central cinema is **UGC/De Brouckère** (⊠*pl. de Brouckère, Lower Town* ☎*0900/10440*).

ART-HOUSE CINEMAS

The **Musée du Cinéma** (⊠*rue Baron Horta 9, Upper Town* ☎*02/507–8370*) shows classic and silent movies, the latter accompanied live by an improvising pianist. It is one of the only places in the world that shows silent movies daily. Buying a ticket to see a film also gains entry to the small but fascinating museum (€2 for separate entry).

The excellent cinema **Arenberg/Galeries** (⊠*Galeries St-Hubert, Upper Town* ☎*02/512–8063*) screens an impressive array of art-house films. Avant-garde **Nova** (⊠*rue d'Arenberg 3, Upper Town* ☎*02/511–2774*) shows a quirky, uncommercial selection of animation, shorts, and sound installations despite its shoestring budget and uncertain tenancy. The slightly run-down **Vendôme** (⊠*chaussée de Wavre 18, Ixelles* ☎*02/502–3700*) puts on regular themed festivals (e.g., Latin American, Jewish cinema).

The **Flagey cinema** (⊠*pl. Sainte-Croix 18, Ixelles* ☎*02/641–1020*) shows a mix of art-house and classic films and has regular mini-festivals. The biggest cinema, with 26 theaters, is the futuristic **Kinepolis** (⊠*av. du Centenaire 1, Heysel* ☎*0900/00555*). In March, the International Festival of Fantasy Film takes over **Auditorium Passage 44** (⊠*blvd. du Jardin Botanique 44, Upper Town* ☎*02/201–1495*) and other venues for a packed program of thrillers and chillers, culminating in a Vampires Ball.

OPERA & DANCE

OPERA

The national and world-renowned opera house, **La Monnaie/De Munt** (⊠*pl. de la Monnaie, Lower Town* ☎*070/23-39-39* ⊕*www.lamon naie.be*), has almost nightly (and some daily) performances of everything from dance to opera. Tickets are resonable, so it's worth checking out the schedule to see if somethind interests you. Visiting opera and dance companies often perform at another large theater, the **Cirque Royal** (⊠*rue de l'Enseignement 81, Upper Town* ☎*02/218–2015*).

DANCE

Dance is among the liveliest arts in Belgium. Its seminal figure, Anne Teresa De Keersmaeker, is choreographer-in-residence at the opera house, but her Rosas company also has its own performance space within her **PARTS school** (⊠*av. Van Volxem 164, Forest* ☎*02/344–5598*). Alternatively, it performs at the **Kaaitheater** (⊠*pl. Sainctelette 20* ☎*02/201–5959*), as do the Royal Flanders Ballet and many other Belgian and international dance troupes. Contemporary dance companies come to the **Halles de Schaerbeek** (✉*rue Royale 22b Upper Town* ☎*02/218–2107*). Innovative provincial company Charleroi–Danses runs **La Raffinerie** (✉*rue de Manchester 21, Molenbeek* ☎*02/410–3341*) in a splendid old sugar refinery. The delightful **Chapelle des Brigittines** (✉*rue des Visitandines 1, Lower Town* ☎*02/506–4300*) welcomes cutting-edge productions.

THEATER

Brussels' theater scene is thriving—and becoming more accessible to English-speakers. Most of the city's 30-odd theaters put on French productions, with the others staging Dutch-language performances. But visits by international companies like the Royal Shakespeare Company are common, and some theaters surtitle occasional works in English.

The best way to keep informed about theater performances is to check the "What's On" section of the English-language *Bulletin,* the Wednesday pull-out section of *Le Soir,* or the Agenda section of *Deze Week.*

The francophone **Théâtre National** (✉*blvd. Emile Jacqmain 111–115, Lower Town* ☎*02/203–4155*) opened spectacular new headquarters in 2005 and stages a reliable, varied mix of plays, bringing international companies to Brussels. Its Dutch-speaking counterpart **KVS** (✉*quai aux Pierres de Taille 7, Lower Town* ☎*02/210–1100*) has also spruced up its theater spaces. Avant-garde performances are often the most rewarding and show at the **Théâtre Les Tanneurs** (✉*rue des Tanneurs 75, Lower Town* ☎*02/512–1784*) and the **Halles de Schaerbeek** (✉*rue Royale 22b, Upper Town* ☎*02/218–2107*). Musicals and international theater play at the **Théâtre de Poche** (✉*chemin du Gymnase 1a, Uccle* ☎*02/649–1727*). Music, debates in Flemish, and a grab-bag of theatrical acts appear at the **Kaaitheater** (✉*pl. Sainctelette 20, Lower Town* ☎*02/201–5959*). The **Royal Flemish Theatre** (✉*rue de Laeken 146* ☎*02/210–1112*) is a neo-baroque venue featuring Flemish-language theater and contemporary dance.

NIGHTLIFE

By 11 PM, many Bruxellois have packed up and gone home—but around midnight, bars and cafés fill up again and roads become congested as night crawlers take over. Sipping a cool beer on an outdoor terrace on a warm night is a simple yet unbeatable pleasure. The club scene is lively, and world-famous DJs as well as homegrown mavericks spin regularly. Many places stay open until dawn. For a rundown on upcoming DJ parties and other late-night events, one resource is the Web site **www.noctis.com.**

NIGHTLIFE KNOW-HOW

Women should avoid walking alone late at night in the narrow streets of the city center and the Marolles district. Even on busy boulevards, women can draw unwelcome, though generally unthreatening, remarks. Men are expected to give doormen or bouncers a small tip of a couple of euros as they leave an establishment—especially if they plan to visit the place again. In the bathrooms of most bars, you'll find a "Madame

Pipi," who'll charge you around 30¢ to use the facilities. These women keep the lavatories clean and are legendary for their ability to catch you if you try to avoid paying—it's better to just cough up.

BARS

There's a café on virtually every street corner, most serving all kinds of alcoholic drinks. Although the Belgian brewing industry is declining as the giant Inbev firm (the brewers of Stella Artois) muscles smaller companies out of the market, Belgians still consume copious quantities of beer, some of it with a 10% alcohol content. Most bars here have artisanal beers along with the major-brand usual suspects. The place St-Géry, rue St-Boniface, and the Grand'Place area draw the most buzz.

DANCE SPOTS

Café de Bruxelles (⊠ *Grand'Place 12A, Lower Town* ☎ *02/503–3325*) changes from a sedate bistro to a 1980s retro-music haven after dark. On Saturday nights, student favorite **Le Corbeau** (⊠ *rue St-Michel 18–20, Lower Town* ☎ *02/219–5246*) becomes the biggest party in town, and it's not long before the entire bar is dancing on the wooden tables. **Havana's** (⊠ *rue de l'Epee 4, Lower Town* ☎ *04/9592–5195*), a Latino restaurant, transforms into a pulsating Latino bar and dance club after hours. **Bazaar** (⊠ *rue des Capucins 63, Upper Town* ☎ *02/511–2600*) plays an eclectic mix—'80s music, today's chart-toppers, and Turkish and Middle Eastern hits. **Les Salons de l'Atalaide** (⊠ *chaussée de Charleroi 89, Ixelles* ☎ *02/537–2154*) is another restaurant that transforms into a nightclub and is perfect for those who like cheesy pop.

FOR THE COOL CROWD

The stylish, Art Deco **Archiduc** (⊠ *rue Antoine Dansaert 6, Lower Town* ☎ *02/512–0652*) attracts a thirtyish, fashionable crowd; it gets smoky up on the balcony. The sidewalk outside **Au Soleil** (⊠ *rue du Marché-au-Charbon 86, Lower Town* ☎ *02/513–3430*) teems with the hip and would-be hip, enjoying relaxed trip-hop sounds and very competitive prices. Another favorite with the arty crowd is Flemish bar **Monk** (⊠ *rue Ste-Catherine 43, Lower Town* ☎ *02/503–0880*), which used to be a schoolhouse. The walls in trendy **Café Central** (⊠ *rue de Borgval 14, Lower Town* ☎ *02/513–7308*) are covered in wooden triangles, perhaps an influence on the angular haircuts of the scruffily cool clientele. **Mappa Mundo** (⊠ *rue du Pont de la Carpe 2–6, Lower Town* ☎ *02/514–0901*), famous for its mojito cocktails, packs two floors with an international mix of partiers and poseurs. **Zebra** (⊠ *pl. St-Géry 35, Lower Town* ☎ *02/511–0901*) manages to be popular yet low-key. **Greenwich** (⊠ *rue des Chartreux 7, Lower Town* ☎ *02/511–4167*) is a city classic that oozes old-world coolness and is famous for its chess-playing regulars. **Kafka** (⊠ *rue de la Vierge Noire 6, Lower Town* ☎ *02/513–5489*) is unpretentious and relaxing with an old-fashioned revolutionist feel.

HOTEL BARS

Among the most popular hotel bars are those in the **Hilton,** the **Conrad, Amigo,** and the **Métropole** (⇨ *Where to Stay, above*).

IRISH PUBS

Like most Western European cities, Brussels has a sizable number of "Irish" bars. **The James Joyce** (⊠*rue Archimède 34, Etterbeek* ☎*02/230–9894*) has rock-bottom prices during happy hour and a lovely beer garden. Eurocrats, politicians, and journalists warm the barstools of **Fabian O'Farrell's** (⊠*pl. du Luxembourg 7, Schuman* ☎*02/230–1887*), a pub in the shadow of the European Parliament. For authentic warmth, head to **Kitty O'Shea's** (⊠*blvd. de Charlemagne 42, Etterbeek* ☎*02/230–7875*), which gets especially lively when major sports matches play on its wide-screen TV. Big and boisterous **O'Reilly's** (⊠*pl. de la Bourse, Lower Town* ☎*02/552–0481*) blasts chart hits to crowds of sports fans and stag-nighters. The **Wild Geese** (⊠*av. Livingstone 2–4, Etterbeek* ☎*02/230–1990*) heaves with expat singles in varying stages of inebriation. **De Valera's** (⊠*pl. Flagey 17, Ixelles* ☎*02/649–8054*) is the latest addition to Brussels' thriving Irish pub scene and stands next to the newly renovated place Flagey.

IXELLES BARS

L'Amour Fou (⊠*chaussée d'Ixelles 185, Ixelles* ☎*02/514–2709*) has a selection of newspapers for the lone visitor and is popular with the

★ student intellectual crowd. The bar-restaurant **L'Ultime Atome** (⊠*rue St-Boniface 14, Ixelles* ☎*02/511–1367*) stays busy day and night; it serves food until 1 AM and is known for having the most stunning waitstaff in town. **Roxy's** (⊠*rue du Bailli, Ixelles*) is a trendy bar with a rooftop balcony perfect for summer nights. **Belga** (⊠*pl. Flagey 18, Ixelles* ☎*02/640–3508*), which has a huge terrace, is a noisy bar popular with students and young, hip Belgians.

TRADITIONAL BARS

Beer is one of Brussels' biggest tourist draws, and the city has a few traditional-style bars where you can sample everything from the sour delights of local Lambic to the six Trappist treasures, brewed by monks in Orval, Chimay, Rochefort, Westmalle, and Westvleteren, and revered the world over. One of the best is **Bier Circus** (⊠*rue de l'Enseignement 57, Upper Town* ☎*02/218–0034*), which has a huge list of brews on its menu, including some excellent organic beers. With its wooden decor and friendly staff, this is a great place to start learning about Belgian beer, and there's good food, too. The grungy **Chez Moeder Lambic** (⊠*rue de Savoie 68, St-Gilles* ☎*02/539–1419*) claims to stock 600 Belgian beers and a few hundred more foreign ones, as well as comic books to read while you sip. **A la Mort Subite** (⊠*rue Montagne aux Herbes Potageres 7, Lower Town* ☎*02/513–1318*) was named after a drinking game established by bankers almost a century ago. Today, it has a fine collection of beers.

Fodor'sChoice For a taste of Brussels' Art Nouveau heritage, head to **De Ultieme Hal-**
★ **lucinatie** (⊠*rue Royale 316, Upper Town* ☎*02/217–0604*), where you can also eat. **Fleur en Papier Doré** (⊠*rue des Alexiens 53, Upper Town* ☎*02/511–1659*) was the hangout for Surrealist René Magritte and his artist friends, and their spirit lingers on.

LIVE MUSIC

Ancienne Belgique (⊠*blvd. Anspach 110, Lower Town* ☎*02/548–2424*) thrums with rock, pop, alternative, and world music. A wide range of concerts and cultural events take place at the **Beursschouwburg** (⊠*rue Auguste Orts 20–28, Lower Town* ☎*02/550–0350*) arts center. The center's *Bal Modernes* are fun mass-dance events where you can go along, learn the steps, and join in. At **Flagey** (⊠*pl. Sainte-Croix 18, Ixelles* ☎*02/641–1020*) you can hear a classical, jazz, or contemporary concert in a wonderful, shiplike Art Deco building. There's also a good art-house cinema.

> ### THE OTHER FOOTBALL
>
> Soccer is Belgium's most popular spectator sport, and the leading club, **Anderlecht** (⊠*av. Theo Verbeeck 2, Anderlecht* ☎*02/522–1539*), has many fiercely loyal fans. Their home field is Parc Astrid. Major international games are played at the **Stade Roi Baudouin** (⊠*av. du Marathon 135, Heysel* ☎*02/479–3654*). For information and tickets, contact the **Maison du Football** (⊠*av. Houba de Strooper 145, Heysel* ☎*02/477–1211*).

Mainstream rock acts and big-league French chansonniers stop off at **Forest-National** (⊠*av. du Globe 36, Forest* ☎*0900/00991*). **Le Botanique** (⊠*rue Royale 236, Upper Town* ☎*02/218–3732*) throws a wide musical net, and it hosts a superb 10-day rock–pop festival, *Les Nuits Botanique,* in September. Though officially the Galician cultural center, **La Tentation** (⊠*rue de Laeken 28, Lower Town* ☎*02/223–2275*), provides a superb venue for a broad selection of world-music performers. Each August, there is a series of free concerts, ranging from opera to pop, in the Grand'Place, as part of the **Euritmix** festival. In June, the three-day **Couleur Café** world-music festival brings top-class performers from Africa and South America to Brussels.

JAZZ

After World War II, Belgium was at the forefront of Europe's modern jazz movement: of the great postwar players, harmonica maestro Toots Thielemans and vibes player Sadi are still very much alive and perform in Brussels. Other top Belgian jazz draws include guitarist Philip Catherine, pianist Jef Neve and the experimental ethno-jazz trio Aka Moon. The city's ultracool Flemish-speakers hang out at **L'Archiduc** (⊠*rue Antoine Dansaert 6, Lower Town* ☎*02/512–0652*), which has regular jazz sessions on Sunday. **The Music Village** (⊠*rue des Pierres 50, Lower Town* ☎*02/513–91345*) hosts a plethora of international jazz musicians. **Sounds** (⊠*rue de la Tulipe 28, Ixelles* ☎*02/512–9250*) dishes up contemporary jazz along with good food. An established jazz club with its own record label and festival, **Travers** (⊠*rue Traversière 11, Upper Town* ☎*02/218–4086*) pulls in aficionados.

DANCE CLUBS

The dance scene is in perpetual mutation: as fast as a promising new outfit sets up, another falls foul of regulations and shuts down. Look out for posters announcing hot nights—sometimes in obscure venues like the bowels of the Gare Centrale or even the Atomium. Action starts at midnight in most clubs.

Recyclart (⊠*rue des Ursulines 25, Lower Town* ☎*02/502–5734*) is a multidisciplinary space near the Grand'Place, and becomes a club on Friday and Saturday nights where DJs spin and bands play house and electronica. It used to be a railway station, and you can still hear trains rattling past overhead.

HOUSE & TECHNO MUSIC

Electronica fans prefer **Fuse** (⊠*rue Blaes 208, Les Marolles* ☎*02/511–9789*), a bunker-style techno haven with monthly gay nights. An affluent set retreats to the **Jeux d'Hiver** (⊠*chemin du Croquet 1, Ixelles* ☎*02/649–0864*), hidden among trees in the Bois de la Cambre, for techno, house, and electro beats. The revolving dance floor at the glitzy **Le Mirano Continental** (⊠*chaussée de Louvain 38, Ixelles* ☎*02/227–3970*) hosts top house and techno DJs, as well as regular theme nights.

SALSA

Salsa addicts can indulge their habit at **Cartagena** (⊠*rue du Marché-au-Charbon 70, Lower Town* ☎*02/502–5908*). Professional dancers mix with enthusiastic amateurs at the salsa club **Montecristo Café** (⊠*rue Henri Maus 25, Lower Town* ☎*02/511–8789*), but be prepared for serious heat as the night wears on.

GAY BARS

Brussels is not nearly as advanced as Amsterdam when it comes to gay culture, but several clubs hold regular gay and lesbian nights. For instance, La Démence is the monthly gay night at **Fuse** (⇨*Dance Clubs, above)*. **Belgica** (⊠*rue du Marché-au-Charbon 32, Lower Town*) is a trendy meeting point at the heart of what passes for the gay quarter. **Tels Quels** (⊠*rue du Marché-aux-Charbon 81, Lower Town* ☎*02/512–4587*) is not only a bar, but also a resource for up-to-date information about the capital's gay scene and the publisher of a monthly magazine.

The two best bars for lesbians are slightly beyond the city center. **Café qu'on sert** (⊠*av. Albert 59, Forest* ☎*02/343–0233*) is a friendly, energetic place. **Le Capricorne** (⊠*rue d'Anderlecht 6, Anderlecht* ☎*02/512–1503*) has a relaxed atmosphere.

SHOPPING

For generations, Brussels has been the place to indulge a taste for some of the finer things in life: chocolate, beer, lace, and lead crystal. Brussels is also heaven for comic book collectors, and there are lots of offbeat shops to tempt magpies. While the city may not be bursting with bargains, there are inexpensive finds to be made in the markets. Value-added tax (TVA) inflates prices, but visitors from outside the EU can obtain refunds. Sales take place in January and July.

SHOPPING DISTRICTS

The stylish, upper-crust shopping area for clothing and accessories spans the upper end of **avenue Louise; avenue de la Toison d'Or,** which branches off at a right angle; **boulevard de Waterloo,** on the other side of the street; **Galerie Louise,** which links the two avenues; and **Galerie de la Toison d'Or,** another gallery two blocks away. The **City 2** mall on place Rogier and the pedestrian mall, **rue Neuve,** are fun and inexpensive shopping areas (but not recommended for women alone after dark).

There are galleries scattered across Brussels, but low rents have made **boulevard Barthélémy** the "in" place for avant-garde art. The **Windows complex** (⊠ *blvd. Barthélémy 13, Upper Town*) houses several galleries. On the **place du Grand Sablon** and adjoining streets and alleys you'll find antiques dealers and smart art galleries.

The **Galeries St-Hubert** is a rather stately shopping arcade lined with posh shops selling men's and women's clothing, books, and objets d'art. In the trendy **rue Antoine Dansaert** and **place du Nouveau Marché aux Grains,** near the Bourse, are a number of boutiques carrying fashions by young designers and interior design and art shops. **Avenue Louise** and its surrounding streets in Ixelles have a number of chic boutiques offering clothes new and vintage, jewelry, antiques, and housewares.

> ### RUN LIKE THE WIND
>
> For an in-town run, use the **Parc de Bruxelles** (⊠ *pl. des Palais,* adjacent to pl. Royale, Upper Town). For more extensive workouts, head for the **Bois de la Cambre** (⊠ *Southern end of av. Louise, Ixelles/Uccle*), a sprawling park that's a favorite among joggers, families, and dog-lovers. The southern end of the Bois de la Cambre merges into the beech woods of the 11,000-acre **Forêt de Soignes,** extending as far south as Genval with its lake and restaurants.

DEPARTMENT STORES

The only comprehensive department store is **Inno** (⊠ *rue Neuve 111, Lower Town* ☎ *02/211–2111* ⊠ *av. Louise 12, Ixelles* ☎ *02/513–8494* ⊠ *chaussée de Waterloo 699, Uccle* ☎ *02/345–3890*). In addition to all kinds of designer clothes, it stocks linens and kitchenware. Cheap and cheerful **Hema** (⊠ *rue Neuve 11, Lower Town* ☎ *02/227–5211*) is the place for kitchen goods, candles, and other miscellany.

SPECIALTY STORES

ANTIQUES

If you're looking for a bargain then don't miss the antiques market in the Sablon area on the weekend. The Sablon also offers many pristine antiques shops that sell expensive African antiquities.

For antique bathroom fittings, go to **Baden Baden** (⊠ *rue Haute 78–84, Les Marolles* ☎ *02/548–9690*). **La Bobine d'Or** (⊠ *rue Blaes 135, Les Marolles* ☎ *02/513–4817*) is crammed with antique lace, vintage

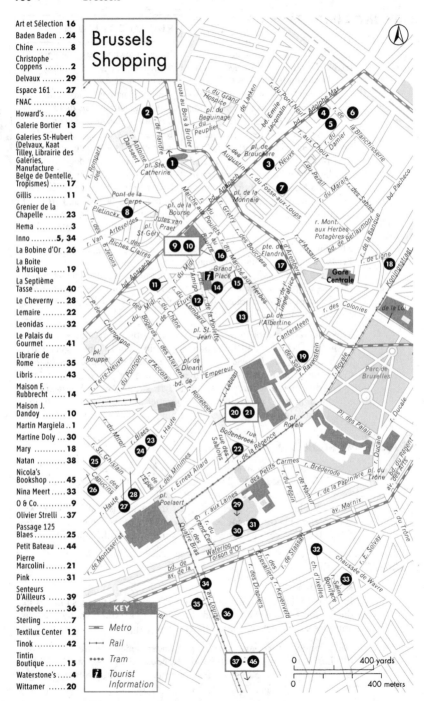

Brussels
Shopping

KEY

Metro

Rail

Tram

Tourist
Information

0   400 yards

0   400 meters

clothes, jewelry, figurines, and just about anything else that can be squeezed in. **Le Cheverny** (⊠*rue Haute 126, Les Marolles* ☎02/511–5495) has a fine selection of Art Nouveau lamps, as well as some Art Deco items. **Espace 161** (⊠*rue Haute 161, Les Marolles* ☎02/502–3164) offers crystal chandeliers and sumptuous furniture. **Grenier de la Chapelle** (⊠*rue Haute 51, Les Marolles* ☎02/513–2955) is the place for rustic wood furniture. **Lemaire** (⊠*rue de la Régence 34, Upper Town* ☎02/511–0513) has an extensive selection of fine porcelain and earthenware. **Passage 125 Blaes** (⊠*rue Blaes 121–125, Les Marolles* ☎02/503–1027) brings together 25 antiques dealers under one roof, with a vast range of goods including chandeliers, bathroom fixtures, art, and furniture in a variety of styles.

BOOKS

The **Galerie Bortier** (⊠*rue de la Madeleine–rue St-Jean, Upper Town*) is a small, attractive arcade devoted entirely to rare and secondhand books. It was designed by the architect responsible for the Galeries St-Hubert. **Librairie des Galeries** (⊠*Galerie du Roi 2, Upper Town* ☎02/511–2412) carries an extensive selection of books in both French and English on art, architecture, and photography. **Libris** (⊠*Espace Louise, Ixelles* ☎02/511–6400) is well stocked with current French-language titles. Shops specializing in comic strip albums include those at chaussée de Wavre Nos. 167, 179, and 198, and the **Tintin Boutique** (⊠*rue de la Colline 13, off Grand'Place, Lower Town*). **Tropismes** (⊠*Galerie des Princes 11, Upper Town* ☎02/512–8852) carries more than 40,000 titles and will help you find out-of-print books.

You won't lack for English-language bookstores here. **Librairie de Rome** (⊠*rue Jean Stas 16A, Ixelles* ☎02/511–7937) has a large selection of foreign newspapers and magazines. The friendly staff at **Sterling** (⊠*rue du Fossé-aux-Loups 38, Upper Town* ☎02/223–6223) exude an infectious enthusiasm for reading. **Waterstone's** (⊠*blvd. Adolphe Max 71–75, Upper Town* ☎02/219–2708), a larger, less personal store, carries pricey hardcovers, paperbacks, and periodicals.

CHILDREN'S CLOTHES

Tinok (⊠*av. Louise 165, Ixelles* ☎02/646–3587) is an upscale store stocking toys, furniture, baby wear, and clothes for children aged up to six. For inexpensive, good quality children's clothes, and soft, flattering cotton shirts for women, try **Petit Bateau** (⊠*av. de la Toison d'Or 50, Ixelles* ☎02/545–7650).

CHOCOLATES

Fodor'sChoice ★ In virtually every neighborhood in the city center, you'll be just a bonbon's throw from an outstanding chocolate shop. *Pralines* (chocolates filled with flavored creams, liqueur, or nuts) were invented here, and many chocolatiers still hand-make these delicious morsels. While Godiva and other brands of mass-produced chocolates are widely available, now's your chance to seek out the work of artisans. **Leonidas** (⊠*blvd. Anspach 46, Lower Town* ☎02/218–0363) is a bit less expensive than its competitors, but still high quality thanks to Belgium's strict controls on chocolate. **Mary** (⊠*rue Royale 73, Upper Town* ☎02/217–4500), the official

CLOSE UP

Chocolate Country

Years ago, visitors to Brussels, stepping out of the Midi train station, would be greeted by the sight of the Côte D'Or chocolate factory. The plumes of smoke rising from its stacks would scent the air with a seductive aroma of freshly made chocolate. Though the factory closed in the late 1970s, you won't lack for reminders of one of the country's signature industries. With nearly 500 large- and small-scale chocolatiers vying for a place at the top, Belgian chocolate making is a prodigious and cutthroat business. The domestic market alone is formidable; Belgium has one of the world's highest chocolate consumption rates, at an average of more than 15 pounds per person per year.

The country's reputation for high quality rests on choice raw materials and meticulous production practices. Belgian companies go after the rare criollo cocoa beans and the trinitario variety (a cross between criollo and the hardier, less subtle forastero cocoa), both of which have complex, nonbitter flavors. The bean roasting and crushing is done with exceptional precision. The best producers conch their chocolate—a refining process of mixing the chocolate with extra cocoa butter or other additions—for days rather than a few hours, as standard manufacturers do. Extended conching creates a smooth, even texture and reduces acid levels, enhancing the chocolate taste.

You can get a full rundown on the production process at the Musée du Cacao et du Chocolat in Brussels. Of course, you should also indulge in a little self-education at some of the local chocolate shops as well.

Belgium's chief contribution to the history of chocolate making came in 1912, when Belgian chocolatier Jean Neuhaus created the first *pralines*, bite-size chocolates filled with a mixture of nuts and sugar. Billed as "individual masterpieces," these hand-crafted delicacies proved an excellent way for chocolatiers to distinguish themselves. Neuhaus's "couverture" chocolate formed a shell that could hold all kinds of fillings: caramels, creams, flavored ganaches, and more. Combining visual elegance with exquisite taste, the praline continues to undergo reinvention by chocolatiers. Classic examples such as gianduja (hazelnut) share display cases with newcomers flavored with ginger, tea, or herbs. Many chocolatiers make seasonal or special-event pralines; and some chocolatiers, such as Pierre Marcolini, are increasingly emphasizing the origins of the cocoa beans, offering chocolates made from beans from a single location, such as Venezuela or Ghana.

So seriously does Belgium take its reputation as a chocolate producer that in 2000 its Ministry of Economic Affairs created a mark of quality assurance, AMBAO ("cocoa" in Swahili). The formation of AMBAO was a quick response to the EU decision earlier that year that ruled that up to 5% of the cocoa butter in chocolate could be replaced by other vegetable fats and the result could still be called chocolate. Members of the AMBAO association, ranging from large international companies to small artisanal producers, use only 100% cocoa butter in their chocolate, and uphold higher overall quality levels than those dictated by the EU bureaucrats.

–Olivia Mollet

purveyor of chocolate to the Belgian court, turns out excellent hand-made pralines. Be sure to try the dark-chocolate mousse, divided into five degrees of cocoa intensity. The flagship store of the chain **Neuhaus** (⊠*Galerie de la Reine 25–27, Upper Town* ☎*02/502–5914*) displays its goodies behind stained-glass windows. The shop windows of **Pierre Marcolini** (⊠*pl. du Grand Sablon 39, Upper Town* ☎*02/514–1206*) are especially colorful and creative, with unusual flavors like tea and thyme. The namesake boy wonder of the chocolate world started out as a pastry chef and is thought to produce the best handmade pralines. At **Wittamer** (⊠*pl. du Grand Sablon 12, Upper Town* ☎*02/512–3742*) you can choose between exquisite chocolates and other gorgeously wrapped boxes of delicacies, such as *marrons glacés* (candied chestnuts) and almond-paste biscuits—all make great gifts.

CRYSTAL

The Val St-Lambert mark is the only guarantee of handblown, hand-engraved lead crystal vases and other glass. You can buy it in many stores; the specialist is **Art et Sélection** (⊠*rue du Marché-aux-Herbes 83, Lower Town* ☎*02/511–8448*).

FOOD

★ **Maison J. Dandoy** (⊠*rue au Beurre 31, Upper Town* ☎*02/511–0326*) has the best biscuits in Brussels, including the Belgian specialty *speculoos,* spiced cookies available in many shapes and sizes. **O & Co.** (⊠*rue au Beurre 28, Lower Town* ☎*02/502–7511*) is stacked to the ceiling with a wide selection of olive oils made by small producers from throughout the Mediterranean, including France, Italy, Spain, Greece, and Israel. Temptations at **Le Palais du Gourmet** (⊠*rue du Bailli 106, Ixelles* ☎*02/537–6653*) include cheeses, condiments, oils and vinegars, foie gras, caviar, and wine. **La Septième Tasse** (⊠*rue du Bailli 37, Ixelles* ☎*02/647–1971*) sells about 100 different kinds of tea, as well as china teapots and gleaming silver urns. You can enjoy a cup of tea in the shop's cozy café, then select loose tea to take home.

HATS

Flemish milliner **Christophe Coppens** (⊠*rue Léon Lepage 2, Ixelles* ☎*02/512–7797*) designs cutting-edge hats. If you're planning a trip to Ascot, this is the place to find that one-of-a-kind creation that will make you stand out in a crowd. The hats at **Gillis** (⊠*rue du Lombard 17, Upper Town* ☎*02/512–0926*) are made using head molds, irons, and steam. If you've lost a favorite hat, the shop can re-create it from a picture.

LACE, LINEN & TAPESTRIES

Lace sold in the souvenir shops is likely to come from East Asia; it's best to ask whether a piece is genuine handmade Belgian lace or machine-made. An introductory visit to the **Musée du Costume et de la Dentelle** (⊠*rue de la Violette 6, Lower Town* ☎*02/512–7709*) is a good idea if you're planning to shop for lace.

Browse samples of local lace craftsmanship at **Maison F. Rubbrecht** (⊠*Grand'Place 23, Lower Town* ☎*02/512–0218*). **Manufacture Belge de Dentelle** (⊠*Galerie de la Reine 6–8, Upper Town* ☎*02/511–4477*) sells contemporary and antique handmade lace. For Belgian linen, try **Martine Doly** (⊠*blvd. de Waterloo 27, Upper Town* ☎*02/512–4628*). For tapestries that are evidence of Belgium's long tradition as a high-quality textiles-producing center, head for **Textilux Center** (⊠*rue du Lombard 41b, Upper Town* ☎*02/513–5015*).

LEATHER GOODS

FodorsChoice **Delvaux** (⊠*Galerie de la Reine 31, Upper Town* ☎*02/512–7198*
★ ⊠*blvd. de Waterloo 27, Upper Town* ☎*02/513–0502*) makes outstanding, classic handbags, wallets, belts, and attaché cases. Be prepared to part with a hefty sum, but the Delvaux products last and last.

MEN'S CLOTHES

Olivier Strelli (⊠*av. Louise 72, Ixelles* ☎*02/512–5607*) is Belgium's Armani equivalent, with its contemporary, minimalist fashion. If you're looking for shirts, head to **Pink** (⊠*blvd. de Waterloo 23, Upper Town* ☎*02/502–0508*). The selection of shirts and ties is vast, and, yes, they come in many colors in addition to pink. There is also a smaller selection of women's shirts.

MUSIC

La Boite à Musique (⊠*rue Coudenberg 74, Upper Town* ☎*02/513–0965*) is the best place in Brussels for classical music—suitably, the store is next to the Palais des Beaux-Arts symphony hall. **FNAC** (⊠*City 2, rue Cendres 16, Lower Town* ☎*02/209–2211*) offers a full range of music, from rap to rock to jazz, in a large store that also has a good selection of books, in English as well as French. You can buy concert tickets here, too.

PERFUME

Senteurs D'Ailleurs (⊠*av. Louise 100, Ixelles* ☎*02/511–6969*) is the Rolls-Royce of perfume shops, with a diverse selection of perfumes, bath products, and candles in scents ranging from floral to thyme and honey from specialized producers.

TOYS

FodorsChoice **Serneels** (⊠*av. Louise 69, Ixelles* ☎*02/538–3066*) is a paradise of
★ toys that is as much fun for adults as for children, although the prices tend to be stratospheric. The stuffed animals, many of them virtually life-size, are the stars of the store. Exquisite wooden rocking horses, wooden soldiers, dolls, and model cars, boats, trains, and airplanes are also hard to resist.

WOMEN'S CLOTHES

Chine (⊠*rue Van Arteveld 2, Upper Town* ☎*02/503–1499*), as the name implies, sells clothes from China, mainly simple silks in softly feminine styles. Flemish designer **Kaat Tilley** (⊠*Galerie du Roi 4, Upper Town* ☎*02/514–0763*) shows fanciful clothes and jewelry in a quirky setting. Antwerp doesn't hoard all the avant-garde clothing design; Brussels claims the flagship boutique of **Martin Margiela** (⊠*rue Leon Lepage 40, Ixelles* ☎*02/223–7520*). The reclusive designer pursues deconstructed clothing; look for his trademark exposed seams and white-stitched labels. Royal favorite minimalist designer Edouard

Vermeulen is the genius behind **Natan** (⊠*av. Louise 158, Ixelles* ☎*02/647–1001*). Natan also has a second location at rue du Namur 78, as well as a men's shop on rue Antoine Dansaert. Designer **Nina Meert** (⊠*rue St-Boniface 1, Ixelles* ☎*02/514–2263*) comes from a family of painters and opened her house of couture in 1979 in Brussels and Paris. She has dressed the likes of actresses Isabelle Adjani and Meryl Streep and Belgium's Queen Paola. For less expensive but still chic Belgian fashion, try **Rue Blanche** (⊠*rue Antoine Dansaert 39, Lower Town* ☎*02/512–0314*).

STREET MARKETS

Bruxellois with an eye for fresh farm produce and low prices do most of their food shopping at the animated open-air markets in almost every commune. Among the best are those in **Boitsfort** in front of the Maison Communal on Sunday morning; on **place du Châtelain,** Wednesday afternoon; and on **place Ste-Catherine,** all day, Monday–Saturday. In addition to fruits, vegetables, meat, and fish, most markets include traders with specialized products, such as cheese or wild mushrooms. The most exotic market is the Sunday morning **Marché du Midi,** where the large North African community gathers to buy and sell foods, spices, and plants, transforming the area next to the railway station into a vast bazaar. You can also join the thousands of shoppers in the meat and produce market in **Anderlecht's,** housed in a 19th-century former abattoir every Friday, Saturday, and Sunday 7–2.

★ From March to October, the Grand'Place's cobbles bloom with color during its **Marché des Fleurs,** or flower market, held every day except Monday. You need to get to the flea market, **Vieux Marché** (⊠*pl. du Jeu de Balle, Les Marolles*), early to pick up real bargains, but it's a pleasant place to drink in the working-class atmosphere of the Marolles all morning. It's open daily 7–1. The **Marché du Sablon** (⊠*pl. du Grand Sablon, Upper Town*), Saturday 9–6 and Sunday 9–2, is frequented by established antiques and rare-book dealers.

SIDE TRIPS FROM BRUSSELS

WATERLOO

19 km (12 mi) south of Brussels.

Waterloo, like Stalingrad and Hiroshima, changed the course of history. The defeat of the French here in June 1815 ended Napoléon's attempt to dominate Europe.

The British army's top officers were at a swanky Brussels ball on the night of June 16, 1815, when they were called to face Napoléon's men. After joining their rank-and-file troops in Waterloo, they garrisoned Hougoumont farm, which still exists today, and spent the night of June 17 being lashed by heavy rain. Their allies, the Prussians, were camped in nearby Wavre.

At midday on June 18, the French soldiers, led by their cancer-stricken emperor, started their offensive at the farm. Heavy fighting raged all day and the bad weather that had soaked the British troops actually came to their defence, hindering the heavy French artillery and lessening the impact of cannonballs. The allies held their positions and eventually the French army were being attacked from all sides. In the early evening, Napoléon and his men retreated, escaping back to France. Later, he surrendered to the British and was exiled to Saint Helena, where he died in 1821. The short, brutal clash, which made a hero of the British Duke of Wellington, took a gruesomely heavy toll on both sides, with 48,000 deaths.

What Victor Hugo once called the *morne plain* (dismal plain) is now a patch of open space in a prosperous suburb complete with large, whitewashed villas and smart boutiques. Home to two American schools for international children, Waterloo has a cosmopolitan feel. More than one-fifth of the population is foreign, including a large percentage of American, French, and Canadian expats.

The battle site itself is rather shabby, with souvenir shops, frites stands, and an abandoned go-cart track. But the regional government, inspired by the Gettysburg site in the United States, is pouring millions of euros into a plan to vastly improve the area. A bypass is being constructed to pedestrianize the area, buildings are being restored to their 19th-century state, and there will be a proper parking lot, along with an access route lined with a memorial wall featuring the names of the regiments that fought in the battle. An underground exhibition space will be filled with scale models, 3-D films attempting to re-create the battlefield experience, and audioguides in 10 languages.

GETTING HERE & AROUND
To reach Waterloo, take bus W from Brussels (on place Rouppe); it runs at half-hour intervals, and the ride takes around 50 minutes. There is also frequent commuter-train service from the Gare du Midi to Waterloo; the trip takes 15 minutes.

WHAT TO SEE
Arthur Wellesley, the Duke of Wellington, spent the night of June 17, 1815, at an inn in Waterloo, where he established his headquarters. When he slept here again the following night, Napoléon had been defeated.

The inn is now the **Musée Wellington.** It presents the events of the 100 days leading up to the Battle of Waterloo, maps and models of the battle itself, and military and Wellington memorabilia in well-laid-out displays. There's some information in English. ⊠*chaussée de Bruxelles 147* ☎*02/354–7806* ⊠*€5* ☼*Apr.–Sept., daily 9:30–6:30; Oct.–Mar., daily 10–5.*

The actual **Champ de Bataille** (battlefield) is south of Waterloo (signposted "Butte de Lion"). Here Wellington's troops received the onslaught of Napoléon's army. A crucial role in the battle was played by some of the ancient, fortified farms, of which there are many in this area. The Hogoumont farm was fought over all day; 6,000 men, out of total casualties of 48,000, were killed here. Later in the day, fierce fighting raged around the farms of La Sainte Haye and Papelotte. In the afternoon, the French cavalry attacked, in the mistaken belief that the British line was giving way. Napoléon's final attempt was to send in the armored cavalry of the Imperial Guard, but at the same time the Prussian army under Blücher arrived to engage the French from the east, and it was all over. The battlefield, made up of rye fields, is best surveyed from the top of the **Butte de Lion,** a pyramid 226 steps high and crowned by a 28-ton lion, which was erected by the Dutch 10 years later.

The **visitor center** offers an audiovisual presentation of the battle, followed by a mood-setting film of the fighting seen through the eyes of children. You can buy souvenirs here, too—from tin soldiers and T-shirts to soft toy lions and model cannons. There are also plenty of books, some highly specialized, about the battle and the men who led the fighting. The adjacent **Panorama de la Bataille,** first unveiled in 1912, contains a vast, circular painting of the charge of the French cavalry, executed with amazing perspective and realism. ⊠*rte. du Lion 252–254* ☎*02/385–1912* ⊕*www.waterloo1815.be* 💳*€12, covering all Waterloo sights* ⊙*Apr.–Sept., daily 9:30–6:30; Oct., daily 9:30–5:30; Nov.–Feb., daily 10:30–4; Mar., daily 10–5.*

From the prevalence of souvenirs and images of Napoléon, you might think that the battle was won by the French. In fact, there were Belgian soldiers fighting on both sides. Napoléon's headquarters during his last days as emperor were in what is now the small **Musée du Caillou** in Genappe, south of the battlefield. It contains the room where he spent the night before the battle, his personal effects, and objects found in the field. ⊠*chaussée de Bruxelles 66* ☎*02/384–2424* 💳*€4* ⊙*Apr.–Sept., daily 10:30–6:30; Nov.–Mar., daily 1–5.*

WHERE TO STAY & EAT

$$$$ ✕**La Maison du Seigneur.** In a peaceful, whitewashed farmhouse with a
FRENCH spacious terrace, Ghislaine de Becker and his son Pilou offer elegant, classical French cuisine. The seasonal menu could include sole with shrimp sauce. ⊠*chaussée de Tervuren 389* ☎*02/354–0750* 🝖*AE, DC, MC, V* ⊙*Closed Sun.–Wed., Feb., and last 2 wks of Aug.*

¢–$ ✕**L'Amusoir.** Popular with resident Americans, this is an unpretentious
STEAK steak house in an old white-walled building in the center of town. It serves mouthwatering filet mignon, prepared with a variety of sauces, and hearty Belgian traditional dishes. ⊠*chaussée de Bruxelles 121* ☎*02/354–8233* 🝖*AE.*

$–$$ ✕**Les 65 Colonnes.** This large, light-filled brasserie turns out Belgian and
FRENCH French staples for great prices. Its speciality is seafood, but you can't go wrong with the steak frites either. ⊠*chaussée de Bruxelles 389* ☎*02/351–5929* 🝖*MC, V.*

$$ 🏨**Hotel Le Côté Vert.** This relaxed hotel is in the center of Waterloo town, but surrounded by greenery. The spacious, spotless rooms are

simply decorated in blue. A buffet breakfast is served on a pretty ter-race. ⊠*chaussée de Bruxelles 200G* ☎*02/354–0105* ➷*30 rooms* ⌂*In-room: safe. In-hotel: restaurant, bar* ▭*AE, DC, MC, V.*

GAASBEEK

15 km (9 mi) west of Brussels.

Visiting Gaasbeek is like stepping inside one of Bruegel's paintings of village life. The area is called Pajottenland, and you may already be familiar with the landscape from his works, many of which were painted here.

GETTING HERE & AROUND
Take the 142 De Lijn bus from the Gare du Midi. The trip takes around 45 minutes.

WHAT TO SEE
From the terrace of the **Kasteel van Gaasbeek,** originally built in 1240, you have a panoramic view of this landscape. The rulers of Gaasbeek once lorded it over Brussels, and the townspeople took terrible revenge and razed the castle in 1388. Restored in Romantic style in the 19th century, it contains outstanding 15th- and 16th-century tapestries. Rubens's will is among the documents in the castle archives. The sur-rounding park is popular with picnickers. A guide booklet is available in Dutch only. ⊠*Kasteelstraat 40* ☎*02/531–0130* ▭*€6* ☽*Apr.–June, Sept., and Oct., Tues.–Thurs. and weekends 10–5; July and Aug., Tues.–Sun. 10–5.*

Brugge & the North Sea Coast

WORD OF MOUTH

"Of all our travels, we found Bruges to be the city we will never forget and would love to return to and share with our adult children. We spent 3 days there and felt those three days were the high-light of the trip. We were so impressed with the elegant simplicity of the old city. No honking cars; gracious, friendly people; easy walking; wonder-ful food; and a wealth of history. Our most magi-cal times were at night, after the day tourists from Brussels returned on their trains. We meandered along the canals, over small bridges photograph-ing the uplit buildings and streets."

—ibailey

Updated by
Tim Skelton

LONG THOUGHT OF AS A Sleeping Beauty reawakened, Brugge is an ancient village whose heritage has been well preserved. However, the contemporary comparison is sometimes closer to Beauty and the Beast—particularly in summer, when visitors flock here in overwhelming numbers. Still, in the quiet, colder seasons, the city offers a peaceful refuge, and you can feel the rhythm of life centuries ago.

Belgians make the most of their wide coastline, known as the North Sea Coast. Resort towns such as Knokke-Heist, Oostende, and Koksijde are packed on summer days when the water warms. Along the coast, children fly kites, teenagers ride pedal cars, horses thunder by along the shore, and lovers walk arm in arm atop the fine, golden sand. Offshore, great yachts with smooth white sails cut through the cold breeze, heading to and from the harbors at Blankenberge, Nieuwpoort, Oostende, and Zeebrugge.

ORENTATION & PLANNING

GETTING ORIENTATED

BRUGGE (BRUGES)

Brugge is compact, like a small island amid the winding waterways, and the twists and turns may lead you to unexpected pleasures. Brugge's historic center is encircled by a ring road that loosely follows the line of the city's medieval ramparts. In fact, the ancient gates—Smedenpoort, Ezelpoort, Kruispoort, and Gentpoort—still stand along this road. Most of Brugge's sights lie inside the ring road. The town center is technically divided up into parishes or *kwartiers* around the local churches: Sint-Gillis, Sint-Anna, Sint-Magdalena, Onze-Lieve-Vrouwekerk, Sint-Salvators, and Sint-Jacobs. In practice, however, the center is so compact that locals rarely use these parish names. Instead, they usually refer to an area by its major landmark. Only the names of the quieter, residential neighborhoods of Sint-Gillis and Sint-Anna are commonly used. Just outside the ring road are the suburban neighborhoods of Sint-Kruis, Sint-Michiels, Sint-Andries, and Sint-Pieters.

NORTH SEA COAST

The cold North Sea wrote the history of Flanders's wealth and politics, linking its ports, protecting its people, and providing crucial natural resources. Today, the North Sea coast is still irresistible to invaders—of a more peaceful kind. Along the northwest coast, simple settlements are strung between summer resorts and seaside business centers with names like Oostende, Koksijde, and Knokke-Heist. Tourists come for the region's fresh air, quiet beaches, and quaint, colorful villages.

PLANNING

TAKE IT ALL IN

1 Day: Get thee to Brugge as early as possible on the first day. Must-see spots include the Begijnhof near Minnewater, as well as the great buildings around Burg and Markt squares. Soak up the artwork, including the Groeninge and Memling museums, and Michelangelo's sculpture in the Onze-Lieve-Vrouwekerk. You might take an afternoon canal ride—or, after dinner, when crowds have thinned, you can wander alongside the water.

3 Days: Follow the previous itinerary but spend two nights in Brugge. On the second day, visit more of the city's sights and museums or take a side trip to Damme. Spend the last day exploring the rural countryside of western Flanders: serene villages and World War I sights, such as the battlefields around Ieper *(see Chapter 2, Historic Battlegrounds)* and the massive British cemetery of Tyne Cot *(see Chapter 2)*. Alternatively, you could head to one of the North Sea coastal towns, such as Oostende or Knokke, for sun (sometimes), fun, and fresh seafood.

EAT RIGHT, SLEEP WELL

There are hundreds of restaurants in Brugge, ranging from taverns offering a quick snack to stylish establishments serving Flemish or international (albeit mostly French) delicacies. Seafood is great here, as the coast is nearby; meals cooked with Belgian beer are a treat as well. While in the Markt, snack like a Belgian with mayonnaise-covered fries.

Unless you're going to a high-class restaurant, casual dress is always appropriate. You should make reservations, especially on weekends and holidays. Otherwise, your best strategy for getting a table is to come just as the restaurant opens or after the main rush. The busiest mealtimes tend to be from noon to 1:30 and 7 to 9. After 10 PM it can be hard to find restaurants that are still serving. Many restaurants serve meals outdoors, even in winter on heated terraces. A 16% service charge and a 19% V.A.T. are always included in the tab, so you don't need to leave a tip, although most people round off upwards.

Brugge is a popular weekend escape, full as it is of romantic suites and secluded hideaways. You'll find old-fashioned accents at most hotels in the "City of Swans." The tourist office can help you make reservations for lodgings in Brugge and the surrounding countryside. On ⊕*www. brugge.be* you'll find an extensive list of hotels. The Bed & Breakfast page has more than 100 entries; staying in these often very picturesque places might be the easiest way to make contact with locals. Rates, which are sometimes higher than in regular hotels, usually include a hearty Belgian breakfast of bread, cereal, cold cuts, cheese, yogurt, eggs, and fruit. Half-board meal plans are also frequently available.

If you'd like to stay in a coastal town in summer, be sure to make arrangements at least a few weeks in advance. Tax (6%) and service are included in all accommodation rates.

Flanders

KEY

⊢⊣ Rail Lines

NETHERLANDS

MER DU NORD (NORTH SEA)
NORDZEE (NORTH SEA)

FRANCE

Kalmhout

Antwerp
Mortsel

Brussels

Vilvoorde

Willebroek

Asse

N1

E19/A1

E40

N17

Schelde

Schelde

N11

Dendermonde

N47

Aalst

N28

N8

St-Niklaas

E17/A14

N49

N403

N60

Zelzate

N253

N252

N61

N49

N58

Lochristi

N70

Laarne

Melle

N17

Herzele

Eeklo

Waarschoot

N9

Gent

R4

E40/A10

N42

Brakel

Geraardsbergen

N8

Oudenaarde

N60

Ronse

Maldegem

N44

Beernem

N499

Leiestreek

Deinze

N35

Zulte

Leie

N43

N36

Kluisbergen

E17/A14

Het
Zwin

Knokke-Heist

Oostkerke

Damme

N376

Brugge
see detail map

N50

Tielt

N31

Zeebrugge

N371

Blankenberge

N34

Jabbeke

Gistel

N33

Torhout

N35

Roeselare

E403

Kortrijk

A19

A17

Passchendaele

N303

Tyne Cot

Zillebeke

Breden

A10

E40/A18

Oostende

N34

Nieuwpoort

Oostduinkerke

Koksijde

N35

N301

Diksmuide

N369

N38

Ieper

Poperinge

N8

Sint-
Idesbald

De Panne

see detail map
North Sea Coast

0   10 miles
0   15 km

TOP REASONS TO VISIT

Walk Back in Time. The planning laws in Brugge have been very strict for many years (it was the first city in Europe—in 1972—to get cable TV, which dispensed with those unsightly antennae), meaning there are few new buildings to spoil the illusion that you've waltzed back to another age.

Float on By. The canals that cut though the center of Brugge are among the most beautiful you will find anywhere. Take a boat trip and travel down them at a pace that befits their grandeur.

A Land in Miniature. If you're looking to experience every cliché about Belgium in one tidy package, Brugge is the place to find it: chocolate, lace, waffles, fries, beer, and Flemish stepped gables. All within steps of one another.

Streching Your Legs. One of the great joys of a trip to Flanders is strolling in the cool, early morning before the crowds amass, or late in the evening when lighted buildings shimmer like gold along the narrow waterways.

Sand Between Your Toes. Belgium may only have 67 km (42 mi) of coastline, but what little there is consists almost exclusively of sandy beach. Resorts like Knokke are the ideal places to take it all in.

WHAT IT COSTS IN EUROS					
	¢	$	$$	$$$	$$$$
Restaurants	under €10	€10–€15	€15–€20	€20–€30	over €30
Hotels	under €75	€75–€100	€100–€150	€150–€225	over €225

Restaurant prices are for a main course at dinner, including tax and tip. Hotel prices are for two people in a standard double room in high season, on the European Plan (EP, with no meals) unless otherwise noted. Costs include 6% tax.

GETTING HERE & AROUND

Ostend-Bruges International Airport is slowly expanding into regular passenger service. However, most flights are still charters, so your best bet is to fly to Brussels and drive or take the train from there.

Considering the flat-as-a-pancake terrain, it's easy to travel on two wheels. You can rent bikes at rental shops or at the ticket windows of train stations. A valid train ticket gets you a discounted rate. Many bike rental companies have both adult bikes (with or without baby seats) and children's bikes. Maps with suggested cycling routes are available at local tourist offices.

The **De Lijn** bus company provides bus, tram, and trolley service throughout Flanders. Roads in this region are well maintained, with good signage. Be sure to watch out for cyclists.

To visit the battlefields from here, driving is definitely the best solution, because the various World War I sights are in different directions from Ieper. The easiest way to reach Ieper is via the A19 from Kortrijk, which peters out north of the city; highway N38 continues to

Poperinge, where you're close to the French highway linking Lille with Dunkirk and Calais.

See By Ferry, in Getting Here & Around in Travel Smart Belgium for information regarding ferry service to and from the United Kingdom.

The Belgian national railway, **NMBS/SNCB** sends two trains each hour to Brugge from Brussels (50 minutes) and three trains an hour from Gent (25 minutes) and from Oostende (15 minutes). Oostende is the terminus of the Cologne–Brussels–Oostende railway line, which connects with the ferry service to Ramsgate and the boat train to London. A train departs every hour from Brussels (1 hour, 10 minutes), from Gent (40 minutes), and from Brugge (15 minutes).

TOURING BRUGGE & ENVIRONS

BIKE TOURS   Brugge-based **Quasimundo Bike Tours** organizes three itineraries: an introduction to Brugge, a nighttime Brugge ride, and a trip out to Damme and Oostkerke. The tours cost €24 per person. **Pink Bear Tours** leads two cycling tours from Brugge at €20 a pop. One does a sightseeing loop of Brugge and the nearby village of Damme; the other focuses on the polderland outside the city. **The Green Bike Tour** follows a similar path, exploring Brugge and then heading out to Damme and Oostkerke. Tours cost €15 per person. All of these bike tours have English-speaking guides; rates include bike rental.

BOAT TOURS   The waterways threading through the center of Brugge make for lovely sightseeing routes. Independent motor launches depart from four jetties along the Dijver and Katelijnestraat and by the Vismarkt as soon as they are reasonably full (every 15 minutes or so) daily March–November and depending on the weather in December and February. The trips take just over a half hour and cost €5.50.

BUS TOURS   **Quasimodo Tours** runs a couple of minibus excursions with English commentary, hosting up to 30 people per trip. Be sure to wear comfortable shoes as both tours involve several stops and some walking. The "Triple Treat" tour refers to Belgium's three great culinary delights: waffles, chocolate, and beer. You'll have a chance to sample all three; this tour is held Monday, Wednesday, and Friday. The other itinerary, offered Sunday, Tuesday, and Thursday, covers the Flanders Fields war grounds, taking you to trenches, war graves, museums, monuments and the preserved battlefield at Hill 60. Both tours cost €55 per person; reservations are essential. **Daytours** offers a similar battlefield tour, Tuesday to Sunday year-round, which costs €59 per person.

WALKING TOURS   **In&Uit Brugge** can set you up with a private English-speaking guide for a minimum cost of €50 for two hours, €25 per extra hour. In July and August, groups are consolidated at the tourist office every day at 3; the cost per person is €5 (children free).

VISITOR INFORMATION

All of the city and regional tourist offices in Flanders have English-speaking staff. **Westtoerisme** provides info on the whole area. Brugge's visitor information bureau is open daily year-round, though it closes for lunch breaks on weekends. In addition to its guides and services, it has a set of lockers where you can store your bags; buy a locker token at the desk for €1. A small branch office, also with lockers, is in the train station.

The opening hours of the coastal tourist offices vary. Some are open daily (Oostende), others are open daily but close for lunch (Knokke-Heist), and a few close on at least one weekend day fall through spring (De Panne, Koksijde). In the peak summer season, most keep slightly longer hours. The regional tourism ministry hosts ⊕*www.dekust.org*, a Web site on the coastal resorts that has pages translated in English and lots of helpful links.

HEALTH & SAFTEY

A duty doctor service is on call for nights, weekends, and holidays in each major town in Flanders. Some pharmacies rotate night and weekend duty; calling the information hotline will give you the name and address of the current 24-hour or late-night pharmacy.

You can feel secure striking out on your own, as petty crime is minimal and Flemings speak enough English to point you in the right direction.

ESSENTIALS

Airport Ostend-Bruges International Airport (☎ *059/55–12–11* ⊕ *www. ostendairport.be*).

Bus De Lijn (☎ *059/56–52–11 West Flanders, 09/210–9311 East Flanders* ⊕ *www. delijn.be*).

National Railway NMBS/SNCB (☎ *02/555–2525* ⊕ *www.b-rail.be*).

Emergency Contacts Ambulance (☎ *100*). **Duty doctors** (☎ *050/36–40–10*). **Night pharmacies** (☎ *050/40–61–62*). **Police** (☎ *101*).

Tours Quasimundo Bike Tours (☎ *050/33–07–75* ⊕ *www.quasimundo.com*). **Pink Bear Tours** (☎ *050/61–66–86* ⊕ *www.pinkbear.freeservers.com*). **The Green Bike Tour** (☎ *0479/97–12–80*). **Quasimodo Tours** (☎ *050/37–04–70* ⊕ *www.quasimodo. be*). **Daytours** (☎ *050/34–60–60* ⊕ *www.visitbruges.org*). **In&Uit Brugge** (✉ *'t Zand 34* ☎ *050/44–46–46* ⊕ *www.brugge.be*). **Westtoerisme** (✉ *Koning Albert I laan 120, Brugge* ☎ *050/30–55–00*).

BRUGGE

Brugge has tangled streets, narrow canals, handsome squares, and old gabled buildings that were such a powerful magnet more than a century ago. Its limits now incorporate the port of Zeebrugge, and it is the administrative center of West Flanders. Although strong in politics, its principal industry remains tourism. Brugge has not only awakened from its centuries-old sleep, but it is also bright-eyed with spruced-up shops and services. The current throngs of admiring day-trippers have definitively overthrown the "despotic" silence that Belgian writer Georges Rodenbach wrote about it his 1892 novel *Bruges-la-Morte* (*Brugge, the Dead*).

Although it is often called Bruges, its French name, the city's official name is indeed Brugge (*bruhg*-guh), and you'll score points with the locals by using the Flemish title.

TIMIMG

You'll need two to three hours to leisurely explore the city, more if you're an art fan or tend to linger at picturesque vistas. The best strategy is to start at dawn with the walkable sights and then to visit the museums as the crowds start to hit the Burg. Alternatively, you could explore the museums first and postpone your stroll until the early evening (a good plan for rainy days). Before setting out, check the carillon schedule so that you can try to be near the Markt in time to hear one of the performances. If you need a rest, consider riding high in a horse-drawn carriage, or hopping a boat for a swan's-eye view of the canals (although the boats are usually crowded and the pilot's spiels clichéd).

It's best to spend at least one night in Brugge so that you can enjoy the city when the day-trippers aren't flooding the streets. Brugge is at its most enchanting at night, when floodlights illuminate the buildings and melt on inky water. Or in the pink of morning, when bells chime and gliding cygnets seem to play hide-and-seek in the mist. Whenever you walk, bring a camera.

Early spring and late fall are good times to tour Brugge; the weather is still mild and there are fewer tourists. Temperatures hover close to freezing in January and February, but you'll have the sights to yourself—note, however, that some restaurants along the coast close in winter. Remember that municipal museums are usually closed Monday.

GETTING HERE & AROUND

Cycling is certainly easier than driving around Brugge's winding streets, as cyclists can go in both directions along more than 50 one-way streets. These streets are marked on the tarmac with an image of a bicycle circled in blue. The Brugge tourist office sells a cycling brochure outlining five different routes around the city; it's available in English and costs €1.50. Flemish-language cycle maps aren't hard to figure out, though, as the routes are well-marked. There are plenty of places to rent bikes and you can get an inexpensive rental at the train station; if you have a valid train ticket for that day, you get a discount.

Most buses run every five minutes (less often on Sundays); minibuses are designed to navigate the narrow streets. Bus stops are clearly marked and dotted frequently around the town; the railway station is the main terminus. Several buslines take you from the station to the city center. Buy your tickets on board (€1.60) or from ticket machines (€1.20) at the terminus. Buses to surrounding towns and the coast also leave from the railway station.

Brugge is 5 km (3 mi) north of the E40 motorway, which links Brussels with Gent and Oostende. It is 126 km (76 mi) from the Le Shuttle terminus at Calais. Access for cars and coaches into Brugge's center is severely restricted. The historic streets are narrow and often one way.

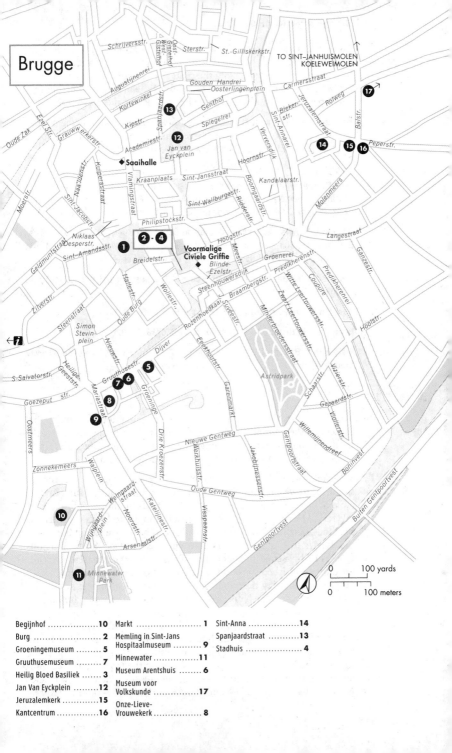

Brugge

TO SINT–JANHUISMOLEN
KOELEWEIMOLEN

Saaihalle

Voormalige
Civiele Griffie
Blinde-
Ezelstr.

100 yards
100 meters

There are huge parking lots at the railway station and near the exits from the ring road, plus underground parking at 't Zand. For those brave enough to face tackling the center's tricky one-way system, there is also underground parking at the Biekorf (behind the public library), Zilverpand, and Pandreitje, as well as parking at the Begijnhof.

Brugge has large taxi stands at the railway station and at the Markt. Taxis are metered and the rates are reasonable, but public transport, only €1.20, is always a cheaper way of getting around.

ESSENTIALS

Bike Rental Bauhaus Bike Rental (⊠ *Langestraat 135* ☎ *050/34–10–93*). **De Ketting** (⊠ *Gentpoortstraat 23* ☎ *050/34–41–96*). **Eric Popelier** (⊠ *Mariastraat 26* ☎ *050/34–32–62*). **Koffieboontje** (⊠ *Hallestraat 4* ☎ *050/33–80–27*).

Car Rentals Avis (⊠ *Koningin Astridlaan 97* ☎ *050/39–44–00* ⊕ *www.avis.be*). **Europcar** (⊠ *Sint-Pieterskaai 48* ☎ *050/31–45–44* ⊕ *www.europcar.be*). **Hertz** (⊠ *Pathoekeweg 25* ☎ *050/37–72–34* ⊕ *www.hertz.be*).

Internet Cafés Bauhaus DNA Cybercafe (⊠ *Langestraat 135* ☎ *050/34–10–93* ⏱ *Daily 9–9*).

Post Office De Post Brugge (⊠ *Markt 5* ☎ *050/47–13–10*).

Train Station Brugge (⊠ *Stationsplein* ☎ *050/38–23–82*).

Visitor Info Brugge (⊠ *In&Uit Brugge, 't Zand 34* ☎ *050/44–46–46* ⊕ *www. brugge.be*).

WHAT TO SEE

You can buy a €15 combination ticket for entry into five municipal museums: the Museum voor Volkskunde, the Groeningemuseum, the Gruuthusemuseum, the Memling, and the Arentshuis. These tickets do not expire and are available at all participating museums.

⑩ Begijnhof. The 13th-century beguinage is a pretty and serene cluster of
★ small, whitewashed houses, a pigeon tower, and a church surrounding a pleasant green at the edge of a canal. The Begijnhof was founded in 1245 by Margaret, Countess of Constantinople, to bring together the Beguines—girls and widows from all social backgrounds who devoted themselves to charitable work but who were not bound by religious vows. Led by a superintendent known as the Grand Mistress, the congregation flourished for 600 years. The last of the Beguines died about 50 years ago; today the site is occupied by the Benedictine nuns, who still wear the Beguine habit. You may join them, discreetly, for vespers in their small church of St. Elizabeth. Although most of the present-day houses are from the 16th and 17th centuries, they have maintained the architectural style of the houses that preceded them. One house has been set aside as a small museum. Visitors are asked to respect the silence. The horse-and-carriage rides around the town have a 10-minute stop outside the beguinage—long enough for a quick look round. ⊠ *Oude Begijnhof, off Wijngaardstraat* ☎ *050/33–00–11* 🎫 *Free,*

house visit €2 ⊙ *Mar.–Nov., daily 9:30–5; Dec.–Feb., Mon., Tues., Fri. 10–noon, Wed. and Thurs. 2–4* Ⓜ *Bus 12.*

② **Burg.** A popular daytime meeting place and an enchanting, floodlit
Fodor'sChoice scene after dark, the Burg is flanked by striking civic buildings. Named
★ for the fortress built by Baldwin of the Iron Arm, the Burg was also the former site of the 10th-century Carolingian Cathedral of St. Donaas, which was destroyed by French Republicans in 1799. You can wander through the handsome, 18th-century law court, the Oude Gerechtshof, the Voormalige Civiele Griffie with its 15th-century front gable, the Stadhuis, and the Heilig Bloed Basiliek *(see below)*. The Burg is not all historic splendor, though—in sharp contrast to these buildings stands a modern construction by Japanese artist Toyo Ito, added in 2002. Public opinion is sharply divided over Ito's pavilion over a shallow pool; you'll either love it or hate it. ⊠ *Hoogstraat and Breidelstraat* Ⓜ *Bus 1 or 12.*

⑤ **Groeningemuseum.** The tremendous holdings of this gallery give you
Fodor'sChoice the makings for a crash course in the Flemish Primitives and their
★ successors. Petrus Christus, Hugo Van der Goes, Hieronymus Bosch, Rogier van der Weyden, Gerard David, Pieter Bruegel (both Elder and Younger), Pieter Pourbus—all are represented here. Here you can see Jan van Eyck's wonderfully realistic *Madonna with Canon Van der Paele,* in which van Eyck achieved texture and depth through multiple layers of oil and varnish. The painter's attention to detail is all-embracing; the canon's pouchy flesh and the nets of wrinkles around his eyes are as carefully depicted as the crimson folds of the Madonna's robe or her waving golden hair. There's also one of Hans Memling's greatest works, the *Moreel Triptych.* The namesake family is portrayed on the side panels, all with preternaturally blank expressions. As if this weren't enough, the museum also encompasses a strong display of 15th- to 21st-century Dutch and Belgian works, sweeping through to Surrealist and contemporary art. The Groeninge is set back from the street in a pocket-size park behind a medieval gate. Although it is blessedly small, its riches warrant a full morning or afternoon. Thoughtfully, there's a play area to keep antsy children busy. An audioguide is available in English. ⊠ *Dijver 12* ☎ *050/44–87–11* 🎟 *€8, includes an audioguide, combination ticket €15* ⊙ *Tues.–Sun. 9:30–5* Ⓜ *Bus 1 or 12.*

NEED A BREAK? At the **Den Comptoir** (⊠ *Dijver 13* ☎ *050/34–41–54*) you can absorb even more art as you linger over a coffee, beer, or snack. The café is decorated with works by Frank Brangwyn, the Belgian-born painter, illustrator, and designer who became Britain's official war artist during World War I.

⑦ **Gruuthusemuseum.** If you want to understand the daily life of 15th-century Brugge, visit this applied arts museum. The collection is housed in the former home of Lodewijk Van Gruuthuse, a prominent Dutch nobleman who financed Edward IV's campaign to regain the throne of England in 1461. The family made its money from toll rights and from *gruut,* an herb used in brewing beer—a sure way to get rich in Belgium. The home features displays of furniture, tapestries, lace, ceramics, kitchen equipment, weaponry, and musical instruments. Room 6 has an attractive Gothic interior with a 15th-century mantelpiece and stained-glass windows. Don't miss the 18th-century guillotine—a piece of equipment that most homes of the era fortunately didn't contain. The audioguides are available in English. ⊠ *Dijver 17* ☎ *050/44–87–11* 🖭 *€6, includes audioguide and entry to Onze-Lieve-Vrouwekerk, combination ticket €15* ۞ *Tues.–Sun. 9:30–5* Ⓜ *Bus 1 or 12.*

❸ **Heilig Bloed Basiliek.** The Basilica of the Holy Blood manages to include both the austere and the ornate under one roof—not to mention one of Europe's most precious relics. The 12th-century Lower Chapel retains a stern, Romanesque character. Look for the poignant, 14th-century Pietà and the carved statue of Christ in the crypt. From this sober space, an elaborate, external Gothic stairway leads to the stunningly lavish Upper Chapel, which was twice destroyed—by Protestant iconoclasts in the 16th century and by French Republicans in the 18th—but both times rebuilt. (Note that the Upper Chapel is closed to visitors during Eucharistic Mass on Sunday 11–noon.) The original stained-glass windows were replaced in 1845, and then again after an explosion in 1967, when they were restored by the Brugge painter De Loddere. The basilica's namesake treasure is a vial thought to contain a few drops of the blood of Christ, brought from Jerusalem to Brugge in 1149 by Derick of Alsace when he returned from the Second Crusade. It is exposed here every Friday in the Lower Chapel 8:30–10 and in the Upper Chapel 10–11 and 3–4. On Ascension Day, it becomes the centerpiece of the magnificent *De Heilig Bloedprocessie* (Procession of the Holy Blood), a major medieval-style pageant in which it is carried through the streets of Brugge. The small **museum** next to the basilica contains the 17th-century reliquary. ⊠ *Burg* ☎ *050/33–67–92* ⊕ *www.holyblood.com* 🖭 *Museum: €1.50* ۞ *Apr.–Sept., Thurs.–Tues. 9:30–noon and 2–6, Wed. 9:30–noon; Oct.–Mar., Thurs.–Tues. 9:30–noon and 2–4, Wed. 9:30–noon* Ⓜ *Bus 1 or 12.*

NEED A BREAK? In an alley off well-worn Breidelstraat you'll find the tiny, two-tier, brick-and-beam coffeehouse and pub De Garre (⊠ *De Garre 1* ☎ *050/34-10-29*). Settle in for some Mozart and magazines with your coffee or beer. You won't lack for a choice of brews; the menu lists more than 100 regional beers, four beers on tap, and five Trappist beers. A plate of cheese, such as Oude Brugge, is a good match with one of the heartier beers. De Garre is open from noon to midnight. No credit cards.

⓬ **Jan van Eyckplein.** This colorful yet low-key square lies at the center of Hanseatic Brugge, marked with a statue of the famed 15th-century painter. It includes the old **Tolhuis** (Customs House), built in 1477, where vehicles on their way to market had to stop while tolls were levied on goods brought from nearby ports. The building is now an information office for the province of West Flanders. The **Poortersloge**, a late-Gothic building with a slender spire, was owned by the guild of porters and used as a meeting place for the burghers. Currently, it's used to store historic documents but it occasionally opens for exhibitions. The bear occupying one niche represents the legendary creature speared by Baldwin of the Iron Arm and later became the symbol of

Medieval Splendor

Glorious buildings and art are highlights of a visit to Flanders. Brugge and Gent, the region's textile and artistic centers, are the major places to observe the incredible flowering of creativity in the late Middle Ages. In the 15th century Flemish artists hit upon new compositions for oil paint, refining it so that wet-on-dry changes could be made. The improved medium unleashed a movement toward scrupulously depicted, realistic detail and vibrant, jewel-like colors. Some of the world's greatest art treasures were painted in this period, including Hans Memling's St. Ursula Shrine and Jan van Eyck's *Adoration of the Mystic Lamb* altarpiece.

Stained glass and religious art including diptychs, triptychs, and polyptychs (altarpieces with two or more painted panels) are numerous in this region. Textile merchants showed off their riches by building magnificent houses and by having their portraits painted by famous artists. Similar building materials and local civic spirit add a homogeneous quality to Brugge and Gent, with Ieper and the lowland villages following a similar style. All have chunky churches and town halls, towering belfries, ornate guildhalls, and splendid burgher's homes, many built of sturdy local brick. The majority of buildings destroyed during the First and Second World Wars were rebuilt in their original style; even today, the Flemings build homes that would seem perfectly in place during medieval times.

---

the city. ✉ *Intersection of Academiestraat, Spiegelrei, and Spanjaardstraat* Ⓜ *Bus 4 or 14.*

⓯ Jeruzalemkerk. The striking, 15th-century Jerusalem Church, with its stained-glass windows, was built by two pilgrims returning from the Holy Land who copied that city's Church of the Holy Sepulchre. The black marble mausoleum of Genoese pilgrim Anselm Adornes and his wife occupies a central position. Anselm became burgomeister of Brugge, but was murdered in Scotland while he was consul there in 1484. ✉ *Jeruzalemstraat 3, Sint-Anna* ☎ *No phone* ✉ *Free* ☽ *Weekdays 10–noon and 2–6, Sat. 10–noon and 2–5* Ⓜ *Bus 4 or 14.*

⓰ Kantcentrum. The Lace Center maintains the quality and authenticity of the ancient Belgian craft of lace making. This foundation includes a lace museum in the Jerusalem almshouses in Balstraat, as well as a school where youngsters are taught the intricate art of the bobbins, and a shop to buy provisions. You can watch lace-making demonstrations every afternoon except Sunday. The building is the former home of the Adornes family, and adjoins their mausoleum in the Jeruzalemkerk. ✉ *Peperstraat 3A, Sint-Anna* ☎ *050/33–00–72* ⊕ *www.kantcentrum. com* ✉ *€2.50* ☽ *Weekdays 10–noon and 2–6, Sat. 10–noon and 2–5* Ⓜ *Bus 4 or 14.*

❶ Markt. Used as a marketplace since ad 958, this square is still one of **FodorsChoice** the liveliest places in Brugge. In the center stands a memorial to the ★ city's medieval heroes, Jan Breydel and Pieter De Coninck, who led the commoners of Flanders to their short-lived victory over the aristocrats of France. On the east side of the Markt stand the provincial government house and the post office, an excellent pastiche of Burgundian Gothic. Old guild houses line the west and north sides of the square, their step-gabled facades overlooking the cafés spilling out onto the sidewalk. These buildings aren't always as old as they seem, though—often they're 19th-century reconstructions. The medieval **Belfort** (Belfry) on the south side of the Markt, however, is the genuine article. The tower dates to the 13th century, its crowning octagonal lantern to the 15th century. Altogether, it rises to a height of 270 feet, commanding the city and the surrounding countryside with more presence than grace. The valuables of Brugge were once kept in the second floor treasury; now the Belfort's riches are in its remarkable 47-bell carillon. (Impressing Belgians with a carillon is no mean feat, as Belgium has some of the best carillons in the world.) If you haven't walked enough, you can climb 366 winding steps to the clock mechanism, and from the carillon enjoy a gorgeous panoramic view. Back down in the square, you may be tempted by the **horse-drawn carriages** that congregate here; a half-hour ride for up to four people, with a short stop at the Begijnhof, costs €30 plus "something for the horse." ⊠ *Intersection of Steenstraat, St-Amandstraat, Vlamingstraat, Philipstockstraat, Breidelstraat, and Wollestraat* ☎ *050/44–87–11* 🎟 *€5* ⊙ *Tues.–Sun., 9:30–5. Carillon concerts: Sun. 2:15–3. June 15–July 1 and Aug. 15–Sept., Mon., Wed., and Sat. 9 PM–10 PM. Oct.–June 14, Wed. and Sat. 2:15–3* Ⓜ *Bus 1 or 12.*

NEED A BREAK?

Tiny pastries, ice cream, and sorbets in exotic flavors can all be found in the tearoom **De Medici** (⊠ *Geldmuntstraat 9* ☎ *050/33-93-41*). You can dine in or take out. For something more substantial, they also serve light lunches including quiche and salads.

⑨ ★ Memling in Sint-Jans Hospitaalmuseum. The collection contains six works, but they are of breathtaking quality and among the greatest—and certainly the most spiritual—of the Flemish Primitive school. Hans Memling (1440–94) was born in Germany, but spent the greater part of his life in Brugge. In *The Altarpiece of St. John the Baptist and St. John the Evangelist,* two leading personages of the Burgundian court are believed to be portrayed: Mary of Burgundy (buried in the Onze-Lieve-Vrouwekerk) as St. Catherine, and Margaret of York as St. Barbara. The "paintings within the painting" give details of the lives of the two saints. The miniature paintings that adorn the St. Ursula Shrine are likewise marvels of detail and poignancy; Memling's work gives recognizable iconographic details about cities, such as Brugge, Cologne, Basel, and Rome. The Memling is housed in **Oud Sint-Janshospitaal,** one of the oldest surviving medieval hospitals in Europe. It was founded in the 12th century and remained in use until the early 20th century. Furniture, paintings, and hospital-related items are attractively displayed; the 13th-century middle ward, the oldest of three, was built in Romanesque style. A fascinating 18th-century painting shows patients arriving by sedan chair and being fed and ministered to by sisters and clerics. There is a short guide to the museum in English, and the audioguide is in English, too. ⊠ *Mariastraat 38* ☎ *050/44–87–11* 🎟 *€8, includes*

audioguide, combination ticket
€15 ⊗ *Tues.–Sun. 9:30–5* Ⓜ *Bus 1 or 12.*

⓫ **Minnewater.** Romantically termed "the Lake of Love," this man-made reservoir was created in the 13th century to expand the city harbor, and it often accommodated more than 100 ships. The swans of Minnewater evoke an etymological legend or perhaps a historical truth: in 1488, six years after his wife's death, Maximilian of Austria was imprisoned by the people of Brugge, and his advisor, Pieter Lanchals, was decapitated. Because the name *Lanchals* is very close to the Dutch word for "long neck," when Maximilian was freed, he ordered Brugge to expiate its crime by keeping swans in the canals of the city in perpetuity. ⊠ *Off Wijngaardplein, by the Begijnhof* Ⓜ *Bus 12.*

❻ **Museum Arentshuis.** The upper floor of this 18th-century building is dedicated to the multitalented artist Frank Brangwyn (1867–1956), born in Brugge to British parents. His works include everything from book illustrations to a mural in New York City's Rockefeller Center, but he is perhaps best known for his World War I posters. He also influenced the reconstruction of many Brugge buildings in a pseudo-Gothic style, and many of his brooding drawings, etchings, and paintings of Brugge are on view here. On the ground floor, special exhibits on a variety of themes (Italian painting, heraldic art, etc.) cycle through every three months. ⊠ *Dijver 16* ☎ *050/44–87–11* 💶 *€3, combination ticket €15* ⊗ *Tues.–Sun. 9:30–5* Ⓜ *Bus 1 or 12.*

⓱ **Museum voor Volkskunde.** A row of 17th-century whitewashed almshouses originally built for retired shoemakers now holds an engaging Folklore Museum. Within each house is a reconstructed historic interior: a grocery shop, a living room, a tavern, a cobbler's workshop, a classroom, a pharmacy, and a kitchen. Another wing holds a tailor's shop and a collection of old advertising posters. Twice a week the museum holds kid-oriented demonstrations on candy making, using natural flavorings such as honey and aniseed. You can end your tour at the museum café, In de Zwarte Kat (the "Black Cat"). In early December, the museum hosts events to mark the feast of Sint-Niklaas, the original Santa Claus. ■ **TIP➜ Although the official address is Rolweg, the entrance is just around the corner at Balstraat 43.** ⊠ *Rolweg 40, Sint-Anna* ☎ *050/33–00–44* 💶 *€3; it's also part of the €15 combination ticket* ⊗ *Tues.–Sun. 9:30–5* Ⓜ *Bus 4 or 14.*

❽ **Onze-Lieve-Vrouwekerk.** The towering spire of the plain, Gothic Church of Our Lady, begun about 1220, rivals the Belfry as Brugge's symbol. It is 381 feet high, the tallest brick construction in the world. While brick can be built high, it cannot be sculpted like stone; hence the tower's somewhat severe look. Look for the small *Madonna and Child* statue, an early work by Michelangelo. The great sculptor sold it to a merchant from Brugge when the original client failed to pay. It was stolen by Napoléon, and during World War II by Nazi leader Hermann Göring; now the white-marble figure sits in a black-marble niche behind an altar at the end of the south aisle. The choir contains many 13th- and 14th-century polychrome tombs, as well as two mausoleums: that of Mary of Burgundy, who died in 1482 at the age of 25 after a fall from her horse; and that of her father, Charles the Bold, killed in 1477 while laying siege to Nancy in France. Mary was as well loved in Brugge as her husband, Maximilian of Austria, was loathed. Her finely chiseled effigy captures her beauty. ⌧ *Dijver and Mariastraat* ☎ *No phone* ⌸ *€6, includes entry to Gruuthusemuseum* ☉ *Weekdays 9–4:50, Sat. 9–4:40, Sun. 1:30–5* Ⓜ *Bus 1 or 12.*

★ **Reien.** The narrow and meandering *reien,* or canals, with their old humpback stone bridges, give Brugge its character, opening up perspective and imposing their calm. The view from the **Meebrug** is especially picturesque. Farther along the Groenerei are the **Godshuizen De Pelikaan,** almshouses dating from the early 18th century. There are several such charitable buildings in the city, tiny houses built by the guilds for the poor, some still serving their original purpose. **Steenhouwersdijk** overlooks the brick rear gables that were part of the original county hall. The Vismarkt (Fish Market) has 19th-century buildings designed in classical style; fresh seafood from Zeebrugge is sold Tuesday–Saturday. Just beyond is the little **Huidenvettersplein** (Tanners' Square), with its 17th-century guild house. Next to it, from the **Rozenhoedkaai** canal, the view of the heart of the city includes the pinnacles of the town hall, basilica, and Belfry—the essence of Brugge.

⑭ **Sint-Anna.** The Sint-Anna neighborhood illustrates how yesteryear's poverty can become today's charm. The small houses that now look so tidy were the homes of the 19th-century's truly needy. The area is now quiet and residential, with a sprinkling of sightseeing spots—a good place to explore when Brugge's main squares get clogged with tourists. In contrast to the modest houses, the 17th-century **Sint-Annakerk** *(St. Anne's Church)* is opulent with sculpted wood, copper, and enormous paintings. The church is open April through September, Monday through Saturday 10–noon and 2–5, and Sunday 2–5. ⌧ *Bordered by Potterierei, Langestraat, and Kruisvest* Ⓜ *Bus 4 or 14.*

NEED A BREAK?

Vlissinghe (⌧ *Blekersstraat 2, Sint-Anna* ☎ *050/34–37–37*) is said to be the oldest pub in Brugge; people have been enjoying the beer here since 1515. It doesn't seem to have changed much over the centuries, with its wood-panel walls and huge Flemish hearth stove. Tourists and locals come together around the big wooden tables or in the sunny enclosed garden. There's a small menu of light meals, including a good lasagna. It's closed on Monday and Tuesday.

☼ **Sint-Janshuismolen and Koeleweimolen.** The outer ramparts of the medieval city of Brugge used to be dotted with windmills; now four remain along the ring road. Of these, two can be visited and are still used to grind flour: the St-Janshuismolen (1770) and the Koeleweimolen (1765). The wooden steps leading up to them are quite steep and not for the faint-hearted. ⊠*Kruisvest, Sint-Anna* 🕾*050/44–87–64* 💷*€2* ⊘*Sint-Janshuismolen: May–Sept., Tues.–Sun. 9:30–12:30 and 1:30–5. Koele-weimolen: June–Sept., Tues.–Sun. 9:30–12:30 and 1:30–5* Ⓜ*Bus 4.*

⑬ Spanjaardstraat. The street leads up to the quay where goods from Spain were unloaded. The house at No. 9 was where St. Ignatius of Loyola stayed when he came to Flanders on holidays from his studies in Paris. Directly ahead are the three arches of the **Augustijnenbrug.** Dating from 1391, it's the oldest bridge in Brugge. On the other side of the canal, **Augustijnenrei** is one of the loveliest quays.

❹ Stadhuis. White sandstone towers with 48 decorated window recesses define the town hall, a jewel of Gothic architecture that marked the transition of power from the nobility to the city aldermen. Built at the end of the 14th century, it's the oldest town hall in Belgium and served as the model for the community centers in every Flemish town. The statues that originally embellished the facade were smashed by the French Republicans and have been replaced by modern replicas. From the balcony, the Counts of Flanders used to take their oaths to affirm civic liberties. Inside, a grand staircase ascends to the Gothic Hall, which has a marvelous, double-vaulted timber roof. Its 19th-century frescoes relate a romantic version of the history of Brugge. ⊠*Burg 12* 🕾*050/44–81–41* 💷*€2.50, includes Museum van het Brugse Vrije in the Voormalige Civiele Griffie and audioguide* ⊘*Daily 9:30–5* Ⓜ*Bus 1 or 12.*

Voormalige Civiele Griffie. Inside this 16th-century Former Recorder's House, a mixture of Gothic and Flemish Renaissance elements, is the **Museum van het Brugse Vrije** (Provincial Museum of the Liberty of Brugge), a remnant of the 15th-century county hall. Its courtroom has a huge oak and black-marble chimneypiece with a large bas-relief depicting a young, robust, nearly life-size Charles V, carved in dark oak and marble by Lanceloot Blondeel. The audioguide is available in English. ⊠*Burg 11a* 🕾*050/44–82–60* 💷*€2.50, includes Stadhuis admission and audioguide* ⊘*Daily 9:30–12:30 and 1:30–5* Ⓜ*Bus 1 or 12.*

WHERE TO EAT

$$–$$$
BELGIAN

✕**Beethoven.** Chef Chantal Mortier built up a substantial local following over the years; she now serves them at her intimate Flemish restaurant off the Markt, with her husband at the front of the house. In winter a fire warms up the dining room and the menu offers comforting favorites like steak (fillet, tournedos, or rib eye) with frieten. In summer the street-front tables become a prime spot for people-watching. The menu lightens up accordingly, with salads such as goat cheese and honey or shrimp and smoked salmon. Though reservations aren't mandatory, they're highly recommended. ⊠*Sint-Amandstraat 6* 🕾*050/33–50–06* ▭*MC, V* ⊘*Closed Tues. and Wed.* Ⓜ*Bus 1 or 12.*

$$–$$$$
BELGIAN

✕**Breydel-De Coninc.** In a plum spot along the route from the Markt to the Burg, this no-frills restaurant is well known among locals. The plain furnishings leave the focus on the fresh seafood for which the establishment is famed. Although eel and steak are available, the res-

Brugge's Medieval History

Brugge's history begins some time in the third century, when it was a Gallo-Roman settlement of farmers and merchants who traded with England and Gaul. It remained relatively rural until the 11th century, when its seaside location along the trade path turned it into an international commercial center. Linked with the estuary of the Zwin on the North Sea by a navigable waterway, Brugge was one of the most active members of the Hanseatic League during the 13th century. Top trade items included Flemish cloth, Scandinavian fish, Russian furs, Gasconian wine, and Venetian silk. Italian merchants from Lombardy, Tuscany, and Venice soon set up shop in Brugge.

In 1301 the French queen Jeanne of Navarre was annoyed by the finery flaunted by the women of Brugge. The men of Brugge, in return, were annoyed at being requested to fund a lavish reception for the French royal couple. One fine morning in May 1302, they fell upon and massacred the French garrison, and then joined the men of Gent and Ieper to defeat the French chevaliers in the epic Battle of the Golden Spurs. It must have been a notable battle, for at that time the population of Brugge alone was around 40,000—twice that of the current city center.

Flanders became a Burgundian state in the 15th century, and an era of unprecedented wealth began in Brugge. The famed Flemish Primitive style of painting evolved at this time, representing a revolution in realism, portraiture, and perspective, bringing the era alive in astonishing detail. Hans Memling, for instance, took portraiture in a new direction with his depiction of the Moreel family in their namesake triptych. (You can see this work in the Groeningemuseum, one of the city's matchless art collections. Most of Memling's best paintings are still in Brugge.)

Jan van Eyck, one of the most renowned Primitive artists, was named court painter to Philip the Good, Duke of Burgundy, who married Isabella of Portugal in a ceremony of incredible luxury in Brugge's Prinsenhof in 1429. It was just one of the lavish celebrations to take place in the city; the last Burgundian feast here was the wedding of Duke Charles the Bold to Margaret of York, sister of England's Edward IV, in 1468.

At the end of the century adversity struck. Flemish weavers had emigrated across the Channel and taught their trade to the English, who became formidable competitors. Even worse, the Zwin began to silt up, and the people of Brugge had neither the will nor the funds to build the canal that might have saved their industry. Instead, trade and fortune and the wool trade switched to Antwerp. The Spaniards conquered Brugge in 1548, and the city fell into poverty.

In the 19th century, British travelers rediscovered Brugge and spread its fame as a perfectly preserved medieval town. Its look is classic, but much of the city was actually redesigned in the 19th century by British architects keen to spread the Gothic Revival. Only two of the original timber medieval houses remain.

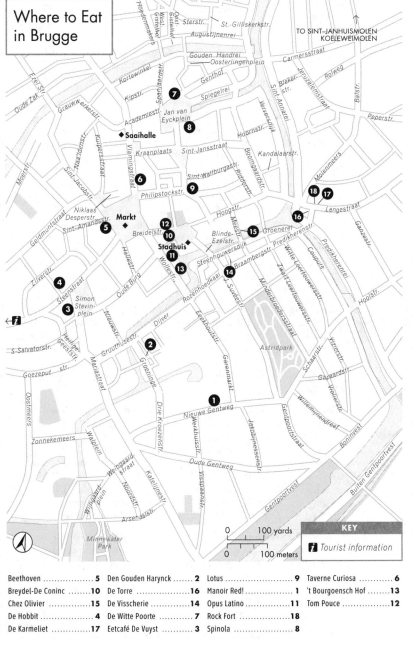

Where to Eat in Brugge

TO SINT-JANHUISMOLEN
KOELEWEIMOLEN

◆ Saaihalle

◆ Markt

Stadhuis

Astridpark

Minnewater Park

| 0 | 100 yards |
| 0 | 100 meters |

KEY

🛈 Tourist information

taurant's biggest draw is mussels—there's nothing more basically, and deliciously, Belgian than a huge crock heaped high with shiny, blue-black shells. ⊠ *Breidelstraat 24* ☎ *050/33–97–46* ⊟ *MC, V* ⊗ *Closed Wed.* Ⓜ *Bus 1 or 12.*

> ### A FAMILY BREW
>
> **De Halve Maan** (⊠ *Walplein, between Wijngaardstraat and Zonnkemeers* ☎ *050/33-26-97* ⊗ *Daily 10–6*), is the only family brewery left in Brugge. One of their beers is Brugse Zot (Fool of Brugge); it owes its name to Maximilian of Austria who was welcomed to the city by a procession of fools and jesters. When asked to donate money to the local asylum, he replied: "Today I have seen nothing but fools!" Work up a thirst by touring the brewery itself for €5, drink included.

$$$–$$$$
FRENCH
✕ **Chez Olivier.** Set above a quiet canal, with white swans gliding below, this French charmer is purely romantic. Chef Olivier Foucad uses impeccably fresh ingredients for "light food," such as scallops in ginger and herbs, duck in rosemary honey, and lightly marbled Charolais beef. Lunches are a bargain and the staff is flexible—if you want one main course or two starters instead of the full prix-fixe menu, just ask. For the best views, request a window seat next to the water. ⊠ *Meestraat 9* ☎ *050/33–36–59* ⊟ *MC, V* ⊗ *Closed Thurs. and Sun. No lunch Sat.* Ⓜ *Bus 1.*

$–$$
SOUTHERN
✕ **De Hobbit.** You're a long way from Memphis but you can still get ribs. Here you can order up a plate of "Hobbit style" (barbecued) or Thai-style ribs then puzzle over the brain-teasers on your placemat. If you're still hungry after your first serving, seconds are on the house. The menu goes beyond pork with pasta, salads, and prawns in garlic butter. ⊠ *Kemelstraat 8 (off Steenstraat)* ☎ *050/33–55–20* ⊟ *AE, DC, MC, V* Ⓜ *Bus 1 or 12.*

$$$$
FRENCH
Fodor'sChoice
★
✕ **De Karmeliet.** This stately, 18th-century house with a graceful English garden is a world-renowned culinary landmark. Owner-chef Geert Van Hecke's inventive kitchen changes the menu every two months; you might be offered goose liver with truffled potatoes or cod carpaccio with asparagus. The waitstaff perfectly choreographs each course with a cool professionalism in keeping with the restaurant's formal ambience. The wine cave plumbs the best of international vintages. ⊠ *Langestraat 19* ☎ *050/33–82–59* ⌂ *Reservations essential Jacket required* ⊟ *AE, DC, MC, V* ⊗ *Closed Sun. and Mon.* Ⓜ *Bus 6.*

$$$$
FRENCH
✕ **Den Gouden Harynck.** Few culinary artists have the depth and natural flair of chef Philippe Serruys. In his unpretentious, airy dining room you are treated to beautifully presented, creative French dishes, though the name of the restaurant, "the golden herring," is hardly a French specialty. Try the pigeon with green apples and onion fondue, or lobster with fig chutney. ⊠ *Groeninge 25* ☎ *050/33–76–37* ⊟ *AE, DC, MC, V* ⊗ *Closed Sun. and Mon. No lunch Sat.* Ⓜ *Bus 1 or 12.*

$$–$$$
BELGIAN
✕ **De Torre.** For traditional Belgian food at honest prices, this is the place. From noon until 10 PM, Flemish stew, tomato with shrimp, mussels, or fillet of sole are served as they are in many Flemish homes. The

18th-century house is decorated in art deco style and the sunny terrace has a lovely view of the reien. ✉ *Langestraat 8* ☎ *050/34–29–46* ☐ *MC, V* ✆ *Closed Wed. Closed Tues. Sept.–June* Ⓜ *Bus 6 or 16.*

$$$$
SEAFOOD
★

✕ **De Visscherie.** To find this popular seafood restaurant overlooking the Vismarkt, look for the modern sculpture of a fisherman and the large fish hanging from its balcony. Business at the busy, outdoor terrace has been going strong for more than 25 years. Try one of the turbot variations, monkfish with Ganda ham and melon, or the langoustines with mozzarella, herbs, and sun-dried tomatoes. If you can't decide, order the restaurant's signature dish: waterzooi with saffron. ✉ *Vismarkt 8* ☎ *050/33–02–12* ☐ *AE, MC, V* ✆ *Closed Tues. and first half of Dec.* Ⓜ *Bus 6 or 16.*

$$$–$$$$
FRENCH
★

✕ **De Witte Poorte.** Cross through a courtyard, under low brick vaults and stone arches, to reach this warm, yet formal French restaurant. The emphasis is on seafood with a contemporary twist, such as monkfish simmered in white wine and saffron and langoustine waterzooi. You can watch your meal being prepared behind a smoked-glass partition or look onto the lush little garden. Save room for the goodies on the dessert cart. ✉ *Jan van Eyckplein 6* ☎ *050/33–08–83* ☐ *AE, MC, V* ✆ *Closed Sun. and Mon., 1st 2 wks in Jan., and 1st 2 wks in July* Ⓜ *Bus 4 or 14.*

$–$$
CONTEMPORARY

✕ **Eetcafé De Vuyst.** The spires of Brugge are dramatically framed within the two-story, glass walls of the popular, light-filled Eetcafé. Go through to the back of the building and you'll come to a lovely garden restaurant, a calm respite from Brugge's busy streets. The café is ideal for a sandwich or light meal with the kids, and also homes in on classic Belgian specialties such as beef braised in beer or Flemish rabbit. ✉ *Simon Stevinplein 15* ☎ *050/34–22–31* ☐ *MC, V* ✆ *Closed Tues.* Ⓜ *Bus 1 or 12.*

¢–$
VEGETARIAN

✕ **Lotus.** The neat dining room, with its lines of flower-topped tables, fills up quickly at this popular vegetarian café. The menu changes weekly but always has small and large plates; you might try a four-cheese quiche, a basil and beetroot salad, or curried veggies. Whatever the combination, it's delicious and well presented. Don't miss the desserts; the lemon pie is particularly good. ✉ *Wapenmakersstraat 5* ☎ *050/33–10–78* ☐ *No credit cards* ✆ *Closed Sun. and last 2 wks in July. No dinner* Ⓜ *Bus 4 or 14.*

$$$–$$$$
FRENCH

✕ **Manoir Red!** High standards are the trademark in the dining room of this small but lavish 18th-century property. The restaurant serves an expert blend of French and Flemish dishes; the exquisite tastes are well worth the price. Look for fresh game and local seafood. Manoir Red! also has beautiful guest rooms. ✉ *Nieuwe Gentweg 53* ☎ *050/33–70–70* ⚐ *Reservations essential* ☐ *AE, DC, MC, V* ✆ *Closed Sun. No lunch Mon.* Ⓜ *Bus 1 or 11.*

$
CAFÉ

✕ **Opus Latino.** Though it's on the busy Burg, this café-restaurant manages to be quiet and secluded. There are two ways of finding it: either through the shopping gallery Ten Steeghere, next to the Heilig Bloed

Basiliek, or via De Garre, the little lane off Breidelstraat. Its terrace overlooking a canal makes a good meeting point and rest stop for a restorative snack—a few tapas, perhaps, or a cheese board. ⊠*Burg 15* ☎*050/34–72–78* ▤*MC, V* ◷*Closed Wed.* Ⓜ*Bus 1 or 12.*

$$–$$$ ╳ **Rock Fort.** There's only room for 22 at this very trendy little restau-
ECLECTIC rant. The menu is adventurous, combining tuna with foie gras (*Tonijn Gioacchino*) and pork jowls with morel juice. The exhaustive wine list covers Europe as well as Australia, New Zealand, and American vintages. Next door is Bar Salon, a lounge-bar offering small snacks and colorful pre-appetizers. ⊠*Langetsraat 15* ☎*050/33–41–13* ◿*Reservations essential* ▤*AE, MC, V* ◷*Closed weekends* Ⓜ*Bus 6 or 16.*

$$$–$$$$ ╳ **Spinola.** This multistory canal-house restaurant by the Jan van Eyck
CONTINENTAL statue is a real charmer. From an intimate main dining room an iron staircase leads to the upper tables; the open kitchen is in back. Here, chef-owners Sam and Vicky Storme cook up rich Burgundian cuisine: fresh game, goose liver, shellfish, and pigeon with truffles. Dinner by candlelight is the ultimate extravagance, with a choice of some 300 wines. ⊠*Spinolarei 1* ☎*050/34–17–85* ▤*DC, MC, V* ◷*Closed Sun. and Mon.* Ⓜ*Bus 4 or 14.*

$$–$$$ ╳ **Taverne Curiosa.** By day, this cross-vaulted, medieval crypt provides
CONTINENTAL a quiet spot for conversation over a light meal and a local beer. In the evening, though, it shifts gears and becomes a busy, high-volume hangout, open until the wee hours. The menu includes omelets, sandwiches, and *visschotel* (smoked fish plates), plus pancakes and ice cream for dessert. The background music hits the right note. ⊠*Vlamingstraat 22* ☎*050/34–23–34* ▤*AE, MC, V* ◷*Closed Mon. and July* Ⓜ*Bus 4 or 14.*

$$$ ╳ **'t Bourgoensch Hof.** Although its weathered timbers and sharp-raked
BELGIAN roofs were rebuilt at the turn of the 20th century, this restaurant, 't Bourgoensch Hof, is housed in one of the most medieval-looking buildings in Brugge. It also has one of the city's most romantic, canalside settings, with the light from the windows shedding kaleidoscopic reflections onto the water. The cuisine is as appealing as the setting, with selections including panfried langoustines with wild mushrooms, salmon tournedos with bacon, and turbot medallions with coriander and caramelized leeks. There are 17 guest rooms upstairs, but as they don't represent great value for money, you'd be better off eating here and sleeping elsewhere. ⊠*Wollestraat 39* ☎*050/33–16–45* ⊕*www. bourgoensch-hof.be* ▤*AE, DC, MC, V* ◷*Closed Tues. and Wed.* Ⓜ*Bus 1 or 11.*

$$$ ╳ **Tom Pouce.** Every afternoon, this friendly tearoom becomes the Burg's
BELGIAN magnet, largely due to the fabulous view from its terrace (although be aware the prices reflect the setting). It feels comfortably frayed and at peak times a bit hectic, with its heavy velour drapes, splashy carpet, cracked crockery, and a noisy open-service bar. Tourists, shoppers, and loyal retirees alike dig into warm apple strudel, freshly made ice cream, and airy waffles. First-timers should order the tour de force: hot *pannekoeken* (light, eggy, vanilla-perfumed pancakes) with a pat of but-

Mussels & More

The backbone of Flanders food is the local produce that's served fresh and presented simply—you won't find painted plates or veggies sculpted beyond recognition. Naturally, this is seafood country, with fresh fish shipped in daily to Brugge; the coastal towns serve authentic North Sea delicacies at terrace restaurants whipped by sand and salt air. Even in landlocked Gent, some 50 km (30 mi) from the coast, locals snack on whelks and *winkles* (sea snails) as if they were popcorn. Flemings are mad about *mosselen* (mussels)—try them steamed, curried, or bathed in a white-wine broth accented with celery, onions, and parsley. Main courses are inevitably accompanied by a mountain of *frieten* (french fries), fried twice, making them especially crisp and delicious. For death by fries, buy them piping hot and salty from a stall, as the Belgians do, and dip them in the big dollop of accompanying mayo.

Paling (eels) are one of the region's specialties. The flesh is firm, fatty, and sweet, and served in long cross-sections with a removable backbone. *Paling in t'groen* is eel served in a green herb sauce, a heady mix of sorrel, tarragon, sage, mint, and parsley. Sole and turbot are also popular main courses, served broiled, poached with a light mousseline sauce, or grilled with a rich béarnaise or mustard sauce. Herring is eaten *maatjes* (raw) in the spring. To sound like a local, try these tongue-twisters when you order: *oostduinkerkse paardevissersoep* (fish soup) and *dronken rog op Nieuwpoortse wijze* (ray).

When the Flemish aren't eating their fish straight or in a blanket of golden sauce, they consume it in the region's most famous dish, *waterzooi* (a thick broth rich with cream and vegetables). The citizens of Gent have a chicken version, as well as *Gentse hutsepot* (a casserole with carrots, onions, potatoes, and meat). For a hearty dish, look for *vlaamse stoverij* (beef or pork stew with onions, braised in beer). *Paardenvlees* (horse meat), with its sweet flavor and beefy texture, is considered a delicacy.

If you visit Flanders in springtime, look for memorably delicious vegetables, such as the tender white *asperge* (asparagus), served either in mousseline sauce or with a garnish of chopped hard-boiled egg and melted butter. These pale stalks are sweeter than the familiar green ones and are called "white gold" because the Flemings snap them up as fast as they arrive during their short season. In March and April, seek out the rare, expensive *jets de houblon* (delicate shoots of the hops plant).

A cheese course is often served before—or in place of—dessert, and there are hundreds of delicious local choices, many runny and pungent. Chocolate and whipped cream are favorite dessert ingredients, and homemade ice cream turns up on all kinds of menus in warm months. Local pastries include *Gentse mokken* (hard sugar cookies), *lierse vlaaikens* (plum tarts), and *speculoos* (sugary ginger cookies), all of which are often accompanied by coffee. Warm pancakes and Belgian *waffelen* (waffles) topped with fruit or syrup are available everywhere from sidewalk stalls to fancy restaurants. The famous crisp waffles, which have a vanilla flavor, are formed in cast-iron molds with pre-sweetened dough.

4

ter and a sprinkle of dark brown sugar. If your appetite dictates a full meal, choose from standbys like lamb cutlets, waterzooi, or rabbit stew. ⊠ *Burg 17* ☎ *050/33–03–36* ▭ *AE, DC, MC, V* Ⓜ *Bus 1 or 12.*

WHERE TO STAY

$$ ⌂ **Anselmus.** Crafted from a 16th-century mansion, this family-run bed-
★ and-breakfast is a find. Rich colors and period accents add romance to otherwise simple, comfortable furnishings, although there are many elegant touches—note the winding staircase in the entryway. **Pros:** friendly staff; historic building. **Cons:** limited parking. ⊠ *Riddersstraat 15* ☎ *050/34–13–74* ⊕ *www.anselmus.be* ⛱ *10 rooms* ♿ *In-room: Wi-Fi. In-hotel: bar, Wi-Fi, parking (paid)* ▭ *AE, MC, V* ۞ *Closed Jan.* ۞|*BP* Ⓜ *Bus 6 or 16.*

$–$$ ⌂ **Bryghia.** This restored German–Austrian trade center is a handsome, 15th-century landmark. Outside, the brick walls are lined with paned windows and flower boxes; inside, the hotel is warmed by pastel floral fabrics and beech cabinets. Bedrooms are simple yet comfortable, and the public rooms include small sitting areas and a beamed, slate-floor breakfast salon. **Pros:** quiet location. **Cons:** a little way from the sights. ⊠ *Oosterlingenplein 4* ☎ *050/33–80–59* ⊕ *www.bryghiahotel. be* ⛱ *18 rooms* ♿ *In-room: safe, minibar. In-hotel: bar, parking (paid)* ▭ *AE, DC, V* ۞|*BP* Ⓜ *Bus 4 or 14.*

$$$$ ⌂ **Crowne Plaza.** On the corner of the Burg, this modern brick building stands at attention with all flags flying. Built on the foundation of the former 12th-century St. Donace Cathedral, it's an archaeological treasure, exhibiting 10th- to 16th-century ramparts, tombs, and other artifacts. The large, bright rooms are cheery, and some are bi-level, with beamed, vaulted ceilings. The attached bar, café, and restaurant are always busy. **Pros:** unbeatable location. **Cons:** expensive; rooms lack character. ⊠ *Burg 10* ☎ *050/44–68–44* ⊕ *www.ichotelsgroup. com* ⛱ *89 rooms, 7 suites* ♿ *In-room: safe, Internet, Wi-Fi. In-hotel: restaurant, bar, pool, gym, parking (paid), no-smoking rooms, Wi-Fi* ▭ *AE, DC, MC, V* Ⓜ *Bus 1 or 12.*

$$$ ⌂ **De Castillion.** This hotel's location reflects its past as the palace for Brugge's bishop, Jean-Baptiste de Castillon—it's right across from the cathedral. The 17th-century buildings are now filled with eclectically stylish guest rooms. The hotel also houses the exquisite (and formal) restaurant Le Manoir Quatre Saisons ($$$$; reservations essential; closed Mon. and Tues. and Sun. dinner). Several special arrangements are possible, combining a one or more night's stay, gastronomic dinners, and excursions. **Pros:** great location. **Cons:** parking limited. ⊠ *Heilige Geeststraat 1* ☎ *050/34–30–01* ⊕ *www.castillion.be* ⛱ *18 rooms, 2 suites* ♿ *In-room: safe, Internet, minibar. In-hotel: restaurant, bar, gym, parking (paid), no-smoking rooms* ▭ *AE, DC, MC, V* Ⓜ *Bus 1.*

¢–$ ⌂ **De Pauw.** From the ivy-covered brick exterior to the fresh flowers
★ and doilies in the breakfast parlor, this is a welcoming little inn, set in

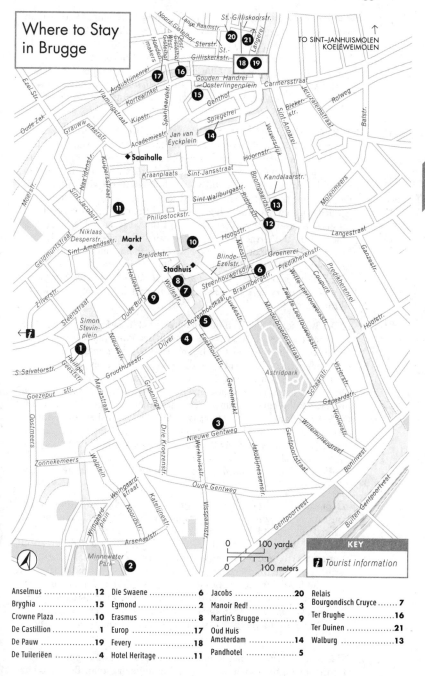

Where to Stay in Brugge

Anselmus	12	Die Swaene	6	Jacobs	20	Relais Bourgondisch Cruyce	7
Bryghia	15	Egmond	2	Manoir Red!	3	Ter Brughe	16
Crowne Plaza	10	Erasmus	8	Martin's Brugge	9	Ter Duinen	21
De Castillion	1	Europ	17	Oud Huis Amsterdam	14	Walburg	13
De Pauw	19	Fevery	18			
De Tuileriën	4	Hotel Heritage	11	Pandhotel	5	

KEY

🛈 Tourist information

a square opposite Sint-Gillis church. Rooms have names rather than numbers to give them a homier feel, and needlepoint cushions and old framed prints add to the warmth. Breakfast, which includes cold cuts, cheese, and six kinds of bread, is served on pretty china. **Pros:** quiet location; good value. **Cons:** limited parking; rooms quite small. ⊠ *Sint-Gilliskerkhof 8* ☎ *050/33–71–18* ⊕ *www.hoteldepauw.be* ➹ *8 rooms, 6 with bath* ⅁ *In-hotel: parking (free)* ⊟ *MC, V* ⦿ *BP* Ⓜ *Bus 4 or 14.*

$$$–$$$$
★
🏨 **De Tuileriën.** Patrician tastes suffuse this 15th-century mansion. The decor is genteel, with reproduction antique furniture, Venetian glass windows, and weathered marble complemented by mixed-print fabrics and wall coverings in celadon, slate, and cream. Rooms are romantic, with marble-accented bathrooms, although those with canal views receive some traffic noise; courtyard rooms are quieter. The firelit bar is filled with cozy tartan wing chairs, and the neo-Baroque breakfast salon features a coffered ceiling. When the weather holds, breakfast is served on the terrace alongside the canal. **Pros:** charming; elegant; historic building. **Cons:** very expensive; on main tourist drag, so can get noisy. ⊠ *Dijver 7* ☎ *050/34–36–91* ⊕ *www.hoteltuilerieen.com* ➹ *22 rooms, 23 suites* ⅁ *In-room: safe, Internet. In-hotel: bar, pool, bicycles, laundry service, parking (paid)* ⊟ *AE, DC, MC, V* ⦿ *BP* Ⓜ *Bus 1 or 12.*

$$$–$$$$
🏨 **Die Swaene.** Hidden behind a painted brick facade along one of the prettiest stretches of canal is this lavishly decorated, family-run hotel. Romantics will swoon at the elegant windows done in swagged tulle, the sparkling crystal accents, and the marble antiques. The gilt-ceiling lounge, built in the late 1700s, was once a guildhall of the tailors. One guest room is set in a converted Flemish kitchen with a stone fireplace and a carved four-poster. The romantic, candlelit restaurant ($$$$) overlooking the garden is noted for fish dishes. Breakfast is served in the sun-filled garden room. **Pros:** central canal-side loction; friendly staff. **Cons:** parking limited. ⊠ *Steenhouwersdijk 1* ☎ *050/34–27–98* ⊕ *www.dieswaene-hotel.com* ➹ *22 rooms, 2 suites* ⅁ *In-room: minibar. In-hotel: restaurant, pool, parking (paid)* ⊟ *AE, DC, MC, V* ⦿ *BP* Ⓜ *Bus 1.*

$$
★
🏨 **Egmond.** Play lord of the manor at this refurbished 18th-century house near the Begijnhof. Public rooms have hearths and chimneypieces, beamed ceilings and dark-wood moldings. Breakfast is served in an oak-beam hall with a Delft-tile fireplace. Each room has a special period feature or two, and all are airy, with garden views. You can stroll the perimeter of the Minnewater park; the hotel is only 10 minutes' walk from the bustle of central Brugge. **Pros:** historic building; quiet location. **Cons:** far from main sights. ⊠ *Minnewater 15* ☎ *050/34–14–45* ⊕ *www.egmond.be* ➹ *8 rooms* ⅁ *In-room: safe, Internet, Wi-Fi. In-hotel: bar, parking (paid), no-smoking rooms* ⊟ *MC, V* ⦿ *BP* Ⓜ *Bus 3 or 12.*

$$–$$$
🏨 **Erasmus.** Crisp geometric lines, wood accents, and copper lighting fixtures make this hotel seem more Scandinavian than Belgian. The

4

guest rooms are plain but comfortable; some have smashing city views. There are a couple of good places to eat here (both closed Monday): the brasserie ($–$$) for a casual snack or light lunch, and the restaurant ($$$), which serves Flemish fare with a twist—usually one that is beer-inspired. More than 150 brews are on the menu as well, making this a popular post-tour stop in the city center. **Pros:** great location; good food available. **Cons:** limited parking. ☒ *Wollestraat 35* ☎ *050/33–57–81* ⊕ *www.hotelerasmus.com* ↪ *9 rooms* ♿ *In-hotel: 2 restaurants, bar* ▭*AE, DC, MC, V* ⫶○⫶*BP* Ⓜ *Bus 1 or 11.*

¢–$ 🏨 **Europ.** Although this updated 18th-century town house could use some loving care, the coveted property overlooks a canal and is a five-minute walk from the town center. Modern, spartan rooms are beneath low, sloped ceilings with dormers, and beds feature Swiss-flex construction mattresses that ensure a sound night's sleep. **Pros:** quiet location. **Cons:** standard rooms quite small. ☒ *Augustijnenrei 18* ☎ *050/33–79–75* ⊕ *www.hoteleurop.com* ↪ *28 rooms* ♿ *In-room: Wi-Fi. In-hotel: bar, parking (paid)* ▭*DC, MC* ⫶○⫶*CP* Ⓜ *Bus 4 or 14.*

¢–$ 🏨 **Fevery.** This child-friendly hotel is part of a comfortable family home in a quiet corner of Brugge. There's enough clutter to make you feel like you never left your own house, and even a baby monitor so parents can relax with a drink downstairs after putting a child to bed. Rooms are small and basic, but provide anything a modest traveller needs. Families of four should ask for the double room for €125. **Pros:** good value; quiet location. **Cons:** parking limited; far from sights. ☒ *Collaert Mansionstraat 3* ☎ *050/33–12–69* ⊕ *www.hotelfevery.be* ↪ *10 rooms* ♿ *In-room: Wi-Fi. In-hotel: bar, parking (paid), no-smoking rooms* ▭*AE, DC, MC, V* ⫶○⫶*BP* Ⓜ *Bus 4 or 14.*

$$$ 🏨 **Hotel Heritage.** Once a private mansion, this 19th-century building has been converted into a lavish hotel. Guest rooms are in keeping with the building's heritage—elegant, with chandeliers, reproduction antique furniture, and warm fabrics in reds and golds. The hotel is just a few steps from the Markt. There's also a sauna and fitness room in the vaulted cellar. **Pros:** great location; friendly staff; historic building. **Cons:** parking somewhat limited. ☒ *Niklaas Desparsstraat 11* ☎ *050/44–44–44* ⊕ *www.hotel-heritage.be* ↪ *20 rooms, 4 suites* ♿ *In-room: minibar, safe, Internet, Wi-Fi. In-hotel: bar, Wi-Fi* ▭*AE, DC, MC, V* ⫶○⫶*BP* Ⓜ *Bus 2 or 12.*

Fodor's Choice ★

¢–$ 🏨 **Jacobs.** The public rooms are plush and accented with crystal, but this is actually quite a casual place. (Breakfast tables are decorated with plastic waste buckets.) Rooms are no-frills but clean. **Pros:** quiet location; good value. **Cons:** basic facilities; some rooms small. ☒ *Baliestraat 1* ☎ *050/33–98–31* ⊕ *www.hoteljacobs.be* ↪ *23 rooms* ♿ *In-hotel: bar* ▭*AE, MC, V* ⫶○⫶*BP* Ⓜ *Bus 4 or 14.*

$$$–$$$$ 🏨 **Manoir Red!** The guest rooms of this 18th-century manor are as luxurious as they are delightful. Every room has its own character, from classic to modern with Italian stylings; two suites have whirlpool tubs and hammam showers. Make sure to dine in the restaurant, decorated with murals from the French occupation, or in the garden beneath the

fountain designed by the Belgian artist Serge Vandercam. **Pros:** quiet location. **Cons:** a little way from the sights. ⊠ *Nieuwe Gentweg 53* ☎ *050/33–70–70* ⤶ *3 rooms, 5 suites* ⚷ *In-room: safe. In-hotel: restaurant, parking (free)* ▤ *AE, MC, V* ⦿ *BP* Ⓜ *Bus 1.*

$–$$ ⌨ **Martin's Brugge.** It would be hard to beat the price for this location, behind the Belfort. While the building dates to the 17th century, the interiors are contemporary. Guest rooms have warm yellow-and-peach furnishings; some have sloped, beamed ceilings. **Pros:** great location; good value. **Cons:** some rooms quite small. ⊠ *Oude Burg 11* ☎ *050/33–03–19* ⊕ *www.tassche.com* ⤶ *20 rooms* ⚷ *In-hotel: bar* ▤ *MC, V* Ⓜ *Bus 1 or 11.*

$$$–$$$$ ⌨ **Oud Huis Amsterdam.** Two noble, 17th-century houses in the elegant
★   Hanseatic district combine the grace of another era with the polish of a modern, first-class property. Parts of this town house date to the 1300s, and owners Philip and Caroline Train have preserved such antique details as tooled Cordoba leather wallpaper, rough-hewn rafters, and Delft tiles. Rooms with canal views overlook the busy street; back rooms with red rooftop views are quieter. Summer concerts are held in the courtyard terrace. **Pros:** great views from front rooms; beautiful historic building. **Cons:** some rooms can be noisy. ⊠ *Spiegelrei 3* ☎ *050/34–18–10* ⊕ *www.oha.be* ⤶ *44 rooms* ⚷ *In-room: Internet. In-hotel: bar, parking (free)* ▤ *AE, DC, MC, V* ⦿ *BP* Ⓜ *Bus 4 or 14.*

$$$–$$$$ ⌨ **Pandhotel.** This 18th-century mansion may have a large dollop of
★   neoclassical grandeur, but it's also permeated with the warmth of the family owners. The impressive public rooms have restored wood paneling and moldings, rough-hewn flooring, and Oriental rugs. Modern touches include a skylight in the breakfast room and gleaming copper accents in the open kitchen, where breakfast is prepared daily. Individually decorated bedrooms are charming, some with canopy beds and marbleized bathrooms. Some rooms overlook the cathedral, others the red roofs of the city skyline. Two- and three-night packages are good deals. **Pros:** centrally located; friendly staff. **Cons:** parking is limited. ⊠ *Pandreitje 16* ☎ *050/34–06–66* ⊕ *www.pandhotel.com* ⤶ *26 rooms* ⚷ *In-room: safe, minibar, DVD, Wi-Fi. In-hotel: room service, bar, Wi-Fi.* ▤ *AE, DC, MC, V* ⦿ *BP* Ⓜ *Bus 1.*

$$$–$$$$ ⌨ **Relais Bourgondisch Cruyce.** This truly magnificent hotel is situated in
Fodor's Choice   one of the most romantic corners of Brugge. Some rooms overlook the
★   canal and all of them, whether with classic or modern furnishings, live up to the highest expectations. Bathrooms are large and well equipped; all rooms have a large flat-screen TV. **Pros:** great location; historic building; friendly. **Cons:** limited parking (reserve in advance). ⊠ *Wollestraat 41–47* ☎ *050/33–79–26* ⊕ *www.relaisbourgondischcruyce.be* ⤶ *16 rooms* ⚷ *In-room: minibar. In-hotel: restaurant, parking (paid)* ▤ *AE, MC, V* Ⓜ *Bus 1 or 11.*

$$–$$$ ⌨ **Ter Brughe.** This renovated, 16th-century, step-gabled house is now a slick, efficient hotel. Although the modern decor is a bit generic, heavy beams, tempera murals, and leaded-glass windows offer glimpses of the building's intriguing former life. The oldest section is the vaulted cellar, originally a warehouse, which opens onto the canal and now serves as the breakfast room. Newer rooms are slightly larger. **Pros:** good value. **Cons:** some rooms quite small. ✉ *Oost-Gistelhof 2* ☎ *050/34–03–24* 🌐 *www.hotelterbrughe.com* ⇨ *46 rooms* ♿ *In-room: minibar, safe. In-hotel: bar, parking (paid)* ▭ *AE, DC, MC, V* 🍽 *BP* Ⓜ *Bus 4 or 14.*

$$ **Ter Duinen.** Near the Duinenbrug (Dunebridge) lies Ter Duinen, a modest hotel in a quiet neighborhood 5 to 10 minutes' walk from the center of town. Rooms are cozy, comfortable, and a good value. The building dates from the beginning of the 19th century and has been well restored. Visitors can enjoy a drink in the newly built orangerie close to the small garden. **Pros:** quiet location. **Cons:** a little way from the sights. ✉ *Langerei 52* ☎ *050/33–04–37* 🌐 *www.terduinenhotel.be* ⇨ *20 rooms* ♿ *In-hotel: bar, parking (free)* ▭ *AE, MC, V* Ⓜ *Bus 4 or 14.*

4

$$$ **Walburg.** One of Brugge's grandest 19th-century town houses is now a hotel, only a few blocks from the Burg. It was built by Isidoor Alderwerelt, the same architect who finished the Palais de Justice in Brussels, and most of its original features were kept when the house was renovated in 1997. The lovely rooms, tastefully decorated in different color schemes with antique furniture and marble bathrooms, are a generous 750 square feet. Classical music welcomes you in the marble lobby and you can easily imagine Viennese-style balls taking place in the dining room. There's also a beautiful garden at the back. **Pros:** quiet location; historic building; large rooms. **Cons:** parking is limited. ✉ *Boomgaardstraat 13–15* ☎ *050/34–94–14* 🌐 *www.hotelwalburg.be* ⇨ *12 rooms, 1 suite* ♿ *In-room: safe, minibar. In-hotel: restaurant, bar* ▭ *AE, DC, MC, V* ⊗ *Closed Jan.* 🍽 *BP* Ⓜ *Bus 6 or 16.*

NIGHTLIFE & THE ARTS

The West Flanders Cultural Service hosts a helpful Web site, **www.tinck.be,** that lists upcoming arts events, museum exhibits, concerts, and the like. The site can be translated into English, and covers all of West Flanders.

THE ARTS

The monthly *Agenda Brugge,* available in English, gives details of all events in the city; you can get a copy at the tourist office. Listings for events and movie screenings are also published in the local Flemish newspaper *Exit,* available at bookstores and in the public library. Movies are invariably screened in their original language with Flemish subtitles, and there are plenty of English-language films on the local screens.

THEATER

The **Concertgebouw Brugge** (✉ *'t Zand 34* ☎ *050/47–69–99* 🌐 *www.concertgebouw.be*) stages music, dance, and theater events with both national and international acts. Ride the elevator to the seventh floor for a view across Brugge that's comparable to that from the Belfry tower—without having to climb up 366 steps. There's a café at the top.

Flemish Festivals

Year-round dances, concerts, parades, celebrations, markets, fairs, and art exhibits loosen up even the most reserved Flemings. The most famous annual celebration is the Festival of Flanders, a variety of musical events that take place in major cities from April to October. In Brugge, the Procession of the Holy Blood on Ascension Day is well worth seeing, and the Gent Festival in July is packed with events. In winter, *Kerstmarkten* (traditional Christmas markets) are held throughout the region. The third week of June brings *Dag van Beiaard* (Day of the Carillon), a celebration of bells and belfries, when chimes echo from city to city. The local tourist boards have calendars of other festive events; check while planning your visit. There are also free summer music festivals in most major cities. In August the rural village of Dranouter (near Ieper, on the French border) welcomes thousands of music lovers during the three-day international folk festival.

The city theater, **Koninklijke Stadsschouwburg** (⊠ *Vlamingstraat 29* ☎ *050/44–30–60*), presents classical music, dance, and theater; most of the major Flemish companies stop off here. In front of the neo-Renaissance theater stands a statue of Papageno the bird-fancier, a character from Mozart's opera *The Magic Flute.*

CONCERTS

The **MaZ** (⊠ *Magdalenastraat 27*) hosts all kinds of concerts. It's behind the train station, outside the historic city center. Most events at the MaZ are organized either by **Cultuurcentrum Brugge** (☎ *050/44–30–40* ⊕ *www.cultuurcentrumbrugge.be*) or by **Cactus** (☎ *050/33–20–14* ⊕ *www.cactusmusic.be*).

FESTIVALS

Fodor'sChoice ★

More than 2,000 locals take part in the colorful, medieval-style **Heilige Bloedprocessie** (*Procession of the Holy Blood* ⊕ *www.holyblood.org*), which dates back to the 13th century and is held annually on Ascension Day. The precious liquid relic is taken from its place in the church of the same name and carried through flag-bedecked streets in the city center, accompanied by horsemen. Scenes are enacted from the Old and New Testament. For seats in the stands erected around town, book your tickets for the event well in advance from the tourist office. Otherwise, you can find a space in the crowds standing along other parts of the route and watch for free.

Among secular events, one of the best is the **Cactusfestival** (⊕ *www.cactusfestival.be*), a three-day, open-air music celebration in July. It's usually held in the Minnewater park. There are several free concerts by local and international artists in Brugge's marketplaces during the **Klinkers festival** in August. The **Reiefeest** (*Festival of the Canals*), held every third August (the next is in 2011), features a sound-and-light show with 600 actors, dancers, and musicians. The **Praalstoet van de Gouden Boom** (*Pageant of the Golden Tree*), commemorating the marriage of Charles the Bold and Margaret of York, is normally held every five years; the next one will take place in 2012.

NIGHTLIFE

Brugge is not the liveliest city at night, but there are a handful of good hangouts.

Pubs, mostly catering to an under-30 clientele, are clustered around the Eiermarkt, at the back of the Markt. There are also several at 't Zand, such as **Ma Rica Rokk** (✉ *'t Zand 7–8* ☎ *050/33–83–58*), where dance beats pound all through the night. A chic, older crowd gravitates toward the clubs at the Kraanplein and the bars on Langestraat.

The **Cactus Club** (✉ *Magdalenastraat 27* ☎ *050/33–20–14*) is the original Brugge venue for pop, rock, folk, and blues acts. It also hosts some comedy nights, occasionally in English.

A somewhat older crowd gathers in **De Stoepa** (✉ *Oostmeers 124* ☎ *050/33–04–54*), a pub and restaurant with a slight Eastern touch in its setting as well as on its menu. Here you can enjoy couscous, beef teriyaki and several spicy dishes.

There are several gay-friendly bars in Brugge. One well-known spot is **Bar Bolero** (✉ *Garenmarkt 32*), which is closed on Thursday. A list of gay-friendly nightspots can be found on ⊕ *www.gaybruges.be*.

Don't miss a trip to **Retsin's Lucifernum** (✉ *Twijnstraat 8, off Philip-stockstraat* ☎ *050/34–16–50*). Ring the bell to enter and follow the dark corridor down to a door, which opens into a bright bar with twinkling chandeliers, bizarre decoration, and often live Hungarian gypsy music. This is a rum-cocktails-and-Russian-champagne kind of place. Things start up around 9 PM and go on well past midnight. It's open Saturday only.

Academie (✉ *Wijngaardstraat 7–9* ☎ *050/33–22–66*) is one of the nicest hotel bars. Hold forth at **The Meeting** (✉ *Spiegelrei 3* ☎ *050/34–18–10*) of the Oud Huis Amsterdam; it's got tables set out in a leafy courtyard.

OUTDOOR ACTIVITIES

For questions about sports services in Brugge, contact the **City Sports Service** (✉ *Koning Leopold III Laan 50, Sint-Andries* ☎ *050/72–70–00*). Based at Olympiapark, a multipurpose sports center with an Olympic-size swimming pool, it's available Monday and Wednesday–Friday 9–noon, and on Tuesday 9–noon and 2–6. There's usually an English-speaking staff member on hand. Also at the site is the Jan Breydel stadium, where **Club Brugge** (☎ *050/40–21–21* ⊕ *www.clubbrugge.be*), the city's premier soccer team, is based. Soccer fans can get match tickets from the club.

GREEN SPACES

The green belt along the old city walls is a good place for jogging; it runs alongside the canals and between the city's medieval gates. You can jog between Ezelpoort and Smedenpoort and on to the railway station, or from Dampoort along Kruisvest to Katelijnepoort.

If you head a little ways beyond the city center you can reach some lovely large parks. The wooded Stedelijk Domein Beisbroek (Beisbroek City Park) in Sint-Andries, for instance, draws people for jogging, walking, or playing with kids. It has picnic areas, a deer park, a castle with a nature center, and even an observatory. To get here, take a bus from 't Zand or the train station. The Provinciaal Domein Tillegembos in Sint-Michiels is another good spot. This woodland estate has playgrounds, a horse mill, and a 14th-century castle. Catch the bus from the Biekorf in the center of Brugge.

SHOPPING

Most shops in Brugge are open Monday–Saturday 9 or 10–6; some souvenir shops are also open on Sunday. Although there are a couple of tacky tourist stores, Brugge has many trendy boutiques and shops, especially along Nordzandstraat, as well as Steenstraat and Vlamingstraat, both of which branch off from the Markt. Ter Steeghere mall, which links the Burg with Wollestraat, deftly integrates a modern development into the historic center. The largest and most pleasant mall is the Zilverpand off Zilverstraat, where 30-odd shops cluster in Flemish gable houses around two courtyards fringed with sidewalk cafés.

MARKETS

The Markt is the setting for the weekly **Woensdag Markt** (Wednesday Market), with vegetables, fruit, flowers, specialty cheeses, and hams. (Occasionally, if there is a major event taking place on the Markt, the market moves to the Burg.) Brugge's biggest market is the **Zaterdag Markt** (Saturday Market) on 't Zand, selling all kinds of cheeses, hams, and cooked meats, as well as some clothing and household items. The **Vismarkt** (Fish Market) is held, appropriately, on the Vismarkt, daily except Sunday and Monday. All three markets are morning events, from 8 to approximately 12:30. On weekends from March 15 through November 15 there's a **flea market** open throughout the day along the Dijver.

SPECIALTY STORES

ART & ANTIQUES

Art and antiques dealers abound. **Guyart** (⊠*Pitsenbosdreef 7* ☎*050/33–21–59*) has a fine arts gallery a little south of the city center. **Papyrus** (⊠*Walplein 41* ☎*050/33–66–87*) specializes in silverware. **'t Leerhuis** (⊠*Groeninge 35* ☎*050/33–03–02*) deals in contemporary art. **Vincent Lebbe's Het Witte Huis** (⊠*Gistelsesteenweg 30* ☎*050/31–63–01*) specializes in furniture and decorative objects from the 18th and 19th centuries.

CHOCOLATE

You can't go far in the city center without seeing a tempting window display of chocolate truffles and pralines. One of the best shops is **The Chocolate Line** (⊠*Simon Stevinplein 19* ☏*050/34–10–90*); along with delicious handmade candy it sells handy cases for packing your chocolates in to take home. Another good source for handmade treats is **Chocolaterie Sukerbuyc** (⊠*Katelijnestraat 5* ☏*050/33–08–87*). Their display is split between chocolates and marzipan; choose your vice. Across the street they run a tearoom where you can nibble a scone or sample a plate of chocolates.

During the 19th century a young couple started selling *babelutten* (hard sweets made of sugar and butter) to the tourists along the beach at the Belgian coast. Two centuries later **Moeder Babelutte** *(Mother Babelutte)* has become a household name with several shops in western Flanders that sell traditional Flanders sweets. Try the one in Katelijnestraat 26, where you'll also find *cuberdons* (red, nose-shaped candy) and an assortment of chocolates.

FOOD

Possibly the smallest shop in the Noordzandstraat, and stuffed with foreign and local delicacies, **De Westhoek** (⊠*Noordzandstraat 39*) is a treat to the palate. Cheese pies, pancakes, quiches, and avocaat (an alcoholic drink made with eggs) are homemade.

LACE

Brugge has been a center for lace making since the 15th century. You can find pieces costing €5–€500 in the many souvenir shops around the Markt, Wollestraat, Breidelstraat, and Minnewater. Handmade lace in intricate patterns, however, takes a very long time to produce, and this is reflected in the price. For work of this type, you should be prepared to part with €250 or more. A good shop for the serious lace lover is in the Sint-Anne quarter, behind the church: **'t Apostelientje** (⊠*Balstraat 11* ☏*050/33–78–60*).

SIDE TRIPS FROM BRUGGE

DAMME

7 km (4 mi) north of Brugge.

A quiet agricultural village with a population of about 10,000 Flemings, Damme lies in a peaceful polder landscape of waving fields and far horizons. Walking its streets today feels much as it would have centuries ago. If you take the miniature paddle steamer *Lamme Goedzak,* which travels along a canal lined with slender poplars, the town is a half hour from Brugge. You could even hike or bike the distance along a common canal path.

Damme owes its place in history to a tidal wave that ravaged the coast in 1134 and opened an inlet from the Zwin to the environs of Brugge. The little town grew up as a fishing village until a canal was dug to connect Damme to Brugge. The former settlement was soon a key port and snapped up exclusive rights to import such treasured commodities as Bordeaux wine and Swedish herring. The "Maritime Law of Damme" thus became the standard for Hanseatic merchants. Later, when the Zwin channel silted up, Damme's fortunes slowly declined; however, its Burgundian architecture remains well-preserved. Today, the town rides a literary wave; it has a large number of antiquarian bookshops and market stalls offering books in a variety of languages. There's an added lure of good restaurants and cafés.

GETTING HERE & AROUND

The road from Brugge to Damme follows the canal and is a short ride (by bike or car) through one of the most beautiful parts of *le plat pays* (the flat country). From Brugge take R30 (the circular road around the city) and follow the Damse Vaart-Zuid. There is no train service, but bus line 43 connects Brugge's train station and Markt with Damme in about 15 minutes; buses run hourly during the middle of the day. You can travel by boat between Easter and the end of September. The river barge *Lamme Goedzak* runs five times a day, and a round-trip costs €7.

ESSENTIALS

Tourist Info Damme (✉ *Huyse de Grote Sterre, Jacob van Maerlantstraat 3* ☎ *050/28–86–10* ⊕ *www.toerismedamme.be* ◷ *Mid-Apr.–mid-Oct., weekdays 9–noon and 2–6, weekends 10–noon and 2–6; mid-Oct.–mid-Apr., weekdays 9–noon and 2–5, weekends 2–5*).

River Barge Contact *Lamme Goedzak* (⊕ *www.bootdammebrugge.be*).

WHAT TO SEE

On a clear day you can see as far as the Netherlands from the top of the tower of the **Onze-Lieve-Vrouwekerk** *(Church of Our Lady)*, which rises high above the surrounding farmland as a symbol of Damme's proud past. Poet Jacob van Maerlant, who lived and worked in Damme during the late 13th century, is buried under the main portal below the tower. Charles the Bold and Margaret of York were married here.

Jacob van Maerlant's statue stands tall and poetic in the center of the **Marktplein**. On the facade of the Gothic Stadhuis (Town Hall) you can see Charles, the noble duke, presenting the wedding ring to his fiancée Margaret, plus other stone effigies of Flemish counts set in niches between the high windows. The step-gabled building's interior moldings and clocktower are especially outstanding. Note the Huyse de Grote Sterre, a 15th-century patrician's residence that was also home to the Spanish military governor in the 17th century; it's now a tourist office and a literary museum.

OFF THE BEATEN PATH

Lissewege. Surrounded by meadows, this settlement is one of the prettiest and best-preserved of the coastal villages. Whitewashed houses cluster around a 13th-century brick church and line a narrow, flower-bordered canal that runs through the village. The former Cistercian Abbey of Ter Doest includes a perfectly preserved, massive 13th-century barn, still supported by original beams. The train from Brugge to Zeebrugge stops in Lissewege, as does the 791 bus from Brugge railway station.

WHERE TO STAY & EAT

$$$$
CONTINENTAL
★

✕**De Waterput.** At this small, whitewashed farmhouse you won't be poring over the menu—chef Willy Bataillie creates delicious daily prix-fixe multicourse meals based on the most tempting market produce. You might be served smoked salmon, John Dory with chives, wild duck with small onions, or crêpes suzette. The out-of-town detour to this small restaurant is worth the time as much for the scenic drive as for the food. ⊠*Rondsaartstraat 1* ☎*050/59–92–56* ▤*DC, MC, V* ☉*Closed Tues.–Thurs. and mid-Dec.–mid-Jan.*

¢–$
BELGIAN

✕**Ter Kloeffe.** Flemings and tourists meet over a light meal and a local beer at this nice little restaurant. Go for crepes (with tuna, chicken, or shrimp) or the abundant *Damse boerenschotel,* a plate crammed with ham, pâté and local charcuterie. ⊠*Jacob van Maerlantstraat 5* ☎*050/35–64–94* ☉*Closed Wed. No dinner Tues.*

$

▦**Hofstede De Stamper.** For a taste of country Flanders, stay at this 18th-century farmstead whose grounds are home to cattle, sheep, and poultry. Basic rooms and shared facilities are not for everyone, but the real treats are meals prepared with fresh farm products—and, on Sunday, warm, fragrant bread and cakes baked in a wood oven. Available on weekends, and on request during the week, this true farm experience is only 2 km (1 mi) from Damme. **Pros:** quiet location; rustic. **Cons:** remote—hard to reach without own transport. ⊠*Zuiddijk 12, border of Brugge and Damme* ☎*050/50–01–97* ➥*3 rooms* ⅃*In-hotel: restaurant* ▤*No credit cards* ⵏ*BP.*

$$

▦**Hotel Wilgenhof.** If you follow the Damme canal out from Brugge, you'll reach this gorgeous mansion on the polder, a good base for excursions in either direction and to the coast, which is 12 km (7 mi) away. The gardens are lovely; you can eat your breakfast outside when the weather permits. There's also an inviting sitting room with a fireplace where you can rehash the day's activities or just put your feet up and read a book. **Pros:** beautiful location; quiet; historic building. **Cons:** remote—hard to reach without own transport. ⊠*Polderstraat 151, Sint-Kruis* ☎*050/36–27–44* ⊕*www.hotel-wilgenhof.be* ➥*6 rooms* ⅃*In-hotel: restaurant, bar* ▤*AE, DC, MC, V* ⵏ*BP.*

EN ROUTE

The tiny polder villages are a delight to explore by foot, bike, or hand-operated ferry along the canals. **Hoeke,** the Zwin port for German merchants, has a 13th-century church and a 19th-century windmill. Head to **Lapscheure,** on the Dutch border, to explore a major 18th-century dike system. **Moerkerke** is the site of the Battle of the Windmill, which took place late in World War II. **Oostkerke,** near Damme, is a whitewashed little village with a 14th-century castle and a 19th-century mill. **Sijsele** features a unique combination of castle and golf-course green scenery. You'll find neo-Gothic architectural treasures in **Vivenkapelle,** including a 19th-century church, rectory, abbey, and school, designed by the architect Jean de Bethune.

4

THE NORTH SEA COAST

Just a century ago, the 65 km (39 mi) stretch from De Panne in the southwest to Knokke (pronounced kuh-nock-kuh) in the northeast was practically unspoiled, with beach dunes connected to the plains beyond by a kilometer or so of moss-covered ground (Ter Streep). The dunes were fortified by dikes as early as the 10th century, but life here remained at the mercy of the sea. Oostende and Nieuwpoort were the only major settlements in 1830, when Belgium achieved independence. Leopold I, Belgium's first king, chose to live here, and royal hangers-on and French-speaking nobility followed. Soon a light railway and seawalls appeared, and the coast became safer, more accessible, and even quite fashionable. With the 1960s came mass tourism and almost the entire coastline fell into the hands of developers. Today, the resort towns are packed so closely that it's difficult to know where one ends and the next begins. Blocks of housing, campgrounds, villas, and hotels line the waterfronts, united much of the way by promenades. You can walk for miles along the dike, flanked by modern apartment houses that grab much of the view.

With its prevailing breeze and wide, sandy beaches, the Belgian coast offers splendid opportunities for water sports. Sailing, swimming, windsurfing, and sand-yachting (skimming along the beach aboard a wheeled platform equipped with a sail) are all popular options. Even horseback riding is a semi-aquatic sport here, with horses splashing along the water's edge.

Note that every coast town has its own character. Knokke is a resort for the well-off; Blankenberge is very popular; Heist and De Haan draw families; Koksijde and De Panne, close to the border, attract French-speaking tourists, and Oostende is considered the capital of the Flemish North Sea Coast.

THE BEACHES

The beach slopes gently to the sea, but for those willing to brave the cold waters, currents can be tricky. A green flag means bathing is safe; yellow, bathing is risky but guards are on duty; red, bathing is prohibited. There are accidents every year, so mind the warnings and swim only at beaches supervised by lifeguards. Many resorts also offer good public outdoor pools. Nudists can skinny-dip in Bredene, next to Oostende. Some prefer the long, wide Belgian sea coast in the off-season, when you can walk quietly along the beach in the pale winter sun and fill your lungs with bracing sea air, then warm up in a cozy tavern with a plate of steaming mussels.

GETTING HERE & AROUND

If you're coming by car, the six-lane E40 from Brussels passes both Gent and Brugge en route to Oostende and Calais in France. Keep in mind that traffic on the E40 can be bumper-to-bumper on summer weekends. At such busy times, a better alternative is the N9; for Knokke, you branch off on N49. From Calais, the E40 has been completed on the French side, but a few kilometers of two-lane road remain

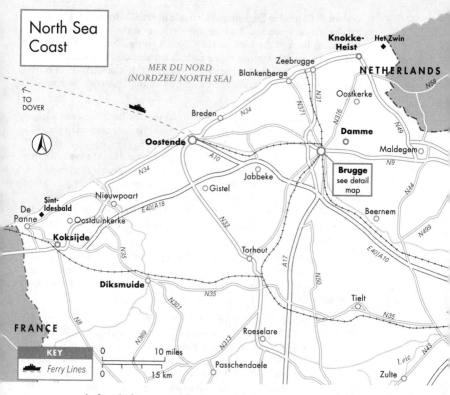

North Sea Coast

MER DU NORD (NORDZEE/ NORTH SEA)

TO DOVER

Knokke-Heist   Het Zwin

Zeebrugge

Blankenberge

NETHERLANDS

N58

Oostkerke

Breden   N34

N371   N31   N376

Damme

N49

Oostende   A70   Maldegem

N9

Brugge
see detail
map

N34   Jabbeke

Gistel

N44

Nieuwpoort

Sint-
Idesbald

De
Panne   E401/A18

Oostduinkerke

Koksijde   N35

Beernem

N499

N33

Torhout   A17   N50   E40/A10

Diksmuide

N301   N35

Tielt

N35

N8   N369   Roeselare   N43

FRANCE   N313   _Leie_

KEY

🚢 Ferry Lines

0 ——— 10 miles

0 ——— 15 km

Passchendaele   Zulte

---

before linking up with the rest of the E40 to Oostende and Brussels. The coastal road, N34, is very busy in summer, so allow ample time for driving between resorts.

Along the coast there's a tram service—a happily preserved relic of another era—all the way from Knokke to De Panne. The trams are modern, and it's a pleasant ride, but don't expect uninterrupted views of the sea; the tram tracks are on the leeward side of the dike. The service runs every 15 minutes Easter–September. Fares start at €1.20 and go up depending on the distance traveled; you can buy tickets on board the tram, but they cost one third more than if bought in advance.

ESSENTIALS

Tram Contact De Lijn (☎ _059/56–52–11 West Flanders, 09/210–9311 East Flanders_ ⊕ _www.delijn.be_).

OOSTENDE

115 km (69 mi) northwest of Brussels, 28 km (17 mi) west of Brugge, 98 km (59 mi) northeast of Calais.

A transportation and fishing center and an old-fashioned, slightly raffish resort, Oostende (pronounced _oh_stender in Flemish), otherwise known as Ostend in English and Ostende in French, leads a double life. It's the largest town and the oldest settlement on the coast, with a history going back to the 10th century. Long a pirates' hideout, Oostende has hosted many a famous rogue and adventurer, and it was from here that Crusaders also set sail for the Holy Land. In the early 17th century, when villagers backed the Protestant cause, Oostende withstood a Spanish siege for three years.

One of Continental Europe's first railways was built between Oostende and Mechelen in 1838, eventually resulting in regular mail packet services to Dover, England, beginning in 1846. (The town remains a favorite day-trip destination for Brits, who ferry across the sea to shop and enjoy the seafood.) A hundred years ago, the town was at its belle epoque height, with a boom of neoclassical buildings dripping with ornamentation. Elegantly dressed ladies shaded under parasols strolled along the Promenade on the arms of gents in spats. But during World War II many of the buildings were bombed; times changed; the glamour dimmed.

Although it might never quite relive its heyday, Oostende has regained much of its grandeur during recent years. Historic buildings have been embellished, dikes renewed, and there's been a revival of cultural activities.

GETTING HERE & AROUND
The six-lane E40 from Brussels passes both Gent and Brugge en route to Oostende and Calais in France. Keep in mind that traffic on the E40 can be bumper-to-bumper on summer weekends. At such busy times, a better alternative is the N9. Hourly trains from Brugge get you there in 15 minutes; from Brussels, it takes an hour.

ESSENTIALS
Visitor Info Oostende (✉ *Monacoplein 2* ☎ *059/70–11–99* ⊕ *www.toeris me-oostende.be*).

WHAT TO SEE
On the elevated **Albert I Promenade** shops and tearooms compete for attention with the view of the wide beach and the sea, popular here with surfers.

At one end stands the **Kursaal** *(Casino)*, which, in addition to gambling facilities, has a vast concert hall and exhibition space. The gaming rooms have striking murals by Surrealist Paul Delvaux. ✉ *Oosthelling* ☎ *059/70–51–11, 070/22–56–00 reservations for shows* ⊕ *www.cko. be* ⊗ *Gaming rooms, 3 PM–dawn.*

Jokingly called "the longest restaurant in Europe," the **Visserskaai** *(Fishermen's Wharf)* overlooking yachts berthed at Montgomery Dock is a row of fish eateries. Nearby in a covered market women hawk seafood in all its forms every day. This picturesque area is crossed with narrow streets. ✉ *Albert 1, Promenade, opposite end from Casino.*

NEED A
BREAK?

James Café (⊠ *James Ensor Galerie 34* ☎ *059/70–52–45*), in a small, refined shopping precinct named after the city's most famous resident, is renowned for its shrimp croquettes.

The **James Ensorhuis** is an introduction to the strange and hallucinatory world of the painter James Ensor (1860–1949), who was recognized late in his life as one of the great artists of the early 20th century. Using violent colors to express his frequently macabre or satirical themes, he depicted a fantastic carnival world peopled by masks and skeletons. The displays in this house, which was his home and studio, include many of the objects found in his work, especially the masks, and copies of his major paintings. ⊠ *Vlaanderenstraat 27* ☎ *059/80–53–35* ⊡ *€2* ☉ *Easter weekend and June–Sept., 10–noon and 2–5; Nov.–May, weekends 2–5.*

Oostende also has a good modern art museum, the **Provinciaal Museum voor Moderne Kunst** *(PMMK)*, with Belgian contemporary artists well represented by Pierre Alechinsky, Roger Raveel, and Paul Van Hoeydonck (whose statuette, *The Fallen Astronaut,* was deposited on the moon by the *Apollo XV* crew), among others. Ceramics, paintings, sculpture, and graphic art are all displayed. The admission fee is increased for special exhibitions. ⊠ *Romestraat 11* ☎ *059/50–81–18* ⊕ *www.pmmk.be* ⊡ *€5* ☉ *Tues.–Sun. 10–6.*

Mercator, the three-masted training ship of the Belgian merchant marine, which sailed from the 1930s to the 1960s, is now moored close to the city center, ready to sail, if needed. Decks, fittings, and the spartan quarters have been kept intact, and there's a museum of mementos brought home from the ship's exotic voyages; during one they hauled back mysterious statues from Easter Island. ⊠ *Mercatordok, Vindictivelaan* ☎ *059/70–56–54* ⊡ *€4, includes audioguide* ☉ *Apr.–June and Sept., daily 10–12:30 and 2–5:30; July and Aug., daily 10–5:30; Oct.–Mar., weekends 10–12:30 and 2–4:30.*

WHERE TO STAY & EAT

$$–$$$
SEAFOOD

✕**Mosselbeurs.** Mussels are the focus at this cheap and cheery restaurant not far from the station. The mustard-color exterior walls are studded with enormous mock mussel shells, while inside the black-and-white-check floor and tidy decor suggest a maritime theme. Deliciously meaty mollusks are served about any imaginable way. ⊠ *Dwarsstraat 10* ☎ *059/80–73–10* ⊟ *AE, MC, V* ☉ *No lunch Sun.*

$$$–$$$$
CONTEMPORARY

✕**Villa Maritza.** Bearing the name of an Austro-Hungarian countess who caught Leopold II's fancy, this 100-year-old villa, furnished in Renaissance Flemish style, serves seafood: monkfish roasted with thyme, fennel, and anise; lobster carpaccio with garlic; and duck's liver served sweet-and-sour with sherry. Take a good look at the outside; it's one of the oldest houses on the coastline. ⊠ *Albert I Promenade 76* ☎ *059/50–88–08* ⌔ *Reservations essential* ⊟ *AE, DC, MC, V* ☉ *Closed Mon. No dinner Sun.*

$$–$$$

🏨**Andromeda.** So close to the casino that you can practically hear the rolling of the dice, this modern luxury hotel has public rooms in black and white and guest rooms in restful colors that match the sea. Some rooms have balconies overlooking the beach. A sunny terrace restaurant serves North Sea fish and lobster dishes. Should the beach not be relaxing enough, hit the spa for a massage. **Pros:** central location; close to beach. **Cons:** rooms with sea view and balcony are expensive. ⊠ *Albert 1 Promenade 60,* ☎ *059/80–66–11* ⊕ *www.andromedahotel. be* ⇆ *94 rooms* ⚴ *In-room: refrigerator (some). In-hotel: restaurant, bar, pool, spa, parking (paid)* ⊟ *AE, DC, MC, V.*

$$$–$$$$ ⊡ **Thermae Palace Hotel.** King Leopold II, who dabbled in architecture, designed this art deco building, the only grande-dame hotel to survive the pummeling of the World Wars. Tile floors, high ceilings, and wide verandas on the sea are some of its charms. Most guest rooms have balconies. Check out the cozy bar and terrace for a beer or something stronger before or after a meal or a brisk walk. Rooms without a sea view are cheaper. **Pros:** quiet spot away from bustling city; beachside location; elegant. **Cons:** a little way from the city center. ⊠ *Koningen Astridlaan 7,* ☎ *059/80–66–44* ⊕ *www.thermaepalace.be* ⇆ *159 rooms* ⚴ *In-room: minibar, Wi-Fi. In-hotel: 2 restaurants, bar, gym, parking (free), Wi-Fi* ⊟ *AE, DC, MC, V.*

NIGHTLIFE & THE ARTS

Oostende's museums and cultural events are covered on the **www.tinck. be** Web site. The site can be translated into English, and includes all the nearby coastal towns as well.

THE ARTS

Check the *Bulletin*'s What's On section under "Other Towns" for cultural activities. There are frequent retrospectives at Oostende's museums. Concerts of all kinds, from classical to rock, pop, and jazz, draw crowds from far away to the 1,700-seat hall at the **Kursaal** (⊠ *Monacoplein* ☎ *070/22–56–00* ⊕ *www.kursaaloostende.be*). Flemish singing superstar Helmut Lotti, the best-selling artist in the country's history, is a frequent performer.

NIGHTLIFE

The closure rate among seasonal nightspots is high; make sure the place you select is still in business. The best bet along the coast is generally the local casino, where gambling underwrites the nightclub entertainment. Blues and jazz clubs are in and around Kapucijnenstaat, and discos are at Carre beach.

The **Lounge Bar** (⊠ *Westhelling* ☎ *0475/76–59–51*), which is run by the Kursaal, is the classiest nightspot in Oostende (entrance costs €5). Young male visitors from across the Channel who arrive bent on a bender head straight for the dowdy **Langestraat,** where there's a wide choice of snack bars, beer joints, pizza houses, topless bars, and disco-clubs.

OUTDOOR ACTIVITIES

GOLF

The 18-hole course at the **Royal Ostend Golf Club** (☎ *059/23–32–38*) in De Haan is picturesquely embedded between the dunes and the polder, 12 km (7 mi) east of Oostende.

HORSE RACING

In Oostende the **Wellington Hippodrome** (✉ *Sportstraat 48* ☎ *059/80– 60–55*) is a top track for flat racing and trotting. Flat racing is July and August, Monday, Thursday, weekends, and bank holidays; trotting races are May–September, Friday at 6:45 PM.

WINDSURFING

Windsurfing is extremely popular, and special areas have been set aside for it along many beaches. In Oostende, there's a **water sports center** (✉ *Vicognedijk 30* ☎ *059/32–15–64 in the afternoon*) on the Spuikom waterway (also used for oystering).

KOKSIJDE

27 km (17 mi) southwest of Oostende.

★ Koksijde and Sint-Idesbald are small resorts, separated by a few kilometers, that offer more than beach life. Koksijde has the highest dune on the coast, the **Hoge Blekker,** 108 feet high.

GETTING HERE & AROUND

From De Panne, take the N34 to Koksijde. By train, Koksijde is one hour from Gent on a direct route, or just under an hour from Brugge (including a change in Lichtervelde).

ESSENTIALS

Visitor Info **Koksijde** (⊕ *www.koksijde.be*).

WHAT TO SEE

Nearby are the ruins of the Cistercian **Duinenabdij** *(Abbey of the Dunes)*, founded in 1107 and destroyed by the iconoclasts in 1566. Traces of the original abbey, the cloisters, and columns from the refectory remain. An archaeological museum shows collections from the digs, as well as interesting examples of regional plants and animals. ✉ *Koninklijke Prinslaan 6–8* ☎ *058/53–39–50* ⊕ *www.tenduinen.be* 🎫 *€5* 🕙 *Tues.–Fri. 10–6, weekends 2–6.*

The architecture of the strikingly modern **Onze-Lieve-Vrouw ter Duinenkerk** *(Our Lady of Sorrows of the Dunes Church)*, north of the abbey, suggests both the dunes and the sea through bold colors, undulating forms, and stained glass. The church was built in 1964. A crypt holds the remains of the first abbot of adjacent Dunes Abbey. ✉ *Jaak Van Buggenhoutlaan.*

Many art lovers head for Sint-Idesbald to discover the **Paul Delvaux Museum** in a reconverted Flemish farmhouse. It is dedicated to the painter, famous for his surrealist mix of nudes, skeletons, and trains, who died in 1994 at the age of nearly 100. This collection has work from the various stages of Delvaux's career, including his later, somewhat eerie female nudes. ⊠ *Paul Delvauxlaan 42* ☎ *058/52–12–29* ⊕ *www.delvauxmuseum.com* 🔢 *€8* ⊗ *Apr.–Sept., Tues.–Sun. 10:30–5:30; Oct.–Dec., Thurs.–Sun. 10:30–5:30.*

KNOKKE-HEIST

33 km (20 mi) northeast of Oostende, 17 km (10 mi) north of Brugge, 108 km (65 mi) northwest of Brussels.

Knokke-Heist (which includes five beach resorts—Knokke, Heist, Alberstrand, Het Zoute, and Duinbergen) is an area of dunes and sea, purple wildflowers and groomed golf courses. Heist, Alberstand, and Duinbergen are sports- and family-oriented beaches, but to young Belgians of ample means, K-H is the beach to show off designer fashions or a buff new beau. Those who inhabit the old-money villas of Het Zoute, inland from the beach, wouldn't flaunt their chauffeurs and butlers; you'd assume they were there.

Along the Kustlaan, on the leeward side of the dike, you'll find branches of virtually every fashionable shop in Brussels, all of them open Sunday. The Casino has an enormous 2,000-light Venetian-crystal chandelier in the foyer, perhaps the largest in Europe. Gaming, however, is for members only. In the late 19th century, painters settled in this coastal pleasure zone, and today there are dozens of galleries with works by Belgian and international artists; the Casino displays treasured murals by René Magritte, and in front is a bronze statue of a poet, cast by Zadkine in 1965. In 2005, Knokke's mayor, Count Leopold, revealed plans to build a giant ship-like building on the roof.

The Albertplein, widely known as the *Place M'as-tu-vu* (Did-You-See-Me Square), is a gathering place for the chic-at-heart.

GETTING HERE & AROUND
Branch off onto the N49 for Knokke-Heist. Direct trains a few times an hour get you from Brugge to Knokke in 20 minutes.

ESSENTIALS
Visitor Info Knokke-Heist (⊠ *Zeedijk 660* ☎ *050/63–03–80* ⊕ *www. knokke-heist.be*).

WHAT TO SEE
★ **Het Zwin** is a remarkable 375-acre nature reserve and bird sanctuary reaching the Netherlands border, preserved thanks to the efforts of naturalist Count Léon Lippens (father of the present mayor) in the early 20th century. The Zwin was once a busy estuary, connecting Brugge with the North Sea. In fact, in 1340 Edward III of England and his Flemish allies sailed here to conquer the French fleet, readying to attack England. But after silting up in the 16th century, the waterway has retreated into quiet marsh and tidal channels, encircled by dunes and dikes—the largest salt marsh in Belgium. Saltwater washes into the soil, making for

some unusual flora and fauna. Visit in spring for the bird migrations and from mid-July for the flowers, especially the native *zwinneblomme,* or sea lavender. Rubber boots are a must, and binoculars can be rented. From the top of the dike there's a splendid view of the dunes and inlets. Storks nest in the aviary, which also holds thousands of aquatic birds and birds of prey, including the red-beaked sheldrake, gray plover, avocet, and sandpiper. A former royal villa, the Châlet du Zwin is now an attractive restaurant. There's a lot to see, but if you aren't sure where to look, you can hire a guide for €50. ⊠ *Graaf Léon Lippensdreef 8* ☏ *050/60–70–86* ⊕ *www.zwin.be* ⊠ *€5.20* ⊙ *Easter–Sept., daily 9–7; Oct., daily 9–5; Nov.–Mar., Thurs.–Tues. 9–5.*

The **Sincfala Museum,** set in a 19th-century former school, is especially fun for children. An old Flanders classroom is re-created completely, from the desks to the wall hangings. Just outside is the fishing boat *Jessica.* ⊠ *Pannenstraat 140* ☏ *050/63–08–72* ⊕ *www.sincfala.be* ⊠ *€3.50* ⊙ *Daily 10–noon and 2–5.*

Hundreds of brightly colored butterflies flit about the **Butterfly Garden** in delicate natural display when the weather is warm enough—a lepidopterist's fantasy. ⊠ *Bronlaan 14* ☏ *050/61–04–72* ⊕ *www.vlinder tuin-knokke.be* ⊠ *€4.80* ⊙ *Late Mar.–Sept., daily 10–5:30.*

WHERE TO STAY & EAT

$$$$
BELGIAN
✕ **Ter Dycken.** Discretion and charm are the bywords at this restaurant, known for its terrace adjoining a magnificent garden. Langoustines with chives au gratin, croquettes of hand-peeled shrimp, and baked potato with caviar are among the favorites here. ⊠ *Kalvekeetdijk 137, Knokke* ☏ *050/60–80–23* ☝ *Reservations essential* ▤ *DC, MC, V* ⊙ *Closed Mon., Tues., and Jan.*

$$$$
⛫ **La Réserve.** This vast hotel, complete with a thalassotherapy (seawater-based) spa and a man-made lake, has a country-club approach to pampering. Flowers and antiques do little to warm the airport-style public spaces, but guest rooms are bright and lovely, with spongepainted pastels. You can create anything from a simple package to an extravagant getaway, including bed-and-breakfast-style arrangements and full spa packages. It's directly opposite the casino, three minutes from the beach. **Pros:** on-site spa, close to beach. **Cons:** large size makes it a bit cold & impersonal. ⊠ *Elizabetlaan 158–160, Albertstrand* ☏ *050/61–06–06* ⊕ *www.la-reserve.be* ➬ *110 rooms, 12 suites* ⛭ *In-hotel: restaurant, bar, tennis courts, pool, parking (free), minibar* ▤ *AE, DC, MC, V* ⧖ *BP, MAP.*

$$$–$$$$
⛫ **Manoir du Dragon.** Fortunately, this romantic hotel is just the opposite of what its name suggests. Individually decorated rooms help make this manor house overlooking the water a unique choice. Sitting on a chaise in the garden you feel more like a guest than a tourist, and you'll appreciate the bountiful buffet breakfast, too. **Pros:** quiet location. **Cons:** hard to reach without own transport. ⊠ *Albertlaan 73,* ☏ *050/63–05–80* ⊕ *www.manoirdudragon.be* ➬ *16 rooms* ⛭ *In-*

4

room: safe, minibar. In-hotel: bar, bicycles, parking (free), Wi-Fi ⊟AE, DC, MC, V ⊠BP.

$$$ ⊡ **Rose de Chopin.** This peaceful, whitewashed villa is shaded by poplars and has a romantic garden. Guest rooms are large, each with its own twist; four have private gardens. The location is very convenient; it's right in the middle of Knokke near the little shopping street, and within 15 minutes' walk of the beach. **Pros:** central location. **Cons:** expensive. ⊠*Elisabethlaan 94,* ☎*050/62–08–88* ⊕*www.hotellugano. be* ⊲*9 rooms* ⊡*In-room: kitchen (some). In-hotel: parking (free), Wi-Fi* ⊟*AE, DC, MC, V* ⊠*BP.*

NIGHTLIFE & THE ARTS

The **Casino** (⊠*Zeedijk 507* ☎*050/63–05–00*) offers gala nights with international stars, theater, movies, ballet, exhibitions, and two discos, **Zuri** (entrance on Zeedijk) and **Prince** (entrance on Canada Square).

SHOPPING

Aside from the high-end shops, boutiques, and galleries clustered around Het Zoute, the **Centre de Bolle** traditional market near the Heist station is the place to find crafts, clothing, and foodstuffs at fair prices. It's open on Thursday in July and August.

SPORTS & THE OUTDOORS

CYCLING

You can bike all or part of a "polder route" from Knokke, past woods, salt marshes, farms, and dikes all the way to Damme and Oosterkerke. This is one of the best bike paths on the coast.

GOLF

Two 18-hole golf courses are available at Knokke-Heist's **Royal Zoute Golf Club** (⊠*Caddiespad 14* ☎*050/60–12–27* ⊕*www.zoute.be*).

WALKING

Walking is a joy in this coastal area, with promenades along the beach, dunes to climb, and nature preserves to explore. You could start with the **promenade des fleurs** (Bloemenwandeling), with 5 signposted mi beside willow-lined avenues, gardens, and mansions. Or walk into the surrounding countryside, a picture-book setting of green fields and whitewashed farmhouses with red-tile roofs. Tourist boards offer mapped walking routes (*wandelroutes*), and you can cycle along signed bike paths or ride on horse trails along the routes as well.

Gent

WORD OF MOUTH

"Gent is a highly overlooked city in my opinion. I spent many days there for years on business and do love the place. It was once one of the most important cities and ports in Europe and the world, and because of that it's steeped in great Flemish art and architecture and modern European ambience."

—PalenQ

"A piece of Gent I really like a lot is the part behind the Castle of the Counts, along the river Lieve. It's very peaceful and quiet."

—stardust

Updated by
Tim Skelton

GENT (ALSO CALLED GHENT IN English, Gand in French) originated at the confluence of the rivers Leie and Schelde. It is said that Gent is the child of Leie (personified as Lise) and Schelde (personified as Scaldus). These two figures have become symbols of the city and often appear on civic buildings, such as the old fish market, the Vismijn. The city's early anchors were two 7th-century abbeys, Sint-Pieter (St. Peter) and Sint-Baafs (St. Bavo), and the 9th-century castle of Gravensteen.

Although set far from the coast, the settlement was still open to foreign marauders, such as Viking raiders who maneuvered canoes along the shallow inland rivers to raid the town's treasures. Baldwin of the Iron Arm, the region's first ruler, built a castle to protect his burgeoning kingdom; thus, Gent became the seat of the counts of Flanders. In the 13th century, Gent and Brugge were joined by canal, and 100 years later Gent had attracted more than 5,000 textile workers.

Wealthy burghers were loyal to the counts of Flanders in the early Middle Ages and owed allegiance to the kings of France. However, the weavers were dependent on wool shipments from England, France's enemy in the Hundred Years' War. In 1302, at the crux of the conflict between nations, the weavers took up arms against the French and defeated them in a battle that, to this day, is vividly recalled by Flemish patriots.

In 1448 the people of Gent refused to pay a salt tax imposed by Philip the Good, Duke of Burgundy. For five years their militia stood firm against Philip's troops, and when they were finally overwhelmed, 16,000 townspeople perished. Gent continued to rebel, again and again, against perceived injustices. The emperor himself, Charles V, who was born in Gent, was not immune to their wrath. He responded by razing the St. Bavo Abbey, tearing down the ancient city gates and walls, and suppressing the rights of Gent's citizens. Religious fervor was added to this volatile mixture when the Calvinist iconoclasts proclaimed the city a republic in 1577, only to be overthrown by Spanish forces seven years later. In the 18th century, French armies marched on Gent on four different occasions. This did little to dampen the conflict between French and Flemish speakers in the city.

Gent was rescued from economic oblivion by a daring young merchant named Lieven Bauwens, who, at the end of the 18th century, smuggled a spinning mule out of Britain in a reversal of what had happened hundreds of years earlier, when Flemish weavers emigrated to England. Bauwens's risky exploit, at a time when industrial spying was punishable by death, provided the foundation for a cotton textile industry that employed 160,000 workers a century later.

To facilitate textile exports, in 1822 a new canal was built to link Gent's inland port with the North Sea at Terneuzen, and Gent again became a major trade center. Today the canal is still vital to modern industrial development, including the automobile assembly plant that uses the canal to transport huge car carriers. Thus, while the city of Brugge emerged as a tourist center renowned for its cultural sights, Gent transformed its historic center into a commercial area of almost

TOP REASONS TO VISIT

Avoid the Crowds. The medieval center of Gent is barely less gorgeous than Brugge, but while tourists swarm over the latter like bees around a honeypot, this is somewhere you won't have to queue all day to see.

Eat, Drink, and Be Merry. When it comes to dining, Gent boasts some of Belgium's best regional specialties. Favorites include *waterzooi* (creamy chicken broth) and *paling in't groen* (eel in green sauce). Wash them down with a glass of the local beer, Karmeliet Tripel, which is pretty good, too.

A Brew with a View. Gent's canalside Graslei is one of the country's prettiest locations, and is lined with cafés and restaurants. In fine weather its terraces provide the perfect place to sit and watch the world literally float past.

5

400,000 residents. The Leie's nickname, the Golden River, took on an unfortunate tinge as it came to reflect the color of the river's chemical pollutants. Things have much improved in the last 10 years; the Leie has been cleaned up, tourism is booming, and the city's prestigious university attracts students from all over the world. This influx of international young people gives Gent an especially vibrant, energetic feel—the city may be historic, but it isn't locked into the past.

ORIENTATION & PLANNNING

GETTING ORIENTED

Located midway between Brugge and Brussels, Gent is the capital of the East Flanders Province. Its canals, gables, castles, beguinages, medieval lanes, art masterpieces, and settings that recall Breugel paintings beautifully mix with modern facades and street-side fashions. In the 16th century, only Paris was a greater European power than Gent, so it isn't surprising that it has more monuments than any other Belgian city or that it's the biggest city in the province.

PLANNING

GETTING HERE & AROUND

By Air Although Ostend-Bruges International Airport may be the nearest airport, it doesn't have regular flights. It's far easier to fly to Brussels (Zaventem) and rent a car or travel by train from there to Gent, which is only 67 km (42 mi) away.

By Bike Maps with suggested cycling routes are available at the tourist office. Biking in Gent is fairly safe: the center is a low-traffic zone and on many other streets the speed limit is only 30 KPH (20 MPH). Be careful when biking outside of town; although most roads have a cycle path, not all of them are safe.

Bikes can be rented at rental shops or the ticket window at Sint-Pieters railway station. (If you have a valid train ticket, you get a discounted rate.) Both adult (with or without baby seats) and children's bikes are available.

By Boat Several companies can take you on 40- to 90-minute boat rides on the waterways of Gent from around €5.50. For trips within Flanders, consider a motorboat afternoon or day trip from Gent along the river Leie to Deurle and Sint-Martens-Latem, the beautiful countryside southwest of the city, with Benelux Boats. The company Minerva Boten allows you to steer your own boat. A two-hour journey for four people costs €52; an eight-hour trip costs €175.

See By Ferry, in Getting Here & Around in Travel Smart Belgium for information regarding ferry service to and from the United Kingdom.

By Bus & Tram De Lijn has one trolley, three trams, and dozens of bus lines. There are stops all over town, and most buses run every 10 to 15 minutes. You can buy a ticket (€1.60) or a day pass (€6) on board, but you will save money if you buy the ticket (€1.20) or pass (€5) in advance from the terminal. If you travel with at least five people, buy a group ticket, which will save even more money. There are buses that run on six routes, every 45 minutes throughout the night on Friday and Saturday evenings.

If you arrive in Gent by train, take tram 1, 11, or 12 for the city center. The fare, which you can buy on the tram, costs €1.60. You can also buy a pass for a day's worth of tram travel for €6. Buy tickets in advance at the machines at the tram terminus by Gent Sint-Pieters train station, and the fares drop to €1.20 or €5, respectively; the machines only take bills of small denominations.

By Car The main highways, situated to the south of the city, are easy to find from the city center. From Brussels, Gent is reached via the E40 highway, which continues to Brugge and the coast; get off at exit 9. From Antwerp, take the E17, which continues to Paris. Both the E40 and E17 take you very close to the city center, which is indicated by a white sign that reads Centrum. Traffic can be heavy on these roads during rush hour, and on summer weekends traffic on both highways can be bumper-to-bumper. Gent's parking lots are clearly indicated as you go into the city; ask which one your hotel is closest to when you make your reservation, and then drive in and follow the signs.

If you'd like to visit the battlefields from Gent, driving is definitely the best option. You can drive to Kortrijk on the E17 or on to Ieper on the A19. Poperinge is another 15 km (9½ mi) to the west on the N38.

By Taxi There are taxi stands at the railway station and at major squares. Taxis are metered and the rates are reasonable, but public transport is always a cheaper way of getting around.

By Train The Belgian national railway, NMBS/SNCB, sends two non-stop trains every hour to Gent from Brussels (35 minutes); they all pass through Brussels' three main stations. There's also a frequent direct train connection from Brussels airport to Gent which takes about an hour. Trains run twice an hour from Antwerp, as well. They take you to Gent in a little less than 50 minutes.

TOURING GENT

For a personal guide, call **Gidsenbond van Gent en Oost-Vlaanderen (Association of Gent Guides)** (☎09/233–0772 ⊕*www.gidsenbond-gent.be* ☉*Weekdays 9–12:30*). The charge is €60 for the first two hours, €30 per additional hour; you can make your own itinerary or choose from several themed walks. **Vizit** (☎09/233–7689 ⊕*www.vizit.be*) organizes lively walks, including a couple of kids-oriented tours, that are full of tales of the city's past and present. Prices are €55–€65.

VISITOR INFORMATION

Gent's tourist bureau has English-speaking staff and is open daily. Tours with the guide association Gidsenbond van Genten can be booked here. Another good resource for Gent is an online "urban dissection kit," **www.use-it.be.** This site (with English translations) is geared for students and other finger-on-the-pulse travelers, with write-ups on Gent's bars, music stores and clubs, cultural institutions, inexpensive restaurants, and the like.

ESSENTIALS

Bike Rental Biker (⊠*Steendam 16* ☎09/224–2903). **Sint-Pieters** (☎09/241–2224).

Boat & Ferry Companies Benelux Boats (⊠*Recollettenlei 32* ☎09/225–1505). **Boat in Gent** (⊠*Kraanlei* ☎0478/63-36-30 ⊕*www.boatingent.be*). **Minerva Boten** (⊠*Lindelei 2a* ☎09/233–7917 ⊕*www.minervaboten.be*). **Norfolk Line** (☎02/719–9092, 0844/499-0007 in U.K. ⊕*www.norfolkline.com*). **P & O Ferries** (☎070/70-77-71, 08716/645-645 in U.K. ⊕*www.poferries.com*). **Seafrance** (☎02/549-0882, 0871/423-7119 in U.K. ⊕*www.seafrance.com*). **Superfast Ferries** (☎50/25-22-52, 01383/608-003 in U.K. ⊕*www.superfast.com*).

Car Rentals Avis (⊠*Kortrijkse Steenweg 676* ☎09/222–0053 ⊕*www.avis.be*). **Europcar** (⊠*Einde Were 1* ☎09/226–8126 ⊕*www.europcar.be*). **Hertz** (⊠*Nieuwewandeling 76* ☎09/224–0406 ⊕*www.hertz.be*).

Emergency Contacts Ambulance (☎100). **Duty doctors** (☎09/236–5000). **Night pharmacies** (☎09/001–0500). **Police** (☎101).

Internet Café The Globetrotter (⊠*Kortrijksepoortstraat 180* ☎09/269–0860 ☉*Mon.–Sat. noon–midnight*).

Post Office De Post Centrum Gent (⊠*Lange Kruisstraat 55* ☎09/269–2750).

Train Contacts NMBS/SNCB (☎02/555-2525 ⊕*www.b-rail.be*).

Train Station Gent Sint-Pieters (⊠*Kon. Maria Hendrikaplein* ☎09/221–4444).

Tram Contacts De Lijn (Oost-Vlaanderen) (☎09/210–9311 *East Flanders* ⊕*www.delijn.be*).

Visitor Info Gent (✉ *Botermarkt 17A, under the Belfry* ☎ *09/266–5660* ⊕ *www. visitgent.be)*. **Toerisme Oost-Vlaanderen** (✉ *Sint-Niklaasstraat 2* ☎ *09/269–2600* ⊕ *www.tov.be)*.

TAKE IT ALL IN

1 Day: Arrive in Gent as early as possible and begin your tour with a classic view of the city's three towers from St. Michael's bridge. Divide the rest of your day between the guild houses of the Graslei district, the Gothic cathedral, and the Gravensteen, the ancient castle of the counts of Flanders. After a dinner in the lively Patershol area, take a walk around the illuminated historic district.

3 Days: Follow the previous itinerary but spend two nights in Gent. On the second day you'll have extra time to visit the city's attractions and museums. You could also explore the Leie river area by bike or motorboat. If you haven't already done so, take the last day to explore the rural countryside of western Flanders, stopping at serene villages and the World War I sights around Ieper *(see Historic Battlegrounds, Chapter 2)*.

EAT RIGHT, SLEEP WELL

In Gent, high-class establishments stand next to modest brasseries where you can enjoy just a drink or a snack. Although many serve food all day long, it's safer to respect regular lunch and dinner hours, which are noon to 2 and 6 to 9. Regional specialties include *waterzooi* (traditional Flemish stew, usually with chicken or seafood) and *paling in't groen* (eel in a green-herb sauce). A 16% service charge and a 19% V.A.T. are always included in the tab. Although tipping is not unknown, you don't need to leave a tip unless you receive exceptional service. Rounding up the bill is sufficient.

Bustling Gent's accommodations are often sleek and modern, and there are several stylish hotels in historic buildings. However, hotels generally target weekend and short-term guests. The tourist office can help you make reservations for some of the inns and B&Bs in Gent as well as in the surrounding countryside. These quirky, moderately priced places are often in historic buildings, and usually include a hearty Belgian breakfast: bread, cereal, cold cuts, cheese, yogurt, eggs, and fruit. Half-board meal plans are also frequently available.

WHAT IT COSTS IN EUROS				
¢	$	$$	$$$	$$$$
Restaurants	under €10	€10–€15	€15–€20	€20–€30	over €30
Hotels	under €75	€75–€100	€100–€150	€150–€225	over €225

Restaurant prices are for a main course at dinner, including tax and tip. Hotel prices are for two people in a standard double room in high season, on the European Plan (EP, with no meals) unless otherwise noted. Costs include 6% tax.

EXPLORING GENT

Getting around Gent has recently gotten easier as the city has formally established neighborhood names for the various historic areas in the city center. You'll find neighborhood signposts and sightseeing brochures (in several languages, including English) as you explore. The designated neighborhoods are generally named for a major landmark and include: Gravensteen, also known as Patershol (around the namesake castle, bounded by Kraanlei, Lange Steenstraat, and Geldmunt); Oud Begijnhof, northwest of the Gravensteen; Minnemeers, around the Museum voor Industriele Archeologie en Textiel; Vrijdagmarkt; Portus Ganda, around the quays on the Leie, east of the center; Torenrij, the area around Sint-Michielsbrug; Kouter, covering the streets around its namesake square; Klein Begijnhof; Bijloke; Sint-Pietersplein, around the train station; and Citadelpark.

One of the nicest neighborhoods to explore is the Gravensteen area, once the residential quarter for the textile workers from the Gravensteen. Its layout is medieval but its spirit is modern—the streets are now crammed with chic cafés and restaurants. It's the in place to live for well-off young couples.

Gent is also pursuing a few major water-based projects. More of the city's waterways are being opened to the public, after several decades spent covered up or built over. A new public marina in Portus Ganda area opened in April 2005. This large marina in the eastern part of the city has a dock for up to 80 boats. It's accessible by canal, so Gent can now be reached by pleasure craft from other Belgian cities as well as Holland, France, and the United Kingdom. **De Gentse Barge,** a reconstruction of an 18th-century barge, was launched in summer 2003. This masterpiece of carving and ornamentation is a close copy of a ship used to ferry kings, ministers, and diplomats between Gent and Brugge. It's now moored at the port at Rigakaai where it can be booked by groups ✉*Gent Port Dept.* ☎*0473/48–26–59* ⊕*www.gentsebarge.be.*

Gent's old town has been almost totally restored to its original form, and it now has the largest pedestrian area in Flanders. You'll have to walk along cobblestone streets and pavements, which can be tricky if you wear high-heeled shoes or open sandals. The city center looks like a puzzle piece, surrounded as it is by the river Leie, its tributaries, and canals. Although many people live and work in this area, most reside in neighboring quarters.

TIMING Remember that municipal museums are usually closed Monday. Also keep in mind that some sights, such as the Gravensteen and the Belfort, stop admitting visitors 30–45 minutes before closing time. Although most sites are closed in the evening, many of the prime buildings are illuminated and the view from the bridge at night is stunning—the best view is via a canal-side stroll in late evening.

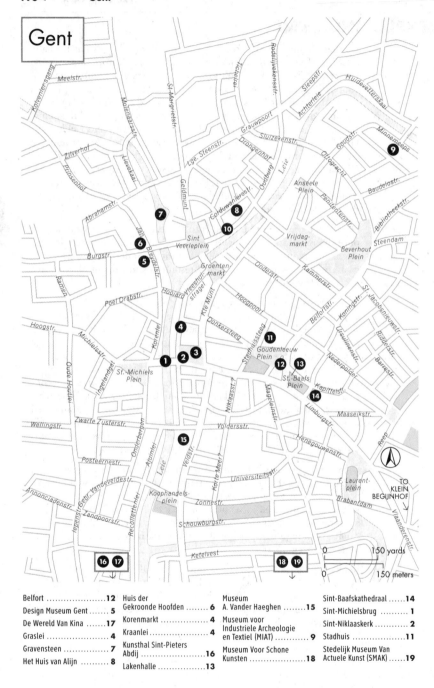

Belfort **12**	Huis der
Design Museum Gent **5**	Gekroonde Hoofden **6**
De Wereld Van Kina **17**	Korenmarkt **4**
Graslei **4**	Kraanlei **4**
Gravensteen **7**	Kunsthal Sint-Pieters
Het Huis van Alijn **8**	Abdij **16**
	Lakenhalle **13**

Museum	Sint-Baafskathedraal **14**
A. Vander Haeghen **15**	Sint-Michielsbrug **1**
Museum voor	Sint-Niklaaskerk **2**
Industriele Archeologie	Stadhuis **11**
en Textiel (MIAT) **9**	Stedelijk Museum Van
Museum Voor Schone	Actuele Kunst (SMAK) **19**
Kunsten **18**	

WHAT TO SEE

⑱ CITADELPARK

Museum voor Schone Kunsten. Built in 1902 at the edge of Citadelp[ark] the neoclassical Museum of Fine Arts is one of Belgium's best. museum's holdings span the Middle Ages to the early 20th century including works by Rubens, Gericault, Corot, Ensor, and Magritte. Its collection of Flemish Primitives is particularly noteworthy, with two paintings by Hieronymus Bosch, *Saint Jerome* and *The Bearing of the Cross*. ⊠ *Fernand Scribedreef 1, Citadelpark* ☎ *09/240–0700* ⊕ *www. mskgent.be* ⌧ *€5* ⊗ *Tues.–Sun. 10–6.*

⑲ Stedelijk Museum van Actuele Kunst (SMAK). Housed in a former casino, the Municipal Museum for Contemporary Art is one of Belgium's most innovative spaces, with constantly morphing displays of post-1945 art. Art by Bacon, Nauman, Panamarenko, Broodthaers, and Long, and the CoBrA (Copenhagen, Brussels, and Amsterdam) group make regular appearances. Performance art is also a highlight. There is some descriptive material in English. ⊠ *Citadelpark* ☎ *09/221–1703* ⊕ *www.smak. be* ⌧ *€5* ⊗ *Tues.–Sun. 10–6.*

5

GRAVENSTEEN/PATERSHOL

❺ Design Museum Gent. Peek into Gent's past in this decorative arts and design museum in an 18th-century burgher's house. Furnished interiors show styles from the Renaissance to the 19th century, including an extensive collection of crafts and designs. In the first-floor wooden room, even the chandelier is made of intricately carved wood. One wing is dedicated to such 20th-century themes as Art Nouveau, Art Deco, and contemporary designs. In the inner courtyard stands a huge flower vase, said to be the largest in the world at 30 feet tall. There are some brochures available in English. ⊠ *Jan Breydelstraat 5, Gravensteen/Patershol* ☎ *09/267–9999* ⊕ *design.museum.gent.be* ⌧ *€2.50* ⊗ *Tues.–Sun. 10–6.*

❹ Graslei. This magnificent row of guild houses in the original port area ★ is best seen from across the river Leie on the **Korenlei** (Corn Quay). The guild house of the **Metselaars** (Masons) is a copy of a house from 1527; the original, which stands near the Sint-Niklaaskerk, has also been restored. The **Eerste Korenmetershuis** (the first Grain Measurer's House), representing the grain weigher's guild, is next. It stands next to the oldest house of the group, the brooding, Romanesque **Koornstapelhuis** (Granary), which was built in the 12th century and served its original purpose for 600 years; this was where the grain claimed by the tax collectors was stored. It stands side by side with the narrow Renaissance **Tolhuis** (Toll House), where taxes were levied on grain shipments. No. 11 is the **Tweede Korenmetershuis** (Grain Measurers' House), a late Baroque building from 1698. The **Vrije Schippers** (Free Bargemen), at No. 14, is a late Gothic building from 1531, when the guild dominated inland shipping. Almost opposite this, across the water at No. 7 Korenlei, is the **Huis der Onvrije Schippers** (Unfree Bargemen), built in 1740 and decorated with a gilded boat. The free bargemen had right of passage along the canals inside the city; the had to unload their cargoes outside the city, and transfer them boats of the guild of free bargemen. Every night the Graslei and other historic monuments are illuminated from sunset to midnight. *Graslei, Gravensteen/Patershol.*

Gravensteen. Surrounded by a moat, the Castle of the Counts of Flanders resembles an enormous battleship steaming down the sedate Lieve Canal. From its windswept battlements there's a splendid view over the rooftops of old Gent. There has been a fortress on this site for centuries. The Gravensteen, modeled after a Syrian crusader castle, was built in 1180 by the Count of Flanders on top of an existing fortress, and has been rebuilt several times since then—most recently in the 19th century to reflect what the Victorians thought a medieval castle should look like. Above the entrance is an opening in the shape of a cross, which symbolizes the count's participation in the Crusades, resulting in his death in the Holy Land.

Today's brooding castle has little in common with the original fortress, built by Baldwin of the Iron Arm to discourage marauding Norsemen. Its purpose, too, changed from protection to oppression as the conflict deepened between feudal lords and unruly townspeople. Rulers entertained and feasted here throughout the Middle Ages, and the Council of Flanders, the highest court in the land, met in chambers here for over 500 years. At various times the castle has also been used as a mint, a prison, and a cotton mill. It was here, too, that the country's first spinning mule was installed after being spirited away from England; soon the castle's chambers echoed with the clattering of looms, and Gent became a textile center to rival Manchester.

The castle also houses a historical weapons museum, with armor, swords, pikes, and crossbows, as well as torture instruments dating from the times of the Council of Flanders. One of the rooms contains a gruesome display of pain-causing implements, and an oubliette is under the building. Spiraling passageways marked by signpost arrows wind through this imposing maze of cold rooms, and the slits in the stones where soldiers launched crossbow arrows and poured boiling oil over unfortunate foes will be of special interest to fans of feudal warfare. If weapons aren't your glass of beer, you can at least enjoy the view from the castle tower. ⊠ *Sint-Veerleplein, Gravensteen/Patershol* ☎ *09/225–9306* ⊠ *€6* ⊗ *Apr.–Sept., daily 9–6; Oct.–Mar., daily 9–5.*

❽ Het Huis van Alijn. The Folklore Museum, the Kraanlei waterfront, and the ancient Patershol district behind it form an enchanting ensemble. The museum includes several settings, including 18 medieval almshouses surrounding a garden, reconstructed to offer an idea of life here 100 years ago. You'll also find a Gent version of Williamsburg, Virginia, with a grocer's shop, tavern, weaver's workshop, and washroom. The chemist's shop features 17th- to 19th-century pharmacy items, and the pipe and tobacco collection has a large selection of snuff, pouches, and tools. The visitors' route takes you from the houses to the chapel and out through the crypt. Children are often drawn to the giant pageant figures, board games, and frequent shows in the beamed-and-brick puppet theater. The star is "Pierke," the traditional Gent puppet. There are some English-language brochures available. ⊠*Kraanlei 65, Gravensteen/Patershol* ☎*09/269–2350* ⊕*www.huisvanalijn.be* ☜*€5* ⊙*Tues.–Sat. 11–5, Sun. 10–5.*

➏ Huis der Gekroonde Hoofden. Busts of the counts of Flanders decorate the facade of the Crowned Heads' House, a distinctive Renaissance building, which dates from 1559. The lowest row includes the sculpted faces of Maximilian, who inherited Flanders through Mary of Burgundy; his son Philip; his grandson Charles V; and Philip of Spain, Charles's son. A plan in the window will tell you who's who. Inside is the popular brasserie **De Gekroonde Hoofden** (evenings only), which serves up tasty steaks and spareribs (¢–$). ⊠*Burgstraat 4, Gravensteen/Patershol* ☎*09/233–3774.*

NEED A BREAK?

Poesjkine (⊠*Jan Breydelstraat 12, Gravensteen/Patershol* ☎*09/224–2919*) is a popular spot for a caffeine fix—or a simple, sinful indulgence. Knowing locals recommend the cream and chocolate desserts. It's closed Tuesday and Wednesday, and the first two weeks of August.

➌ Korenmarkt. The main Corn Market square is fringed with gabled buildings, cafés, and shops; it's also the site of one of the city's busiest tram stops. Adjoining the square, along Korte Munt, is the Groentenmarkt, the former vegetable market and site of the infamous pillory used in the Middle Ages. ⊠*Next to Sint-Niklaaskerk, Gravensteen/Patershol.*

NEED A BREAK?

Drop by **Het Groot Vleeshuis** (*Great Meat Hall* ⊠*Groentenmarkt 7, Gravensteen/Patershol* ☎*09/223–2324*) for coffee or lunch and a spot of toothsome shopping. The wood-beamed hall dates from the early 15th century and was used as a covered meat market. Today it is used as a covered market for regional products. It's an impressive blend of ancient and modern; the metal-and-glass restaurant and promotional center inside have been cleverly constructed without affecting the old hall itself. Both shop and restaurant focus on East Flemish specialties such as Ganda ham, local mustard, and O'de Flandres jenever. It is also a good place to try the local specialty waterzooi. The hall is open from 10–6 and closed Monday.

You could also look for a table on the pleasant terrace of **Het Waterhuis aan de Bierkant** (⊠*Groentenmarkt 9* ☎*09/225–0680*), which overlooks the canal. The menu lovingly if eccentrically describes 150 different beers. Simple, inexpensive snacks include a selection of pungent local cheeses. It opens at 11 and stays open as long as "serious people keep walking the streets," as the owners say.

➓ Kraanlei. At the top of the narrow waterfront, medieval Crane Lane is the guild house of the Kraankinders (men of small stature who worked the cranes to unload the barges). Opposite, above a former wine merchant's house, is Gent's version of the *Manneken Pis,* a cute, pudgy statue relieving himself. Locals claim this figure is older than its coun-

CLOSE UP

Beguinages & Belfries

Composer Cole Porter may have popularized the beguine (a vigorous dance of Martinique and St. Lucia) in the splendor of the tropics, but here the word refers to a single woman who resided independently of her family in a peaceful, secular garden complex called a *begijnhof* (in Flemish) or beguinage. Beguinages date from the 13th century, but today, those who live in the dozen or so beguinages found in the region are most often widows and orphaned daughters. Some have also become homes for low-income families. Beguinages were founded during the Crusades by a priest named Lambert le Begue and were found throughout Europe until the Reformation. The best beguinages are in Flanders, including in Gent and Brugge—and, increasingly, many are occupied by female artisans rather than beguines.

Flanders also has numerous belfries, many of which are centrally located civic towers with carillons. The imposing towers once functioned as brick storehouses where medieval merchants protected their goods and kept their records. They were also used as lookout towers to watch for enemy attacks. In current times, citizens still use them as meeting places, and many are landmark tourist sites. Brugge, Gent, Ieper, and many smaller villages have outstanding old belfries, usually on large squares.

terpart in Brussels. Farther along the street, you can see two Baroque houses with elaborately decorated facades. A figure of a flute player crowns the old No. 79 (present-day No. 55); the house dates from 1669 and has panels representing the five senses. The panels of old No. 77 (present-day No. 57) illustrate six acts of mercy; hospitality to travelers was considered the seventh act of mercy, as the building was once an inn. ⊠ *Kraanlei at the corner of Rodekoning, Gravensteen/Patershol.*

KLEIN BEGIJNHOF

Klein Begijnhof. Founded in 1234 by Countess Joanna of Constantinople, the Small Beguinage is the best preserved of Gent's three beguinages. Protected by a wall and portal, the surrounding petite homes with individual yards were built in the 17th and 18th centuries, but are organized in medieval style. Each house has a statue of a saint and a spacious lawn; a few are still occupied by genuine Beguines leading the life stipulated by their founder 750 years ago. You can walk quietly through the main building and peek into the stone chapel—the houses, however, are off-limits. ⊠ *Lange Violettestraat 71, Klein Begijnhof.*

KOUTER

⑮ Museum Arnold Vander Haeghen. Three of Gent's favorite locals are honored in this 18th-century former governor's home. Nobel Prize–winning playwright and poet Maurice Maeterlinck (1862–1949) kept a library in this elegant, neoclassical building, and it still contains his personal objects, letters, and documents. A cabinet showcases work by the artists Stuyvaert, who illustrated Maeterlinck's publications, and the painter Doudelet. Look for the exceptional 18th-century silk wall decorations in the Chinese salon. There's no descriptive informa-

tion in English. ✉ *Veldstraat 82, near Kouter* ☎ *09/269–8460* 🎫 *Free*
🕐 *Weekdays 9:30–noon and 2–4:30.*

MINNEMEERS

⑨ **Museum voor Industriele Archeologie en Textiel (MIAT).** The Industrial
Archaeology and Textiles Museum occupies a Lancashire-style textile
mill—appropriately enough, as it holds the famous spinning mule spirited from Lancashire, England to Flanders by Gent native Lieven Bauwens, sparking a rival textile industry. The "mule-jenny" can be seen
on the museum's fifth floor, from which there are stunning views of the
rooftops and spires of Gent. This floor is also the best place to start
following the exhibits on the Industrial Revolution and subsequent
technological innovations. The cotton mill area is filled with spinning
wheels and weaving machines; there are demonstrations every Tuesday
and Thursday. (At other times, ask one of the staff.) You can pick up an
English-language explanatory brochure at the front desk. The gift shop
sells items spun and woven on-site. The museum also has a wonderful
little Cinepalace, a theater showing classic films on the second Sunday
of every month. In the garden in front of the museum stands a statue
of Pierre de Geyter, a Gent native who composed the "Internationale,"
the song of the international labor movement. Red flowers are placed
at his feet every May 1. ✉ *Minnemeers 9, Minnemeers* ☎ *09/269–4200*
⊕ *www.miat.gent.be* 🎫 *€2.50* 🕐 *Tues.–Sun. 10–6.*

SINT-PIETERSPLEIN

⑰ **De Wereld van Kina (Kind en Natuur).** This natural history museum shares
an ancient abbey with the Kunsthal Sint-Pieters Abdij *(see below).* Here
you'll find "school subjects" on geology, the evolution of life, human
biology and reproduction, and a diorama room of indigenous birds.
There's an Internet station and a sound-and-light show about Gent and
Emperor Charles V, featuring a large-scale model of 17th-century Gent.
✉ *Sint-Pietersplein 14, Sint-Pietersplein* ☎ *09/244–7373* 🎫 *€2.50*
🕐 *Weekdays 9–5, Sun. 2–5:30.*

⑯ **Kunsthal Sint-Pieters Abdij.** There has been an abbey on this site since
the 7th century, and during the Middle Ages it was one of the richest
and most important Flemish abbeys. Most of the Baroque buildings
you see today were built in the 17th century, however, and now house
the St. Peter's Abbey Arts Center. You can walk around the abbey, the
ruined gardens, and the cellars, where there is an exhibition about the
checkered history of the abbey and its monks. ✉ *Sint-Pietersplein 9*
☎ *09/243–9730* ⊕ *www4.gent.be/spa* 🎫 *€5* 🕐 *Tues.–Sun. and some
public holidays 10–6.*

TORENRIJ

⑫ **Belfort.** Begun in 1314, the 300-foot belfry tower symbolizes the power
of the guilds and used to serve as Gent's watchtower. Since 1377, the
structure has been crowned with a gilded copper weather vane shaped
into a dragon, the city's symbol of freedom. (The current stone spire
was added in 1913.) Inside the Belfort, documents listing the privi-
leges of the city (known as its *secreets*) were once kept behind triple-
locked doors and guarded by lookouts who toured the battlements

hourly to prove they weren't sleeping. When danger approached,
bells were rung—until Charles V
had them removed. Now a 53-bell
carillon, claimed by experts to be
one of the best in the world, is set
on the top floor. One of the original bells, the Triumphanta, cast in
1660 and badly cracked in 1914,
rests in a garden at the foot of the

> ### A GOOD TIP
>
> If your feet get tired, take one of
> the horse-drawn carriages that
> line up in the cathedral square,
> just outside the Belfort; a half-
> hour trip for up to four people
> costs €25.

tower. The largest original bell, Klokke Roeland, is still sung about in
Gent's anthem of the same name. The view from the tower is one of
the city's highlights. ⊠ *Sint-Baafsplein, Torenrij* ☎ *09/233–0772* ☒ *€3*
☺ *Mid-Mar.–mid-Nov., daily 10–6; mid-Nov.–mid-Mar., guided visits
on request only.*

⑬ Lakenhalle. Built as the center for the cloth trade in the 15th century,
the Cloth Hall was still unfinished when the trade collapsed. Its vaulted
cellar was used as a prison for 150 years; currently it houses the tourist
information center and serves as the entrance to the Belfort. From the
Lakenhalle you can enter a small adjacent building, formerly the prison
warder's lodging. Take a look at the ceiling, which dates from 1741; a
sculptured bas-relief depicts the ancient Roman story of Cimon who,
condemned to death by starvation, was visited daily by his daughter,
who breast-fed him. Locals call the building *De Mammelokker* ("The
Suckler"). ⊠ *Sint-Baafsplein, Torenrij.*

⑭ Sint-Baafskathedraal. St. Bavo's Cathedral, begun in the 13th century but
Fodor'sChoice finished in the 16th in the ornate Brabantine Gothic style, dramatically
★ rises from a low, unimposing entryway. It contains one of the greatest
treasures in Christendom: *De aanbidding van het Lam Gods* (*see The
Adoration of the Mystic Lamb*).

Emperor Charles V was christened here more than 500 years ago. The
cathedral was originally dedicated to St. John and it became the site
for the veneration of St. Bavo, Gent's own saint, after Charles V had
the old Abbey of St. Bavo razed. The Order of the Golden Fleece,
instituted in Brugge by Philip the Good in 1430, was convened here
in 1559 by Philip II of Spain. It is still in existence, currently presided
over by King Juan Carlos of Spain as grand master. The coats of arms
of the 51 knights who first belonged to the Order still hang in the south
transept. The cathedral's ornate pulpit, made of white Italian marble
and black Danish oak, was carved in the 18th century by the sculptor Laurent Delvaux. Angels, cherubs, massive trees, flowing robes,
and tresses combine to create a masterwork. A Rubens masterpiece,
Saint Bavo's Entry into the Monastery, hangs in one of the chapels.
Other treasures include a baroque-style organ built in 1623 and a crypt
crammed with tapestries, church paraphernalia, and 15th- and 16th-
century frescoes. ⊠ *Sint-Baafsplein 4, Torenrij* ☒ *Cathedral free, De
Villa Chapel €3, audiotape €0.50* ☎ *09/269–2065* ⊕ *www.visitgent.
be* ☺ *Cathedral: Apr.–Oct., Mon.–Sat. 8:30–6, Sun. 1–6; Nov.–Mar.,
Mon.–Sat. 8:30–5, Sun. 1–5. Chapel: Apr.–Oct., Mon.–Sat. 9:30–4:15,*

CLOSE UP

Adoration of the Mystic Lamb

Now in the De Villa Chapel of St. Bavo's Cathedral, in a glass case where you can see the back as well, this stupendous 12-paneled polyptych by Jan van Eyck and his brother was completed on May 6, 1432. Its history is as tumultuous as that of Gent itself: when the iconoclasts smashed St. Bavo's stained-glass windows and other treasures, the painting with its 24 oaken panels was hidden in the tower, and Napoléon later had it carried off to Paris. Joseph II of Austria found the panels of Adam and Eve prurient because of their naturalistically depicted human bodies—consequently, they disappeared and remained lost for 100 years. The other side panels were sold and hung in a Berlin museum.

In 1920 the masterpiece was again complete, but 14 years later a thief removed the panels on the lower left side. He returned the St. John the Baptist panel, but apparently died while waiting for a ransom for the panel of the Righteous Judges. The lost panel has never been recovered, but most people believe it is hidden somewhere in Gent, possibly even in the cathedral. (The current panel, on the far left, is a copy.) The whole altarpiece was sent to France for safekeeping during World War II, but the Germans located and stole it. American troops eventually discovered it in an abandoned salt mine in Austria.

Today it is yours to enjoy at leisure, accompanied if you wish by an excellent explanation on audiotape. The central panel is based on the Book of Revelations: "And I looked, and, lo, a Lamb stood on the mount Sion, and with him an hundred forty and four thousand, having his Father's name written in their foreheads." There are not quite that many people in the painting, but it does depict 248 figures and 42 different types of flowers, each botanically correct. But statistics do not even suggest its grandeur. It uses a miniaturist technique to express the universal; realism to portray spirituality; and the blood of the sacrificial lamb mixes with the fountain of life to redeem the world. To the medieval viewer, it was an artistic *Summa Theologica,* a summation of all things revealed about the relationship between God and the world. An old tradition identifies the horseman in the foreground of the panel, to the immediate left, as Hubert van Eyck, Jan's brother, while the fourth figure from the left is believed to be Jan himself. It is now thought by art historians that Hubert, once believed to be co-creator of the luminous oil panels, was merely the carver of the imposing wooden frame of the altarpiece. As for the paintings themselves, Jan used brushes so delicate that the finest consisted of a single boar's bristle.

5

Sun. 1–4:15; Nov.–Mar., Mon.–Sat. 10:30–3:15, Sun. 1–3:15 ☞*No visits to cathedral or chapel during services.*

❶ ★ **Sint-Michielsbrug.** The view of Gent from this spot is so perfect it should be patented as the Three Towers from St. Michael's Bridge. You'll see the three medieval towers of Sint-Niklaaskerk, the Belfort, and Sint-Baafskathedraal. This vantage point is the best place to begin a tour of the city; the bridge leads from the Korenmarkt to the Korenlei. ✉*Torenrij.*

② **Sint-Niklaaskerk.** St. Nicholas's Church was built in the 11th century in Romanesque style, but was destroyed a century later after two disastrous fires; it was later rebuilt by prosperous merchants. The tower, one of the many soaring landmarks of this city's famed skyline, dates from about 1300 and was the first belfry in Gent. During the French Revolution the church was used as a stable, and its treasures were ransacked. Further restoration began in the 1960s and was completed in 2000, renewing Belgian's best example of Scheldt-Gothic once again. ⊠ *Cataloniestraat, Torenrij* ☑ *Free* ⊘ *Mon. 2–5, Tues.–Sun. 10–5.*

⑪ **Stadhuis.** The Town Hall is an early example of what raising taxes can do to a city. In 1516 Antwerp's Domien de Waghemakere and Mechelen's Rombout Keldermans, two prominent architects, were called in to build a town hall that would put all others to shame. However, before the building could be completed, Emperor Charles V imposed new taxes that drained the city's resources. The architecture thus reflects the changing fortunes of Gent: the side built in 1518–60 and facing Hoogpoort is in Flamboyant Gothic style; when work resumed in 1580, during the short-lived Protestant Republic, the Botermarkt side was completed in a stricter and more economical Renaissance style; and later additions include Baroque and rococo features. The tower on the corner of Hoogpoort and Botermarkt has a balcony specifically built for making announcements and proclamations; lacelike tracery embellishes the exterior. This civic landmark is not usually open to the public, but you can arrange a tour through the Gidsenbond van Genten or see it on a guided tour offered through the city's tourist office. Look for the glorious Gothic staircase, the throne room, and the spectacularly decorated halls—the Pacificatiezaal hall is where the Pacification Treaty of Gent between Catholics and Protestants was signed. ⊠ *Botermarkt 1, Torenrij* ☎ *09/266–5111* ☑ *Tour €4* ⊘ *Tours May–Oct., Mon.–Thurs. at 2:30.*

NEED A BREAK?

Visit a Gent institution and waft into **Etablissement Max** (⊠ *Goudenleeuwplein 3, Torenrij* ☎ *09/223-9731*) for crispy yet soft-centered Belgian waffles. Try one topped with ice cream, whipped cream, and fruit (no guilt allowed). The informal, light-filled faux–art-nouveau dining room is always busy, awash in the scent of waffle batter and the aromas of Flemish specialties. Salads and sandwiches are also available if you want a light meal.

WHERE TO EAT

CITADELPARK

$$$–$$$$
BELGIAN
Fodor'sChoice
★

✕ **Jan van den Bon.** With room for 30, this distinguished restaurant is a local favorite for French and classic Belgian dishes, particularly seafood and seasonal specialties. White asparagus, for instance, is cooked and sauced to perfection. Sip your aperitif on the terrace overlooking the garden, which supplies the herbs used in the kitchen. ⊠ *Koning Leopold II Laan 43, Citadelpark* ☎ *09/221–9085* ⚏ *Reservations essential Jacket and tie* ⊟ *AE, DC, MC, V* ⊘ *Closed Sun. No lunch Sat.*

GRAVENSTEEN/PATERSHOL

¢–$
VEGETARIAN

✕**Avalon.** Head to this lunch spot near the Gravensteen for delicious organic, vegetarian meals—or soup or a snack. The menu features pasta, stews, and quiches. In good weather, try for a table on the terrace. Be sure to get here early, though—it's only open until 2 PM. ✉*Geldmunt 32, Gravensteen/Patershol* ☎*09/224–3724* ▭*No credit cards* ☺*Closed Sun. No dinner.*

COMING SOON

The **Stadsmuseum Gent (STAM)**, situated in a former 13th-century Cistercian abbey, closed its doors in September 2005. It will reopen in 2009, changing its name to STAM, an abbreviation of Stadsmuseum (city museum). The new museum will cover Gent's cultural history. ✉*Godshuizenlaan 2, Bijloke* ☎*09/225–1106*

$$–$$$
BELGIAN
Fodor'sChoice
★

✕**Belga Queen.** A magnificent restaurant in a magnificent location. The former corn warehouse bordering the Leie has been redesigned by the chef himself, Antoine Pino. The large terrace leads to the ground floor's impressive bar, high tables, and cozy leather seats. The menu has daily fresh suggestions and a three-course lunch is €16. There's a cigar bar with occasional live jazz on the top floor. ✉*Graslei 10, De Kuip* ☎*09/280–0100* ⚐*Reservations essential* ▭*AE, DC, MC, V.*

$$$
ECLECTIC

✕**De 3 Biggetjes.** The name means "the three little pigs," and you'll definitely be tempted to wolf down the wonderful food at this tiny, step-gabled building set on the cobbled Zeugsteeg, or Sow Lane. Even if you huff and puff a bit to get there, the cooking makes the trip worthwhile. The menu combines Belgian, Vietnamese, and French influences. Seafood dishes are a highlight; chef Ly Chi Cuong relies on the daily market for turbot, sole, and the like, while other ingredients are flown in from all over the world, even the Seychelles. There's also a small garden terrace at the back, open in summer. The set menus are a very good value. ✉*Zeugsteeg 7, Gravensteen/Patershol* ☎*09/224–4648* ⚐*Reservations essential* ▭*MC, V* ☺*Closed Wed. and Sun. No lunch Sat.*

$$$–$$$$
BELGIAN

✕**Jan Breydel.** A gardenlike setting makes this little bistro a great place to stop while exploring the historic town center. Proprietors Louis and Pat Hellebaut oversee the preparation of each dish, and the food is as fresh as the atmosphere. Regional ingredients are complemented by delicate sauces and seasonings. The sole with lime butter is excellent; for the more adventurous, there are veal kidneys and sweetbreads with mustard. The three-course set menu includes wine, and represents good value for money. ✉*Jan Breydelstraat 10, Gravensteen/Patershol* ☎*09/225–6287* ▭*AE, DC, MC, V* ☺*Closed Sun. and Mon.*

$$–$$$
BELGIAN

✕**'t Buikske Vol.** This cozy, popular, and chic restaurant is well suited to special occasions, as you're virtually guaranteed a sophisticated meal—and one with a dash of the pleasingly unpredictable. While the service and presentation are dependably good, the menu has some adventurous flavors, such as *fillet de biche* (doe steak), Angus beef with onion confit, and rabbit served with sweetbreads. ✉*Kraanlei 17, Gravensteen/Patershol* ☎*09/225–1880* ⚐*Reservations essential on weekends* ▭*AE, MC, V* ☺*Closed Wed., Sun., Easter wk, and 1st 2 wks of Aug.*

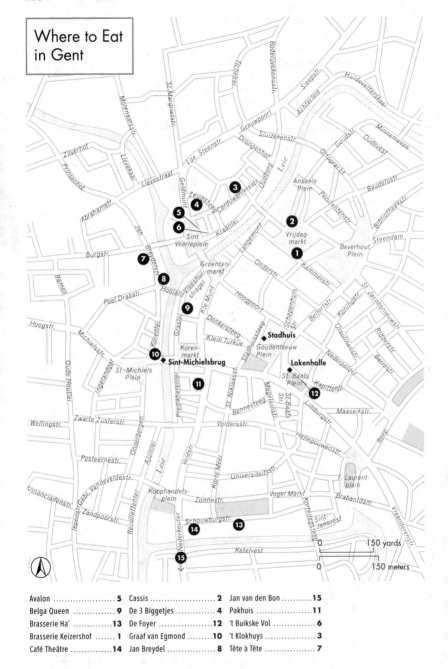

Where to Eat in Gent

$–$$
BELGIAN
✗ **'t Klokhuys.** The name "clockhouse" is already a clue, but once inside, the host of timepieces that occupy every spare inch of wall leave you in no doubt as to the theme. Curiously, however, they all seem to display different times. Elsewhere this traditional brasserie has tiled floors, marble tables, and leather banquettes, while dried hops hang from the ceiling. The food is hearty and delicious, and focuses on local specialties. Or for a splurge, why not select one of the lobsters from the tank? ⊠*Corduwaniersstraat 65, Gravensteen/Patershol* ☎*09/223–4241* ▤*AE, MC, V* ⊘*Closed Mon. No lunch Tues.*

$$–$$$
FRENCH
✗ **Tête à Tête.** Though memorably good, this restaurant doesn't get a lot of press—locals want to keep it for themselves. It's situated unassumingly on busy Jan Breydelstraat, so people tend to pass by without noticing. The kitchen draws on both French and Flemish cooking, with such specialties as bouillabaisse, salmon with a lime-inflected sauce, and duck in green-peppercorn sauce. Be sure to save room for one of the outstanding desserts. ⊠*Jan Breydelstraat 32–34, Gravensteen/ Patershol* ☎*09/233–9500* ⚓*Reservations essential* ▤*MC, V* ⊘*No lunch Mon.–Thurs.*

KOUTER

$$–$$$
CONTEMPORARY
✗ **Brasserie Ha'.** The building may be old—the 1739 Handelsbeurs, once the headquarters for the Imperial Guards of Empress Marie-Thérèse—but the interior is now cutting-edge, and unabashedly stylish. The food is equally chic—and tasty, too, with choices such as roast duck breast with wild mushrooms and a red wine sauce. Before or after a trip to the Sunday morning flower market on the Kouter square, come for the popular breakfast buffet (reservations essential) between 9 and 11. ⊠*Handelsbeursgebouw, Kouter 29, Kouter* ☎*09/265–9181* ▤*AE, MC, V* ⊘*No lunch or dinner Sun.*

$$–$$$
CONTEMPORARY
✗ **Café Theatre.** A persistent social buzz permeates this cosmopolitan brasserie in the shadow of the opera house. The huge bi-level space is decorated with columns, wrought iron, and whimsy (check out the restrooms). Luckily, the food is as good as the people-watching; you might try duck breast with caramelized figs or a stellar steak tartare—the house specialty, and supposedly the best in all of Flanders. After the meal, relax next door in the lounge bar, where you can taste 11 kinds of jenever. The restaurant closes during the annual Gent Festival, held between mid-July and mid-August; check ahead for the summer schedule. ⊠*Schouwburgstraat 5, Kouter* ☎*09/265–0550* ▤*AE, DC, V* ⊘*No lunch Sat.*

TORENRIJ

$$–$$$
BELGIAN
✗ **De Foyer.** The balcony terrace of this theater brasserie is a great place to retreat after visiting Sint-Baafskathedraal—you can watch the passersby on the square and listen to the cathedral's carillon. Inside, you can either sit at a small table or at the large, communal table at the bar, giving you the opportunity to chat with other visitors. The menu plays to the tried-and-true with light snacks, seafood, and steak frites, but also has more intricate dishes such as guinea fowl with Kriekbeer (cherry beer). All wines can be ordered by the glass. The large Sun-

day brunches, served between 9 and 11 AM, are well worth checking out. This is the rare place that's open on public holidays, plus there's free Wi-Fi access in the restaurant. ⊠*Sint-Baafsplein 17, Torenrij* ☎*09/225-3275* ▤*AE, MC, V* ⊘*No dinner Tues.*

$$-$$$
BELGIAN
✕**Graaf van Egmond.** Gaze at the famed spires of Gent from this 13th-century riverside house, then turn your attention to the menu. (Ask for the special Egmond menu for the best selection.) Choose from such dishes as lobster salad, grilled lamb, or *Gentse stoverij* (a traditional dish of beef stewed in beer). The restaurant's interior is lovely, with beamed ceilings, antique and reproduction pieces, and sparkling chandeliers. ⊠*Sint-Michielsplein 21, Torenrij* ☎*09/225-0727* ▤*AE, DC, MC, V.*

$$-$$$
BELGIAN
✕**Pakhuis.** At peak times, this enormously popular brasserie in an old warehouse off the Korenmarkt crackles with energy. A giant Greek statue makes an incongruous counterpoint to the marble-top tables, parquet floors, and long oak bar. Locals rave about the seafood and the oyster bar; there's also more robust fare such as ham knuckle with sharp Gent mustard. The Pakhuis has become even more popular since it was featured in a popular Belgian TV series. ⊠*Schuurkenstraat 4, Torenrij* ☎*09/223-5555* ▤*AE, DC, MC, V* ⊘*Closed Sun.*

VRIJDAGMARKT

$-$$
BELGIAN
✕**Brasserie Keizershof.** When you're looking for a change from the familiar waterzooi, but are still in the mood for comfort food, try this inexpensive, touristy tavern. Light meals and snacks are available all day—toasted sandwiches, spaghetti—but bring an appetite, because portions are huge. There's always an inexpensive daily special, often the kind of food you would expect on a typical Flemish table. It can get quite busy, especially at noon, since the restaurant's size makes it a favorite of tour groups. ⊠*Vrijdagmarkt 47, Vrijdagmarkt* ☎*09/223-4446* ▤*MC, V* ⊘*Closed Sun. and Mon.*

$$-$$$
BELGIAN
★
✕**Cassis.** In a tranquil setting combining beamed ceilings, light wood, and wicker chairs, Cassis offers both traditional and modern Belgian specialties, as well as huge, inventive salads (for example, asparagus, shrimp, smoked salmon, and goat cheese) presented as artfully as a Flemish still life. For the best people-watching, sit on the terrace overlooking the Vrijdagmarkt while the market's in swing. ⊠*Vrijdagmarkt 5, Vrijdagmarkt* ☎*09/233-8546* ▤*AE, MC, V.*

WHERE TO STAY

GRAVENSTEEN/PATERSHOL

¢
▦**De Draeke Youth Hostel.** With its location on the edge of the Lieve canal, near the Gravensteen, this hostel makes a terrific base for city explorations. There are a half-dozen twin-bedded rooms, three rooms with three beds apiece, and the rest are dorm-style with four to six beds per room. Each room has its own bathroom. You need to pay an extra €3 per person if you're not a youth-hostel member, but the rates include breakfast and bedding. **Pros:** historic old building; waterside location;

close to sights. **Cons:** no elevator. ✉ *Sint-Widostraat 11, Prinsenhof* ☏ *09/233–7050* ⊕ *www.jeugdherbergen.be* ⤳ *27 rooms* ♿ *In-room: no a/c, no phone, no TV. In-hotel: restaurant, bar, Wi-Fi* ☰ *MC, V* ⦿ *BP.*

$$-$$$ ⬚**Gravensteen.** Steps from its namesake, this handsome 19th-century mansion exudes atmosphere—at least, from most angles. The public areas are ornate with carved stucco, a marble staircase, and a cupola. Hallways wind to small rooms with a more modern look; some have castle or canal views. Note that some rooms are in a newer, less attractive building at the back and that bathrooms are small, some with showers only. **Pros:** historic old building; close to center; friendly staff. **Cons:** on noisy street. ✉ *Jan Breydelstraat 35, Gravensteen/Patershol* ☏ *09/225–1150* ⊕ *www.gravensteen.be* ⤳ *49 rooms, 2 suites* ♿ *In-room: no a/c (some), Wi-Fi. In-hotel: bar, parking (paid)* ☰ *AE, DC, MC, V.*

> ## A YUMMY WALK
>
> For an original way to visit the city, contact **Vizit** (☏ *09/233–7689* ⊕ www.vizit.be), a private organization that also operates in Brugge, Oostende, and Brussels. Every Saturday they organize a "yummy" walk for €10, or an extensive walking dinner through town for €55–€75, which takes you to four different restaurants. One course from a four-course menu awaits you at each stop. Reservations are essential.

PORTUS GANDA

$$ ⬚**The Boatel.** Get a different perspective on Gent by staying aboard this 1953 riverboat docked on the Leie since Portus Ganda opened. A roughly 10-minute walk from the city center, the rebuilt vessel shows off sections of the original woodwork. Cabins are large and bright, particularly the two master bedrooms above the sea line. The wood floor of the sunny breakfast room can double as the evening gathering spot or even a small meeting room. Free parking is available on the road nearby. Even though it is tightly roped to the shore, remember that boats tend to rock a bit. **Pros:** friendly staff; your hotel is an actual riverboat. **Cons:** far from the sights. ✉ *Voorhoutkaai 44, Portus Ganda* ☏ *09/267–1030* ⊕ *www.theboatel.com* ⤳ *7 rooms* ♿ *In-room: no a/c* ☰ *AE, MC, V.*

SINT-PIETERSPLEIN/BIJLOKE

$ ⬚**Astoria.** That this brick building with large, shuttered windows was once a home won't surprise you once you see the bright rooms, breezily comfortable with cane chairs and tables, colorful bedspreads, and large wooden wardrobes. Public areas are done in warm colors, with wall sconces and accents of polished wood. The hotel is in a clean but somewhat bland residential area near train and tram stations. **Pros:** all rooms non-smoking; quiet location; good value. **Cons:** far from sights. ✉ *Achilles Musschestraat 39, behind Sint-Pieters station* ☏ *09/222–8413* ⊕ *www.astoria.be* ⤳ *18 rooms* ♿ *In-room: no a/c. In-hotel: parking (free)* ☰ *AE, DC, MC, V.*

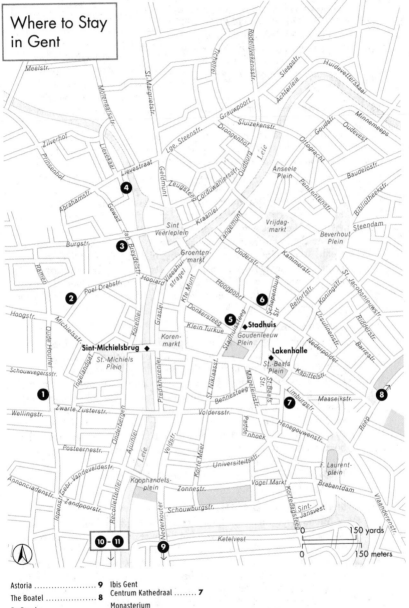

Where to Stay in Gent

$ ⛽ **Europahotel.** If you'd like to be within easy reach of outdoor activities and don't mind staying a mile away from the city center, consider this midsize pension. It's near the waterfront and the Blaarmeersen recreation center so you'll have water sports, windsurfing, and tennis close at hand. The large rooms are modern. In good weather, evening drinks are served on the lawn. The hotel is about half a mile from Sint-Pieters station and a quick tram ride away from the city center. **Pros:** quiet location; good value. **Cons:** far from sights; building lacks character. ✉ *Gordunakaai 59, Blaarmeersen, west of Bijloke* ☎ *09/222–6071* ⊕ *europahotel-gent.be* ⇌ *37 rooms* ⟳ *In-room: no a/c. In-hotel: bar, parking (free)* ▤ *AE, MC, V* ⍩ *BP.*

$$–$$$ ⛽ **NH Gent.** A cool, white exterior belies the warmth inside this central, midsize hotel. There's a grand piano in a comfortable lounge, paintings by local artists punctuate the walls, and a skylight in the breakfast room lets the light pour into the space. Executive rooms have large baths, as well as dining and sitting areas; two suites include fireplaces, CD players, and private terraces. **Pros:** comfortable rooms; friendly staff. **Cons:** a little way from the sights. ✉ *Koning Albertlaan 121, between Sint-Pieters station and Bijloke* ☎ *09/222–6065* ⊕ *www.nh-hotels.com* ⇌ *49 rooms, 2 suites* ⟳ *In-room: no a/c, safe, minibar, Wi-Fi. In-hotel: restaurant, room service, bar, laundry service, parking (free), Wi-Fi* ▤ *AE, DC, MC, V* ⍩ *BP.*

TORENRIJ

$$ ⛽ **Erasmus.** From the flagstone and wood-beam library-lounge to the
★ stone mantels in the individually decorated bedrooms, every inch of this noble 16th-century town house has been scrubbed, polished, and decked with period ornaments. Even the tiny garden has been carefully manicured. Peter Broos, who runs this distinctive hotel near the Korenlei takes care of everything from answering the room service bell pull at night to serving a delicious breakfast in the parlor. **Pros:** central location; friendly staff; personalized service. **Cons:** street noise can be a problem. ✉ *Poel 25, Torenrij* ☎ *09/224–2195* ⊕ *www.erasmushotel. be* ⇌ *12 rooms* ⟳ *In-room: no a/c. In-hotel: bar* ▤ *AE, MC, V* ⊗ *Closed mid-Dec.–mid-Jan.*

$–$$ ⛽ **Ibis Gent Centrum Kathedraal.** Location is this hotel's trump card: it's close to the cathedral. As in most branches of this popular European chain, rooms have cookie-cutter modern decor and requisite amenities. This Ibis has a dependable level of service and comfort, but lacks local character. Triples are available. There's another branch, Ibis Gent Centrum Opera, close to the Flemish Opera building; some of its rooms are a tad cheaper. **Pros:** close to sights; good value for location. **Cons:** part of a chain, so lacks character; there's a charge for parking. ✉ *Limburgstraat 2, Torenrij* ☎ *09/233–0000* ⊕ *www.ibishotel.com* ⇌ *120 rooms* ⟳ *In-room: no a/c. In-hotel: restaurant, bar, parking (paid), Wi-Fi* ▤ *AE, DC, MC, V* ⍩ *BP.*

$–$$ ⛽ **Monasterium PoortAckere.** A complex comprising a former abbey, convent, and beguinage now provides a serene place to stay in a central neighborhood. Some sections date back to the 13th century; most of the buildings, though, are 19th-century Gothic Revival. There are large, comfortable rooms in the Monasterium, the former convent, while in the adjacent convent former cells have been transformed into small guest rooms with a washbasin, shared showers, and toilets. You can take breakfast and dinner in the chapter house. **Pros:** quiet location; beautiful old building. **Cons:** some rooms have shared bathroom; some rooms have no elevator access as one wing has no elevator. ⊠*Oude Houtlei 56, Torenrij* ☎*09/269–2210* ⊕*www.monasterium.be* ⬅*56 rooms, 13 without bath* ♿*In-room: no a/c, no phone, Internet (some). In-hotel: restaurant, bar, parking (paid)* ⊟*AE, DC, MC, V* ⎮O⎮*BP.*

$$$$ ⊞**NH Gent–Belfort.** In the heart of the old city, this grand hotel mirrors the elegance of the renowned Spanish chain. The hotel has undergone a complete redecoration since NH inherited the property from the Sofitel group in 2007. Warming red with sandy-beige color schemes in the rooms, and chic modern styles throughout, help it stick to a business-friendly look. Spacious rooms are well-equipped; some are bi-level, with a second TV. Great weekend deals are available if you book in advance. **Pros:** great location; friendly staff; all-modern luxuries. **Cons:** it's part of a chain, albeit a very good one. ⊠*Hoogpoort 63, Torenrij* ☎*09/233–3331* ⊕*www.nh-hotels.com* ⬅*171 rooms, 3 suites* ♿*In-room: safe, minibar, Wi-Fi. In-hotel: restaurant, bar, gym, parking (paid), Wi-Fi* ⊟*AE, DC, MC, V.*

$$$ ⊞**Novotel Gent Centrum.** This modern hotel is not a shy, retiring type; the interior is done in bold colors and scads of white marble. Guest rooms, which are soundproof, have white laminate furniture, sofa beds, and large bathrooms. Specify your preferred view when you book; some windows overlook a landscaped courtyard with a pool, while others have city vistas. Some rooms have cathedral views. Check out the only element of the past: a medieval crypt, which now houses meeting area. Elsewhere, there's also a small fitness area and a sauna. **Pros:** centrally located; friendly staff. **Cons:** modern building lacks character; local one-way road system makes it difficult to find by car; limited parking. ⊠*Gouden Leeuwplein 5, Torenrij* ☎*09/224–2230* ⊕*www.novotel. com* ⬅*113 rooms, 4 suites* ♿*In-room: minibar, Wi-Fi. In-hotel: restaurant, bar, pool* ⊟*AE, DC, MC, V.*

NIGHTLIFE & THE ARTS

Check the "What's On" and "Other Towns" sections of the *Bulletin* to find schedules of the latest art shows and cultural events. You can find issues of the *Bulletin* in local newsstands and bookstores.

THE ARTS

CONCERTS

De Handelsbeurs (⊠*Kouter 29, Kouter* ☎*09/265–9160* ⊕*www.handels beurs.be*) is a concert hall for all kinds of music, from jazz, to folk, to world, to classical. **De Vlaamse Opera** (⊠*Schouwburgstraat 3, Kouter* ☎*09/225–2425* ⊕*www.vlaamseopera.be*) shares its name—and many opera productions—with a sister company in Antwerp; if you go, note the splendid ceiling and chandelier. Head for the **Kunstencentrum Vooruit**

($\boxtimes$ *Sint-Pietersnieuwstraat 23, Het Zuid* ☎ *09/267–2828* ⊕ *www. vooruit.be*) for top-quality dance, theater, and jazz programs; the venue also hosts rock and contemporary classical concerts. Grab a drink or quick meal in the cafeteria of this former cultural center of the Social-ist Party.

FESTIVALS

★ Gent has several marvelous celebrations. A town crier rings in activities for the 10-day **Gentse Feesten,** which takes place around the third week of July. Street theater, music, costume balls, banquets, an international techno festival, and parades take place around the inner city. Although there are a lot of cultural events, this is primarily a popular feast. Part of these festivities is **De Stroppendragersstoet,** or the Procession of the Rope Wearers, in which a barefoot troop dressed in tabards, with rope nooses around their necks, reenact the events of 1540 when Charles V suppressed the Gent rebellion and made prominent townspeople do a "walk of shame." Today the actor playing Charles V is booed by onlookers and the barefoot townspeople cheer; you can buy commem-orative nooses in many shops around the town at this time. Tradition-ally, the feast closes with "the day of the empty wallets." (After 10 days of partying, who has any money left?)

In August, the three-day **Patersholfeesten** fills the historic Patershol quarter with all kinds of music and parades. Other cultural festivities include the **Festival van Vlaanderen,** a classical- and world-music festival in the major Flemish cities, which usually starts in the second half of September, and the **Internationaal Filmfestival van Vlaanderen,** held during the first half of October.

NIGHTLIFE

As in most Belgian towns, nightlife in Gent centers around grazing and drinking and talking with friends through the wee hours. The stu-dent population generates a much busier, more varied nightlife than you'll find in Brugge or other towns in Flanders. The area around Oude Beestenmarkt and Vlasmarkt, near Portus Ganda, is mainly where young people gather for dancing and partying.

There are special dance nights, several gay bars, and lots of gay and lesbian organizations providing help and advice. The tourist office even provides a gay and lesbian city map. You can get more information at **Casa Rosa** ($\boxtimes$ *Kammerstraat 22, Het Zuid* ☎ *09/269–2812*).

BARS

De Dulle Griet ($\boxtimes$ *Vrijdagmarkt 50, Vrijdagmarkt* ☎ *09/224–2455*) is a quintessential Gent pub. It has more than 250 kinds of drinks but specializes in the 1.2-liter *Kwak* beer, complete with a collector's stein and stand—ask for a "Max." If you brave this beer, though, you must leave one of your shoes as deposit when you order. The pub is open from noon until 1 or 2 AM, apart from Sunday evening when it closes early. A little way southeast of the center, but worth checking out, the **Hopduvel** ($\boxtimes$ *Rokerelstraat 10, Bijloke* ☎ *09/225–3729*) is in a grubby residential street, but don't be deterred by the exterior: inside is a spa-

The City of Flowers

Every five years, Gent becomes awash with color as it host the "Gentse Floraliën"—the Floralies of Gent. This huge botanical exhibition is what earns Gent it's nickname—"City of Flowers"—and it gives the region's gardeners a chance to place their wares in an international shop window. Azaleas are a particular local specialty, and the best examples of these are exported around the globe.

The first event in 1809 filled an exhibition space of just 500 square feet, but since then it has grown beyond recognition. Today's **Floraliën** (⏲ *Daily 8–6:30* ⛶ *€17* ⊕ *www.floralien.be*) attracts hundreds of thousands of visitors from around the world. It will be held for the 34th time April 16–25, 2010.

cious old-style brick café with a warming open fireplace in winter and a large leafy garden terrace in summer. To taste a potent Belgian specialty, head to **'t Dreupelkot** (⊠ *Groentenmarkt 12, Gravensteen/Patershol* ☎ *09/224–2120*), which produces its own jenever in a multitude of different flavors, including vanilla and chocolate.

The **Town Crier** (☎ *09/222–6743* ⊕ *www.towncriers.be*), who spends his days walking the streets making announcements and tolling his bell, can also take you on a pub crawl. You'll need a reservation, though.

DANCING

Gent's top hot spot is **Culture Club** (⊠ *Afrikalaan 174, Dampoort* ☎ *09/267–6440* ⊕ *www.cultureclub.be*). This former warehouse close to the harbor is now a danceteria with a different atmosphere and style on each level, from languishing lounge to pounding techno. If you're lucky, the Dewaele brothers, DJs who have hosted parties for artists like Madonna and David Bowie, will be there doing a set.

The club **Democrazy** (⊠ *Penitentenstraat 17, Vrijdagmarkt* ☎ *09/227–5196*) angles toward alternative underground music. Check out their Web site, www.democrazy.be (in English), for details on the bands they schedule.

JAZZ

The busy late-night jazz café **Jazz Café Damberd** (⊠ *Korenmarkt 19, Gravensteen/Patershol* ☎ *09/329–5337*) occupies one of the most historic pubs in Gent. Jazz musicians from all over the world play here. **Lazy River Jazz Café** (⊠ *Stadhuissteeg 5, Torenrij* ☎ *09/223–2301*) is a friendly, intimate place beloved by locals and the older crowd. **Backstage** (⊠ *Sint-Pietersnieuwstraat 128, Het Zuid* ☎ *09/233–3535*), a café-restaurant near the Kunstencentrum Vooruit, presents occasional classical and jazz concerts.

There are concerts as well as dance nights at **Muziekcafé Charlatan** (⊠ *Vlasmarkt 6, near Portus Ganda* ☎ *09/224–2457*). It's open every day from 4 PM; music starts up at 10 or 11. Their lineup covers alt-rock, funk, and lots of DJ nights.

OUTDOOR ACTIVITIES

Just minutes from the city, the 250-acre **Blaarmeersen** (✉ *Zuiderlaan 5* ☎ *09/221–1414*) is Gent's large sports and recreation center. Here you'll find tennis courts, squash courts, a roller-skating track, jogging and cycling tracks, and facilities for windsurfing, sailing, canoeing, and camping. There are also several green areas at the edge of town: the Citadel park and De Bijloke to the south; the Koning Albert Park and the Klein Beginhof (small beguinage) to the east.

BIKING

For cycling routes, pick up a bicycle map from the tourism office; it's in Flemish but easily deciphered. You can rent bikes at the train station or at **Biker** (✉ *Steendam 16* ☎ *09/224–2903*), open daily.

5

BOATING

Boating is popular along the river and canals; you can take a boat tour or rent your own vessel. You can rent a motorboat or "mini-yacht" from the **Minerva Boat Company** (☎ *03/233–7917* 🌐 *www.minervaboten.be*) and sail around Gent or to Deurle and Sint-Martens-Latem. Boats take four to five people and no special license is required. The embarkation and landing stage is at Coupure, on the corner of Lindenlei.

SHOPPING

Langemunt and **Veldstraat** are the major shopping streets, while the smart fashion boutiques cluster along **Voldersstraat.** Gent also has several exclusive shopping galleries where fancy boutiques are surrounded by upscale cafés and restaurants; try the **Bourdon Arcade** (Gouden Leeuwplein) and **Braempoort,** between Brabantdam and Vlaanderenstraat.

MARKETS

The largest market is the attractive and historic **Vrijdagmarkt,** held Friday 7–1 and Saturday 1–6. This is where leaders have rallied the people of Gent from the Middle Ages to the present day. The huge square is dominated by a turret that was part of the tanner's guild house, and the statue in the middle is of Jacob van Artevelde, who led a rebellion from here in 1338, defending the neutrality of the city and Flanders during the Hundred Years' War. You can take home a supply of *Gentse mokken,* syrup-saturated biscuits available from any pastry shop, or famously strong Gent mustard. On Sunday mornings, also visit the **flower market** on the Kouter, where there is often a brass band playing, and sample oysters and a glass of champagne at **De Blauwe Kiosk,** a booth on the edge of the market at the corner of Kouter and Vogelmarkt.

SPECIALTY STORES

FOOD

Scoop up the best chocolates in town, perhaps even in Flanders, at the family-run **Chocolaterie Van Hoorebeke** (✉ *Sint-Baafsplein, Torenrij*

☎09/221–0381). You can look through a plate of glass set into the shop floor and see the chocolates being made by hand below.

At **Het Hinkelspel** (✉ *F. Lousbergskaai 33, Dampoort* ☎09/224–2096) you can buy five types of homemade cheeses. Be sure to try the Pas de Bleu, the only Belgian blue cheese. A good old-fashioned sweet shop, with tempting large jars of sweets on its shelves, can be found at **Temmerman** (✉ *Kraanlei 79, Gravensteen/Patershol* ☎09/224–0041). For something savory, visit Gent's famous mustard maker **Tierenteijn** (✉ *Groentenmarkt 3, Gravensteen/Patershol* ☎09/225–8336).

LINENS
The linens, lace, and lavender items at **Kloskanthuis Home Linen** (✉ *Korenlei 3, Torenrij* ☎09/223–6093) are a good bargain—the prices here are lower than those in Brugge shops.

SIDE TRIP FROM GENT

LEIESTREEK

10 km (6 mi) southwest of Gent.

Bucolic Leiestreek (Leie Region) has attracted many painters, and it's especially pleasant to discover their work in its original setting. The best way to enjoy the willow-lined banks of the meandering Leie is by rented motorboat or bike. Sint-Martens-Latem, with its 15th-century wooden windmill, drew several important artists in the years before World War I. Among these were Gustave van de Woestyne and Constant Permeke; Permeke went on to become a leading Expressionist painter.

GETTING HERE & AROUND
Sint-Martens-Latem lies 14 km (9 mi) southwest from Gent. Deinze is another 11 km (7 mi). By car from Gent, take the E40 motorway and get off at exit 14; follow the N43, which will take you to the nicest areas in the Leie region. From Gent several De Lijn (lines 34, 35, and 36) buses will take you to Latem within a half hour. There are two trains every hour from Gent to Deinze; the trip takes 12 minutes.

WHAT TO SEE
In the village of **Deurle** is the **Museum Dhondt-Dhaenens,** a 1967 complex built by Jules and Irma Dhont-Dhaenens to house their large art collection. The museum has rotating exhibits focusing on the work of contemporary artists. ✉ *Museumlaan 14* ☎09/282–5123 ⊕ *www.museumdd.be* ✒€3 ☉ *Tues.–Sun. 11–5.*

Around the corner, the house of artist Gust de Smet has been turned into the **Museum Gust de Smet.** About 100 of his paintings line the walls of his living room, workshop, and bedroom, which have all been kept intact. ✉ *Gust de Smetlaan 1* ☎09/282–7742 ⊕ *www.sint-martens-latem.be* ✒€2.75 ☉ *Apr.–Sept., Wed.–Sun. 2–6; Oct.–Mar., Wed.–Sun. 2–5.*

The 14th-century **Sheldt-Gothic Church of Our Lady** in the village of **Deinze** has a steeple carillon that chimes in major thirds—the world's first (originally, carillons only chimed in minor thirds).

Next to the river stands the spacious **Museum van Deinze en de Leiestreek,** which has an important collection of painting by artists who lived and worked in Sint-Martens-Latem. There are works by Emile Claus, Minne, Permeke, Servaes, De Smet, and Raveel. It's a must-see for art lovers. ✉ *Lucien Matthyslaan 3–5* ☎ *09/381-9670* ⊕ *www.museumdeinze. be* ✆€2.75 ⊙ *Tues.–Fri. 2–5:30, weekends 10–noon and 2–5.*

WHERE TO STAY & EAT

$$$–$$$$ ✕ **Auberge du Pêcheur.** A lovely half-hour drive (or a somewhat lon-

FRENCH ger bicycle ride) from Gent brings you to this riverside inn, which houses no less than two great restaurants. For a casual bite try the Green, a brasserie where the menu leans to hearty dishes, such as dark, meaty spareribs. Meanwhile, the formal Orangerie restaurant serves six-course meals that might include grilled turbot, pigeon served with sweetbreads, or eel baked in a cream sauce. If weather permits, ask for a table on the terrace; the magnificent view of the river is one you'll never forget. Both restaurants offer a daily prix fixe menu. If you are overcome by the sumptuous spread, there are tasteful guest rooms ($$) available upstairs, some with a view of the Leie. ✉ *Pontstraat 41, Sint-Martens-Latem* ☎ *09/282-3144* ⊕ *www.auberge-du-pecheur.be* ⌕ *Reservations essential for Orangerie* ▤ *AE, DC, MC, V* ⊙ *Closed Mon. No lunch Sat. No dinner Sun.*

¢–$ ▦ **Charl's Inn.** A wrought-iron arch welcomes you to this country bed-and-breakfast near Sint-Martens-Latem, within a reasonable biking distance of Gent. The guest rooms are airy and comfortable (except for the cramped "nook" rooms). Breakfast is by a brick hearth, and the large, groomed grounds and gardens are perfect for strolling and cycling. **Pros:** quiet location; friendly staff. **Cons:** far from anywhere, which could also be a plus if that's what you're looking for. ✉ *Autoweg Zuid 4, Afsnee* ☎ *09/220-3093* ⇗ *9 rooms* ⌂ *In-hotel: bar, bicycles, parking (free)* ▤ *AE, MC, V* ⏱*BP.*

Antwerp

WORD OF MOUTH

"Antwerp's cathedral houses four Rubens altar-pieces. I'm not Catholic, nor an art expert, but it had me motionless for quite a while."

—stfc

Updated by
Tim Skelton

ANTWERP IS EUROPE'S SECOND-LARGEST PORT and has much of the zest often associated with a harbor town. But it also has an outsized influence in a very different realm: that of clothing design. Since the 1980s, Antwerp-trained fashion designers have become renowned for experimental styles paired with time-honored workmanship. Several designers, such as Dries Van Noten and Véronique Branquinho, stay firmly rooted in the city; others have filtered into major European couture houses. On their home turf, you can experience the fascinating mix of tradition and innovation that influences their work.

In its heyday, Antwerp (Antwerpen in Flemish, Anvers in French) played second fiddle only to Paris. Thanks to artists such as Rubens, Van Dyck, and Jordaens, it was one of Europe's leading art centers. Its printing presses produced missals for the farthest reaches of the Spanish empire. It became, and has remained, the diamond capital of the world. Its civic pride was such that the Antwerpen *Sinjoren* (patricians) considered themselves a cut above just about everybody else. They still do.

ORIENTATION & PLANNING

GETTING ORIENTED

North of Brussels on the banks of the Scheldt river, Antwerp is the largest city in Flanders. Once a major port town, today it's home to the country's fashion industry. Its central neighborhoods are easily explored on foot, but you'll need to hop on a tram or bus if you want to go farther afield.

OUDE STAD

Antwerp's bustling city center is concentrated in the Oude Stad on the right bank of the Scheldt River. East of the Oude Stad is Quartier Latin, a neighborhood filled with antiques stores and boutiques. Pedestrian streets and narrow cobblestone alleyways open onto lively, terrace-filled squares. Here you'll find the Grote Markt, a tribute to Flanders's Golden Age with its elaborate town hall and guild houses. Nearby is the Onze-Lieve-Vrouwekathedraal, Antwerp's finest cathedral, and the city's favorite son's home, Rubenshuis.

THE MEIR, DIAMANTWIJK & CENTRAAL STATION

The Meir, the main shopping thoroughfare, leads east from the Oude Stad to Centraal Station and the predominantly Jewish Diamantwijk area. North of the Meir is Stadswaag, and above that, Het Eilandje. Antwerp's maritime past and present infuse both of these neighborhoods; you'll find docks, the Hogere Zeevaartschool (Antwerp's School of Navigation), and many businesses that cater to shipping and yachting. Immediately south of the Meir is Sint-Andrieskwartier, known for its clothing and bric-a-brac shops.

TOP REASONS TO VISIT

Shop 'Til You Drop. Antwerp is a sophisticated shopper's paradise, with a center that's crammed with trendy stores and designer boutiques showing off the latest creations by the region's top fashionistas. Although you may need fresh air when you catch a glimpse of some of the price tags.

Diamonds Are Forever. Shiny rocks are not just a girl's best friend in Europe's largest center of diamond trading. If you can't afford to buy,

you can still admire, and watch them being cut at Diamondland.

No Struggling Artist. Vincent van Gogh may have had to barter his paintings in exchange for meals, but it's clear from a visit to Peter Paul Rubens's home that the Flemish master had no such problems earning a crust. The lovingly restored home re-creates what it would have been like when the 17th-century court painter to Archduke Albrecht was in his prime.

BEYOND CENTRAL ANTWERP

South of the city center is Het Zuid (which you'll often see abbreviated as 't Zuid), popular for its trendy restaurants, cafés, and clubs. Its main drags are Amerikalei, Kronenburgstraat, and Waalsekaai. The residential area of Middelheim, south of Het Zuid, is full of parks. Art Nouveau homes make Zurenborg, southeast of the city center past Centraal Station, one of Antwerp's most beautiful neighborhoods.

PLANNING

Although you can "do" Antwerp in a day, you would do much better with two or three days, allowing time to sample some of the great restaurants and the lively nightlife and to properly explore the rich collections of the Koninklijk Museum voor Schone Kunsten and other museums. This is a walking city, so take the time to explore side streets and squares. Avoid limiting your visit to a Monday, when the museums are closed, for they are an integral part of the experience. Keep in mind that many museums are free on Friday. Local markets are at their best (and busiest) on weekends.

TAKE IT ALL IN

1 Day: Wander the narrow streets of the Oude Stad, window-shopping and perhaps sampling some local beer along with a lunch of the ubiquitous mussels and french fries. Then head to Rubenshuis to see a faithful and rich re-creation of the famous painter's own house and studio. Afterwards, make a trip to see the Bruegels at the Museum Mayer Van den Bergh. Next stop is the Plantin-Moretus Museum, the home and printing plant of a publishing dynasty that spanned three centuries. The museum overlooks a tranquil square, just the place for a restful café visit at day's end.

3 Days: Follow the suggestions above for Day 1. On Day 2, start with a walk along the river Scheldt to appreciate Antwerp's centuries-long tradition as a major European port. If you've made an early start, you could take a boat tour to see the modern, working harbor. Absorb a sense of the city's religious history by visiting some of its churches, including Sint-Pauluskerk and Sint-Jacobskerk, where Rubens is buried. Take a break from history with a trip to the Zoo Antwerpen or visit Aquatopia. Indulge your covetous streak with a trip to the Diamantwijk and the Provinciaal Diamantmuseum. If it's peace and quiet you're after, head to the Begijnhof, an almost hidden 13th-century convent. On your last day, use the morning to take advantage of Antwerp's ranking as a key European fashion center. First hit the Mode Museum, then window-shop along the smaller streets radiating off the Meir. After that, head south to greener areas and stop at the Openluchtmuseum Middelheim for a welcome break to enjoy the sculptures in this open-air museum. Finish with dinner and a nightcap in the chic Het Zuid neighborhood.

EAT RIGHT, SLEEP WELL

Antwerp cuisine understandably focuses on fish, presented with few frills in even the finest restaurants, often poached or steamed, and reasonably priced. From the chilled whelks and periwinkles (marine snails) picked out of their shells with pins, to piles of tender little *grijze garnalen* (small shrimp), to the steamy white flesh of the mammoth *tarbot* (turbot), the scent of salt air is never far from your table. The ubiquitous *mosselen* (mussels) and *paling* (eels), showcased in midpriced restaurants throughout the city center, provide a heavier, heartier version of local fish cuisine. Bought live from wholesalers, the seafood is irreproachably fresh.

Antwerp has a high number of restaurants for a city its size. Many of the traditional places, both formal and casual, are clustered in Oude Stad. There are plenty of tourist-focused restaurants on the Grote Markt, but if you look along the smaller streets around the square you'll find some excellent local favorites. Het Zuid, meanwhile, is known for trendier cafés and restaurants. Peak dining hours are generally from noon until 3 and from 8 PM to 11 or midnight. Since the dining scene is quite busy, it's best to make reservations.

Antwerp's hotels with the most character are generally found in the Oude Stad and its adjacent neighborhoods. There are several intimate boutique hotels, but as these can fill up far in advance, be sure to make reservations as early as possible. Some hotels have set prices throughout the year but many offer weekend rates. All hotels include taxes (6%) in their room rates.

The city's tourism bureau, Toerisme Antwerpen, keeps track of the best hotel prices and can make reservations for you up to a week in advance. Write or e-mail (✉ *toerisme@stad.antwerpen.be*) for a reservation form. It also maintains a list of some 25 recommended bed-and-breakfast accommodations from €35 to €55 per night.

WHAT IT COSTS IN EUROS					
	¢	$	$$	$$$	$$$$
Restaurants	under €10	€10–€15	€15–€20	€20–€30	over €30
Hotels	under €75	€75–€100	€100–€150	€150–€225	over €225

Restaurant prices are for a main course at dinner. Hotel prices are for two people in a standard double room in high season, on the European Plan (EP, with no meals) unless otherwise noted. Costs include 6% tax.

GETTING HERE & AROUND

By Air Only one carrier, VLM, serves Antwerp's Deurne Airport. It's generally easier to fly into Brussels's Zaventem airport. Zaventem serves many airlines and has convenient transportation connections to Antwerp.

By Bus De Lijn operates Antwerp's city bus service; it's an easy system to use. Most lines begin outside Centraal Station on the Koningin Astridplein. All stops are clearly marked with a yellow pole. Single-ride tickets cost €1.60 when bought on the bus, or €1.20 bought in advance at metro stations. Other options include a day pass (€6 on board, €5 bought in advance), which are good on all forms of public transportation. These are available at De Lijn offices, the tourist office, and at some metro stops. Ask for a transit route map at the tourist office or metro stations. Buses run frequently, roughly from 6 AM to midnight.

By Car Antwerp is surrounded by a ring road from which expressways shoot off like spokes in a wheel. At this writing, the ring road was being renovated, so you may run into some roadwork delays. The city is 48 km (29 mi) north of Brussels on the E19; 60 km (36 mi) northeast of Gent on the E17; 119 km (71 mi) northwest of Liège on the A13.

A car isn't necessary—and is more often than not a burden—when exploring Antwerp's central area. The city's streets may not be quite as busy as those in Brussels, but they're crowded enough to make driving difficult. An ongoing construction project along the connected thoroughfares known as "de Leien" (Italielei, Frankrijklei, and Amerikalei) makes things even more snarly. Avoid rush hours, generally 6:30–9:30 AM and 4–7 PM, and keep a sharp eye out for one-way streets and aggressive drivers. Remember that drivers have priority from the right. Street parking is rare but there are several central parking lots, including some near Grote Markt and Groenplaats.

By Public Transport Antwerp's tram and metro public transit system is extensive and reliable. Some segments operate as the pre-metro system, which is basically a tram running underground for part of its route. The most useful subway line for visitors links Centraal Station (metro: Diamant) with the left bank, which is the other side of the river (Linkeroever), via the Groenplaats (for the cathedral and Grote Markt). A €1.20 (€1.60 bought on board) ticket is good for one hour on all forms of public transport, including buses; a €5 (€6 bought on board) pass buys unlimited travel for one day. Tickets are available at De Lijn offices, the tourist office, and at the Diamant, Opera–Frankrijklei, and

Groenplaats metro stops. The metro system is open 6:30 AM–midnight. Stations are marked by large arrows indicating the entrances.

By Taxi There are taxi stands marked with a "taxi" sign at every principal point in the city center, such as Groenplaats and in front of Centraal Station, but it's often easier to call for one. All taxis are metered, starting with a base rate of €2.70 plus €1.20 per km. The rates are higher at night (10 PM–6 AM).

By Tour Flandria operates 50-minute boat trips on the river Scheldt, departing from the Steenplein pontoon, next to the Steen. These run Easter weekend and daily May–September. The company also offers 2½-hour boat tours of the port, which leave from Quay 14 near Londonstraat. These tours run Easter weekend, daily from May through August, and September through October on weekends. Both tours have English-speaking guides.

Touristram operates hour-long tram tours with cassette commentary in the Oude Stad and old harbor area. Tickets are sold on the tram, and tours leave on the hour. Departure is from Groenplaats. From mid-February to mid-March, and November to mid-December, tours run only on weekends 11–4; from mid-March to September they run daily 11–5; in October, daily 1–4.

You can arrange for a personal English-speaking guide through the Toerisme Antwerpen (the city tourist office). This requires two days' to three weeks' notice, depending on the season. You can ask your guide to show you any part of the city that interests you, either by neighborhood or by theme (fashion, history, architecture, etc.). The tourism bureau also sells booklets that sketch out walks through the city focusing on fashion and architecture.

By Train NMBS/SNCB, the national railway, connects Antwerp with several trains a day to all other major Belgian cities. There are four to five trains an hour between Antwerp and Brussels, and hourly trains make the 15-minute trip between Antwerp and Lier. International Thalys trains arrive and leave only from Berchem Station, south of the city center, rather than using the downtown Centraal Station. Among other routes, the Thalys trains run seven times a day between Antwerp and Paris and six times a day to and from Amsterdam.

ESSENTIALS

Bus Station (⊠ *Franklin Rooseveltplaats, Meir* ☎ *070/22–02–00*).

Emergency Contacts Ambulance (☎ *100*). **Emergency room** (⊠ *Algemeen Centrum Ziekenhuis OCMW Antwerpen Campus Sint-Elisabeth, Leopoldstraat 26, Oude Stad* ☎ *03/223–4111*). **Police** (☎ *101*). **Red Cross** (☎ *03/541–0023*).

Internet Café 2zones (⊠ *Wolstraat 15, Oude Stad* ☎ *03/232–2400* ⊕ *www.2zones. be*).

Rental Cars Avis (⊠ *Centraal Station* ☎ *03/218–9496* ⊕ *www.avis.be*). **Budget** (⊠ *Het Eilandje* ☎ *03/213–7960* ⊕ *www.budget.be*). **Hertz** (⊠ *Deurne Airport* ☎ *03/239–2921* ⊕ *www.hertz.be*).

Taxis Antwerp Tax (☎03/238–3838 ⊕www.antwerp-tax.be). **Metropole Taxi** (☎03/231–3131 ⊕www.metropole.be). **Star Taxi** (☎03/257-5757 ⊕www.startaxi-nv.be).

Tour Companies Flandria (☎03/231–3100 ⊕www.flandriaboat.com). **Toerisme Antwerpen** (✉Grote Markt 13, Oude Stad ☎03/232–0103 ⊕www.antwerpen.be). **Touristram** (☎03/480–9388).

Train Stations Berchem Station (✉Burgemeester Ryckaertplein 1, Berchem ☎03/204–2040). **Centraal Station** (✉Koningin Astridplein, Meir ☎03/204–2040). **Lier** (✉Leopoldplein 32, Lier ☎03/229–5502).

Visitor Info Toerisme Provincie Antwerpen (Antwerp Provincial Tourist Office ✉Koningin Elisabethlei 16, Middelheim ☎03/240–6373 ⊕www.tpa.be ⊙Weekdays 8:30–4:30). **Toerisme Antwerpen** (Antwerp City Tourist Office ✉Grote Markt 13, Oude Stad ☎03/232–0103 ⊕www.antwerpen.be ⊙Mon.–Sat. 9–5:45, Sun. 9–4:45).

EXPLORING ANTWERP

The area that surrounds Centraal Station, Antwerp's magnificent railway station, is in the commercial center of the city, but is not representative of its character. Hop on the subway to Groenplaats and walk past the cathedral and then into the Grote Markt. This is where Antwerp begins.

OUDE STAD

The Oude Stad is where visitors and locals alike go to find the essence of Antwerp. The narrow, winding streets, many of them restricted to pedestrian traffic, are wonderful for strolling, the squares are full of charm, and the museums and churches are the pride of the city.

After centuries as an industrial port, Antwerp is now developing another identity as a cruise-ship port. A cruise terminal opened in 2003 under the historic hangars. The mooring site for cruise ships and charter-boat tours has given the Steenplein, the area between the terminal and the Steen fortress, a new burst of energy.

WHAT TO SEE

❷ **Etnografisch Museum.** This fascinating ethnographic museum explores the art, myths, and rites of the native peoples of Africa, the Americas, Asia, and the South Seas. André Malraux described some of its thousands of masks, tools, weapons, sculptures, and other objects in his work La Musée Imaginaire, a compilation of the world's most important art and artifacts. Look for such rare pieces as a Wayard Aparai dance costume worn during a boy's initiation ceremony. A detailed pilgrimage painting on cloth entitled Lhasa and surrounding is one of only two such paintings known in the world. Ask to borrow the free English-language museum guidebook. ✉Suikerrui 19, Oude Stad ☎03/220–8600 ⊕museum.antwerpen.be €4, free on Fri. ⊙Tues.–Sun. 10–5 Ⓜ Metro 2, 3, or 5.

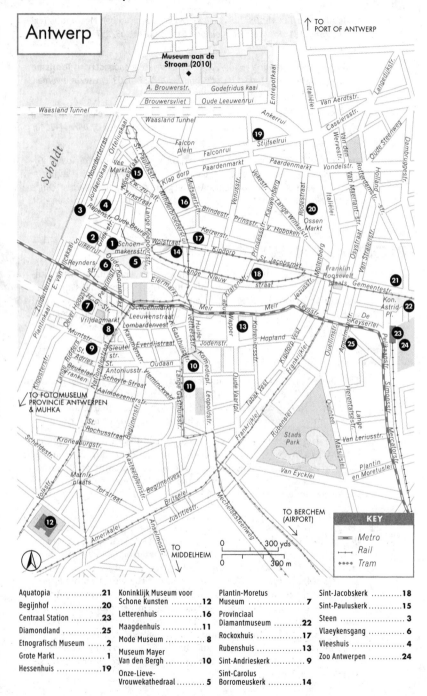

Antwerp

TO
PORT OF ANTWERP

Museum aan de
Stroom (2010)

KEY
Metro
Rail
Tram

0   300 yds
0   300 m

TO MIDDELHEIM

TO BERCHEM
(AIRPORT)

❶ Grote Markt. The heart of the Oude Stad, the Grote Markt is dominated by a huge fountain splashing water onto the paving stones. Atop the fountain stands the figure of the legendary Silvius Brabo, who has been poised to fling the hand of the giant Druon Antigon into the river Scheldt since the 19th century. Another famous monster slayer, St. George, is perched on top of a 16th-century guild house at Grote Markt 5, while the dragon appears to be falling off the pediment.

The triangular square is lined on two sides by guild houses and on

> **DID YOU KNOW?**
>
> Antwerp is often called the City of the Madonnas. On almost every street corner in the old section, you'll see a high niche with a protective statuette of the Virgin. People tend to think that because Belgium is linguistically split it is also religiously divided. This emphatically is not so. In fact, the Roman Catholic faith appears to be stronger and more unquestioning in Flanders than in Wallonia.

the third by the Renaissance **Stadhuis.** Antwerp's town hall was built in the 1560s during the city's Golden Age, when Paris and Antwerp were the only European cities with more than 100,000 inhabitants. In its facade, the fanciful fretwork of the late-Gothic style has given way to the discipline and order of the Renaissance. The public rooms are suitably impressive, though the heavy hand of 19th-century restoration work is much in evidence. You can see the interior only by reserving a guided tour; these are available in English. ⊠ *Grote Markt, Oude Stad* ☎ *03/220–8020* 💶 *€0.75* Ⓜ *Metro 2, 3, or 5.*

⓳ Hessenhuis. This historic warehouse built for German merchants in the 16th century is the last surviving example of such storehouses, which marked the expansion of the *Nieuwstad* (New town). For years it lay dormant, then was rediscovered in the 1950s by a group of artists who held avant-garde art exhibitions and heated debates. Now it's only open during exhibitions but merits a visit simply for its architectural importance, boasting Brabant Gothic brick and sandstone, with arched portals and marble reflecting Italian Renaissance influences. ■**TIP**➜ The site's café is open daily if you need to rest weary limbs as you admire the building. ⊠ *Falconrui 53, Oude Stad* ☎ *03/231–1356* ⊕ *museum.antwerpen. be* 💶 *Varies depending on exhibition* ☉ Ⓜ *Tram 1.*

⓫ Maagdenhuis. Originally a foundling hospital for children of the poor, the Maagdenhuis (Maidens' House) opened in 1552 and remained in operation until 1882. A boys' orphanage, the Knechtjeshuis, which had opened nearby in 1558, also closed in 1882 when more modern institutions became available. The Maagdenhuis chapel and entrance gateway were constructed from 1564 to 1568; the rest of the building, including the somewhat austere but tranquil court, with its Baroque columns and Virgin Mary statuary, dates from 1634 to 1636. The Maagdenhuis Museum houses a collection of objects from the orphanages, including clothes, workbooks, and needlework. The museum also displays paintings and statuary, as well as a collection of rare 16th-century Antwerp pottery, including a complete set of porridge basins. Although the collection includes one Rubens, the most important paintings were lent to

A GOOD WALK

The **Grote Markt** ❶ is a good place to start your walk, with its impressive fountain of the city's mythical hero Silvius Brabo commanding its center, while the Stadhuis and Flemish guild houses form a triangle on this marketplace. Head down Suikerrui toward the river, stopping en route at the **Etnografisch Museum** ❷. At the end of the street, turn right to the waterfront fortress, the **Steen** ❸. Walk up the blocklong Repenstraat to the step-gabled **Vleeshuis** ❹. Proceed along Oude Beurs to Schoenmakersstraat, which will bring you to the cathedral. Walk down Blauwmoezelstraat in the direction of the Grote Markt, going around the cathedral to its entrance on Handschoenmarkt. The Gothic **Onze-Lieve-Vrouwekathedraal** ❺ contains some of Rubens's greatest paintings. A few steps to the left from the front of the cathedral, and you're in Oude Koornmarkt. At No. 16 begins the **Vlaeykensgang** ❻, an old cobblestone lane. It merges into Pelgrimstraat. Turn right, then right again on Reynderstraat, past the Baroque house of the painter Jacob Jordaens; then left on Hoogstraat and left again on Heilige Geeststraat, and you're at the **Plantin-Moretus Museum** ❼, the printer's stately home and workshops. Walk along Oever with its many antiques shops and make a left on to Muntstraat, coming along to **Sint-Andrieskerk** ❾. Muntstraat changes to Augustijnenstraat; when you reach Nationalestraat you'll find the fashionista mecca, the **Mode Museum** ❽. Continue on Sleutelstraat, which with a slight jag right on Kammenstraat leads to Oudaan. Follow Oudaan to Lange Gasthuisstraat to the **Museum Mayer Van den Bergh** ❿, on the left, to see its outstanding Bruegels. A few doors down on Lange Gasthuisstraat is the **Maagdenhuis** ⓫, a museum displaying artifacts from its days as an orphanage as well as Flemish art. From here you can catch a No. 8 tram to the **Koninklijk Museum voor Schone Kunsten** ⓬, with its stellar collection of Flemish art. Take a walk through the residential area around the museum; on the corner of Plaatsnijderstraat and Schilderstraat you'll see a ship's prow jutting from a corner balcony. This Art Nouveau house was commissioned by a local shipbuilder; it's called "The Five Continents."

the Royal Museum of Fine Arts in 1890. In addition to the museum, the building now houses some offices of the Public Center for Social Welfare. ⊠ *Lange Gasthuisstraat 33, Kruidtuin* ☎ *03/223–5620* 💶 *€3* ⊙ *Mon. and Wed.–Fri. 10–5, weekends 1–5* Ⓜ *Tram 8.*

❽ **Mode Museum (MoMu).** To get up to speed on the latest clothing designers, head to MoMu for a fashion crash course. Inside the early-20th-century building you'll find comprehensive exhibits, some highlighting the avant-garde work of contemporary Flemish designers. Rotating exhibits also make the most of the museum's collections of clothing, accessories, and textiles dating back to the 18th century; you can ponder the workmanship of delicate antique lace alongside deconstructed blouses from the late 1990s. Also in the museum's complex are the Flanders Fashion Institute, the fashion academy of the Royal Academy of Fine Arts (the designer wellspring), a brasserie, library, reading room, and a boutique. You can pick up a brochure with information in English. ⊠ *Nationalestraat 28, Sint-Andrieskwartier* ☎ *03/470–2770* ⊕ *www.momu.be* ☞ *€6* ☉ *Tues.–Sun. 10–6, every first Thurs. of the month 10–9* Ⓜ *Tram 8.*

⑩ Museum Mayer Van den Bergh. Pieter Bruegel the Elder's arguably greatest
Fodor'sChoice and most enigmatic painting, *Dulle Griet,* is the showpiece here (room
★ 9). Often referred to in English as "Mad Meg," it portrays an irate woman wearing helmet and breastplate—a sword in one hand, and food and cooking utensils in the other—striding across a field strewn with the ravages and insanity of war. There is no consensus on how to read this painting. Some consider it one of the most powerful antiwar statements ever made. Others claim that it denounces the Inquisition. Either way, nothing could be further from the Brueghelian villages than this nightmare world. In 1894, Mayer Van den Bergh bought *Dulle Griet* for 480 Belgian francs. Today it is priceless. The museum also has a set of Bruegel's witty, miniature illustrations of *Twelve Proverbs,* based on popular Flemish sayings.

Mayer Van den Bergh was a passionate art connoisseur who amassed a private collection of almost 4,000 works in the 19th century. The collection includes treasures such as a life-size polychrome statue from about 1300 of St. John resting his head on Christ's chest (room 6). It is, however, the Bruegels that make this small museum a must. There's an English-language pamphlet on sale for €2.50 that reviews part of the collection. ⊠ *Lange Gasthuisstraat 19, Kruidtuin* ☎ *03/232–4237* ⊕ *museum.antwerpen.be/mayervandenbergh* ☞ *€4, €6 for combination ticket with Rubenshuis* ☉ *Tues.–Sun. 10–5* Ⓜ *Tram 8.*

NEED A BREAK?

De Foyer (⊠ *Komedieplaats 18, Kruidtuin* ☎ *03/233–5517*) occupies the ornate rotunda of the mid-19th-century Bourla Theater. The decor alone is worth a visit, but the café serves buffet lunch and light snacks and is open noon–midnight. It's popular with locals, especially on Sunday, when the buffet breakfast is booked weeks in advance.

⑤ Onze-Lieve-Vrouwekathedraal. A miracle of soaring Gothic lightness, the
Fodor'sChoice Cathedral of Our Lady contains some of Rubens's greatest paintings
★ and is topped by its 404-foot-high north spire—now restored to its original gleaming white and serving as a beacon that can be seen from far away. Work began in 1352 and continued in fits and starts until 1521. Despite this, it is a homogeneous monument, thanks to a succession of remarkable architects, including Peter Appelmans, Herman and Domien de Waghemakere, and Rombout Keldermans the Younger. The tower holds a 49-bell carillon played at various times throughout the year.

The cathedral's art treasures were twice vandalized, first by Calvinists in 1566 and again by the French revolutionary army at the end of the 18th century. The French even broke up the floor so that their horses would not slip on it. The masterpieces were either sold at auction or carried off to Paris. Some, but by no means all, have subsequently

Architecture of Antwerp

The architectural character of Antwerp was defined during its two great eras of prosperity, in the 16th and 19th centuries. The relative lack of building at other times means that the city is unusually harmonious, with four- and five-story brick buildings mostly undisturbed by skyscrapers and steel-and-glass cubes. Traditional Flemish Gothic architecture pervades Antwerp, from its impressive Grote Markt to the many small, unsung buildings that line the narrow streets of the old town. The style continued to influence construction in the 19th century, but that period also brought the richly ornamented buildings that line Antwerp's main shopping street, as well as the fanciful extravaganzas of the Antwerp zoo. The combination makes a walk through Antwerp an aesthetic delight.

been returned. Other works, either donated or purchased, make up an outstanding collection of 17th-century religious art, including four Rubens altarpieces, glowing with his marvelous red, allegedly fortified by pigeon's blood. The panels of *De Kruisafneming* (*The Descent from the Cross*) triptych—Mary's visit to Elizabeth (with the painter's wife as Mary) and the presentation of Jesus in the temple—are among the most delicate and tender biblical scenes ever painted. *De Hemelvaart van de Maagd Maria* (*The Assumption of the Virgin Mary*), painted for the high altar, shows the Virgin being carried upward by massed ranks of cherubs toward the angel waiting to crown her Queen of the Angels. *De Hemelvaart* (*The Assumption*) is skillfully displayed so that the rays of the sun illuminate it exactly at noon. ⊠ *Handschoenmarkt, Oude Stad* ☎ *03/213–9951* ⊕ *www.dekathedraal.be* ⊠ *€2* ⊙ *Weekdays 10– 5, Sat. 10–3, Sun. 1–4* Ⓜ *Metro 2, 3, or 5.*

➐ **Plantin-Moretus Museum.** This was the home and printing plant of an ★ extraordinary publishing dynasty. For three centuries, beginning in 1576, the family printed innumerable bibles, breviaries, and missals; Christophe Plantin's greatest technical achievement was the *Biblia Regia* (in room 16): eight large volumes containing the Bible in Latin, Greek, Hebrew, Syriac, and Aramaic, complete with notes, glossaries, and grammars.

The first three rooms were the family quarters, furnished in 16th-century luxury and containing several portraits by Rubens. Others remain as they were when occupied by accountants, editors, and proofreaders, while many contain Bibles and religious manuscripts dating back to the 9th century, including one owned by King Wenceslas of Bohemia. The workshops are filled with Plantin's 16 printing presses. Two typefaces designed here, Plantin and Garamond, are still in use. The presses are in working order—you can even purchase a copy of Plantin's sonnet, *Le Bonheur de ce monde (An ode to contentment),* in any of seven European languages, printed on an original press. There's a free information brochure available in English. ⊠ *Vrijdagmarkt 22–23, Sint-Andrieskwartier* ☎ *03/221–1450* ⊕ *museum.antwerpen.be/plan-*

tin_moretus ⊠€6, *free last Wed. of the month* ⏱*Tues.–Sun. 10–5* Ⓜ*Tram 8.*

⑨ Sint-Andrieskerk. This late-Gothic church dedicated to St. Andrew dates to 1514 but reflects substantial Baroque influences from its extension during the 18th century. The church is notable for the magnificence of its Baroque high altar, stained-glass windows, and columns. Its most striking feature is the pulpit depicting Peter and his brother Andrew, created by Jan-Baptist Van Hoof and Jan-Frans Van Geel in 1821. The church is closed to visitors during services. ⊠*Sint-Andriesstraat 5, Sint-Andrieskwartier* ☎*03/232-0384* ⊠*Free* Ⓜ*Tram 8.*

⑭ Sint-Carolus Borromeuskerk. Like so much of Antwerp, the Jesuit St. Charles Borromeo Church bears the imprint of Rubens. The front and tower are generally attributed to him, and his hand can certainly be seen in the clustered cherubim above the entrance. The church's facade suggests a richly decorated high altar, inviting the observer inside. The interior was once magnificent, but most of Rubens's frescoes were destroyed by fire, and other works were carted off to Vienna when the Austrians banned the Jesuits in the 18th century. The square is one of the most attractive in Antwerp, flanked by the harmonious Renaissance buildings of the Jesuit convent, now occupied by the City Library. Ask to see their lace collection (€1.50). ⊠*Hendrik Conscienceplein 12, Oude Stad* ☎*03/231-3751* ⊠*Free* ⏱*Mon.–Sat. 10–12:30 and 2–5, Sun. mass* Ⓜ*Tram 10 or 11.*

NEED A BREAK? Its name, **Het Elfde Gebod** (⊠*Torfbrug 10, Oude Stad* ☎*03/289-3466*), means the 11th Commandment, and the place is crammed with more than 600 plaster saints and angels salvaged from old churches. It's tucked into a tiny street between the Grote Markt and the cathedral. The food and drink are straightforward but hearty, and you can sit on the terrace.

⑮ Sint-Pauluskerk. The late-Gothic St. Paul's Church, built 1530–71, is a repository of more than 50 outstanding paintings. There are three by Rubens, including a visceral depiction of Jesus's flagellation, as well as early works by Jordaens and Van Dyck. The church is further enriched by more than 200 17th- and 18th-century sculptures, including the confessionals attributed to Peeter Verbruggen the Elder. A Baroque altar completed in 1639 towers over the more somber Gothic nave. Sint-Pauluskerk was restored in 1968 after damage from a major fire. There's a series of walking tours and presentations—available in English, French, and Dutch—on the church's history, art, and artifacts. ⊠*Sint Paulusstraat 20, Oude Stad* ☎*03/232-3267* ⏱*May–Sept., daily 2–5* Ⓜ*Tram 4 or 7.*

③ Steen. The Steen is more than 1,000 years old and looks it. A 9th-century waterfront fortress, it was built to protect the western frontier of the Holy Roman Empire. It was partially rebuilt 700 years later by Emperor Charles V. You can distinguish the darker, medieval masonry extending midway up the walls from the lighter upper level of 16th-century work. The only survivor of the original waterfront, the Steen was used as a prison for centuries. Opposite the entrance is a cross where those sentenced to death said their final prayers. Many houses were torn down in the 19th century to make room for the wide, straight quays that today are practically deserted, the port having moved north of the city. The **Noorderterras,** a promenade starting at the Steen, is a popular place for a Sunday stroll along the Scheldt, which here is 550 yards wide. "God gave us the river," say Antwerpers, "and the river gave us all the rest." ⊠*Steenplein, Oude Stad* ☎*03/201–9340* ⊕*museum.antwerpen.be* Ⓜ*Metro 2, 3, or 5.*

❻ **Vlaeykensgang.** A quiet cobblestone lane in the center of Antwerp, the
FodorśChoice Vlaeykensgang seems untouched by time. The mood and style of the
   ★ 16th century are perfectly preserved here. There is no better place to linger on a Monday night when the carillon concert is pealing from the cathedral. The alley ends in Pelgrimsstraat, where there is a great view of the cathedral spire. **Jordaenshuis,** nearby, was the home of Jacob Jordaens (1593–1678), the painter many saw as the successor of Rubens. Unfortunately, it's no longer open to the public, but you can see the exterior. ⊠*Reyndersstraat 6, Oude Stad* Ⓜ*Metro 2, 3, or 5.*

NEED A BREAK?   **De Groote Witte Arend** (⊠ *Reyndersstraat 18, Oude Stad* ☎*03/223–5033*), in a secret courtyard near the Jordaens house, is in a former convent. The background music tends to be Vivaldi or Telemann, the atmosphere is genteel without being snobbish, and there's a good selection of draft beers and tasty sandwiches.

Vleeshouwersstraat. The Vleeshuis *(⇨below)* is the most prominent landmark of the residential neighborhood that has arisen in this historic district. Many ancient buildings remain, among them **De Spieghel** (The Mirror) off Oude Beurs at Spanjepandsteeg. Originally built for the archers' guild, it was bought in 1506 by Pieter Gillis, a leading humanist. ⊠*Bounded by Oude Beurs, Kuipersstraat, Jordaenskaai, Doornikstraat, and Veemarkt, Oude Stad* Ⓜ*Metro 2, 3, or 5.*

❹ **Vleeshuis.** Over the centuries, the Gothic Butcher's Hall (1501–04) has morphed from a meat market to a refined museum. Antwerp's oldest remaining public building was once the only place in the city where meat could be sold. The museum focuses on the musical life of the city. ⊠*Vleeshouwersstraat 38–40, Oude Stad* ☎*03/233–6404* ⊕*museum. antwerpen.be/vleeshuis* 🎟*€5* ⊙*Tues.–Sun. 10–5* Ⓜ*Metro 2, 3, or 5.*

THE MEIR, DIAMANTWIJK & CENTRAAL STATION

Here you'll find two of Antwerp's defining elements: Peter Paul Rubens (represented by his home and numerous works found in the surrounding neighborhood), and the Diamantwijk, world center of the diamond trade. The Centraal Station and adjacent zoo at the hub of the bustling district are both architectural gems.

TIMING & PRECAUTIONS

It's best to visit the Diamantwijk Tuesday–Friday, as on Saturday some shops close for the Jewish Sabbath; others close on Sunday. The zoo, on the other hand, is busiest on weekends. Keep in mind that most museums are closed Monday.

WHAT TO SEE

㉑ Aquatopia. Mother Earth's mystical underwater world never ceases to amaze. Two floors offer visitors a fascinating journey into an array of water habitats; submarine, mangrove, corals, reefs, lush vegetation, swamps, and rain forests accommodate more than 250 different species of animals and a striking array of marine life. Children can touch snakes, interact with an iguana that roams free, and watch ray- and shark-feeding shows. ✉ *Koningin Astridplein 7, Centraal Station* ☎ *03/205–0740* ⊕ *www.aquatopia.be* 💶 *€13.95* ⊙ *Daily 10–6, last entry at 5* Ⓜ *Tram 3 or 5.*

㉒ Begijnhof. The convent dates from the 13th century, but by the 1960s there was only one Beguine nun left. Redbrick buildings surrounding a courtyard garden (which is closed to the public) give a sense of tranquillity as you stroll the roughly cobbled walk. Furniture from the convent can be seen in house No. 38. ✉ *Rodestraat 39, Stadswaag* 💶 *Free* ⊙ *Daily 10–5* Ⓜ *Bus 1 or 13.*

㉓ Centraal Station. The neo-Baroque railway terminal was built at the turn of the 20th century during the reign of Leopold II of Belgium, a monarch not given to understatement. The magnificent exterior and splendid, vaulted ticket-office hall and staircases call out for hissing steam engines, peremptory conductors, scurrying porters, and languid ladies wrapped in boas. Today most departures and arrivals are humble commuter trains, but the station still inspires. W. G. Sebald's acclaimed 2001 novel *Austerlitz,* for instance, opens in the main hall. Its narrator recalls, "When I entered the great hall of the Centraal Station with its dome arching nearly sixty meters high above it, my first thought, perhaps triggered by my visit to the zoo . . . was that this magnificent although then severely dilapidated foyer ought to have cages for lions and leopards let into its marble niche . . . just as some zoos, conversely, have little railway trains in which you can, so to speak, travel to the farthest corners of the earth." The station has undergone major redevelopment work in recent years, and two new underground levels have been added to accommodate high-speed trains. This has turned the track areas into an impressively vast open space. ✉ *Koningin Astridplein, Centraal Station* Ⓜ *Metro 2, 3, or 5.*

COMING SOON . . .

Museum aan de Stroom (MAS) (⊕ *www.mas.be*), the newest addition to Antwerp's museum parade, will occupy a brand-new dockside building just north of the old town when it opens in 2010. MAS will cover the history of Antwerp, as well as feature art and historical artifacts that were previouosly housed in other museums. Pride of place will go to the former Maritime Museum's collection of models, figureheads, instruments, prints, and maps.

6

CLOSE UP   Antwerp, and How it Got that Way

The Flemish Antwerpen is very close to the word *handwerpen,* which means "hand throwing," and that, according to legend, is exactly what the Roman soldier Silvius Brabo did to the giant Druon Antigon. The giant would collect a toll from boatmen on the river and cut off the hands of those who refused, until Silvius confronted him, cut off the giant's own hand, and flung it into the river Scheldt. That's why there are severed hands on Antwerp's coat of arms.

Great prosperity came to Antwerp during the reign of Holy Roman Emperor Charles V. Born in Gent and raised in Mechelen, he made Antwerp the principal port of his vast domain. It became Europe's most important commercial center in the 16th century, as well as a center of the new craft of printing. The Golden Age came to an end with the abdication of Charles V in 1555. He was succeeded by Philip II of Spain, whose ardent Roman Catholicism brought him into immediate conflict with the Protestants of the Netherlands. In 1566, when Calvinist iconoclasts destroyed paintings and sculptures in churches and monasteries, Philip II responded by sending in Spanish troops. In what became known as the Spanish Fury, they sacked the town and killed thousands of citizens.

The decline of Antwerp had already begun when its most illustrious paint-ers, Peter Paul Rubens, Jacob Jordaens, and Anthony Van Dyck, reached the peak of their fame. Rubens's tie to the city is a genial, pervasive presence. The artist's house, his church, and the homes of his benefactors, friends, and disciples are all over the old city. His wife also seems to be everywhere, for she frequently posed as the model for his portraits of the Virgin Mary. Rubens and fellow Antwerper Van Dyck both dabbled in diplomacy and were knighted by the English monarch. Jordaens, less widely known, stayed close to Antwerp all his life.

The Treaty of Munster in 1648, which concluded the Thirty Years' War, further weakened Antwerp's position, for the river Scheldt was closed to shipping—it was not to be active again until 1863, when a treaty obliged the Dutch, who controlled the estuary, to reopen it.

The huge and splendid railway station, built at the close of the 19th century, remains a fitting monument to Antwerp's second age of prosperity, during which it hosted universal expositions in 1885 and 1894. In World War I, Antwerp held off German invaders long enough for the Belgian army to regroup south of the IJzer. In World War II, the Germans trained many V-1 flying bombs and V-2 rockets on the city, where Allied troops were debarking for the final push.

Diamantwijk. The diamond trade has its own quarter in Antwerp, where the skills of cutting and polishing the gems have been handed down for generations by a tightly knit community. Multimillion-dollar deals are agreed upon with a handshake, and the Antwerp Diamond High Council was established in 1975 to further the industry. Some 85% of the world's uncut diamonds pass through Antwerp. Twenty-five million carats are cut and traded here every year, more than anywhere else in the world. The district occupies a few nondescript city blocks west of Centraal Station. A large part of the community is Jewish, so you'll see shop signs in Hebrew and Hasidic men with traditional dark clothing and side curls. Below the elevated railway tracks, a long row of stalls and shops gleams with jewelry and gems.

Diamond cutting began in Brugge but moved to Antwerp in the 16th century, along with most other wealth-producing activities. When a flood of rough diamonds from South Africa hit the markets in the 19th century, Antwerp rose to the top of the field. Today the industry employs some 18,000 people, divided among 1,500 independent firms. Jewish establishments close on Saturday for the Sabbath but there are still enough shops open in the neighborhood to have a good browse. ⊠ *Bounded by De Keyserlei, Pelikaanstraat, Lange Herentalsestraat, and Lange Kievitstraat* Ⓜ *Metro 2.*

> ### BRUEGEL TO BAROQUE
>
> Seventeenth-century painter Peter Paul Rubens, arguably Flanders's most famous son, casts a long shadow over Antwerp. His brooding portraits and intense religious depictions are on exhibit throughout the city. They hang not only in Antwerp's art museum and Rubens's own house, but also in churches and other smaller sites. Other Flemish artists with close ties to Antwerp, including stellar painters such as Pieter Bruegel the Elder, and the Baroque artist Van Dyck, captured the region's rich history and its dark, northern atmosphere in works that rank among the world's finest.

6

㉕ **Diamondland.** A spectacular showroom, Diamondland was created to enable visitors to get a sense of the activity that goes on behind closed doors in the security-conscious Diamantwijk. All explanations are in English and you can watch several diamond cutters at work. Many of the hundreds of jewelry pieces on display (and for sale) are specially designed by an in-house jeweler. ⊠ *Appelmansstraat 33A, Diamantwijk* ☎ *03/229–2990* ⊕ *www.diamondland.be* ⊙ *Nov.–Mar., Mon.–Sat. 9:30–5:30; Apr.–Oct., Mon.–Sat. 9:30–5:30, Sun. 10–5* Ⓜ *Metro 2.*

⑯ **Letterenhuis.** Worth a stop if you're curious about Flemish authors, the Archive and Museum of Flemish Cultural Life provides an overview of the past 200 years of art and culture in Flanders, including posters, photos, manuscripts, arts-related publications, and historical documents. You'll get much more out of it if you understand Flemish or a related language; there are no explanatory materials in English. There is an extensive library open to the public. ⊠ *Minderbroedersstraat 22, Stadswaag* ☎ *03/222–9320* ⊕ *museum.antwerpen.be/amvc_letterenhuis* ⊡ *€3* ⊙ *Tues.–Sun. 10–4:30* Ⓜ *Tram 10 or 11.*

㉒ **Provinciaal Diamantmuseum.** Enter the world of a "girl's best friend"
★ through the high-tech interactive displays in this diamond museum. The visit begins on the third floor where interesting lighting, touchscreen computers, and amazing exhibits illustrate the entire production process, from mining to gem cutting. There's also general information on diamond sources and qualities that will prime your understanding of the precious stones. A free English-language audioguide explains the

CLOSE UP

Antwerp's Brilliant Industry

Knowing that 80% of rough diamonds pass through Antwerp and 50% are sold in the city, it's hard to imagine that India dominated the diamond trade from the 4th century BC to the 18th century. In the 13th century, Venice was a shipping point for Indian goods (including diamonds) to the West. Strategic cities in Northern Europe maintained trading routes with Venice during the Middle Ages and eventually diamond traders made their way to Brugge. In fact, it was Lodewijck van Bercken, a Brugge resident, who invented the technique of polishing diamonds with diamonds. The silting up of Brugge's harbor meant the gradual relocation of the diamond industry to Antwerp in the 15th century, and Antwerp's liberal and welcoming atmosphere encouraged immigrants to settle here.

Today, Antwerp's diamond sector maintains its unique multicultural atmosphere. Indians, Jews, Belgians, Australians, Russians, Lebanese, Africans, and Japanese contribute to the hub of activity found here. The heavily guarded Diamond Square Mile is the headquarters of 1,500 firms, four diamond exchanges, 350 workshops, specialized diamond banks, security and transport firms, brokers, consultants, and diamond schools, employing some 30,000 people.

The bourse is the meeting point for buyers, sellers, and brokers. Individuals must become members and adhere to strict rules. Transactions are conducted in a traditional and informal way. There are no written contracts. A handshake and the phrase *Mazal U'Brach* (may the deal bring you luck) closes a deal. Trade disputes are handled in-house, where two members are commissioned each week to solve conflicts.

Large windows illuminate the four large trading rooms in which sellers and buyers wheel and deal. Twenty years ago the floor bustled with activity but now business is largely conducted in private offices.

The HRD is the customs office for all diamonds moving in and out of Belgium. Each day, the council checks 1,000 diamonds with strict anonymity and objectivity, confirming their authenticity based on the characteristics of each stone using the 4Cs (carat, color, clarity, cut).

The global trade in diamonds has come under a great deal of scrutiny in recent years, particularly in the wake of the Hollywood movie *Blood Diamond,* which drew attention to so-called "conflict diamonds." Dealers in Antwerp are understandably keen to distance themselves from this tarnished image, and the strict checks carried out by the HRD are there to ensure that all gems passing through the city are ethically correct.

See the Shopping section for store recommendations.

wonderful collections of jewelry, which range from 16th-century pieces to contemporary creations. ⊠ *Koningin Astridplein 19–23, Centraal Station* ☎ *03/202–4890* ⊕ *www.diamantmuseum.be* 🎫 €6 ☉ *Feb.– Dec., Thurs.–Tues. 10–5:30* Ⓜ *Metro 2, 3, or 5.*

⓱ Rockoxhuis. This was the splendid Renaissance home of Rubens's friend and patron Nicolaas Rockox, seven times mayor of Antwerp. A humanist and art collector, Rockox moved here in 1603. The art on display includes two of Rubens's works. One is *Madonna en Kind* (*Madonna and Child*), a delicate portrait of Rubens's first wife, Isabella, and their son, Nicolaas; the other is a sketch for the *Kruisiging* (*Crucifixion*). The collection also includes works by Van Dyck, Frans Snijders, Joachim Patinier, Jordaens, and David Teniers the Younger. The setting makes visiting this collection an exceptional experience. Rather than being displayed on museum walls, the paintings are shown in the context of an upper-class Baroque home, furnished in the style of the period. A documentary slide show in English describes Antwerp at that time. ✉ *Keizerstraat 10–12, Stadswaag* ☎ *03/201–9250* 🌐 *www.rockoxhuis.be* 🎫 *€2.50* 🕙 *Tues.–Sun. 10–5* Ⓜ *Tram 10 or 11.*

13 ★ **Rubenshuis.** A fabulous picture of Rubens as painter and patrician is presented here at his own house. Only the elaborate portico and temple, designed by Rubens in Italian Baroque style, were still standing three centuries after the house was built. Most of what's here is a reconstruction (completed in 1946) from the master's own design. It represents Rubens at the pinnacle of his fame, a period during which he was appointed court painter to Archduke Albrecht and, with his wife, was sent on a diplomatic mission to Madrid, where he also painted some 40 portraits. He conducted delicate peace negotiations in London on behalf of Philip IV of Spain, and while in London he painted the ceiling of the Whitehall Banqueting Hall and was knighted by Charles I of Great Britain. The most evocative room in Rubens House is the huge studio, where drawings by Rubens and his pupils, as well as old prints, help to re-create the original atmosphere. In Rubens's day, visitors could view completed paintings and watch from the mezzanine while Rubens and his students worked. Rubens completed about 2,500 paintings, nearly all characterized by the energy and exuberance that were his hallmark. A few Rubens works hang in the house, including a touching sketch in the studio of the Annunciation and a self-portrait in the dining room. Unfortunately, his young widow promptly sold off some 300 pieces after his death in 1640. ✉ *Wapper 9, Meir* ☎ *03/201–1555* 🌐 *museum.antwerpen.be/rubenshuis* 🎫 *€6, includes admission to Museum Mayer Van den Bergh* 🕙 *Tues.–Sun. 10–5* Ⓜ *Metro 2, 3, or 5.*

18 **Sint-Jacobskerk.** Peter Paul Rubens is buried in the white sandstone St. Jacob's Church. A painting depicting him as St. George posed between his two wives, Isabella Brant and Helena Fourment, hangs above his tomb. The three-aisle church blends late-Gothic and Baroque styles; the tombs are practically a who's who of prominent 17th-century Antwerp families. ✉ *Lange Nieuwstraat 73, Meir* ☎ *03/232–1032* 🕙 *Apr.–Oct., daily 2–5* Ⓜ *Tram 10 or 11.*

24 **Zoo Antwerpen.** Antwerp's zoo houses its residents in style. Giraffes, ostriches, and African antelopes inhabit an Egyptian temple; a Moorish villa is home to the rhinoceroses; and a thriving okapi family grazes around an Indian temple. In part, this reflects the public's taste when the zoo was created 150 years ago. Today animals are allowed maximum space, and much research is devoted to endangered species. The zoo also has sea lions, an aquarium, and a house for nocturnal animals. ✉ *Koningin Astridplein 26, Centraal Station* ☎ *03/202–4540* 🌐 *www.*

6

zooantwerpen.be ☎€17.50 ⊗*Jan., Feb., Nov., and Dec., daily 10–4:45; Mar., Apr., and Oct., daily 10–5:30; May, June, and Sept., daily 10–6; July and Aug., daily 9–6:30* Ⓜ*Metro 2, 3, or 5.*

BEYOND CENTRAL ANTWERP

Middelheim is south of the city, above the tunnel for the expressway to Brussels. Berchem is south of the Centraal Station, a few minutes away by train or tram. Het Zuid is a trendy area 15 minutes' walk southwest of the Grote Markt, close to the banks of the Scheldt. The Port of Antwerp stretches for miles to the north and northwest of the city, and you'll need your own wheels to visit this vast area.

WHAT TO SEE

Berchem. In this neighborhood southeast of Antwerp's city center, the 19th-century entrepreneur Baron Edouard Osy and his sister, Josephine Cogels, inherited an old castle, demolished it, and built some refreshingly eccentric houses reflecting the eclectic tastes of the era. There are houses in Renaissance, Greek classical, and Venetian styles, but most of all, there are Art Nouveau buildings, especially at the southern end of Cogels Osylei and Waterloostraat. Berchem is the first stop on the railway line to Brussels.

FotoMuseum Provincie Antwerpen. In fall 2004, this photography museum reopened with a new wing designed by architect Georges Baines. The new section includes two spaces for temporary exhibits, two auditoriums for films, a café, and a shop. The collection here celebrates the likes of Henri Cartier-Bresson, William Klein, and Man Ray. There's also a display tracing the history of photography, from the "miragioscope" of the early 19th century to a James Bond camera disguised as a gun. Temporary exhibits, lectures, and workshops enhance the permanent shows. ⊠*Waalse Kaai 47, Het Zuid* ☎*03/242-9300* ⊕*www.fotomuseum. be* ☎€6 ⊗*Tues.–Sun. 10–5* Ⓜ*Bus 6 or Tram 8.*

NEED A BREAK?

Pakhuis (⊠*Vlaamse Kaai 76, Het Zuid* ☎*03/238-1240*), a crowded former warehouse, is dominated by a series of shiny vats used to brew the café's three beers; the Antwerp Blond in particular is vastly superior to mass-produced brews. The building's conversion is slightly sterile, but the ales, well-prepared snacks, and professional service can't be faulted.

⑫ ★ Koninklijk Museum voor Schone Kunsten. A must for the student of Flemish art, the Royal Museum of Fine Arts collection is studded with masterworks from Bruegel to Ensor. Paintings recovered from the French after the fall of Napoléon form the nucleus of a collection of 2,500 works of art. Room H is devoted to Jacob Jordaens; Room I, mostly to monumental Rubens; and Room G, to Bruegel. The collection of Flemish Primitives includes works by van Eyck, Memling, Roger van der Weyden, Joachim Patinir, and Quinten Metsys. On the ground floor there's a representative survey of Belgian art of the past 150 years—Emile Claus, Rik Wouters, Permeke, Magritte, Delvaux, and especially James Ensor. Ask for the audioguide in English. To get here from the city center, you can take tram 8. ⊠*Leopold de Waelplaats 2, Het Zuid* 🕿*03/238–7809* ⊕*museum.antwerpen.be/kmska* 🎫*€6* 🕙*Tues.–Sat. 10–5, Sun. 10–6* Ⓜ*Tram 8.*

Museum van Hedendaagse Kunst (MuHKA). Here you'll find contemporary paintings, installations, video art, and experimental architecture from both Belgian and international artists, including works by the mysterious Flemish theater director/choreographer/artist Jan Fabre, whose sculptures and installations, often based on or involving insects, have established him as a leading figure in the Belgian art world. The museum is in a renovated grain silo in the trendy Waalse Kaai street. ⊠*Leuvenstraat 32, Het Zuid* 🕿*03/260–9999* ⊕*www.muhka.be* 🎫*€5* 🕙*Tues.–Sun. 10–5* Ⓜ*Bus 6 or 23, or Tram 8.*

Openluchtmuseum Middelheim. The Middelheim Open Air Sculpture Museum puts all kinds of sculptures, from Rodin to Henry Moore, out to pasture in a park. There are more than 300 pieces on the attractive grounds, including works by Alexander Calder and Ossip Zadkine. A pavilion houses smaller and more fragile sculptures. ⊠*Middelheimlaan 61, Middelheim* 🕿*03/827–1534* ⊕*museum.antwerpen.be/ middelheimopenluchtmuseum* 🎫*Free, except for special exhibitions* 🕙*Tues.–Sun. 10–sunset* Ⓜ*Bus 17 or 22.*

OFF THE BEATEN PATH

Port of Antwerp. Although the Port of Antwerp is 88 km (53 mi) from the sea, it is Europe's second-largest port (after Rotterdam). Giant locks facilitate navigation up the river Scheldt; the largest measures 550 yards by 75 yards. Every year, 100 million tons of goods are shipped here, serving a vast area stretching across half of Europe. Surprisingly, in the midst of all this hustle and bustle is a traditional fishing village, Lillo, nestled among the enormous refineries, the tankers, and the buildings of the chemical industries. ▮**TIP➔ You'll need your own car to get here. Take Havenweg A12.** ⊠*Scheldelaan, on the banks of the river 20 km (12 mi) north of town.*

WHERE TO EAT

OUDE STAD

$$$
MEDITERRANEAN
★

✕ **De Kleine Zavel.** Wooden crates filled with bottles evoke this building's history; it was once a hotel for people in the shipping industry. Peer up at the ceiling's original intricate carvings before weighing the choices on the constantly changing menu. ⊠*Stoofstraat 2, Oude Stad* 🕿*03/231– 9691* ▤*AE, MC, V* 🕙*No lunch Sat.* Ⓜ*Metro 2, 3, or 5.*

$$$$
CONTEMPORARY

✕ **Gin Fish.** In a house on a narrow street, this tiny two-level restaurant serves some of the best, most sophisticated fish dishes in the city. Chef Didier Garnich serves four-course meals in a relaxed environment—in fact, you don't even have to decide among dishes. There's no menu; instead, the daily meal is driven by the morning's market purchases. You might be served langoustines in a light curry sauce or sea scallops cooked in a mushroom-sorrel stock. The crème brûlée is outstanding.

Antwerp's Local Dining Traditions

Belgium's kinship to brewing figures high in the country's culture and regional differences give way to local flavors. Antwerp has its own brewery, De Koninck (The King), and its light-amber beer is drunk in a special 8 oz. glass. Some prefer the beer in a smaller glass called a *prinske* (prince).

In the past, every household had a bottle of *Elixir d'Anvers* in its medicine cabinet, a homemade remedy respected for its healing properties. Touted as strong enough to cure a horse, its use was endorsed by Louis Pasteur. It consists of 32 different kinds of herbs; saffron gives it a yellow color. Nowadays, it's simply a popular aperitif.

Worstenbrood (sausage in bread) is typically eaten the Monday following January 6th. Tradition dictated that corporations and guilds hold annual meetings at the beginning of the year, after which people didn't return to work, leading to *verloren maandag* (Lost Monday). The butcher offered employees sausages and the baker, bread—hence, worstenbrood was born. Over time, it became a ritual among laborers.

Turning to the more exotic, *paling in 't groen* (eel in green sauce) is cooked in a special sauce with an assortment of herbs. *Fricadellen met krieken* (meatloaf smothered with sour cherries and a lot of sugar) is popular during holidays or feasts.

✉ *Haarstraat 9, Oude Stad* ☎ *03/231–3207* ♿ *Reservations essential* ▤ *AE, DC, MC, V* ⊗ *Closed Sun., Mon., and June. No lunch* Ⓜ *Metro 2, 3, or 5.*

$$–$$$
CONTEMPORARY

✕ **Hecker.** Choose one or two bottles of wine out of a selection of 120 and leave it to Danish chef Kasper Kurdahl to serve up a scrumptious concoction to enhance the wine's flavor. He constantly reinvents traditional dishes and unapologetically combines tastes and textures you would never imagine for fabulous results. ✉ *Kloosterstraat 13, Oude Stad* ☎ *03/234–3834* ▤ *AE, DC, MC, V* ⊗ *Closed Wed. No lunch Mon.* Ⓜ *Bus 6 or 34.*

$–$$
ECLECTIC

✕ **Het Hemelse Gerecht.** In this cozy nook behind the cathedral, the daily menu is written on a three-panel chalkboard that seems to be bigger than the restaurant itself. Up on the board you'll find an eclectic mix, from tapas to jambalaya to a solid rendition of the classic *waterzooi* (traditional Flemish stew with chicken or seafood). With five tables, this is a small gem. You're wise to phone ahead for a table, as hours of operation are sometimes dictated by the reservation book. ✉ *Lijnwaadmarkt 3, Oude Stad* ☎ *03/231–2927* ▤ *No credit cards* ⊗ *Closed Wed.* Ⓜ *Tram 10 or 11.*

$$$–$$$$
SEAFOOD

✕ **Het Nieuwe Palinghuis.** The name means The New Eelhouse, and sweet-fleshed eel, prepared in a variety of ways, is the house specialty, along with grilled turbot, grilled scallops, and sole in lobster sauce. Fittingly for an Antwerp landmark, the restaurant has dark wood and a comfortable, deep-rooted air. ✉ *St-Jansvliet 14, Oude Stad* ☎ *03/231–7445* ▤ *AE, DC, MC, V* ⊗ *Closed Mon., Tues., and June* Ⓜ *Bus 6 or 34.*

$$-$$$ ✕**Hungry Henrietta.** Though near the busy shopping stretch of the Meir,
BELGIAN   this stylish Antwerp institution is on a quiet, calm square, making it a
good place to retreat if you're feeling fashion fatigue. When weather
permits, try for a seat on the terrace, then decide between such dishes
as salmon fillet and loin of lamb. ✉*Lombardenvest 19, Oude Stad*
☎*03/232–2928* ▤*DC, MC, V* ⊘*Closed weekends and first 3 wks in
Aug.* Ⓜ*Metro 2, 3, or 5.*

$$-$$$ ✕**In de Schaduw van de Kathedraal.** Cozier and more traditional than
BELGIAN   the wave of contemporary restaurants dominating the scene, this little
place makes good on its name: it has a dining room facing the cathedral
square and a terrace where you can take your meal in the cathedral's
shadow. Try the delicious North Sea crab gratiné. ✉*Handschoenmarkt
17–21, Oude Stad* ☎*03/232–4014* ▤*AE, DC, MC, V* ⊘*Closed Tues.*
Ⓜ*Metro 2, 3, or 5.*

$$$ ✕**Neuze Neuze.** Five tiny houses have been cobbled together to create
CONTINENTAL   this handsome, split-level restaurant with plenty of nooks and cran-
Fodor's Choice   nies on different levels, whitewashed walls, and dark-brown beams.
★   Look for grilled scallops with Belgian endive and bacon in a wheat-
beer sauce, and ham with truffles and "spaghetti" made of thinly cut
vegetables. ✉*Wijngaardstraat 19, Oude Stad* ☎*03/232–2797* ▤*AE,
DC, MC, V* ⊘*Closed Sun., 2 wks in Aug., and 1 wk in Jan. No lunch
Wed. and Sat.* Ⓜ*Tram 10 or 11.*

$$$-$$$$ ✕**P. Preud 'Homme.** In a location that has served as a pastry shop and a
CONTEMPORARY   gun shop, this exquisite restaurant mixes Art Nouveau design, antiques,
and a 400-year-old Spanish ceiling. The food is on a par with the decor,
and includes lobster and oysters. Other house specialties include such
delicacies as terrine of duck liver, fried scallops in leek sauce, and ice
cream with hot-chocolate sauce. ✉*Suikerrui 28, Oude Stad* ☎*03/233–
4200* ▤*AE, DC, MC, V* ⊘*Closed Jan.* Ⓜ*Metro 2, 3, or 5.*

$$$-$$$$ ✕**Sir Anthony Van Dijck.** You used to find well-respected haute cuisine
FRENCH   here, but the owner has made the transition to a more relaxed estab-
★   lishment. Now the monthly changing menu offers brasserie fare such
as salad *liègeoise* (with beans, boiled potatoes, and morsels of bacon),
duck à l'orange, and tuna steak. Under high, massive beams supported
by stone pillars, you sit surrounded by flowers and carved wood, at
tables overlooking an interior courtyard. There are two seatings a night.
✉*Vlaeykensgang, Oude Koornmarkt 16, Oude Stad* ☎*03/231–6170*
▤*AE, DC, MC, V* ⊘*Closed Sun., Aug., Dec. 25–Jan. 1, and Easter
wk* Ⓜ*Metro 2, 3, or 5.*

¢–$ ✕**Spaghettiworld.** The pasta is good, but the people-watching is even
CAFÉ   better at this hip joint where Keith Haring drawings set the mood.
The young and the style-conscious fuel up here before a night on the
town. ✉*Oude Koornmarkt 66, Oude Stad* ☎*03/234–3801* ▤*AE,
DC, MC, V* ⊘*Closed Mon. and Tue. No lunch Wed.–Fri. and Sun.*
Ⓜ*Tram 2 or 15.*

$–$$ ✕**'t Brantyser.** This old, two-level bistro with dark rafters, brick, and
INTERNATIONAL   stucco, serves a range of meal-size salads and affordable specials of

meat and veg. It has an open fire, lighted in winter. ✉*Hendrik Conscienceplein 7, Oude Stad* ☎*03/233–1833* ▭*AE, MC, V* Ⓜ*Tram 10 or 11.*

$$$$
FRENCH
Fodor'sChoice
★

✕**'t Fornuis.** In the heart of old Antwerp, this cozy restaurant, decorated in traditional Flemish style with heavy oak chairs and beamed ceilings, serves some of the best (and priciest) food in the city. Chef Johan Segers likes to change his French-accented menu at regular intervals, but roasted sweetbreads with a wild-truffle sauce are a permanent fixture. Take a look at the wonderful collection of miniature stoves while you're waiting to be seated. ✉*Reyndersstraat 24, Oude Stad* ☎*03/233–6270* ⚑*Reservations essential Jacket and tie* ▭*AE, DC, MC, V* ✆*Closed weekends, last 3 wks in Aug., Dec. 25–Jan. 1* Ⓜ*Metro 2, 3, or 5.*

$–$$
BELGIAN

✕**'t Hofke.** It's worth visiting here for the location alone, in the Vlaeykensgang alley, where time seems to have stood still. The cozy dining room has the look and feel of a private home, and the menu includes a large selection of salads and omelets, as well as more substantial fare. Try for a table in the courtyard. ✉*Vlaeykensgang, Oude Koornmarkt 16, Oude Stad* ☎*03/233–8606* ▭*AE, MC, V* Ⓜ*Tram 2, 3, or 5.*

$–$$
BELGIAN

✕**Zuiderterras.** A stark, glass-and-black-metal construction, this riverside café and restaurant was designed by avant-garde architect bOb (his spelling) Van Reeth; it resembles a docked cruise ship. You're virtually assured a good view, since large windows stretch on all sides. You'll have the river traffic on one side and, on the other, a view of the cathedral and the Oude Stad. The food is as modern as the surroundings, with dishes such as salmon lasagna with fresh basil. ✉*Ernest Van Dijckkaai 37, Oude Stad* ☎*03/234–1275* ▭*AE, MC, V* Ⓜ*Bus 6 or 34.*

THE MEIR, DIAMANTWIJK & CENTRAAL STATION

$$–$$$
CONTEMPORARY

✕**Flamant Dining.** In keeping with the celebrated style of the home-design shop of the same name, the freshness and tastefulness of the interior here transfers fluently to its meals. Chef Eric Somers creates sensational salads, perfect for lunch, or spectacular plates like sea bass with tomato confit and black olives. Presentation is the key and dishes are as pleasing to look at as the diluted colors and romantic patterns of the restaurant. The splendid terrace is a real haven from hectic city life. ✉*Lange Gasthuisstraat 12, Kruidtuin* ☎*03/227–7441* ▭*AE, MC, V* ✆*Closed Sun.* Ⓜ*Tram 8.*

$$–$$$
CONTEMPORARY

✕**Horta.** The iron framework of the 18th-century Maison du Peuple, a building designed by the famed Art Nouveau architect Victor Horta, now supports this brasserie. It siphons a hip crowd from trendy Hopland Street and keeps a sunny feel with large mustard-yellow industrial beams and windows all around. The kitchen sends out such tempting contemporary dishes as roasted perch with asparagus, shiitake mush-

Where to Stay & Eat in Antwerp

KEY

⇌ Metro

⊢⊣ Rail

•••• Tram

Restaurants ▼

De Kleine Zavel **13**

Dome/Dome Surmer **33**

Euterpia **37**

Flamant Dining **27**

Gin Fish **4**

Hecker **14**

Het Hemelse Gerecht **10**

Het Nieuwe Palinghuis **11**

Het Pomphuis **1**

Horta **26**

Hungry Henrietta **24**

In de Schaduw van
de Kathedraal **9**

Neuze Neuze **20**

O'Kontreir **34**

P. Preud 'Homme **6**

Sir Anthony Van Dijck **7**

Spaghettiworld **16**

't Brantyser **21**

't Fornuis **15**

't Hofke **8**

Zuiderterras **5**

Hotels ▼

Antwerp Hilton **17**

Best Western Classic
Hotel Villa Mozart **18**

Crowne Plaza
Antwerp **35**

De Witte Lelie **22**

Hotel Firean **36**

Hotel Julien **19**

Hotel Rubens **3**

Hyllit **25**

Ibis Antwerpen Centrum ..**29**

International
Zeemanshuis **2**

Plaza Hotel **31**

Prinse **23**

Radisson SAS
Park Lane Hotel **32**

Ramada Plaza Antwerp **38**

Rubenshof **39**

Scoutel **30**

t'Elzenveld **28**

t'Sandt **12**

rooms, and artichokes with a warm rouille. ⊠*Hopland 2, Oude Stad* ☏*03/232–2815* ▤*AE, DC, MC, V* Ⓜ*Tram 2, 3, or 5, or Bus 9.*

BEYOND CENTRAL ANTWERP

$$$–$$$$ ✕**Dome.** Architecture and food aficionados will appreciate the classic
FRENCH French cuisine and somber decor in this splendid Art Nouveau build-
ing. This former teahouse, sewing school, and police office maintains
its original floor mosaic, and the whitewashed walls and dome-shaped
roof parallel its haute cuisine. French chef Julien Burlat and wife Sophie
Verbeke, former stylist for Dries Van Noten, set up this restaurant (and
its marine version, Dome sur Mer, just a stone's throw away) in the
upscale Zurenborg neighborhood. Enjoy the monkfish with fresh spin-
ach, pumpkin oil, and red-wine sauce, or saddle of lamb and eggplant
caviar in wild-thyme sauce. The sign by the front door here is so discreet
you may well walk straight past without realizing. ⊠*Grote Hondstraat
2, Zurenborg* ☏*03/239–9003* ▤*AE, DC, MC, V* ✆*Closed Sun. and
Mon. No lunch Sat.* Ⓜ*Bus 9.*

$$$–$$$$ ✕**Euterpia.** Owners Marc and Marijke Tombeur turned this gorgeous
CONTEMPORARY Art Nouveau building into a restaurant favored by a chic, arty set.
★ House specialties include *coucou de Malines*, chicken in puff pastry
with truffle sauce and wild mushrooms. Try for a table in the garden,
but if the weather's not cooperating you can still dine alfresco on the
closed terrace. ⊠*Generaal Capiaumonstraat 2, Berchem* ☏*03/235–
0202* ▤*AE, DC, MC, V* ✆*Closed Mon., Tues., and 3 wks in Aug. No
lunch* Ⓜ*Bus 34 or Tram 11.*

$$$ ✕**Het Pomphuis.** The name translates to the Pump House, and in its
CONTEMPORARY heyday it drained the neighboring dry dock to allow for ship mainte-
nance. And it still looks the part. Boasting an eclectic style with Art
Nouveau features, the vast interior has an impressive 23-foot pit with
iron parapets and round arch windows with original metal rods. Today,
it has no loftier purpose than to provide an impressive interior, the
better to savor goose-liver terrine with shallot compote and a fine herbes salad. Make a trip to the washroom to view the heavy steel pump
doors. ⊠*Siberiastraat Z/N, Het Eilandje* ☏*03/770–8625* ▤*AE, MC,
V* Ⓜ*Bus 31 or 35.*

$$ ✕**O'Kontreir.** This stark, minimalist-style restaurant offers sweet and
CONTEMPORARY spicy fare like great garlic spareribs and shrimp scampi. The menu
is seasonal, but steaks are a fixture. ⊠*Isabellalei 145, Middelheim*
☏*03/281–3976* ⟟*Reservations essential* ▤*AE, MC, V* ✆*Closed
Mon., Tues., and 2 wks in June* Ⓜ*Bus 14.*

WHERE TO STAY

OUDE STAD

$$$$ ⊞**Antwerp Hilton.** This five-story complex incorporates the fin-de-siècle facade of what was once the Grand Bazar department store. Mahogany doors open onto spacious guest rooms with duvet-topped beds and flat-screen TVs. The bathroom mirrors are even heated so they won't steam up when you most need them. Multiple telephones, data ports, and Wi-Fi access make each room business-friendly; the neutral color scheme won't distract you from your work. Afternoon tea is served in the marble-floor lobby. **Pros:** luxurious; large rooms; centrally located. **Cons:** such luxury doesn't come cheap. ✉*Groenplaats, Oude Stad* ☎*03/204–1212* ⊕*www.hilton.com* ↘*193 rooms, 18 suites* ♿*In-room: safe, Wi-Fi. In-hotel: 2 restaurants, bar, gym, parking (paid), no-smoking rooms, Wi-Fi* ▤*AE, DC, MC, V* Ⓜ*Tram 2 or 15. The hotel has an entrance in the Groenplaats metro station.*

$$ ⊞**Best Western Classic Hotel Villa Mozart.** This small, modern hotel, a part of the Best Western chain, is ideally situated in the pedestrian zone next to the cathedral. The rooms feel a bit cramped, but they have the amenities you'd expect from an international chain, and many have cathedral views. In fair weather you can take breakfast on the terrace facing the cathedral. **Pros:** great location. **Cons:** small rooms; no private parking. ✉*Handschoenmarkt 3–7, Oude Stad* ☎*03/231–3031* ⊕*www.bestwestern.be/classichotelvillamozart* ↘*25 rooms* ♿*In-room: safe. In-hotel: restaurant, bar* ▤*AE, DC, MC, V* Ⓜ*Metro 2, 3, 5, or 15.*

$$$ ⊞**Hotel Julien.** Informality is the trademark of this elegant hotel in a 16th-century renovated historic house, which spills over into a quiet patio. Despite its city location, the peaceful setting makes it feel like a relaxing refuge. Enjoy breakfast on porcelain dishes made exclusively for the hotel. Spacious rooms are tastefully decorated with contemporary designs including wooden ceilings and terra-cotta floors, which effortlessly provide a comfort level like home. A room with a view of the cathedral is worth the extra expense. There's a DVD and CD library as well. **Pros:** friendly staff; historic building. **Cons:** no private parking. ✉*Korte Niewstraat 24, Oude Stad* ☎*03/229–0600* ⊕*www.hotel-julien.com* ↘*11 rooms* ♿*In-room: safe, Wi-Fi. In-hotel: room service, Wi-Fi* ▤*AE, MC, V* ⍩*CP* Ⓜ*Tram 10 or 11.*

$$ ⊞**Hotel Rubens.** A peaked tower marks this small, colorful hotel directly behind the Grote Markt. The tower is said to be the oldest in Antwerp, and was part of the original city walls. The room decor may not be terribly original, but the deep bathtubs make for a good soak at the end of the day. **Pros:** friendly staff; great location; quiet courtyard garden. **Cons:** parking limited. ✉*Oude Beurs 29, Oude Stad* ☎*03/222–4848* ⊕*www.hotelrubensantwerp.be* ↘*36 rooms* ♿*In-room: safe, Wi-Fi. In-hotel: bar, parking (paid), Wi-Fi* ▤*AE, DC, MC, V* ⍩*CP* Ⓜ*Tram 10 or 11.*

6

$ 🏨 **Ibis Antwerpen Centrum.** What this centrally located chain hotel lacks in individuality and character, it more than makes up for in value for money and its central location, just a few minutes' walk from the Grote Markt. Rooms are basic, but clean and modern, and popular with business travelers. Some good deals are available in summer. **Pros:** great location; good value for money. **Cons:** part of a chain, so lacking character; some rooms small; bathrooms are small. ⊠*Meistraat 39, Oude Stad* ☎*03/231–8830* ⊕*www.accorhotels.com* ⬗*150 rooms* ♿*In-room: Wi-Fi. In-hotel: bar, parking (paid), Wi-Fi* ▤*AE, DC, MC, V* Ⓜ*Tram 12.*

$$ 🏨 **'t Elzenveld.** An oasis of peace and quiet in the heart of the city, 't Elzenveld is a cultural center located in the medieval buildings of the former St. Elisabeth General Hospital. The tranquil, cloistered gardens, dating from 1804, are gorgeous with trees, shrubs, and exotic plants. The old convent has been renovated into guest rooms but still gives a glimpse of its former life with parquet floors and period furniture. Rooms range from small to spacious but aren't air-conditioned. **Pros:** quiet location; historic building. **Cons:** some rooms small. ⊠*Lange Gasthuisstraat 45, Oude Stad* ☎*03/202–7770* ⊕*www.elzenveld.be* ⬗*26 rooms, 8 suites, 6 apartments* ♿*In-room: Wi-Fi, no a/c* ▤*AE, DC, MC, V* ⦿|*BP* Ⓜ*Tram 8.*

$$$ 🏨 **'t Sandt.** A former soap factory is now one of Antwerp's classiest
Fodor'sChoice hotels. Each guest room has a unique configuration; simple back-
★ drops of white walls and beamed ceilings set off rich furnishings. Some rooms have antique furnishings. A handful of others have a view of the cathedral. You can also get a cathedral view from the tranquil garden. **Pros:** great location; friendly staff; quiet garden. **Cons:** limited parking. ⊠*Zand 13–19, Oude Stad* ☎*03/232–9390* ⊕*www.hotel-sandt. be* ⬗*30 suites, 6 apartments* ♿*In-room: safe, Wi-Fi, minibar* ▤*AE, DC, MC, V* Ⓜ*Metro 2, 3, or 5.*

THE MEIR, DIAMANTWIJK & CENTRAAL STATION

$$$$ 🏨 **De Witte Lelie.** Three step-gabled 16th-century houses have been com-
Fodor'sChoice bined to make the "White Lily," Antwerp's most exclusive hotel. As
★ soon as you enter the grand lobby, a stylish blend of old and new, it's clear that personal service is the watchword. As the name suggests, the hotel's decor is mostly white, punctuated with colorful carpets and modern art. Elegant salons have grand fireplaces, and breakfasts are served on a loggia that opens onto the inner courtyard. **Pros:** large rooms; friendly, attentive service. **Cons:** some rooms have no elevator access. ⊠*Keizerstraat 16–18, Stadswaag* ☎*03/226–1966* ⊕*www. dewittelelie.be* ⬗*4 rooms, 6 suites* ♿*In-room: safe, Wi-Fi. In-hotel: parking (paid)* ▤*AE, MC, V* Ⓜ*Tram 10 or 11.*

$$$ 🏨 **Hyllit.** Here you can roll out of bed and hit the stores. The Hyllit stands on the corner of De Keyserlei, a high-end shopping street, with its entrance on Appelmansstraat (reception on second floor), the gateway to the Diamantwijk. Rooms are decorated in muted colors and equipped with office-style desks. There's a rooftop buffet break-

fast room. **Pros:** convenient for station and Diamantwijk. **Cons:** modern and lacking character. ☒*De Keyserlei 28–30, Centraal Station* ☏*03/202–6800* ⊕*www.hyllithotel.be* ➲*71 rooms, 56 suites* ⚴*In-room: Internet. In-hotel: restaurant, room service, pool, gym, parking (paid)* ▤*AE, DC, MC, V* Ⓜ*Tram 2, 3, 5 or 15.*

¢ ★ 🏨**Internationaal Zeemanshuis.** Originally established as a hotel for sailors, the Seamen's House is now open to all. (Sailors make up nearly half of the clientele, though, and they reap a significant discount.) Standard single and double rooms have showers; deluxe rooms have full baths, refrigerators, and in-room safes. The self-service restaurant carries on the tradition of a friendly meeting place. **Pros:** good value. **Cons:** limited facilities; ugly building. ☒*Falconrui 21, Stadswaag* ☏*03/227–5433* ⊕*www.zeemanshuis.be* ➲*114 rooms* ⚴*In-room: refrigerator, safe. In-hotel: restaurant* ▤*AE, MC, V* Ⓜ*Bus 9.*

$$ 🏨**Prinse.** Set well back from the street, this 400-year-old landmark with an interior courtyard was once the home of 16th-century poet Anna Bijns. Now it has a modern look, with black leather chairs, soft blue curtains, and tile bathrooms. Exposed beams give top-floor rooms more character. Soothing music resounds in the lobby. **Pros:** quiet location; friendly staff; historic building. **Cons:** limited parking. ☒*Keizerstraat 63, Stadswaag* ☏*03/226–4050* ⊕*www.hotelprinse.be* ➲*35 rooms* ⚴*In-room: Internet (some), minibar* ▤*AE, DC, MC, V* �◎*BP* Ⓜ*Tram 10 or 11.*

¢ 🏨**Scoutel.** This hotel, owned by the Boy Scouts and Girl Guides but open to all ages, is in a modern building five minutes' walk from Centraal Station. The double and triple rooms are simple but adequate; all have toilets and showers. Rates are lower for people under 25, and most of the guests *are* young people. Sheets are included; towels can be rented. Guests are provided with front-door keys. **Pros:** good value. **Cons:** basic; noisy due to proximity to mainline railway. ☒*Stoomstraat 3, Centraal Station* ☏*03/226–4606* ⊕*www.scoutel.be* ➲*22 rooms* ⚴*In-room: no a/c, no phone. In-hotel: no elevator* ▤*MC, V* �◎*BP* Ⓜ*Bus 16.*

BEYOND CENTRAL ANTWERP

$$$ 🏨**Crowne Plaza Antwerp.** On the ring road outside of the city center, the Crowne Plaza caters primarily to business travelers. Rooms are clean and comfortable, though not long on character, and the staff is first-rate. The fitness center has extensive facilities, including a tanning bed, sauna, Turkish steam bath, and pool. Excellent deals are available if you book ahead through the Web site. **Pros:** easy access for vehicles. **Cons:** far from the sights. ☒*Gerard Le Grellelaan 10, Middelheim* ☏*03/259–7500* ⊕*www.ichotelsgroup.com* ➲*262 rooms* ⚴*In-room: Wi-Fi. In-hotel: restaurant, bar, pool, gym, parking (paid)* ▤*AE, DC, MC, V* Ⓜ*Bus 17 or 22.*

$$$ ★ 🏨**Hotel Firean.** This art deco gem, built in 1929, embodies not only the architectural style but also the grace of a bygone era. The setting,

a residential neighborhood on the tram line into town, reinforces the tranquillity inside, expressed by fresh flowers, rich fabrics, and a tasteful mix of antiques and reproductions. The service is what you'd hope for from a family-owned and -operated establishment. There's scrupulous attention to detail; breakfast eggs come in floral-print cozies, for instance, and jazz piano is discreetly piped into public areas. The owner's son runs a restaurant a few doors away. **Pros:** family–run; historic building; full of character. **Cons:** far from the sights. ⊠ *Karel Oomsstraat 6, Middelheim* ☎ *03/237–0260* ⊕ *www.hotelfirean.com* ⤴ *9 rooms, 6 in annex next door* ⟨ *In-room: safe, Internet. In-hotel: bar* ⊟ *AE, DC, MC, V* ☾ *Closed last wk of July–Aug.15, Dec. 24–1st weekend after Jan. 6* ⦿ *CP* Ⓜ *Tram 2.*

$$$　𝖜 **Plaza Hotel.** Like its (unrelated) namesake in New York, the Plaza in Antwerp is near Central Park (Stadspark), a brisk walk from the city center. It has a handful of traditional grace notes, such as cherrywood paneling in the public spaces, comfy lounge chairs in the lobby, and a marble entrance. The rooms are good-size by local standards, with walk-in closets. Ask about special weekend rates. **Pros:** friendly staff. **Cons:** on a noisy street. ⊠ *Charlottalei 49, Zurenborg* ☎ *03/287–2870* ⊕ *www.plaza.be* ⤴ *80 rooms* ⟨ *In-room: safe, minibar, Wi-Fi. In-hotel: bar* ⊟ *AE, DC, MC, V* ⦿ *BP* Ⓜ *Bus 14 or 16.*

$$$　𝖜 **Radisson SAS Park Lane Hotel.** Amazing views of the Stadspark are a key draw for the city's only five-star hotel. Spacious rooms are bright and fitted with all the amenities of a large chain hotel. The atrium bar is very airy with a lot of plants, and makes a nice place for a drink. **Pros:** good location opposite park. **Cons:** modern and lacking character. ⊠ *Van Eycklei 34, Middelheim* ☎ *03/285–8585* ⊕ *www.radissonsas. com* ⤴ *156 rooms, 14 suites* ⟨ *In-room: Wi-Fi. In-hotel: restaurant, bar, pool, gym* ⊟ *AE, DC, MC, V* Ⓜ *Bus 9.*

$$$　𝖜 **Ramada Plaza Antwerp.** Sharp angles and a minimalist design distinguish this glass-and-steel structure set in a park 10 minutes south of the city center. Rooms are equipped for business travelers, with conveniences like desks and hair dryers, and the service is consistently good. **Pros:** easy access for vehicles. **Cons:** far from the sights. ⊠ *Desguinlei 94, Middelheim* ☎ *03/244–8211* ⊕ *www.ramadaplaza-antwerp.com* ⤴ *213 rooms* ⟨ *In-room: safe, Wi-Fi. In-hotel: 2 restaurants, bar, gym, Wi-Fi* ⊟ *AE, DC, MC, V* Ⓜ *Bus 17 or 22.*

$　𝖜 **Rubenshof.** Once a cardinal's residence, this hotel shows remnants of its former glory with a mixture of turn-of-the-20th-century styles. The breakfast room, for instance, is a terrific example of the Jugendstil (Art Nouveau) style. The hotel is owned by a friendly Dutch couple, and it's close to the Koninklijk Museum voor Schone Kunsten. Rooms are simple, with wooden furniture and basic amenities. Those on the top floor are geared toward backpackers and share a bathroom; these are cheaper, in the ¢ range. **Pros:** good value for money; historic building. **Cons:** some rooms share bathrooms; no elevator; furnishing showing their age. ⊠ *Amerikalei 115–117, Het Zuid* ☎ *03/237–0789* ⊕ *www.*

rubenshof.be 🛏*22 rooms* ♿*In-hotel: no elevator* ▤*AE, DC, MC, V* Ⓜ*Tram 4, 12, or 24.*

NIGHTLIFE & THE ARTS

THE ARTS

Check the *Bulletin*, a weekly English-language newsmagazine, for details on arts events in Antwerp. You can pick up a copy at bookstores and newsstands.

DANCE

Antwerp is home to a host of innovative and exciting ballet and dance troupes, and its school is internationally renowned. The major ballet company is the **Koninklijk Ballet van Vlaanderen** (*Royal Flanders Ballet* ✉*Kattendijkdok Westkaai 16, Het Eilandje* ☎*03/234–3438* ⊕*www.koninklijkballetvanvlaanderen.be*), whose productions tour regularly across Belgium. The companies of leading Belgian choreographers, including Anne Teresa De Keersmaeker, Wim Vandekeybus, and Alain Platel, frequently perform at **deSingel** (✉*Desguinlei 25, Middelheim* ☎*03/248–2828* ⊕*www.desingel.be*).

OPERA & CONCERTS

Antwerp's opera company is **Koninklijke Vlaamse Opera** (*Royal Flanders Opera* ✉*Frankrijklei 3, Centraal Station* ☎*03/233–6685*), which has a sister company in Gent. The **Koninklijk Philharmonisch Orkest van Vlaanderen** (Royal Flanders Philharmonic) most frequently performs at **deSingel** (✉*Desguinlei 25, Middelheim* ☎*03/248–2828*). A regular venue for classical music is the **Koningin Elisabethzaal** (✉*Koningin Astridplein 26, Centraal Station* ☎*0900/00–311* ⊕*www.elisabethzaal.be*).

Major rock concerts are held at the **Sportpaleis** (✉*Schijnpoortweg 113, Merksem* ☎*03/400–4040*), although Antwerp is inexplicably not on the regular gig circuit.

THEATER

The flagship of the more than two dozen theaters in Antwerp is the **Bourla Theater** (✉*Komedieplaats 18, Kruidtuin* ☎*03/224–8844*), a marvelously restored 19th-century facility, which is now the home of the **Koninklijke Nederlands Schouwburg** (Royal Dutch-speaking Theater). This troupe presents both classic and contemporary plays. Contemporary productions by international companies appear regularly at the multipurpose **deSingel** (✉*Desguinlei 25, Middelheim* ☎*03/248–2828*). The **Poppenschouwburg Van Campen** (*Van Campen Puppet Theater* ✉*Lange Nieuwstraat 3, Oude Stad* ☎*03/237–3716*) presents traditional puppet performances September–May. Shows are in Flemish, and the stories can be hard to puzzle out if you're not familiar with Flemish or Dutch.

NIGHTLIFE

There are 2,500 taverns in Antwerp—one for every 200 inhabitants—and the city is the club-going capital of Belgium, which means that the centers of nightlife are abuzz until the wee hours of the morning. The **Grote Markt** area attracts many tourists as well as locals with a range of traditional Belgian alehouses and some small discos, especially in the narrow, winding streets around the cathedral. **Leuvenstraat,** particularly around the Museum van Hedendaagse Kunst (MuHKA), teems with cafés and pool halls. Some of the cafés even have small acting troupes that perform nightly. The small, hidden square of **Stadswaag** has a cluster of bars and discos. Along the waterfront at **Vlaamse Kaai** and **Waalse Kaai** there's a large parking square where you'll find some of Antwerp's biggest clubs as well as a group of smaller pubs. Be advised, though, that they share the area with Antwerp's red-light district.

BARS

Bar Tabac (⊠ *Waalse Kaai 43, Het Zuid* ☎*No phone*) is a studiously seedy mock-Gallic truckers' café. **Beveren** (⊠*Vlasmarkt 2, Oude Stad* ☎*03/231–2225*) is boisterous and old-fashioned. **Bierhuis Kulminator** (⊠*Vleminckveld 32–34, Oude Stad* ☎*03/232–4538*) pours 550 different kinds of beer, including EKU-28, known as the strongest beer on earth; some of the beers are 30 years old. Facing the main square's fountain, **Den Engel** (⊠*Grote Markt 3, Oude Stad* ☎*03/233–1252*) draws an eclectic clientele. African-theme **L'Entrepot du Congo** (⊠ *Vlaamse Kaai 42, Het Zuid* ☎*03/238–9232*) attracts a refined crowd; music varies, and food is available. The atmospheric **Pelgrom** (⊠*Pelgrimsstraat 15, Oude Stad* ☎*03/234–0809*) is in the vaulted brick cellars of a 16th-century tavern. **Vagant** (⊠*Corner of Pelgrimsstraat and Reyndersstraat, Oude Stad* ☎*03/233–1538*) is a late-night haunt. Try one or more of their 200 kinds of jenevers.

DANCE CLUBS

Café d'Anvers (⊠*Verversrui 15, Stadswaag* ☎*03/226–3870*), in the red-light district, is the city's flagship house and techno venue, attracting ravers from across Europe to its friendly dance floors. **Café Local** (⊠*Waalse Kaai 25, Het Zuid* ☎*03/238–5004*) imaginatively re-creates pre-Castro Cuba, although the music is uninspired chart dance. **Red and Blue** (⊠*Lange Schipperskapelstraat 11 and 13, Het Eilandje* ☎*03/213–0555*) can pack in up to 1,000 people. The gay night on Saturday pulls in plenty of internationals, while locals hit the house and garage-rock dance night on Friday.

GAY BARS

Antwerp has a more upfront gay scene than most Belgian cities; Van Schoonhovenstraat, near the Centraal Station, is clustered with gay bars, and there are plenty dotted around the city center. Ask in the tourist office for their "gay map" of Antwerp, detailing gay and gay-friendly clubs, bars, restaurants, saunas, and clinics. The **Het Roze Huis & Café Den Draak** (⊠*Draakplaats 1, Zurenborg* ☎*03/288–0084* ⊕*www.hetrozehuis.be*) is Antwerp's gay and lesbian community house, with a café (whose name means "The Dragon") on the ground floor.

JAZZ CLUBS

There's a handful of good jazz venues in town, but they don't host music every night so be sure to check the schedules in advance. **Antwerpse Jazz Club** (☎*03/238–8479*), which celebrated its 70th anniversary in 2008, hosts occasional jazz evenings at locations around the city. Call for times and locations. **De Hopper** (✉*Leopold De Waelstraat 2, Het Zuid* ☎*03/248–4933*) sporadically presents jazz performances in a rather formal environment. **De Muze** (✉*Melkmarkt 15, Oude Stad* ☎*03/226–0126*) has train-station decor and good jazz sounds. **DeSingel** (✉*Desguinlei 25, Middelheim* ☎*03/248–2828*), one of Antwerp's leading performing-arts venues, sometimes features jazz.

SPORTS & THE OUTDOORS

BICYCLING

The best places to cycle are along the left bank of the Scheldt or through one of the many parks scattered throughout the city. You can also bike through the city streets; though some streets are narrow or otherwise a bit tricky to navigate, the city has made itself more bicycle-friendly by marking designated bike paths in red. **De Windroos** (✉*Steenplein 1a, Oude Stad* ☎*03/480–9388*) rents bikes by the hour (€2.50) or by the day (€12.50). Rentals do not include helmets.

GOLF

The **Brasschaat Open Golf Club and Country Club** (✉*Miksebaan 248, Brasschaat* ☎*03/653–1084*) is just 15 km (9 mi) from the city center. It has an 18-hole golf course and admits nonmembers for €35 on weekdays and €50 on weekends.

SKATING

The most popular skating rink is **Antarctica** (✉*Moerelei 119, Wilrijk* ☎*03/828–9928*), in a suburb about 5 km (3 mi) from the city center, reachable by bus. You can rent skates for €2 an hour and use the indoor or outdoor rink. If you're in Antwerp during the winter holidays, be sure to hit the skating rink that's set up in the Grote Markt, **Antwerp on ice** (☎*03/232–0103*). You can rent skates (€2 per hour) and glide past the old guild houses—this is especially lovely in the evening, when the buildings are illuminated. The rink also hosts evening concerts and other special events.

SHOPPING

Much of Antwerp's reputation for edgy chic comes from its clothing designers; dedicated followers of fashion consider the city in a league with Milan and Paris, and Antwerp-based couturiers regularly appear in the international glossies. Credit for this development goes to the so-called Antwerp Six (students of Linda Loppa from the class of 1981 at Antwerp's Fashion Academy) and in equal measure to the new wave of talent that has more recently stormed the catwalks. Ready-to-wear by stalwarts Ann Demeulemeester, Dirk Bikkembergs, Dries Van Noten, and relative newcomers Raf Simons, Véronique Branquinho, and Wim Neels command high prices. However, in the shopping area south of Groenplaats, prices are less astronomical. And, of course, the Diamantwijk is prime territory for glittering precious stones.

SHOPPING STREETS

The elegant **Meir,** together with its extension to the east, **De Keyserlei,** and at the opposite end, **Huidevettersstraat,** is where you will find high-street standbys and long-established names. Shopping galleries branch off from all three streets—**Century Center** and **Antwerp Tower** from De Keyserlei, **Meir Square** from Meir, and **Nieuwe Gaanderij** from Huidevettersstraat. The area in and around the glamorous **Horta Complex,** on Hopland, the street parallel to the Meir between Centraal Station and the Oude Stad, is also a popular shopping hub.

Many boutiques cater to more avant-garde tastes. The best-known area is **De Wilde Zee,** which straddles the Meir and Oude Stad, consisting of Groendalstraat, Lombardenstraat, Wiegstraat, and Korte Gasthuisstraat. The nearby Schuttershofstraat, Kammenstraat, and Nationalestraat are also fizzing with new spots. Another pedestrian area for general shopping is **Hoogstraat,** between Grote Markt and Sint-Jansvliet, with its appendix, **Grote Pieter Potstraat.** Here you find good second-hand bookshops and all kinds of bric-a-brac.

CLOTHING

AVANT-GARDE FASHION

The explosive success of the Antwerp Six put Belgium firmly on the fashion map, and Antwerp in particular is a haven for cutting-edge women's and men's ready-to-wear fashions. **Louis** (✉ *Lombardenstraat 2, Sint-Andrieskwartier* ☎ *03/232–9872*) was one of the first places to sell the work of Antwerp's top designers in the late 1980s. Today, it sells the collections of the city's more recent talent—Martin Margiela, Ann Demeulemeester, A. F. Vandervorst, and Raf Simons.

Most of the original six now have their own stores. **Ann Demeulemeester** (✉ *Verlatstraat 38, Het Zuid* ☎ *03/216–0133*) sells her clothes in an elegant corner store close to the Koninklijk Museum voor Schone Kunsten.

The work of Dries Van Noten is in the splendid renovated **Modepaleis** (✉ *Kammenstraat and Nationalestraat 16, Sint-Andrieskwartier* ☎ *03/470–2510*), a men's and women's outfitter. Owned by Walter Van Beirendonck and Dirk Van Saene, **Walter** (✉ *Sint-Antoniustraat 12, Sint-Andrieskwartier* ☎ *03/213–2644*) sells the best of their collections against a futuristic backdrop.

The next wave of designers has promptly opened up boutiques as well. The tiny white building now occupied by **Anna Heylen** (✉ *Lombardenvest 44, Oude Stad* ☎ *03/203–0298*) is not far from the Meir. The clothes aren't too stern, lightened with lace, an occasional deco-

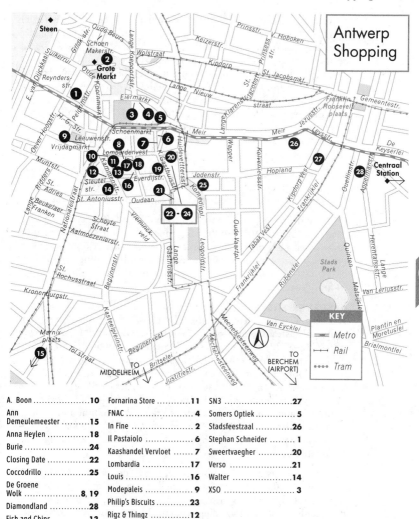

Antwerp
Shopping

KEY

===== *Metro*

⊢—⊣ *Rail*

●●●● *Tram*

rative trim, or perhaps a thought-provoking statement. Anna herself stands behind the counter once a week. Creations by Belgian designer **Kaat Tilley** (✉*Schuttershofstraat 4, Oude Stad* ☎*03/231–1497*) can be found in a pleasant old building where the romantic interior is enhanced with light, feminine clothes in soft fabrics. **Stephan Schneider** (✉*Reyndersstraat 53, Oude Stad* ☎*03/226–2614*) uses the same fabrics for his men's and women's collections; his boutique is sharply designed, with stock stashed away in drawers. The beautifully draped men's and women's lines of **Véronique Branquinho** (✉*Nationalestraat 73, Sint-Andrieskwartier* ☎*03/232–8972*) are shown in a former jewelry store.

Shoe shop **Coccodrillo** (✉*Schuttershofstraat 9, Kruidtuin* ☎*03/233–2093*) has fashionable footwear for adults and children by the likes of Ann Demeulemeester, Dirk Bikkembergs, and Martin Margiela.

Children from five years old to their teens can find the latest attire from Max & Lola, Inge Van den Broeck, Anne Kuris, and Simple Kids at **De Groene Wolk** (✉*Korte Gasthuisstraat 20, Oude Stad* ☎*03/234–1847*). Proving you're never too young to be fashionable, a branch at 66 Lombardenvestraat sells Quincy, the trendy threads for the three-months-to-four-years set.

DESIGNER LABELS

Antwerp also has plenty to offer the fashion lover with more conventional tastes. **Closing Date** (✉*Korte Gasthuisstraat 15, Kruidtuin* ☎*03/232–8722*) stocks pieces by Vivienne Westwood and D2. **SN3** (✉*Frankrijklei 46–48, Meir* ☎*03/233–8633*), in a former cinema, is worth a look for women's wear by Chanel, Prada Sport, Miu Miu, and Sonia Rykiel. A longtime presence on the designer-clothing scene, **Verso** (✉*Lange Gasthuisstraat 9–11, Kruidtuin* ☎*03/226–9292*), located in a former bank, carries such labels as Prada, Paul Smith, and Armani for men and women. **XSO** (✉*Eiermarkt 13, Oude Stad* ☎*03/232–5801*) is the place for clothes by Issey Miyake, Dolce & Gabbana, and Bikkembergs.

Built in 1908 as an exhibition space, the **Stadsfeestzaal** (✉*Meir 78, Oude Stad* ☎*03/202–3100*) was gutted by a major fire in 2000. Now fully restored, it houses an upscale shopping mall, featuring 40 chic designer-label stores including Tommy Hilfiger and Olivier Strelli. There's also a champagne bar in the vast main hall, and even if you're not in the mood for retail therapy, it's worth dropping by just to marvel at the spectacular neoclassical architecture.

STREET SCENE

Kammenstraat is where it's at for less expensive street fashion, as well as record stores. The best-known clothes shop is **Fish and Chips** (✉*Kammenstraat 36–38, Sint-Andrieskwartier* ☎*03/227–0824*); it has a bargain-basement feel, with '60s to '70s decor, a slide from the second to first floor, and limited-edition books and designer toys. **Fornarina Store** (✉*Oudaan 1b, Sint-Andrieskwartier* ☎*03/213–2025*)

CLOSE UP

Antwerp a la Mode

Antwerp is now an established part of the international fashion scene. Yet its homegrown (or at least home-trained) designers have persistently avoided any flashy antics: this is not the place for lurid diva tantrums or vampy collections. Instead, the passion for fashion manifests itself with a particularly Belgian sensibility: thoughtful, deliberate, well-crafted, inventive.

Credit for bringing the world's attention to the phenomenon goes to the so-called Antwerp Six, and in equal measure to the designer who trained them, Linda Loppa. (Some contend the label "Antwerp Six" stuck because it was easier for non-Flemings to pronounce than the designers' names). As the story goes, six graduates of the Antwerp Academy from the years 1980 and 1981 rented a truck, drove to the London fashion week, and took the show by storm. The reality may not be quite that dramatic, but in just a few years the Academy crew had made a serious impact. These days, style arbiters are fixtures at the Academy's annual spring show for design graduates. You can check coverage of the show on the Academy's Web site, ⊕ www.antwerp-fashion.be.

The original Six are Dries Van Noten, Dirk Bikkembergs, Dirk Van Saene, Ann Demeulemeester, Walter Van Beirendonck, and Marina Yee; although they shared the same training ground, their styles are distinctly different.

Van Noten, for instance, creates an "East meets West" fusion of classic looks with exotic fabrics, inspired by countries like India, Morocco, and Egypt. Van Beirendonck consistently pushes the conceptual envelope with futuristic ideas; through most of the 1990s he designed a label called Wild and Lethal Trash. Demeulemeester, on the other hand, has developed a pared-down, fluid aesthetic, turned out mainly in black and white—perfect for the Patti Smith music that often plays at her shows.

Designer Martin Margiela also graduated from the Academy, along with the Antwerp Six pack. So private that he's been compared to reclusive authors J.D. Salinger and Thomas Pynchon, Margiela nevertheless has an avid following. In addition to his past work with Jean-Paul Gaultier and Hermès in Paris, he devotes his own line to his signature deconstructions, clothes with seams, stitching, and hems exposed.

The next wave of designers promises similarly intriguing innovations. Véronique Branquinho often looks to Jane Birkin for inspiration; Bernhard Willhelm takes a playful, pop-culture-inflected approach; and Raf Simons delves into youth culture for his men's clothing. Stephan Schneider, Anna Heylen, and Wim Neels are other names to watch.

6

sells the Italian club-clothes brand of the same name. **Ringz & Thingz** (⊠ *Kammenstraat 65–67, Sint-Andrieskwartier* ☎ *03/226–8588*) has a collection of clothing and accessories with a skate-punk feel aimed squarely at the youth market. There is also a second store directly across the street at No. 58.

DIAMONDS

The heart of the city's diamond industry is in and around Appelmansstraat, near the Centraal Station. Here merchants from the world over have dealt in diamonds for 500 years. The **Diamond High Council** (⊠ *Hovenierstraat 22, Centraal Station* ☎ *03/222–0511* ⊕ *www.hrd.be*), also known by the acronym HRD, provides a directory of diamond-related businesses and a rundown on key diamond-buying points like the "four Cs" (color, carat, clarity, cut). It can also, for a fee, certify the quality of submitted diamonds, including fancy-color stones. For advice on buying diamonds at the retail level, you can contact the **Antwerp Diamond Jewellers Association** (⊠ *Hoveniersstraat 22, Centraal Station* ☎ *03/222–0545* ⊕ *www.adja.be*), which operates under the umbrella of the Diamond High Council. It has a brochure listing the addresses of its members' shops. If you buy a loose stone and plan to set it, be sure to choose a reputable establishment for the work, so that your diamond is not switched for an inferior one.

The largest diamond showroom is **Diamondland** (⊠ *Appelmansstraat 33a, Diamantwijk* ☎ *03/229–2990*), where tours of polishers, goldsmiths, and setters at work can be arranged before you settle down to business. Loose diamonds can be set while you wait.

FOOD SHOPS

Upscale takeout and specialty-food shops are clustered around the fashionable De Wilde Zee district on Wiegstraat, Schrijnwerkersstraat, and Korte Gasthuisstraat. Fabulous Italian provisioner **Il Pastaiolo** (⊠ *Wiegstraat 18, Oude Stad* ☎ *03/233–8631*) sells ready-to-eat pasta dishes, filled panini, and pizzas to go. **Kaashandel Vervloet** (⊠ *Wiegstraat 28, Oude Stad* ☎ *03/233–3729*) is the best address for regional cheeses. Try juice bar **Lombardia** (⊠ *57 Lombardenvest, Oude Stad* ☎ *03/233–6819*) for excellent fresh-fruit cocktails to drink on-site as well as health food products.

If you're after an edible souvenir from Antwerp, head for the old-fashioned biscuit and cake store **Philip's Biscuits** (⊠ *Korte Gasthuisstraat 11, Oude Stad* ☎ *03/231–2660*). *Speculaas* (spiced honey cookies), *macarons* (coconut cookies), and *peperkoek* (gingerbread) are best and can be ordered in attractive tins—a good gift alternative to chocolate. Founded in 1884, **Goossens** (⊠ *Korte Gasthuisstraat 31, Oude Stad* ☎ *03/226–0792*) is a popular bakery and an old favorite with locals. If only chocolate will do, try family-run **Sweertvaegher** (⊠ *Groendalstraat 8, Kruidtuin* ☎ *03/226–3691*), which has been selling the stuff since the 1930s. **Burie** (⊠ *Korte Gasthuisstraat 3, Oude Stad* ☎ *03/232–3688*) is a top source for handmade chocolates. There is a second outlet at No. 41 on the same street.

OTHER SPECIALTY STORES

For a fascinating glimpse of how shopping used to be, stop by **A. Boon** (⊠*Lombardenvest 2–4, Oude Stad* ☎*03/232–3387*), which stocks old-fashioned leather gloves that would appeal to your grandparents. The shop was opened in 1929 and still has the original fittings inside. The window display looks like it hasn't been changed since the 1950s. Eyeglass wearers should pop into **Somers Optiek** (⊠*Eiermarkt 41, Oude Stad* ☎*03/233–4758*), where cutting-edge designer frames by Belgians Theo Somers and Patrick Hoet are stocked. For attention-grabbing eyewear, this place is a must. **In Fine Maison de Parfum** (⊠*Grote Markt 19, Oude Stad* ☎*03/288–5388*) has an amazing selection of perfumes and a nice display of glass bottles, but it's discovering the secret alchemy between perfume and personality that makes a visit to this shop unique. Prices range from €54 for 50 ml to €79 for 100 ml. **FNAC** (⊠*Groenplaats, Oude Stad* ☎*03/213–5611*), an all-purpose shop, is a staple in many large Belgian cities; Antwerp's version stocks a good selection of English-language books with a noteworthy collection of novels, coffee-table books, classics, contemporary thrillers, and blockbusters.

STREET MARKETS

Though you can shop for antiques on Kloosterstraat throughout the week, there's a special antiques market on **Lijnwaadmarkt** (Easter–Oct., Sat. 9–5), north of the cathedral. The **Rubensmarkt** (Rubens Market, Aug. 15 annually) is held on the Grote Markt, with vendors in 17th-century costumes hawking everything under the sun. Public auction sales of furniture and other secondhand goods are held at **Vrijdagmarkt** (Fri. 9–noon). On Theater-Plein (a block south from Rubenshuis on Wapper), there is a general weekend market (Sat. 8–3, Sun. 8–1) selling flowers and produce. Many locals still refer to the Sunday market as **Vogelenmarkt** (bird market), in spite of the fact that the sale of live animals at street markets is now banned.

SIDE TRIPS FROM ANTWERP

LIER

17 km (10 mi) southeast of Antwerp, 45 km (27 mi) northeast of Brussels.

★ The small town of Lier may seem a sleepy riverside settlement, but it has long attracted poets and painters and has even known its moment of glory. It was here in 1496 that Philip the Handsome of Burgundy married Joanna the Mad of Aragon and Castile, daughter of King Ferdinand and Queen Isabella of Spain. From that union sprang Emperor Charles V and his brother and successor as Holy Roman Emperor, the equally remarkable Ferdinand I of Austria.

Lange Wapper

There are myriad 16th-century legends surrounding Lange Wapper, the water devil, but all agree he lived near water. That's why a bronze statue of this famous demon trickster, built by Albert Poels, was placed by the Scheldt river in front of the Steen Castle, now the National Maritime Museum.

Lange Wapper could change his size—he could make himself as small as a baby or as large as a giant. As a formidable giant, he would stand with a foot planted on either side of the canal and frighten drunks during the night. Many men who stayed too long at the bars used Lange Wapper's antics as an excuse for lateness.

Virile and cheeky, he garnered the reputation of a fertility god—it's claimed that young women who visit the statue after marriage go on to bear many children. Himself a philanderer, he used every ploy possible to get close to women. One story tells how he turned himself into a newborn baby and waited on a public bench. A woman who had just given birth pitied the foundling and proceeded to breast-feed him, only to receive the fright of her life when he transformed into a grown man!

GETTING HERE & AROUND

Lier is a short drive from Antwerp on the N10. From Brussels, take the E19/N14 via Mechelen.

WHAT TO SEE

The **Sint-Gummaruskerk,** where Philip and Joanna were wed, is a product of the De Waghemakere–Keldermans architectural partnership that worked so well in building the cathedral in Antwerp. The church is notable for its stained-glass windows from the 15th and 16th centuries—those in the choir were the gift of Maximilian of Austria (father of Philip the Handsome), who visited in 1516 and is depicted in one of the windows, along with his wife, Mary of Burgundy. ⊠ *Kardinaal Mercierplein, follow Rechtestraat to Kerkstraat* ☎ *03/480–0721* ⊙ *Daily 10–noon and 2–5.*

The Kleine Nete flows straight through the heart of Lier; the Grote Nete and a canal encircle the center. Along the riverside, willows bend over the water. Across the river stands the **Zimmertoren,** a 14th-century tower renamed for Louis Zimmer, who designed its astronomical clock with 11 faces in 1930. His studio, where 57 dials show the movements of the moon, the tides, the zodiac, and other cosmic phenomena, is inside the tower. ⊠ *Zimmerplein 18* ☎ *03/491–1395* ⊕ *www.zimmertoren. com* ⊠ *€2.50* ⊙ *Tue.–Sun. 9–noon and 1:30–5:30.*

NEED A BREAK?   **Van Ouytsels Koffiehoekje** (⊠ *Rechtestraat 27* ☎ *03/480–2917*) still roasts its own coffee. Drop by from 9 to 6 Tuesday through Sunday for the delicious syrup-filled biscuits, *Lierse Vlaaikens,* which are the local specialty.

The **Begijnhof** differs from most other beguinages in that its small houses line narrow streets rather than being grouped around a common. A Renaissance portico stands at the entrance, and on it is a statue of St. Begge, who gave his name to this congregation and who probably derived his own from the fact that he was *un begue* (a stammerer). Beguines were members of ascetic or philanthropic communities of women, not under vows, founded in the Netherlands in the 13th century. ⊠ *Begijnhofstraat.*

Stedelijk Museum Wuyts-Van Campen en Baron Caroly, a lovely provincial museum, is home to the extraordinary *Vlaamse Gezegdan (Flemish Proverbs)*, painted in 1607 by Pieter Bruegel the Younger. In it you can find representations of some 85 Flemish proverbs. One such adage warns about the woman who's "carrying water in one hand and fire in the other," meaning someone who's fickle and cannot be trusted. Also on display is Jan Steen's splendid *Vechtender Boeren (Squabbling Peasants)*, as well as works by such artists as Maurice De Vlaminck and Henri De Braekeleer. ⊠ *Florent Van Cauwenberghstraat 14* ☎ *03/480–1196* ⌘ *€1* ⊗ *Tues.–Sun. 10–noon and 1–5.*

If the weather's nice, and you fancy sitting down while the sights glide past you, then take a 40-minute **cruise on the Nete River** in a traditional Flemish fishing boat. Pickup and drop off are at the Sint-Jansbrug bridge, behind the Zimmertoren. ☎ *03/800–0553* ⌘ *€2.50* ⊗ *May–Sept., Sun. 2–6.*

WHERE TO STAY & EAT

$$–$$$ ✕ **De Fortuin.** At this romantic restaurant and tavern, the tavern is less
BELGIAN expensive. Shrimp croquettes are a specialty, and the service is friendly. In summer you can eat on the terrace overlooking the river. ⊠ *Felix Timmermansplein 7* ☎ *03/480–2951* ▭ *AE, MC, V* ⊗ *Closed Mon. Oct.–Apr.*

$–$$ ⊞ **Hotel Hof Van Aragon.** The oldest hotel in Lier is situated alongside a small canal. The rooms have all been renovated, and are welcoming and comfortable. **Pros:** quiet neighborhood; friendly staff. **Cons:** some rooms are quite small. ⊠ *Aragonstraat 6,* ☎ *03/491–0800* ⊕ *www.hva.be* ⇌ *20 rooms* ▭ *AE, DC, MC, V.*

KALMTHOUT

18 km (11 mi) north of Antwerp.

GETTING HERE & AROUND

Kalmthout is a short ride from Antwerp along the N11/N22 via Kapellen.

WHAT TO SEE

The **Kalmthoutse Heide** is a vast heath of pines, sand dunes, and ponds, with flourishing birdlife, crossed by marked paths. The **Arboretum** contains more than 6,000 trees in a 25-acre park, where you can wander freely across the lawns. It's a peaceful oasis with a varied range of colors every season, the presence of wildflowers providing a special accent. ⊠ *Heuvel 2* ☎ *03/666–6741* ⌘ *€4* ⊗ *Mid-Mar.–mid-Nov., daily 10–5.*

The Meuse & the Ardennes

WORD OF MOUTH

"Liege is an industrial city but one of the most fantastic things to do is to visit La Batte, the weekend market along the river. The market is about a mile long and has everything—fresh foods, produce, used goodies, and antiques. Going with a French speaking person is a must. We felt a little at a loss with our high school French. The merchants are very nice but talk so fast that you miss half of what they are saying, especially when it comes time to talk money."

—yy4me

Updated by
Karina Hof
and Cillian
Donnelly

TO ACQUIRE THE WALLONIA HABIT, start by leaving the highway, stopping off in a town, or driving around the countryside—and arriving at your final destination a few hours, or a couple of days, late.

Natives of the area by and large speak French (though there is a pocket of German-speakers to the east, along the border with Germany). One in three also understands Walloon, a dialect descended from demotic Latin. The linguistic frontier corresponds roughly to the northern boundary of the Roman empire, and "Walas" was the name given to the Romanized Celts of the region. Today, the economy of rust-belt Wallonia has been overtaken by that of high-tech Flanders. The coal mines are a thing of the past, and the steel industry is fighting a tenacious battle to remain competitive. The Walloons are highly conscious of their culture and linguistic heritage and take pride in their separate identity within the framework of the nation.

The Meuse comes rushing into Belgium from France, foaming through narrow ravines. In Dinant it is joined by the Lesse and flows, serene and beautiful, toward Namur, Wallonia's capital city. At Namur comes the confluence with the Sambre, tainted from its exposure to the steel-manufacturing plants of Charleroi. Here, the river becomes broad and powerful, and gradually the pleasure craft are replaced by an endless procession of tugboats and barges. It passes through Liège, the region's largest city, then up through Holland, where, under a different name, the Maas, it reaches the sea.

From the name of the river is derived the adjective "Mosan," used to describe an indigenous style of metalworking of extraordinary plasticity. It reached its finest flowering during the 12th and 13th centuries with masters such as Renier de Huy, Nicolas de Verdun, and Hugo d'Oignies. They worked with brass, copper, and silver to achieve artistic heights equal to those of the Flemish painters two centuries later.

ORIENTATION & PLANNING

GETTING ORIENTED

This part of Belgium is marked by contrasts. The bigger cities of Namur and Liège mix a bit of cosmopolitan bustle with the historical appeal of ages-old European towns. In the countryside, major roads lead to tiny hamlets, and hills give way to deep river valleys. There's a vast territory to cover, and plenty to see and do, whether you're driving along rustic back roads or strolling down city streets.

The Meuse river valley and the wooded plateau of the Ardennes are popular travel destinations for Belgians and foreign visitors alike; the hilly, even mountainous, terrain is a great draw for nature lovers who enjoy hiking, biking, and canoeing. The region stretches over Wallonia's three eastern provinces, Namur, Liège, and, to the south, Belgian Luxembourg.

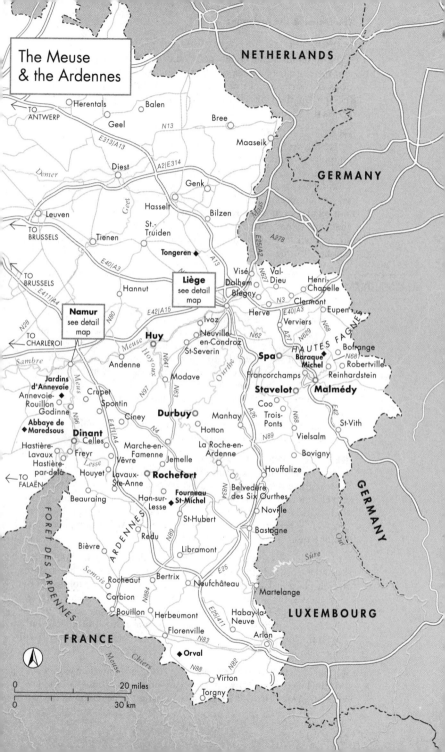

NAMUR

The city stands at the confluence of the Meuse and the Sambre rivers, and these strategic waterways neatly divide it into three distinct sections: the partly pedestrian historic center on the banks of the Sambre; the spur of the Citadelle; and the residential Jambes neighborhood across the Meuse.

LIÈGE

Liège, the area of Wallonia most influenced by the French, is a good jumping-off point for exploration of the Ardennes, a largely wooded region that stretches into the Grand Duchy of Luxembourg to the south. There's a medieval air to the Ardennes; the small towns interspersed among the woods are dominated by centuries-old castles and abbeys and even older Roman ruins. The twisting roads are often a challenge to navigate. Here, as in the Meuse valley and perhaps more so, outdoor activities amid the deciduous forests, rocky escarpments, and fast-flowing rivers are an ever-popular pastime.

PLANNING

WHEN TO GO

The best months for touring the Meuse and the Ardennes are April–June, September, and October, when the weather is warm and pleasant. Fall brings a colorful backdrop and excellent game to restaurant menus. But if you're visiting the Ardennes in the low season (November–March), you are sure to be rewarded with traditional festivals and carnivals. You also have more of the region's natural splendor to yourself in winter and early spring, when there are far fewer tourists than in summer. Note that the Ardennes region is very popular with Belgian and Dutch vacationers, especially during the school holidays in July, August, October, and February or March.

GETTING HERE & AROUND

By Bus From train stations in Liège, Verviers, Eupen, Trois-Ponts, and Namur there is bus service to other cities in the Ardennes. By far, bus travel is not the easiest way to get around. Buses depart infrequently, and connecting usually involves long waits. The national bus company TEC (Transports En Commun) serves the Ardennes region. In the major cities, TEC buses also provide local service.

In Liège, buses serve the downtown area, along the main boulevards, from the Coeur Historique to the train station. The main bus stations are on place St-Lambert, rue Léopold, place de la République Française, and at the Guillemins train station. Bus stops are clearly marked with a yellow TEC sign, and tickets can be purchased on the bus, in TEC kiosks, or in stations. Service maps are free. A single trip on a bus in the inner city costs €1.30 (two zones), and eight-trip cards sell for €6.30.

By Car The most convenient way of getting around the Meuse valley and the Liège region is by car, especially since public transportation services are scant. The E411 highway cuts through the region. Elsewhere,

TOP REASONS TO VISIT

Back to Nature. Belgium's reputation for being flat and featureless is gloriously disproved on even the briefest of trips to the Ardennes; even townscapes, such as Namur and Liège are surrounded by thick greenery and hilltops perfect for surveying the surrounding countryside. Venture out farther and you'll discover clandestine forest walkways and rugged trails. And even though the summer months attract the majority of tourists, winter visits can prove most rewarding, when, between November and March, the place is sprinkled with a covering of snow that makes for some marvelous scenic splendor.

A Place of Learning. Most towns offer much in the way of local history, from museums and ancient churches to ruins and battlegrounds and provide much insight into the region's sometimes turbulent history.

Small Town Variety. The Belgian countryside is more densely populated than is often expected and you'll be pleasantly surprised at the variety of small towns and villages. The area around Malmédy is especially rewarding.

Keep Active. Set up camp in one of the local towns and spend a day hiking or biking in the hills and forests of the surrounding area. If you find yourself here during the snowbound period, cross-country skiing resorts cater to the adventurous.

Step it up a Gear. Held annually around the beginning of September, the Belgian Grand Prix at Francorchamps is one of the most internationally renowned race circuits and what it lacks in length it more than makes up for in excitement. Make sure you book your tickets in advance.

you travel chiefly on pleasant, two-lane roads through lovely scenery. Getting lost on the back roads of Wallonia is a true pleasure.

In the Meuse valley, Rochefort is close to the E411 highway, which links Brussels with Luxembourg and runs south and east. Namur is close to the intersection of the E411 with the E42, which links Liège with Charleroi, Mons, and Paris, as well as with Tournai, Lille, and Calais. To get to Tongeren from Brussels take the E40 to Exit 29 for the N69.

Liège is almost halfway to Cologne from Brussels on the E40. The city is also linked with Paris by the E42, which merges with E19 from Brussels near Mons; with Antwerp by the E313; and with Maastricht and the Dutch highway system by E25, which continues south to join the E411 to Luxembourg.

If you want to rent a car, most car-rental agencies in Liège and Namur are open weekdays and Saturday morning. In Liège, the majority of agencies have offices either on boulevard de la Saveniée or boulevard d'Avroy. In Namur there are agencies on avenue des Combattants and avenue de Luxembourg.

By Train Two NMBS/SNCB trains an hour link Brussels with Namur (one hour from Brussels' Gare du Midi, 50 minutes from the Gare du Nord). They connect with a local service to Dinant (25 minutes).

Two trains run every hour from Brussels to Liège's Gare des Guillemins (one hour by express train from Brussels Nord, one hour and 10 minutes from Brussels Midi; local trains are 10 minutes slower). Thalys high-speed trains cut 15 minutes off travel time from Brussels Midi. All express trains from Ostend to Cologne stop at Liège, as do international trains from Copenhagen and Hamburg to Paris.

Direct trains run hourly to Tongeren. There are local train services from Liège via Verviers to Eupen, and to Trois-Ponts (near Stavelot). The high-speed TGV train runs from points in France and Germany to Liège.

EAT RIGHT, SLEEP WELL

This part of Belgium is full of atmospheric gray-stone inns serving dishes redolent of forest and farm. Game meats, like venison and wild boar, figure prominently on restaurant menus, especially in fall. Autumn is also a good time for attractive hotel-restaurant packages, and many city dwellers venture into the country for *les weekends gastronomiques,* which include two or three lavish meals with two nights' lodging. Chefs dabble with various ingredients and cuisines, but most tend toward the French tradition and rely on fresh regional produce. Restaurants generally begin serving lunch at 12:30 and dinner at 7:30 or 8, and casual attire is the norm.

Hotel rooms in this region tend to be low-price, even if there's an outstanding restaurant downstairs. They usually fill up on weekends and during high season, June–August. If you prefer to eat somewhere other than in the hotel you've booked, clear it with the management: you're often expected (and sometimes obliged) to eat in their restaurant. Many hotels offer *demi-pension* (half-board) arrangements, as well as *les weekends gastronomiques,* which include a few elaborate meals for a set rate. Farmhouse accommodations and B&Bs are widely available and especially popular with families.

WHAT IT COSTS IN EUROS					
	¢	$	$$	$$$	$$$$
Restaurants	under €10	€10–€15	€15–€20	€20–€30	over €30
Hotels	under €75	€75–€100	€100–€150	€150–€225	over €225

Restaurant prices are for a main course at dinner, not including tax or tip. Hotel prices are for two people in a standard double room in high season, on the European Plan (EP, with no meals) unless otherwise noted. Costs include 6% tax.

PLANNING YOUR TIME

1 Day: As the regional capital, Namur is the heart of Wallonia. Spend the day meandering through the old city, discovering its charms and treasures—visits to the Musée Félicien Rops, the Musée Archéologique, and the Eglise St-Aubain are musts. Sunset at the Citadelle, followed by dinner at L'Essentiel, is a perfect way to end an enchanting day.

3 Days: Spend Day 1 in Namur as described above. On the following day, either explore the picturesque area in and around Durbuy or leave Namur heading south toward Dinant, stopping at the Jardins d'Annevoie—a horticultural masterpiece—en route. In Dinant you can walk through the historic center, hike to the fort, or venture out, kayaking along the Meuse or climbing the château ruins in nearby Freyr, taking in the charms of the region as you go. Pick up a *flamiche* or a *croque de Dinant* and stop for a beer at Brasserie du Bocq or the Caracole Brewery. An evening picnic at L'Abbaye de Maredsous is a relaxing way to end the day. The next day, explore the region's famous caves at Grotte de Rochefort and Han-sur-Lesse near Rochefort, or drive a little farther on into Belgian Luxembourg to visit some of the moving World War II Battle of the Bulge sites in the region *(see Chapter 2 for more information)*.

7 Days: A week will allow you to explore the area's natural beauty and cultural traditions fully. Spend Day 1 in Namur and devote Days 2 and 3 to Dinant and Rochefort or Durbuy, as described above. Take a long but gorgeous drive to the famous Abbaye d'Orval and reward yourself with one of its delicious Trappist beers or a sample of cheese *(see Chapter 1 for more information)*. Spend the night in or around Orval. On Day 5, meander through the Belgian Ardennes to La Roche-en-Ardenne, where you can lunch on outstanding *jambon d'Ardennes*, or visit World War II sights either here or a little farther south in Bastogne. Then head back to the city, spending Days 6 and 7 in Liège; try to schedule your visit so that you're there on Sunday for La Batte, the weekly flea market.

VISITORS INFO

Regional tourism offices are generally open weekdays 9–4 or 5, with a one-hour lunch break between 12:30 and 1:30. Town tourism offices are open daily without a break from about 9 to 5 or 6. Some may close at 3 or 4 on weekends.

ESSENTIALS

Bus Contacts TEC (⊕ *www.infotec.be*).

Emergency Contacts Police (☎ *101*). **Ambulance** (☎ *100*).

Regional Tourism Offices Province of Liège Tourist Office (✉ *blvd. de la Sauvenière 77 Liège B4000* ☎ *04/237–9526* ⊕ *www.ftpl.be*). **Province of Namur Tourist Office** (✉ *Parc Industriel, av. Reine Astrid 22, boîte 2, Namur* ☎ *08/174–9900* ⊕ *www.paysdesvallees.be*). **Wallonia Office de Promotion du Tourisme** (✉ *rue Saint-Bernard 30, Brussels* ☎ *07/022–1021, to request brochures 02/509–2400* ⊕ *www.belgique-tourisme.net*).

Rental Agencies Avis (✉ *blvd. d'Avroy 238 B, west of Nouvelle Ville, Liège* ☎ *04/252–5500* ✉ *av. des Combattants 31, Namur* ☎ *081/735–780* ⊕ *www.avis.be*). **Europcar** (✉ *chaussée de Marche 601, Namur* ☎ *081/31–32–56* ⊕ *www.europcar.com*). **Hertz** (✉ *blvd. d'Avroy 60, west of the Nouvelle Ville, Liège* ☎ *04/222–4273* ⊕ *www.hertz.be*).

Train Stations Gare des Guillemins (⌧ *pl. des Guillemins 2, south of the Nouvelle Ville, Liège* ☎ *02/528–2828* ⊕ *www.euro-liege-tgv.be*). **Gare Namur** (⌧ *pl. de la Station* ☎ *081/25–22–22*). **Tongeren** (☎ *01/223–1032* ⌧ *Stationplein 1, Tongeren*).

Train Lines NMBS/SNCB (☎ *02/528—2828 in Liège and Namur* ⊕ *www.b-rail. be*). **TGV** (☎ *04/225–1958 in Liège* ⊕ *www.tgv.com*). **Thalys** (☎ *02/548–0600* ⊕ *www.thalys.be*).

NAMUR

64 km (38 mi) southeast of Brussels, 61 km (37 mi) southwest of Liège.

In Namur, remnants of the Roman empire stand side by side with the contemporary regional seat of government. The majority of the city's points of interests lie in the historic center, and the best way to discover them is on foot. However, no visit to Namur is complete without a trip up to the Citadelle. It overlooks Namur's characteristic 17th-century Mansard rooftops (made from *pierre de Namur*, a bluish-gray stone quarried in the area) and the river valleys beyond. At sunset, the view is magical. From this vantage point you can observe Namur's rapid growth since it was designated the seat of government for all of Wallonia in 1986. The population of 105,000 is now spread among 25 neighboring townships.

GETTING HERE & AROUND

Trains run twice every hour from Brussels to Namur. The journey time is about one hour from Gare du Midi, or 50 minutes from Gare du Nord.

ESSENTIALS

Hospitals Clinique CHR (⌧ *av. Albert 1è 185* ☎ *081/72–61–11* ⊕ *www.chrn.be*).

Tourism Offices Namur (⌧ *Esplanade de l'Hôtel de Ville* ☎ *08/124–6211* ⊕ *www. ville.namur.be*).

TIMING & PRECAUTIONS

Remember that most museums are closed on Monday. If you would like to explore one of the city's lively markets, head for the town center on a Saturday or to Jambes on the left side of the Meuse River on Sunday. The Feast of Wallonia takes place the third week in September at the Citadelle. On New Year's Eve, the Citadelle hosts a light show. You can also ask the staff at the tourist office on place de l'Europe Unie if there are any local festivals happening during your stay.

WHAT TO SEE

☾ **Citadelle.** Over the past 1,000 years, this fortification overlooking
Fodor's Choice Namur has been sieged and occupied more than 20 times. Today you
★ can reach it by the cobblestone, cherry tree–lined route Merveilleuse;

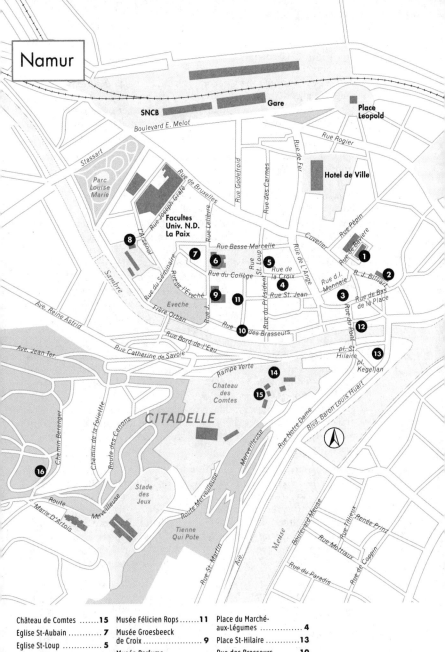

Namur

SNCB

Gare

Place Leopold

Boulevard E. Melot

Stassart

Parc Louise Marie

Rue de Bruxelles

Rue Joseph Grafé

Rue Letièvre

Rue Godefroid

Rue des Cames

Rue de Fer

Rue Rogier

Hotel de Ville

Facultes Univ. N.D. La Paix

Rue Pépin

Rue de Bavière

Cuvelier

8

Rue du Séminaire

La Sambre

Rue de l'Eveché

Rue Basse Marcelle

7

6

Rue du Collège

Rue du Président St. Loup

5

Rue de la Croix

4

Rue de l'Ange

R. J. Billiart

1

2

Rue d.l. Monnaie

3

Rue de Bas de la Place

Sambre

Eveche

9

11

Rue St. Jean

Ave. Reine Astrid

Frère Orban

Rue J.

Rue J.

Rue de Pont

10

Rue des Brasseurs

12

Rue Bord-de-l'Eau

Rue Catherine de Savoie

pl. St. Hilaire

13

pl. Kegeljan

Ave. Jean Ferr.

Rampe Verte

14

Château des Comtes

15

Blvd. Baron Louis Huart

CITADELLE

Chemin Berenger

Chemin de la Follette

Route des Canons

Merveilleuse

Rue Notre-Dame

Meuse

16

Route Marie-D'Artois

Merveilleuse

Stade des Jeux

Route Merveilleuse

Rue St-Martin

Ave.

Meuse

Boulevard-Meuse

Rue Tillieux

Rue Renée Prinz

Tienne Qui Pote

Rue Mottiaux

Rue de Cognn.

Rue du Paradis

each curve in the road affords a magnificent view of the city. From April through September, you can take a guided tour in English of the Citadelle. If you'd rather explore on your own, take a copy of the brochure "Storming the Citadel of Namur," which describes five self-guided walks that you can take around the property. Your €6 ticket to the Citadelle gets you a 50¢ discount at the other on-site attractions, and it includes the train ride around the property. The Citadelle is open April–October, daily 11–6, and November–March, weekends 11–5.

⑮ One of the complex of buildings that make up the Citadelle is the ruins of the **Château de Comtes** (⊠*rte. Merveilleuse 8* ☎*08/165–4500* ⊕*www.citadelle.namur.be* ⊠*€5* ☉*first half of Mar: weekends; late Mar.–late Sept., daily 11–5*), which has been converted into a Namur history museum. Upstairs is a small but amusing exhibit about the area's early history as told through cartoons. Downstairs, the former kitchen has historic artifacts and an exhibit about iron forging (Namur's first industry) where kids can mint their own coins. There are several other decidedly nonmilitary attractions at the Citadelle.

⑭ The **Musée Parfums Guy Delforge** (⊠*rte. Merveilleuse 60* ☎*081/22–12–19* ⊕*www.delforge.com* ⊠*€3*), at the Château de Comtes, is in the former officers' mess hall. It's a fragrance factory that allows you to witness the steps of isolating and combining the aromas involved in creating a fine perfume. A shop upstairs exhibits the work of local artists and sells the factory's products. The factory is open Tuesday–Saturday 9:15–5:30, and Sunday 2:15–5:30. In July and August, it's open additionally Monday 9:15–5:30. Tours, some in English, are generally held Tuesday–Saturday at 3:30, or by appointment. **⑯** The **Parc Reine Fabiola** (⊠*Rond Point Thonar 1* ☎*081/73–84–13* ⊠*€5*) on the Citadelle grounds, includes a large playground with miniature golf, go-carts, and electric cars. Hours change seasonally, but it's generally open until 6 PM (but closed on Sundays in April and early May). ☎*081/22–68–29* ⊕*www.parf.be*.

❼ **Eglise St-Aubain.** After floodwaters from the Sambre receded out of Namur in 1751, construction began on this Italian Baroque–style church, made from Belgian marble. Inside, a statue of Notre Dame de la Paix protects the city, and St. Aubain is discreetly represented at the base of the altar, holding his head in his hands. If you're interested in religious relics, take note of the double cross atop the church dome, signifying that a piece of the holy cross is stored on the premises. ⊠*pl. St-Aubain* ☎*081/22–03–20* ⊕*www.ville.namur.be* ⊠*Free* ☉*Daily 10–5*.

❺ **Eglise St-Loup.** Designed by Brother Pierre Huyssens and built in the late 16th century by the Jesuits, this formidable building, now used as a cultural center, is considered part of Wallonia's "Grand Heritage." The marble for the impressive black-and-red columns was quarried from the Ardennes, and the limestone for the carved ceiling is from Maastricht. It's been undergoing painstaking renovations for over 20 years. The building next door was also built by the Jesuits as a college and is now a state school. ⊠*rue St-Loup* ☎*081/22–80–85* ⊕*www.ville.namur.be* ⊠*Free* ☉*Daily 10–5*.

Tours

BY BOAT

Boat tours, from short excursions to all-day trips, are available in both Dinant and Namur. **Bateau Ansiaux** (☎ 082/22-23-25 ⊕ www.ansiaux. be) offers a classic Dinant discovery cruise, plus cruises to the castle and the rock of Freyr. Round trips are 50 minutes for €5.50 per person or 90 minutes for €9.50 per person. **Companie Des Bateaux** (☎ 082/22-23-15 ⊕ www.bateaux-meuse.be) schedules round-trip, 50-minute cruises of the Sambre and the Meuse for €5.50 per person. Round-trip cruises between Namur and Wépion last an hour and 45 minutes and cost €9.50, while round-trip cruises between Namur and Dinant last nine hours and cost €20. **Bateau Bayard** (☎ 082/22-22-10 ⊕ www.dinantourism.com) offers round-trip, 45-minute cruises from Dinant to Anseremme for €5.50 and round-trip, three-hour cruises to Givet, the first French town across the border, for €15. With some advance planning, you could probably arrange to sail the entire length of the Meuse from France to the Netherlands on sightseeing boats.

From Liège, **Blegny-Mine** (☎ 04/387-4333 for reservations ⊕ www.blegnymine.be) offers one-day sightseeing boat excursions to Maastricht in the Netherlands on Friday July and August. A visit to the Blegny Coal Mine and museum is included. Departures are from the Passerelle on the right bank of the Meuse and cost €12.25.

ON FOOT

In Namur, walking tours of the old city and the Citadelle, plus tours with a theme, such as local painters or gardens in the city, take place every day during July and August, starting at the tourism bureau. Request an English-speaking guide. The price, per person, is €3.45.

You can also hire a personal English-speaking guide from the Liège City tourist office. Rates are €39.65 for two hours, €58.25 for three hours. If your French is up to it, you're welcome to join a guided walking tour with French commentary, starting from the city tourist office, July and August, Wednesday–Sunday at 2, for €3.45.

7

❷ **Institut des Soeurs de Notre-Dame.** When you enter the small exhibition
★ room that contains the **Trésor Hugo d'Oignies,** you are immediately engaged by the sight of glowing glass cases of brightly lit gold and bejeweled objets d'art. This prize collection of crosses, medallions, reliquaries, and other religious artifacts is considered one of the seven treasures of Belgium. The relics were created by Brother Hugo d'Oignies for the monastery in nearby Oignies at the beginning of the 13th century. Between the French Revolution and World War II, the collection was protected by the Sisters of Notre Dame. Look for a tiny portable altar, once belonging to Cardinal Jacques de Vitry, and a book of gospels containing parchment painted with gold leaf. Labels are in French but an English-speaking nun is usually on hand to provide information. ⊠ *rue Billiart 17* ☎ *081/23-03-42* ☜€*1.50* ☉ *Closed Sunday mornings, Mondays, and holidays.*

NEED A BREAK? Relive Namur's brewing legacy at **La Cuvé à Bière** (⊠ *rue des Brasseurs 108* ☎ *081/26–13–63* ⊘ *Tues.–Sat. 2–5 and 5–late)*. The popular tavern is a fine spot to rub elbows with the locals over a game of darts and a hearty beer.

❽ L'Arsenal. The Arsenal is perhaps the best-preserved work of French architect Sébastien Vauban in all of Europe. Originally built under orders from Louis XIV in 1692 as a munitions depot, the building was restored in the early 1980s and now houses a student center for Namur's university. ⊠ *rue Bruno 11.*

⓲ Musée Archéologique. This museum contains fine Roman and Merovingian antiquities from the Namur region, including a magnificent collection of jewelry from the 1st to the 7th centuries. Some of the artifacts are taken from Namur's archaeological sites and others were found in the Sambre and Meuse rivers. One of the more curious artifacts is a model of the city, fashioned by Louis XV's spies. (The original is at Versailles.) The museum is on the waterfront in the handsome 16th-century Butchers' Hall. Brochures in English are available at the entrance. ⊠ *rue du Pont 23* ☎ *081/23–16–31* ⊕ *www.ciger.be/namur/ musees/archeo* 🎫 *€2* ⊘ *Tues.–Fri. 10–5, weekends 10:40–5.*

⓫ Musée Félicien Rops. Considered a scandal in his day, surrealist artist and Namur native Félicien Rops (1833–98) is now heralded as an artistic treasure. This museum houses a large collection of his drawings, engravings, and prints, which are by turns surreal, erotic, and whimsical. Rops spent time in Paris, mingling with the likes of Charles Baudelaire and Stéphane Mallarmé. ⊠ *rue Fumal 12* ☎ *081/22–01–10* ⊕ *www.ciger.be/rops* 🎫 *€3, €5 for temporary exhibitions* ⊘ *Nov.–Easter, Tues.–Sun. 10–5; Easter–June and Sept., Tues.–Sun. 10–6; July and Aug., daily 10–6.*

❾ Musée Groesbeeck de Croix. Ring the bell to enter this comfortable 18th-century house; inside you'll find an extensive collection of Walloon decorative arts. View regional artifacts such as hand-painted Spanish-leather wallpaper, a collection of cutlery, an 18th-century handmade parlor board game, and one of the city's first water closets. Ask for the small brochure in English, which explains the collection. ⊠ *rue Saintraint 3* ☎ *081/23–75–10* ⊕ *www.ciger.be/namur/musees/croix* 🎫 *€2* ⊘ *Tue.–Sun. 10–noon and 1:30–5.*

❻ Palais Provinçal. This handsome 18th-century manor house was built by Namur's Bishop de Strickland; now the Walloon Parliament meets in what was once the bishop's private chapel. The interior walls of the house are lined with art, including an Italian stucco of the four seasons in the foyer and a Félicien Rops–drawn caricature and a painting by Rops's own teacher, the Flemish-inspired Marinous, in the meeting room. In the receiving room, which was originally the billiard hall, look for the portrait of the handsome man in blue, the bishop himself. ⊠ *pl. St-Aubain 2* ☎ *081/25–68–68* ⊕ *www.province.namur.be* 🎫 *Free* ⊘ *Open by appointment only.*

❸ Place d'Armes. This square has played a part in the economic history of Belgium, for here during the 18th century, when the city was under

Austrian rule, the Department of Commerce met and money was minted. It has also felt the brunt of Belgium's position as a European battleground—it was leveled in World War I and again in World War II. Today the square consists of an immense, hardwood platform—a sunny local meeting place—surrounded by modern buildings containing a conference center and shops. The annual Christmas Market takes over the square in early December. Look for the 18th-century **Beffroi,** a tower that was never a belfry, despite its name. ⊠*rue de Marchovelette and rue de Monnaie* ☎*081/24–11–33.*

❹ **Place du Marché-aux-Légumes.** Originally a Roman graveyard, this is Namur's liveliest square. The statue of an overflowing fruit basket in the middle of the square symbolizes the vendors who have come here for centuries to sell their produce. On Saturday mornings, the tradition continues. During the annual fall Festival de Wallonie, food, drink, and fun fill the plaza. **Eglise St-Jean,** which fronts the square, was completed in 1890 and took more than 200 years to build. ⊠*rue St-Jean and rue de President* ☎*081/23–06–33.*

⓭ **Place St-Hilaire.** At the base of the Citadelle, this spot seems like an unassuming parking lot. In fact it's one of Belgium's most important archaeological sites. In 1992 archaeologists unearthed a corpse dating from 100 BC, and in 2000 a well-preserved body of a 10-year-old boy from the 18th century was found. Peer down into the roped off area of the dig to see remnants of Roman walls, which fuel the theory of many local historians that Julius Caesar himself visited Namur. ⊠*pl. St-Hilaire, at base of rue du Pont at rue de Grognon and pl. Kegeljan.*

⓾ **Rue des Brasseurs.** In the 18th and 19th centuries, brewers flocked to this street paralleling the Sambre River for its easy access to water. It quickly became one of Namur's wealthiest strips. Now, old breweries and warehouses have been converted into elegant, fashionable residences.

❶ **Théâtre Royal de Namur.** This regal theater was first built in 1860 and has burned to the ground and been rebuilt in the same 19th-century Italianate style three times. It's now home to the Namur Orchestra and Wallonia Orchestra, as well as plays, dance, poetry readings, lectures, and film screenings. To find out what's happening, stop by or look for listings in *La Meuse* or *Vers L'Aenier,* the city's two papers. ⊠*pl. du Théâtre 2* ☎*081/22–60–26* ⊕*www.theatredenamur.be.*

OFF THE BEATEN PATH

L'Abbaye de Maredsous. Take the N92 to Yvoir and go east on N971 for about 10 km (6 mi) to reach this abbey, built in the late 19th century as a cloister for a small order. A school, library, fromagerie, brewery, ceramics studio, and farm were eventually added. Now the sprawling complex dominates the hill, but it remains an idyllic spot for picnics, meditative walks, or evening vespers. The visitor center has exhibitions about the abbey, a snack bar serving the abbey's famous beers and cheeses, and a gift shop selling the ceramics and other products that are made by the monks in residence. Information pamphlets in English are available. ⊠*rue de Maredsous 11, Denee* ☎*082/69–82–11* ⊕*www. maredsous.com* ☜*Free* ☉*Daily 9–6.*

WHERE TO EAT

$$$ ✕**Biétrumé Picar.** Eating is serious business in this white house in the
CONTINENTAL suburb of Les Plantes, 3 km (2 mi) south of central Namur. (It's a bit
difficult to find, so call ahead for directions.) Chef Charles Jeandrain
focuses his attention on seafood, offering a changing menu that might
include oyster soup, salmon wrapped in phyllo, veal ratatouille, and
crème brûlée made with fresh goat cheese. After your meal, settle in the
salon for a cigar or a cognac. ⊠*Tienne Macquet 16* ☎*081/23–07–39*
Jacket and tie ⊟*AE, DC, MC, V* ⊘*Closed Mon. lunch, and Sun. din-*
ner, 1st wk of Jan., 2 wks late July–early Aug.

$$–$$$ ✕**La Petite Fugue.** In an unassuming redbrick house on a quiet street off
FRENCH the place du Marché-aux-Légumes, this classy restaurant with a deli-
Fodor's Choice cate musical motif lives up to its name. (In addition to being a musical
★ term, *le petit fugue* also means "the small escape.") The menu, which
changes daily, promises haute cuisine emphasizing regional ingredients,
such as locally caught trout and locally raised lamb. The subtly flavored
dishes perfectly match the restaurant's gentle interior. ⊠*pl. Chanoine*
Descamps 5 ☎*081/23–13–20* ⚞*Reservations essential* ⊟*AE, MC,*
V ⊘*Closed Sun.*

$$$ ✕**L'Essentiel.** White petals casually strewn over the table settings give
CONTEMPORARY you a hint of the artistry and elegance found at this secluded country
★ farmhouse 10 km (6 mi) outside of Namur. You could start your meal
with Parmesan cheese crème brûlée or white asparagus dappled with
caviar, followed by succulent veal with carrots and parsley or a perfectly
poached salmon on a bed of shiitake mushrooms. Desserts include a
dark-chocolate fudge beignet in a ginger-spiced golden biscuit mesh.
The surrounding garden is suitably exquisite. ⊠*rue Roger Clément*
32, Temploux ☎*081/56–86–16* ⊕*www.lessentiel.be* ⚞*Reservations*
essential; Jacket and tie ⊟*AE, MC, V* ⊘*Closed Sat. and Mon.*

$–$$ ✕**Le Temps des Cerises.** On a narrow street in the city center, this cozy,
BELGIAN Old Belgium–themed café serves hearty regional food amid cherry-red
furniture, lace curtains, and lots of antique bric-a-brac. A red-tinted
mannequin leans against a wall marked with childish writings and
drawings. The kitchen prepares reliable regional food, such as farm
ham with mustard sauce. ⊠*rue des Brasseurs 22* ☎*081/22–53–26*
⊟*MC, V* ⊘*Mon.–Sat. 9:30–6:30. No lunch Sat.*

WHERE TO STAY

$$ ⬚**Beauregard.** Built into a wing of the Namur Casino, this is a busi-
ness hotel, with identical rooms in bright color schemes (lime, salmon,
teal). Several rooms have wide views of the river. A breakfast buffet is
served in a vast hall overlooking the river on the Citadelle side. **Pros:**
casino on premises, nice views. **Cons:** security lines to enter hotel, no
private parking. ⊠*av. Baron de Moreau 1* ☎*081/23–00–28* ⊕*www.*
hotelbeauregard.be ⇄*47 rooms* ⚷*In-room: no a/c. In-hotel: no eleva-*
tor, restaurant, bar, Wi-Fi. ⊟*AE, DC, MC, V* ⎆*CP.*

$ ⛫**Château de Namur.** Some of the spacious rooms in this 1930s mansion atop the Citadelle's bluff have balconies and splendid views—both of which more than compensate for the somewhat minimalist interiors. The L'Ermitage restaurant ($$$) has a handsome brick-vaulted ceiling and a French menu. You might order grilled shrimp or clam skewers. Even if you're not dining here, it's a lovely place to have a drink, for the view. **Pros:** impressive setting; excellent resraurant. **Cons:** must book dinner in advance; room decor can feel impersonal. ⊠*av. de l'Ermitage 1* ☎*081/72–99–00* ⊕*www.chateaudenamur.com* ⇴*29 rooms* ⓘ*In-room: no a/c. In-hotel: restaurant, bar, tennis court, Wi-Fi* ⊟*AE, DC, MC, V.*

¢ ⛫**Grande Hôtel de Flandre.** Namur's oldest hotel has been in business for nearly a century, and its grand entrance celebrates its Victorian heritage. Although the spare but adequate rooms could use some renovation, the location (directly across from the train station) puts you in the heart of the city. Rooms in the back tend to be quieter. **Pros:** free Wi-Fi throughout entire hotel; affordable parking nearby. **Cons:** rooms hot in summer; some beds are short. ⊠*pl. de la Station 14* ☎*081/23–18–68* ⊕*www.province.namur.be* ⇴*33 rooms* ⓘ*In-room: no a/c. In-hotel: restaurant, parking (fee), Wi-Fi* ⊟*AE, DC, MC, V.*

$$-$$$ ⛫**La Source Fleurié.** Once a restaurant known for an extensive Austrian wine list, this villa is now a charming bed and breakfast with a beautiful flower garden. There are three rooms, each with their own bathroom and a fully-furnished apartment with kitchen, bathroom, and barbecue-ready terrace. The property is situated 7 km (4 mi) south of Namur in a woodsy area with a nearby brook. **Pros:** rooms each have private bathroom; apartment available; free Wi-Fi. **Cons:** breakfast only meal served on premises; rooms lack minibar. ⊠*av. General Gracia 11, Profondville* ☎*081/41–21–86* ⊕*http://source-fleurie.be* ⇴*3 rooms, 1 apartment* ⓘ*In-hotel: Wi-Fi, no elevator, pets allowed* ⊟*AE, D, MC, V.*

$$ ⛫**Leonardo Hotel Namur.** This Israeli chain hotel is on the river before you reach Namur coming from Dinant, in the heart of the strawberry-growing region. Twenty-five modern conference rooms may give the place a strong business vibe, but its riverfront location and proximity to many historical sites make this an appealing spot for holidayers. There's also an impressive selection of games and recreational facilities (indoor and outdoor pool, volleyball, table tennis, and pool). **Pros:** river view; access to jogging and cycling paths. **Cons:** free Wi-Fi only in lobby; no elevator. ⊠*chaussée de Dinant 1149, Wépion-* ☎*081/46–08–11* ⊕*www.leonardo-hotels.com* ⇴*110 rooms* ⓘ*In-room: Internet. In-hotel: restaurant, room service, bar, pools, laundry service, parking (no fee), no-smoking rooms, some pets allowed, no elevator, Wi-Fi* ⊟*AE, DC, MC, V.*

$$-$$$ ⛫**Les Tanneurs.** This exquisite boutique hotel is the creation of Christian Bouvier, who defied developers prepared to demolish a row of ancient buildings in the heart of Namur. The sleek, contemporary rooms are individually decorated—yours might have marble flooring,

brick walls, oak furniture, and abstract paintings. The least expensive rooms are far more plain than the expensive ones. There are two restaurants: L'Espièglerie ($$$–$$$$), serving such delicacies as quail stuffed with sweetbreads and roast duck with figs; and Le Grill des Tanneurs ($$), one flight up, which serves a simpler menu at a fraction of the cost. L'Espièglerie is closed Saturday at lunch and Sunday at dinner. **Pros:** uniquely styled rooms; quality dining; good location. **Cons:** some rooms inaccessible by elevator; no a/c. ⊠*rue des Tanneries 13* ☎*081/24–00–24* ⊕*www.tanneurs.com* ⊅*28 rooms* ⌂*In-room: no a/c, Internet. In-hotel: 2 restaurants, bar, Wi-Fi* ⊟*AE, DC, MC, V.*

$$ ⊡ **Villa Gracia.** Proprietors Gisèle Dabeux and Michel Vandenberghen take great pride in their transformation of General Gracia's former mansion on the Meuse into a small, luxurious inn. The immense rococo-style rooms have sitting areas, crystal chandeliers, river views, and enormous marble bathrooms. The beds are wonderfully plush, right down to the sheets washed in specially softened water. Mornings start on a plant-filled, glass-enclosed terrace overlooking the river, where you're served a breakfast made to order. Right on the bus line to downtown Namur, Villa Gracia is also accessible by car, boat, or helicopter. **Pros:** river view; spacious rooms. **Cons:** no dinner service; no a/c. ⊠*chaussée de Dinant 1445, Wépion* ⌖*8 km (5 mi) south of Namur* ☎*081/41–43–43* ⊕*www.villagracia.com* ⊅*8 rooms* ⌂*In-room: no a/c. In-hotel: parking (no fee), Internet terminal* ⊟*AE, DC, MC, V.*

FodorśChoice
★

NIGHTLIFE

Namur is a quiet town when it comes to nightlife, but if you want to go out for a drink after dinner, there are a few pubs and cafés to check out. **Le Piano Bar** (⊠*pl. Marché aux Légumes 10* ☎*081/23–06–33*) has a good selection of beers and hosts live jazz, blues, and rock concerts Friday and Saturday night.

SHOPPING

The heart of Namur's shopping district is along rue de l'Ange and rue de Fer, which are lined with clothing boutiques, music stores, and other shops catering to a predominantly student crowd. To pick up a gift unique to the Walloon region, head to **La Cave de Wallonie** (⊠*rue de la Halle 6* ☎*081/22–06–83*). The small store's shelves are lined with Wallonian food products such as pâtés, sausages, jams, honey, and liqueurs. There are also more than 300 Belgian beers in stock, plus stemware from each of the breweries. The shop is open Monday–Saturday 10:30–6.

EN
ROUTE   Between Namur and Dinant, the **Château et Jardins d'Annevoie** *(Château and Gardens of Annevoie)* present a happy blend of 18th-century French landscaping and romantic Italian garden design. The grounds are particularly remarkable for their naturally occurring, spring-fed waterfalls, fountains, and ponds, interspersed among flower beds, lawns, grottoes, and statues. The water displays function without mechanical aids

and have remained in working order for more than two centuries. The château blends perfectly with the gardens; the furniture, paneling, and family portraits all contribute to the refined elegance of the property. ⊠*rue des Jardins 37a* ☎*082/67–97–97* ⊕*www.jardins.dannevoie.be* 🎫*€7.80* ⊘*Apr.–end June and Sept.–early Nov., daily 9:30–5:30; July and Aug., daily 9:30–6:30.*

NAMUR PROVINCE

Roman legions commanded by Julius Caesar marched up the Meuse valley through present-day Namur Province 2,000 years ago and made it one of the principal routes to Cologne. Later, it served a similar purpose for Charlemagne, linking his Frankish and German lands. Little wonder that massive forts were built on the rocks overlooking the invasion routes. Even so, the French came through here under Louis XIV and again under Napoléon. The Dutch, who ruled here for little more than a decade after Waterloo, expanded these fortifications. A century later, the Germans broke through here, pushing west and south in World Wars I and II.

This martial past seems altogether out of proportion to the pleasant, peaceful Meuse valley of the present day. South of the city of Namur, the Meuse meanders through the rolling countryside to lovely Dinant, a perfect base for exploring the region by foot, boat, or bicycle. Farther south still, Rochefort and neighboring Han-sur-Lesse are known for their magical caves. Throughout the province castles, gardens, abbeys, churches, and charming towns will reward your attention.

DINANT

29 km (17 mi) south of Namur, 93 km (56 mi) southeast of Brussels, 80 km (48 mi) southwest of Liège.

Simultaneously hanging off and tucked under spectacular cliffs on the Meuse, Dinant's dramatic setting has been the stage for a turbulent history. The town has been attacked more than 200 times in the course of eight centuries. A few of the more notable assaults include when Charles the Bold sacked the town in 1466 and threw 600 men, tied in pairs, into the river; when Henri II took the town in 1554; when Louis XIV stormed through in 1675, and again 17 years later; and most recently when the Germans burned Dinant in World War I and then returned twice during World War II.

The Rocher Bayard rock formation on the southern edge of town aptly illustrates how Dinant's natural wonders are linked to its military and folkloric past. Legend has it that the rock got its distinctive needle's-eye–shaped hole when a steed named Bayard—the property of the four Aymon brothers, Charlemagne's foes—split it with his hoof. Allegedly Louis XIV's troops widened the passage when they invaded the city.

Dinant also has a rich industrial past. Between the 12th and 15th centuries, copper production, known as *dinanderie,* boomed. Eventually the metal-working industry gave way to mining and textiles, which governed the local economy up until the beginning of the 20th century. Now Dinant (population 12,500) caters to the tourists who flock here to discover the city's historic ruins, natural beauty, and culinary pleasures. If you're interested in Belgian beer, seek out the two breweries within 10 km (6 mi) of the city. Music lovers, especially those who fancy jazz, have an additional reason to visit Dinant. Its most famous son is Adolphe Sax (born here in 1814), inventor of the saxophone. Belgium honored Sax by using his image on the 200-franc note.

GETTING HERE & AROUND

An hourly train service snakes along the Meuse river valley between Namur and Dinant. This picturesque trip takes approximately 30 minutes.

ESSENTIALS

Internet Cafés Hotel Ibis (⊠ *Remparts d'Albeau 16,* ☎ *082/21-15-00* ⊕ *www. ibishotel.com*).

Tourism Office Dinant (⊠ *Av. Cadoux 8* ☎ *08/222-2870* ⊕ *www.dinant-tour isme.be*).

WHAT TO SEE

The **Citadelle** is on the cliff top, towering directly over Dinant's city center. You can reach it by cable car or by climbing the 400 steps that were cut into the rock face in the 16th century. The fortress is not as old as you might suspect—the ancient fortification was razed in 1818 by the Dutch, who replaced it with the current structure before being ousted. The view is splendid, and there is an arms museum with cannons and cannonballs. The **Dinanderie Museum,** also in the Citadelle, has a collection of weather vanes and all manner of household utensils, products of the town's metalworking past. ⊠ *pl. Reine Astrid 3–5* ☎ *082/22-36-70* ⊕ *www.citadellededinant.be* ⚑ *€6.80, including cable car (only available during high season)* ☉ *Apr.–Oct., daily 10–6; Nov.–Mar., Sat.–Thur. 10–5.*

The town's keystone is the Gothic **Eglise Notre-Dame de Foy.** It dates from the 13th century; its distinctive blue onion-dome tower was a 17th-century addition. Legend has it that a woodcutter found a statue of the virgin in a nearby tree trunk, and the church has been a pilgrimage site ever since. ⊠ *rue du Village 4* ☎ *082/22-62-84* ⚑ *Free* ☉ *Daily 10–5.*

Co-founded by the Association Internationale Adolphe Sax and the city's Maison de la Culture, the **Maison de la Pataphonie** invites children to explore, invent, and make music as part of a two-hour guided tour. Demonstrations show you how to make music without professional instruments, simply using ordinary items like water and bits of copper and wood. At the end of the session, would-be musicians compose their own symphony. ⊠ *rue en Rhée 51* ☎ *082/21-39-39* ⊕ *www.dinant. be/index.htm?lg=3&m1=30&m2=185* ⚑ *€5* ☉ *Tours Wed. at 2:30, Mon. and holidays at 2 and 4:30.*

La Merveilleuse, a cave whose many stalactites are remarkably white, is on Dinant's left bank, about 490 yards from the bridge, on the road toward Philippeville. Tours depart hourly and a visit takes about 50 minutes. ⊠*rte. de Philippeville 142* ☎*082/22–22–10* ⌂*€6.50* ☉*Apr.–end Oct., daily 11–5; July and Aug., daily 10–6; Nov., Mar., and during school vacation, weekends 1–4; Dec.–Feb. during school vacation, 1–4.*

The Belot family has been brewing at **Brasserie du Bocq** since 1858. Their specialties include La Gauloise (blonde, brown, amber), Blanche de Namur, and St-Benoit. You can take an informative tour in English, then visit the small village of Purnode next door. ⊠*rue de la Brasserie 4, Purnode* ✛*10 km (6 mi) southwest of Dinant* ☎*082/61–07–90* ⊕*www.bocq.be* ⌂*€4* ☉*Tours: Mar.–June, Sept.–Oct., Sat.–Sun. at 2 and 4; July and Aug., daily at 2 and 4.*

Brasserie Caracole, in an old mill 7 km (4 mi) south of Dinant, heats its beer in a traditional wood stove and spices it with such surprising flavors as orange peel and coriander. Its signature snail mascot is a whimsical allusion to Namur province's reputation for being slow-paced. Even if you don't drink, the distinctive cavernous tasting room lined with old brewing equipment is worth a visit; admission includes a tasting. ⊠*Côte Marie Thérèse 86, Falmignoul* ☎*08/274–4080* ⊕*www.brasserie-caracole. be* ⌂*€5* ☉*July and Aug., daily 1–7; Sept.–June, Sat. 2–7.*

The drive south of Dinant is filled with stunning views from the road of towering rock formations across the river. The town of **Freyr,** on the left bank, is considered the best rock-climbing center in Wallonia.

The **Château de Freyr** is an impressive Renaissance building with beautiful interiors decorated with 17th-century woodwork and furniture, including a restored children's coach. Louis XIV visited here during the siege of Dinant in 1675. Its park has been laid out in accordance with the design principles of Le Nôtre, the French landscape architect. Guided tours and documentation in English are available. ⊠*Domaine de Freyr, Waulsort* ☎*082/22–22–00* ⊕*www.freyr.be* ⌂*€6* ☉*Oct.–Mar., Sun. 2–4:30; Apr.–June and Sept., weekends and holidays 10:30–12:45 and 2–5:45; July and Aug., Tues.–Sun. 10:30–12:45 and 2–5:45.*

WHERE TO EAT

$–$$$
FRENCH
✕**Centre Mosan.** This grand mansion overlooking the Meuse is the cooking school where the next generation of Belgian chefs learn the art of cuisine. The traditional French food, such as the chicken cooked with cream and potatoes, and formal service are of high standard. Though the dining room is rather plain, it has a beautiful view of the river. ⊠*av. Winston Churchill 36* ☎*082/21–30–53* ⌂*Reservations essential* ▤*AE, MC, V* ☉*Closed Sat.–Mon. No dinner.*

$$$–$$$$
CONTINENTAL

✕ **Le Jardin de Fiorine.** An unassuming gray facade belies the elegant interior and pretty garden of this ambitious restaurant. Specialties include lobster and sweetbread salad, fillet of sole with apple and truffle, and roast pigeon with corn cakes. ⊠ *rue Georges Cousot 3* ☎ *082/22–74–74* ⊕ *www.jardindefiorine.be* ⊟ *AE, DC, MC, V* ☻ *Closed Wed., 2 wks Feb. and 2 wks July. No dinner Sun.*

$$–$$$
ITALIAN

✕ **Les Amourettes.** With pink-and-red walls and a bright-red awning, this adorable restaurant shines out from its spot in a little Dinant square. Painted portraits and pictures of pumpkins and apples decorate the walls, and paper lanterns and big flowers are scattered throughout. The menu is strong on seafood—try the grilled fresh fish or langoustines—but also lists veal and chicken dishes. ⊠ *pl. St-Nicholas 11* ☎ *082/22–57–36* ⊟ *MC, V* ☻ *Closed Mon.*

$$$
CONTINENTAL

✕ **Le Vivier d'Oies.** This country inn is in a lovely stone farmhouse with a modern stone-and-glass wing. The cuisine is sophisticated: goose liver sautéed with caramelized pears, crayfish with artichoke hearts, and a spring asparagus menu. ⊠ *rue Etat 7, Dorinne* ♦ *northeast of Dinant, about 10 km (6 mi) east of Yvoir* ☎ *083/69–95–71* ⊕ *www. levivierdoies.be* ⊟ *AE, DC, MC, V* ☻ *Closed Wed. and Thurs., 2 wks June–July, 2 wks Sept.–Oct.*

WHERE TO STAY

$

🏨 **Hôtel de la Couronne.** Seemingly built into the Citadelle's cliffs, this no-frills hotel couldn't be more centrally located. It's been in the same family for four generations and offers many lodging options. Some rooms have bunk beds, some have three beds, some have views, and some have connecting suites. The same-named restaurant serves local fare and there's a lively local bar scene well into the night. **Pros:** great central location; bar and restaurant specialize in Belgian food and Trapist beer. **Cons:** outdated decor; no a/c. ⊠ *rue de Sax 1* ☎ *082/22–24–41* ⊕ *www.hotellacouronne.com* 🛏 *20 rooms, 8 with bath* ♿ *In-room: no a/c. In-hotel: restaurant, parking (no fee)* ⊟ *MC, V.*

¢

🏨 **Les Cretiás.** The glorious garden and tremendous valley views more than compensate for the smallish rooms, narrow hallways, and somewhat dusty decor of this home-style inn in the tiny village of Falmignoul. The restaurant ($–$$$; closed Monday and Tuesday) serves well-respected traditional French cuisine. Try the risotto St. Jacques with lobster butter, or tongue in phyllo served with mushrooms. The tasting, seasonal, and daily menus also feature an extensive cheese selection. **Pros:** beautiful garden; lovely view. **Cons:** rather small rooms; no elevator. ⊠ *rue des Cretiás 99, Falmignoul* ♦ *7 km (4 mi) south of Dinant* ☎ *082/74–42–11* ⊕ *www.lescretias.be* 🛏 *11 rooms* ♿ *In-room: no a/c, no TV. In-hotel: restaurant, no elevator* ⊟ *AE, MC, V* ☻ *Closed Jan., June 21–July.*

$–$$
Fodor'sChoice
★

🏨 **Moulin de Lisogne.** The husband-and-wife team of Alan Blondiaux and Martine Legrain have created a sensualist's dream at their romantic inn. The restaurant ($$–$$$; closed Monday and Tuesday, no dinner Sunday) serves goose, veal, and beef raised on the premises, vegetables from the garden, bread baked by M. Blondiaux in the skylighted bakery off the enormous kitchen, and wine from his own vineyard in France. Mme. Legrain has decorated the lodgings with equally elegant flair. Ask to stay in the Tower, which has beautiful oak furniture and an oversize tub sunken into the pale pink marble bathroom. M. Blondiaux doubles as the head of Dinant's tourist office and can help with any questions about the area. **Pros:** picturesque premises; fantastic dinner. **Cons:** disappointing breakfast; not all rooms have TV. ⊠*rue de la Lisonette 60, Lisogne ✛7 km (4 mi) northeast of Dinant* ☎*082/22–63–80* ⮐*10 rooms* ⚘*In-room: no a/c. In-hotel: restaurant* ▤*AE, MC, V* ⊘*Closed mid-Dec.–mid-Feb.*

SPORTS & THE OUTDOORS

KAYAKING Kayaking or boating on the Meuse, or its lively tributary, the Lesse, is a great way to see the landscape: forested valleys, rocky cliffs, and countless streams. To tackle the lower Lesse, try the 12-km (8-mi) or 21-km (13-mi) ride from Houyet, through two rapids and past the high cliffs holding Walzin Castle, to Anseremme on the Meuse, south of Dinant. The season runs April–October. Rentals start at around €10 per person.

Ansiaux Kayaks (⊠*rue du Velodrome 15* ☎*082/22–23–25* ⊕*www.ansiaux.be*), a branch of Les Kayaks Bleus, offers guided kayak trips from Houyet to Anseremme (about five hours, 21 km [13 mi]) and from Gendron to Anseremme (about three hours, 12 km [7.4 mi]). Rental prices for a single-seat kayak are €15 (weekday) or €16 (weekend) for the Houyet route and €14 (weekday) or €15 (weekend) for the Gendron route. They also run day-long cruises along the Meuse and lead all-terrain biking and rock-climbing trips.

Bateaux Bayard (⊠*rte. de Phillipville* ☎*082/22–22–10* ⊕*www.dinantourism.com*) offers guided kayak and caving trips that last 45 minutes to an entire day. Kayak rentals cost €12 or €16 for a single-person boat, €24 or €32 for a double. **Compagnie des Bateaux** (⊠*rue Daoust 64B* ☎*082/22–23–15* ⊕*www.bateaux-meuse.be*), affiliated with Les Kayaks Bleus, guides kayak trips from Houyet and Gendron to Anseremme. **Kayaks Libert** (⊠*quai de Meuse 1* ☎*082/22–61–86 or 081/22–22–10* ⊕*www.dinantourism.com*) organizes trips for individuals and groups; the routes for individuals go between Houyet and Dinant and Gendron and Dinart. Kayak rentals cost €12 or €16 for a single-person boat, €24 or €32 for a double. They also have boat tours on the Meuse, starting with a 45-minute run for €5.50. **Les Kayaks Bleus** (⊠*pl. d'Eglise 2* ☎*082/22–43–97* ⊕*www.lessekayaks.be*), affiliated with Ansiaux Kayaks, offers guided kayak trips from Houyet and Gendron to Anseremme at the same prices. They also offer caving, rock climbing, and "aerial" or "bridge-walking" tours. You can combine two different tours for a full day of activities.

BIKING **Les Draisines de la Molignee** (⊠*rue de la Gare 82, Falaën* ☎*082/69–90–79* ⊕*www.molignee.be/draisines/draisines_gb.htm*) organizes rail-biking trips on special five-seater cycles that run along abandoned railroad tracks in the valley of Molignee between Falaën and Mardesous.

Celles (☎ *Celles tourism office: 08/266–6267* ⊕*www.celles.org*) about 10 km (6 mi) southeast of Dinant on N94, is one of the most beautiful villages in Wallonia. Make sure to visit the **Eglise St-Hadelin,** in the center of this tiny town.

ROCHEFORT

35 km (22 mi) southeast of Dinant, 128 km (79 mi) southeast of Brussels, 55 km (34 mi) southwest of Liège.

In the 12th century, the Count of Rochefort had the most important feudal estate in the province of Liège. Today, Rochefort is a quiet tourist town on the border of the Namur and Luxembourg provinces. The name Rochefort means "strong rock" and comes from the prominent rock castle, the Château Comtal, which anchors the town center. Rochefort is known for its delicious Trappist beer and cheese, plus a number of interesting sights in town and in the vicinity, most notably the Grottes de Han. The Rochefort tourist office has developed a series of walking tours intended to illustrate the town's motto: "On the tracks of a land born from the union of water, earth, and mankind." The office also sells reduced-price package tickets to the region's archaeological sites and caves.

GETTING HERE & AROUND

The nearest railway station to Rochefort is in Jemelle, about 3 km (2 mi) east. Direct trains run hourly to Jemelle from both Namur (40 minutes) and Liège (75 minutes). From Jemelle, bus #29 and #166a make the short journey to Rochefort in about 5 minutes. Both run approximately once each hour. Bus #29 continues on to the Grottes de Han caves, a further 5 km (3 mi) west. If you are driving, the trip from Namur takes about 45 minutes, or 75 minutes from Liège.

ESSENTIALS

Tourism Office Rochefort (⊠*rue de Behogne 5* ☎*08/434–5172* ⊕*www. valdelesse.be*).

WHAT TO SEE

While in Rochefort, be sure to visit the little **Chapelle de Lorette.** Josine de la March, Countess of Rochefort, built the chapel in 1620 in hopes that it would hasten the return of her son—who, so the story goes, had been kidnapped by a monkey, and was returned upon the chapel's completion.

The **Grotte de Lorette** sits in the center of town. Carved by the Lomme River, the cave maintains a constantly warm temperature. The most remarkable of its many halls is the *Salle de Sabat* (Hall of the Witches' Sabbath), which is more than 250 feet high. ⊠*Drève de Lorette* ☎*084/21–20–80* ⊕*www.grotte-de-han.be* 🎫€7.25 ☉*Apr.–Nov., daily 10–5.*

Come for the majestic view and explore ruins dating from the 11th through the 19th centuries at the **Château Comtal** *(Castle of the Counts),* situated on a rise overlooking Rochefort's town center. There is also an active archaeological dig and a small archaeological museum on-site. ⊠*rue Jacquet* ☏*0496/61–71–45* ⊑*€2* ⊙*Apr.–Nov., daily 10–6; Dec.–Mar., by appointment.*

Ꮸ Built to incorporate the ruins of a Gallo-Roman villa, the 1,240-acre **Malagne Archeo-Park** has nature trails, regional exhibits, historical reenactments, and an abundance of events specifically for kids. Call ahead for a schedule of events. ⊠*Malagne 1* ☏*084/22–21–03* ⊕*www. malagne.be* ⊑*€4.20* ⊙*Mar.–Nov., daily 11–6.*

Fodor'sChoice The magnificent **Grottes de Han** *(Han Caves)*, which had provided ref-★ uge for threatened tribes since neolithic times, were rediscovered in the mid-19th century. To tour them, board an ancient tram in the center of Han-sur-Lesse that carries you to the mouth of the caves. There multilingual guides take over, leading groups on foot through 3 km (2 mi) of dimly lighted chambers. You get occasional glimpses of the underground river Lesse as you pass giant stalagmites and eventually enter the vast cavern called the Dome, 475 feet high, where a single torchbearer dramatically descends the sloping cave wall. The final part of the journey is by boat on the underground river. The trip takes about 90 minutes. The cave is 13°C (55.4°F), with 90% humidity, all year long, so consider bringing a sweater with you. ⊠*rue Joseph Lamotte 2, Han-sur-Lesse* ✦*6 km (4 mi) southeast of Rochefort* ☏*084/37–72–13* ⊕*www.grotte-de-han.be* ⊑*€11.50.*

Ꮸ The **Réserve d'Animaux Sauvages,** in the domain of Han, is a 625-acre wildlife reserve filled with animals native to the region, such as wild boars, brown bears, bison, wolves, and lynx. A coach takes you through the park, where you can observe the animals in their natural habitat. The trip takes an hour and 15 minutes. ⊠*rue Joseph Lamotte 2, Han-sur-Lesse* ✦*6 km (4 mi) southeast of Rochefort* ☏*084/37–72–13* ⊕*www.grotte-de-han.be* ⊑*€9.50.*

Ꮸ **Domaine Provincial de Chevetogne,** 10 km (6 mi) northeast of Rochefort, has glorious gardens, a pool, tennis courts, horseback riding, paddle-boats, and miniature golf. In summer there are weekend afternoon jazz and classical concerts. ⊠*Chevetogne* ✦*15 km (9.5 mi) northeast of Rochefort* ☏*083/68–72–11* ⊕*www.companyevent.eu* ⊑*€10 (only during Apr.–Nov.)* ⊙*Park: end March–beginning Nov., daily 9–8. Gardens: daily (swimming pool only open Apr.–Nov.).*

LIÈGE

61 km (37 mi) northeast of Namur, 97 km (58 mi) east of Brussels, 122 km (73 mi) southwest of Cologne.

The bustling city of Liège—Luik to the Flemish and Dutch, Lüttich to the Germans—sits deep in the Meuse valley at the confluence of the Meuse and Ourthe rivers. After Belgian independence in 1830, Liège was a leader in a countrywide upsurge of industrial activity, and that, for good and bad, has marked its character ever since. The first European locomotive was built in Liège, and the Bessemer steel production method was developed here; it is to the burning furnaces that Liège owes its nickname, *la cité ardente* (the Fiery City). The surrounding hills and rivers were rich in minerals, including potassium, calcium, iron, and sand, and these resources were heavily mined. Drawing on a centuries-old tradition of weapons manufacturing, the Fabrique Nationale started to build precision firearms, and Val St-Lambert began to produce glassware that has gained worldwide recognition. Liège's port, one of the biggest inland waterways in Europe, was busy with barges and other commercial vessels. In August 1914 the forts of Liège kept the German invasion force at bay long enough for the Belgian and French troops to regroup; in 1944–45, more than a thousand V1 and V2 missiles exploded in the city.

Liège's outskirts are still lined with industrial facilities—some operational, some (notably **Val St-Lambert** and Blegny) transformed into innovative museums, and others closed. Although the views may not be beautiful, you shouldn't let this deter you from giving Liège its due. A soot-covered old building may house a historic treasure, a delicious meal, or a glorious flower shop. (Liège has many talented florists whose windows brighten up the city streets.) An inconspicuous cobblestone alley could be home to busy cafés and architectural gems.

The Liègeois have a reputation for friendliness and are clearly proud of their city. Blue and white plaques are visible on the portals of the many buildings that have been designated Wallonian heritage sights. Walloon can still be heard on the streets and is taught at the local university, where students have been known to say, *"Po brêre on èst chal, po bêure!"* (We are not here to complain, we are here to drink!) Tchantchès, Liège's beloved puppet with his red nose and indefatigable attitude, is the town mascot. Pèkèt, a regional genever made from juniper berries and consumed straight up, is plentiful. And, every Sunday morning, as has happened for centuries, the quai is transformed into **La Batte,** one of Europe's biggest weekly street markets.

In addition to its own merits, Liège is a good urban base from which to explore forests, parks, and other pleasures that lie to its south.

GETTING HERE & AROUND

Trains to Liège run from Brussels at least twice every hour, taking between an hour and an hour and a half, depending on the number of interim stops. Hourly regional trains run directly between Antwerp Central and Liège, taking 2¼ hours to complete the journey. However, you can shave 30 minutes off this trip by taking the faster intercity trains in the direction of Brussels, and connecting in Brussels North.

Although not commonly used in the other towns, taxis are plentiful in Liège. They can be picked up at cab stands in the principal squares or summoned by phone. Fares are €2.11 plus €1.10 per km in the city and €2.40 per km when you leave the city.

ESSENTIALS

Taxi Contacts Liège Tax (☎ *0800/32–200 toll free*). **Melkior** (⊕ *www.melkior.be*).

Hospitals Hôpital Citadelle (⊠ *blvd. du 12è de Ligne 1, northwest of the Coeur Historique* ☎ *04/225–6111* ⊕ *www.chrcitadelle.be).*

Tourism Office Liège (⊠ *En Féronstrée 92* ☎ *04/221–9221* ⊕ *www.liege.be).*

TIMING

The walk itself takes about 90 minutes, but with visits to the museums and shops, plus a stop for lunch, you can fill a day. On weekends, the streets are crowded with locals and visitors, and the exciting market at La Batte takes place on Sunday. Most museums are closed Monday.

EXPLORING LIÈGE

The city is roughly divided into four sections. **Le Carré,** bordered by rue de l'Université and boulevard de la Sauvenière, is the city's commercial district. It was originally a small island surrounded by river-fed canals, but the canals were dredged and filled in the 19th century to accommodate street traffic. Now these same streets, some of which are limited to pedestrians only and lined with cafés and boutiques, pulsate with shoppers, workers, and tourists. The **Coeur Historique** is chock-full of museums, churches, and cobblestone streets, testament to Liège's long, rich history. Within the historic center, the 373 steps of the Montagne de Bueren lead up to the remains of the Citadelle. There have been fortifications at the Citadelle for several centuries; during the World Wars it was used as a barracks and a prison camp. Most of the Citadelle was torn down in the late 1960s and early 1970s, leaving only some ramparts. A hospital now occupies the site. East of Le Carré on the north side of the river is the **Nouvelle Ville,** or New Town, where many 18th-century homes have been restored. The rejuvenation and gentrification of this area may eventually push out the red-light district, which is still operational in a few of the smaller alleys off the quai. **Outremeuse,** across the river, is up-and-coming. Mostly quiet, it has a few streets lined with ethnic restaurants, bars, and Liège's own unique *cafés chantant* (singing cafés). More establishments are opening regularly. This neighborhood is home to Liège's two most famous sons: Georges Simenon (the writer) and Tchantchès (the puppet).

WHAT TO SEE

❽ Cour St-Antoine. In a clever example of urban renewal, what was formerly a slum is now a beautifully restored residential square with a small-village feel. The facade of the red house at the north end of the square resembles a church and is connected by a small channel to a pyramid-like structure replicating Tikal, a Mayan ruin in Guatemala. ⊠ *Between rue des Brasseurs and rue Hors-Château, Coeur Historique.*

❾ Eglise St-Barthélemy. This church contains Liège's greatest treasure and one of the Seven Religious Wonders of Belgium: the Baptismal Font of Renier de Huy, which dates from between 1107 and 1118. The brass masterpiece of Art Mosan, weighing half a ton, is decorated in high relief with figures of the five biblical baptismal scenes. They're depicted with an extraordinary suppleness, and the font rests on 10 oxen, which

Fodor'sChoice
★

are also varied and interesting. During the French Revolution the font was hidden by the faithful, but the cover has disappeared. The church, consecrated in 1015, is one of the rare Romanesque churches to escape transformation into the Gothic style, retaining its austerity. The nave, however, has been retouched in baroque fashion. In the square outside the church, the 1992 metal sculpture *Les Principautres* by local artist Mary Andrien playfully celebrates Liège's religious and industrial history. ⊠*pl. St-Barthélemy, Coeur Historique* ⊕*www.liege.be* ⌨€1.24 ☉*Mon.–Sat. 10–noon and 2–5 except during services, Sun. 2–5.*

⑰ Eglise St-Denis. This is one of the oldest churches in Liège; its outer walls once formed part of the city's defenses. It has a handsome reredos portraying the suffering of Christ. ⊠*pl. St-Denis, rue de la Cathédrale, Nouvelle Ville* ☎*04/223–5756* ⊕*www.liege.be* ☉*Mon.–Sat. 9–noon and 1:30–5, Sun. 9* AM*–noon.*

⑮ Eglise St-Jacques. The grimy exterior of this minicathedral a few blocks southwest of Liège's center, near the place St-Jacques, belies a wonderful interior. Marble, stained glass, and polished wood achieve an outstanding visual harmony. The glory of the church is the Gothic vault, decorated in intricate patterns of vivid blue and gold and containing myriad sculpted figures. ⊠*pl. St-Jacques, south of Nouvelle Ville* ☎*04/222–1441* ⊕*www.liege.be* ☉ *Weekdays 8–noon, Sat. 4–6.*

⑫ Grand Curtius. Due to reopen in 2009, this complex will house five of Liège's top museums. The 13,000-piece collection of the **Musée d'Armes** (☎*04/221–9416* ⊕*www.museedarmes.be* ⌨€1.25) recalls the city's prominence as an arms-manufacturing town beginning in the Middle Ages. (Now the main weapons factory is in Herstal, north of Liège.) Among the many rare and beautifully executed pieces are a Lefaucheux pinfire revolver and the Velodog hammerless revolver. Exhibits describe the technical aspects of manufacturing as well as engraving and inlaying.

The **Musée d'Archéologie et d'Arts Décoratifs** holds rare Belgo-Roman and Frankish works, such as Bishop Notger's *Evangelistery,* an exquisite 10th-century manuscript of the Gospels. The small **Musée du Verre,** or glass museum, will exhibit Venetian glass and Val St-Lambert crystal.

⑦ Impasses. These narrow mews were where servants had their tiny houses in the days of the prince-bishops. Prominent citizens lived along neighboring En Hors-Château. As late as the 1970s, it was believed that the best approach to urban redevelopment was to tear down these houses. Luckily, common sense prevailed. The **Impasse de l'Ange** and **Impasse de la Couronne** are two examples of the six such well-restored impasses in town. Duck under the *ârvô,* the bridge over the alleyway, to discover lush gardens, finely restored Tudor homes, and a number of *potales* (wall chapels), devoted mostly to the Virgin or to St. Roch, who was venerated as the protector against disease epidemics. ⊠*Off En Hors-Château, Coeur Historique.*

❹ Montagne de Bueren. This stairway of 373 steps ascends from Hors-Château toward Liège's Citadelle. It honors the memory of Vincent van Bueren, a leader of the resistance against Charles the Bold. In 1468 he climbed the hill with 600 men, intending to ambush the duke and kill him. Betrayed by their Liègeois accents, they lost their lives and the city was pillaged and burned. Charles the Bold, a superstitious man, made sure the churches remained untouched while the city was in flames so he wouldn't be sent to hell. At the base of the stairs is a former nunnery, now a compound for antiques dealers. ⊠ *Hors-Château, Coeur Historique.*

🔟 **Musée d'Ansembourg.** The sculptures, tapestries, marble fireplaces, painted ceilings, and ceramics in this mansion evoke the opulent lifestyle of its original owner, 18th-century merchant and banker Michel Willems. It was converted into a decorative and fine arts museum in 1903. Look for Willems's carved-oak cupboard in the dining room and the Hubert Sarton six-face mantel clock. Brochures in English are available. ⊠ *En Féronstrée 114, Coeur Historique* 🕾 *04/221–9402* 💳 *€4.50* ⊙ *Tues.–Sat. 1–6, Sun. 11–4:30.*

⑭ **Musée d'Art Moderne et Contemporain.** Almost all the big names are represented in this collection of 700-odd French and Belgian paintings dating from the 1850s on. Some of the stars are Emile Claus' *Le Vieux Jardinier* (*The Old Gardener*) and Paul Gauguin's *Le Sorcier de Hiva-Oa* (*The Sorcerer of Hiva-Oa*). The museum stands in the attractive Parc de la Boverie, about 3 km (2 mi) southeast of the town center, favored by the Liègeois for a stroll far away from the traffic. You can walk partway along the riverfront to get there. Inquire about English-language brochures. ⊠ *Parc de la Boverie 3* 🕾 *04/343–0403* ⊕ *www.mamac.org* 💳 *€5* ⊙ *Tues.–Sat. 1–6, Sun. 11–4:30.*

⑤ **Musée d'Art Religieux et d'Art Mosan.** There are many pieces here, including an 11th-century *Sedes Sapientiae* (*Seat of Wisdom*), a stiff and stern-faced seated Virgin, clearly the product of an austere age. Printed guides in English are available. ⊠ *rue Mère Dieu 11, Coeur Historique* 🕾 *04/221–4279* ⊕ *www.multimania.com/maramliege* 💳 *€2.50* ⊙ *Tues.–Sat. 11–6, Sun. 11–4.*

⑪ **Musée de l'Art Wallon.** The museum showcases works by Walloon artists from the 17th century to the present day, including Surrealists René Magritte and Paul Delvaux. Twelve dilapidated buildings were taken apart, brick by brick, and put together again to form an appealing architectural whole. There's no explanatory information in English. Note next door is the **Ilôt St-Georges,** an interesting example of urban archaeology. ⊠ *En Féronstrée 86, Coeur Historique* 🕾 *04/221–9231* ⊕ *www.liege.be* 💳 *€5* ⊙ *Tues.–Sat. 1–6, Sun. 11–4:30.*

③ **Musée de la Vie Wallonne.** In an old Franciscan convent, carefully reconstructed interiors give a vivid and varied idea of life in old Wallonia, from coal mines to farm kitchens to the workshops of many different crafts. The museum even includes a court of law, complete with a guillotine. Life-size statues in carnival costumes greet you in the entrance hall. And one gallery is populated by the irreverent marionette Tchantchès and his band, who represent the Liège spirit. There isn't any explanatory information in English. ⊠ *Cour des Mineurs*

1, Coeur Historique ☎04/237–9040 ⊕www.viewallonne.be ☒€5 ⊙Tues.–Sat. 9:30–6, Sun. 10–4.

⓭ **Musée Tchantchès.** Discover the mystique and mishaps of Liège's most
☾ beloved marionette at this museum in the Outremeuse district. Here
you can learn the answers to such burning questions as: How did
Tchantchès meet his girlfriend Nanesse? Why did he have to eat an
iron shoe to fight the measles at the age of three? Was he really designed
by an Italian puppeteer? See Tchantchès in action October through
April for their Sunday morning puppet shows at 10 or by appointment. There's no explanatory information available in English. ⊠*rue
Surlet 56, Outremeuse* ☎04/342–7575 ⊕www.tchantches.be ☒€3
⊙*Museum visits: Tues. and Thur. 2–4.*

⓰ **Place de la Cathédrale.** This is Liège's version of a central park. A busy
★ square, it bubbles over with the sounds of families shopping, students
gossiping, and other Liègeois just hanging out. Street musicians, mimes,
and other performers are common, adding to the mix of sounds and
sights. The square is flanked by the north wall of the Gothic **Cathédrale
St-Paul.** Inside are handsome statues by Jean Delcour, including one of
St. Paul. (Other graceful works by this 18th-century sculptor dot the
old city.) The cathedral's most prized possessions are in the Treasury,
especially the *Reliquaire de Charles le Téméraire* (*Reliquary of Charles
the Bold*), with gold and enamel figures of St. George and the bold
duke himself on his knees; curiously, their faces are identical. This reliquary was presented to Liège by Charles the Bold in 1471 in penance
for having had the city razed three years earlier. ⊠*rue Bonne-Fortune
6, Nouvelle Ville* ☎*Cathedral: 04/232–6131, Treasury: 04/232–6132*
⊕www.ulg.ac.be/trecatlg ☒*Cathedral: free. Treasury €4* ⊙*Cathedral:
daily 8:30–5 except during services; Treasury: Tues.–Sun. 2–5; guided
tours daily at 3* ☞*Ring bell next to cloister door.*

■ NEED A
BREAK?
Pollux (⊠*rue de la Cathédrale 2* ☎*04/223–6781*) **is a popular bakery
where you can pick up a freshly baked** *gauffre* **(Belgian waffle), topped with
powdered sugar and perhaps a bit of melted chocolate.**

❻ **Place du Marché.** This bustling square is as old as Liège itself. For centuries it was where the city's commercial and political life was concentrated. The 18th-century Hôtel de Ville is here, with its two entrances:
one for the wealthy and one for the common people. A number of
the old buildings surrounding it were among the 23,000 destroyed
by German bombs. In the center stands the **Perron,** a large fountain
sculpted by Jean Delcour, topped with an acorn—the symbol of Liège's
liberty. ⊠*Bordered by rue du General Jacques, rue des Mineurs, and
En Féronstrée, Coeur Historique* ☎04/ 221–9221 ⊕www.liege.be.

❷ **Place St-Lambert.** Now a vibrant, bustling focal point, this square went
through a long period of neglect after the Cathedral of St. Lambert,
the largest cathedral in Europe, was destroyed during the French
Revolution. At its center proudly stands a sculpture honoring both
the murdered 8th-century saint and the future of Liège. Archaeological evidence indicates that the area may have been populated for as

many as 10,000 years; an underground exhibition hall displays the finds unearthed in recent excavations. On one side of the square stands the enormous **Palais des Princes-Evêques,** which has been rebuilt at different stages since the days of the first prince-bishops. The present facade dates from 1734. The 16th-century courtyard with individually decorated columns has remained unchanged. ■**TIP**➔**Tours can be booked in advance by contacting the Palais de Justice.** ⊠*Junction of rue de Bruxelles, rue Léopold, rue Joffre, rue du General Jacques, and rue Souverain Pont, Nouvelle Ville* ☎*04/222–4105.*

❶ **Théâtre Royal** is a handsome 18th-century performing-arts venue in the center of the city. Legend has it that the local composer Grétry had his heart buried underneath the pit. His statue stands outside the building. The well-respected Opéra Royal de Wallonie is based here, and L'Orchestra Philarmonique often performs at the theater. Call for schedule and ticket information. ⊠*pl. de la République Française at Boulevard de la Sauvenière and rue Joffre, Nouvelle Ville* ☎*04/221–4720* ⊕*www.orw.be* ☉*Box office Mon.–Sat. 10:30–6 PM, performance nights only.*

OUTSIDE LIÈGE

There are a few World War II sites of interest near Liège, such as the Cimetière Américain des Ardennes, the Fort de Battice, the Fort de Loncin, and the Henri-Chapelle cemetery. *For more information, see Chapter 2.*

Complexe Touristique de Blegny. The highlight of a visit to this complex east of Liège is a trip down the former Blegny Coal Mine, which produced 1,000 tons of coal a day at its peak. Liège's wealth was based on coal, which was mined from the Middle Ages until 1980. An audiovisual presentation illustrates this history, and former miners lead tours of the surface and underground facilities. Make an appointment to take the tour in English. A coal mine tour takes 2 hours, though you can spend at least half a day here with the kids because there's also a museum, playground, restaurant, and café. ⊠*rue Lambert Marlet 23, Blegny* ✛*15 km (9 mi) northeast of Liège* ☎*04/387–4333* ⊕*www.blegnymine.be* ☒*€8.50.*

★ **Cristalleries du Val St-Lambert.** In 1826 the Val St-Lambert factory opened in a restored 13th-century abbey at Seraing, on the Meuse south of Liège, and began producing crystal that became the pride of Belgium and the subject of worldwide acclaim. Eventually production was cut back; now what was once a humming factory is a museum that explores the history of glass manufacturing through clever interactive exhibits and glass-blowing demonstrations. Val St-Lambert crystal is available at the gift shop, which can also mend broken pieces you've brought from home or custom-etch your new treasure. ⊠*rue du Val 245, Seraing* ✛*12 km (7½ mi) from Liège* ☎*04/330–3800* ⊕*www.val-saint-lambert.com* ☒*€6.*

Château du Val St-Lambert. Just across a little square from the Cristalleries du Val St-Lambert, is a castle, which houses the Glass Museum of Liège and contains pieces of Charles Graffart, one of the great creators in Val

St-Lambert. The two-story complex also offers a high-tech interactive glass-and-crystal factory where you can see glass-blowing demonstrations and ogle one-of-a-kind pieces. ⊠*rue du Val 245, Seraing* ✛*12 km (7½ mi) from Liège* ☎*04/330–3800* ⊕*www.val-saint-lambert. com* ⊠*€6* ⊙*Showroom: 9–5; Tours: Mon.–Thur. 10:30 and 2:30, Friday 10:30, and every second weekend of the month except Aug. hourly from 10:30–3:30.*

Préhistosite de Ramioul. The world of early humans is on display at this speculative re-creation of prehistoric dwellings. You can get a sense of your ancestors' technical aptitude while trying your own hand at making pots and polishing stones. The museum is next to the **cave of Ramioul**, where the lighting system brings out the beauty of the rock formations. Guides explain in English the cave's animal life and its use by humans. Tours are led April–October on Saturday and Sunday at 2. ⊠*rue de la Grotte 128, Flémalle* ✛*near Seraing, 15 km (9 mi) south of Liège* ☎*04/275–4975* ⊕*www.ramioul.org* ⊠*€3 and €9 for tour* ⊙*Mon.–Tues. 9–5, Sat.–Sun. 10–6.*

WHERE TO EAT

$ **BELGIAN**

✕ **Amon Nanesse.** Playful like the puppet Tchantchès, the bar La Maison du Pèkèt concocts cocktails using *pèkèt*—Liège's local liquor—in every way imaginable. When you've had your fill of pèkèts with passion fruit, head next door to the attached restaurant, A Mon Nanesse. Named after Tchantchès's girlfriend, this friendly joint serves hearty Belgian fare made with, of course, pèkèt. Ten rooms in two 17th-century town houses comprise the restaurant and bar, and a disco is slated to open next door. ⊠*rue de l'Epée 4, Coeur Historique* ☎*04/250–6783* ⊕*www.maison dupeket.be* ⚠*Reservations essential* ⊟*No credit cards.*

$-$$ **BELGIAN**

✕ **As Ouhès.** This stylish spot on the place du Marché is one of celebrity chef Robert Lesenne's most popular restaurants. Violet walls highlight old black and white photographs of Liège. You can expect large portions of Walloon specialties, such as rabbit stewed in beer, and succulent *boulets* (traditional Liège pork-and-beef meatballs flavored with a fruit syrup) served with mounds of frites. Tables are often hard to come by; try for one outside when weather permits. ⊠*pl. du Marché 21, Coeur Historique* ☎*04/223–3225* ⊕*www.as-ouhes.be* ⊟*AE, DC, MC, V.*

¢-$$ **BELGIAN**

✕ **Au Parc des Moules.** Ask Liège natives about this institution hidden on a pedestrian alley and watch their eyes light up. You'd be hard pressed to find a longer or more creative menu of mussels. More than 50 different dishes involving mussels tempt seafood lovers. Try the *moules flambé* with cognac, or *moules mexicane* with tequila. ⊠*rue Tête de Boeuf 19, Le Carré* ☎*04/223–7149* ⊟*AE, DC, MC, V.*

¢-$ **CONTEMPORARY**

✕ **Bruit Qui Court.** This regal restaurant is discreetly tucked in a handsome courtyard next to one of Liège's most beautiful flower shops. The chic interior has a cast-iron staircase leading to a mezzanine, and the menu offers French-inspired contemporary cuisine. The specialties are meal-size salads—try the warm chicken salad or the smoked-salmon salads with fresh herbs. The early-bird special is a tasty, light way to begin a night at the opera. ⊠ *blvd. de la Sauvenière 142, Nouvelle Ville* ☎ *04/232–1818* ⊕ *www.bruitquicourt.be* ⊟ *MC, V* ⊗ *No lunch Sun.*

¢–$ ✕ **Café Lequet.** Known as a Simenon family haunt, this wood-pan-
BELGIAN eled neighborhood standby serves unbeatable boulets smothered in Liège's special date-and-apple syrup and classic moules piled high with the inevitable frites. The place is filled with regulars, young and old. ⊠ *Quai sur Meuse 17, Nouvelle Ville* ☎ *04/22–22–134* ⊟ *No credit cards* ⊗ *No dinner Sun. and Tues.*

$–$$$ ✕ **Concordia.** A block from the train station, this dinerlike Liège institu-
BELGIAN tion has been here since 1943. It serves all day and has a varied menu. If you order the steak tartare—the house specialty—one of the chefs will prepare it right in front of your eyes. You can also come in for a cup of coffee and to watch Madame Somens, the proud proprietor, tempt the neighborhood children with irresistible chocolates as the regulars come and go. ⊠ *rue des Guillemins 114, near the Guillemins train station* ☎ *04/252–2915* ⊟ *AE, DC, MC, V* ⊗ *Closed 15 June–15 July.*

$$–$$$ ✕ **Le Bistro d'en Face.** Checkered banquettes and tiles with roosters (the
FRENCH symbol of Wallonia) decorate this rustic bistro. The menu lists regional meat specialties such as Ardennes sausage, as well as dishes from else-where in Europe, like hot pistachio sausage from Lyon with potatoes and mustard. ⊠ *rue de la Goffe 8–10, Coeur Historique* ☎ *04/223–1584* ⚏ *Reservations essential* ⊟ *AE, MC, V* ⊗ *Closed Mon. and Tues. No lunch Sat.*

$$$$ ✕ **Le Thème.** You'll always be surprised and seldom disappointed at this
FRENCH whimsical, colorful den. The fixed-price menu (with or without wine) changes five times per year; duck arrives in hunting season. Hidden on a residential *impasse*, it's very much a part of the vibrant neigh-borhood. ⊠ *Impasse de la Couronne 9, Coeur Historique* ☎ *04/222–0202* ⊕ *www.letheme.com* ⚏ *Reservations essential* ⊟ *MC, V* ⊗ *No lunch Sun.*

¢–$ ✕ **L'Oeuf Au Plat.** This quai-side restaurant specializes, as its name sug-
BELGIAN gests, in egg dishes. Try the house specialty, the Liège tradition *laf-ricassette*, an egg-based fondue. A handsome wooden cabinet displays a collection of culinary objects, all related to the egg. ⊠ *Quai de la Batte 30, Coeur Historique* ☎ *04/222–4032* ⊟ *AE, DC, MC, V* ⊗ *Closed Tues.*

¢–$$ ✕ **Vaudree II.** The beer selection is the draw here—there are more than
CAFÉ 980 to choose from. The simple menu lists sandwiches served with frites. Last call is 1 AM during the week and 3 AM on the weekends. ⊠ *rue St-Gilles 149, 1 km (⅔ mi) west of the Nouvelle Ville* ☎ *04/223–1880* ⊕ *www.vaudree-concept.be* ⊟ *AE, MC, V.*

7

CLOSE UP

For Meat Lovers

Eating in the Ardennes is one of the most straightforward pleasures Belgium has to offer. The region's charcuterie is some of the best in Europe. Ardennes sausage, neat and plump, is made with a blend of veal and pork and is smoked over smoldering oak; its flavor is somewhere between simple American summer sausage and the milder Italian salamis. The real charcuterie star is *jambon d'Ardennes*, ham that is salt-cured and delicately smoked so that its meat—as succulent as its Parma and Westphalian competitors—slices up thin, moist, and tender, more like a superior roast beef than ham. Restaurants offer generous platters of it, garnished with crisp little gherkins and pickled onions or, if you're lucky, a savory onion marmalade. Native river trout makes a slightly lighter meal, though once poached in a pool of butter and heaped with toasted almonds, it may be as rich as red-meat alternatives. One pleasant low-fat alternative, though not always available, is *truite au bleu* (blue trout). Plunged freshly killed into a boiling vinegar stock, the trout turns steely blue and retains its delicate flavor.

WHERE TO STAY

$ **Best Western Univers Hotel.** This landmark property on a bright, busy street in the town center has all the functional, contemporary furnishings and modern-day business needs that one would expect of a Best Western. Its friendly efficient staff, however, makes it a cut above most train-station hotels. The on-site bar downstairs is open from 7 AM until midnight. Most of Liège's city center sights are within walking distance. **Pros:** close to train station; fully complimentary breakfast; accommodating staff. **Cons:** 20-minute walk from city center; surroundings can be unpleasant at night. ⊠*rue des Guillemins 116, near the Guillemins train station, Liège* ☎*04/254–5555* ⊕*www.comfortinn. be* ⇆*51 rooms* ♿*In-hotel: restaurant, bar, parking (fee), Wi-Fi* ⊟*AE, DC, MC, V.*

$$$ **Holiday Inn.** Next to the Palais des Congrès, this modern, well-maintained hotel is a favorite choice for European Congress delegates and businesspeople. Many rooms have a view of the river, and within walking distance is a riverside park with a children's playground. **Pros:** clean rooms; inviting pool and sauna. **Cons:** 20-minute walk from city center; Internet access from rooms is only via cable and costs €12.50 per day. ⊠*Esplanade de l'Europe 2, 4 km (2 ½ mi) south of Outremeuse* ☎*04/342–6020* ⊕*www.holiday-inn.com* ⇆*214 rooms, 5 suites* ♿*In-room: Internet. In-hotel: bar, pool, gym, laundry service, parking (fee), no-smoking rooms, some pets allowed, Internet terminal* ⊟*AE, DC, MC, V.*

$$$ **Hôtel Mercure.** In the center of town, this modern, full-service hotel is near to all of Liège's major sights. The rooms are spacious, contemporary, and comfortable, and the restaurant and lobby, full of bustle, are great places for people-watching. The helpful concierge can answer

all your Liège-related questions. Ask about weekend rates. **Pros:** close to city center; spacious rooms. **Cons:** front rooms can be noisy; Wi-Fi costs €10 per hour. ⊠*Blvd. de la Sauvenière 100, Nouvelle Ville* ☎*04/221–7711* ⊕*www.mercure.com* ⇆*105 rooms* ⌂*In-room: Internet. In-hotel: 2 restaurants, room service, bar, gym, laundry service, parking (fee), some pets allowed, Wi-Fi* ▤*AE, DC, MC, V.*

¢ 🏠**Le Cygne D'Argent.** Gentle pastels and discreet, simple furnishings **Fodor'sChoice** characterize this welcoming, family-run boutique hotel. Each room is ★ slightly different, though all are bright and carpeted, with modern, white-tile bathrooms. Some baths have only showers, others only tubs, so be sure to state your preference. Rooms in front overlook Mosan-style residential rooftops, while those in the back have views onto gardens. Breakfast is available, though not inclusive of the room price, and can be ordered as room service. **Pros:** good location; clean rooms. **Cons:**no free parking; bathing facilities differ from room to room. ⊠*rue Beeckman 49, 2 km (1¹/₃ mi) southwest of the Nouvelle Ville* ☎*04/223–7001* ⊕*www.cygnedargent.be* ⇆*21 rooms* ⌂*In-room: minibar, safe. In-hotel: bar, parking (fee), Wi-Fi* ▤*AE, DC, MC, V.*

¢ 🏠**Passerelle Hôtel.** In an animated part of Outremeuse, this modest hotel with threadbare but functional rooms is a favorite with the actors who perform at the theater around the corner. The big windows in the bright, airy breakfast room look onto the bustling street. **Pros:** very central location; friendly staff; free Wi-Fi throughout hotel. **Cons:** can get noisy at night; some rooms feel run-down. ⊠*chaussée des Prés 24, Outremeuse* ☎*04/341–2020* ⇆*16 rooms* ⌂*In-room: no a/c. In-hotel: Wi-Fi* ▤*AE, DC, MC, V.*

$$$$ 🏠**Ramada Plaza Liège City.** This property on the banks of the Meuse is a few blocks from major museums, the historic center, and not far from the airport. The chain hotel is fit for accommodating conferences, so it may have a high business clientele, but there are still charming touches of antiquity. The brasserie-style restaurant is housed in a former 17th-century convent overlooking a garden. **Pros:** free parking; good breakfast. **Cons:** far from city center; surroundings less than picturesque. ⊠*Quai St-Léonard 36, 3 km (2 mi) east of the Coeur Historique* ☎*04/228–8111* ⊕*www.ramadaplaza-liege.com* ⇆*149 rooms* ⌂*In-hotel: restaurant, bar, gym, parking (no fee)* ▤*AE, DC, MC, V.*

NIGHTLIFE & THE ARTS

The *Bulletin*'s What's On section lists events scheduled to take place in Liège. For tickets, call the tourism office Monday through Saturday 9–5 and Sunday 9–3, or go to **Infor-Spectacles** (⊠*En Féronstrée 92* ☎*04/222–1111* ⊕*www.technomedia.be/liegeagenda/agenda.asp*).

THE ARTS

MUSIC & OPERA

Liège has an excellent opera company, the **Opéra Royal de Wallonie** (⊠*rue des Dominicains 1, Le Carré* ☎*04/221–4722* ⊕*www.operaliege. be*), considered the country's most innovative. The city's symphony orchestra, **Orchestre Philharmonique de Liège** (✉*blvd. Piercot 25, Le Carré* ☎*04/220–0000* ⊕*www.opl.be*), has recorded prize-winning CDs and tours internationally with a largely contemporary repertoire. The ticket office and reservation line are open Mon.–Fri. 12:30–5:30. The **Orchestre Royal de Chambre de Wallonie** (✉*Jardin du Maïeur, Hôtel de Ville, Mons* ☎*06/584–7044* ⊕*www.orcw.be*) and other ensembles participate in the annual Festival de la Wallonie in Liège in September, with concerts also in Spa and Stavelot. The **Festival de Musique de Stavelot** (✉*Abbaye, Salon Arthur Grumiaux, Stavelot* ☎*080/86–27–34* ⊕*www.festivalstavelot.be*) is held every August, with classical concerts in the old abbey.

PUPPET THEATER

From October through April, on Wednesday at 2:30 and Sunday morning at 10:30, you can see traditional, informal puppet shows starring the irrepressible Tchantchès at the **Musée Tchantchès** (✉*rue Surlet 56, Outremeuse* ☎*04/342–7575* ⊕*www.tchantches.be*). During the same months, you can visit the museum on Tuesday and Thursday between 2 and 4, and also request special guided visits and mini shows. Tchantchès and other characters also appear in puppet theater productions at the **Musée de la Vie Wallonne** (✉*cour des Mineurs, Coeur Historique* ☎*04/237–9040* ⊕*www.viewallonne.be*). Shows are in French and Liègeois dialect, and they typically involve some political humor. The **Théâtre Al Botroule** (✉*rue Hocheporte 3, Nouvelle Ville* ☎*04/223–0576*) has puppet shows for adults (Saturday at 8:30) and for children (Saturday and Wednesday at 3). Call to confirm seasonal productions.

THEATER

Successful, well-known touring companies perform at the **Théâtre de la Place** (✉*pl. de l'Yser 1, Outremeuse* ☎*04/342–0000* ⊕*www.theatre delaplace.be*). Most shows are in French or Walloon. It's worth checking out what's on at **Les Chiroux** (✉*pl. des Carmes 8, Le Carré* ☎*04/223–1960* ⊕*www.chiroux.be*), which hosts local and international art exhibits and theater groups. The **Festival du Théâtre de Spa** (✉*rue de la Poste 2, Spa* ☎*087/77–17–00* ⊕*www.festivaldespa.be*) is a showcase for young actors and directors. Programs and information about the three-week August season are available starting in early June.

NIGHTLIFE

The Liègeois have an amazing ability to stay up until all hours, and nightlife is booming on both sides of the Meuse. Le Carré quarter, on the left bank, is favored by students and those who go to a show first and out afterward. In the narrow, cobble-laned Roture quarter in Outremeuse there's hardly a building without a café, club, ethnic restaurant, or jazz hangout.

CAFÉS & CLUBS

First Class (✉*rue du Parc 39, south of the Nouvelle Ville, Outremeuse* ☎*04/344–3888* ⊕*www.firstclassliege.be*), near the Holiday Inn, is a swanky bar where you can sample liquors and good cigars. It opens at 8 Tuesday through Thursday evenings, and 4 on Friday afternoons.

At **Les Olivettes** (✉*rue Pied-du-Pont des Arches 6, Coeur Historique* ☎*04/221–1251* ⊕*www.lesolivettes.eu*), a specialty-beer bar, locals have the tendency to get up and sing in front of everyone. **Café Tchantchès** (✉*rue Grande-Beche, Outremeuse* ☎*04/343–3931* ⊕*www.taverne-tchant ches.be*), a true Liège institution, offers evenings of puppet entertainment along with beer and cocktails.

SPORTS & THE OUTDOORS

BICYCLING

You can rent bikes to tour Liège at your own pace at **La Maison des Cyclistes** (✉*rue de Gueldre 3, Gomzé-Andoumont* ☎*04/222–9954* ⊕*www.provelo.org* ☾*Mon., Tues., and Fri. 3–6*). Day rates are €12 and helmets are included. You can also join an organized bike tour.

SHOPPING

MARKETS

Fodor's Choice ★ By far the most exciting shopping experience Liège has to offer is at **La Batte,** one of Europe's biggest weekly street markets. Traffic is diverted away from the quai de la Batte every Sunday morning, when vendors and shoppers pour onto the quai for a day of serious browsing. Some shoppers drive in all the way from France, Germany, and the Netherlands for a chance to buy something among the exotic goods that turn up at this international market. You can see anything from live birds, flowers and plants, and antique books and furniture, to spiced sausage, aged cheese, and Moroccan carpets and clothing. Plan to spend a few hours here. A word of advice and a word of caution: be prepared to bargain, and be on the lookout for pickpockets.

SHOPPING NEIGHBORHOODS

In Liège, **Le Carré** is almost exclusively a pedestrian area, with boutiques, cafés, and restaurants. The most important shopping arcade is **Galerie Opera** (✉*pl. de la République française*), which caters to a young crowd with chain clothing stores and cafés. The **Passage Lemonnier** (✉*Between Vinâve d'Ile and rue de l'Univérsité*) is more upscale with small designer boutiques.

SPECIALTY SHOPS

Glassware from Val St-Lambert can be found in a number of shops and most advantageously at the **Cristalleries du Val St-Lambert factory shop** (✉*rue du Val 245, Seraing* ☎*04/337–0960*). Firearms, an age-old Liège specialty, are still handmade to order by some gun shops, notably **Lebeau-Courally** (✉*rue St-Gilles 386* ☎*04/252–4843* ⊕*www.lebeau-courally. com*). Visits by appointment only. Keep in mind that only a licensed arms importer may carry arms into the United States.

LIÈGE PROVINCE

The history of Liège Province differs fundamentally from that of the rest of the country. For 8 of its 10 centuries it was an independent principality of the Holy Roman Empire. At the end of the 10th century the controlling bishop, Notger, transformed his bishopric into a temporal domain. His successors had to devote as much time to the defense of the realm—much larger than the present province—as to pastoral concerns. The power of the autocratic prince-bishops was also hotly contested by the increasingly independent-minded cities. The end was brought about by the French Revolution, which many Liègeois joined with enthusiasm. The ancient Cathédrale St. Lambert in Liège City was razed, and the principality became a French *département* in 1815, after Napoléon.

In the 19th and 20th centuries, Belgium's industrial economy relied heavily on the natural resources of the region. Much of the area's natural beauty has remained intact, however, and today hiking, biking, canoeing, and kayaking are major draws. Spa—from which all other spas derive their name—is still a popular resort, with regal old buildings and curative waters. And in the easternmost area of the country, where German is spoken, the Haute Fagnes national park possesses an eerie beauty.

TONGEREN

20 km (12 mi) east of Sint-Truiden, 20 km (12 mi) southeast of Hasselt, 87 km (52 mi) east of Brussels, 19 km (11 mi) northwest of Liège.

Tongeren (Tongres in French) started life as a Roman army encampment. It is one of Belgium's two oldest cities (the other being Tournai) and is visibly proud of the fact. This is where Ambiorix scored a famous but short-lived victory over Julius Caesar's legions in 54 BC. (There's a statue of the strapping warrior in the Grote Markt square.) The Roman city was considerably larger than the present one; over the centuries, it was repeatedly sacked and burned. By the end of the 13th century, the city had retreated within its present limits and enjoyed the occasionally burdensome protection of the prince bishops of Liège. The Moerenpoort gate and sections of the ramparts remain from that period. These days, Tongeren is regularly invaded by vendors and browsers for its weekly **antiques market**. The selection of antiques and *brocante* (vintage goods and collectibles) draws people from all over the country, as well as Germany and the Netherlands. The dealers set up shop in the town's main squares and thoroughfares. It's held on Sunday, starting at 6 AM.

GETTING HERE & AROUND

Hourly trains from Liège Guillemins take 40 minutes to reach Tongeren. Trains also run hourly from Brussels, taking one hour 50 minutes.

ESSENTIALS

Tourism Office **Tongeren** (⊠ *Stadhuis, Stadhuisplein 9* ☎ *01/239–0255* ⊕ *www. tongeren.be*).

WHAT TO SEE

Fodor's Choice
★

The elaborate **Onze-Lieve-Vrouwebasiliek** is one of the most beautiful medieval monuments in the world. The original church was built on Roman foundations in the 4th century and was the first stone cathedral north of the Alps. A siege in 1213 destroyed everything but the 12th-century Romanesque cloister; soon afterward construction of the present-day Basilica of Our Lady began, a project that would take three centuries to complete. It is open daily from 8–6 (entrance is free). The Chapter House contains the **schatkamer** *(treasury)*, the richest collection of religious art in the country, including a 6th-century ivory diptych of St. Paul, a Merovingian gold buckle from the same century, and a truly magnificent head of Christ sculpted in wood in the 11th century. The central nave, up to the pulpit, the choir, and the south transept, dates from 1240. The candlesticks and lectern, from 1372, are the work of Jehan de Dinant, one of a number of outstanding metalworkers who flourished in the Meuse valley at that time. The basilica has excellent acoustics and is often used for symphony concerts. ⊠ *Grote Markt* ☎ *012/39–40–34* ⊕ *www.tongeren.be* ☎ *€2.50* ⊘ *1 Apr.–Sept. 3, Mon. 1:30–5, Tues.–Sun. 10–noon and 1:30–5.*

NEED A BREAK?

De Pelgrim (⊠ *Brouwerstraat 9* ☎ *012/23–83–22*) is an old-fashioned tavern, open late, that serves light and simple meals such as *omelette paysanne* (omelet with bacon and potatoes) and cheese croquettes.

Tongeren Prison Near the grounds of the Provinciaal Gallo-Romeins Museum, visitors can get an eery glimpse of more recent history. Established in 1844 and vacated as recently as 2005, the Tongeren *gevangenis* is Belgium's oldest prison. ⊠ *Wijngaardstraat 65* ☎ *012/67–03–30* ⊕ *www.gevangenistongeren.be* ☎ *free* ⊘ *Tues.–Fri., 1–5; weekends and holidays 10–6.*

WHERE TO STAY & EAT

$$$
BELGIAN
Fodor's Choice
★

✕ **Clos St-Denis.** An enormous 17th-century farmhouse with attached barns is the home of one of Belgium's top restaurants. Chef Christian Denis serves extravagant fare: lobster tartare with chives; gratin of oysters in champagne and caviar; ravioli of *foie d'oie* (goose liver) in truffle cream. Four dining rooms outdo each other for period luxury—burnished parquet, Persian runners, chinoiserie. ⊠ *Grimmertingenstraat 24, Vliermaal* ☎ *012/23–60–96* ⊕ *www.closstdenis.com* ♧ *Reservations essential* ▤ *AE, DC, MC, V* ⊘ *Closed Tues. and Wed.; Jan. 1–15, July 1–15.*

$–$$
Ⅲ **Ambiotel.** Location is this basic hotel's trump card; it's right next to the cathedral and on one of the squares that fills up with antiques dealers for the Sunday market. The beige-painted rooms are small and functional; some have showers instead of full baths. **Pros:** proximity to anqtiue market; free Wi-Fi. **Cons:** check out at 10 am.parking on Sunday can be a challenge ⊠ *Veemarkt 2* ☎ *012/26–29–50* ⊕ *www.*

7

ambiotel.be ↻*22 rooms* ▤*AE, DC, MC, V* ⚒*In-hotel: restaurant, bar, parking (no fee), Wi-Fi* ⍩*EP.*

HUY

33 km (20 mi) southwest of Liège, 32 km (19 mi) east of Namur, 83 km (50 mi) southeast of Brussels.

Huy (pronounced we), where the Hoyoux joins the Meuse, is a workers' town, and the main employer is the power industry. It dates back to 1066 and contains some sights of historical interest.

GETTING HERE & AROUND

Three trains every hour make the short trip between Namur and Huy. The fastest ones cover the distance in under 20 minutes. Two trains an hour run from Liège, also taking 20 minutes.

ESSENTIALS

Tourism Office Huy (✉*Grand'Place 1* ☎*08/521-7821* ⊕*www.huy.be*).

WHAT TO SEE

The first stone of the Gothic **Eglise Collégiale de Notre-Dame** *(Collegiate Church of Our Lady)* was laid in 1311. It has a rose window, the so-called Rondia, 30 feet in diameter. Its treasury contains several magnificent reliquaries, two of them attributed to Godefroid de Huy, who followed in the footsteps of Renier, also a native of Huy and a master of the Mosan style. ✉*rue de Cloître* ☎*085/21-20-05* ⊕*www.pays-de-huy. be* ⌨*€3* ☽*Daily 9–noon and 2–5.*

Huy's **Grand'Place** centers on a remarkable fountain, the **Bassinia**, a bronze cistern decorated with saints that dates from 1406. In the 18th century, the Austrians topped it with their double eagle. ✉*Grand Place 16* ☎*08/523-5048* ⊕*www.pays-de-huy.be.*

From the square you can wander through winding alleys to the old Franciscan monastery, which is now the **Musée Communal,** a mine of local folklore and history with an exceptional Art Mosan oak carving of Christ. ✉*rue Vankeerberghen 20* ☎*085/23-24-35* ⊕*www.musee-huy. be* ⌨*€3* ☽*Mon.–Fri. 2–4; May 17–Sept. 28, Sat.–Sun. 2–6.*

For a great view of the town and the surrounding countryside, take a mile-long ride on the cable car from the left bank of the Meuse across the river to the cliff-top **Citadelle,** part of the defenses built by the Dutch in the early 19th century. During World War II, the Germans used it as a prison for resistance members and hostages. It now contains a **Musée de la Résistance** with photographs, documents, and scale models. Visitors can also ride a cable car. ✉*chaussée Napoléon* ☎*085/21-53-34* ⊕*www.fortdehuy.be* ⌨*€4* ☽*Easter weekend–Sept. 30, weekdays 9–12:30 and 1–4:30 weekends and holidays 11–6; July and Aug., daily 10–7; last entry one hour before closing.*

DURBUY

40 km (24 mi) southwest of Spa, 51 km (31 mi) south of Liège, 119 km (71 mi) southeast of Brussels.

Fodor'sChoice ★ Surrounded by deep forests in the Ourthe river valley, an 11th-century castle towers over this tiny, picture-perfect town. Ever since John the Blind deemed it a city in 1331, Durbuy has taken pride in promoting itself as "the smallest city in the world." Allegedly, Durbuy derives its name from a pre-Latin dialect in which *duro bodions* translates as "dwellings near the fortress." Durbuy's narrow streets, never more than a stone's throw from the main square, are lined with amazingly well-preserved 16th- and 17th-century architecture. During the summer season they fill with tourists.

GETTING HERE & AROUND

Getting to Durbuy via public transport can be problematic. The nearest railway station is in Barvaux, 4 km (2 mi) to the east, and if you don't fancy walking from there, bus and taxi options are very limited. Things are a little easier if you have a car; the drive from Liège should take around 50 minutes.

ESSENTIALS

Tourism Office Durbuy (⊠ *pl. aux foires 25* ☎ *08/621–2428* ⊕ *www.durbuyinfo. be*).

WHEN TO GO For such a small town, Durbuy hosts a surprising number of festivals and markets. In March, chocoholics flock to the **marché du chocolat.** The last Sunday in August is the **marché des fleurs,** where florists carpet the main square in vibrant blossoms. Each Saturday in July there is a classical music concert in the church, and on the second Saturday of the month between April and September a **marché des antiquités** comes to town, setting out all kinds of vintage and antique wares.

WHAT TO SEE

The **Parc des Topiaries** on the bank of the Ourthe offers a lighthearted variation on the concept of a formal European garden. Here, more than 250 box trees have been patiently pruned into a variety of shapes and sizes. Look for the dancing elephant, the sunbathing Pamela Anderson, and the re-creation of Brussels' Manneken Pis. The café terrace commands an excellent view of the village. ⊠ *rue Haie Himbe 1* ☎ *086/21–90–75* ⊕ *www.topiairesdurbuy.be* ⊠ *€4.50* ⊙ *Mid-Mar.–mid-Nov., daily 10–6; mid-Nov.–mid-Mar., weekends 10–6.*

WHERE TO STAY & EAT

¢–$ BELGIAN ✕ **Ferme au Chêne.** Otherwise known as the "Marckloff," this small artisanal brewery makes 350 liters of beer every 10 days. Brew masters Jacques and Michel Trine calculate that this permits each Durbuy resident one liter of beer during each brew cycle. But there's always some left for visitors to the brewery's restaurant, which specializes in traditional Ardennes sausage and other local cuisine. Entry is free, though tasting cost €2.80. The brewery is always closed Wednesdays and, except for in July and August, on Thursdays. ⊠ *rue Cte. d'Ursel 36*

☎086/21–10–67 ⊕*www.durbuy info.be* ⊘*Closed Jan.*

$$ ▣**Le Clos Des Récollets.** This 17th-century home in the heart of Durbuy takes its name from the religious order that resided there at one time. The beauty of the house and grounds, the excellent menu of the restaurant ($$$), and the hospitality of proprietors Frédéric and Thérèse Bruneel make this inn a perfect country getaway. Frédéric is also the chef and brings the experience he gained from SAS Sea Grill in Brussels to his tables in Durbuy. Oven-baked cod and lamb medallions crusted with bread crumbs are regular treats, and guests can order fixed price menus for the entire table. The restaurant is closed Tuesday and Wednesday.

> **A LOVELY DRIVE**
>
> Take N841 8 km (5 mi) southeast out of town to **Weris** (designated one of the "most beautiful villages of Wallonia"). Continue south on N841 to 807 east toward **Soy**, home of the **Fantome**, a small artisanal brewery. Farther along the 807 in **Hotton**, climb through caves lined with calcium deposits. Follow N86 to **Barvaux**, a perfect place to swim in the Ourthe River, rent a boat, or play tennis or golf. On the way back to Durbuy, notice the signs for the **Château de Petite Somme**, an 18th-century castle, now home to members of the Hare Krishna.

Pros: homemade jams and *jambon d'Ardennes* at breakfast; free Wi-Fi. **Cons:** some rooms are small; nearest train station (Barvaux) is 5 km (3 mi) away. ⊠*rue de la Prévôté 9* ☎086/21–29–69 ⊕*www.closdes recollets.be* ⇆*8 rooms* ⌂*In-hotel: restaurant, a/c, no elevator* ⊟*AE, DC, MC, V* ⊙*EP.*

$$ ▣**Le Sanglier des Ardennes.** Dominating the center of town, this inn–cum–luxury restaurant has a stone fireplace, wood beams, and public spaces punctuated by glass cases with perfume, leather, and French scarves for sale. Rooms are classic pastel-modern, and the bathrooms are large. The restaurant ($$$–$$$$) offers grand French cooking with some regional touches, all beautifully presented. You might find roast, herbed chicken with a salt crust, and beef with wild forest mushrooms. Back windows overlook the Ourthe River. If there are no rooms available, ask about one of the other three hotels in town under the same ownership. Note that the restaurant here is closed Thursday and in January. **Pros:** highly regarded restaurant; central location. **Cons:** no minibar or refrigerators in rooms; narrow breakfast selection ⊠*rue Comte d'Ursel 14* ☎086/21–32–62 ⊕*www.sanglier-des-ardennes.be* ⇆*50 rooms* ⌂*In-room: a/c. In-hotel: restaurant, bar, Wi-Fi* ⊟*AE, DC, MC, V* ⊘*Closed Jan.* ⊙*EP.*

¢ ▣**Le Vieux Pont.** M. and Mme. Stourbes, an affable young couple, have cleverly renovated the attic of this charming 19th-century house (once the residence of the town-drawbridge operator) into a series of homey guest rooms. (Some rooms have a shower only, others a bathtub only.) Downstairs, the bright yellow walls of the brasserie ($–$$) are adorned with historic photographs of old Durbuy. You may also dine on the large outdoor terrace overlooking the town square. Fish from the Ourthe and ham from Ardennes are menu highlights. The restaurant is

CLOSE UP

Outdoors on the High Moors

Exploring the landscape is one of the great attractions of Wallonia. Hiking here is an undemanding activity that attracts even the most sedentary. You need to be in somewhat better shape to shoot the rapids in a kayak, but you can pick your river in accordance with skill and the number of watery thrills and spills you think you can handle. Mountain bikes are readily available for hire, and in winter there's generally enough snow for a handful of ski lifts

to stay open for a few hopeful weeks. Even from a car, you can discover the real Wallonia along rural routes. You crest a hill, and there's an unexpected vista of miles and miles of woods and lakes and fields; you turn a corner and find yourself in a village where every house has slate walls and roof. You roll down the window and the fresh air is so incredible you have to stop.

closed Wednesday and January. **Pros:** quaint atmosphere; restaurants offer delicious local faire. **Cons:** bathing facilities differ from room to room; narrow breakfast selection. ⊠*pl. aux Foires 26* ☎*086/21–28–08* ⊕*www.levieuxpont.be* ☞*13 rooms, 9 with shower, 4 with bath* ♿*In-room: no a/c. In-hotel: restaurant, bar, Wi-Fi, no elevator* ▤*MC, V* ⊘*Closed Jan.*

SPORTS & THE OUTDOORS

Durbuy Adventure (⊠*Domaine des Closeries, allée du Val 62, Barvaux–St-Ourthe* ☎*086/21–28–15* ⊕*www.durbuyadventure.be*) can arrange kayaking, mountain biking, rafting, and even paint-ball experiences. **Durbuy Discovery** (⊠*Warre 72* ☎*086/21–44–44* ⊕*www.fermededurbuy.com*) can arrange nature walks, horseback riding, kayaking, and spelunking, plus full-day tours that combine several activities.

SHOPPING

Artisanal products are plentiful in Durbuy. The **Confiture Saint Amour** (⊠*rue St-Amour 13* ☎*086/21–12–76*), 2 km (1 mi) south of town, sells homemade lotions, potions, jams, honey, and vinegars. A demonstration room lets you discover how fruit from the forest is transformed into delicious jams.

SPA

38 km (23 mi) southeast of Liège, 18 km (11 mi) north of Stavelot, 139 km (83 mi) southeast of Brussels.

★ The Romans came here to take the waters, and they were followed over the centuries by crowned heads, such as Marguerite de Valois, Christina of Sweden, and Peter the Great. Less welcome was Kaiser Wilhelm II, who established his general headquarters in Spa before fleeing to Holland in November of 1918 to abdicate control of Germany. By then the town was already past its prime. During the 18th and 19th centuries, it had been the watering place of international high society, and many gracious houses remain from that period. The pleasures of "taking the cure" in beautiful surroundings were heightened in those days by high-stakes gambling, playing *pharaon* or *biribi* for rubles, ducats, piastres, or francs. The **Casino** dates from 1763, making it the oldest in the world. Now, the glamorous gaming rooms support a number of cultural activities in addition to gambling. Those age 18 and older can pick up a casino pass at the tourist office, which allows for free admission into the casino. To get from the casino to the water springs, hop on the **tourist train,** which stops at all of the springs in town. The circuit takes 45 minutes and costs €4.

The casino is only one of the many architectural gems that line the streets of Spa. These glorious buildings, and the rest of the town, are being lovingly restored, and this small city of splendor is once again becoming a destination for people of all ages and interests.

Check the well-stocked **Tourist Office** (⊠*pl. Royale 41* ☎*087/79–53–53* ⊕*www.spa-info.be*) for information about walking tours, hikes, sports activities, and special events around town.

GETTING HERE & AROUND
To reach Spa from Liège, take the hourly train in the direction of Verviers and change in Pepinster. The total journey time is about 50 minutes.

ESSENTIALS
Internet Cafés Let's Go Video (⊠*rue Schaltin 37* ☎*087/77–38–89* ⊕*http://letsgovideo.be*).

Tourism Office Spa (⊠*rue Royale 41* ☎*08/779–5353* ⊕*www.spa-info.be*).

WHAT TO SEE
The **Musée de Cheval et Musée de la Ville D'eaux** are two institutions in one. The first hosts a permanent exhibit on Spa's waters and fountains, and includes a collection of *jolites,* painted figurines fashioned from local wood. The Horse Museum contains an extensive display of equestrian paraphernalia. ⊠*av. Reine 77 B* ☎*087/77–44–86* ⊕*www.spavillaroyale.be* ⊠*€3* ⊙*July–Sept. and school holidays, Wed.–Mon. 2–6; Mar.–Nov, weekends 2–6.*

☾ Elephants, camels, lions, and kangaroos live at **Monde Sauvage.** Don't forget to visit the pool, which is home to sea lions and polar bears. The park is easily accessible from downtown Spa by foot, car, or the **Tourist Train,** which tours town daily June–September. ⊠*Fange de Deigné 3, Aywaille* ☎*04/360–90–70* ⊕*www.mondesauvage.be* ⊠*€15* ⊙*mid-Feb.–mid-Nov., daily 10–6:30.*

The charming **Musée de la Lessive** *(Laundry Museum)* is dedicated to the art and science of keeping clothes clean—not a task to be taken lightly, particularly when royalty and nobility come to town to sweat away their maladies. ⊠*rue de la Geronstere 10* ☎*087/77–14–18* ⊠*€2* ⊙*Sun. 2–6; July, Aug. and school vacation daily 2–6.*

NEED A
BREAK?
Settle into a booth at **La Gâterie Tea Room** (⊠*pl. du Monument 18* ☎*087/77–48–80* ☼*Closed Fri.*) for waffles, crepes, homemade ice cream, or a fresh-baked tart.

The best-known of Spa's water sources—locally known as *pouhons*—is the **Pouhon Pierre Le Grandé,** which can be visited by tourists as well as *curistes* (people taking the cure). The price for a glass straight from the source is a modest €0.20. In past times, pregnant women came to drink the iron-rich water. Nowadays, the source draws those with poor circulation, anemia, and arthritis. ⊠*pl. Royale 41, Spa* ☎*087/79–53–53* ⊕*www.spa-info.be* ⊠*Free* ☼*Baths: Easter–Oct., daily 10–noon and 1:30–5; Nov.–Easter, weekdays 1:30–5, weekends 10–noon and 1:30–5.*

At the **Spa Monopole** you can take a tour of the factory that produces the famous Spa brand mineral water, as well as the adjoining museum, with exhibits of old Spa bottles and crates. There isn't much in the way of English-language explanatory material, but there are interesting historic photos and the tour ends with a drink of the water. ⊠*rue Auguste Laporte 34* ☎*087/79–41–11* ⊕*www.spa.be* ☼*Weekdays 9–4* ⊠*Free.*

SPA

Les Thermes de Spa is a testament to Spa's recent rejuvenation. The ultra-modern thermal center has a full menu of relaxation treatments, plus fitness facilities, hot tubs, two swimming pools, a sauna, and even a funicular link to the city and the Radisson SAS Palace Hotel. A slew of restaurants, shops, and terrace lounges leave nothing to be desired. ⊠*Colline d'Annette et Lubin* ☎*08/777–2560* ⊕*www.thermesdespa. com* ☼*Indoor and outdoor baths: Mon.–Sat. 10–9; Sun. 10–8; treatments by appointment.*

FESTIVALS

Book early if you plan to visit Spa around July 21, Belgium's national holiday. For six days around that time, the annual **Francofolie Festival** (⊠*rue Rogier 2B, Spa* ☎*08/777–6381* ⊕*www.francofolies.be*) transforms this quiet thermal center into a nonstop bubbling cauldron of French music. A sister festival happens in Quebec City, Canada, at the same time.

WHERE TO EAT

$$$
BELGIAN
FodorsChoice
★

✕ **L'Art de Vivre.** Jean-François Douffet's fresh approach in the kitchen contrasts pleasantly with the old-fashioned gentility of his competitors. Sautéed goose liver accompanied by a potato pancake, pike perch with deep-fried basil leaves, roast pigeon with a balsamic vinegar sauce, and ice cream with figs are among his creations. ⊠*av. Reine Astrid 53* ☎*087/77–04–44* ⊕*www.artdevivre.be* ▤*AE, DC, MC, V* ☼*Closed Tues. and Wed.*

$$–$$$
BELGIAN
★

✕ **La Brasserie du Grand Maur.** This graceful 200-year-old city mansion houses a lovely restaurant with a loyal clientele. Tartare of salmon, lamb infused with tomato and thyme, and duck's breast with raspberries and red currants are special favorites. The setting is all polished wood, linens, and antiques. ⊠*rue Xhrouet 41* ☎*087/77–36–16* ▤*AE, DC, MC, V* ⊗*Closed Mon.*

$-$$ ✕**Le Clair Obscur.** This informal hangout features a wide selection of
CAFÉ   salads and delectable desserts. The building itself is an example of how Spa is renovating its architectural gems. Once a discotheque, its brick was restored and the main room brightened up for its transformation into a well-loved eatery. In fair weather, the expansive deck is equally inviting. ⊠*rue Delhasse 32* ☎*087/77–51–38* ▤*MC, V* ⊗*Closed Mon. and Tues.*

WHERE TO STAY

$$ ⌧**Best Western Premiere Hôtel Villa des Fleurs.** Fresh flowers abound in
★   this splendid 1880 beaux arts mansion, once the private home of the director of the Spa Casino. The entry foyer's enormous chandelier and grand staircase set the tone for the rooms' thick draped decor, mammoth beds, and marble bathrooms. Rooms in the back have views of the beautiful garden. **Pros:** ideally situated; classy decor; free Wi-Fi. **Cons:** restaurant is off-premise; only some rooms have garden views. ⊠*rue Albin Body 31* ☎*087/79–50–50* ⊕*www.villadesfleurs.be* ➟*12 rooms* ⌕*In-room: Internet. In-hotel: bicycles, parking (free)* ▤*AE, DC, MC, V* �Ⓞ*CP.*

$ ⌧**Cardinal.** Offering a real taste of old Spa, this grand urban resort hotel opened in 1924. Its period architecture and styling are fresh and intact, although the rooms have taken on the functional simplicity of a chain hotel. Have tea in the muraled salon, hot chocolate in the beautiful oak café, or dinner in the swanky chandeliered dining hall. **Pros:** proximity to thermal center and casino; common areas have Old World charm. **Cons:** no internet; rooms lack character. ⊠*pl. Royale 21–23* ☎*087/77–10–64* ⊕*www.hotel-cardinal.be* ➟*29 rooms* ⌕*In-room: no a/c. In-hotel: parking (fee)* ▤*AE, DC, MC, V.*

¢   ⌧**Le Relais.** Although right in the center of town, this small, friendly hotel seems like a simple country inn. Each room has a different name and style, such as the Spa Room, with its decorative water bottles and photographs of various attractions in Spa, and the Stavelot Room, with pictures of the Stavelot abbey and people celebrating Carnival. The restaurant ($$) has a warm decor of olive-green walls and red tablecloths; its menu changes seasonally. **Pros:** great location; quality restaurant. **Cons:** shabby rooms; poor breakfast. ⊠*pl. du Monument 22* ☎*087/77–11–08* ⊕*www.hotelrelais-spa.be* ➟*11 rooms* ⌕*In-room: no a/c. In-hotel: restaurant* ▤*AE, DC, MC, V* ⊗*No dinner Sun.*

$$$ ⌧**Radisson SAS Hôtel Balmoral.** Up the hill from downtown Spa, this handsome 1905 landmark was where King Leopold II routinely hosted opulent banquets. Its dark-wood accents and rich maroon hues are reminiscent of an old-fashioned gentleman's club. You can test your skills in the billiards room or linger over the grand piano for a song and a drink. The indoor pool is fed by Spa's own waters. Rooms range from single efficiency units with kitchenettes to sleek executive suites. The chic restaurant Entre Terre et Mer (Between Earth and Sea) uses

ingredients from the sea and the Haute Fagne area. A shuttle can take you into town. **Pros:** brand-new wellness center; walk-in humidor; will organize Ardennes forest barbecues for group. **Cons:** outside town; can feel somewhat impersonal. ✉*av. Leopold II 40* ☎*087/79–21–41* ⊕*www.radisson.com/spabe* ➾*89 rooms* ♿*In-room: dial-up. In-hotel: restaurant, tennis courts, pool, gym, no-smoking rooms, Wi-Fi* ▤*AE, DC, MC, V* ⏀*CP.*

$$$ 🏨**Radisson SAS Palace Hôtel.** The Palace was built in 2003 to accommodate some of the expected 150,000 yearly visitors to the Thermes de Spa to which the hotel has a direct link via a funicular. Rooms are contemporary, with pale wood furnishings; they have a view of the forest or the city. Spa's tourist office and railway station are within walking distance. **Pros:** convenient access to Thermes de Spa; free Wi-Fi. **Cons:** fee to use pool; no free parking. ✉*pl. Royal* ☎*087/79–21–54* ⊕*www.radissonsas.com* ➾*126 rooms* ♿*In-room: Internet. In-hotel: restaurant, bar, gym, spa, Wi-Fi* ▤*AE, DC, MC, V.*

SPORTS & THE OUTDOORS

For those wanting a lift, the **Spa Airfield** (✉*rue de la Sauvèniere 8* ☎*087/79–52–60* ⊕*www.skydivecenterspa.com*) offers high-flying opportunities, including a parachuting center. Helicopter rides cost €50 per person for 15 minutes or €118 for 35 minutes. A tandem jump costs €180.

RACING

Motor-sports fans know **Francorchamps** (near Spa) as one of the world's top racing circuits, where Formula 1 drivers zig and zag with astounding speed and precision. The annual Grand Prix race takes place in late August or early September, and there are other events throughout the year. Contact **Intercommunale du Circuit de Spa-Francorchamps** (✉*rte. du Circuit 55, Francorchamps* ☎*087/27–51–38* ⊕*www.spa-francorchamps. be*) for information.

HAUTE FAGNES

20 km (13 mi) northeast of Spa, 40 km (25 mi) east of Liège, 137 km (85 mi) southeast of Brussels.

Fodor'sChoice
★
Twenty-one kilometers (13 mi) northeast of Spa sits Eupen, the gateway town for the Haute Fagnes. Here, in the heart of the German-speaking part of Belgium, is a marvelous 722 square km (279 square mi) ecological expanse of peat bogs, heath, and marshland. This is Belgium's largest area of protected wilderness, and it also happens to be the country's wettest, coldest, and most bizarre terrain. Foggy mists, sometimes dense, make navigating a path through the park's wilderness difficult. The saturated bogs hide quagmires just waiting to pull down unsuspecting feet—thus, explorations are confined to wooden boardwalks. Don't let the somewhat forbidding circumstances deter you; the Haute Fagnes is one of Belgium's natural wonders.

GETTING HERE & AROUND

To fully appreciate the wilds of the Hautes Fagnes you'll need your own transport. Driving from Liège via Eupen, it takes approximately 30 minutes to reach the northern edge of the park. The park can also be reached from Spa in about 15 minutes by heading northeast.

WHAT TO SEE

As is appropriate for such wild and mist-covered terrain, the area is also shrouded in mystery and lore. For example, two 19th-century lovers wandered to their death in the shifting landscape; the **Croix des Fiances** near the Baraque Michel Resthouse commemorates their tragic slip into the netherworld. At the **Centre Nature Botrange** nature center, you can get a professional introduction to the flora and fauna of the park. Parts of the area can only be visited with a guide, particularly the peat bogs and the feeding areas of the *capercaillies* (large and very rare woodland grouse—the park's symbol). You can book an individual guide in advance, and you can also rent boots and bikes, or arrange for a horse-drawn wagon ride. ⊠*rte de Botrange, Robertville* ☎*080/44–03–00* ⊕*www.centrenaturebotrange.be* ⌸*€2.50* ⊘*Daily 10–6.*

Reinhardstein, the loftiest and possibly the best-preserved medieval fortress in the country, is reached by a mile-long hike through the Hautes Fagnes. It sits on a spur of rock overlooking the river Warche and has been in the hands of such illustrious families as the Metternichs, ancestors of Prince Metternich, the architect of the Congress of Vienna in 1815. The Hall of Knights and the Chapel are gems. Guided tours, lasting a little over an hour, are available in English upon request, provided there is a minimum of 20 participants. ⊠*Chemin du Cheneux 50, Robertville* ☎*080/44–68–68* ⊕*www.reinhardstein.net* ⌸*€6* ⊘*Tours: July–Aug., Tues., Thur. and weekends; Sept.–Oct. weekends only.*

MALMÉDY

57 km (34 mi) southeast of Liège, 156 km (94 mi) southeast of Brussels, 16 km (10 mi) southeast of Spa.

Malmédy and its neighbor, Stavelot, formed a separate, peaceful principality, ruled by abbots, for 11 centuries before the French Revolution. The Congress of Vienna, redrawing the borders of Europe, handed it to Germany, and it was not reunited with Belgium until 1925. In a scene straight out of *Catch 22*, the center of Malmédy was destroyed by American bombers in 1944 after the town had been liberated. Still, there's enough left of the old town for an interesting walk. And either of the twin towns is an ideal place to stay while exploring the Haute Fagnes.

GETTING HERE & AROUND

The nearest railway station to Malmédy is Trois-Ponts. There are around a dozen daily departures from Liège Guillemins (50 minutes to one hour). Bus #745 connects with train arrivals and takes a further 25 minutes to reach Malmédy, passing through Stavelot en route.

ESSENTIALS

Tourism Office Malmédy (✉ *rue Jules Steinbach 1, Malmedy* ☎ *08/079–9666* ⊕ *www.malmedy.be*).

FESTIVAL

Malmédy's long-standing, extremely lively carnival, beginning on the Saturday before Lent, is among the most famous in Belgium. To learn more about it, you can visit the newly renovated **Musée du Cwarmê** (☎ *08/068–5536* ⊕ *www.malmedy.be*) expected to open in May 2009 with its bright collection of costumes, masks, and models of *cwarmê* (carnival) floats.

WHERE TO STAY & EAT

$$ 🏨 **Hostellerie Trôs Marets.** Up the hill on the road toward Eupen, this inn offers a splendid view over the wooded valley. In fall, the fog hangs low over the nearby Haute Fagnes; in winter, cross-country skiing beckons. The main building contains the restaurant and rustic rooms. A modern annex has suites furnished in contemporary English style with fireplaces, plus a large indoor pool. The restaurant ($$$$) serves such specialties as duck's liver with caramelized apples, asparagus in truffle vinaigrette, grilled duckling with honey, and Herve cheese soufflé with Liège liqueur. Half-board is a good value. **Pros:** free Wi-Fi throughout hotel; bathrobes and slippers in each room; L'Occitane bath products. **Cons:** No on-site spa. ✉ *rte. des Trôs Marets 2, Bévercé* ⚓ *3 km (2 mi) north on N68 from Malmédy* ☎ *080/33–79–17* ⊕ *www.trosmarets. be* 🛏 *7 rooms, 4 suites* ⚒ *In-room: Wi-Fi. In-hotel: restaurant, pool* ☰ *AE, DC, MC, V* ⊙ *Closed mid-Nov.–Dec. 23.*

¢ 🏨 **Ferme Libert.** This rustic inn is on the edge of a mystical forest a few
★ miles north of town on the road to Eupen. The rooms vary—some are modern, others old-fashioned, with sturdy wood furniture. In the restaurant ($$$$), you can gaze across a valley as you await your meal. The menu is long on meat of all kinds, including ostrich, bison, and springbok. Ferme Libert feels much like an Alpine resort, with skiing in winter (at least for a few weeks) and bracing walks the rest of the year. Half-board is required on weekends. **Pros:** enchanting natural surroundings; restaurant is a carnivore's delight. **Cons:** hard to reach without a car; Wi-Fi available in only some areas of hotel. ✉ *rue de la Ferme Libert 33, Bévercé* ☎ *080/33–02–47* ⊕ *www.fermelibert.be* 🛏 *18 rooms with bath, 22 with shower* ⚒ *In-hotel: restaurant, no elevator, Wi-Fi* ☰ *AE, MC, V* 🍽 *MAP.*

SPORTS & THE OUTDOORS

The **Worriken Sports Center** (✉ *rue Worriken 9, Bütgenbach* ☎ *080/44–69–61* ⊕ *www.worriken.be*) offers horseback riding in the Hautes Fagnes region.

STAVELOT

15 km (9 mi) southwest of Malmédy, 59 km (37 mi) southeast of Liège, 158 km (95 mi) southeast of Brussels.

Although Stavelot is practically a twin town of Malmédy, its traditions differ. Here Carnival is celebrated on the fourth Sunday in Lent and is animated by about 2,000 *Blancs-Moussis* (White Monks), dressed in white with long capes and long bright-red noses, who swoop and rush through the streets. The Blancs-Moussis commemorate the monks of Stavelot, who in 1499 were forbidden to participate in Carnival but got around it by celebrating Laetare Sunday (three weeks before Easter). Stavelot was badly damaged in the Battle of the Bulge, but some picturesque old streets survive, particularly rue Haute, off place St-Remacle.

GETTING HERE & AROUND

The nearest railway station to Stavelot is Trois-Ponts. There are around a dozen daily departures from Liège Guillemins (50 minutes to one hour). Bus #745 connects with train arrivals and takes a further 10 minutes to reach Stavelot, before continuing on to Malmédy.

ESSENTIALS

Tourism Office Stavelot (⊠ *Abbaye de Stavelot, pl. St-Remacle 32* ☎ *08/086–2706* ⊕ *www.abbayedestavelot.be).*

WHAT TO SEE

Stavelot's square is named for St. Remacle, who founded a local abbey in 647. His reliquary, now in the **Eglise St-Sébastien,** is one of the wonders of Art Mosan. Dating from the 13th century, it is 6½ feet long and decorated with statuettes, of the apostles on the sides and of Christ and the Virgin on the ends. ⊠ *rue de l'Eglise 7* ☎ *080/88–0160* ☏ *free; €4 for tour (only available during high season)* ⊙ *July–end Sept. and during Christmas and Easter vacation, Thur.–Sun. 2–6; Oct.–June, by appointment.*

Only a Romanesque tower remains of the original buildings that formed the **Ancienne Abbaye** *(Old Abbey).* Inside this grand rose-color building are three museums and a cultural arts center. The **Musée du Circuit** is dedicated to racecars and the Spa-Francorchamps racetrack. Monoplace and Brigatti race cars are on display, and one of several films on racing draws you into a virtual ride on the track. The high-tech **Musée de la Principauté de Stavelot-Malmedy** displays archaeological remains and religious objects found in and around the region. The **Musée Guillaume Apollinaire** is the only museum devoted to the life and work of the French poet and essayist, who spent time here during his youth. Some of his original manuscripts are on display. ⊠ *pl. St-Remacle* ☎ *080/88–08–78* ⊕ *www.abbayedestavelot.be* ☏ *€7.50 for a visit to all three museums* ⊙ *Daily 10–6.*

WHERE TO STAY & EAT

$$ ★ **Le Romantik Hotel Le Val d'Amblève.** In an unassuming whitewashed main house, spacious, plush, traditional-contemporary guest rooms look out on gorgeous grounds with century-old trees. Inside, the sophisticated restaurant ($$$; reservations essential) serves such delicacies as pigeon with a pear and truffle sauce and lobster with celery. Retire to the pink salon for an after-dinner drink. The restaurant is closed Monday and three weeks in January. **Pros:** romantic setting; good deal for fixed-price lunch and dinner menus. **Cons:** need a car to reach property; nearest train station (Trois Pont) is a 15-minute drive away. ✉ *rte. de Malmédy 7* ☎ *080/28–14–40* ⊕ *www.levaldambleve.com* ⇆ *24 rooms* ♿ *In-hotel: restaurant, tennis courts, parking (no fee), some pets allowed, Wi-Fi, no elevator* ▭ *AE, DC, MC, V.*

$ **Hostellerie La Maison.** This small, charming spot in the center of town has upstairs rooms overlooking place St-Remacle and a downstairs restaurant ($$$) with a French menu. The rooms are bright and spacious, with Victorian-style flowered wallpaper and antique or reproduction furniture. Chandeliers and floor-to-ceiling drapes decorate the chic, little dining room. Try the lobster soup with scallops and crayfish. The restaurant is closed Sunday evening and Monday, though serves dinner every other day of the week. **Pros:** restaurant has fine wine selection; assortment of package deals. **Cons:** no Sunday dinner; no a/c. ✉ *pl. St-Remacle 19* ☎ *080/88–08–91* ⊕ *www.hotellamaison.info* ⇆ *12 rooms* ♿ *In-room: no a/c, Internet. In-hotel: restaurant, bar* ▭ *AE, MC* ⦿ *BP.*

$ **Hôtel d'Orange.** A former post house, this apricot-color hotel has been in the same family since 1789. The charming, individually decorated rooms reflect a Victorian sensibility, with upholstered chairs and sofas, while the bathrooms are completely up to date. Downstairs, the restaurant ($$–$$$) offers several fixed-price menus, including one for kids. Quail, ever popular in these parts, chicken *à l'estragon* (with tarragon) and lamb are staples on the menu. The restaurant is closed for lunch on Wednesday. **Pros:** Sunday champagne breakfast buffet; free connection to hotel from Trois Ponts or Verviers train stations. **Cons:** closed Jan.–mid-Feb.; modest accommodations. ✉ *Devant les Capucins 8* ☎ *080/86–20–05* ⊕ *www.hotel-orange.be* ⇆ *16 rooms* ♿ *In-room: no a/c. In-hotel: restaurant, no elevator, Wi-Fi, parking (fee)* ▭ *AE, DC, MC, V.*

SPORTS & THE OUTDOORS

Virtually all the rivers of the Ardennes are great for canoeing, and the meandering Amblève is one of the best. Single or double kayaks can be rented April–October at **Cookayak** (✉ *Stavelot* ☎ *04/7370–4584* ⊕ *www.cookayak.be*) for a 9-km (5-mi) ride from Coo to Cheneux (about 1½ hrs) or a 23-km (14-mi) ride to Lorcé (about 3½ hrs). Bus service back to the starting point is provided.

UNDERSTANDING
BELGIUM

CHRONOLOGY

55 BC	Julius Caesar's legions extend Roman control to the Meuse and Waal rivers.
ca. AD 300	Inundation of the Frisian plain causes Rome to abandon it.
ca. 400	Roman rule retreats before invading Frisians in the north and Franks in the south.
481–511	Under their king, Clovis, the Frankish Merovingians extend their rule north.
800	Charlemagne, king of the Franks, is crowned Emperor of the Romans by the pope. His domains extend from the marches of Denmark to Spain.
843	The Treaty of Verdun divides Charlemagne's empire into three. Belgium is divided at the Scheldt River between France and Lotharingia. Viking attacks begin along the coast.
862	Baldwin Iron-Arm establishes himself as first count of Flanders, but rule of the Lotharingian lands is constantly disputed.
ca. 1200	With the rise of towns, the collection of duchies and counties that constitutes the Low Countries gains economic power.
1302	The men of Flanders revolt against French attempts at annexation and defeat Philip the Fair's army at the Battle of the Golden Spurs, near Kortrijk. Flanders remains a desirable prize.
1361	Philip the Bold, son of John II of France, establishes the great duchy of Burgundy, which, by Philip's marriage in 1369 to Marguerite, heiress of the count of Flanders, grows to include Flanders, Artois, Limburg, and Brabant.
1419–67	Philip's grandson Philip the Good extends Burgundian rule over Holland, Zeeland, and Hainaut and presides over the golden age of the Flemish Renaissance. Painters include the van Eycks, Hans Memling, and Rogier van der Weyden.
1464	Philip calls the deputies of the states—nobles, merchants, and churchmen—to meet together, thus beginning the States-General, the Dutch representative assembly.
1477	The death of Philip's son Charles leaves his granddaughter Mary of Burgundy as heiress. Mary marries the Habsburg heir, Maximilian of Austria; their son Philip marries Juana, heiress to the throne of Spain.
1500	Birth in Gent of Charles, son of Philip and Juana, who inherits the collective titles and holdings of Burgundy, Spain, and Austria as Charles V, Holy Roman Emperor.
ca. 1520–40	Protestantism spreads through the Netherlands.
1549	By the Pragmatic Sanction, Charles declares that the 17 provinces constituting the Netherlands will be inherited intact by his son Philip.

CHRONOLOGY

1555 Charles V abdicates, dividing his empire between his brother Ferdinand and his son Philip, who inherits Spain and the Netherlands. A devout Catholic, Philip moves to suppress Protestantism in the Netherlands.

1566 Revolt in Antwerp against Spanish rule provokes ruthless suppression by the Spanish governor, the duke of Alva.

1568 Beginning of 80 years of warfare among the 17 provinces and Spain.

1572 The "Sea Beggars" under William of Orange take to the natural Dutch element, water, and harass the Spanish.

1579 The Spanish succeed in dividing the Catholic south from the Protestant north with the Treaty of Arras. The seven Protestant provinces in the north—Holland, Friesland, Gelderland, Groningen, Overijssel, Utrecht, and Zeeland—declare themselves the United Provinces, under the hereditary *stadtholder* (city elder), William the Silent of Orange.

1585 Antwerp falls to the Spanish, and the division of the Netherlands between north and south is effectively completed; the Dutch close the Scheldt to navigation, depriving Antwerp of its egress to the sea and leading to its rapid decline.

1609 The Twelve Years' Truce temporarily ends fighting between the United Provinces and Spain.

1648 By the Treaty of Westphalia, the Spanish finally recognize the independence of the United Provinces. What will become Belgium remains under Spanish control but is a battleground between the ambitions of France and a weakening Spain.

1701–17 The War of the Spanish Succession ends with the Treaty of Utrecht, which transfers the Spanish Netherlands to Austria. Depleted of men and money, the Netherlands declines in the 18th century.

1789–90 Inspired by events in France, the Brabançonne revolution succeeds in overthrowing Austrian rule in Belgium, but divisions between conservatives and liberals allow the Austrians to regain their territory.

1795 The French defeat the Austrians and annex the Belgian provinces and Luxembourg.

1806–10 Napoléon establishes the Kingdom of Holland, ruled by his brother Louis Bonaparte, but finally annexes the Netherlands to France.

1815 Napoléon is defeated at Waterloo, near Brussels. By the terms of the congress of Vienna, the Netherlands and Belgium are reunited under William I, but the union proves an unhappy one. Luxembourg is divided between William and Prussia.

1830 Again inspired by a revolution in France, the Belgians rise against William I and declare their independence.

CHRONOLOGY

1831 With the guarantees of the great powers, the Belgians draw up a constitution and elect as king Leopold of Saxe-Coburg (an uncle to soon-to-be-Queen Victoria of England).

1839 The Netherlands finally recognizes Belgium as an independent, neutral state. Luxembourg is again divided, with 60% going to Belgium while the rest remains a duchy, with William I of the Netherlands as grand duke.

1865 Leopold II succeeds his father as king of the Belgians; begins reign as empire builder in Africa and rebuilder of Brussels at home. By the terms of an international agreement, the Prussian garrisons withdraw and Luxembourg's independence and neutrality are guaranteed.

1885 The establishment of the Congo Free State brings Belgium into the ranks of colonial powers.

1893 Victor Horta completes the first Art Nouveau building in Brussels, launching Belgium as one of the earliest Art Nouveau hotbeds. He continues to design buildings in this style through the 1920s.

1898 Birth of René Magritte (d. 1967), famed Surrealist artist.

1903 Birth of Georges Simenon (d. 1989), creator of Inspector Maigret and Belgium's most widely read author.

1908 Congo Free State annexed to Belgium.

1909 Albert succeeds Leopold II of Belgium; leads Belgian resistance from exile during World War I.

1914 In violation of the terms of the 1839 treaty, Germany invades and conquers Belgium at the outset of World War I.

1914–18 The area around Ieper (Ypres) remains a brutal battlefield for the duration of World War I. Use of poison gas introduced.

1919 The Franco-Belgian alliance ends Belgian neutrality and signals the dominance of the French-speaking Walloons. Universal male suffrage is granted.

1934 Albert dies in a rock-climbing accident. Leopold III succeeds him on the Belgian throne.

1940 May 10: Nazi Germany launches blitzkrieg attacks on Belgium, Luxembourg, and the Netherlands. The Dutch army surrenders May 14, the Belgians May 28. Grand Duchess Charlotte and Queen Wilhelmina flee; King Leopold III remains in Belgium, where he is eventually imprisoned. The Nazi occupation leaves lasting imprints on all three countries.

1947 The Marshall Plan helps rebuild devastated areas. Belgium, the Netherlands, and Luxembourg form a customs union.

1948 Women gain the vote in Belgium.

CHRONOLOGY

1951   Amid controversy over his wartime role and continued ethnic dissension, King Leopold III of Belgium abdicates in favor of his son, Baudouin.

1957   Belgium is a charter member of the European Economic Community (EEC).

1960   A 50-year treaty establishes the Benelux Economic Union. The Belgian Congo gains independence.

1967   Already the center of the EEC, Brussels becomes host to NATO.

1974   Eddy Merckx, regarded by many as the greatest cyclist of all time, wins his fifth Tour de France. While leading the tour the following year, he is attacked by a French spectator who didn't want to see him break the record for wins, then held by Frenchman Jacques Anquetil. Despite this setback and a later crash that breaks his jaw, he carries on to finish second.

1980   The Belgian national soccer team reaches the final of the European Championships, but is beaten 2-1 by West Germany.

1988   The American Mark Morris Dance Group becomes the official dance company of the Théâtre National de la Monnaie (the National Opera House) in Brussels—a controversial move for conservative Belgian tastes.

1991   Belgium becomes one of the last European monarchies to abolish the *Lex Salica* (Salic law), which stipulates that only male heirs can ascend to the throne. The Maastricht Treaty is adopted, marking the beginning of the European Union. André Cools, former deputy prime minister and Socialist Party leader, is assassinated.

1992   The artistic director, Jan Hoet, Belgium's art enfant terrible, curates "Documenta IX in Kassel," firmly placing Belgium at the forefront of contemporary European art.

1993   King Baudouin of Belgium dies and is succeeded by his brother, Albert II.

1994   Belgium becomes a confederation of three semi-autonomous regions: Flanders, Wallonia, and Brussels.

1999   Gent's Stedelijk Museum voor Aktuele Kunst (Municipal Museum of Contemporary Art) opens, asserting Belgium's commitment to experimental contemporary art.

2001   Princess Elisabeth Thérèse Marie Hélène is born on October 25. As a result of the abolition of the Salic Law, she is the first princess to be in line for the throne.

2002   The Belgian franc is officially replaced by the euro.

2003   Top-ranked tennis players Kim Clijsters and Justine Henin-Hardenne meet for an all-Belgian French Open final—a first in the history of the competition. Henin-Hardenne goes on to win the title three more times, in 2005, 2006, and 2007.

2007 After a record 192 days of political deadlock, a temporary coalition government is formed on December 19. Following a general election on June 10, the leading parties had been unable to agree on the divisive issues of the economy, increased autonomy for Flanders and Wallonia, and the boundaries of the Brussels voting district. Most Belgians, however, agreed that the country ran more efficiently without effective leadership.

2008 Having failed to carry out promised political reforms, Prime Minister Yves Leterme tenders his government's resignation on July 15, threatening to plunge the country back into turmoil. King Albert II however averts a crisis by refusing to accept the resignation and forcing the government to carry on. At this writing the key disagreements between the main Flemish and Wallonian political parties remain as unresolved as ever.

—Anita Guerrini, Olivia Mollet, and Tim Skelton

BATTLE SCARS FROM THE BULGE

The first thing the sleepy American soldiers noticed was light—pinpoints of light blinking to the east, distinct in the pitch-black of an early midwinter morning. Close on the heels of these lights came the roar of a thousand exploding shells, the pounding percussion of heavy artillery. As rockets and mortars screamed overhead, German foot soldiers poured through five well-spaced points in the sparsely protected front line, their way lit by searchlights that bounced off the clouds, flooding the land with eerie, artificial "moonlight."

It was 5:30 AM on December 16, 1944, along the eastern border of Belgium and Luxembourg. The Allied armed forces had let its guard down after several grueling, exhausting months of combat. After landing at Normandy in June and southern France in August, they had pressed steadily inland, pushing the German armies back to the old Siegfried line and liberating France, Belgium, and Luxembourg by September. They fought viciously, died in droves, and spent weeks at a time hungry, filthy, and sleepless. In the relatively calm days before Christmas they basked in the role of heroes. That morning they were caught with their pants down in one of the most massive and successful surprise attacks in World War II. It was Hitler's last, desperate effort to regain western Europe, and it was one of the greatest failures of Allied intelligence in the war.

In September 1944, when Hitler first announced secret plans for an all-out attack on the western front, his army could scarcely have been in more desperate straits. More than 3½ million German men had died over the preceding five years, and devastating Allied bombing raids were leveling German cities each day. Not only had the Allies driven the Wehrmacht out of France, Belgium, and Luxembourg, but Italy was being lost in bitter fighting as well, and Russia had

penetrated west to Warsaw and Bucharest. The Third Reich was in danger of being choked off from all sides, and Hitler, dismissing the advice of his more prudent commanders, saw no option but to strike out offensively. His goal: to take the all-important port at Antwerp, from where the River Schelde flowed from Belgium through the Netherlands and into the North Sea. By closing in on Antwerp, the Germans would not only cut off the most likely source of new supplies, but also surround and capture some 1 million remaining Allied forces. His strategy: to surprise the Allies by attacking through the improbably rough, virtually impassable forest terrain of the Ardennes in southeastern Belgium and northern Luxembourg. He intended to overwhelm the Allies with massive artillery fire as German forces pressed on to take the strategic bridges of the River Meuse, then reinforce his position with a second wave of troops while closing out defenders with strong flanks at the north and south. Antwerp could be reached in a week, he insisted, and the Allies would be crippled by winter fog, snow, and mud.

In an attempt to inspire his bitter, war-weary army for what seemed even then to be a suicidal mission, Hitler named the aristocratic Gerd von Rundstedt commander in chief in the West. In a decision that was to set the tone for one of the most vicious and bloody conflicts in the war, he then placed Joseph "Sepp" Dietrich in charge of the Sixth Panzer Army. Dietrich was an early Nazi loyalist and SS commander, chief executioner in the 1934 Nazi Party purge (the Night of the Long Knives), and notorious for ordering the execution of more than 4,000 prisoners taken over three days at the Russian front. SS Lt. Col. Joachim Peiper, a kindred spirit of Dietrich's in his brutal executions in Russia, was given command of the SS Panzer Division called Leibstandarte Adolf Hitler. It was Dietrich who passed on Hitler's inspirational message that this was "the decisive hour of the German people," that the attacking army was to create a "wave of terror and fright" without "humane inhibitions."

While the Germans built up staggering quantities of materiel along the Siegfried line—tanks, artillery, rafts, and pontoons—and moved in men from all corners of the shrinking Reich, the Allied command remained remarkably unperceptive. Reconnaissance pilots flew over unwonted activity near Bitburg, Trier, and Koblenz—trains, truck convoys, heaps of equipment along the roads. Messages were intercepted and deciphered, some asking for increased forces, some for more detailed information on Ardennes and Meuse terrain. Yet Generals Bradley, Eisenhower, Middleton, and Patton continued to misinterpret Hitler's intentions, anticipating instead a predictable counterattack around Aachen and Cologne, well north of the Ardennes. In fact, such a misinterpretation was part of Hitler's plan, and he went so far as to strut a visible buildup of forces in the north while secretly preparing to attack elsewhere. On December 12, an optimistic Allied intelligence summary described the vulnerability and "deathly weakness" of German forces in the area.

On the evening of December 15, the German soldiers, who had been as unaware of the plan as the Allies, were finally told what morning would bring. A message came from von Rundstedt: "We gamble everything . . . to achieve things beyond human possibilities for our Fatherland and our Führer!" Some, convinced the cause was lost, faced the news of further carnage with dismay; others saw a final opportunity to avenge the civilian death toll in German cities. Members of the SS, the greatest believers in the Nazi effort and thus the least restrained by the niceties of the Geneva Convention, welcomed the "holy task" with a blood lust that was to be more than sated in the weeks to come.

That night, across the border in Luxembourg, German-born film star Marlene Dietrich performed for American soldiers and went to bed early.

The Germans attacked at 5:30 AM with a thoroughness and a ruthlessness that impressed the Allied soldiers even through their bewilderment. The assault crippled Allied communications, and word moved as slowly as in the era before telegraph. A mere 20 mi from one prong of the attack, General Omar Bradley had breakfast at the Hotel Alfa in Luxembourg City and, blithely unaware of the change in situation, headed toward Paris for a meeting with Eisenhower, who had that very day been promoted to five-star General of the Army. Neither heard of the conflict until late afternoon; neither believed, at first sketchy report, that it was anything more than a flash in the pan.

It was. From the first wave of "artillery-prepared" assaults characterized by a barrage of shells followed by a surge of infantry attacks, to the sharp, startled, and for the most part instinctive defense of the Allies, the offensive was to escalate quickly into a battle of staggering scale. The Americans surprised the Germans in their tenacity, while the Germans amazed the Americans with their almost maniacal dedication.

Over the next month and a half, the two sides bludgeoned each other, struggling through harsh terrain and winter muck, reducing medieval castles to smoking rubble, and razing villages that had been liberated only months before. The ferocious tone of the fight was set early on: On December 17, SS officers of Lieutenant Colonel Peiper ordered the execution of 130 American prisoners outside Malmédy. The victims were left where they fell, periodically kicked for signs of life, and shot again. A few who survived, hiding the steam of their breath, crawled away when night fell and told their stories, and the massacre at Malmédy became a rallying point for the bitter Allies. Prisoners of war were murdered on both sides, and at times the gunfights took on a guerrilla aspect, with those in danger of capture, fearing execution, dissolving into the dense forest to go it alone.

And not only soldiers were killed. On December 18, in and near Stavelot, Peiper's SS troops ordered whole families of civilians from their cellars—women, children, elderly men—and shot them methodically; the toll reached 138. On December 24, SS security men assembled all the men of Bande, screened out those over 32, stripped them of watches and rosaries, and executed them one by one. The sole survivor, before he slugged his way free and dashed for the forest, noticed that his would-be executioner was weeping.

And on December 23, Americans wrought their own kind of horror in Malmédy when Army Air Corps Marauders, headed for the German railroad center of Zulpich, mistakenly emptied 86 bombs on the village center, killing as many of its own troops as innocent citizens. As the people dug out from the rubble on December 24, another misguided swarm of American bombers dropped an even more lethal load, leveling what was left of the center. On December 25, four more planes mistook Malmédy for St. Vith and 64 more bombs were dropped. Civilian victims—refugees and residents alike—were laid in rows in the school playground.

It wasn't a very merry Christmas on either side of the Ardennes that year. Sleepless, shell-shocked, often out of touch, soldiers from both sides huddled in icy pillboxes and snowy foxholes. Both sides drew up propaganda flyers carefully phrased in the recipients' mother tongue. For the Americans, the not-so-inspirational message admon-ished them: "Why are you here? What are you doing, fighting somebody else's war? You will die and your wife, your mother, your daughters will be left alone. Merry Christmas!" For the Germans, the American pamphlets simply assured them they were losing the war, and that they'd long since lost the battle.

But in truth, neither side held a clear upper hand until well into January. By the time the carnage slowed and the tide turned, the Germans had pressed deep into Belgium, their central thrust "bulging" west to within miles of the Meuse and Dinant. Though Hitler grudgingly ordered retreat from the farthest point of the Bulge on January 8, the Germans continued to fight through January 28, as they were driven all the way back to the Siegfried line.

By the battle's end, some 19,000 American soldiers had died, as had at least as many Germans. Hundreds of Belgian and Luxembourg citizens were dead as well, and survivors came back to find their villages flattened, their churches gaping shells, their heretofore impervious castles reduced to heaps of ancient stone. In Luxembourg, the towns of Diekirch, Clervaux, Vianden, and Echternach had been prime battle zones and were left charred and crumbled. In Belgium, St. Vith, Houffalize, and myriad Ardennes resort towns like La Roche were wasted by artillery "preparation" and the gun-and-grenade battles that ensued. And Bastogne, surrounded, besieged, and pounded by artillery for days, had lost what was left of its town center in the concentrated bombing Hitler ordered for Christmas Eve.

Today, throughout the Ardennes region, the faces of monuments and main streets are incongruously new and shiny, their resourceful owners having taken charred, roofless, windowless shells and made the best of the worst by installing new plumbing, modern wiring, efficient windows, central heat. Yet there are scars, visible and invisible. Behind the caulked shrapnel holes, which pock foundations and farmhouse walls, lurk bitter memories that weren't altogether appeased at Nuremburg. And the ugliness of the conflict, distorted by a new generation, occasionally rears its head: On the stone memorial at the crossroads outside Malmédy, where the names of the victims of the massacre have been carved, someone has spray-painted a swastika.

The cultural chasm between the two sides of the battle seems embodied in the two military cemeteries outside Luxembourg City. The American plot at Hamm is a blaze of white-marble glory, its 5,000 graves radiating in graceful arcs under open sun, its well-tended grass worn by the shoes of visitors. Just down the road at Sandweiler, however, is German plot, heavily shaded and concealed from view, with a few hundred low, dark-stone crosses marking the graves of some 5,000 men. Yet another 5,000, gathered in battle by the U.S. Army Burial Service and dumped unceremoniously in mass graves, were transferred here and buried under one heavy cross, with as many as possible identified in fine print crowded on a broad bronze plaque. Those graves are tended today by busloads of German schoolchildren, who visit in the name of a concept long overdue: *Versöhnung über den Gräbern—Arbeit für den Frieden* (reconciliation over the graves—work for peace).

—Nancy Coons

FABLED FINE ARTS

Belgium's position at the heart of Western Europe put it squarely in the way of marauding armies, dynastic ambitions, conflicting religions, and lucrative trade routes as far back as Roman times. As a Flemish identity began to solidify, between the 9th and 11th centuries, these forces joined to create the conditions under which Flemish pictorial art would flourish five centuries later. The roots of the first great age of Flemish art lie in medieval trades: manuscript illumination, miniature painting, weaving tapestries for castle walls, and stonework and decorative arts for the Church. The medieval guild system, with its high standards and demanding apprenticeships, established a tradition of technical and artistic expertise.

The skills honed in these conditions came to the fore in the early 15th century, when relative economic prosperity, an upwardly mobile court nobility, and the enlightened patronage of the ruling dukes of Burgundy allowed Flanders-Brabant to emerge as a rival to Italy for artistic pre-eminence in Western Europe. The Flemish painters known as the Primitives moved painting resolutely out of the Middle Ages by recording the world around them with what we would now call a painter's eye. Jan and Hubert van Eyck, Rogier van der Weyden, Petrus Christus, Gerard David, Hans Memling, and their colleagues set out to find the universal in the particular. They came from a tradition of meticulous technique, close attention to line-based detail, and the use of brilliant color (weak color went unnoticed in the dark interiors for which most paintings were destined). In their contemplative, harmonious paintings, they used gradations of color to record light, objects, and the human body in astonishingly realistic detail. Portraits, in particular, convey a lifelike depth of character. The face of a burgher may remind you of a man you passed in the street that day, or that of a saint may resemble the young woman who sold you your museum ticket. For all its fascinating detail, however, the Primitives' work is static, their subjects caught in a timeless stillness.

Most of the 15th-century masters clustered in the major cities, particularly Brugge, training up-and-comers in their busy studios. (Memling, for instance, is thought to have worked with Rogier van der Weyden.) The exception was Hieronymous Bosch, who painted his elaborately inventive visions of Hell in the second half of the 15th century; he lived off the beaten track in s'Hertogenbosch (a Dutch town since 1629). Although Bosch's painting contains harbingers of the pictorial realism to come, he seems to have had almost no contact with contemporary artists.

It is often claimed, though not undisputed, that the Flemish Primitives, and Jan van Eyck in particular, invented oil painting. Oil-based paint was, in fact, used long before the 15th century, but the Flemish artists devised new binders that made the paint easier to handle and popularized its use. Van Eyck's work exemplifies this revolution. The new paint composition allowed for wet-on-dry changes, making his incredible modeling and detail possible. As for the color, one theory holds that such intense, durable hues were achieved by applying a white base layer of chalk and glue, followed by single layers of mineral pigment mixed with egg yolk and egg white. The foundation layer brightened the colors, the mineral pigments created an enamel-like durability, and the egg white hardened to the consistency of horn.

The Calvinist turbulence of the 16th century temporarily calmed the runaway creativity. The 1585 division of the Low Countries into the independent Calvinist north and the Spanish Catholic south, however, set the scene for the Catholic Counter-Reformation, several decades of Habsburg-nurtured prosperity in the south, and another Flemish surge to artistic prominence. This exuberant second golden age was dominated by the Antwerp-based painter Peter Paul Rubens.

Though Flemish by birth, Rubens established himself as an artist during an eight-year stint in Italy. His art reflected his time—energetic, colorful, and voluptuous. Greek and Roman sculpture and paintings by Italian masters such as Tintoretto, Correggio, Caravaggio, and Titian made their mark; Rubens incorporated these influences into the Flemish tradition. He tempered his Italian-taught dynamism with sustained attention to detail, color, and modeling. By combining dramatic Italian composition with Flemish realism, Rubens fused the two leading Western European artistic styles.

Rubens returned to Antwerp in 1608, where his fame drew other young painters to study and work at his hyper-productive studio. Commissions poured in from princes and crowned heads across Europe, and the studio's output was huge. Assistants such as the young Anthony van Dyck collaborated with Rubens on paintings that ranged from portraits of Italian nobles to religious triptychs, intimate family portraits to monumental ceiling work for King Charles I in London.

Van Dyck took things a step further by working quickly and freely, giving his portraits a craggy, emotional feel that Rubens's polished classical forms initially lacked. The styles of both van Dyck and Rubens became softer and more sensual, with a more agile use of color, in their later years. (Rubens died in 1640, van Dyck in 1641.) Jacob Jordaens followed closely in their wake; he also worked in Rubens's studio and became one of the 17th century's best figure painters. Pieter Bruegel the Elder and his son Jan were other notable contemporaries. Bruegel the Elder was and is considered the best of the family artists for his exceptionally precise and evocative depictions of village life, parables, landscapes, and allegories. Their enduring popularity is evinced by the work of his grandson, Pieter Bruegel III, who made a comfortable living copying the Elder's work.

The second Flemish golden age ended in 1648 with the definitive partition of the Low Countries, and it was not until the early 20th century that Belgium again had a significant impact on the international art scene. James Ensor paved the way in the late 19th century with avant-garde paintings and drawings; his use of sinister carnival masks recalls Bosch's disturbing fantasies. The Surrealists, in turn, paid tribute to Ensor during their intra-war heyday of experimental work. The Belgian painter René Magritte became one of the most renowned Surrealists, with his extraordinary images based on ordinary objects. In true Belgian form, though, he avoided a tight alliance with an authoritative group. Rather than join the Surrealist circle in France, Magritte worked in Brussels for most of his life. On a visit to his long-time home there, you can see the bourgeois interiors he transformed with his groundbreaking imagination.

BOOKS & MOVIES

BOOKS

ART & ARCHITECTURE

Flemish Primitives. For a hefty, illustrated study of the Flemish Primitives, including Rogier van der Weyden, Dirk Bouts, Hans Memling, and Hieronymus Bosch, look up *The Flemish Primitives* by Cyriel Stroo (1996–2002). This has the imprimatur of the Royal Museum of Fine Arts of Belgium, but as it's an expensive, three-volume commitment, it may be best to seek it out in a library. Curator Dirk de Vos's *Flemish Primitives: The Masterpieces* (2003) is a more manageable illustrated tome. (De Vos also published a catalog on Rogier van der Weyden, now out of print but worth looking up in libraries.) Translations of the work of Otto Pächt include: *Van Eyck and the Founders of Early Netherlandish Painting* (2000) and *Early Netherlandish Painting from Rogier van der Weyden to Gerard David* (2002). There are also many studies of individual artists available, such as Wilhelm Fraenger's *Hieronymus Bosch* (2003), which analyzes Bosch's imagery and ties it to the painter's personal tribulations. *Bruges and the Renaissance* (1999), by Maximiliaan P.J. Martens, focuses on the 16th century, picking up where the Primitives left off.

Rubens. Paul Oppenheimer mines the life of 17th-century master Peter Paul Rubens for his biography *Rubens: A Portrait* (2002). Unfortunately, many of the catalogs of Rubens's work are out of print; your library may have some on its shelves. Sabine van Sprang and Joost Vander Auwera's in-depth study *Rubens: A Genius at Work* (2007) analyzes the artist's techniques using modern technology, putting his methods and materials into historical context.

Art Nouveau. In one of a series of illustrated books on major architects, the publisher te Neues outlines Victor Horta's contributions to the Art Nouveau style in *Victor Horta* (2003). You can read about Art Nouveau in the context of other artistic developments in *Brussels Fin de Siècle* (1999), edited by Philippe Roberts-Jones.

20th Century. Check out Jacques Meuris's *René Magritte: 1898–1967* (1998), an inclusive retrospective of Magritte's work, including little-known photographs, short films, and sculptures. Suzi Gablik's *Magritte* (1985) investigates Magritte's paintings through his repeated images, such as the bowler-hatted man.

In *Christ's Entry Into Brussels in 1889* (2002), Patricia G. Berman examines James Ensor's coming of age as he painted one of the most striking pieces of artistic social commentary of 19th-century Europe. For a more general overview of Ensor's oeuvre, look for *James Ensor, 1860–1949: Masks, Death, and the Sea* (1999), by Ulrike Becks-Malorney.

General. In its Masters of Art series, publisher Harry N. Abrams Inc. counts Bruegel the Elder, Bosch, and Magritte in its topic roster. Phaidon produces two introductory series on art history with Belgium-related (and reasonably priced) titles; the Colour Library series has books on Bruegel and Magritte, and the Art and Ideas series includes a study on Rubens.

For the Kids. Anders Shafer's illustrated story *The Fantastic Journey of Peter Bruegel* (2002) is an imaginary diary of Bruegel's trip from Antwerp to Rome in the 16th century. For more on Bruegel, try *Tower of Babel: The Builder With The Red Hat* (1998), by Nils Jockel, which uses one of the characters depicted in Bruegel's painting to introduce life in 16th-century Antwerp. The rhymes and rhythms of *Pish, Posh, Said Hieronymus Bosch* (1991), written by Nancy Willard and illustrated by Diane and Leo Dillon, make for great reading aloud. Filled with creatures both absurd and fantastic, this dreamy story pairs the infectious text with Bosch-inspired drawings.

FICTION

Two of the most famous French-language 19th-century novels about Belgium are available in English translations: Georges Rodenbach's *Bruges-la-Morte* (*Bruges the Dead*), which sparked an enormous wave of interest in Brugge; and Charles de Coster's picaresque *La légende d'Uylenspiegel* (*The Legend of the Uylenspiegel*), which captures the spirit of Belgian defiance of outside authority.

Charlotte Brontë's time in a Belgian school is reflected in her novels *The Professor* and *Villette*. *The Professor* addresses the Belgians more directly, but both take a disparaging line, often tied to the religious divide between the staunchly Protestant Brontë and her Catholic schoolmates.

For a fictional account of the devastating World War I battle zone around Ieper, Winston Groom's *A Storm In Flanders: The Ypres Salient, 1914–1918: Tragedy and Triumph on the Western Front* (2002) is a must-read. Groom describes in startling, realistic detail the relentless years of combat. Also of note is Siegfried Sassoon's *Memoirs of an Infantry Officer*, originally published in 1930. Sassoon, best known for his war-related poetry, wrote one of the most enduring, evocative accounts of trench warfare; ostensibly fiction, *Memoirs* draws heavily on Sassoon's own experience on the Western Front.

William Wharton's *A Midnight Clear* (1983) is a fictional account of an Ardennes battle in World War II as seen by American GIs. Hugo Claus's *Het Verdriet van België* (*The Sorrow of Belgium*), an outstanding coming-of-age novel of life during the Occupation, was republished in English in 2003.

The extraordinarily prolific Georges Simenon is best known for creating the indomitable Inspector Maigret, Belgium's clear-headed and witty answer to Sherlock Holmes. Seventy-nine of the Maigret stories have been translated into English from their original French, and many have been made into movies and TV dramas. Simenon also penned 120 of what he considered to be more literary works, his *romans durs,* or "tough novels." Though Simenon died in 1989, his works continue to receive international acclaim.

Maurice Maeterlinck and Marguerite Yourcenar are two other exceptional Belgian writers who worked in French. Awarded the Nobel Prize for Literature in 1911, the playwright and poet Maeterlinck was closely identified with the French Symbolist literary movement. While earlier works such as *L'Intruse* (*The Intruder*) and *Les Aveugles* (*The Blind*) have strong fatalistic overtones, his best known play, *L'Oiseau bleu* (*The Blue Bird*), is an allegorical children's tale about the search for happiness. Marguerite Yourcenar gained literary acclaim with her metaphysical historical novels; she was the first woman elected to the prestigious Académie Française. Her most famous work, *Mémoires d'Hadrien* (*Memoirs of Hadrian*), deals with the emperor's musings from his deathbed. English translations of both Maeterlinck and Yourcenar are readily available.

Of contemporary Belgian writers, Amélie Nothomb is the best known to anglophone readers; her work often involves questions of Belgian identity. *Stupeurs et tremblements* (*Fear and Trembling,* 2001) is a semi-autobiographical glimpse into her adventures in Japan's business culture, and was made into a French film in 2003. *Métaphysique des tubes* (*The Character of Rain,* 2003) takes a more metaphysical approach toward the discovery of a distinct sense of self.

Hergé set many of the *Tintin* cartoon adventures in foreign lands, but Tintin himself remained always the quintessential *bon petit Belge.*

FOOD & DRINK

Ruth van Waerebeek's *Everybody Eats Well in Belgium* (1996) presents an in-depth yet manageable introduction to Belgian cuisine. Covering such traditional favorites as waterzooi, Belgian waffles, and mussels and fries, van Waerebeek accentuates each chapter with family recipes and sidebars on historical notes of interest. There's also an entire chapter devoted to beer.

One of the most informative books on Belgian beer is Pierre Rajotte's *Belgian Ale* (1996). Rajotte mixes historical background and categorical expertise with his own brewing tips. *The Good Beer Guide to Belgium* (2005), by Tim Webb, offers a travel-oriented overview of the country, its pubs, and its potent products. Though broader in scope, *Michael Jackson's Great Beer Guide* (2000) has plenty to say about Belgian brews, categorizing them by flavor and body. The late Jackson, who died in 2007, also produced several other beer guides that cover Belgian and Trappist beers, including *Michael Jackson's Great Beers of Belgium* (1998), *Ultimate Beer* (1998), and a couple of editions of his *Beer Companion*.

HISTORY

For a broad look at the historical backdrop that informs contemporary Belgian culture, look to J.C.H. Blom's *History of the Low Country* (1999), which spans Dutch and Belgian political, social, and religious sagas from the Roman era to the 20th century. It does an excellent job explaining Belgium's sources of pride and of persistent concern.

A painfully accurate report on the misrule of King Leopold II of Belgium over the Congo, Adam Hochschild's *King Leopold's Ghost* (1998) relates the sorry case of Leopold's colonial regime. As the Congo River basin was essentially the king's private property, his cruelty went unchecked for over 20 years. Hochschild's book reminds us of Leopold's brutality and the efforts of those who resisted. For a more personal account, read *Back to the Congo* (1992) by Flemish journalist Lieve Joris. Prompted by her missionary uncle's stories, Joris travels to Zaire (now the Democratic Republic of the Congo) and slowly comes to grips with the country's current struggles and Belgium's colonial past.

Luc Sante's *Factory of Facts* (1998) is ostensibly a memoir, but it's foremost a keenly observed examination of Belgian (particularly Wallonian) sensibilities; it's also one of the rare English-language books about Belgium that isn't also about war.

John Keegan's *The Face of Battle* (1983) includes a brilliant analysis of the Battle of Waterloo. Drawing upon firsthand accounts from all sides, Mark Adkin's *The Waterloo Companion* (2002) complements the soldiers' stories with detailed maps and photographs of this famous battle-site. Barbara Tuchman's *A Distant Mirror* (1978), describing 14th-century European affairs, gives valuable insights, illuminated by memorable vignettes, into the conflicts between Flemish towns and the Crown of France. *The Guns of August* (1982) applies Tuchman's narrative technique to the events, largely in Belgium, of the first month of World War I.

Leon Wolff's *In Flanders Fields* (1984) is a classic account of the catastrophic campaign of 1917, while John Toland's *No Man's Land* (1985) covers the events on the Western Front in 1918. *Major and Mrs. Holt's Battlefield Guide to Ypres Salient* (1997) is a valuable resource for visiting the region ravaged during World War I.

For a voyeuristic view inside a 17th-century Belgian convent, track down *The Burdens of Sister Margaret* (2001), by Craig Harline. Culled from a collection of letters written by a nun from a convent in Leuven, this book explores the daily life of a tight-knit religious community, delving into everything from demonic possession and sexual harassment to the continued pursuit of faith.

TRAVEL

For a hilarious account of Belgium's many cultural idiosyncrasies, look up to *A Tall Man in a Low Land* (2000). Harry Pearson, a Brit who lived for a time in Belgium, covers everything from the passionate differences between Wallonia and Flanders to the now-defunct Underpants Museum in Brussels.

MOVIES

The brothers Jean-Pierre and Luc Dardenne won rare international attention for Belgian cinema with their tough, thought-provoking films of the late 1990s. *La Promesse* (*The Promise,* 1996) examines the lives of a group of immigrants surviving (or not) on the edge of Belgian society and a boy who becomes involved with them. *Rosetta* (1999), the story of a young woman scrambling to retain menial jobs, won the Palme d'Or at Cannes and made the brothers household names in Europe.

Their latest film, *L'Enfant* (2005) tells the story of a young couple's efforts to regain their newborn son after he is sold by the derelict father.

But not all Belgian films are so bleak. In *Ma Vie en Rose* (*My Life in Pink,* 1997), directed by Alain Berliner, comfortable bourgeois culture is challenged by a little boy who truly believes he will turn into a girl. A forerunner on reality "mockumentaries," the dark *C'est arrivé près de chez vous* (*Man Bites Dog,* 1992) follows a serial killer as he goes through his day and expounds on subjects as varied as art and the beauty of death. In the blackly comic *Toto the Hero* (1991), director Jaco Van Dormael transforms an old man's recollections into a somewhat suspect universal portrait of modern man. *Pauline & Paulette* (2001), a sweet tale about a mildly mentally handicapped elderly woman and her sister, won the Special Mention at Cannes.

While not a Belgian movie as such, the British thriller *In Bruges* (2008), starring Colin Farrell and Ralph Fiennes, is set and filmed almost entirely in that city, and features a host of scenic locations to get you in the travel mood.

—Updated by Tim Skellton

FLEMISH VOCABULARY

Flemish is a Germanic language; though it may look daunting at first, most of its sounds correspond to sounds in English. Flemish has two forms for "you": U/Uw (formal) and jij/je/jou (casual). When addressing an adult you don't know, it's always best to use the formal term.

Each consonant in double-consonant pairings is usually pronounced separately. The toughest to pronounce is the ch, a gutteral sound which may remind you of the ending of "loch." G is also soft and gutteral, while j is pronounced like the y in "yes." W sounds like a v, as in "vast," and v is softened with an f-like sound, as in "fast."

Doubled vowels extend the vowel sound: aa, for instance, is pronounced like the a in "father," ee sounds like the a in "date," and oo sounds like the o in "vote." There are a couple of tricky pairings, such as eeu, which combines long vowel sounds like the ay in "hay" and the oo of "hoot." Ei and ij are both pronounced the same way, but fluctuate depending on regional accent; they could sound like the ey in "they" or like a strong i, as in "time."

	ENGLISH	FLEMISH	PRONUNCIATION
BASICS			
	Yes/no	Ja/nee	yah/nay
	Please	Alstublieft	**ahls**-too-bleeft
	Thank you	Dank u	**dahnk** ew
	You're welcome	Niets te danken	neets tuh **dahn**-kuh
	Excuse me, sorry	Pardon	pahr-**don**
	Good morning	Goede morgen	**khoo**-duh **mohr**-khuh
	Good evening	Goede avond	**khoo**-duh **ah**-fohnt
	Goodbye	Dag	dakh
NUMBERS			
	one	een	ayn
	two	twee	tvay
	three	drie	dree
	four	vier	veer
	five	vijf	vaif
	six	zes	zehss
	seven	zeven	**zhay**-fuh
	eight	acht	ahkht
	nine	negen	**nay**-khuh

ENGLISH	FLEMISH	PRONUNCIATION
ten	tien	teen
eleven	elf	elf
twelve	twaalf	tvahlf
thirteen	dertien	**dehr**-teen
fourteen	veertien	**feer**-teen
fifteen	vijftien	**faif**-teen
sixteen	zestien	**zehss**-teen
seventeen	zeventien	**zay**fuh-teen
eighteen	achttein	**ahkht**-teen
nineteen	negentien	**nay**-khuh-teen
twenty	twintig	**tvin**-tukh
twenty-one	eenentwintig	**ayn**-en-tvin-tukh
thirty	dertig	**dehr**-tukh
forty	veertig	**feer**-tukh
fifty	vijftig	**fehf**-tukh
one hundred	honderd	**hohn**-durt
one thousand	duizend	**douw**-zuhnt

DAYS OF THE WEEK

Sunday	zondag	**zohn**-dakh
Monday	maandag	**mahn**-dakh
Tuesday	dinsdag	**dinns**-dakh
Wednesday	woensdag	**voons**-dakh
Thursday	donderdag	**don**-der-dakh
Friday	vrijdag	**vrai**-dakh
Saturday	zaterdag	**zah**-ter-dakh

USEFUL PHRASES

Do you speak English?	Spreekt U engels?	spraykt ew **ehng**–uhls
I don't speak Dutch.	Ik spreek geen nederlands.	ik sprayk **khayn nay**-der-lahnds
I don't understand (it).	Ik begrijp (het) niet.	ik buh-**khraip** (uht) neet

ENGLISH	FLEMISH	PRONUNCIATION
I don't know (it).	Ik weet (het) niet	ik **vayt** (uht) neet
I'm American/English.	Ik ben amerikaans/ engels	ik ben ah-mer-ee-**kahns**/ehng-uhls
Where is . . .	Waar is . . .	vahr iss . . .
the train station?	het station?	heht stah-**shohn**
the post office?	het postkantoor?	heht **pohst**-kahn-tohr
the hospital?	het ziekenhuis?	heht **zee**-kuh-howss
Where are the restrooms? (men/women)	Waar is de WC? (heren/dames)	**vahr** iss duh **vay-say** (hay-ruh/dah-muh)
Left/right	Links/rechts	links/rekhts
Straight ahead	Rechtdoor	rehkht-dohr
How much is this?	Hoeveel kost dit?	hoo-FAYL kohst dit
Do you accept credit cards?	Neemt U krediet-kaarten aan?	**naymt** ew kray-**deet**-kahr- tuh-**ahn**?
I am ill/sick.	Ik ben ziek	ik ben zeek
I want to call a doctor.	Ik wil een dokter bellen	ik vil uhn **dohk**-ter **behl**-luh
Help!	Help!	help
Stop!	Stoppen!	**stop**-puh

DINING OUT

I'd like	Ik wil graag . . .	ik vil khrahkh . . .
. . . to reserve a table.	. . . een tafel reserveren	. . . uhn **tah**-full ray-sayr-vay-ruh
. . . the wine list.	. . . de wijnkaart	. . . duh **vain**-kahrt
. . . the menu	. . . de menu/kaart	. . . duh muh-**new**/ **kahrt**
. . . the bill/check	. . . de rekening	. . . duh **ray**-kuh-ning
beer	bier	beer
mineral water	mineraalwater	meen-eh-**raahl-vah**-ter
napkin	een servet	uhn ser-**veht**
fork	een vork	uhn fork
knife	een mes	uhn mehs
spoon	een lepel	uhn **lay**-puhl
bread	brood	broht

ENGLISH	FLEMISH	PRONUNCIATION
butter	boter	**boh-**ter
pepper	peper	**pay-**per
salt	zout	zowt
sugar	suiker	**zow-**kuhr
Cheers!	Proost!	**prost!**

FRENCH VOCABULARY

One of the trickiest French sounds to pronounce is the final nasal n sound (whether or not the n is the final letter of the word). You should try to pronounce it as a sort of nasal grunt—as in "huh." The vowel that precedes the n will govern the vowel sound of the word, and in this list we precede the final n with an h to remind you to be nasal.

Another difficult sound is the untransliterable eu, as in neuf (nine), and the very similar sound in je (I) and de (of). The closest approximate sound might be the vowel in "put," but rounded. The famous rolled r is a glottal sound. Consonants at the ends of words are usually silent; when the following word begins with a vowel, however, the two are run together by sounding the consonant. There are two forms of "you" in French: vous (formal and plural) and tu (a singular, personal form). When addressing an adult you don't know, vous is always best.

	ENGLISH	FRENCH	PRONUNCIATION
BASICS			
	Yes/no	Oui/non	wee/nohn
	Please	S'il vous plaît	seel voo play
	Thank you	Merci	mair-**see**
	You're welcome	De rien	deh ree-**ahn**
	Excuse me, sorry	Pardon	pahr-**dohn**
	Good morning	Bonjour	bohn-**zhoor**
	Good evening	Bonsoir	bohn-**swahr**
	Goodbye	Au revoir	o ruh-**vwahr**
	Mr. (Sir)	Monsieur	muh-**syuh**
	Mrs. (Ma'am)	Madame	ma-**dam**
NUMBERS			
	one	un	uhn
	two	deux	deuh
	three	trois	twah
	four	quatre	**kaht**-ruh
	five	cinq	sank
	six	six	seess
	seven	sept	set
	eight	huit	wheat
	nine	neuf	nuf
	ten	dix	deess

ENGLISH	FRENCH	PRONUNCIATION
eleven	onze	ohnz
twelve	douze	dooz
thirteen	treize	trehz
fourteen	quatorze	kah-torz
fifteen	quinze	kanz
sixteen	seize	sez
seventeen	dix-sept	deez-**set**
eighteen	dix-huit	deez-**wheat**
nineteen	dix-neuf	deez-**nuf**
twenty	vingt	vehn
twenty-one	vingt-et-un	vehnt-ay-**uhn**
thirty	trente	trahnt
forty	quarante	ka-**rahnt**
fifty	cinquante	sang-**kahnt**
one hundred	cent	sahn
one thousand	mille	meel

DAYS OF THE WEEK

Sunday	dimanche	dee-**mahnsh**
Monday	lundi	luhn-**dee**
Tuesday	mardi	mahr-**dee**
Wednesday	mercredi	mair-kruh-**dee**
Thursday	jeudi	zhuh-**dee**
Friday	vendredi	vawn-druh-**dee**
Saturday	samedi	sahm-**dee**

USEFUL PHRASES

Do you speak English?	Parlez-vous anglais?	par-lay **voo ahn**-glay?
I don't speak French.	Je ne parle pas français.	zhuh nuh parl pah frahn-**say**
I don't understand.	Je ne comprends pas.	zhuh nuh kohm- **prahn** pah
I don't know.	Je ne sais pas.	zhuh nuh say **pah**

ENGLISH	FRENCH	PRONUNCIATION
I'm American/English.	Je suis américain/anglais.	zhuh sweez a-may-ree-**kahn**/ahn-**glay**
Where is . . .	Où est . . .	oo ay
the train station?	la gare?	la gar
the post office?	la poste?	la post
the hospital?	l'hôpital?	Lo-pee-**tahl**
Where are the restrooms?	Où sont les toilettes?	oo sohn lay twah-**let**
(men/women)	(hommes/femmes)	(**oh**-mm/**fah**-mm)
Left/right	A gauche/à droite	a goash/a drwaht
Straight ahead	tout droit	too drwah
How much is this?	C'est combien?	say comb-bee-**ehn**
Can I pay with a credit card?	Puis-je payer carte de crédit?	**pweezh** payay ahvehk ewn kahrt duh **kray**-dee?
I am ill/sick.	Je suis malade.	zhuh swee ma-**lahd**
I want to call a	Je veux appeler un	zhuh veuh a-play
doctor.	docteur.	uhn dohk-**tehr**
Help!	Au secours!	o suh-**korr**
Stop!	Arretez!	A-reh-**tay**

DINING OUT

I'd like	Je voudrais	zhuh voo-**dray**
. . . to reserve a table.	. . . réserver une table.	ray-zehr-vay ewn **tah**-bl
. . . the wine list.	. . . la carte des vins.	lah kahrt day va(n)
. . . the menu	. . . la carte.	la cart
. . . bill/check	. . . l'addition.	la-dee-see-**ohn**
beer	une bière	ewn **byehr**
mineral water	l'eau minérale	**loh** meen-ay-rahl
napkin	une serviette	ewn sair-vee-**et**
fork	une fourchette	ewn four-**shet**
knife	un couteau	uhn koo-**toe**
spoon	un cuillière	uhn kwee-**air**

ENGLISH	FRENCH	PRONUNCIATION
bread	le pain	luh pan
butter	le beurre	luh burr
pepper	le poivre	luh **pwah**-vruh
salt	le sel	luh sell
sugar	le sucre	luh **sook**-ruh
Cheers!	Santé!	Sahn-**tay**!

Travel Smart Belgium

PLANNING TOOLS, EXPERT INSIGHT, GREAT CONTACTS

WORD OF MOUTH

"I adore the charming, smaller scale of the Belgian cities and I love the French joie de vivre meets Dutch practicality that Belgium offers. Belgium isn't Rome (or Paris for that matter) but that's precisely why I enjoy it so much."

—global_guy

GETTING HERE & AROUND

UPDATED BY TIM SKELTON

▌ BY AIR

Flying time to Belgium is about seven hours from New York and 8½ hours from Chicago. Depending upon your routing and transit time, flights from Dallas last approximately 13 hours and flights from Los Angeles, approximately 16 hours. Because of its small size, there are no scheduled domestic flights within Belgium.

Belgium has no quarantine requirements, so it isn't difficult to travel with pets. However, you must provide an antirabies vaccination certificate for your cats and dogs dated at least 30 days prior to flight.

Airlines & Airports Airline and Airport Links.com (⊕www.airlineandairportlinks.com) has links to many of the world's airlines and airports.

Airline Security Issues Transportation Security Administration (⊕www.tsa.gov) has answers for almost every question that might come up.

Air Travel Resources in Belgium European Consumer Centre Belgium (☎02/542–3346 ⊕www.eccbelgium.be) is an EU-sponsored organization that dispenses free consumer advice including handling complaints about air travel.

AIRPORTS

The major international airport serving Belgium is Brussels Airport at Zaventem, 14 km (9 mi) northeast of Brussels. Sometimes called Zaventem for short, the airport has nonstop flights from the United States and Canada and is easy to navigate, with signs in English as well as French and Dutch. There are plenty of facilities, including airport hotels, rental-car agencies, shops, a bank, a travel agency, a post office, Internet stations for last-minute

e-mail, restaurants, and bars, including ones specializing in Belgian beer.

Ryanair uses the smaller Brussels South Charleroi Airport, 46 km (29 mi) south of Brussels, as a hub. Though farther out of the city, it's connected to Brussels by a regular bus service. A new terminal building opened in 2008, doubling the airport's capacity and greatly improving the available range of dining and shopping options.

There's a third, smaller international airport, Antwerp Airport, otherwise known as Deurne, 5½ km (3 mi) southeast of Antwerp.

Services at these airports are more limited, but lower costs make them worth investigating.

Airport Information Brussels Airport (BRU) (☎02/753–7753 ⊕www.brusselsairport. be). **Brussels South Charleroi Airport** (CRL) (☎071/25–12–29 ⊕www.charleroi-airport. com). **Antwerp Airport** (ANR) (☎03/285–6500 ⊕www.antwerp-airport.be).

GROUND TRANSPORTATION

Trains run up to four times each hour from Brussels Airport to the city center, taking around 15 minutes. A one-way ticket costs €2.90. The railway station is directly accessible from the terminal building. Direct services also run from the airport to several other Belgian cities. There are also bus connections to the city leaving from outside the terminal, level 0. These cost about the same, but take longer and have limited space for luggage, so are only convenient if your destination is in the northern suburbs. Taxis offer the best door-to-door service, but will cost around €35 to the city center. Many companies serve the airport, but Taxi Hendriks has vehicles suitable for wheelchair users if you call in advance.

Autocars l'Elan operates an hourly shuttle-bus service between Brussels South Charleroi Airport and Brussels South railway station. The journey takes 40 minutes and costs €13 one way, €22 return. There are also direct services to Brugge, which cost €20 one way (€38 round-trip) and take around 90 minutes. For other destinations, TEC buses link the airport with Charleroi railway station. Bus tickets cost €2.50 one way, or a combined bus-and-rail ticket to anywhere in Belgium costs €10.50 one way. Taxi rides from Charleroi have a preset fare for each destination and are not metered. To be on the safe side, make sure you know what this is beforehand (the information desk will tell you).

Antwerp city bus 14, operated by De Lijn, connects Antwerp airport with both Berchem (10 minutes) and Centraal (20 minutes) stations on a regular basis. The one-way fare to Centraal Station is €2 if bought in advance, or €2.70 bought from the driver. A taxi will cost around €20, depending on destination.

TRANSFERS BETWEEN AIRPORTS

There are no specific shuttle services between Belgian airports. If you need to connect, use one of the services listed above. Taking a taxi is an option, but will cost in excess of €100.

Contacts Autocars l'Elan (⊕ www.voyages-lelan.be). **De Lijn** (☎ 070/22-02-00 ⊕ www.delijn.be). **SNCB/NMBS** (☎ 02/528-2828 or 02/555-2525 ⊕ www.b-rail.be). **Taxi Hendriks** (☎ 02/752-9800 ⊕ www.hendriks.be). **TEC** (☎ 071/23-41-15 ⊕ www.tec-wl.be).

FLIGHTS

After the 2001 bankruptcy of Sabena, Belgium's national airline, SN Brussels Airlines became the country's foremost carrier, with routes to the United States, Africa, and all over Europe. In the United States, there are direct services to Brussels from Atlanta, Chicago, New York (JFK and Newark), Orlando, Philadelphia, and Washington (Dulles). Many European airlines have teamed up with American carriers in an effort to give more consistent service; for example, KLM (Royal Dutch Airlines) has partnered with Northwest Airlines.

Low-cost carrier Ryanair operates an ever-expanding network of routes out of its hub at Brussels South Charleroi Airport. This can be a very economical way of getting around Europe, and you'll get the best deals if you book well ahead.

You are not required to reconfirm flights from Brussels, but you should reconfirm departure time by telephone if you have made your reservation considerably in advance, as flight schedules are subject to change without notice. Check in for long-haul flights to and from Belgium two hours prior to departure—and don't forget your passport. If you are flying within Europe, check-in time is forty minutes to one hour prior to departure, depending on the airline. There is no curbside check-in at airports in Belgium.

A European Union regulation has standardized the rights of passengers to compensation in the event of flight cancellations or long delays. The law covers all passengers departing from an airport within the European Union, and all passengers traveling into the EU on an EU carrier, unless they received assistance in the country of departure. Full details are available from the airlines, and are posted prominently in all EU airports.

To Belgium American Airlines (☎ 800/433-7300 ⊕ www.aa.com). **Brussels Airlines** (☎ 516/622-2248 in U.S. ⊕ www.brusselsairlines.com). **Continental Airlines** (☎ 800/231-0856 for international reservations ⊕ www.continental.com). **Delta Airlines** (☎ 800/241-4141 for international reservations ⊕ www.delta.com). **Northwest Airlines** (☎ 800/225-2525 ⊕ www.nwa.com). **United Airlines** (☎ 800/538-2929 for international reservations ⊕ www.united.com). **USAirways** (☎ 800/622-1015 for international reservations ⊕ www.usairways.com).

Within Europe **Air France** (☎800/237–2747 in U.S., 070/22–24–66 in Belgium ⊕www.air france.us). **British Airways** (☎800/247–9297 in U.S., 02/717–3217 in Belgium ⊕www. britishairways.com). **Brussels Airlines** (☎516/622–2248 in U.S., 0870/735–2345 in U.K., 02/200–6234 in Belgium ⊕www.brussels airlines.com). **KLM (Royal Dutch Airlines)** (☎800/447–4747 in U.S., 070/22–27–47 in Belgium ⊕www.klm.com). **Ryanair** (⊕www. ryanair.com).

▌BY BIKE

Travel by bicycle is popular and easy in Belgium; bike paths border its scenic canals and seaside roads. Many towns provide special lanes parallel to main streets for bicycles, and bicycle racks are available to the public.

Cycling in cities is less pleasant, as traffic is dense, bicycle paths are scarce, and drivers are less hospitable about sharing the road with cyclists.

You can rent bicycles at Belgium's seaside resorts by the hour, half day, or day, with daily prices usually ranging from €9 to €12. If you are traveling in a group, consider another popular seaside rental option, a bicycle built for six pedalers.

You can also **rent bicycles as part of a train-bike package** at 16 train stations in the country's most popular tourist destinations. The package includes one round-trip one-day ticket and bike rental at your destination station, with a total cost ranging from €12 to €22. You are required to make a deposit, which is reimbursed when you return your bicycle. A booklet called *B-Excursions,* available at major train stations, lists participating stations.

Géocarte mapmakers produce bicycle guides with maps for nine Belgian regions. They are for sale in bookstores such as La Route de Jade, for about €10 per region. You can also pick up bicycle maps from national and local tourist information

centers. *See Visitor Info, in Essentials below for contact information.*

■**TIP**➜ Most airlines accommodate bikes as luggage, provided they're dismantled and boxed.

Bike Maps **La Route de Jade** (✉Rue de Stassart 116, Brussels ☎02/512–9654).

Bike Tours **Euro-Bike Tours** (☎800/321–6060 ⊕www.eurobike.com). **Vermont Bicycle Touring** (☎800/245–3868 ⊕www.vbt.com).

▌BY BUS

Belgium has an extensive network of reasonably priced urban and intercity buses. STIB/MIVB (Société des Transports Intercommunaux de Bruxelles/Maatschappij voor het Intercommunaal Vervoer te Brussel) covers service around Brussels and to other towns in the region. De Lijn runs buses in Flanders, including Antwerp, Brugge, and Gent, while TEC buses connect towns in Wallonia.

International bus travel is generally eclipsed by train service in terms of both convenience and price, but some bus companies do offer connections between Brussels and nearby capitals. Eurolines has up to three daily express services between Brussels and Amsterdam, Berlin, Frankfurt, Paris, and London, and offers multipass discounts and student fares.

Smoking on all buses, both national and international, is prohibited.

■**TIP**➜ If you're planning to travel extensively in Europe, it may make sense to invest in a Eurolines Pass for unlimited travel among 40 cities including Brussels. At this writing, a 30-day Eurolines Pass costs €439 for high-season travel, €299 for off-season travel. The Eurolines Coach Station is at CCN Gare du Nord.

Fares and schedules are available at the STIB, De Lijn, TEC, and Eurolines sales offices or at local travel agencies. Bus transit companies accept major credit cards and cash.

Bus Information De Lijn (☎070/22–02–00).
Eurolines (☎02/274–1350 ⊕www.eurolines.
com). **STIB/MIVB** (☎0900/10–310 ⊕www.
stib.be). **TEC** (☎071/23–41–15 ⊕www.
tec-wl.be).

▌ BY CAR

Belgium is a small country and driving distances are not great. Most destinations are not more than two hours from Brussels. There are no tolls, but the major highways can get very congested, especially around Brussels and Antwerp. Driving within cities can be a nightmare if you're not used to Belgian roads. You may have to compete with trams, or taxi drivers with a death wish, for space, and city centers often have narrow roads with unfathomable one-way systems.

Belgium is covered by an extensive network of four-lane highways. Brussels is 204 km (122 mi) from Amsterdam on E19; 222 km (138 mi) from Düsseldorf on E40; 219 km (133 mi) from Luxembourg City on E411; and 308 km (185 mi) from Paris on E19.

From Calais, the fastest route to Gent, Brugge, and Antwerp is along the coast; for Brussels either follow this route or head inland via Lille and Tournai; use the inland route for Mons, Namur, Liège, and Luxembourg.

GASOLINE

Gasoline stations are plentiful throughout Belgium. Major credit cards are widely accepted. If you pay with cash and need a receipt, ask for a *reçu* (French) or *ontvangstbewijs* (Flemish). Unleaded gas and diesel fuel are available at all stations. Costs vary between €1.50 per liter for diesel fuel and €1.55 per liter for unleaded gas, but with global oil prices spiraling these may rise. Drivers normally pump their own gas, but full service is available at a few stations. Unless you have a debit card from a Belgian bank, you must pay an attendant during open hours. On Sundays and late at night, drivers should

---

FLEMISH? FRENCH? ENGLISH?

If you're traveling outside of Brussels, be prepared to see city names in French or Flemish, depending upon whether you are in the south or the north, respectively. So, you need to know that Antwerp is Antwerpen in Flemish and Anvers in French; likewise, Bruges is Brugge in Flemish and Bruges in French; Brussels is Bruxelles in French and Brussel in Flemish; Ghent is Gent in Flemish and Gand in French. Even more confusing, Liège and Luik are the same place, as are Louvain and Leuven, and Namur and Namen. Yet more difficult is Mons (French) and Bergen (Flemish), or Tournai (French) and Doornik (Flemish). If you're heading south, remember that the nearby French city of Lille is signposted as Rijssel in Flemish areas.

---

look for a gas station on a major highway, which should be open and manned around the clock.

PARKING

With the narrow streets in many cities, on-street parking can be problematic, and often restricted to residents only. Every city center has at least one and usually several multistory parking lots. Some are pay-as-you-leave (pay at coin machines by the entry-exit); others are pay in advance and you display your ticket in your car window. Ticket machines accept all euro coins. Prices vary, but start from around €1.50 per hour.

RENTAL CARS

The major car rental firms have booths at the airports. This is convenient, but the airports charge rental companies a fee that is passed on to customers, so you may want to rent from the downtown locations of rental firms. Consider also whether you want to get off a transatlantic flight and into an unfamiliar car in an unfamiliar city.

Rental cars are European brands and range from economy, such as a Ford Ka, to luxury, such as a Mercedes. It is also possible to rent minivans. Rates in Belgium vary from company to company; daily rates for budget companies start at approximately €35 for an economy car including collision insurance. This may not include mileage, airport fee, and 21% V.A.T. tax. Weekly rates often include unlimited mileage.

It is usually less expensive to reserve your car before your departure, through your local travel agent or online. For a good deal, book through a travel agent who will shop around. Look into wholesalers, companies that do not own fleets but rent in bulk from those that do and often offer better rates than traditional car-rental operations. Prices are best during off-peak periods. Rentals booked through wholesalers often must be paid for before you leave home.

You can drive your own car or rent one in Belgium with a valid driver's license from most English-speaking countries or from other European nations. You must also produce a national identity card or passport. If in doubt that your license will be recognized outside your home country, get hold of an international driving permit (IDP), available from AAA. These international permits, valid only in conjunction with your regular license, may save you a problem with local authorities.

You must be at least 21 years old to rent cars from most agencies. Some agencies require renters to be 25.

There's usually a surcharge for adding a driver to your rental agreement. Before you pick up a car in one city and leave it in another, ask about drop-off charges or one-way service fees, which can be substantial. Also inquire about early-return policies; some rental agencies charge extra if you return the car before the time specified in your contract while others give you a refund for unused days. Most agencies note the tank's fuel level on your contract; to avoid a hefty refueling fee,

return the car with the same tank level. If the tank was full, refill it just before you turn in the car, but be aware that gas stations near rental outlets may overcharge. It's almost never a good deal to buy a tank of gas with the car when you rent it; the understanding is that you'll return it empty, but some fuel usually remains.

Rental Agencies Alamo (☎800/522-9696 ⊕www.alamo.com). **Avis** (☎800/331-1084 ⊕www.avis.be). **Budget** (☎800/472-3325 ⊕www.budget.com). **Hertz** (☎800/654-3001 ⊕www.hertz.be). **National Car Rental** (☎800/227-7368 ⊕www.nationalcar.com).

ROAD CONDITIONS

A network of well-maintained, well-lit highways (*snelweg* in Flemish, *autoroute* in French) and other roads covers Belgium, making car travel convenient. There are no tolls. Under good conditions, you should be able to travel on highways at an average of about 120 KPH (75 MPH).

Directions to the major highways are indicated on blue signs that include the number of the highway and the direction in terms of destination city rather than "north," "south," "east," or "west." On the Brussels–Liège/Luik motorway, signs change language with alarming frequency as you crisscross the Wallonia–Flanders border. *Uitrit* is Flemish for exit; the French is *sortie*.

Traffic can be heavy around the major cities, especially on the roads to southern Europe in July and August, when many Belgians begin their vacations, and on roads approaching the North Sea beaches on summer weekends. Summer road repair can also cause some traffic jams on highways and in town.

Rush hour traffic is worst from September until June. Peak rush hour traffic is 7 AM–9:30 AM and 4 PM–7:30 PM, Monday–Friday. You are most likely to encounter traffic jams as you travel into cities in the morning, out of cities in the afternoon, and on ring roads around major cities in the morning and in the afternoon. The ring road around Antwerp is notoriously busy at all times.

City driving is challenging because of chronic double parking and lack of street-side parking. Beware of trams in some cities, and of slick cobblestone streets in rainy weather.

ROADSIDE EMERGENCIES
If you break down on the highway, look for emergency telephones located at regular intervals. The emergency telephones are connected to an emergency control room that can send a tow truck. It's also possible to take out an emergency automobile insurance that covers all of your expenses in case of a breakdown on the road.

Emergency Services Europ Assistance (☎02/533–7575). **Touring Secours** (☎070/34–47–77).

RULES OF THE ROAD
Be sure to observe speed limits. On highways in Belgium, the limit is 120 KPH (75 MPH), though the cruising speed is usually about 130 KPH (about 80 MPH). The speed limit on other rural roads is 90 KPH (55 MPH), and 50 KPH (30 MPH) in urban areas. Speed limits are enforced, sometimes with hidden cameras, and speeding penalties are a hefty €65–€150. If you're stopped by the police, fines are issued on the spot, and refusal to pay may result in your vehicle being impounded.

Drivers in Belgium can be impatient with slower drivers using the left lanes, which are considered strictly for passing. For safe highway driving, go with the flow, stay in the right-hand lane unless you want to pass, and make way for faster cars wanting to pass you. If you forget this rule of the road, drivers will remind you by flashing their high beams.

Fog can be a danger on highways in late fall and winter. In such cases, it's obligatory to use your fog lights.

In cities and towns, approach pedestrian crossings with care. Stop signs are few and far between. Instead, white triangles are painted on the road of the driver who must yield. Priority is given to the driver coming from the right, and drivers in Belgium exercise that priority fervently.

Using a handheld mobile phone is illegal while driving, but you're allowed to drive while using a headset or earpiece.

Use of seatbelts is compulsory in Belgium, both in front and rear seats, and there are fines for disobeying. Turning right on a red light is not permitted.

Your car must carry a red warning triangle in case of breakdown. All cars rented in Belgium will already have these.

Drinking and driving is prohibited. Breathalyzer controls are routine on highways on weekend nights, and common throughout Belgium over holiday weekends, Christmas, and New Year's Eve. Drunk drivers are fined at least €100 and their cars are confiscated until the following day.

Illegally parked cars are ticketed, and the fines start from €15. If you park in a tow-away zone, you risk having your car towed, paying a fee of at least €100, and receiving a traffic ticket.

▌BY CRUISE SHIP

The cruise lines listed below occasionally include Antwerp or Brugge (docking in Zeebrugge) as part of a European cruise itinerary.

Cruise Lines Celebrity Cruises (☎800/647–2251 ⊕www.celebrity.com). **Cunard Line** (☎800/728–6273 ⊕www.cunard.com). **Holland America Line** (☎206/281–3535 or 877/932–4259 ⊕www.hollandamerica.com). **Silversea Cruises** (☎800/722–9955 ⊕www.silversea.com).

▌ BY FERRY

Transeuropa Ferries has services between Ramsgate, England, and Oostende, with four daily round-trips. P & O Ferries operates overnight ferry services once daily from Hull, England to Zeebrugge. Superfast Ferries also makes overnight crossings, connecting Zeebrugge and Rosyth (Edinburgh), Scotland. Both companies have fairly comfortable ferries for the crossing, and you can take your car.

To get between Belgium and southern England, you need to connect through the French ports of Dunkerque or Calais, a 30-minute drive from the Belgian border, where you can take the ferry to Dover with one of a number of ferry companies: Seafrance, Norfolk Line, and P & O Ferries.

Ferry schedules and fares fluctuate between low (winter) and high (summer) season. Travel agencies in the United Kingdom and in Belgium sell ferry tickets and provide exact fares and schedules. Five-day excursion fares are significantly less expensive than last-minute bookings. They must be booked at least seven days in advance.

Contacts Norfolk Line (☎02/719-9092, 0844/499-0007 in U.K. ⊕www.norfolkline. com). **P & O Ferries** (☎070/70-77-71, 08716/645-645 in U.K. ⊕www.poferries.com). **Seafrance** (☎02/549-0882, 0871/423-7119 in U.K. ⊕www.seafrance.com). **Superfast Ferries** (☎050/25-22-52, 01383/608-003 in U.K. ⊕www.superfast.com).**Transeuropa Ferries** (☎059/34-02-60, 01843/595-522 in U.K. ⊕www.transeuropaferries.com).

▌ BY TRAIN

The easiest mode of transportation within Belgium is train travel. Belgian National Railways (SNCB/NMBS) maintains an extensive network of prompt and frequent services. Intercity trains have rapid connections between the major towns and cities, while local and regional trains also stop at all smaller towns and villages in between. The exception is in the southeast of Belgium, particularly in the Ardennes. Tourist hubs such as La Roche-en-Ardenne are connected to the nearest rail stations only by infrequent buses. If you plan to do a lot of exploring in this region, renting a car can save you a lot of time and effort.

Domestic trains use the capital's three stations: Gare du Midi, Gare Centrale, and Gare du Nord. National service is extensive and frequent. For example, four to five trains an hour link Antwerp with Brussels; the trip takes about 45 minutes. There are several train connections every hour between the Brussels Airport and Brussels, from early morning until late evening. A few trains continue on to Gent, but for all other destinations you'll need to transfer in Brussels.

An expanding network of high-speed trains puts Brussels within commuting distance of many European cities. Eurostar trains, which leave from Brussels's Gare du Midi, take 2 hours, 20 minutes to get to London's Waterloo station. At this writing, fares were €232.75 for a fully flexible one-way economy fare and €323.50 for a fully flexible one-way first-class ticket. A number of promotional round-trip fares are available; if you book in advance and waive the right to make changes to your itinerary, rates drop as low as €80 for a return second-class fare to London, or €55 for a round-trip second-class ticket to Paris. Seat reservations are required for both Eurostar and Thalys trains.

Thalys high-speed trains to Paris, Bordeaux, Avignon, Marseille, Liège, Cologne, Aachen, Amsterdam, Rotterdam, and The Hague also leave from the Gare du Midi. a standard one-way ticket from Brussels to Paris costs about €82 in economy and €128 in first class. The trip lasts 1.3 hours. Thalys trains also run to Amsterdam and Cologne, taking around 2½ hours. A cheaper, but slower, hourly train travels between Brussels and Amsterdam, via Antwerp. The service is called the "Hi-Speed," but take this name with a grain of salt. Reservations are not required for this.

Train travel is available in first or second class. First-class seats are slightly more spacious and are upholstered. First-class passengers on Thalys trips to Paris and on Eurostar trips to London are served beverages and a complimentary light meal.

Smoking is prohibited on all trains in Belgium.

RAIL PASSES

To save money, look into rail passes. But be aware that if you don't plan to cover many miles, you may come out ahead by buying individual tickets. If you're traveling in a group of two to five people, the Belgian railway offers discounted prices for two one-way trips or one return trip. If you're under 26 years old, a Go Pass allows you 10 one-way second-class train trips to any destination in Belgium for €46. The tickets are valid for one year. If you're between 26 and 65, you can buy a Rail Pass, which is identical to a Go Pass, but more expensive: €71 in second class, or €109 in first. People over 65 should ask for a senior ticket (*seniorenbiljet* in Flemish, *billet seniors* in French), which entitles you to second-class round-trip travel anywhere in Belgium for only €4. You'll have to provide proof of age for this, and the tickets are not valid weekdays before 9 AM. There are also reduced fares for weekend trips to the Belgian seaside or the Ardennes. You can pick up a booklet of Belgian railway package excursions, *B-Excursions,* available at Belgium's major train stations.

For travel between Belgium, the Netherlands, and Luxembourg, consider the *Billet Benelux Weekend* and *Carte Benelux Tourrail,* which offer significant discounts for weekend travel and travel within one month, respectively.

Belgium is among the 20 countries in which you can use EurailPasses, which provide unlimited first-class rail travel, in all of the participating countries, for the duration of the pass. If you plan to rack up the miles, get a standard pass. These are available for 15 days ($795), 21 days ($1,029), one month ($1,279), two months ($1,809), and three months ($2,235). If your plans call for only limited train travel, look into a Eurail Select-pass, which can cost less than a EurailPass. Unlike EurailPasses, however, you get a limited number of travel days, in a limited number of adjoining countries, during a specified time period. For example, a two-month pass ($505) that includes the whole of Benelux—which in this instance counts as a single country—allows 5 days of rail travel. Whichever pass you choose, remember that you must purchase your pass before you leave for Europe.

Many travelers assume that rail passes guarantee them seats on the trains they wish to ride. Not so. You need to book seats ahead even if you are using a rail pass; seat reservations are required on some high-speed trains. You will also need a reservation if you purchase sleeping accommodations.

Major train stations have an information office for information about fares and schedules. All train stations post complete listings, by time, of arrivals and departures, including the track number. You can also get maps and timetables through the national rail line.

To avoid crowds, don't travel by train to the Belgian coast on Saturday morning or return from there on Sunday afternoon in the summer. Belgium's national holiday, July 21, also draws train travelers from Brussels to the seaside and the Ardennes.

Train tickets bought in Belgium can be paid for using currency or a major credit card—American Express, Diners Club, MasterCard, or Visa. You cannot pay for train tickets with traveler's checks, but currency exchange booths in the stations can cash your checks. For international travel, you may pay and reserve with a credit card by telephone, at the train station itself, or through a local travel agency.

Short of flying, taking the Channel Tunnel is the fastest way to cross the English Channel: 35 minutes from Folkestone to Calais, 60 minutes from motorway to motorway. The Belgian border is just a short drive northeast of Calais. High-speed Eurostar trains use the same tunnels to connect London's St. Pancras Station directly with Midi Station in Brussels in around two hours.

Reservations are obligatory on the Eurostar train to London and on the Thalys train to Paris. Reservations are not required for domestic trains.

Train Contacts **CIT Tours Corp** (☎800/248–7245 in U.S.). **DER Travel Services** (☎800/782-2424). **Eurorail** (⊕www.eurorail.com). **Eurostar** (☎02/528-2828 ⊕www.eurostar.com). **Rail Europe** (☎888/382-7245 in U.S. ⊕www.raileurope.com). **SNCB/NMBS** (☎02/528-2828 or 02/555-2525 ⊕www.b-rail.be).

Thalys (☎0900/10-177 ⊕www.thalys.be).

Channel Tunnel Car Transport **Eurotunnel** (☎0870/535-3535 in the U.K., 070/22-32-10 in Belgium, 03-21-00-61-00 in France ⊕www.eurotunnel.com).

ESSENTIALS

■ ACCOMMODATIONS

Belgium offers a range of options, from the major international hotel chains and small, modern local hotels to family-run restored inns and historic houses. Prices in metropolitan areas are significantly higher than those in outlying towns and the countryside.

Most hotels that cater to business travelers will grant substantial weekend rebates. These discounted rates are often available during the week as well as in July and August, when business travelers are thin on the ground. Moreover, you can often qualify for a "corporate rate" when hotel occupancy is low. The moral is, always ask what's the best rate a hotel can offer before you book. No hotelier was ever born who will give a lower rate unless you ask for it.

The lodgings we list are the cream of the crop in each price category. We always list the facilities that are available—but we don't specify whether they cost extra: when pricing accommodations, always ask what's included and what costs extra.

CATEGORY	COST
¢	Under €75
1	€75–€100
2	€100–€150
3	€150–€225
4	Over €225

All prices are for a standard double room in high season, based on the European Plan (EP) and including tax and service charges.

■**TIP→** Assume that hotels operate on the European Plan (EP, no meals) unless we specify that they use the Breakfast Plan (BP, with full breakfast), Continental Plan (CP, Continental breakfast), Full American Plan (FAP, all meals), Modified American Plan (MAP, breakfast and dinner) or are all-inclusive (AI, all meals and most activities).

APARTMENT & HOUSE RENTALS

If you want a home base that's roomy enough for a family and comes with cooking facilities, consider a furnished rental. These can save you money, especially if you're traveling with a group. Home-exchange directories sometimes list rentals as well as exchanges.

Apartment and villa rentals and *gîtes* (farmhouse rentals) are easy to find in popular vacation areas, such as the Belgian coast and the Ardennes countryside. Rentals from private individuals are usually for a one- or two-week minimum. Sheets and towels are not provided.

You can also rent vacation villas within Belgium's vacation parks. These self-contained parks, in rural or seaside settings, consist of residences and facilities such as swimming pools, hiking and bicycling trails, restaurants, and activities for children. There is usually a one-week minimum, although it's often possible to rent for shorter periods during the winter months.

Listings with photos and details of local vacation parks and vacation villa rentals are available from the national tourism office of Belgium. Listings of local rental agents are also available at local tourist information centers at seaside towns along the Belgian coast. Local rentals by individuals in Belgium can be found in the classified section of French-language *Le Soir* and Flemish *De Morgen* daily newspapers or in *Vlan* weekly.

Contacts Forgetaway (⊕ www.forgetaway. weather.com). **Home Away** (☎ 512/493–0382 ⊕ www.homeaway.com). **Interhome** (☎ 800/882–6864 ⊕ www.interhome.us). **Villas International** (☎ 800/221–2260 ⊕ www. villasintl.com).

Local Agents Gîtes de Wallonie (☎081/31–18-00 ⊕www.gitesdewallonie.be). **Hoeve-en Plattelandstoerisme in Vlaanderen (Farm and Country Tourism in Flanders)** (☎016/28-60-35 ⊕www.hoevetoerisme.be). **Vacation Villas** (⊕www.vacationvillas.net).

BED & BREAKFASTS

Bed-and-breakfast accommodations (*chambres d'hôtes* in French or *gastenkamers* in Flemish) are less common in Belgium than in Great Britain or the United States; the ones you do find usually need to be reserved in advance. Most are in rural or residential areas. Although clean, B&Bs are very simple, often without private bathrooms.

Listings are available at local tourist information centers, but you must make your own reservations directly with the proprietor. *Taxistop,* a company that promotes inexpensive lodging and travel deals, sells a B&B guide to Belgium and makes reservations.

Reservation Services Taxistop (☎070/22-22-92 ⊕www.taxistop.be).

HOME EXCHANGES

If you want to swap homes with a Belgian family for a week or two, it can be organized via Taxistop. Taxistop is the local operator for HomeLink International, the world's largest home exchange organization.

Exchange Clubs HomeLink International (☎800/638-3841 ⊕www.homelink.org). **Taxistop** (☎070/22-22-92 ⊕www.taxistop.be).

HOSTELS

Hostels in Belgium are well organized and clean. Rooms with 1–10 beds are available and hostels are suitable for family stays. Many are near train stations. The Auberges de Jeunesse and Vlaamse Jeugdherbergen associations are affiliated with the International Youth Hostel Federation.

Contacts Auberges de Jeunesse de la Belgique Francophone (☎02/219-5676 ⊕www.laj.be). **Hostelling International—**

USA (☎301/495–1240 ⊕www.hiusa.org). **Vlaamse Jeugdherbergen** (☎03/232-7218 ⊕www.vjh.be).

HOTELS

Hotels in Belgium are rated by the Benelux Hotel Classification System, an independent agency that inspects properties in Belgium, the Netherlands, and Luxembourg. The organization's star system is the accepted norm for these countries; one star indicates the most basic hotel and five stars indicates the most luxurious. You'll find star rankings posted at hotel entrances or at check-in desks. Stars are based on detailed criteria—mainly facilities and amenities, such as private baths, specific items of furniture in guest rooms, and so on. Rooms in one-star hotels are likely not to have a telephone or television, and two-star hotels may not have air-conditioning, or elevators. Four- and five-star hotels have conference facilities and offer amenities such as pools, tennis courts, saunas, private parking, dry-cleaning service, and room service. Three-, four-, and five-star hotels are usually equipped with hair dryers and coffeemakers.

All hotels listed have private bath unless otherwise noted. Single rooms in one-to three-star hotels often have a shower (*douche* in French and Flemish) rather than a bathtub (*bain* in French, *bad* or *ligbad* in Flemish). A double room includes either one double bed (*lit double* in French, *tweepersoonsbed* in Flemish) or two single beds. A single room includes one single bed (*lit simple* in French or *eenpersoonsbed* in Flemish). Three people who wish to room together should ask about the possibility of adding a small bed in a double room. Rooms that accommodate four people are rare, except in five-star hotels.

Taking meals at a hotel's restaurant usually provides you with a discount. Some restaurants, especially country inns, require that guests take half board (*demi-pension* in French, *half-pension* in Flemish), at least lunch or dinner, at the hotel. Full pension (*pension complet* in French, *volledig pension* in Flemish) entitles guests to both lunch and dinner. Guests taking either half or full board also receive breakfast. If you take a *pension,* you pay per person, regardless of the number of rooms. If you are not taking half or full pension, ask if breakfast is included in the price of the room.

It's wise to reserve your hotel in advance. Rooms fill up quickly at the Belgian coast and in the Ardennes in July and August, during the period around Easter, and on May 1. Throughout the year conventions can fill up business hotels in Brussels.

You may reserve your room by telephoning or writing in English, as all hoteliers and reservations services in Belgium understand the language, and increasingly online via the hotel's own Web site. Be specific about your wishes or requirements. If you reserve a double room, be sure to specify whether you want two single beds or one double bed. Inquire about possibilities for more than two people in one room. Specify if you want a room with a bathtub, shower, or both. Ask if breakfast is included and specify if you wish to take half or full board. If you are traveling in summer, ask if the property is air-conditioned. If you're arriving by car, inquire about parking facilities. If the hotel is in a city, consider asking for a high floor or a room away from the street in order to avoid noise.

Hotels prefer that you confirm your reservation by fax or e-mail. If you are having an extended stay, the property commonly asks for a deposit either in the local currency or billed to your credit card.

Among the reservations services in Belgium are Belsud, which can arrange self-catering accommodations and B&Bs in Brussels and Wallonia, and Toerisme Stad Antwerpen, which makes hotel and B&B reservations in Antwerp and Flanders.

Contacts Belsud Réservation (☎070/22–10–70 ⊕www.belsud.com). **Toerisme Stad Antwerpen** (☎03/232–0103 ⊕www.antwerpen.be).

▌COMMUNICATIONS

INTERNET

If you're traveling with a laptop, take a spare battery and an electrical-plug adapter with you, as new batteries and replacement adapters are expensive and not all brands are available in Belgium. Almost all hotels are equipped with jacks for computers with Internet connections and many also have Wi-Fi hot spots. Sometimes these services are offered free; or a fee may be charged. You can find cybercafés in most major cities. Apple computers are uncommon in Belgium, so finding assistance for a Mac-related problem is difficult.

Contacts Cybercafes (⊕www.cybercafes.com) lists over 4,000 Internet cafés worldwide.

PHONES

The good news is that you can now make a direct-dial telephone call from virtually any point on earth. The bad news? You can't always do so cheaply. Calling from a hotel is almost always the most expensive option; hotels usually add huge surcharges to all calls, particularly international ones. In some countries you can phone from call centers or even the post office. Calling cards usually keep costs to a minimum, but only if you purchase them locally. And then there are mobile

LOCAL DO'S & TABOOS

GREETINGS
Belgians greet friends and family with three superficial kisses—right cheek, left cheek, right cheek. Less intimate greetings are made with a handshake.

SIGHTSEEING
Observe common-sense dress rules when sightseeing—don't wear beach clothes to a house of worship for example—and you won't cause offense. Food and drinks are generally not allowed in museums. There are laws about jaywalking, but these are widely ignored. Belgians have some of the worst driving habits in Europe, so take care of other road users, both when behind the wheel, and as a pedestrian. You may see a fair number of beggars on the streets, particularly in Brussels. Follow your own conscience here, but most people do not give them money.

OUT ON THE TOWN
If you're invited to a home, bring a gift; flowers and a box of pralines or a bottle of wine are appropriate gifts. If the host has young children, offer a small toy or book. You should arrive about 10 minutes late, to allow your host time for last-minute preparations. With before-dinner drinks, allow your host to serve you, rather than helping yourself. During the meal, keep both hands above the table.

DOING BUSINESS
It's acceptable to arrive up to 10 minutes late for business appointments. Even so, expect a short wait once you've been announced. Exchange business cards as introductions are made. Shake hands and use last names. The pace of business meetings is more relaxed than in the United States, so don't rush into business too promptly; instead spend a few minutes chatting about weather or travel. If you've met your associate's family previously, ask about them.

Business lunches are far more popular than breakfast meetings. If you initiate the lunch, you're expected to select the wine and pay for the meal. If you're unfamiliar with restaurants, menus, or wines, ask your guest to make suggestions. Allow yourself and your guest to order and enjoy the meal, conversing about neutral topics such as vacations or the food itself before engaging in business. Leave your props and handouts in your briefcase until after the meal.

LANGUAGE
Belgium has three official languages: Flemish, French, and German (spoken by a small minority). There are four language regions: Flanders (Flemish), Brussels (bilingual), Wallonia (French), and the scant eastern sections (German). The vehement allegiances of the French- and Flemish-speakers to their respective languages date back to the mid-19th century. Soon after Belgium won its independence from Holland, a revival of the Flemish language was met with the imposition of French as the official language. Linguistic hostilities continued for more than a century; distinct linguistic regions were fixed only in the mid-20th century.

Regional languages are taken very seriously. Many Flemish-speaking Belgians understand French, but the reverse is often not the case and emotions may run high if you make that assumption. Fortunately, most Belgians are capable and more than willing to speak English, especially to anglophones. So, speak the language of the region if you know it, or use English. Written Flemish has been standardized and follows the same grammatical rules as neighboring Dutch, but the spoken language has regional flavors and accents that differ from city to city, and even from hamlet to hamlet. The same applies to the French spoken in the southern part of the country, which is why francophone Belgians are often the butt of French jokes. Except in bilingual Brussels, street and road signs only appear in one language, so make sure to keep the translations handy.

phones (⇨*below*), which are sometimes more prevalent—particularly in the developing world—than landlines; as expensive as mobile phone calls can be, they are still usually a much cheaper option than calling from your hotel.

In Belgium, phone numbers have nine digits: either a six-digit local number preceded by a three-digit area code, or a seven-digit local number preceded by a two-digit area code. The dial tone is a constant flutelike sound.

The country code (used when calling from abroad) for Belgium is 32; the country code for the United States is 1. In Belgium, the two- or three-digit area code (called a city code when applied to metropolitan areas) will always begin with zero; the zero is dropped when calling Belgium from abroad. The city code for Brussels is 02; for Antwerp, 03; for Liège, 04; for Gent, 09; and for Brugge, 050.

Toll-free numbers begin with 0800. Premium rate calls begin with 0900.

CALLING WITHIN BELGIUM

All calls within the country must include the regional telephone code.

Unlike in the United States, the cost of local calls in Belgium increases depending upon the duration of the call.

If you're making a call from city to city within Belgium, the number you dial will have a total of nine digits, either a two-digit area code and a seven-digit local number or a three-digit area code and a six-digit local number.

Avoid making lengthy long-distance telephone calls directly from your hotel room, as hefty surplus charges are added. Instead use a phone card or use a long-distance provider.

Public pay phones are easy to find, but require a phone card or credit card. After the dial tone, insert either your phone or credit card, then dial.

For English-language telephone assistance, dial 1405.

CALLING OUTSIDE BELGIUM

For international calls, dial 00, followed by the country code, followed by the area code and telephone number.

Access Codes AT&T Direct (☎0800/100–10 in Belgium, 800/435–0812 other areas). **MCI WorldPhone** (☎0800/100–12 in Belgium, 800/444–4141 other areas). **Sprint International Access** (☎0800/100–14 Belgium, 800/877–7746 other areas).

CALLING CARDS

Coin-operated public telephones in Belgium have been replaced by card-operated phones. Telephone cards (*télécarte* in French, *telefoonkaart* in Flemish) good for both domestic and international calls, are sold at post offices, newspaper stands, and many train stations. The minimum card costs €5.

MOBILE PHONES

Cell phones are called GSMs, or mobiles. British standard cell phones work in Belgium, but American and Canadian standard (nonsatellite or non-GSM) cell phones do not. If you'd like to rent a cell phone while traveling, reserve one at least four days before your trip, as most companies will ship it to you before you travel. CellularAbroad rents cell phones packaged with prepaid SIM cards that give you a Belgian cell phone number and calling rates. Planetfone rents GSM phones, which can be used in more than 100 countries. The Belgian company Locaphone has offices in the Brussels airport where you can pick up or drop off rental phones; it rents GSM phones and satellite phones. Cell phone telephone numbers are preceded by 0475, 0477, 0495, or 0497, followed by six digits.

Contacts CellularAbroad (☎800/287–5072 ⊕www.cellularabroad.com). **Locaphone** (☎32/2/652–1414 ⊕www.locaphone.be). **Planetfone** (☎888/988–4777 ⊕www. planetfone.com).

■ CUSTOMS & DUTIES

Americans and other non-EU members are allowed to bring in no more than 200 cigarettes, 50 cigars, 1 liter of spirits, 2 liters of wine or sparkling wine, 50 grams of perfume, and .25 liters of toilet water. EU members may bring in 800 cigarettes; 200 cigars; 10 liters of spirits; 90 liters of wine, of which 60 liters may be sparkling wine; 50 grams of perfume; and .25 liters of eau de toilette.

Information in Belgium Brussels Airport Customs Office (☎02/753–2910).

U.S. Information U.S. Customs and Border Protection (⊕www.cbp.gov).

■ EATING OUT

Belgium's better restaurants are on a par with the most renowned in the world. Prices are similar to those in France and Great Britain. The Belgian emphasis on high-quality food filters down to more casual options as well, from main-square cafés to the street vendors you'll find in towns large and small. The restaurants we list in this book are the cream of the crop in each price category.

Most restaurants are open for lunch and dinner only. Restaurants and hotel pension packages serve hot three-course meals including a starter or soup, a main course, and dessert. A set-price, three-course menu for lunch (*déjeuner* in French, *lunch* in Flemish) is offered in many restaurants. Dinner (*dîner* in French, *diner* in Flemish) menus are very similar to lunch menus. Diners aren't commonly given a choice of vegetables or salad.

Some large hotels serve buffet breakfast (*petit déjeuner* in French, *ontbijt* in Flemish) with cooked American fare. Smaller hotels and bed-and-breakfasts serve bread, rolls, butter, jam, and cheese with juice and coffee or tea and occasionally a hard-boiled egg.

Cafés and snack bars are open in the morning and serve coffee, tea, juice, and rolls, but don't serve a full American-style breakfast. You can also order a quick sandwich lunch or a light one-course meal at cafés, pubs, cafeterias, and snack bars.

Smoking in Belgian cafés and restaurants is prohibited. However, some bars above a certain size, and with adequate ventilation, have an exemption from this ruling.

MEALS & MEALTIMES

Most of Belgium's restaurants show a marked French influence on their menus. But there are also many specialties that are distinctively Belgian. Steamed North Sea mussels is what pops into most people's minds when they think of Belgian cuisine; they're served throughout the country. A longstanding Flemish dish, now popping up on menus throughout the country, is *waterzooi*, a creamy stew made with chicken, rabbit, or fish. *Carbonnades* or *stoverij*, a beef stew cooked in beer, also shows up in all regions. *Stoemp* is a filling mixture of mashed potatoes and vegetables. Eel is another Flemish specialty; the firm white flesh is often smoked or served in a cream-based sauce, and most notably as *paling in 't groen* (Flemish) or *anguilles au vert* (French), with a green herb sauce. Belgian endive (*chicons* in French, *witloof* in Flemish) is usually cooked with ham, braised, and topped with a cheese gratin. A popular first course is tomato filled with tiny gray shrimp (*crevettes grises* in French, *grijze garnaaltjes* in Flemish), fresh from the North Sea. During fall hunting season, restaurants and inns in the countryside turn out special game dishes with *sanglier* or *everzwijn* (wild boar) and *faisan* or *fazant* (pheasant). Complete your meal with *frites* or *frieten* (french fries), which Belgians proudly claim to have been invented not in France but in Belgium. The secret to Belgian fries is that they are fried twice—

usually in animal fat, so they don't always meet vegetarian standards.

Belgium produces several noteworthy cheeses; some of the best are handmade in monasteries, such as Maredsous.

Throughout Belgium, roadside french fry stands (*friterie* in French or *frituur* in Flemish) offer servings of french fries with a selection of condiments. Another favorite snack is the famous Belgian waffle (*gaufres* in French, *wafels* in Flemish), which you can buy at waffle stands in cities. Waffles here are a dessert, not a breakfast food. There is a distinct difference between the waffles sold at waffle stands, often called *gaufres liègeoises* after Liège, their city of origin, and those that are sold in cafés and tea salons. The former are usually very sweet and more substantial while the latter are lighter and fluffier, and topped with powdered sugar and a dollop of whipped cream. Other popular sweets include macaroons, *speculoos* (ginger cookies), and fruit tarts. It's a point of pride that classic Belgian dessert recipes haven't changed for centuries. *For details on Belgian chocolate, see "Chocolate Country" in Chapter 3.*

Breakfast is served in hotels from about 7 to 10. Lunch is served in restaurants noon–2, and dinner 7–9. Pubs and cafés often serve snacks until midnight. Many restaurants are closed Sunday for dinner, and restaurants in cities often close Saturday for lunch.

Unless otherwise noted, the restaurants listed in this guide are open daily for lunch and dinner.

PAYING

Major credit cards are accepted in most restaurants. Visa and MasterCard are the most widely accepted credit cards. Smaller establishments often don't accept American Express or especially Diners Club, because of high commission charges, and some pubs and cafés won't accept credit cards at all. Don't rely on traveler's checks for paying restaurant bills.

Tipping 15% of the cost of a meal is not common practice in Belgium. Nonetheless, it is customary to round off the total, adding a small amount for good service.

For guidelines on tipping see Tipping below.

CATEGORY	COST
¢	Under €10
1	€10–€15
2	€15–€20
3	€20–€30
4	Over €30

All prices are per person in € for a main course at dinner including 21% tax and service.

RESERVATIONS & DRESS

Regardless of where you are, it's a good idea to make a reservation if you can. We only mention them specifically when reservations are essential (there's no other way you'll ever get a table) or when they are not accepted. For popular restaurants, book as far ahead as you can (often 30 days or more), and reconfirm as soon as you arrive. (Large parties should always call ahead to check the reservations policy.) We mention dress only when men are required to wear a jacket or a jacket and tie.

Belgians tend to favor crisp but relatively casual dress when dining out; men in button-down shirts are more common than a dining room full of suits. When in doubt, check ahead with the restaurant in question.

WINES, BEER & SPIRITS

Belgium is a beer-lover's paradise. Artisanal breweries produce around 800 types of beer, many of which are offered in Belgian pubs and cafés. Kriek, a fruit-flavored beer, and Duvel, a very strong blond beer, are Belgian favorites. Some of Belgium's Trappist monasteries still produce their own brews, such as Orval, Westmalle, Rochefort, and Chimay (⇨ *See Chapter 1, Belgian Beer*). Popular mass-produced brands are Stella Artois, Jupiler, and Maes.

Keep in mind that many Belgian beers have a high alcohol content; 8%–9% alcohol per volume is not unusual. (Conventional beers have a 5%–6% alcohol content.) Different types of beer are served in different kinds of glasses; each shape is geared to best showcase a certain brew's particular characteristics. Here's a tip about sedimented beer: while the sediment is drinkable, it isn't usually poured into the glass. Inexperienced staff in nonspecialist beer bars are not always aware of this, and may try to empty the entire bottle into your glass. If in doubt, it's perfectly acceptable to ask to pour the beer yourself.

Licenses are not required for sale of beer or wine in dining establishments. As a result, beer is served at virtually all restaurants, snack bars, pubs, and cafés, and wine is served at all restaurants and most other establishments. There is no legal minimum age for consumption of beer or wine. Sale of hard liquor does require a license, and the legal age for consumption of liquor is 18. The cost of beer and wine in dining establishments is very reasonable. Liquor and mixed cocktails are considerably more expensive.

Be sure to try locally produced *genièvre* or *jenever*, a strong, ginlike spirit taken neat. Sometimes its edge is taken off with sweeter fruit flavors like apple, lemon, and red currant. In some bars, bartenders fill the small glass to the brim, so that only surface tension keeps it from overflowing. Faced with such a delicate balance, you have to lean over and take the first sip from the bar, rather than pick up the glass.

Belgians tend not to drink their own tap water. It's perfectly safe to do so, but water aficionados don't like the taste. If you decide to follow their lead, the locally produced Spa mineral water brands

WORD OF MOUTH

Was the service stellar or not up to snuff? Did the food give you shivers of delight or leave you cold? Did the prices and portions make you happy or sad? Rate restaurants and write your own reviews in Travel Ratings or start a discussion about your favorite places in Travel Talk on www.fodors.com. Your comments might even appear in our books. Yes, you too can be a correspondent!

are an excellent and reasonably priced alternative.

■ ELECTRICITY

The electrical current in Belgium is 220 volts, 50 cycles alternating current (AC); wall outlets take Continental-type plugs, with two round prongs. Grounded plugs have the same configuration as those in France, with an extra pin. This means you will need an adapter even if using appliances from neighboring Germany and the Netherlands, for example. Nongrounded plug sockets are compatible.

Consider making a small investment in a universal adapter, which has several types of plugs in one lightweight, compact unit. Most laptops and mobile phone chargers are dual voltage (i.e., they operate equally well on 110 and 220 volts), so require only an adapter. These days the same is true of small appliances such as hair dryers. Always check labels and manufacturer instructions to be sure. Don't use 110-volt outlets marked FOR SHAVERS ONLY for high-wattage appliances such as hair dryers.

Contacts Steve Kropla's Help for World Travelers (⊕ www.kropla.com) has information on electrical and telephone plugs around the world. Walkabout Travel Gear (⊕ www.walkabouttravelgear.com) has a good coverage of electricity under "adapters."

■ EMERGENCIES

In case of medical emergencies, call an ambulance, which will take you to the nearest hospital or clinic's emergency center. Ambulance personnel and police are very cooperative and can speak some English. If you call from a public phone, these hotline calls are free. The Community Help Service operates an English-speaking help line, which provides professional counseling services to the English-speaking community in Belgium.

Foreign Embassies United States Embassy to Belgium (⊠ Blvd. du Régent 25–27, Brussels ☎ 32/2–508–2111 ⊕ belgium. usembassy.gov).

General Emergency Contacts Police (☎ 101). **Medical emergencies, fire, accidents, ambulance** (☎ 100). **Poison control** (☎ 070/24–52–45). **English-speaking help line** (☎ 02/648–4014).

■ HEALTH

Beligum is relatively disease-free and you are unlikely to encounter problems. If you do, the Belgian health service is regarded by many as the best in the world, so you'll be in safe hands.

MEDICAL INSURANCE

Consider buying trip insurance with medical-only coverage. Neither Medicare nor some private insurers cover medical expenses anywhere outside of the United States. Medical-only policies typically reimburse you for medical care (excluding that related to pre-existing conditions) and hospitalization abroad, and provide for evacuation. You still have to pay the bills and await reimbursement from the insurer, though.

Another option is to sign up with a medical-evacuation assistance company. A membership in one of these companies gets you doctor referrals, emergency evacuation or repatriation, 24-hour hotlines for medical consultation, and other assistance. International SOS Assistance Emergency and AirMed International provide evacuation services and medical referrals. MedjetAssist offers medical evacuation.

Medical Assitance Companies AirMed International (⊕ www.airmed.com). **International SOS Assistance Emergency** (⊕ www. intos.com). **MedjetAssist** (⊕ www.medjetassist.com).

Medical-Only Insurers International medical Group (⊕ www.imglobal.com). **International SOS** (⊕ www.internationalsos.com). **Wallach & Company** (⊕ www.wallach.com).

OVER-THE-COUNTER REMEDIES

For diarrhea or intestinal problems, Ercéfuryl is very effective and is sold in capsules or liquid without prescription in pharmacies. For indigestion, Rennie tablets are also sold without prescription in pharmacies. Aspirin (*aspirine* in both French and Flemish) and vitamins (*vitamine* in both French and Flemish) are sold only in pharmacies.

SPECIFIC ISSUES IN BELGIUM

English-speaking medical help is easy to find in Belgium. Most doctors have a basic English vocabulary and are familiar with English medical terms.

Pharmacies (*pharmacie* in French, *apotheek* in Flemish) are clearly identified by a green cross displayed over the storefront.

Belgium is relatively insect-free. Nonetheless, country rivers and canals attract mosquitoes in the summertime. Air-conditioning is rare and screens are not used, so if you sleep with open windows, turn off lights, which attract mosquitoes. For reasons unknown, there seem to be more mosquitoes in Antwerp than in other cities.

Belgians are not disciplined in curbing their dogs, so beware of droppings, particularly if you're walking in a residential area or near a park or a cemetery. Dogs are permitted in restaurants. They are not permitted in supermarkets.

■ HOURS OF OPERATION

Banks in Belgium are open weekdays 9–4. Some branches are also open Saturday 9–noon. Smaller branches close between noon and 2. Office hours are generally weekdays from 9 until 5:30. Some offices close for lunch between 12:30 and 2, although post offices do not. Government offices are open weekdays from 9 until 5.

Gas stations are generally open from 7 AM until 7 PM. In small villages, gas stations often close on Sunday and for lunch from 12:30 until 2. Gas stations on highways don't close for lunch and are usually open until midnight.

Most museums in Belgium are closed on Monday, Christmas Day, New Year's Day, Labor Day (May 1), All Saints' Day (Nov. 1), and Armistice Day (Nov. 11). Museum hours are generally from 10 until 5. Many museums stop admitting visitors after 4:15 PM or so. National museums stay open during lunchtime. Smaller private museums may close between 12:30 and 2.

Most pharmacies are open until 7 on weekdays and are closed on weekends. For urgent prescriptions, closed pharmacies post signs indicating the nearest open pharmacies (*pharmaciens de garde* in French or *dienstdoende apothekers* in Flemish). In cities where security is a problem, rather than keep the entire shop open, pharmacists use a small window for filling prescriptions at night.

Except for stores in tourist areas, bakeries, and some delicatessens and flower shops, all shops are closed on Sunday. The rest of the week, shops are open 10–6. Small neighborhood shops often close for lunch between 1 and 2. Bakeries, delicatessens, and other small grocery stores remain open until 7. Supermarkets are open 9–8, and the larger ones remain open until 9 on Friday. Duty-free shops at Brussels Airport are open daily 6 AM–9 PM. "Night" shops, for newspapers, tobacco, drinks, and limited grocery items, are open seven days a week 6 PM–dawn. These *magasins de nuit* (in French) or *nachtwinkels* (in Flemish) are in all major cities and tourist destinations.

HOLIDAYS

All government and post offices, banks, and most shops are closed on Belgium's national day, July 21. Businesses are also closed on Easter Monday, Labor Day (May 1), the Ascension (May), Pentecost (June), the Assumption (Aug. 15), All Saints' Day (Nov. 1), Armistice Day (Nov. 11), Christmas Day, and New Year's Day. If a holiday falls on a weekend, offices sometimes close the preceding Friday or following Monday, but this isn't universal.

■ MAIL

A post office is known as a *bureau de poste* (in French) or *postkantoor* (in Flemish). The central post office, near Brussels Midi Station, is open weekdays from 7 AM until 7 PM, and Saturday from 10 AM until 3 PM, from September to June. In July and August it remains open until 10 PM Monday to Saturday, and is open Sunday from 11 AM until 7 PM.

Most other post offices are open on weekdays 9–5.

From Belgium, first-class (airmail) letters and postcards to the United States cost €0.90. Airmail letters and postcards to the United Kingdom cost €0.80.

Your hotel is the best address to use for having shipments sent to you. The address should include your name and the date of your arrival at the hotel. Be sure that customs formalities are in order. Advise your hotel in advance if you expect to receive mail or deliveries that require a signature upon receipt.

Post Office Central Post Office (✉ Av. Fonsny 1, Brussels). **Centre Monnaie** (✉ Pl. de la Monnaie, Lower Town, Brussels ☎ 02/226–2111).

ADDRESSES

Addresses in Belgium are segregated by language throughout the country; they hew to the official language of each destination. The only place where the street names are in both French and Flemish is the officially bilingual capital, Brussels. In some Flemish cities where francophone history still lingers, such as Gent and Antwerp, elderly people may refer to places in French, but street signs are only in Flemish.

Addresses are written with the street name first, followed by the number. Some common terms include: for street, *straat* in Flemish and *rue* in French; for square, *plein* or *place*. *Laan* or *avenue* means avenue as does *dreef* or *drève*. *Grote markt* or *grand place* indicates a market square, usually at the historic center of town.

SHIPPING PACKAGES

Express delivery services are available in major cities throughout Belgium. Deliveries can be made to the United Kingdom in one day, to the United States in one or two days, and to Australia and New Zealand in two to three days. There are no drop-off boxes; however, pickup service from major cities is prompt and efficient. Cost for sending a document express to the United States is about €100.

For your convenience, ask shops about shipping purchases back home. Neuhaus chocolate shops, for example, often provide this service for a minimal surcharge.

Express Services DHL (☎02/715–5050 ⊕www.dhl.be). **FedEx** (☎0800/135–55 or 02/752–7111 ⊕www.fedex.com).

▌ MONEY

Costs in Brussels are roughly on a par with those in London and New York; Antwerp and other major tourist centers are nearly as dear. Less-traveled areas are significantly less expensive. All taxes and service charges (tips) are included in hotel and restaurant bills and taxi fares.

Gasoline prices are steep, but highways are toll-free.

Prices throughout this guide are given for adults. Substantially reduced fees are almost always available for children, students, and senior citizens. *For information on taxes, see Taxes below.*

ITEM	AVERAGE COST
Cup of Coffee	€1.50–€2
Glass of Wine	about €2.50
Glass of Beer	€2–€3
Baguette	€1.25
single bus/ metro/tram ride	€1.20–€2
Theater Ticket	about €25

▌TIP➜ Banks never have every foreign currency on hand, and it may take as long as a week to order. If you're planning to exchange funds before leaving home, don't wait till the last minute.

ATMS & BANKS

ATMs (*distributeur automatique* in French, *geldautomaat* in Flemish) are in banks throughout Belgium, either inside the bank itself or on the facade of the bank building. They are accessible 24 hours a day, seven days per week, but are occasionally guarded and inaccessible, usually for about an hour, when cash is being transferred from the machines. The distributors themselves determine with which networks they work. For example, BBL works with Maestro, Fortis also works with Maestro and Cirrus, and CGER-ASLK works with Maestro, Cirrus, and Plus. To be sure, inquire at your home bank about use of its network in Belgium.

CREDIT CARDS

Throughout this guide, the following abbreviations are used: **AE,** American Express; **DC,** Diners Club; **MC,** Master-Card; and **V,** Visa.

It's a good idea to inform your credit-card company before you travel, especially if you're going abroad and don't travel internationally very often. Otherwise, the credit-card company might put a hold on your card owing to unusual activity—not a good thing halfway through your trip. Record all your credit-card numbers—as well as the phone numbers to call if your cards are lost or stolen—in a safe place, so you're prepared should something go wrong. Both MasterCard and Visa have general numbers you can call (collect if you're abroad) if your card is lost, but you're better off calling the number of your issuing bank, since MasterCard and Visa usually just transfer you to your bank; your bank's number is usually printed on your card.

If you plan to use your credit card for cash advances, you'll need to apply for a PIN at least two weeks before your trip. Although it's usually cheaper (and safer) to use a credit card abroad for large purchases (so you can cancel payments or be reimbursed if there's a problem), note that some credit-card companies *and* the banks that issue them add substantial percentages to all foreign transactions, whether they're in a foreign currency or not. Check on these fees before leaving home, so there won't be any surprises when you get the bill.

■ TIP ➡ Before you charge something, ask the merchant whether or not he or she plans to do a dynamic currency conversion (DCC). In such a transaction the credit-card *processor* (shop, restaurant, or hotel, not Visa or MasterCard) converts the currency and charges you in dollars. In most cases you'll pay the merchant a 3% fee for this service in addition to any credit-card company and issuing-bank foreign-transaction surcharges.

Dynamic currency conversion programs are becoming increasingly widespread. Merchants who participate in them are supposed to ask whether you want to be charged in dollars or the local currency,

but they don't always do so. And even if they do offer you a choice, they may well avoid mentioning the additional surcharges. The good news is that you *do* have a choice. And if this practice really gets your goat, you can avoid it entirely thanks to American Express; with its cards, DCC simply isn't an option.

Major credit cards are accepted in most hotels, gas stations, and restaurants in Belgium. Smaller establishments, shops, and supermarkets often accept Visa cards only.

Reporting Lost Cards American Express (☎02/676–2121). **Diners Club** (☎02/626–5004). **MasterCard** (☎070/34–43–44). **Visa** (☎0800/183–97).

CURRENCY & EXCHANGE

With Brussels proud of its status as the honorary capital of Europe, it came as no surprise that Belgium was in the first wave of countries adopting the euro as their national currency in 2002. Belgian francs have been withdrawn from circulation, but if you have any old franc notes lurking in a drawer from a previous visit, you can exchange them for euros, for an indefinite period, at branches of the Banque Nationale. Franc coins, however, can no longer be exchanged. The euro comes in bills of 5, 10, 20, 50, 100, 200, and 500. Coins come in 1, 2, 5, 10, 20, and 50 cents, and 1 and 2 euro. At press time the exchange rate was US$1.58 to €1.

Currency exchange booths are widely available throughout the large cities in Belgium, at major train stations, and at major tourist destinations. There is a surcharge for each transaction, regardless of the amount exchanged.

■ TIP ➡ Even if a currency-exchange booth has a sign promising no commission, rest assured that there's some kind of huge, hidden fee. (Oh . . . that's right. The sign didn't say no *fee*.). And as for rates, you're almost always better off getting foreign currency at an ATM or exchanging money at a bank.

Currency Conversion Google (⊕www. google.com).**Oanda.com** (⊕www.oanda.com). **XE.com** (⊕www.xe.com).

▌ PACKING

The best advice for a trip to Belgium in any season is to pack light, be flexible, bring an umbrella (and trench coat with a liner in winter), and always have a sweater or jacket available. For daytime wear and casual evenings, turtlenecks and flannel shirts are ideal for winter, alone or under a sweater, and cotton shirts with sleeves are perfect in summer. Blue jeans are popular and are even sometimes worn to the office; sweat suits, however, are never seen outside fitness centers. For women, high heels are nothing but trouble on the cobblestone streets of Brussels and other old cities, and sneakers or running shoes are a dead giveaway that you are an American tourist; a better choice is a pair of dark-color walking shoes or low-heeled pumps.

Women here wear skirts more frequently than do women in the United States, especially those over 35. Men need include a jacket and tie only if you're planning to visit one of the upper-echelon restaurants.

In your carry-on luggage, pack an extra pair of eyeglasses or contact lenses and enough of any medication you take to last a few days longer than the entire trip. You may also ask your doctor to write a spare prescription using the drug's generic name, as brand names may vary from country to country. In luggage to be checked, never pack prescription drugs, valuables, or undeveloped film.

To avoid customs and security delays, carry medications in their original packaging. Don't pack any sharp objects in your carry-on luggage, including knives of any size or material, scissors, nail clippers, and corkscrews, or anything else that might arouse suspicion.

To avoid having your checked luggage chosen for hand inspection, don't cram bags full. The U.S. Transportation Security Administration suggests packing shoes on top and placing personal items you don't want touched in clear plastic bags.

▌ PASSPORTS & VISAS

When traveling internationally, carry your passport even if you don't need one, for example if traveling between Belgium and other countries within the European Schengen agreement (which includes the Netherlands, France, and Germany, but not the United Kingdom). Not only is it the best form of ID, but it's also being required more and more. You will often have to show a passport when checking into a hotel, for example.

All U.S. citizens, even infants, need a valid passport to enter Belgium for stays of up to 90 days.

U.S. Passport Information U.S. Department of State (☎877/487–2778 ⊕http://travel. state.gov/passport).

U.S. Passport & Visa Expediters A. **Briggs Passport & Visa Expeditors** (☎800/806–0581 or 202/338–0111 ⊕www. abriggs.com).**American Passport Express** (☎800/455–5166 or 800/841–6778 ⊕www. americanpassport.com).**Passport Express** (☎800/362–8196 ⊕www.passport express.com).**Travel Document Systems** (☎800/874–5100 or 202/638–3800 ⊕www. traveldocs.com).**Travel the World Visas** (☎866/886–8472 or 301/495–7700 ⊕www. world-visa.com).

▌ RESTROOMS

Carry some small change with you if you get caught short in Belgium. Public restrooms (*toilettes* in French, *toiletten* in Flemish, but also referred to as *WC*) in train stations, tourist spots, beaches, and highway restaurants are frequently manned by attendants, who will charge you about €0.30–€0.50 per visit, and will scowl menacingly at you if you ask them to change a large note. Pay on the way out. Nevertheless, thanks to the attendant, these restrooms are always clean and equipped with toilet paper. Similarly, some cafés, restaurants, and theaters also hire attendants who charge even patrons per visit.

Other restrooms in cafés and pubs are free to patrons. Therefore, even if your visit is expressly to use the restroom, you are expected to buy a drink. If you don't have the time or inclination to drink, ask first—they're required by law to allow you to use their facilities. A few older cafés and bars may only have one unisex restroom. Women shouldn't be surprised to find a urinal, possibly in use, beside the washbasin in such establishments.

Gas stations along highways usually have a unisex restroom. For access you need not buy gas, just ask the gas station attendant for the key. Unattended restrooms are often not up to the same standards as those manned by attendants, so take tissues with you.

Find a Loo The Bathroom Diaries (⊕www. thebathroomdiaries.com) is flush with unsanitized info on restrooms the world over—each one located, reviewed, and rated.

▌ SAFETY

Don't wear an external money belt or a waist pack, both of which peg you as a tourist. Distribute your cash and any valuables (including your credit cards and passport) between a deep front pocket, an inside jacket or vest pocket, and a hidden money pouch. Don't reach for the money pouch once you're in public.

Belgium is relatively safe, even at night. Nonetheless, it is wise to avoid highway rest stops and sparsely populated metro stations at night. Although they aren't likely to assault, tramps and derelicts tend to make train stations unsavory at night.

Beware of pickpockets, especially around tourist attractions, in public transportation, and in airports and train stations. Men shouldn't carry wallets in back pants pockets. When in restaurants, don't hang bags or purses on the backs of chairs or tuck them under tables; put them in a safe place, such as your lap or firmly between your feet. Lock your car, and never leave anything of value inside. Don't expect a great deal of sympathy if you have been pickpocketed or burglarized. Local police make reports but usually investigate no further.

Women can travel, check in at hotels, and relax at cafés and restaurants with virtually the same ease as men. Some underground parking lots in major cities reserve spaces for women that are close to the exit; these are marked with the international "woman" symbol either on the pavement or on a sign. Women traveling alone should nonetheless avoid lingering around neighborhoods near train stations, as these neighborhoods are traditionally where prostitutes operate.

If you carry a purse, choose one with a zipper and a thick strap that you can drape across your body; adjust the length so that the purse sits in front of you at or above hip level. (Don't wear a money belt or a waist pack.) Store only enough money in the purse to cover casual spending. Distribute the rest of your cash and any valuables between deep front pockets, inside jacket or vest pockets, and a concealed money pouch.

As in other destinations around the world, avoid buying "leather" goods, or "wool" carpets from vendors selling out of car trunks, in metro stations, or other makeshift stores.

In popular tourist areas, beware of restaurant personnel beckoning tourists on the street and luring prospective diners with a complimentary glass of champagne. At the end of the meal, the "compliments" are reflected in the tab.

Although begging is against the law in Belgium, it is common to encounter beggars, often using children as props, in busy shopping areas and on metros. Because Belgium provides social assistance to the truly destitute, consider beggars' tales of woe with skepticism.

Safety Transportation Security Administration (TSA; ⊕www.tsa.gov).

▌TAXES

Airport taxes and passenger service charges levied in Belgian airports are always included in the total fare charged at the time of your ticket purchase.

All hotels in Belgium charge a 6% Value-Added Tax (TVA), included in the room rate; in Brussels, there is also a 9% city tax.

In Belgium, TVA ranges from 6% on food and clothing to 33% on luxury goods. Restaurants are in between; 21% V.A.T. is included in quoted prices.

To get a V.A.T. refund you need to reside outside the European Union and to have spent €125 or more in the same shop on the same day. Provided that you personally carry the goods out of the country within 30 days, you may claim a refund. When making a purchase, ask for a V.A.T. refund form and find out whether the merchant gives refunds—not all stores do, nor are they required to. Have the form stamped like any customs form by customs officials when you leave the country or, if you're visiting several European Union countries, when you leave the EU. After you're through passport control, take the form to a refund-service counter for an on-the-spot refund (which is usually the quickest and easiest option), or mail it to the address on the form (or the envelope with it) after you arrive

home. You receive the total refund stated on the form, but the processing time can be long, especially if you request a credit-card adjustment.

Global Refund is a Europe-wide service with 225,000 affiliated stores and more than 700 refund counters at major airports and border crossings. Its refund form, called a Tax Free Check, is the most common across the European continent. The service issues refunds in the form of cash, check, or credit-card adjustment.

V.A.T. Refunds Global Refund (☎800/566–9828 ⊕www.globalrefund.com).

▌TIME

Belgium is in the same time zone as France, Germany, Italy, and Spain and is one hour ahead of England, Ireland, and Portugal. It is six hours ahead of New York, seven hours ahead of Chicago, nine hours ahead of Los Angeles, and either eight hours (April to October) or ten hours (November to March) behind Sydney.

Time Zones Timeanddate.com (⊕www.time anddate.com/worldclock).

▌TIPPING

In Belgium, a tip (*service compris* or *service inclusief*) may be included in restaurant and hotel bills; if it is, you'll see a clear indication on the bill. If service is not included, people often round up a bit when paying, but it isn't offensive to pay the exact amount. Taxi drivers also appreciate a rounding up of the bill, but again, paying the exact amount is perfectly acceptable. Railway porters expect €0.75 per item on weekdays and €1 on weekends. For bellhops and doormen at both hotels and nightspots, €2.50 is adequate. Bartenders are tipped only for notably good service; again, rounding off is sufficient.

▌ TOURS

Belgium is an easy place to get around as an independent traveler, but if time is limited you may want to sign up for a tour, which will allow you to pack more in. Guided visits can also provide you with insight you may otherwise have missed out on, and can be a good idea if you have a special interest in mind.

SPECIAL-INTEREST TOURS

BARGE/RIVER CRUISES

Belgium's rivers and canals provide an interesting perspective for sightseeing. In some cities such as Brugge and Gent, a river- or canal-boat tour is a must and allows you to glimpse sites that would not be accessible otherwise. See the relevant chapters for details of operators there. A variety of half-day and full-day cruises are available from May to September. Reservations are usually required.

Rivertours arranges guided cruises along Belgium's canals and rivers, and charters boats to larger groups for special occasions. Savoir Faire runs cruises on a 12-berth barge from Amsterdam to Paris, calling in Antwerp, Gent, and Brugge. Le Boat has cruises in the Brugge region on boats with one to four cabins.

Contacts in Belgium Rivertours (☏053/72–94–40, or 02/218–5410 ⊕www.rivertours.be).

Contacts in the U.S. Savoir Faire (⊕www.cruise-savoir-faire.com). **Le Boat** (☏800/734–5491 ⊕www.leboat.com).

BATTLEFIELDS

In Ieper, several companies organize half- or whole-day tours by minibus through Flanders Fields. These can be booked daily and there are various options. Expect to pay at least €25 per person for a basic tour taking you to the major cemeteries and monuments around the town.

From Brugge, Quasimodo runs minibus excursions with English commentary, hosting up to 30 people per trip. On Sunday, Tuesday, and Thursday, they offer a trip that covers the Flanders Fields war grounds, taking you to trenches, war graves, museums, and monuments. The tour costs €55 per person, € 45 under 26; reservations are essential.

Brugge-based Daytours run two trips for up to seven people: Flanders Inside Out and Last Post, at €59 and €40, respectively. Flanders Inside Out includes the In Flanders Fields museum, Menenpoort in Ieper, Tyne Cot cemetery, and the Flemish polders. The Last Post trip takes you to the Last Post bugle ceremony at the Menenpoort.

Muziekcentrum 't Folk, located in the village of Dranouter, offers four different tours, some of them focusing on the role of music during the war. The only motorized tours of Bastogne are in an original army jeep. Contact Willy's Jeep Tour for further information. Tours cost €40.

Companies Salient Tours (☏057/21–46–57 ⊕www.salienttours.com). **Flanders Battlefield Tour** (☏057/36–04–60 ⊕www.ypres-fbt.be). **Private Guided Tours Annette** (☏057/44–69–33 ⊕www.visit-ypres.be). **Muziekcentrum 't Folk Dranouter** (☏057/21–78–62 ⊕www.folkdranouter.be). **Daytours** (☏050/34–60–60). **Quasimodo Tours** (☏050/37–04–70 ⊕www.quasimodo.be). **Willy's Jeep Tour** (☏063/60–10–75).

BEER

Although you'll find beer cafés on almost every street corner, there are surprisingly few organized beer tours. Most visitors create their own itineraries based on particular interests. Two companies do organize minitrips for tourists. City Tour Leuven takes you on a short tour of the Hoegaarden brewery for €20. Reservations are essential. In Brussels, Qualiguides organizes two-hour walks to beer sites in the capital for groups of at least 10; the cost is €15 per person. Beer Trips.com runs a variety of guided beer-tasting trips to Belgium, with several departures each year.

Contacts **Beer Trips.com** (☎406/531–9109 ⊕beertrips.com). **Qualiguides** (☎02/466–0585 ⊕www.qualiguides.be).

DAY TOURS & GUIDES

English-language sightseeing tours are routinely organized in tourist cities such as Brussels and Brugge. You can find information about reliable tours, guides, and schedules through national tourism offices (⇨ Visitor Information). Museums and special exhibits often offer English-language guides or headphones with explanations in English.

GARDENS

Since 1984, Coopersmith's had been offering garden tours throughout contineneHal Europe and the United States. The package to the Lowlands includes gardens, castles, and museums of Holland and Belgium.

Contacts **Coopersmith's** (☎415/669–1914 ⊕www.coopersmiths.com).

VISITOR INFORMATION

Every town in Belgium has an official tourist office with key visitor's information, maps, and calendars of events. The helpful staff is usually trilingual (English, French, and Flemish). The offices might close for an hour at lunchtime, but during the high season they might stay open past 6. Offices in the main tourist destinations are open on weekends as well as weekdays, but they often close for lunch.

In the U.S. Visit Belgium (✉220 E 42nd St., Suite 3402, New York, NY ☎212/758–8130 ⊕www.visitbelgium.com).

Within Belgium Brussels and Flanders (✉Rue Marché aux Herbes 61–63, Brussels ☎02/504–0390 ⊕www.visitflanders.com). **Brussels and Wallonia** (✉Rue Saint-Bernard 30, Brussels ☎070/221–021 ⊕www.opt.be).

ONLINE TRAVEL TOOLS

Virtually all cities and towns have individual tourism Web sites; see the Essentials sections at the end of each chapter, but here are some regional ones:

The Belgian federal government maintains a good Web site of general information on the country. The Brussels regional site covers everything from historical anecdotes to city transit to cultural events. A nonprofit tourist bureau, Brussels International, hosts a site that focuses on the capital. Among its features are a directory of hotel discount offers and photos of the city. The Tourism Flanders organization's Web site includes events listings, introductions to the region's attractions, and contact information for tourism-related companies. The Office of Tourism Promotion for Wallonia has a similarly wide-ranging site.

Expatica, a source for English-language news, events listings, and commentary on various countries, has a link to Belgium-specific information on its site. Some of the articles are less than fresh, but this can be a good way to catch up on events of the past few months. The Bulletin, the online arm of Brussels' weekly English-language magazine, has lists of what's on in the capital, and occasional restaurant reviews. For a little humor, Frites.be has a grab bag of cultural, political, and french-fry lore, with pages translated into English. The official Hergé site lists all of the famous Tintin comic books, details the entire cast of characters, and posts Tintin-related news nearly every month.

The Web site for the Royal Museums of Fine Arts of Belgium provides contact information for The Museum of Ancient Art, the Modern Museum of Art, the Wiertz Museum, and Meunier Museum, as well as information on collections, exhibitions, activities, and more. The Flanders Fashion Institute's Web site can give you a leg up on the latest work by young Belgian designers. It also has a great shopping directory for Antwerp.

To learn more about Belgium's beers, the so-called "Belgian Beer Escort" gives you tasting notes, descriptions of Belgium's types of beer, and audio clips of the correct pronunciations of various brew terms.

All About Belgium Belgian Beer Escort (⊕belgianstyle.com/mmguide). **Belgian Fed-** **eral Government** (⊕www.belgium.be). **Brussels International** (⊕www.brusselsdiscovery. com). **Brussels regional Web site** (⊕www. bruxelles.irisnet.be). **The Bulletin** (⊕www.the bulletin.be). **Expatica** (⊕www.expatica.com). **Flanders Fashion Institute** (⊕www.ffi.be). **Frites.be** (⊕www.frites.be). **Hergé** (⊕www. tintin.com). **Office of Tourism Promotion for Wallonia** (⊕www.opt.be). **Royal Fine Arts Museums** (⊕www.fine-arts-museum.be). **Tourism Flanders** (⊕www.visitflanders.com).

INDEX

Photo Credits: 6, *Jan Kranendonk/Shutterstock.* 7 (left), *Peter Adams/age fotostock.* 7 (right) and 9
(left), *Belgian Tourist Office NYC/USA, www.visitbelgium.com.* 9 (right), *Kurt De Bruyn/Shutterstock.*
10, *LOOK Die Bildagentur der Fotografen GmbH/Alamy.* 11, *Belgian Tourist Office NYC/USA, www.*
visitbelgium.com. 12, *Soca/Shutterstock.* 13 (right) and 14-18, *Belgian Tourist Office NYC/USA, www.*
visitbelgium.com.

NOTES

NOTES

Tim Skelton was born in England, but has lived in the Netherlands since 1994, working as a freelance writer and editor. A dedicated fan of Belgian beer for two decades, whenever possible he heads south of the border to indulge his passion in some of Gent and Antwerp's many delightful cafés. For this edition Tim updated the Brugge & the North Sea Coast, Gent, Antwerp and Travel Smart chapters. He has also contributed to Fodor's Amsterdam & the Netherlands and Fodor's Germany, and is the author of Luxembourg—the Bradt Travel Guide.

Nicola Smith has lived in Brussels for nine years after graduating from Glasgow University with a degree in French and German. She has worked as a political researcher at the European Parliament in Brussels and as a journalist for the past six years, for local magazines and mainstream newspapers including *The Scotsman* and *The Sunday Times*.

Cillian Donnelly was born and raised in Dublin. He worked in local media for the best part of a decade before finally taking the plunge and moving to Brussels in 2005, where he found gainful employment as a freelance news reporter for several publications. He now spends most of his time drinking gratis Champagne in the European Parliament, but still remains overwhelmed by the efficiency of the Belgian public transport system.

Karina Hof has lived in Amsterdam since 2003, the year she left her native New Amsterdam to attend graduate school. After completing MA degrees in linguistics and cultural analysis, she began writing about life in the Benelux. She eats quiche in Brussels regularly.